Communications in Computer and Information Science 1378

Satish Kumar Singh · Partha Roy ·
Balasubramanian Raman ·
P. Nagabhushan (Eds.)

Computer Vision and Image Processing

5th International Conference, CVIP 2020
Prayagraj, India, December 4–6, 2020
Revised Selected Papers, Part III

Editors
Satish Kumar Singh
Indian Institute of Information
Technology Allahabad
Prayagraj, India

Balasubramanian Raman
Indian Institute of Technology Roorkee
Roorkee, India

Partha Roy
Indian Institute of Technology Roorkee
Roorkee, India

P. Nagabhushan
Indian Institute of Information
Technology Allahabad
Prayagraj, India

ISSN 1865-0929 ISSN 1865-0937 (electronic)
Communications in Computer and Information Science
ISBN 978-981-16-1102-5 ISBN 978-981-16-1103-2 (eBook)
https://doi.org/10.1007/978-981-16-1103-2

This Springer imprint is published by the registered company Springer Nature Singapore Pte Ltd.
The registered company address is: 152 Beach Road, #21-01/04 Gateway East, Singapore 189721, Singapore

Preface

The 5th IAPR International Conference on Computer Vision & Image Processing was focused on image or video processing and computer vision. This year CVIP 2020 was held at the Indian Institute of Information Technology Allahabad, Prayagraj, India. We received submissions on topics such as biometrics, forensics, content protection, image enhancement/super-resolution/restoration, motion and tracking, image or video retrieval, image, image/video processing for autonomous vehicles, video scene understanding, human-computer interaction, document image analysis, face, iris, emotion, sign language and gesture recognition, 3D image/video processing, action and event detection/recognition, medical image and video analysis, vision-based human gait analysis, remote sensing, multispectral/hyperspectral image processing, segmentation and shape representation, image/video security, visual sensor hardware, compressed image/video analytics, document, and synthetic visual processing and Datasets and Evaluation, etc. CVIP is now one of the flagship conferences in the field of Computer Science and Information Technology.

CVIP 2020 received 352 submissions from all over the world from countries including Poland, United Kingdom, United States, Norway, Sweden, Russia, Germany, China, and many others. All submissions were rigorously peer reviewed and 134 papers were finally selected for presentation at CVIP 2020. The Program Committee finally selected all 134 high-quality papers to be included in this volume of Computer Vision and Image Processing (CVIP) proceedings published by Springer Nature.

The conference advisory committee, technical program committee, and faculty members of the Indian Institute of Information Technology Allahabad, Prayagraj, India made a significant effort to guarantee the success of the conference. We would like to thank all members of the program committee and the referees for their commitment to help in the review process and for spreading our call for papers. We would like to thank Ms. Kamya Khatter from Springer Nature for her helpful advice, guidance, and continuous support in publishing the proceedings. Moreover, we would like to thank all the authors for supporting CVIP 2020; without all their high-quality submissions the conference would not have been possible.

December 2020 Satish Kumar Singh

Organization

Patron

Bidyut Baran Chaudhuri	ISI Kolkata, India

General Chair

P. Nagabhushan	IIIT Allahabad, India

General Co-chairs

Balasubramanian Raman	IIT Roorkee, India
Shekhar Verma	IIIT Allahabad, India

Conference Chairs

Partha Pratim Roy	IIT Roorkee, India
Sanjeev Kumar	IIT Roorkee, India
Satish K. Singh	IIIT Allahabad, India
Vrijendra Singh	IIIT Allahabad, India

Local Organizing Committee

Shirshu Varma	IIIT Allahabad, India

Conference Conveners

K. P. Singh	IIIT Allahabad, India
Mohammed Javed	IIIT Allahabad, India
Pritee Khanna	IIITDMJ, India
Shiv Ram Dubey	IIIT Sri City, India

Publicity Chairs

Subrahmanyam Murala	IIT Ropar, India
Shiv Ram Dubey	IIIT Sri City, India
Ashwini K.	GAT Bangalore, India

International Advisory and Programme Committee

Ajita Rattani	Wichita State University, USA
Alireza Alaei	Southern Cross University, Australia

Ankit Chaudhary	The University of Missouri – St. Louis, USA
Ashish Khare	University of Allahabad, India
B. H. Shekhar	Mangalore University, India
Bunil Kumar	Balabantaray NIT Meghalaya, India
Debashis Sen	IIT Kharagpur, India
Emanuela Marasco	George Mason University, USA
Gaurav Gupta	Wenzhou-Kean University, China
Guoqiang Zhong	Ocean University of China, China
J. V. Thomas (Associate Director)	STA ISRO Bangalore, India
Juan Tapia Farias	Universidad de Chile, Chile
Kiran Raja	NTNU, Norway
M. Tanveer	IIT Indore, India
Munesh C. Trivedi	NIT Agartala, India
P. V. Venkitakrishnan (Director CBPO)	ISRO Bangalore, India
Prabhu Natarajan	DigiPen Institute of Technology Singapore, Singapore
Pradeep Kumar	Amphisoft, India
Puneet Gupta	IIT Indore, India
Rajeev Jaiswal	EDPO, ISRO HQ (Bangalore), India
Sahana Gowda	BNMIT, Bengaluru, India
Sebastiano Battiato	Università di Catania, Italy
Sharad Sinha	IIT Goa, India
Somnath Dey	IIT Indore, India
Sule Yildirim Yayilgan	Norwegian University of Science and Technology (NTNU), Norway
Surya Prakash	IIT Indore, India
Thinagaran Perumal	Universiti Putra Malaysia, Malaysia
Watanabe Osamu	Takushoku University, Japan
Mohan S. Kankanhalli	National University of Singapore, Singapore
Ananda Shankar Chowdhury	Jadavpur University, India
Anupam Agrawal	IIIT Allahabad, India
Aparajita Ojha	IIITDM Jabalpur, India
B. M. Mehtre	IDRBT Hyderabad, India
B. N. Chatterji	IIT Kharagpur (Past Affiliation), India
Bir Bhanu	University of California, Riverside, USA
Chirag N. Paunwala	SCET, Surat, India
D. S. Guru	University of Mysore, India
Daniel P. Lopresti	Lehigh University, USA
G. C. Nandi	IIIT Allahabad, India
Gaurav Sharma	University of Rochester, USA
Gian Luca Foresti	University of Udine, Italy
Jharna Majumdar	Nitte Meenakshi Institute of Technology, India
Jonathan Wu	University of Windsor, Canada
Josep Lladós	Universitat Autònoma de Barcelona, Spain

K. C. Gowda (Former VC)	Kuvempu University, India
K. R. Ramakrishnan	IISC Bangalore, India
Manoj K. Arora	BML Munjal University, India
Massimo Tistarelli	University of Sassari, Italy
Michal Haindl	Czech Academy of Sciences, Czech Republic
N. V. Subba Reddy	MIT Manipal, India
O. P. Vyas	IIIT Allahabad, India
Paula Brito	University of Porto, Portugal
Rajeev Srivastava	IIT BHU, India
Ramakrishnan Ganesan Angarai	IISc Bangalore, India
S. N. Singh	IIT Kanpur, India
Sanjay Kumar Singh	IIT BHU, India
Sudeep Sarkar	University of South Florida, USA
Suman Mitra	DA-IICT Gandhinagar, India
Suneeta Agarwal	MNNIT Allahabad, India
Susmita Ghosh	Jadavpur University, India
U. S. Tiwari	IIIT Allahabad, India
Umapada Pal	ISI Kolkata, India
Wei-Ta Chu	National Chung Cheng University, Taiwan
Xiaoyi Jiang	University of Münster, Germany
Sushmita Mitra	ISI Kolkata, India

Contents – Part III

U-Net-Based Approach for Segmentation of Tables from Scanned Pages

Ravish Kumar Sharma[1](✉), Romit Bhattacharrya[1](✉), Ratna Sanyal[2](✉), and Sudip Sanyal[2](✉)

[1] BML Munjal University, Gurugram, Haryana, India
[2] NIIT University, Neemrana, Rajasthan, India
{Ratna.Sanyal,Sudip.Sanyal}@niituniversity.in

Abstract. The purpose of Table Segmentation, which is a part of document layout analysis (DLA), is to identify and segment the region of interest from the document while ignoring the rest of the page. We present a deep learning approach for segmentation of tables from a rich variety of documents and explain the effect of preprocessing, distortion correction on the output of deep learning model. Our method is based on the U-net architecture wherein convolution operations extract features from the image and de-convolution operation creates a new image with the desired segmentation. The robustness of our model is verified by testing the proposed system on the ICDAR 2013, ICDAR 2019, Marmot datasets and some randomly clicked images. Our model outperforms all the other methods presented in ICDAR 2019 table segmentation competition with an F score of 0.9694.

Keywords: Convolution neural network · Document layout analysis · Deep learning · Semantic segmentation

1 Introduction

Due to the boom of the internet and its availability to a large section of the population around the world, a huge amount of data is put on the web every second and it is increasing rapidly. A big chunk of this data is available as images. Thus, we need to perform segmentation of different elements of the document viz. text, graphics, tables in order to index these files in the search engine, monitor illegal activity, perform information retrieval, effective compression and storage. This is required so that all these components could be dealt with separately and properly digitized. However, segmentation of tables is still a vital issue in document layout analysis due to varying layout like ruled and unruled tables, different length of text within the table. These layouts could be found in a variety of documents available like magazines, newspapers, scanned pages, comics and

Supported by organization BML Munjal University.

S. K. Singh et al. (Eds.): CVIP 2020, CCIS 1378, pp. 1–11, 2021.
https://doi.org/10.1007/978-981-16-1103-2_1

more. In practice these types of data are noisy, skewed, deformed and most of the time obtained from multilingual and multi-script documents which have irregular textures and scripts. All these anomalies make the segmentation process very difficult. Table segmentation is an extensively researched field and is equally challenging as an algorithm needs to take care of a variety of documents which may contain the noise and distortions. Our firm belief is that we have reached a saturation level in the digital image processing techniques to handle such kind of problem and with the recent improvement in the machine learning domain, a generic architecture can be created that will be more suited to handle this task. Most of the work that is already done in table segmentation involves the use of heuristics while the use of data-driven approach is quite recent but it has outperformed other methods in terms of accuracy as well as the generalization on a variety of documents.

In this paper, we have used semantic segmentation approach for segmentation of the table from the rest of the page. Semantic segmentation is pixel by pixel segmentation of the region of interest from the rest of the image. Our method involves the use of deep learning architecture based on the concepts of U-net [1], wherein convolution operations extract features from the image and de-convolution operation creates a new image with the desired segmentation. In order to prove that our model is robust and can generalize effectively, we trained our model on the training data of Marmot [2], ICDAR 2013 [3], ICDAR 2019 [4] table segmentation dataset. The trained model was then tested on the testing data of these datasets and some randomly clicked images containing tables. We have compared the performance of our model with the participants of ICDAR 2013 and ICDAR 2019 table segmentation competition.

ICDAR 2013 table detection dataset contains PDF of US and European documents along with ground truth in XML format. It has pages with and without tables and some pages with more than two tables that makes the detection task complex. ICDAR 2019 dataset contains a scan of both handwritten documents with tables and printed documents. Marmot dataset comprises of pages in PDF format gathered from research papers. The dataset has English and Chinese documents. We have used only English documents for training our model and developed scripts to convert all PDF documents, XML to images.

The rest of the paper is structured in the following manner, Sect. 2 reviews the work that has been done in this field. Section 3 explains the method used in the present work. Section 4 discusses the results and Sect. 5 concludes the paper.

2 Related Work

Most of the work done on text/table segmentation involved the use of heuristics. These methods were developed by examining the properties of a table like the presence of horizontal and vertical lines, the gap between columns of table and words in normal lines. Performance of these methods is mostly tested on pages that did not have skew, noise and warps. The use of data-driven approaches is quite recent in this field but has the potential to show good performance in all kinds of documents and has outperformed most of the heuristics-based methods in terms of accuracy.

T Kasar et al. [5] present a method to detect a table by extracting features from an image and then feeding these features to an SVM classifier to test if these features belong to a table or not. Features are drawn by identifying horizontal and vertical lines and then using connected components to find intersection points of these lines. They used a set of 26 equations each calculating a feature from each connected component. Minimum three intersecting vertical and horizontal lines are used for feature extraction. This method is restricted to ruled tables without skew.

S. Mandal et al. [6] presented an algorithm based on the observation that the columns of the table have a large gap between fields than the words in a line. Their method involved two-steps: First, the words are clustered together to form a block using connected component method. The results of the first step are then employed to find a set of lines that form a table. This is done by converting lines into rectangular blocks while rows of the table would have multiple blocks due to a large gap. Their algorithm is tested on the University of Washington's document image database and their custom-made dataset, so it cannot be compared directly with our model.

In [7], L. Hao et al. used a hybrid approach. In the first step, they use a hand-engineered method to find areas looking like a table and then use CNN to verify the presence of the table in that area. The table area identification method is restricted to a ruled line table and non-ruled line table with one column.

Schreiber S. et al. presented a Fast RCNN based architecture in [8] for table segmentation. Their method uses a region proposal network that generates regions where the table is expected and then a classifier confirms the presence or absence of a table in the proposed region. They tested their method on the ICDAR table competition dataset and achieved an outstanding F1 score of 0.967. RCNN is also used by Gilani et al. in [9], but with a slightly different approach. Their method involves two modules: image transformation and table detection. Image transformation involves the use of distance transform (Euclidean, Linear and Max distance transform) to extract some initial features. These transformed images are the input to FRCNN model. The model achieved an F1 score of 0.8629 on UNLV dataset.

A combination of deep learning and graphical algorithms for segmentation of charts, bars, line graphs and tables from documents have been employed in [10]. Their method involved the use of Deep Convolutional Neural Network (DCNN) that takes an image as input and outputs binary mask for each class. These maps are then concatenated with input images and passed to a classifier that segments different parts of the documents. To improve the saliency maps Conditional Random Field algorithm is used [11]. Their model performs better than all other recorded methods for ICDAR 2013 dataset with an F score of 0.978, but it does not mention anything about the performance of the model on any other dataset or random images.

We have used a semantic segmentation approach based on the architecture of U-net in the present work. We would also like to mention that information gathered from papers mentioned in this section were extensively employed in tuning the hyper-parameters and experimenting with different preprocessing techniques.

3 Methods

The architecture used by us is based on the concepts of U-net architecture. U-net was a choice because it is simple, fast and has already shown outstanding results in Kaggle competitions and other research work [12–15]. The model starts with a series of convolution operations that learns both high-level and low-level features just like a normal CNN. Subsequently, a de-convolution operation recreates a new image of required segmentation. Skip connections are used to pass the activations of initial layers to the latter part of the network. This avoids the loss of information while training a deep network. Batch normalization is used after every convolution operation. The dimensions of the image used for training are (256, 256, 1). The input image is normalized before being fed into the network. Figure 1 gives an overview of the architecture.

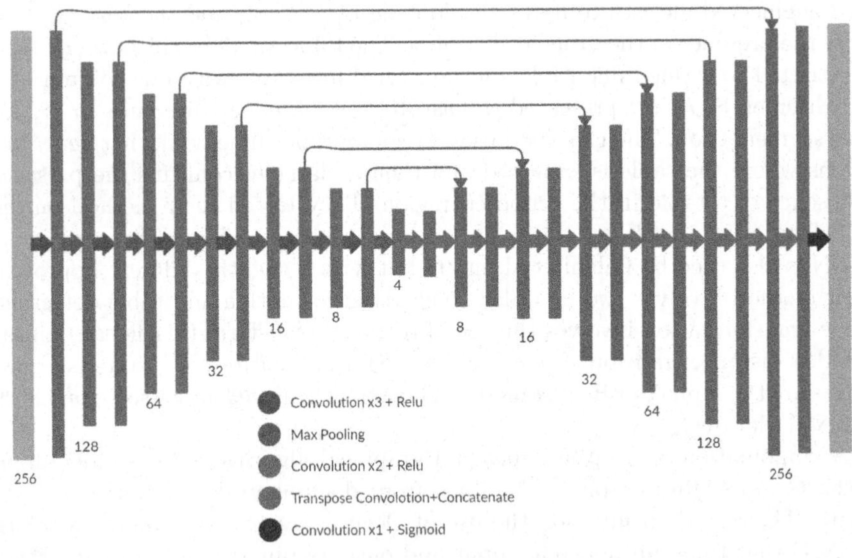

Fig. 1. Overview of the architecture, number written below each block are the dimension of image, height and width of the image are the same in each layer. Yellow bar shows the input and output image respectively. (Color figure online)

Dice coefficient loss was used as the loss function for training and all the hidden layers had a Relu activation function. Equation 1 shows the formula of the dice coefficient. We have also experimented with combinations of binary cross entropy loss and dice coefficient loss by taking average and giving different weightage to each loss. But the best results were obtained by using the dice coefficient as the loss function.

$$\text{Dice Coefficient} = \frac{2 \; * \; Y\_true \; * \; y\_pred}{Y\_true \; + \; y\_pred} \tag{1}$$

Initially, the model was trained with the ICDAR 2013 dataset but the model did not yield satisfactory results due to the inadequate number of training images i.e. 238. Data augmentation did not add much value to the performance. In order to increase the size of the dataset and to make a generic model, the training data of ICDAR 2019, ICDAR 2013 and Marmot dataset were combined. All three datasets belong to different distributions and the number of training images in each dataset was different. In order to maintain the balance of images, we created copies of images in minority dataset by flipping them horizontally. Although the training and testing data of all the three datasets contain noise-free images, adding noise in the training images will make the neural network to perform on noisy data.

While training the network, we experimented with a number of preprocessing techniques like binarization, histogram equalization, and used different morphological operators but these techniques did not have any significant impact on the output of the neural network. A probable reason for this might be that the convolution filters learn the features they want during the training process. So, we used grayscale images normalized by subtracting the images by means of the dataset and dividing the result by the standard deviation of the dataset. Normalization increased the training process as the whole dataset comes under a common scale centered around 0.

4 Results

ICDAR 2013 and ICDAR 2019 table datasets have already provided both training and testing data, but this was not available for the Marmot dataset. We used 450 images for training and 50 for testing from this dataset. We used the F score as an evaluation metric for our model, which is also used as a performance measure in the ICDAR 2013 and ICDAR 2019 datasets. Equation 2 is the formula for F score.

$$\text{F Score} = \frac{2 \; * \; precision \; * \; recall}{precision \; + \; recall} \tag{2}$$

The the F score of our model on ICDAR 2013, ICDAR 2019 and Marmot dataset are 0.9379, 0.9694 and 0.9642, respectively. The results clearly indicate that the model generalizes well on all three datasets.

Figure 2, Fig. 3, and Fig. 4 show some sample output from ICDAR 2013, ICDAR 2019 and Marmot testing data, respectively. Table 1 and Table 2 contains a comparison of the accuracy of our model with participants of the ICDAR 2013 [16] competition, ICDAR 2019 [17] dataset, respectively. We could not find any benchmark on the Marmot dataset. Also, DeepDeSRT [18] and TableNet [19] in Table 1 are deep learning models.

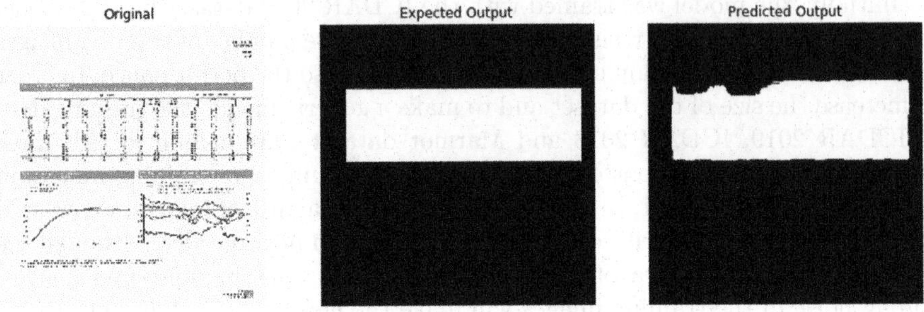

Fig. 2. Sample output from testing data of ICDAR 2013 dataset.

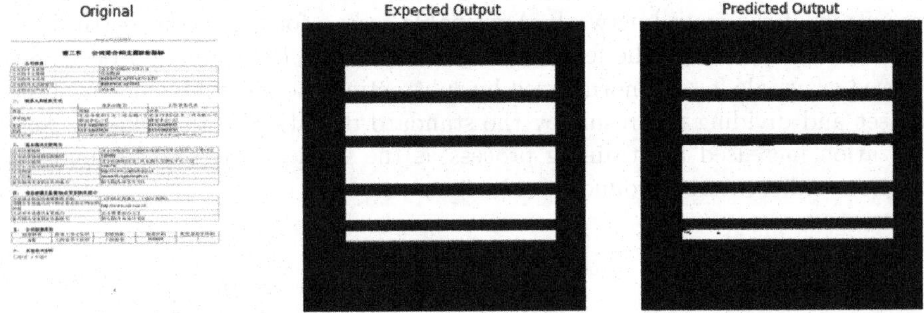

Fig. 3. Sample output from testing data of ICDAR 2019 dataset.

We also tested our model on a dataset of 85 images taken by phone from journals, magazines, and books. Unlike the training dataset, these images contain warps, skew, turn, distortions. The model is still able to predict the tables with an F1 score of 0.8047. Figure 5 shows a sample.

4.1 Observations

1. As can be observed from Table 1 and Table 2, the accuracy of our approach increased significantly from 0.9379 (in ICDAR 2013) to 0.9694 (in ICDAR

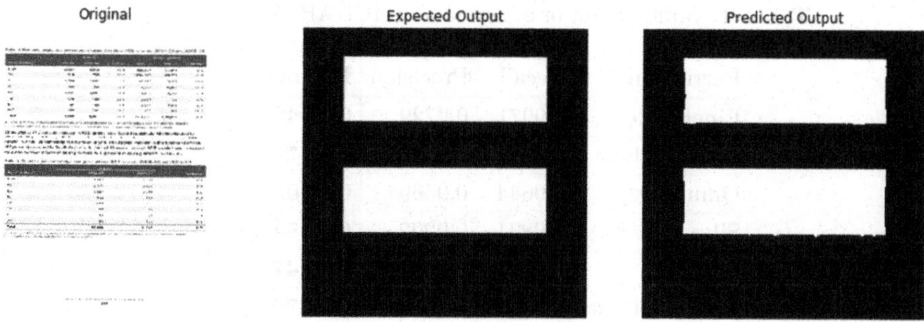

Fig. 4. Sample output from testing data of Marmot dataset.

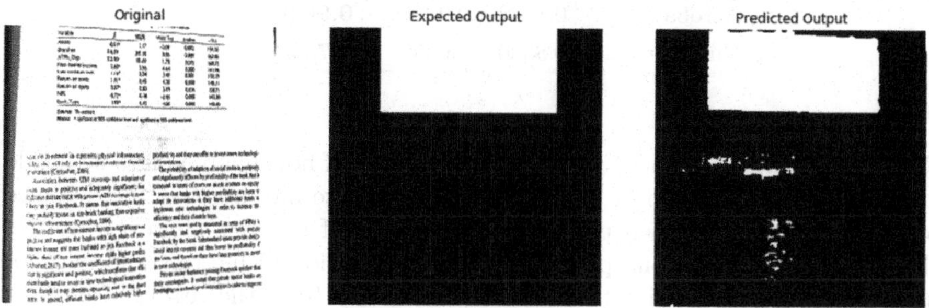

Fig. 5. Sample output from a randomly clicked image.

2019). This is due to the difference in the number of training images available for ICDAR2013 and ICDAR 2019 and kind of images present in both the datasets. The amount of training images in ICDAR 2013 are 238 while in ICDAR 2019 are 1123. The imbalance was reduced by adding augmentation images of ICDAR 2013 in the training data.
2. The accuracy is almost same at all threshold in ICDAR 2019 results, a probable reason for this is the use of sigmoid activation function at the output layer that converges the gradients to its extreme ends that is 0 and 1.
3. The effect of image corrections was also examined. The image dataset created by us contained different types of distortions like skew, brightness difference, warps etc. We used Photoshop to remove distortions in some of the images and tested these new images on our Deep Learning model. This improved the accuracy of our model. Figure 6 shows the output of our neural network on a sample image without corrections and Fig. 7 depicts the results on the same image after applying corrections.

Apart from the above observations, we feel that that the metric used for measuring accuracy, i.e. F-score, can be improved. The F1 score is a standard metric for testing accuracy model in both the ICDAR 2013 and ICDAR 2019 dataset.

Table 1. Comparison of our model on ICDAR 2013 dataset.

Participant	Recall	Precision	**F1 measure**
FineReader	0.9971	0.9729	**0.9848**
DeepDeSRT	0.9615	0.9740	**0.9677**
OmniPage	0.9644	0.9569	**0.9606**
Silva	0.9831	0.9292	**0.9554**
TableNet	0.9501	0.9547	**0.9547**
Our Method	**0.9428**	**0.9331**	**0.9379**
Nitro	0.9323	0.9397	**0.9360**
Nurminen	0.9077	0.9210	**0.9143**
Acrobat	0.8738	0.9365	**0.9040**
Yildiz	0.8530	0.6399	**0.7313**

While, it calculates the accuracy only on the basis of how many points lie inside and outside of the region of interest, it does not take into account the distance of an incorrectly predicted point from the region of interest. However, we feel that a point predicted one pixel away from the region of interest and another incorrectly predicted point that is 100 pixels away from the region of interest should not be penalized the same. Thus, some form of weighted F score would be a better measure of accuracy.

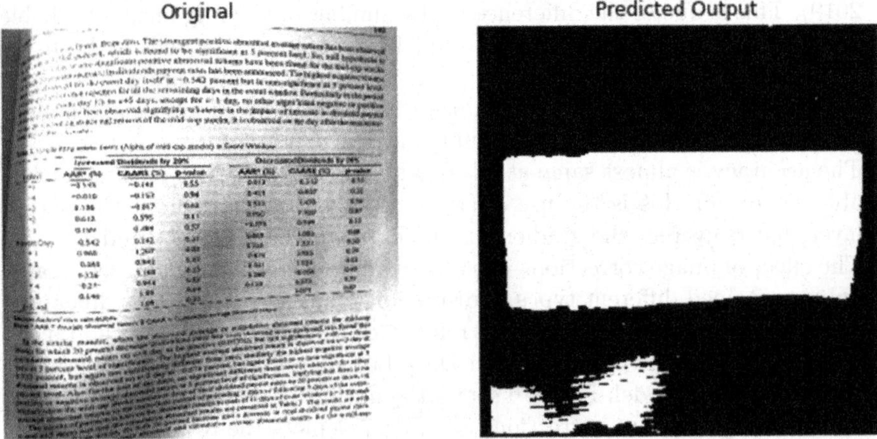

Fig. 6. Output of proposed method on image without removing distortions.

Table 2. Comparison of our model on ICDAR 2019 dataset.

Teams	IoU@0.6	IoU@0.7	IoU@0.8	IoU@0.9	WAvg. F1
Our Method	**0.9703**	**0.9698**	**0.9692**	**0.9684**	**0.9694**
TableRadar	0.9697	0.9599	0.9514	0.9022	0.9423
NLPR-PAL	0.9728	0.9616	0.9379	0.8667	0.9291
Lenovo Ocean	0.9097	0.8999	0.8773	0.8223	0.8773
ABC Fintech	0.8268	0.8165	0.7959	0.7266	0.7861
Applica-robots	0.9020	0.8824	0.8249	0.5448	0.7697
Table Fan	0.8931	0.8648	0.8054	0.5775	0.7684

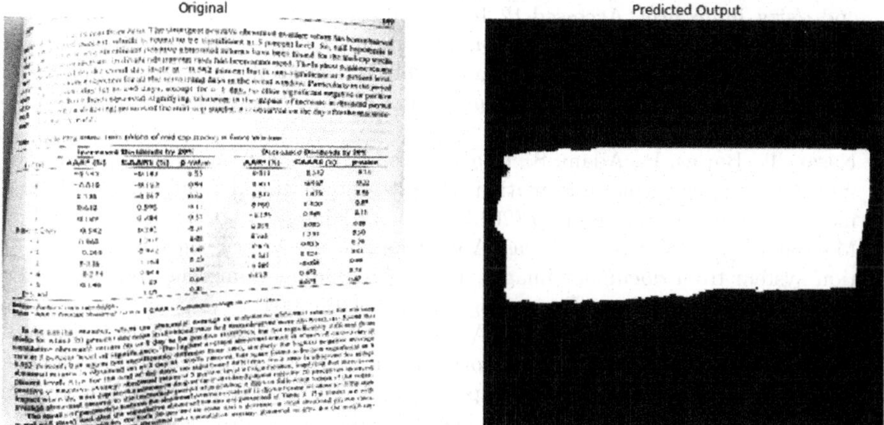

Fig. 7. Output of proposed method on image after removing distortions.

5 Conclusions

This paper presents a deep learning-based method to segment tables from digital documents. U-net based architecture was used that involves the use of convolution operations to extract features from image followed by de-convolution operations to create a new image of desired results. In order to increase the amount of training data and create a generic model, the training data of ICDAR 2013, ICDAR 2019 and Marmot datasets were mixed. The trained model has been tested on the testing dataset of the ICDAR 2013, ICDAR 2019, Marmot table recognition dataset. The F1 on each dataset was 0.9379, 0.9694 and 0.9642, respectively. The model outperforms all the methods used in ICDAR 2019 dataset. To check the robustness of the model, the model was also tested on 85 randomly clicked images from books, journals, and magazines with different types of noise. The F1 score on this dataset was 0.8047. The deep learning based methods yield good results without depending on any hand-engineered features, but are sensitive to distortions. Although the proposed method yields good results without depending on any hand-engineered features, it still requires post-processing for removal of false positives and large amount of dataset is needed with images containing all types of distortions and tables to create a robust model.

References

1. Ronneberger, O., Fischer, P., Brox, T.: U-Net: convolutional networks for biomedical image segmentation. In: Navab, N., Hornegger, J., Wells, W.M., Frangi, A.F. (eds.) MICCAI 2015. LNCS, vol. 9351, pp. 234–241. Springer, Cham (2015). https://doi.org/10.1007/978-3-319-24574-4_28
2. Dataset for table recognition. In: Marmot Dataset. http://www.icst.pku.edu.cn/cpdp/sjzy/index.htm. Accessed 12 June 2020
3. Ground-truthed datasets of PDF tables. In: Tamir Hassan - PDF Table Recognition Dataset. http://www.tamirhassan.com/html/dataset.html. Accessed 12 June 2020
4. Competitions. In: ICDAR2019. https://icdar2019.org/competitions-2/. Accessed 12 June 2020
5. Kasar, T., Barlas, P., Adam, S., et al.: Learning to detect tables in scanned document images using line information. In: 12th International Conference on Document Analysis and Recognition (2013). https://doi.org/10.1109/icdar.2013.240
6. Mandal, S., Chowdhury, S.P., Das, A.K., Chanda, B.: A very efficient table detection system from document images. In: Fourth Indian Conference on Computer Vision, Graphics & Image Processing, pp. 411–416 (2004)
7. Hao, L., Gao, L., Yi, X., Tang, Z.: A table detection method for PDF documents based on convolutional neural networks. In: 12th IAPR Workshop on Document Analysis Systems (DAS) (2016). https://doi.org/10.1109/das.2016.23
8. Schreiber, S., Agne, S., Wolf, I., et al.: DeepDeSRT: deep learning for detection and structure recognition of tables in document images. In: 14th IAPR International Conference on Document Analysis and Recognition (ICDAR) (2017). https://doi.org/10.1109/icdar.2017.192
9. Gilani, A., Qasim, S.R., Malik, I., Shafait, F.: Table detection using deep learning. In: 14th IAPR International Conference on Document Analysis and Recognition (ICDAR) (2017). https://doi.org/10.1109/icdar.2017.131
10. Kavasidis, I., et al.: A saliency-based convolutional neural network for table and chart detection in digitized documents. In: Ricci, E., Rota Bulò, S., Snoek, C., Lanz, O., Messelodi, S., Sebe, N. (eds.) ICIAP 2019. LNCS, vol. 11752, pp. 292–302. Springer, Cham (2019). https://doi.org/10.1007/978-3-030-30645-8_27
11. Lafferty, J.C.N., McCallum, A.C.N., Pereira, F.C.N.: Conditional random fields: probabilistic models for segmenting and labeling sequence data. In: Proceedings of the 18th International Conference on Machine Learning, pp. 282–289 (2001)
12. Cao, H., Liu, H., Song, E., et al.: Two-stage convolutional neural network architecture for lung nodule detection. IEEE J. Biomed. Health Inform (2019). https://doi.org/10.1109/JBHI.2019.2963720
13. Topcoders, 1st place solution. In: Kaggle. https://www.kaggle.com/c/data-science-bowl-2018/discussion/54741. Accessed 12 June 2020
14. Li, M., Yu, S., Zhang, W., et al.: Segmentation of retinal fluid based on deep learning: application of three-dimensional fully convolutional neural networks in optical coherence tomography images. Int. J. Ophthalmol. (2019). https://doi.org/10.18240/ijo.2019.06.22

15. Waldner, F., Diakogiannis, F.I.: Deep learning on edge: extracting field boundaries from satellite images with a convolutional neural network. Remote Sens. Environ. **245**, 111741 (2020). https://doi.org/10.1016/j.rse.2020.111741
16. Gobel, M., Hassan, T., Oro, E., Orsi, G.: ICDAR 2013 table competition. In: 12th International Conference on Document Analysis and Recognition (2013). https://doi.org/10.1109/icdar.2013.292
17. Competition Results. In: ICDAR2019. http://sac.founderit.com/results.html. Accessed 26 Nov 2019
18. Schreiber, S., Agne, S., Wolf, I., et al.: DeepDeSRT: deep learning for detection and structure recognition of tables in document images. In: 14th International Conference on Document Analysis and Recognition (2017). https://doi.org/10.1109/icdar.2017.192
19. Paliwal, S.S., Vishwanath, D., Rahul, R., et al.: TableNet: deep learning model for end-to-end table detection and tabular data extraction from scanned document images. CoRR. abs/2001.01469 (2020)

Air Writing: Tracking and Tracing

Jyotsana Mall[1], Komal Rani[1](✉), and Deepak Khatri[2]

[1] Department of Computer Engineering, Netaji Subhas University of Technology, New Delhi 110078, India

[2] Department of Biotechnology, Netaji Subhas University of Technology, New Delhi 110078, India

Abstract. Writing is an integral part of learning. Its value is quintessential in the development of cognitive understanding which aids in absorbing and demystifying the world around us. Air writing as a concept has been prevalent in education systems all across the world; teachers and parents have been training children to gesture the shapes of letters and spell out words in the air to build the habit of writing, but its technology is relatively recent. In this paper, we have introduced a method to implement air writing which allows users to trace linguistic characters in a pen-up pen-down motion of finger or hand thereby eradicating the need to write continuously. The proposed method is not frustrated by the requirement of extra hardware like a data glove or a specialized camera. The implementation makes use of the in-built camera in personal computers, detects the hand region, and traces or tracks the hand trajectory as per the user's requirement. The implementation is broadly divided into two parts: (i) Detection of hand region; and (ii) Tracking and tracing hand movements. We propose the use of Single Shot Multibox Detector (SSD) with MobilenetV1 as the base network to detect the hand region. For the second half of the implementation, we have used the deque data structure and OpenCV. We have also included the option of complete/partial erasing of the screen to simplify the process of air writing and make it more intuitive.

Keywords: Air Writing · Noncontinuous writing · Single shot multibox detector

1 Introduction

The key concept behind air writing is the ability to utilize a user's hand as a stylus which can interact with a computer via gestures. Air writing allows a user to trace out a letter, word, or even a diagram without having the person interact physically with the computer. Air writing is not an exhaustive process and requires minimum focus. In scenarios where writing using a physical/virtual keyboard or a trackpad is not feasible, air writing is a viable alternative.

A majority of the research done on air writing emphasizes the use of "Graffiti alphabets" which is a writing technique that allows a user to write the English alphabets from A to Z, in capital, using a single stroke. This limits the usability of the program as

S. K. Singh et al. (Eds.): CVIP 2020, CCIS 1378, pp. 12–24, 2021.
https://doi.org/10.1007/978-981-16-1103-2_2

the user is first expected to learn and practice the writing system in order to attain a certain level of efficiency and accuracy.

Conventional writing, on the other hand, is gratifying for two main reasons: (i) the person is in complete control of the ink; and (ii) real-time progress is visible, which aids in avoiding errors and inaccuracies. Therefore, in order to implement an effective and user-friendly way of air writing, we believe the implementation must incorporate these features. In our proposed method, we have introduced an intuitive approach to air writing using non continuous movements and selective erasing. These are two aspects of air writing which have very limited research.

In this paper, we endeavor to reduce the disparity between air writing and conventional writing. Closely mimicking conventional writing entails that our implementation has the capability to distinguish meaningful strokes from the superfluous hand movements while writing a letter or word. We make use of hand gestures to address this challenge.

In our proposed method, air writing is executed over a real-time video taken from the inbuilt camera of the device. We use SSD with MobilenetV1 for faster and accurate hand detection and identify the gesture made by the user to differentiate between the track and trace feature. We draw a reference pointer at the tip of the finger to guide the writing motion of the user. Armed with the knowledge of where to begin the next letter or finish an existing one, the proposed air writing implementation becomes more intuitive.

We further compliment the usability of our air writing implementation by allowing users to write in a pen-up-pen-down manner with the help of motion gestures and also partially/completely erase the air drawn characters in case the user makes an error. These gestures had to be set up such that they do not disrupt the flow of the user while maintaining the simplicity of use. In our implementation, an open hand gesture would result in tracing of the meaningful hand movements, whereas, a closed fist or open hand with fingers spread out would result in tracking only.

This paper is organized in the following manner. In Sect. 2, we discuss the related works of hand detection and air writing. Section 3 describes the workings of SSD with MobilenetV1 and the implementation of noncontinuous air writing and erasing (partial and complete). Section 4 evaluates the performance of the methods used, and Sect. 5 concludes the work done.

2 Related Work

For air writing, the initial step is the detection of the hand. Hand detection has been enforced in different ways to enable gesture recognition which has proved to be a blessing for avenues like robotics, human computer interaction, and a proverbial crutch for the deaf and dumb. One such method includes using extra hardware devices like data gloves that contain sensors or light-emitting diodes to detect the hand [1]. These hardware devices are predominantly expensive, and people are not too keen on buying extra hardware. Shah et al. [2] proposed the gesture recognition method in which a specific color is painted on the finger to aid in tracking hand movements. In this method the marker color is predefined for each frame thereby making finger detection using thresholding faster than plain finger tracking. This method invariably fails when the background color matches the marker color. Various vision-based techniques have also been used for hand gesture recognition. In [3–9] vision-based techniques, there is no requirement for any extra hardware (glove or color marker). The naked hand of the user is captured using the camera and is analyzed using various computer vision techniques like detecting the shape, motion or color of the hand. In general, using color to detect a hand poses a problem if background objects have color similar to skin. To resolve this, a method based on background subtraction was proposed which assumes that the device camera is immobile with respect to a static background. In [3] and [4], the distinctive color range of the hand is used for detection. The RGB color space of the captured image is changed to the YCbCr color space. Next, the skin color range is used to identify the hand region. However, detection using only the skin color can prove to be very challenging as lighting conditions can cause a variance in the color of the objects. Also there exists a great variance in the skin color in the human race and no concrete solution has been proposed to account for this variability. Deepa et al. [5] proposed a gesture recognition and fingertip detection method in which the hand region is discovered using a region growing algorithm followed by morphological operations. The fingertips are then detected using the convex hull algorithm. Singha et al. [9] proposed a method in which they first detect and subtract the face of the user followed by skin filtering to find objects having skin color. Alongside face detection, 3-frame differencing for both colored and grayscale frames followed by morphological operations is performed. The result of skin filtering combined with the result of the 3-frame differencing gives the hand region in the frame.

The next step in air writing involves tracking of the hand to create a trail on the screen. Chen et al. [10] proposed a method to use 6-DOF (six degrees of freedom) motion tracking and a specialized handheld device with a button to mark the beginning and end of air writing. They later published a part 2 [11] in which they redressed the shortcomings of finger tracking from their previous paper. In the newly proposed method, controller-free hand tracking is enabled through Leap [12] and by pressing the Ctrl key the essential writing is distinguished from the redundant ones. Authors of [13] also used the Leap Motion device along with computer vision techniques to recognize written words in air gestures by the user's hands. Amma et al. [14] proposed a method of using a wearable device consisting of inertial sensors and accelerometer to keep track of the hand movement for air writing. However, the need for a special device makes the proposed system unhandy. In [15, 16], Microsoft Kinect depth camera is used to propose an air writing method to identify the characters. All the above-mentioned methods have an implementation for tracking continuous air writing by the user which in general writing is not applicable.

There is a raft of air writing implementations in a continuous fashion with external devices but a paucity of noncontinuous implementations. To make air writing more intuitive, linguistic characters need to be written in a noncontinuous motion. For instance, the English character 'A' cannot be written using a single stroke. This is where the need for noncontinuous motion arises. In addition to the use of uni-strokes, most of the previous work in air writing focuses on completely erasing the screen, which is to get the clean canvas back. It should not be expected of the user to write or draw without aberrations. Thus, the requirement for partial erasing of the screen is essential. A solution to the aforementioned problems has been proposed in this paper.

3 Proposed Method

The implementation's flow of control is explained in the block diagram shown in Fig. 2. The rudimentary steps include capturing the video using the in-built camera of the user's device and extracting frames one at a time for processing. We then detect the hand region in the frame and draw a reference point (RP) on the screen. This helps the users to have a clear idea of where to begin their writing. We divide the screen into two regions - A and B as shown in Fig. 1.

Fig. 1. Frame divided into two regions

Region A contains the drawing toolkit consisting of options - clear all, erase, and a color palette with four choices. Region B is where the actual writing takes place. This UI design is inspired from [17]. If the RP is found in region B, we find the aspect ratio (AR) of the hand gesture detected. This helps to determine whether the user wants to write or simply track the hand movements. If AR is greater than the threshold, meaning the hand gesture was for tracing, we add the coordinates of the current RP to a deque. Finally, we use the deque and OpenCV techniques to either draw or erase lines on the frame.

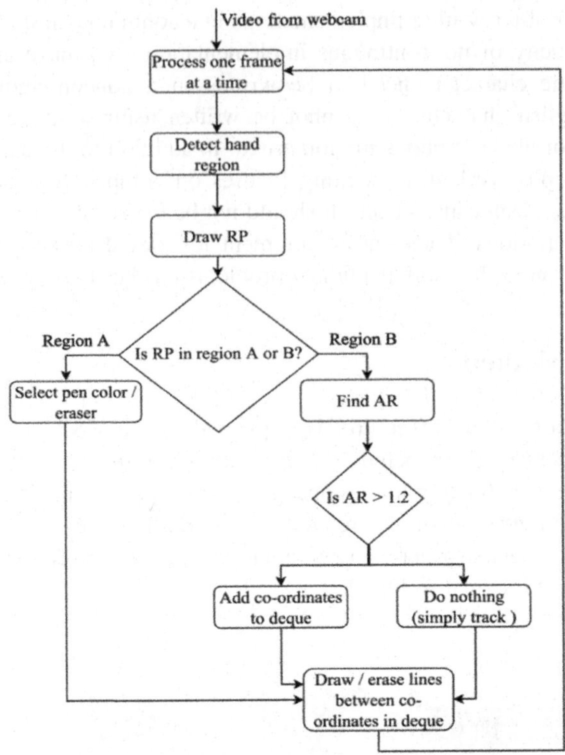

Fig. 2. Proposed method

3.1 Hand Detection with SSD

There was a dearth for faster object detection as compared to existing algorithms like YOLO (You Only Look Once). Thus, SSD, a single shot detector for multiple categories was introduced [18]. SSD is specifically designed for detecting objects in real-time. This algorithm is built on the concept of a feed forward convolution network which gives an output a collection of (predefined size) bounding boxes and confidence scores for the existence of instances of object category in those boxes. The confidence scores are calculated in the range of 0 to 1. Higher the confidence score more will be the probability of the existence of an object class in the bounding box. The network layers at the start of the SSD model are based on conventional architecture used for classifying an image, generally known as the base network. In our implementation, for the base network, we use the MobilenetV1 network. SSD adds additional convolutional feature layers after the base network. The size of these layers keeps on decreasing, unlike YOLO where size remains constant, to make more accurate predictions. In SSD, non-maximum compression is also performed to eliminate the duplicate bounding boxes.

We are using Tensorflow's object detection API for training SSD with MobilnetV1 [19]. The dataset of hands required for gesture detection to train the SSD model is taken from [17]. The model upon detection returns a set of bounding boxes and confidence scores for the object on the frame. We can choose a ground truth value for the confidence score. For our model, we have kept the ground truth value as 0.4, which means if the confidence score is greater than 0.4, only then algorithm detects the object as a hand. For choosing ground truth value, we need to make a tradeoff between accuracy and speed of the model. If this value is high, then the model predicts hands with very high accuracy but will not serve the purpose of continuous writing as it will mark very few bounding boxes as hands. If this value is kept too low, then the accuracy will be compromised. We have used Tensorflow object detection API for the detection of hand trained on custom hand data. It supports only the SSD models which provide a good Mean Average Precision in comparison to Fast and Faster R-CNN models as shown in Table 1. The SSD model also provides good FPS (Fig. 5) performance making it a real time algorithm. We got ~9FPS while running on a i7 5660 CPU, with a GPU we can have a true real time performance with the algorithm.

Table 1. SSD performance in comparison to other novel algorithms. This table is a courtesy of Wei Liu et al. [18]

Method	mAP (mean average precision)	FPS
Faster R-CNN	73.2	7
YOLO	63.4	45
SSD	76.8	22

3.2 Noncontinuous Air Writing

For all confidence scores greater than the threshold value, we find the four corners of the corresponding bounding box and the centroid of hand using (1) and (2).

$$\begin{aligned}(\text{left, right, top, bottom}) = (&\text{boxes[i][1]} * \text{im\_width}, \text{boxes[i][3]} * \text{im\_width}, \text{boxes[i][0]} \\ &* \text{im\_height}, \text{boxes[i][2]} * \text{im\_height})\end{aligned} \tag{1}$$

$$\begin{aligned}\text{y} &= (\text{bottom} + \text{top})/2 \\ \text{x} &= (\text{right} + \text{left})/2\end{aligned} \tag{2}$$

(left, right, top, bottom) denote the four sides of the bounding box encompassing the detected hand. *Boxes* contain all the bounding boxes returned by the SSD model. *im_width, im_height* are the width and height respectively of the frame. *(x, y)* denote the x and y coordinates of the centroid of the hand. *(x, top)* denote the x and y the coordinates of the RP and we draw a circle at this position for better visualization while writing. We then check whether the user is in region A or B. If the user is in region A and selecting the 'clear all' option, we clear the deque. This essentially clears the screen, and anything written by the user is erased. As for the other options in our drawing toolkit, we keep track of the color or eraser option selected. We use two terms - trace and track frequently to describe the hand movements of the user. Tracing refers

to the actual writing done by the user whereas tracking refers to the arbitrary hand movements while writing that we do not want to render on the screen. We have used various hand gestures to differentiate between these two aspects of air writing. AR helps to determine the various gestures made by the user to either track or trace their movements. We find the value of AR using (3).

$$\text{aspect\_ratio} = (\text{top} - \text{bottom})/(\text{left} - \text{right}) \tag{3}$$

The value of the AR is lesser than the threshold value when the user is either making a fist or showing jazz hands as shown in Fig. 3(b) and 3(c). These two gestures are used while tracking the RP to the desired starting point. In such a scenario, we do not need to keep track of the RP, that is, we do not need to trace these points, simply show their position on the frame. The value of AR is greater than the threshold value when the user has their palm facing the camera with fingers together as shown in Fig. 3 (a). If such is the case while the user is present in region B, indicating that the user wishes to write, we add the coordinates of the RP along with the selected color or erasing option to a deque. Finally, we loop through the deque to draw lines between the coordinates with the color selected by the user using the OpenCV library.

3.3 Selective Erasing

Ever since we were children, erasers have been an important constituent in our day to day proceedings. We can simply expunge our imperfections and start over. Writing becomes undeniably easier if we have the option of using an eraser every time we make a mistake. Thus, we introduce the concept of adding a ‘selective erasing’ tool, something which has not been actively worked upon in the air writing field. When the user selects the eraser option from the toolkit, our algorithm erases a default pixel square of area with RP as the center of the square. The default size is calculated according to the dimensions of the frame which differs from device to device. The erasing algorithm works in the following manner - we initially keep a copy of the frame from when the user begins writing. This unaltered frame is blank and has no writing on it. On the modified frame, the square area of pixels that needs to be erased is overlaid with the cropped image of the same square area from the unaltered frame. We have implemented alpha blending technique to overlay the cropped image on the modified frame. We keep the alpha value equal to 1 since we do not want transparency. The user has the additional choice to either increase or decrease the size of the eraser with a maximum and minimum size defined, just like in Microsoft Paint. This can be achieved by hovering over the ‘+’ or ‘−’ sign to increase or decrease the size respectively on the erase toolbox. We display the size of the eraser while it is increasing or decreasing in number format as well as a square box so that visualizing the size of the eraser becomes easier. To erase, the user simply must trace the eraser displayed on the screen over the desired areas. Similar to writing, the eraser can also be either tracked or traced as per the user’s demand.

4 Evaluation

We have implemented an air writing method that processes the real-time video frame by frame. We detect the hand of the user using SSD with MobilenetV1. For testing our model, we have used a Dell webcam. Figure 3 (a), (b), (c) show different hand gestures being detected with their confidence score.

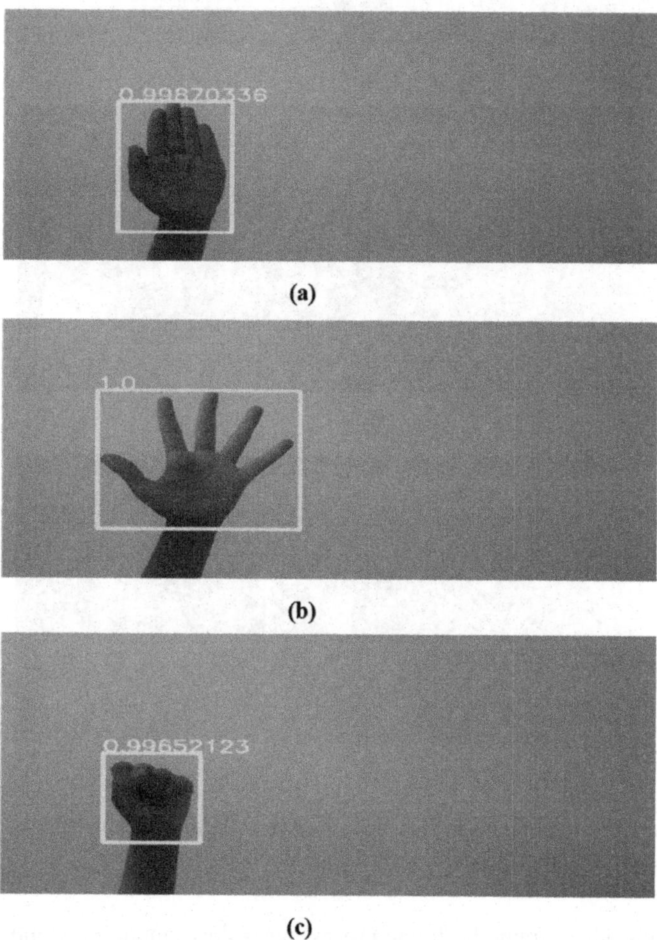

Fig. 3. (a) Detecting hand for tracing. (b) Detecting hand for tracking. (c) Detecting hand for tracking

We use the gesture shown in Fig. 3 (a) for tracing or actual writing. Gestures showed in Fig. 3 (b) and 3 (c) are used for tracking because their aspect ratio is less than 1.2 - the threshold value. Figure 4 (a), (b), (c) show hand detection in a noisy background as is the case in real world scenarios.

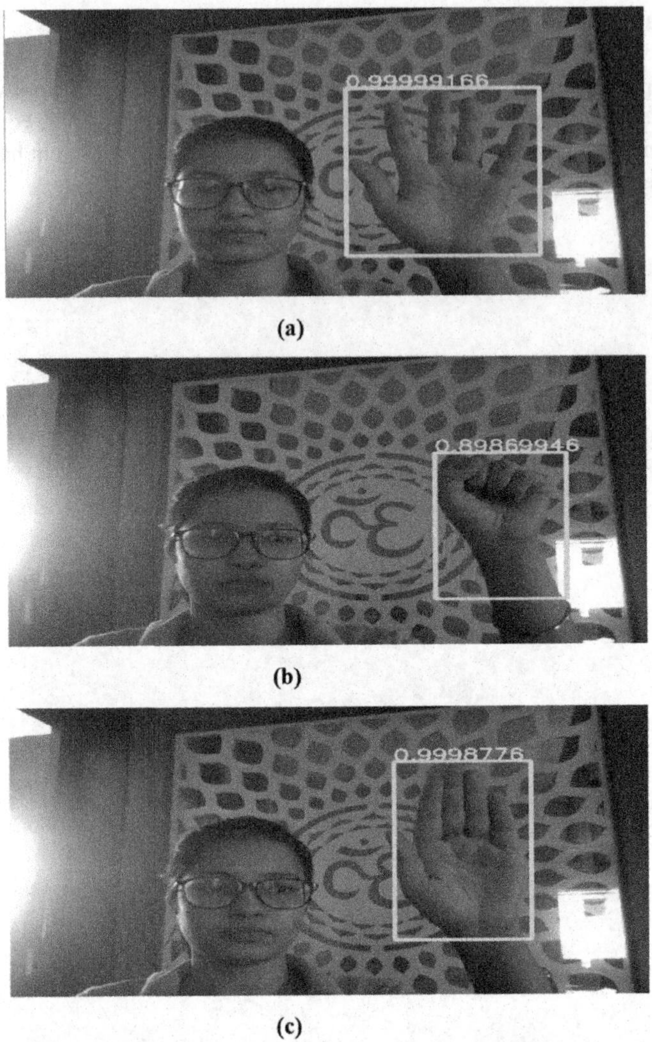

Fig. 4. (a) Detecting hand for tracing in a noisy background. (b) Detecting hand for tracking in a noisy background. (c) Detecting hand for tracking in a noisy background

In methods where frame by frame processing is done, more the number of frames processed per second, and smoother the actions will be performed. In our approach, even without using a GPU, we can process 9 frames per second as shown in Fig. 5. Pseudo code for calculating fps:

```
begin
  fps = 1
  start_time = now()
  num_frames = 0

  while true:
    num_frames += 1
    elapsed_time = seconds(now() - start_time)
    fps = num_frames / elapsed_time

    if fps > 0:
      draw fps
    end If
  end While
end
```

Fig. 5. Figure showing fps while air writing

We are successfully able to write and erase as per the user's desire. Figure 6 (a) and (b) show a demo of air writing and partial erasing.

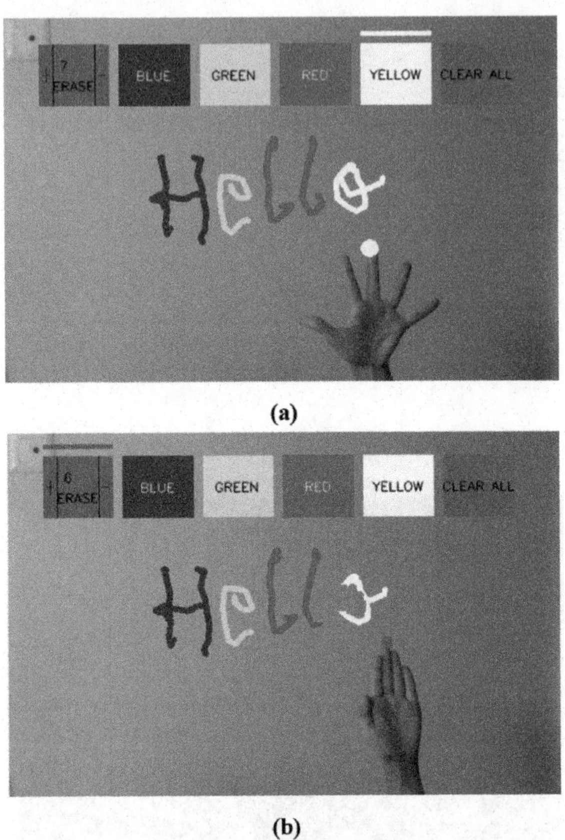

Fig. 6. (a) Demo of air writing. (b) Demo of partial erasing

5 Conclusion

In this paper, we have implemented an air writing approach where tracing and tracking can be accomplished fluently along with adding additional features like an eraser and a color palette to make air writing more intuitive. This air writing method precludes the need for an extra device making it easier and inexpensive for the user. With our proposed method, the user can scribble as well as write linguistic characters or words on the screen without being hampered by the need to write in a continuous motion. The user can use the pen-up-pen-down movements as seen in conventional handwriting comfortably. We divide air writing into two sections: detecting the hand region and tracking and tracing the hand movements. SSD is used to detect the hand of the user. We use the TensorFlow API for training SSD with MobilenetV1. Various hand gestures are used to differentiate between the tracing and the tracking task. We separate the video frames into two parts, one for selecting the air writing tools and the other for actual writing. We process the frames one at a time, use deque to keep track of the coordinates while tracing and either draw or erase the lines as per the user's selection. The person writing can select from four color options. While erasing the size of the eraser can be altered. The "clear all" feature clears the entire writing section and returns a proverbial blank canvas.

Despite the obvious use of air writing: where keyboards cannot be used as an input device, air writing has many other practical applications. For example, classroom and office presentation sessions can be made more interactive. Parents and teachers can use this tool to make their children and students respectively learn writing letters since writing letters in the air can help develop muscle memory for the shape of those alphabets. Also, it is a lot more fun to write with different colors in the air.

References

1. El-Sawah, A., Georganas, N., Petriu, E.: A prototype for 3-D hand tracking and gesture estimation. IEEE Trans. Instrum. Meas. **57**(8), 1627–1636 (2008)
2. Shah, M.N., Rathod, M.R., Agravat, M.J.: A survey on human computer interaction mechanism using finger tracking. Int. J. Comput. Trends Technol. **7**(3), 174–177 (2014)
3. Stenger, B.: Template-based hand pose recognition using multiple cues. In: Narayanan, P.J., Nayar, S.K., Shum, H.-Y. (eds.) ACCV 2006. LNCS, vol. 3852, pp. 551–560. Springer, Heidelberg (2006). https://doi.org/10.1007/11612704_55
4. Park, H.: A Method for Controlling the Mouse Movement Using a Real Time Camera. Brown University, Providence, RI, USA, Department of Computer Science (2008)
5. Prakash, R.M., Deepa, T., Gunasundari, T., Kasthuri, N.: Gesture recognition and fingertip detection for human computer interaction. In: International Conference on Innovations in Information, Embedded and Communication Systems (ICIIECS), pp. 1–4 (2017)
6. Garg, P., Aggarwal, N., Sofat, S.: Vision based hand gesture recognition. Int. J. Comput. Electr. Autom. Control Inf. Eng. **3**(1) (2009)
7. Rautara, S.S., Agrawal, A.: Vision based hand gesture recognition for human computer interaction: a survey. Artif. Intell. Rev. **43**(1), 1–54 (2012)
8. Gupta, R.K.: A comparative analysis of segmentation algorithms for hand gesture recognition. In: 2011 Third International Conference on Computational Intelligence, Communication Systems and Networks (2011)
9. Singha, J., Roy, A., Laskar, R.: Dynamic hand gesture recognition using vision-based approach for human–computer interaction. Neural Comput. Appl. **29**(4), 1129–1141 (2016). https://doi.org/10.1007/s00521-016-2525-z
10. Chen, M., AlRegib, G., Juang, B.-H.: Air-writing recognition, part 1: modeling and recognition of characters, words and connecting motions. IEEE Trans. Hum. Mach. Syst. **46**, 403–413 (2015)
11. Leap motion (2015). https://www.leapmotion.com
12. Chen, M., AlRegib, G., Juang, B.-H.: Air-writing recognition, part 2: detection and recognition of writing activity in continuous stream of motion data. IEEE Trans. Hum. Mach. Syst. **46**, 436–444 (2015)
13. Khan, N.A., Khan, S.M., Kanji, S.J., Iltifat, U.: Use hand gesture to write in air recognize with computer vision. Int. J. Comput. Sci. Netw. Secur. **17**, 51 (2017)

14. Amma, C., Georgi, M., Schultz, T.: Airwriting: a wearable handwriting recognition system. Pers. Ubiquit. Comput. **18**(1), 191–203 (2013). https://doi.org/10.1007/s00779-013-0637-3
15. Mohammadi, S., Maleki, R.: Real-time Kinect-based air-writing system with a novel analytical classifier. Int. J. Doc. Anal. Recogn. (IJDAR) **22**(2), 113–125 (2019). https://doi.org/10.1007/s10032-019-00321-4
16. Islam, R., Mahmud, H., Hasan, Md.K., Rubaiyeat, H.A.: Alphabet recognition in air writing using depth information. In: The Ninth International Conference on Advances in Computer Human Interactions (2016)
17. Github Repository (2018). https://github.com/acl21/Webcam_Paint_OpenCV
18. Liu, W., et al.: SSD: Single Shot MultiBox Detector. Cornell University (2015)
19. Tensorflow Object Detection API Tutorial. https://pythonprogramming.net/introduction-use-tensorflow-object-detection-api-tutorial

Mars Surface Multi-decadal Change Detection Using ISRO's Mars Color Camera (MCC) and Viking Orbiter Images

Indranil Misra[1(✉)], Mukesh Kumar Rohil[2], S. Manthira Moorthi[1], and Debajyoti Dhar[1]

[1] Optical Data Processing Division, Signal and Image Processing Group, Space Applications Centre (ISRO), Ahmedabad 380015, India
[2] Department of Computer Science and Information Systems, Birla Institute of Technology and Science, Pilani, Pilani, Rajasthan, India

Abstract. Mars is a dynamic and active planet in our solar system, which attracts humans due to different geological events continuously reshaping its surface. ISRO's Mars Color Camera (MCC) onboard Mangalyaan spacecraft send more than thousand images of planet Mars at varying spatial resolution, which is of utmost importance for doing surface change detection over Mars. In this paper, we have described a methodology for automated change detection using MCC and Viking images having more than decade separation in image acquisition. The processing steps includes geometric transformation of Viking color image to the same size as MCC, image registration using SIFT based feature matching technique and automated change detection using multi-variate alteration detection (MAD). The workflow chain developed is tested in bi-temporal images from MCC and Viking having more than 20 years' time span difference covering Esylum and Amentia quadrangles of Mars. The result shows the change detection map generated using MCC and Viking images, which focus the changing landscape of Mars due to wind streaks, dust deposits, landslides, lava flows and new impact craters formation.

Keywords: Change detection · SIFT · MAD · MCC · Mars

1 Introduction

To solve the unsolved mysteries of planet Mars ISRO sent Mangalyaan spacecraft on 5th November 2013 from India's spaceport Sriharikota and subsequently Mangalyaan is inserted successfully in Martian orbit on 24th Sep 2014. Mangalyaan contains five instruments for scientific observation over Mars. Mars Color Camera (MCC) onboard Mangalyaan was a RGB bayer pattern camera operates in visible region and capable of imaging Mars at different spatial resolution from 4 km to 15 m due to elliptical orbit of Mangalyaan [1, 2]. The raw bayer data is demosaicked to reconstruct a full color image from the spatially under sampled color channels [3], compute areographic co-ordinates using orbit and attitude information to identify the imaging location on Mars. The processed MCC data is packed and archived as per planetary data system (PDS) standard for dissemination. More than 1000 unique images of MCC are processed that can

S. K. Singh et al. (Eds.): CVIP 2020, CCIS 1378, pp. 25–33, 2021.
https://doi.org/10.1007/978-981-16-1103-2_3

increase the present understanding of Mars in many aspects that include geomorphological analysis, change detection, dust devil/clouds detection at different locations.

The paper highlights processing steps required for automated change detection using MCC and Viking datasets that includes geometric transformation, image registration and multi-variate statistical change detection. MCC PDS data product and Viking Merged Color Mosaic is taken as input to the processing chain. Bi-temporal datasets taken into consideration have more than a decade imaging time difference. The output is change detection map, which automatically infers the surface changes taken place over Mars due to different geological processes.

2 Data Processing Steps

The data processing is triggered with input MCC geometrically corrected data over particular region of Mars and corresponding Viking Color Merged Global Mosaic of Mars having spatial resolution of 920 m is extracted [4]. Digital Image Processing techniques are involved at various stages for the processing of the planetary datasets. The processing steps involved are:

2.1 Overlap Region Extraction

The areographic bounding corners are fetched from MCC geometrically corrected data stored as Geo Tagged Image File Format (Geotiff) [5] and a polygon can be constructed using the corner points. Viking Global Color Mosaic is areo-cut using polygon intersection to get the overlap region as viewed by input MCC data.

2.2 Geometric Transformation

MCC multi date images are captured at varying spatial resolutions due to highly elliptical orbit of Mangalyaan spacecraft. At global scale, MCC large area coverage images are used which are actually obtained in perspective view. These images have been rectified using geometric correction procedure including a map projection step. The extracted Viking image need to be geometrically transformed to MCC map projection such that both MCC and Viking images are into same projection system and need to be resampled to same pixel size as of MCC using standard resampling technique [6].

2.3 SIFT Based Image Registration

Input MCC image need to be aligned at sub-pixel level over geometrically transformed Viking image using image registration process. Feature matching in planetary remote sensing images is a challenging job because of lack of texture and contrast information. The multi-decadal shift in datasets creates additional problem due to lot of change in surface features. Feature Detection is possible with robust operators such as Harris [7], SURF [8] and SIFT [9]. Harris is popular but it is not found optimal for planetary remote sensing images. SURF is fast and reliable than Harris but lacks in extracting stable keypoints in multi sensor images. Scale Invariant Feature Transform (SIFT) is not only a powerful feature detector but also describe the extracted keypoint with 128 element size vector which is subsequently used for feature matching. Experimentally, it is found that SIFT works well for planetary images and can detect relatively stable keypoints.

The SIFT algorithm starts with construction of scale space extrema using Gaussian Kernel [9]. It has been found that Laplacian of Gaussian (LOG) is able to provide stable features and give excellent notion of scales but it is computationally costly. So the Difference of Gaussian (DOG) pyramid is created which is considered to be the close approximation of Laplacian of Gaussian (LOG). Outlier matched points are rejected using mode seeking base technique [10]. Affine transformation model is established with final pruned matched points and MCC image is resampled to generate co-registered data product [11, 12].

2.4 MAD Based Change Detection

In literature, many change detection techniques are found to be applied over remote sensing data to detect changes [13] and we select Multivariate Alteration Detection (MAD) as the one of the most efficient algorithm to detect changes in multispectral bi-temporal satellite images. MAD transformation is based on canonical correlation analysis [14], which is invariant to linear scaling of input data, and is less subject to noise contamination in the image. MAD is also not sensitive to the offset or gain setting of measuring device or to radiometric and atmospheric correction schemes that shows linear relationship with brightness counts. Thus if one uses MAD for change detection on multi-temporal planetary images, preprocessing for radiometric normalization is superfluous [15, 16].

MAD accurately determine the effective magnitude and spatial distribution of the changes by determining the spatially coherent patterns of the major change in an image sequence by retaining the spatial context of the neighborhood pixels. Physical phenomenon observed in remote sensing images generally occupy many pixels in a scene. It is always desirable to estimate the change from the image data itself and MAD provides a statistically rigorous way to retain the spatial context of the data. Thus, MAD performs better than simple image differencing and Principal Component Analysis (PCA).

MAD transformation defined as:

$$\begin{bmatrix} X \\ Y \end{bmatrix} \rightarrow \begin{bmatrix} a_p^T X - b_p^T Y \\ \vdots \\ a_1^T X - b_1^T Y \end{bmatrix} \tag{1}$$

a_i and b_i are the defining coefficients from standard CCA, X and Y are vectors, p is the dimension of the vectors.

MAD transform consists of the variates when we subtract corresponding canonical variates in reverse order. The dispersion matrix of the MAD variates is

$$D\{a^T X - b^T Y\} = 2(I - R) \tag{2}$$

where I is the p × p unit matrix and R is the p × p matrix containing the sorted canonical correlations on the diagonal and zeros off the diagonal.

3 Comparison with Other Techniques

To compare MAD with other change detection techniques, a small simulation is exercised. MCC and Viking image same region is extracted of size 1050 * 1050 pixels. Centre patch of 1000 * 1000 pixels of MCC and corresponding Viking image padded with zero value in all bands, which is geometrically central to a 1050 * 1050 pixels background. Change between two 1050 * 1050 scenes is estimated by computing mean of Image Differencing [17, 18], Principal Component Analysis (PCA) [19, 20] and MAD [15]. Change detected in the region with no changes as indicated with standardized values of the results from different change detection techniques is shown in Table 1. Results shows that MAD performs better than PCA in this kind of situation.

Table 1. Change Detected in No change Region for MCC data

Channels/Components	1	2	3
Image differencing	0	0	0
PCA	0.86	1.62	1.24
MAD	−0.08	−0.12	−0.02

Simple image differencing provides point by point rate of change of the quantity under study but affected significantly by the absolute accuracy and temporal stability of the calibration of the instrument of the satellite. PCA performs better than image differencing but it is not invariant to a linear scaling and affine transformation of the input data sets, which may results in not capturing properly the spatial context information in change detection output. MAD based on canonical variates had better retain the spatial context of the data in the change detection output than PCA and simple image differencing.

4 Processing Workflow Developed

The data processing steps described in step-2 is converted into processing pipeline. The input to the pipeline is MCC geometrically corrected data product in PDS standard. Overlap region is extracted from Viking Merged Color Mosaic and geometrically transformed to reproject the Viking image into same projection system and pixel size as of input MCC. Mars Digital Image Model (MDIM 2.1) is a 231 m spatial resolution global base map of Mars that has improved the absolute accuracy using globally distributed ground control points [21]. MDIM 2.1 act as a ground truth for our change detection workflow and used to validate the final change detection map. The transformed Viking and MCC images are co-registered using SIFT based feature matching technique. Finally MAD based change detection module generates the change detection map for interpretation and analysis. The complete automated processing workflow is shown in Fig. 1.

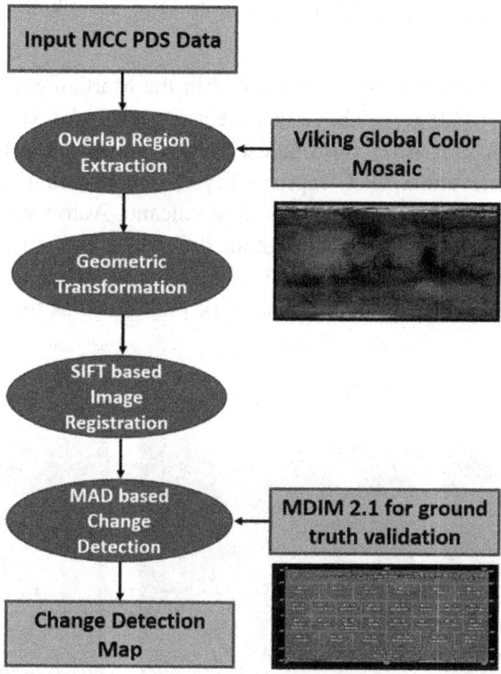

Fig. 1. Automatic processing workflow

5 Results Achieved

The processing workflow is tested in Elysium and Amenthes Quadrangles of Mars which cover large surface area contains mons, impact craters, dust devils and clouds. The input MCC dataset cover this region in Jan/April/July 2016 at varying spatial resolutions and corresponding two decade older Viking Color Mosaic is transformed with the processing workflow shown in Fig. 1. The Fig. 2 shows the transformed Viking Mosaic, input registered MCC image and change detection map covering a large region in a single image shot of MCC. The pink color in change detection map denotes the maximum change happens in impact basin, mons and near Amenthes Fossae.

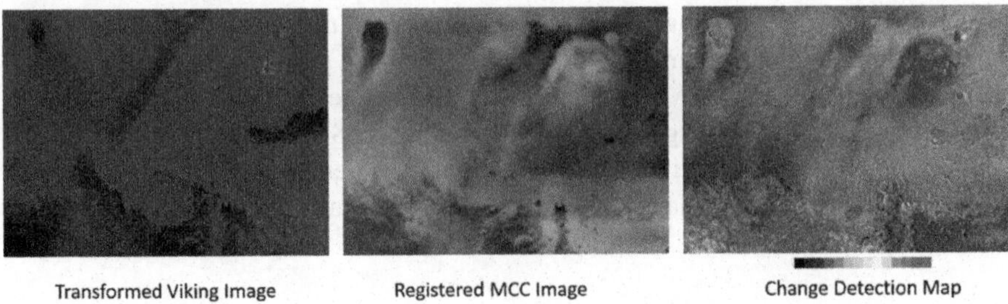

Fig. 2. Large area change detection from MCC and viking images

Elysium mons is a volcano on Mars located in the Martian eastern hemisphere. It stands about 12.6 km (41,000 ft.) above its base, and about 14.1 km (46,000 ft.) above the Martian datum, making it the third tallest Martian mountain in terms of relief and the fourth highest in elevation. MCC captures Elysium mons and it surrounding on 25th April 2016 having clouds over the high standing volcano. Automated change detection map from MCC and Viking shows maximum difference over Elysium mons due to cloud cover and dust devil formation. The Fig. 3 shows the change detection map over Elysium mons, which shows light pink and dark pink color as the maximum surface changes locations.

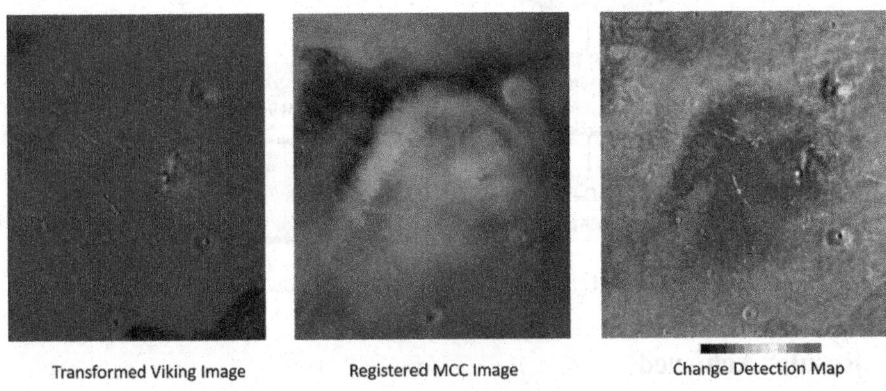

Fig. 3. Change detection over Elysium mons and its surrounding

Utopia basin is the largest easily recognizable impact structure in the northern hemisphere of Mars and exhibits a distinct large scale impact structure. MCC covers this region and compare with older Viking image a big change is identified in this region. The Fig. 4 shows the change detection map over Utopia basin.

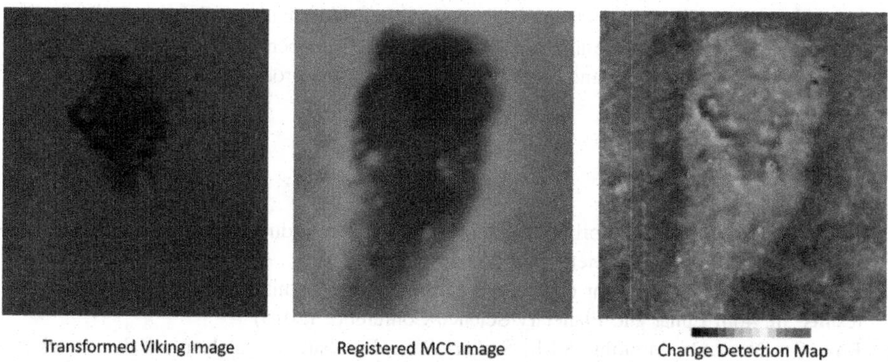

Fig. 4. Change detection over Utopia basin

New impact crater formation found in latest acquisition of MCC image near Amenthes Fossae, which is system of troughs in Amenthes quadrangle of Mars. Such formation is not present in more than two decade older Viking image. The light pink color in change detection map (as in Fig. 5) shows the identified new impact crater (shown in yellow tile) and other changed geological processes.

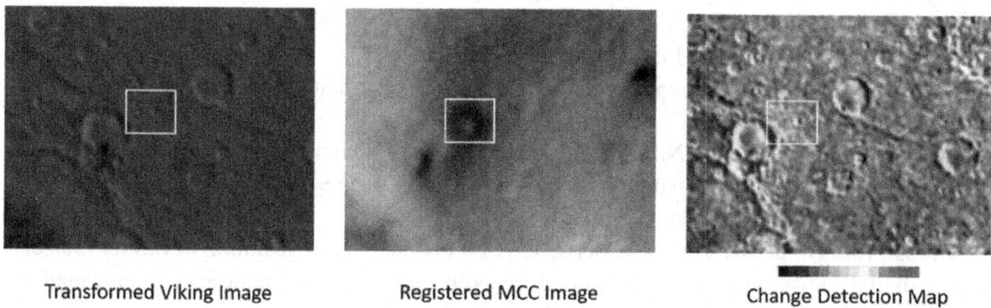

Fig. 5. Change Detection shows new impact crater formation near Amenthes Fossae (Color figure online)

6 Conclusion

Mars Color Camera (MCC) images at varying scales is very useful for understanding the morphological changes over Mars. Multi-temporal images having more than a decade separation helps us to establish a consistent history of a suspected surface change. Automated change detection processing chain described in the paper already shown promising results in identifying changes automatically. The huge MCC image archive can be utilized for change detection studies at different regions of Mars, which finally helps us to monitor the dynamic behavior of dust devils/streaks, clouds and new impact crater formation.

Acknowledgement. The author thanks Director, Space Applications Centre ISRO for his encouragement and support. The author also thanks other members of optical data processing team for carrying out this work and providing feedback on the procedure developed.

References

1. Moorthi, S.M., et al.: Mars orbiter mission: science data products and archive pipeline. In: 46th Lunar and Planetary Science Conference (2015)
2. Arya, A.S., et al.: Mars color camera onboard mars orbiter mission: initial observations & results. In: 46th Lunar and Planetary Science Conference (2015)
3. Roy, S., Dhar, D., Moorthi, S.M., Sarkar, S.S.: Comparative analysis of demosaicking techniques for mars colour camera data. In: IEEE International Conference on Contemporary Computing and Informatics (2014)
4. Mars Viking Global Color Mosaic 925 v1. https://astrogeology.usgs.gov/search/map/Mars/Viking/Color/Mars_Viking_ClrMosaic_global_925m. Accessed 05 Oct 2020
5. Ritter, N., Ruth, M.: GeoTiff Format Specification Document (1995)
6. Misra, I., Moorthi, S.M., Dhar, D.: Techniques developed for large area mars image mosaic using ISRO's mars color camera (MCC) data. Indian J. Geomat. **13**(1), 174–179 (2019)
7. Rublee, E., Rabaud, V., Konolige, K., Bradski, G.: ORB: an efficient alternative to SIFT or SURF. In: 2011 International Conference on Computer Vision, pp. 2564–2571. IEEE, November 2011
8. Bay, H., Tuytelaars, T., Van Gool, L.: Surf: speeded up robust features. In: Leonardis, A., Bischof, H., Pinz, A. (eds.) ECCV 2006. LNCS, vol. 3951, pp. 404–417. Springer, Heidelberg (2006). https://doi.org/10.1007/11744023_32
9. Lowe, D.G.: Object recognition from local scale-invariant features. In: International Conference on Computer Vision, pp. 1150–1157 (1999)
10. Kupfer, B., Netanyahu, N.S., Shimshoni, I.: An efficient SIFT-based mode-seeking algorithm for sub-pixel registration of remotely sensed images. IEEE Geosci. Remote Sens. Lett. **12**(2), 379–383 (2014)
11. Xin, X., Liu, B., Di, K., Jia, M., Oberst, J.: High-precision co-registration of orbiter imagery and digital elevation model constrained by both geometric and photometric information. ISPRS J. Photogramm. Remote. Sens. **144**, 28–37 (2018)
12. Misra, I., Sharma, V., Manthira Moorthi, S., Dhar, D.: An approach for generation of multi temporal co-registered optical remote sensing images from Resourcesat-2/2A sensors. Indian J. Geomat. **13**(1), 174–179 (2019)
13. Singh, A.: Review article digital change detection techniques using remotely-sensed data. Int. J. Remote Sens. **10**(6), 989–1003 (1989)
14. Hotelling, H.: Relations between two sets of variates. York, Biometrika **XXVIII**, 321–377 (1936)
15. Canty, M.J., Nielsen, A.A., Schmidt, M.: Automatic radiometric normalization of multitemporal satellite imagery. Remote Sens. Environ. **3–4**, 441–451 (2004)
16. Nielsen, A.A., Conradsen, K., Simpson, J.J.: Multivariate alteration detection (MAD) and MAF postprocessing in multispectral, bitemporal image data: New approaches to change detection studies. Remote Sens. Environ. **64**(1), 1–19 (1998)
17. Deng, J.S., Wang, K., Deng, Y.H., Qi, G.J.: PCA-based land-use change detection and analysis using multitemporal and multisensor satellite data. Int. J. Remote Sens. **29**(16), 4823–4838 (2008)

18. Fung, T., LeDrew, E.: Application of principal components analysis to change detection. Photogram. Eng. Remote Sens. **53**(12), 1649–1658 (1987)
19. Ridd, M.K., Liu, J.: A comparison of four algorithms for change detection in an urban environment. Remote Sens. Environ. **63**(2), 95–100 (1998)
20. Fung, T., LeDrew, E.: For change detection using various accuracy. Photogram. Eng. Remote Sens. **54**(10), 1449–1454 (1988)
21. Archinal, B.A., et al.: A new Mars digital image model (MDIM 2.1) control network. Int. Arch. Photogram. Remote Sens. **35**, B4 (2004)

Deep over and Under Exposed Region Detection

Darshita Jain(✉) and Shanmuganathan Raman

Indian Institute of Technology, Gandhinagar, Gandhinagar, India
{darshita.jain,shanmuga}@iitgn.ac.in

Abstract. The camera sensors often fail to capture all the brightness intensities present in the visible spectrum of light. This is due to the limited dynamic range of the sensor elements. When bright light falls on a camera sensor, it is not appropriately measured. The recorded brightness values that fall outside the sensor's dynamic range are stored as the minimum or maximum value depending on the bit-depth of the sensor. This results in a loss of information and undesirable artifacts in the form of blown-out areas, referred to as over- and under-exposed regions. In this study, we propose to detect these areas in an image using deep learning tools. Our approach uses semantic segmentation to mark the under, over, and correctly exposed regions in the image. We have created a new dataset containing 4928 images to train and test the performance of the model using a pre-trained state-of-the-art model architecture and re-trained it on our custom dataset. To the best of our knowledge, this is the first attempt to use semantic segmentation and transfer learning methods to identify these regions in an end-to-end fashion. We obtain a Dice score and a Jaccard score of 0.93 and 0.86, respectively, which are better than the state-of-the-art methods. The quantitative and qualitative results show that the proposed method outperforms several existing methods for identifying the over and the under-exposed regions. We will make the dataset public for research work.

Keywords: Camera response function · DeepLabv3 · High dynamic range · Semantic segmentation · Under exposure · Over exposure

1 Introduction

The dynamic range of a real world scene is defined as the ratio of the brightest intensity value to the darkest intensity value, and it is considerably high i.e. 100000:1 [2]. Unlike the human eye, the dynamic range of an optical device is physically limited by its bit-depth, that is the number of bits used for storing the captured scene information, and therefore, it cannot record the entire range of light intensities present in the real world [3]. Whenever the exposure of any part of the image falls outside the dynamic range of the camera sensor, then the pixels corresponding to that region get saturated and appear white (overexposed) or black (underexposed) in the image. These regions lack complete scene

S. K. Singh et al. (Eds.): CVIP 2020, CCIS 1378, pp. 34–45, 2021.
https://doi.org/10.1007/978-981-16-1103-2_4

information and result in undesirable artifacts in the captured images. The over-exposed pixels are characterized by high brightness, low chromaticity and loss of details [15]. A single image taken by a camera cannot contain the entire scene detail because different regions of the scene require different camera exposure settings in order to be captured accurately. Therefore, most of the imaging data available online is having a low dynamic range. Figure 1 shows a scene captured with different camera exposures.

(a) (b) (c)

Fig. 1. (a) Original scene (b) Under-exposed image (c) Over-exposed image.

The concept of HDR imaging was introduced to reproduce a greater dynamic range of luminous intensities than what is possible with the standard optical devices. The HDR images are encoded as a 32-bit floating-point image, which can store more information than the 8-bit RGB images. The camera response function (CRF), plays an important role in HDR imaging and by providing a relationship between the actual scene irradiance and the captured brightness value in an image [5]. Ideally, there should be a linear relationship between the scene irradiance and the brightness values in the image. However, this is not the case in the real world scenario because of the limited dynamic range and bit-depth of the camera.

The exposure correction and HDR imaging deals with recovering the lost details in the under-exposed and over-exposed regions [6–8]. However, we need to identify the boundaries of these regions to process them in prior. The results of the exposure correction methods can be improved if the over and under-exposed regions are detected accurately. We have proposed a deep learning method that uses semantic segmentation and transfer learning to detect the over-exposed, under-exposed, and correctly-exposed regions in a given image.

The use of semantic segmentation is inspired by its usage in applications like object detection [9], medical imaging [10], and land coverage area detection using satellite images [11]. In our case, the pixels that belong to over-exposed regions will share similar properties like high brightness and low chromaticity and can be grouped using semantic segmentation. The proposed method can help distinguishing the white color and the blown-out region, that appears to be white in an image. Transfer learning enables training a deep-learning model even with a smaller dataset. Given a pre-trained model trained on a large dataset, we can either use it as a feature extractor for our task or use the pre-trained weights for initializing the weights of a new model [12].

The following are the key contributions of our work.

1. Detection and generation of segmentation maps corresponding to over, under, and correctly exposed regions. The results of this model can potentially aid the process of exposure correction.
2. A threshold independent method to detect over- and under-exposed regions in an image.
3. A new dataset of 4928 images that can be used for other tasks like exposure correction, object detection, segmentation, etc.

We start by discussing some of the existing approaches in Sect. 2. Section 3.1 describes the details of dataset collection, augmentation and annotation. The network architecture is described in Sect. 3.2. The experimental settings are given in Sect. 3.3. The results and discussion are detailed in Sect. 4, followed by the conclusion in Sect. 5.

2 Related Work

The existing methods for exposure correction attempts to first detect the over-exposed regions in an image. Over-exposure region detection (OER) detection involves identifying pixels having high brightness levels and fewer details or chromaticity. In [6,7], authors have defined specific thresholds to determine these bright regions. An assumption was made that if the brightness value of a pixel is high then the corresponding chromaticity value of the pixel will be low. If a pixel's brightness value exceeds the threshold value, then it is classified as overexposed. Guo's method [8] makes use of the pixel's color and brightness values in the CIELAB color space to generate an overexposed map of the image. Thresholding is later applied on this map to detect the associated regions. This method gave better results than the previous thresholding methods because it took into account both the brightness and the chromaticity value of the pixel. Some methods deploy thresholds for all the three RGB color channels to detect the OERs [13,14]. This leads to an increase in the number of false positives because the correctly exposed pixels are classified as over-exposed because of using a single threshold value for all the images. In all these works, a fixed threshold was used to determine the over-exposure. Due to this, the method was not able to distinguish between the actual white-colored and the blown-out regions, with the latter being classified as white. In [15], a human perception-based method is introduced to detect the OERs in which each pixel's saturation value is thresholded. There exists a deep learning method [16], which can directly covert LDR images into HDR in an end-to-end manner. In [17], a convolutional neural network model is proposed for exposure correction. In both of these deep learning-based approaches, there is no intermediate step of detecting the over and under-exposed regions. Therefore, in some cases, it modifies the intensity of unsaturated regions. Hence, it is necessary to adequately mark the regions which need to be processed to enhance the quality of the results.

A deep learning approach for semantic segmentation made use of a fully connected convolutional network as proposed in [18]. This method was capable of generating segmentation maps for any size of images and was faster than the patch-based method. Further, almost every other segmentation model was based on this paradigm. One challenge associated with using CNN was the use of pooling layers. They are capable of reducing the spatial dimension of the input while increasing the field of view [19]. However, during this process, it discards the location from where the useful features were extracted. For generating segmentation maps, we need to preserve this information. UNet model [19] has an encoder-decoder architecture. The encoder layer reduces the input's spatial information while the decoder layer reconstructs the object details to generate the segmentation maps. SegNet architecture [4] stored the max-pooling indices during the encoder phase and forwarded them to the decoder to enhance the segmentation output resolution. Google Research have proposed several effective models for segmentation task [1,20,21], which make use of atrous convolution, atrous spatial pyramid pooling, and encoder-decoder architecture using ResNet [22] in the encoder phase. One such model is DeepLabv3. It is trained on the subset of the COCO dataset [28]. We have used the weights of the pre-trained model as the starting weights and re-trained the entire network on our custom dataset because our segmentation classes were different from the segmentation classes used in the pre-trained model. While atrous convolution allows us to capture essential features from a larger effective field of view without increasing the number of parameters, The encoder-decoder architecture helps in the effective reconstruction of the object details.

3 Method

Our approach is to divide an image into over, under, and correctly exposed regions by grouping the pixels with similar properties. We show that this can be accomplished by using semantic segmentation. Transfer learning enabled us to use the state-of-the-art network for performing the semantic segmentation task. Instead of training an entire network from scratch, we started with the weights of the pre-trained network and modified its weights by re-training the model on our dataset. Figure 2 depicts the workflow of our approach.

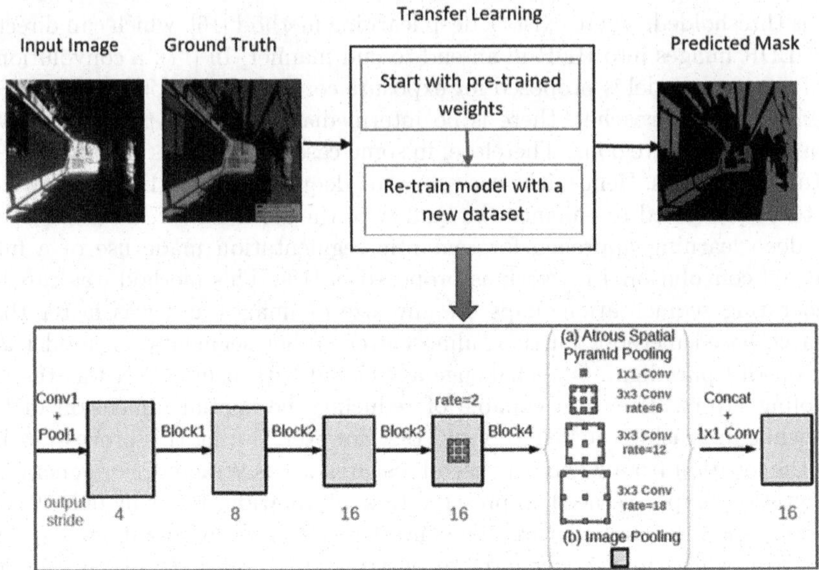

Fig. 2. Block diagram depicting our approach.

3.1 Dataset

We require a dataset consisting of images with both over- and under-exposed regions for this task. To create the dataset, we have collected around 352 HDR images from various sources like [23]. LDR images with different exposure times can be generated from a given HDR image, if the corresponding camera response function (CRF) [5] is known. The CRF provides a mapping of the image irradiance at the image plane to the measured intensity values. As the HDR images were collected from different sources, it was essential to derive a generalized CRF. The CRF was estimated by interpolating one of the irradiance and intensity mappings given in the Database of Response Function (DoRF) [5]. Consider the following equation.

$$I = f(Et) \tag{1}$$

Here, I is the intensity, f is the CRF, E is the irradiance and t is the exposure time. Equation 1 was used to generate LDR images with 14 different exposure times by varying the value of t. Hence, the dataset contains a total of 4928 (352×14) images.

Our segmentation task is different from the usual segmentation tasks because the over and under-exposed regions do not have a predefined shape or boundary. We used an online image annotation tool, called Labelme [24], for manually annotating these images. Instead of annotating all the 4928 images manually, we have selected those images in which both white-colored, as well as overexposed regions, are present. By using the tone mapped HDR images as a reference, we were able to distinguish between the two regions and annotate them accordingly. For the rest of the images, a mix of thresholds was used to annotate the images because when only the over-exposed regions are present in an image then the thresholding methods work fine.

The segmentation masks generated by the LabelMe tool assign a separate color for each of the predefined classes. Thus, we created a mapping between the colors and the corresponding class representation. We have used thresholding to generate the masks of images having only over-exposed regions and no white-colored areas [6]. Figure 3 shows an annotated image using the LabelMe tool.

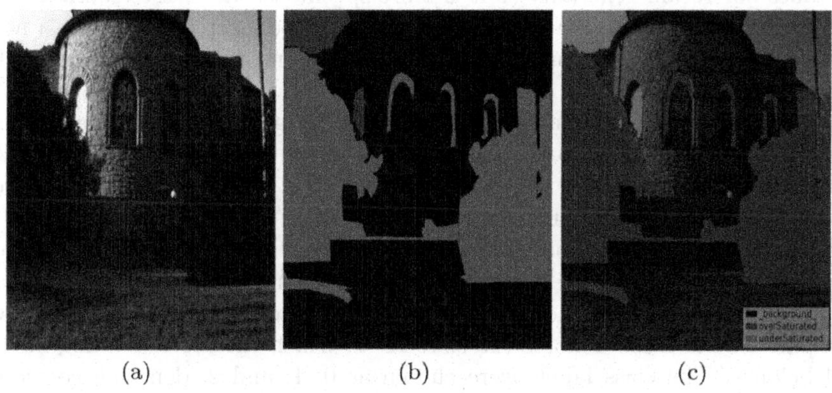

Fig. 3. (a) Input image (b) Ground truth segmentation mask annotated by using LabelMe tool (c) Segmentation mask overlaid on the input image.

3.2 Network Architecture

There are several deep learning methods for performing semantic segmentation. We have deployed the DeepLabv3 model. Two powerful concepts used in DeepLabv3 [1,20,21] were (a) Atrous Convolution (b) Atrous Spatial Pyramid Pooling, as shown in Fig. 2. Atrous convolution is a generalized form of convolutional operation. It introduces a parameter r for controlling the field of view and provides a global view of the image, keeping the number of parameters fixed. Equation 2 illustrates how to perform atrous convolution. The rate r denotes the dilation rate. The kernel is generated by inserting $r - 1$ holes along each spatial dimension. The input x is convolved with the generated kernel. Note that when $r = 1$, it is the regular convolution operation. The atrous spatial pyramid pooling combines atrous convolution having different dilation rates with spatial pyramid pooling [25] to extract multi-scale features effectively.

$$y[i] = \sum_{k} x\left[i + r \cdot k\right] w\left[k\right] \tag{2}$$

3.3 Implementation

The Torchvision [26] package of PyTorch [27] contains a pre-trained DeepLabv3 model with a Resnet-101 [22] encoder. This model is trained on a subset of the COCO dataset [28], which contains the 20 categories present in the Pascal VOC 2012 dataset [29]. We started with the pre-trained weights and gradually updated them by re-training the model with the hand curated dataset. The last layer does not retain generality as it is more specific to the classes contained in the original dataset [30]. We replaced the last fully-connected layer with a new classification layer with 3 output nodes corresponding to the three differently exposed regions.

In the preprocessing of the dataset, only those images were chosen for training in which pixels belonging to all the three categories were present. Out of 4928 total images, 3450 images satisfied this criteria. The DeepLabv3 model was re-trained by optimizing the cross-entropy loss using Adadelta optimizer with a learning rate of 10^{-4} and batch size of 4. A small learning rate was used to ensure we did not distort the pre-trained weights. The train-test split ratio was 0.7. The input images and the corresponding masks were of dimension 480×480. Each pixel of the mask denotes the class ID to which the corresponding image pixel belongs. The class labels were chosen as 0, 1, and 2, denoting correctly exposed, underexposed, and overexposed pixels, respectively. Hence, for a batch size of 'N', the input dimension will be (N × 480 × 480). The network output consists of three channels, each corresponding to the probabilities of a particular class. The overall dimension of the output was (N × 480 × 480 × 3). By taking the $argmax$, we selected the class labels out of 0, 1, and 2, with the maximum probability. We have trained the model on Google Colaboratory notebook using the standard GPU runtime environment.

4 Experimental Results and Discussion

In order to evaluate the performance of the model on our dataset, we deployed the two widely used metrics: the Dice score (F1 score), and the Jaccard score (Intersection over Union score). These two metrics also works with imbalanced data where the number of pixels belonging to one class dominates the number of pixels belonging to other classes. For some images in our dataset, over-exposed regions were more than the under-exposed regions, and vice versa. After re-training the model for 30 epochs, we obtained a Dice score of 0.93 and a Jaccard

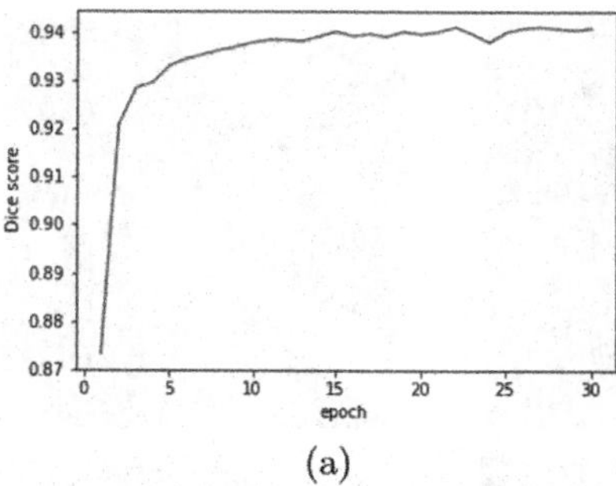

(a)

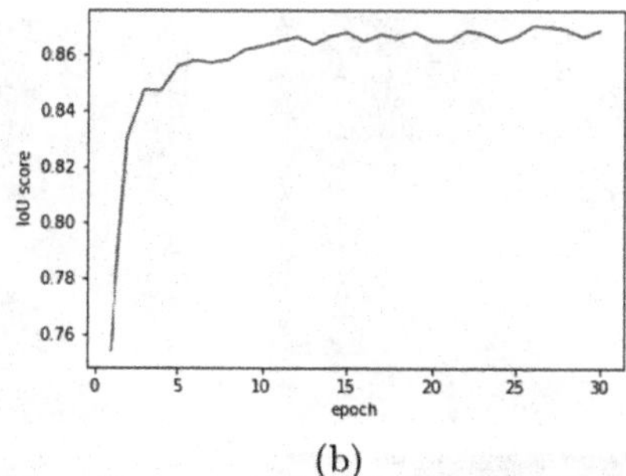

(b)

Fig. 4. (a) Dice Score and (b) Intersection over Union Score vs Epochs during training on validation set.

Table 1. Quantitative comparison among Brightness thresholding method [7], Over-exposed map method [8], and the proposed method using Jaccard score and Dice score.

Evaluation metric	Brightness thresholding [7]	Over-exposed map [8]	Our method
Jaccard score	0.77	0.83	**0.86**
Dice score	0.60	0.76	**0.93**

score of 0.86 on our test dataset. Figure 4 shows the training curve for the Dice and the Jaccard coefficient. As the pre-trained weights of the DeepLabv3 were pretty accurate, most of the learning happened in the initial five epochs and the model converged after completing 30 epochs. The output of our model is shown in Fig. 5. The colors yellow, green, and black denote the over-exposed, under-exposed, and correctly exposed regions.

Table 1, shows that our method clearly outperforms both the brightness thresholding [7] and the Over-exposed map method [8]. We have tested all the three methods on the hand-curated dataset. The previous methods gave accurate results when the input image did not contain both whites and highlights. However, for an input image with both whites and highlights, these methods failed to distinguish between the two. This accounts for their comparatively lower score.

Both the methods mentioned above first detect OERs. However, they can not correctly classify whether a pixel is white colored or an over-exposed one. From Fig. 6, it can be seen that our proposed method is able to distinguish between white colored and an over-exposed pixel to a great extent when compared with the other two methods. It is important to note, that after post-processing, we have extracted only the overexposed regions from our final output. This is done to compare the overexposed regions detected by the previous methods and avoid confusion while examining them.

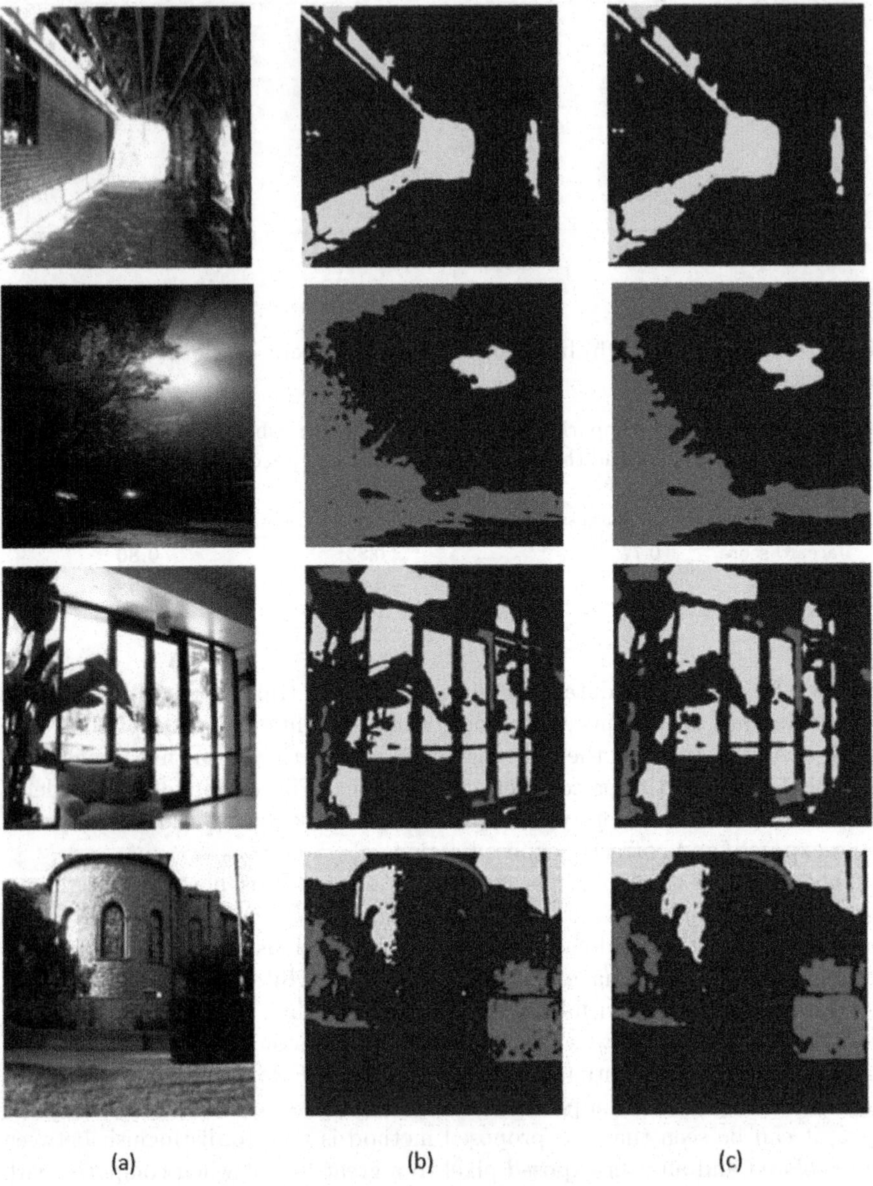

Fig. 5. (a) Input image (b) Ground truth segmentation mask (c) Predicted segmentation mask.

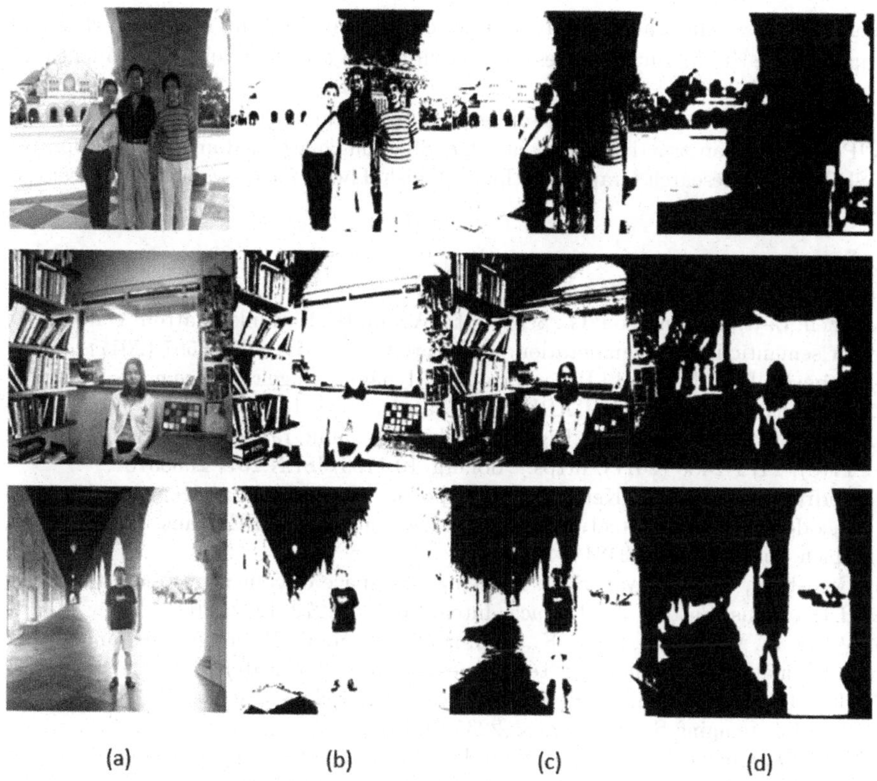

(a) (b) (c) (d)

Fig. 6. (a) Input Test Image, (b) OER detected by [7], (c) OER detected by [8], (d) OER detected by our approach.

5 Conclusion

We have proposed a deep network based transfer learning approach to detect over, under, and correctly exposed regions in an image. This is the first time where semantic segmentation is used to identify these regions. Unlike the previous methods [6,7], our approach is independent of the usage of any threshold value to classify pixels of the image as over- and under-exposed. As the pixel values in an over-exposed region are clipped at the maximum value (255 for an 8-bit image), simple thresholding methods fail to distinguish between the clipped values and the color denoted by the value 255. Our work can also aid the exposure correction task in which the first step is to primarily identify the saturated regions. The proposed method can be used even in the scenarios where ground truth images are not available.

Our approach can also work with other existing segmentation models like UNet [19], SegNet [4], etc. We would like to extend this work to detect the over- and under-exposed regions in a video. The output of our model can be fed to an exposure correction module to recover the lost details in the over-exposed input image. Further, the dataset can be expanded to include images from different domains, like the medical images, to contribute to different related applications.

Acknowledgement. The authors are grateful to the area chairs and the reviewers of CVIP for their constructive comments. Dr. Shanmuganathan Raman was supported by SERB Core Research Grant. We thank Ashish Tiwari for his valuable discussions.

References

1. Chen, L.-C., Papandreou, G., Schroff, F., Adam, H.: Rethinking atrous convolution for semantic image segmentation. arXiv preprint arXiv:1706.05587 (2017)
2. Debevec, P.E., Malik, J.: Recovering high dynamic range radiance maps from photographs. In: ACM SIGGRAPH 2008 Classes, pp. 1–10 (2008)
3. Griffiths, D.J., Wicks, A.: High speed high dynamic range video. IEEE Sens. J. **17**(8), 2472–2480 (2017). https://doi.org/10.1109/JSEN.2017.2668378
4. Badrinarayanan, V., Kendall, A., Cipolla, R.: SegNet: a deep convolutional encoder-decoder architecture for image segmentation. IEEE Trans. Pattern Anal. Mach. Intell. **39**(12), 2481–2495 (2017)
5. Grossberg, M.D., Nayar, S.K.: Modeling the space of camera response functions. IEEE Trans. Pattern Anal. Mach. Intell. **26**(10), 1272–1282 (2004)
6. Wang, L., Wei, L.-Y., Zhou, K., Guo, B., Shum, H.-Y.: High dynamic range image hallucination. In: Rendering Techniques, pp. 321–326 (2007)
7. Hou, L., Ji, H., Shen, Z.: Recovering over-/underexposed regions in photographs. SIAM J. Imaging Sci. **6**(4), 2213–2235 (2013)
8. Guo, D., Cheng, Y., Zhuo, S., Sim, T.: Correcting over-exposure in photographs. In: 2010 IEEE Computer Society Conference on Computer Vision and Pattern Recognition, pp. 515–521. IEEE (2010)
9. Salscheider, N.O.: Simultaneous object detection and semantic segmentation. arXiv preprint arXiv:1905.02285 (2019)
10. Taghanaki, S.A., Abhishek, K., Cohen, J.P., Cohen-Adad, J., Hamarneh, G.: Deep semantic segmentation of natural and medical images: a review. Artif. Intell. Rev. **54**, 1–42 (2020)
11. Schmitt, M., Prexl, J., Ebel, P., Liebel, L., Zhu, X.X.: Weakly supervised semantic segmentation of satellite images for land cover mapping-challenges and opportunities. arXiv preprint arXiv:2002.08254 (2020)
12. Pan, S.J., Yang, Q.: A survey on transfer learning. IEEE Trans. Knowl. Data Eng. **22**(10), 1345–1359 (2009)
13. Di, X., Doutre, C., Nasiopoulos, P.: Correction of clipped pixels in color images. IEEE Trans. Visual Comput. Graph. **17**(3), 333–344 (2010)
14. Rouf, M., Lau, C., Heidrich, W.: Gradient domain color restoration of clipped highlights. In: 2012 IEEE Computer Society Conference on Computer Vision and Pattern Recognition Workshops, pp. 7–14. IEEE (2012)
15. Yoon, Y.-J., Byun, K.-Y., Lee, D.-H., Jung, S.-W., Ko, S.-J.: A new human perception-based over-exposure detection method for color images. Sensors **14**(9), 17159–17173 (2014)
16. Marnerides, D., Bashford-Rogers, T., Hatchett, J., Debattista, K.: ExpandNet: a deep convolutional neural network for high dynamic range expansion from low dynamic range content. In: Computer Graphics Forum, vol. 37, pp. 37–49. Wiley Online Library (2018)

17. Gao, Z., Edirisinghe, E., Chesnokov, S.: OEC-CNN: a simple method for over-exposure correction in photographs. Electron. Imaging **2020**(10), 182-1 (2020)
18. Long, J., Shelhamer, E., Darrell, T.: Fully convolutional networks for semantic segmentation. In: Proceedings of the IEEE Conference on Computer Vision and Pattern Recognition, pp. 3431–3440 (2015)
19. Ronneberger, O., Fischer, P., Brox, T.: U-Net: convolutional networks for biomedical image segmentation. In: Navab, N., Hornegger, J., Wells, W.M., Frangi, A.F. (eds.) MICCAI 2015. LNCS, vol. 9351, pp. 234–241. Springer, Cham (2015). https://doi.org/10.1007/978-3-319-24574-4_28
20. Chen, L.-C., Papandreou, G., Kokkinos, I., Murphy, K., Yuille, A.L.: Semantic image segmentation with deep convolutional nets and fully connected CRFs. arXiv preprint arXiv:1412.7062 (2014)
21. Chen, L.-C., Papandreou, G., Kokkinos, I., Murphy, K., Yuille, A.L.: DeepLab: semantic image segmentation with deep convolutional nets, atrous convolution, and fully connected CRFs. IEEE transactions on pattern analysis and machine intelligence **40**(4), 834–848 (2017)
22. He, K., Zhang, X., Ren, S., Sun, J.: Deep residual learning for image recognition. In: Proceedings of the IEEE Conference on Computer Vision and Pattern Recognition, pp. 770–778 (2016)
23. Liu, S., et al.: Switchable temporal propagation network. In: Proceedings of the European Conference on Computer Vision (ECCV), pp. 87–102 (2018)
24. Russell, B.C., Torralba, A., Murphy, K.P., Freeman, W.T.: LabelMe: a database and web-based tool for image annotation. Int. J. Comput. Vis. **77**(1–3), 157–173 (2008)
25. He, K., Zhang, X., Ren, S., Sun, J.: Spatial pyramid pooling in deep convolutional networks for visual recognition. IEEE Trans. Pattern Anal. Mach. Intell. **37**(9), 1904–1916 (2015)
26. Marcel, S., Rodriguez, Y.: Torchvision the machine-vision package of torch. In: Proceedings of the 18th ACM International Conference on Multimedia, pp. 1485–1488 (2010)
27. Ketkar, N.: Introduction to PyTorch. In: Ketkar, N. (ed.) Deep Learning with Python, pp. 195–208. Springer, Heidelberg (2017). https://doi.org/10.1007/978-1-4842-2766-4_12
28. Lin, T.-Y., et al.: Microsoft COCO: common objects in context. In: Fleet, D., Pajdla, T., Schiele, B., Tuytelaars, T. (eds.) ECCV 2014. LNCS, vol. 8693, pp. 740–755. Springer, Cham (2014). https://doi.org/10.1007/978-3-319-10602-1_48
29. Everingham, M., Van Gool, L., Williams, C.K.I., Winn, J., Zisserman, A.: The pascal visual object classes (VOC) challenge. Int. J. Comput. Vis. **88**(2), 303–338 (2010)
30. Minhas, M.S.: Transfer Learning for Semantic Segmentation using PyTorch DeepLab v3. GitHub.com/msminhas93, 12 September 2019. https://github.com/msminhas93/DeepLabv3FineTuning

DeepHDR-GIF: Capturing Motion in High Dynamic Range Scenes

Chandan Kumar(✉), Ameya Deshpande(✉), and Shanmuganathan Raman(✉)

IIT Gandhinagar, Gandhinagar, Gujrat, India
chandan.kumar@alumni.iitgn.ac.in, shanmuga@iitgn.ac.in

Abstract. In this work, we have proposed a novel computational photography application to generate a Graphics Interchange Format (GIF) image corresponding to High Dynamic Range (HDR) scene involving motion. Though HDR image and GIF image are prevalent in the computational photography community for a long time, according to our literature survey, this is the maiden attempt to combine them in a single framework. Like most other HDR image generation algorithms, the first step in the proposed framework is to capture a sequence of multi-exposure (−2EV, 0EV, 2EV) low dynamic range (LDR) images. The decided exposures (−2EV, 0EV, 2EV) are varied in a round-robin fashion, and continuous frames are captured to get adequate information about the motion of the scene. The next step is to combine sets of three consecutive multi-exposure LDR images to generate HDR images. Further, we take two successive HDR images and produced three in-between frames in a binary-search manner. At last, generated HDR frames and interpolated frames are merged in to a GIF image, which depicts the motion in the scene without losing out on the dynamic range of the scene. The proposed framework works on different types of dynamic scenes, Object movement or Camera Movement, and the results are observed to be visually pleasing without any noticeable artifacts.

Keywords: Computational photography · HDR imaging

1 Introduction

With the advancement in image sensors, cameras can capture images with increasingly more details. However, the amount of information preserved in an image mainly depends on the illumination in the scene. The dynamic range of a real-world scene is 10^6: 1 [3]. We can not capture such a wide range of intensity levels by a standard low dynamic range camera (LDR) because of sensor saturation. The bit-depth of commonly available off-the-shelf cameras is 8. Hence, it maps a vast range of intensity levels to only one of the 255 levels. Therefore, the contrast and some of the essential details present in the scene are lost in the captured image [3]. There are two ways to overcome this problem. Firstly, we can use a high dynamic range camera having a large photon capturing ability

S. K. Singh et al. (Eds.): CVIP 2020, CCIS 1378, pp. 46–57, 2021.
https://doi.org/10.1007/978-981-16-1103-2_5

of the sensor. Therefore, we can capture all the details present in the image in a single attempt. However, this approach is expensive and impractical, as well. Thus, the utility of such a camera is very limited to research purposes only. The alternate method is to take a series of images having different exposures by the off-the-shelf camera. It fuses these images to generate an HDR image broader contrast range present in the real scene. This way, the over-exposed image brings the information from the darker part of the scene while the under-exposed image highlights the information from the brighter part of the scene [15].

In a real-world scenario, things are not always static. Therefore, we have to pay a special care for the HDR image corresponding to a dynamic scene. The position of the object of interest may change while capturing a series of LDR images corresponding to the dynamic scene. We select one reference image from this set of frames and then align the remaining images to the reference image. Finally, the set of LDR frames are fused to generate an HDR image. In this way, the final generated HDR image has the same positions of objects as that of the reference image without any ghosting artifacts.

If only the objects present in a scene are of our concern, we can opt for an HDR image. However, sometimes, we also want to capture their motion. In this case, an HDR video comes in handy. Compared to HDR Imaging, HDR video has got less attention because of the complexity of the problem. It requires heavy cameras that use complex optical systems [16] and sensors [21] for shooting directly. However, we can still describe a dynamic scene by HDR-GIF. We have proposed an approach to generate HDR-GIF with the help of an LDR camera only. We have taken a series of LDR images with different exposures (under, normal, over) by a DSLR camera corresponding to a dynamic scene. We merge three successive LDR images considering the middle one as the reference image and generate HDR images. After that, between each successive HDR image, we generate three intermediate temporally coherent frames in a binary search fashion. Finally, we merge them to form an HDR-GIF image. The primary contributions of this work are:

1. We have generated temporally coherent HDR-GIF images for different scenes by combining all the HDR images from the HDR stack and the in-between generated HDR frames for that particular scene.
2. We are the first ones to attempt this problem, to the best of our knowledge.

In Sect. 2, we mention some of the works related to HDR imaging. We also explain some trivial methods to generate an HDR image and some deep learning techniques that can create HDR images. Section 3 describes all the steps involved in the generation of HDR-GIF from a stack of multi-exposure images. In Sect. 4, we evaluate the generated tone-mapped HDR frames using a no-reference quality metric. In Sect. 5, we see the limitation and future work for the proposed HDR-GIF work.

2 Related Work

In computational photography, HDR imaging is one of the challenging areas of research. There are many breakthroughs in this domain. The popularity of HDR imaging comes after the advancement in digital cameras. Most of the software-based techniques require LDR stack, exposure information, and shutter speed or relative exposure values (EV) to generate an HDR image. In HDR, many works use conventional computational photography as well as deep learning approaches.

One of the initial works is [4]. In this work, they recover the radiance maps from multi-exposure photographs. In [18], the author has taken care of the translation motion of the handheld camera while taking a stack of multi-exposure LDR images. The generated HDR image can be displayed on a typical display after tone mapping the HDR image [2,8,14]. Mertens *et al.* proposed the algorithms to directly combine the LDR stack images and produce a high contrast LDR image [10]. Li and Kang used a median filter and a recursive filter, which helps to improve the weight map used to decide the weight of pixels from different images [7]. There are many algorithms proposed for the dynamic scenes as well, where the main challenge is to handle the ghosting artifacts [6,9,13]. There is another category of deghosting algorithms which employs some method of image alignment. The primary advantage of these algorithms is to gather information from dynamic pixel locations. The initial attempts in this category produce promising results but work only for rigid object motions in the scenes [1,17,20].

There are deep-learning approaches for generating HDR images, from single and multiple images. In [5], they have used a convolution neural network (CNN) to generate an HDR image from a single exposure. In [19], the authors use three parallel encoders for the three input images with skip connection andbased techniques require LDR stack, exposure information, and shutter speed or training the model end to end. In [12], the author uses an encoder-decoder architecture with a skip connection. This model is trained on a video dataset where the network learns to predict the intermediate frames from two consecutive frames.

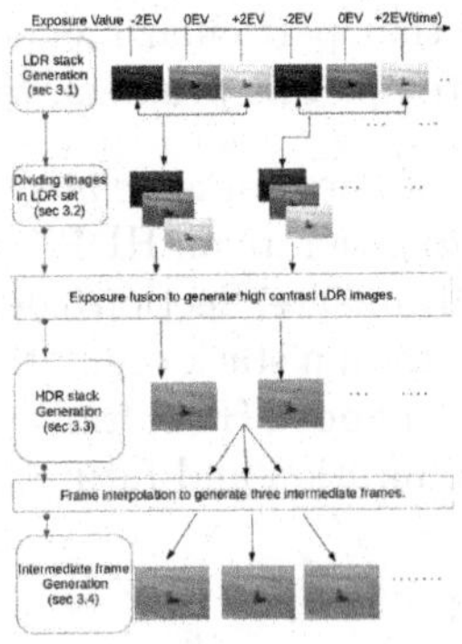

Fig. 1. Flow diagram of the proposed approach.

3 Method

Figure 1 shows the flow diagram of the proposed framework. In this section, we discuss our approach to generating HDR-GIF. Our method has four major components. Each successive subsection provides the details of crucial steps followed in the proposed framework. Since the proposed framework requires the knowledge of camera settings, these aspects are also elaborated.

3.1 LDR Stack Generation

As mentioned earlier, we are considering a commonly available DSLR. Most of these cameras have the functionality of Auto Exposure Bracketing (AEB, captures a scene with multiple exposures) and burst mode (captures images continuously). In our experiments, we use Canon EOS 80D DSLR, which supports AEB with three different exposures. Further, to capture motion in different frames, we place the camera on a tripod and set it into the burst mode. We choose the following setting for our DSLR before shooting the LDR stack.

1. Number of different exposures - Ideally, the number of different exposures can be chosen similar to that of any other HDR generation algorithm. Low-end DSLR cameras support three exposures, and this number can go beyond nine for higher-end DSLR cameras. The camera used in the experiments allows the user to select the spread of 3 exposures in terms of relative exposure value (EV).
2. Number Of Images in LDR stack - After selecting a range of exposures, we need to choose how many frames we want in the final HDR-GIF image. The final GIF consists of the tone-mapped HDR image from the LDR stack and the interpolated HDR frames. Our LDR stack consists of mostly 18, 15, and 12 images for different dynamic scenes.

3.2 Dividing Images in LDR Set

After the generation of LDR stack, we have taken three consecutive images from the stack, having different exposures and calling them an LDR set. Each LDR set consists of 3 images with exposure value -2EV, 0EV, and 2EV, respectively.

3.3 HDR Stack Generation

We have different LDR sets, and each set consists of three images with different exposure values (-2EV, 0EV, 2EV). The scene is dynamic, so the placement of the object in each image in the LDR set might have changed. Hence we have created a tone-mapped HDR image corresponding to each LDR set using the approach mentioned in the paper [19]. For example, consider the size of the

LDR stack to be 12, which means there is a sequence of 12 frames of under, normal, and over-exposure. We generate ($12/3 \rightarrow 4$) 4 HDR images from this stack, which assumes the normally exposed image (0EV) as the reference image. Hence, our HDR images are aligned with respect to the reference image.

The architecture used for generating a sequence of HDR images is a simple encoder-decoder architecture with skip connections which forwards the output of each encoder layer to the corresponding decoder layer [19]. These two inputs are concatenated channel-wise and then sent through the decoder. The overall architecture has three significant components encoder, merger, and decoder. Here we use three different exposure images for generating the final HDR image. Hence, we have three parallel encoders to extract the relevant information from three different exposures. In the next set of layers, the network learns to merge all the pieces of information obtained from the previous layer. In the final set of layers, the network learns to decode the features of the final HDR images.

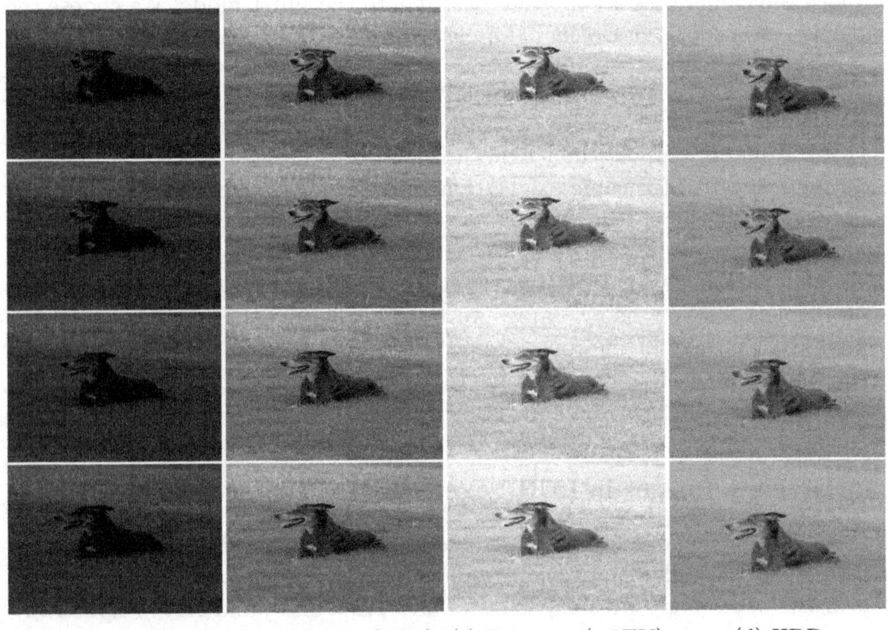

(a) Exposure(-2EV) (b) Exposure(0EV) (c) Exposure(+2EV) (d) HDR

Fig. 2. The first column is the under-exposed, second column is normal-exposed, and the third column is the over-exposed image. The fourth column is the final tonemapped HDR image output corresponding to each row

3.4 Intermediate Frame Generation

We are generating a sequence of tone-mapped HDR images corresponding to a dynamic scene. Hence there will be a significant movement of the object throughout the generated tone-mapped HDR images. To make the motion of the object smoother, we need to generate some in-between frames. Therefore we have used the architecture from the paper [12] to generate the intermediate frames between them. We have generated three in-between frames in a binary search fashion.

A binary search is a well-known algorithm that tells the presence of a key element in a sorted list. The intuition of our binary search fusion algorithm is somewhat similar to this algorithm. Let the generated tone-mapped HDR frames be H1, H2, H3, and so on. We generate a tone-mapped intermediate HDR frame between H1 and H2 say I1 and then we generate between H1 and I1 say H1I1 and between I1 and H2 say I1H2 and so on. We generate three intermediate HDR frames between H1 and H2 namely I1, H1I1, and I1H2. Similarly, we did for H2 and H3, and so on.

Hence, if there are four HDR images, between each successive HDR images, we generate three HDR images. Firstly, we generate a middle HDR image between the first and the second HDR image. Further, we generate between first and middle and then between middle and second, similar to a binary-search. Hence, in this case, we have a total of 13 HDR images ($4 + 3 \times 3 \rightarrow 13$). This set of 13 HDR images best depicts the motion of this scene.

The architecture designed in this paper [12] is for generating the intermediate frames in a video sequence. However, it also works well for generating intermediate HDR frames in our case. The architecture is similar to an encoder-decoder architecture with skip connections. This model is trained on video dataset using L_1 loss and L_f loss. The parameters of the network are learned to predict the video frames. The input to the network is two frames, and the network learns the parameters to produce the intermediate frames. Here the encoders work as a contracting component to extract features, and the decoder works like an expanding network, which comprises of upsampling layers.

Algorithm 1: Generation of Sequence of HDR Images.

Data: Sequence of multi-exposure LDR images
Result: Sequence of HDR images
$n \leftarrow$ total number of input images with different exposures;
$I_j \leftarrow j^{th}$ image in the LDR stack
$i \leftarrow 0$
while $i - 2 <= n$ **do**
  $output \leftarrow [I_i, I_{i+1}, I_{i+2}](Using$ [19]);
  $i \leftarrow i + 1$;
end

Algorithm 2: Intermediate HDR Frame Generation.

Data: Sequence of HDR images
Result: sequence of generated HDR intermediate images
$n \leftarrow$ total number of HDR images;
$I_j \leftarrow j^{th}$ HDR image
$i \leftarrow 0$
while $i - 1 <= n$ **do**
  $I_g \leftarrow [I_i, I_{i+1}](Using[12])$;
  $I_{g1} \leftarrow [I_i, I_g]$;
  $I_{g2} \leftarrow [I_g, I_{i+1}]$;
  $i \leftarrow i + 1$;
end

4 Result

The result for the final HDR image from a sequence of multi-exposure LDR stack is shown in Fig. 2, 4 and 6 for three different scenes, respectively. Here the middle column (normally-exposed) image is used as the reference image. Therefore, the final tone-mapped HDR image is aligned with respect to the reference image. For this dataset, we have generated four tone-mapped HDR images from a sequence of 12 LDR images, which can be seen in Fig. 2.

Now, we have a stack of tone-mapped HDR images. Hence, we have taken each two successive tone-mapped HDR images and generated three intermediate frames. The result of frame interpolation is shown in Figs. 3, 5 and 7 for three different scenes, respectively. In Fig. 3 and 5, we denote the second column as Frame 0, third column as Frame 1, and fourth column as Frame 2. The first and last column is the input HDR frames. Figure 5 shows the quality of Frame 0 and Frame 2 better than the quality of Frame 1 because Frame 0 and Frame 2 are closer to the input frames.

We neither have the reference image for the images in HDR stack nor the generated intermediate frames. Hence, we have used Blind/Referenceless Image Spatial Quality Evaluator (BRISQUE) [11] as our quality metrics. Lower the BRISQUE score, the more the image resembles to a natural scene. In Table 1, we have shown the BRISQUE scores for the 8 different scenes. The entire datasets will be made publically available.

In Table 1 the first column is the scene number, and the second column is the average BRISQUE score for all the tone-mapped images from the HDR stack corresponding to that particular scene. Frame 1 column is the average score of all the middle frames generated between the two consecutive images from the HDR stack. Frame 0 and 2 columns represent the average score for all the frames generated between the first and middle and middle and second HDR image for

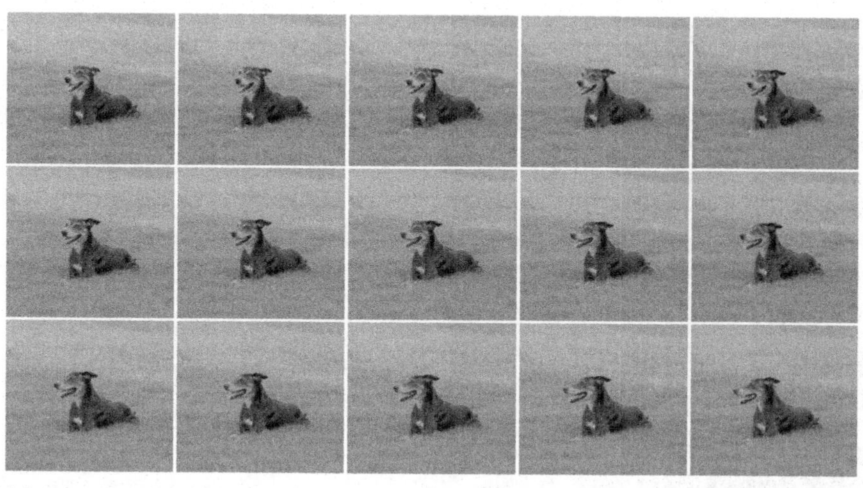

(a) Input Frame (b) Frame 0 (c) Frame 1 (d) Frame 2 (e) Input Frame

Fig. 3. First and the last column are the input HDR image and second, third, and fourth are the generated frames corresponding to each row in binary search fashion

Table 1. BRISQUE score for the generated frames.

Scene ID	HDR image	Generated intermediate frames		
		Frame 0	Frame 1	Frame 2
1	33.1911	35.7319	**36.6094**	36.5195
2	31.5778	36.8537	**36.9426**	36.7345
3	13.3133	**29.0388**	27.8709	26.4833
4	15.2556	34.3949	**34.3949**	31.1909
5	13.6727	29.4127	29.4207	**30.1737**
6	21.5047	45.1340	**45.6646**	45.1148
7	16.2117	36.9045	**37.5481**	36.9194
8	28.6212	30.5786	**30.5786**	31.1362

that particular scene. Table 1 shows that in most cases, the BRISQUE score for Frame 1 is higher(shown in bold) than Frame 0 and Frame 2 because Frame 0 and Frame 2 are more close to the input HDR images. The score for the input HDR image is lowest in each row.

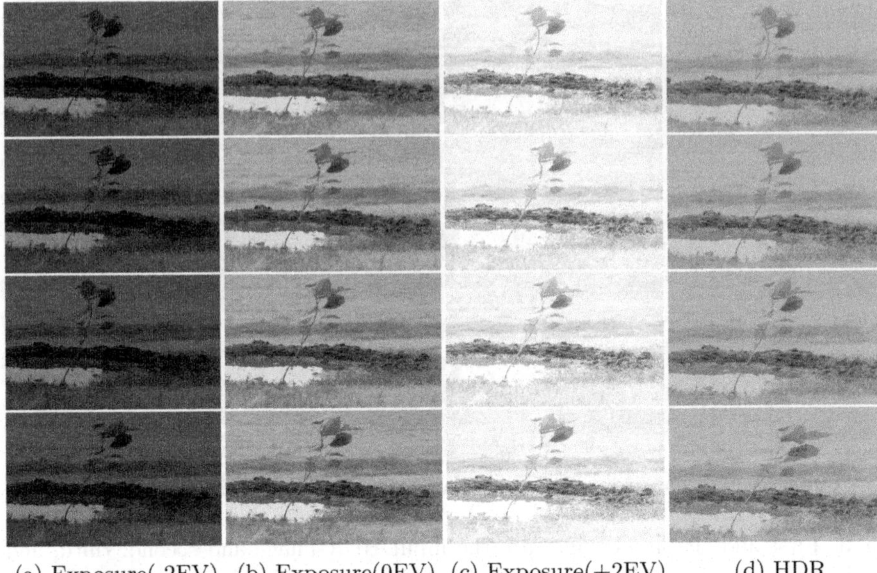

(a) Exposure(-2EV) (b) Exposure(0EV) (c) Exposure(+2EV) (d) HDR

Fig. 4. The first column is the under-exposed, second column is normal-exposed, and the third column is the over-exposed image. The fourth column is the final tonemapped HDR image output corresponding to each row

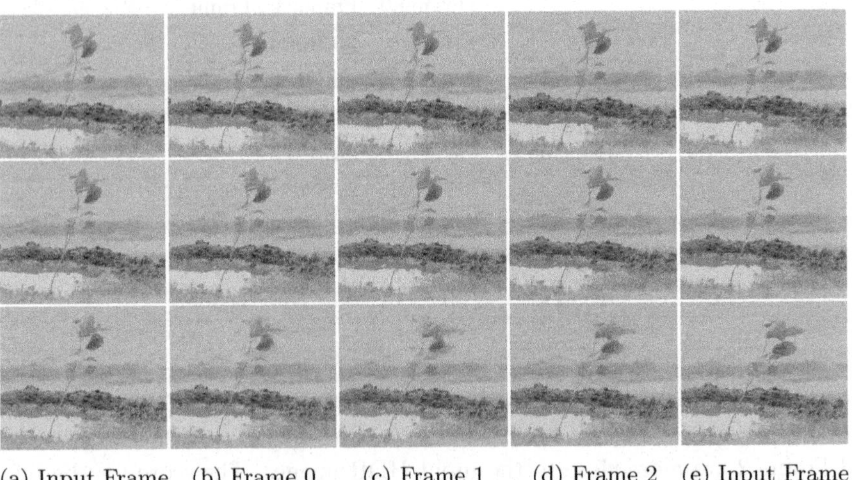

(a) Input Frame (b) Frame 0 (c) Frame 1 (d) Frame 2 (e) Input Frame

Fig. 5. First and the last column are the input HDR image and second, third, and fourth are the generated frames corresponding to each row in binary search fashion

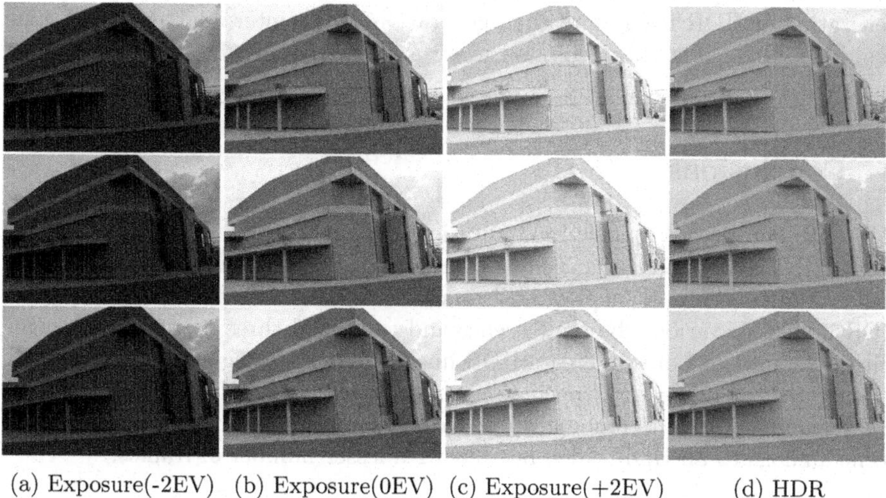

(a) Exposure(-2EV) (b) Exposure(0EV) (c) Exposure(+2EV) (d) HDR

Fig. 6. The first column is the under-exposed, second column is normal-exposed, and the third column is the over-exposed image. The fourth column is the final tonemapped HDR image output corresponding to each row

5 Limitations and Future Work

The network for generating the intermediate frame is trained on videos where the network learns to predict the in-between frames. In videos, the two consecutive frames are very close in terms of object placements in the frame. Therefore, the network learns the linear motion of the objects. It can generate an intermediate frame properly if the motion is not so complex and the frames are not too far from each other. Trying to predict temporally coherent intermediate frames between two images that are little away in terms of object placement is still an interesting area of future work. We have divided our work in two phases like

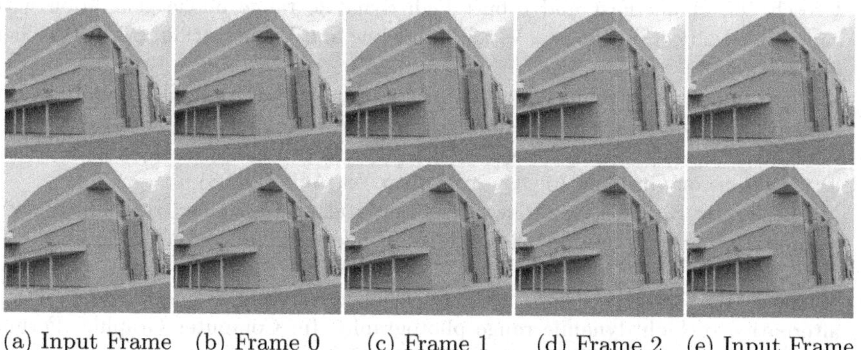

(a) Input Frame (b) Frame 0 (c) Frame 1 (d) Frame 2 (e) Input Frame

Fig. 7. First and the last column are the input HDR image and second, third, and fourth are the generated frames corresponding to each row in binary search fashion

generation of HDR image and then generation of the interpolated frames. One could combine these two steps and make a single model which can be trained end-to-end.

6 Conclusions

We have proposed a new computational photography application called DeepHDR-GIF, which is an excellent combination of high dynamic range imaging and a relatively new concept of GIF images. We have taken the multi-exposure LDR images of various dynamic scenes and combined three consecutive images with different exposures to create HDR images. After getting a sequence of HDR images corresponding to a specific scene, we have generated three intermediate HDR frames. We can combine all of them to create the motion of the entire scene analogs to an HDR video but having a lesser number of frames.

Acknowledgement. This research was supported by the SERB Core Research Grant.

References

1. Akyüz, A.O.: Photographically guided alignment for HDR images. In: Eurographics (Areas Papers), pp. 73–74 (2011)
2. Ashikhmin, M.: A tone mapping algorithm for high contrast images. In: Proceedings of the 13th Eurographics Workshop on Rendering, pp. 145–156. Eurographics Association (2002)
3. Chaurasiya, R.K., Ramakrishnan, K.: High dynamic range imaging. In: 2013 International Conference on Communication Systems and Network Technologies, pp. 83–89. IEEE (2013)
4. Debevec, P.E., Malik, J.: Recovering high dynamic range radiance maps from photographs. In: ACM SIGGRAPH 2008 Classes, p. 31. ACM (2008)
5. Eilertsen, G., Kronander, J., Denes, G., Mantiuk, R.K., Unger, J.: HDR image reconstruction from a single exposure using deep CNNs. ACM Trans. Graph. (TOG) **36**(6), 178 (2017)
6. Grosch, T., et al.: Fast and robust high dynamic range image generation with camera and object movement. Vision, Modeling and Visualization, RWTH Aachen **277284** (2006)
7. Li, S., Kang, X.: Fast multi-exposure image fusion with median filter and recursive filter. IEEE Trans. Consum. Electron. **58**(2), 626–632 (2012)
8. Mantiuk, R., Daly, S., Kerofsky, L.: Display adaptive tone mapping. In: ACM Transactions on Graphics (TOG), vol. 27, p. 68. ACM (2008)
9. Masiá Corcoy, B., Gutiérrez Pérez, D.: Computational imaging: combining optics, computation and perception. Ph.D. thesis, Universidad de Zaragoza, Prensas de la Universidad
10. Mertens, T., Kautz, J., Van Reeth, F.: Exposure fusion: a simple and practical alternative to high dynamic range photography. In: Computer Graphics Forum, vol. 28, pp. 161–171. Wiley Online Library (2009)
11. Mittal, A., Moorthy, A.K., Bovik, A.C.: No-reference image quality assessment in the spatial domain. IEEE Trans. Image Process. **21**(12), 4695–4708 (2012)

12. Niklaus, S., Mai, L., Liu, F.: Video frame interpolation via adaptive separable convolution. In: Proceedings of the IEEE International Conference on Computer Vision, pp. 261–270 (2017)
13. Raman, S., Chaudhuri, S.: Reconstruction of high contrast images for dynamic scenes. Vis. Comput. **27**(12), 1099–1114 (2011)
14. Reinhard, E., Stark, M., Shirley, P., Ferwerda, J.: Photographic tone reproduction for digital images. In: ACM Transactions on Graphics (TOG), vol. 21, pp. 267–276. ACM (2002)
15. Reinhard, E., Ward, G., Pattanaik, S., Debevec, P.: High Dynamic Range Imaging: Acquisition, Display, and Image-Based Lighting (The Morgan Kaufmann Series in Computer Graphics). Morgan Kaufmann Publishers Inc., San Francisco (2005)
16. Tocci, M., Kiser, C., Tocci, N., Sen, P.: A versatile HDR video production system. ACM TOG **30**(4), 41:1–41:10 (2011)
17. Tomaszewska, A., Mantiuk, R.: Image registration for multi-exposure high dynamic range image acquisition (2007)
18. Ward, G.: Fast, robust image registration for compositing high dynamic range photographs from hand-held exposures. J. Graph. Tools **8**(2), 17–30 (2003)
19. Wu, S., Xu, J., Tai, Y.-W., Tang, C.-K.: Deep high dynamic range imaging with large foreground motions. In: Ferrari, V., Hebert, M., Sminchisescu, C., Weiss, Y. (eds.) ECCV 2018. LNCS, vol. 11206, pp. 120–135. Springer, Cham (2018). https://doi.org/10.1007/978-3-030-01216-8_8
20. Yao, S.: Robust image registration for multiple exposure high dynamic range image synthesis. In: Image Processing: Algorithms and Systems IX, vol. 7870, p. 78700Q. International Society for Optics and Photonics (2011)
21. Zhao, H., Shi, B., Fernandez-Cull, C., Yeung, S.K., Raskar, R.: Unbounded high dynamic range photography using a modulo camera. In: 2015 IEEE International Conference on Computational Photography (ICCP), pp. 1–10. IEEE (2015)

Camera Based Parking Slot Detection for Autonomous Parking

Upendra Suddamalla(✉), Anthony Wong, Ravichandiran Balaji, Banghyon Lee, and Dilip Kumar Limbu

MooVita Pte. Ltd., Singapore, Singapore
{upendra,anthonywong,balaji,josephlee,diliplimbu}@moovita.com

Abstract. Autonomous parking is one of the primary functionalities of intelligent vehicles. This requires the accurate detection of a free parking slot and its dimensions. Here we propose a method using a novel combination of computer vision techniques on the camera data mounted on sides of a car. Our occupancy check method is based on perspectivity guided motion segmentation, which makes it a generic approach for handling random obstacles without prior knowledge. When tested on our dataset collected in environments such as shadows, wet surface, indoors and outdoors with obstacles including cars, motorbikes, cones, carton boxes and trees, this method achieved a promising performance with F1 score higher than 97%. With the ability to run on low computational devices such as CPU, this method is adaptable to practical solutions for both AD and aftermarket ADAS systems.

Keywords: Self parking · Motion segmentation · Occupancy check · Autonomous Driving (AD) · Intelligent transportation

1 Introduction

Autonomous Driving (AD) and Driver Assistance Systems (ADAS) are emerging areas to enhance human safety and driving experience. This is achieved by mounting a variety of sensors to capture data, running advanced data processing algorithms to evaluate the vehicle surroundings and making appropriate decisions for navigation. Autonomous parking is a salient functionality of AD, as a vehicle needs to find a suitable parking space while not in operation or for charging. To park a vehicle autonomously, it is required to understand the parking slot position, dimension and occupancy status. Various sensors used for this functionality include Lidars, Ultrasonic range detectors, Radars and/or cameras. These sensors are used in combination or independently to understand the parking environment. Techniques based on Lidar sensors [1] analyze point cloud data to check for the presence of obstacles and suitability of available space for parking based on the dimensions of the subject vehicle. Ultrasonic range finder sensors, associated with wheel encoder, [2–4] measure the free space information as the vehicle navigates while searching for a suitable location. These techniques

S. K. Singh et al. (Eds.): CVIP 2020, CCIS 1378, pp. 58–69, 2021.
https://doi.org/10.1007/978-981-16-1103-2_6

can find a suitable free space for parking but have limitations in providing the accurate markings and boundary of the parking slot. For example, these methods work decently well when a free parking slot is available next to an occupied slot or any physical object such as a pillar. These methods use the object as a reference to estimate the free slot dimension and propose an area for parking. If all the parking slots are free and there is no object for reference, these methods may propose an area which occupies more than one demarcated parking slot and the proposed orientation may not match with the designated parking slot orientation. The demarcation of a parking slot indicates the area allocated for each vehicle. Failure in detection of the accurate boundary of the parking slot may lead to an improper parking manoeuvre and end up in occupying more than one slot and/or in a wrong orientation. Using cameras as the primary sensors can help in addressing this issue, as cameras provide high-resolution information of the environment. [20] and [21] present techniques using a combination of camera and ultrasonic sensors, where cameras are used for slot marking detection and ultrasonic sensors are used for occupancy check. Figure 1 depicts sample images of parking slots under different conditions.

Fig. 1. Sample parking slots

Several techniques are proposed which use camera data to determine a parking slot and further check for occupancy. Wang et al. [5] proposed a method using vision sensors and heuristic-based gradient analysis to determine free slots. This method uses gradient edges to find the boundaries of a slot and uses edge pixel count to decide on occupancy status. This approach works well for parking floors with uniform gradients such as concrete or asphalt, with no shadows or dirt. However, this gives poor results for slots with brick flooring, shadows, dirt or parking signs on the floor as some examples shown in Fig. 1. Houben et al. [6] proposed a method using Linear Discriminant Analysis (LDA) using an image as input. This method performs well in near ideal conditions with no noise. In real-world scenarios with lots of variations in parking zones and illumination conditions, collecting the data with all variations and fine-tuning this method is a challenge. Other state-of-art methods [7] use machine learning for locating and guiding for autonomous parking. Rathour et al. [8] proposed a deep learning network which operates on front and rearview camera data and provides steering angle for end-to-end parking. Deep learning based general object detection techniques such as YOLO [9,10] can help in detecting objects in parking slots. Jensen et al. [11], Amato et al. [12] and Acharya et al. [13] presented a specialized deep learning network for detecting free slots of a large parking area using static cameras mounted at a high position such as the roof of a building. With very good generalization capabilities, learning-based methods show promising results in solving computer vision problems such as object detection. However, the performance of these methods depends on the size and variation of the training dataset covering all possible variations of shape, color, obstacle types and illumination conditions. Based on the complexity of network architecture, machine learning methods demand high computational resources such as GPUs (Graphics Processing Units). This may limit their application for a low-cost real-time solution. Due to these limitations of the existing methods [5,6,8,9,11–13], we define the requirements for parking slot detection algorithm as below: 1. A generic approach which can handle dynamic parking environments and random obstacles 2. Accurately detect parking slot boundary and occupancy status, at par with learning-based methods 3. Real-time performance 4. Low-cost sensor and computing system.

In this work, we discuss a novel method to address these requirements. We propose to solve the problem of detecting a free slot in two steps using a camera image. The first step, detection of parking slots using gradient and structure of the parking lines; and second step to check for occupancy based on motion analysis which provides reliable occupancy status under varying conditions. Similar to the methods based on ultrasonic, this algorithm makes an assumption that the vehicle is in motion (this is required for motion flow estimation). We believe that this is a valid assumption as the vehicle navigates at low speeds in the process of searching for a suitable parking slot. The main contributions of our work include 1. A novel motion segmentation method by considering perspective homography of the camera. 2. A real-time and generic occupancy check method which does not require prior training of the obstacles. 3. Formulation for detecting the valid pair of parking slot corners based on spatial and geometric characteristics.

The organization of the paper is as follows. Section 2 briefs the camera calibration process. Section 3 deals with the detection of parking slot marks. Section 4 talks about the occupancy check method. Section 5 presents the complete system, experiments and Results followed by Conclusions in Sect. 6.

2 Camera Setup and Calibration

To address the problem of detecting parking slots, a camera with a wide-angle lens is mounted on one or both sides of the vehicle as shown in Fig. 2. Pitch angle and mounting position of the camera is selected in such a way that an area between 0.3 m to 5 m from the camera are covered in the image view. Camera calibration is performed by placing a reference planar marker on the ground at a known distance. The calibration process generates a homography matrix h, which helps in mapping image to world coordinates and vice-a-versa. For the benefit of faster performance, we generate and store reference lookup tables for image-to-world coordinate mapping and world-to-image coordinate mapping. We also compute the perspectivity ratio map (PR) at each row in the image, which indicates the scaling effect of perspectivity on a unit length in the world system at each row of the image.

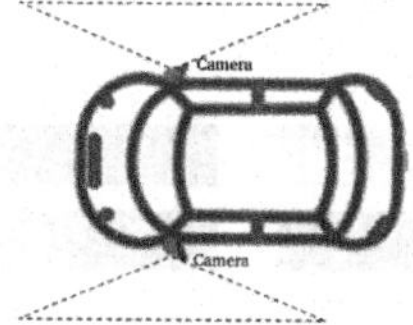

Fig. 2. Camera setup on vehicle (Better viewed in color) (Color figure online)

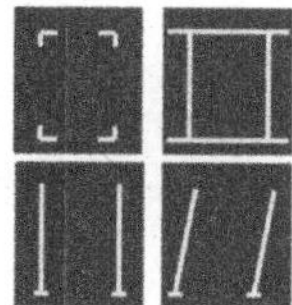

Fig. 3. Various types of parking slot markings

3 Parking Slot Marks Detection

Parking slots, in general, are represented by a set of line-markings in red, yellow or white color. These markings indicate the length, width and orientation of the parking slot allocated for each vehicle. Figure 3 indicates a few variants of parking slot markings that are commonly used. Accurate detection of a parking slot is the first step for successful autonomous parking. The structural characteristics of parking slot markings have similarity with road lane markings in a narrow zone which can be extracted using characteristics such as edge, structure [14] and intensity thresholding [15]. Here we propose to use the gradient to locate the markings and validate by structural characteristics.

We define a pair of 1-D image filters of length $(2N + 1)$, as shown in Fig. 4. These filters help to compute rising (Fig. 4 a) and trailing (Fig. 4 b) edges in the image. Each of these filters f is applied on every pixel x in the input gray image I as shown in Eq. 1, to determine the candidate rising and trailing edge pixels. A valid parking line mark is a combination of rising and trailing edge pixels separated by a distance similar to line mark thickness. So the rising and trailing edge pixels are validated by the condition that rising pixel followed by trailing pixel within a distance less than a threshold value. Then the center pixel of the line mark is computed by averaging each rising and trailing pixel position. This operation creates a binary image, where the bright pixels indicate the centerline of markings. These pixels are processed to compute approximate line segments [16], which are used for further processing. The output of applying 1-D filters and determining center pixel is shown in Fig. 5.

$$foI(x) = \sum_{i=-N}^{N} f(i)I(x+i) \tag{1}$$

The filters shown in Fig. 4 help in determining vertical line-markings. Horizontal line-markings are determined by rotating the input image by 90° and running the same filters. The resultant line segments are rotated by −90° to create horizontal line segments. Alternatively, horizontal lines can be detected by applying a set of vertical 1-D column filters. The approximate line segments are mapped to world coordinates using the homography information h created during the calibration process explained in Sect. 2.

Fig. 4. 1-D filters a. Rising b. Trailing

Fig. 5. a. Gray Image b. Edge of vertical line mark c. Edge of horizontal line mark and d. Combined vertical and horizontal edge

These line segments in world coordinates are then checked for a set of valid intersecting pairs of a vertical line and a horizontal line (V-H). This is done by shortlisting the V-H pairs with the shortest distance between vertical and horizontal line segments is less than a predefined distance threshold d_{thd}. The offset d_{thd}, which is typically equal to the thickness of the line marking, is considered to allow small gaps between V-H line segments due to pixel rounding off in edge detection and line fitting methods. For the shortlisted V-H pairs, we perform the inner product of each vertical line segment with each horizontal line segment as shown in Eq. 2. Here we do not limit the angle of the V-H pair to $90°$ to support slots that are at different orientations with respect to the horizontal boundary (as shown in the 4th sample in Fig. 3).

$$\theta = arccos(V.H/|V||H|) \times 180/\pi \tag{2}$$

Each of the valid V-H pairs is considered as a candidate parking slot corner. It is observed that some of the objects in the scene have similar intensity and geometric pattern and produce the V-H pairs. Examples of part of a vehicle forming a false V-H pair is shown in Fig. 6. To handle the false V-H pairs and to find a correct set of two V-H corners we compute a confidence score which evaluates the geometrical relationship between the set of two corners. The confidence score uses three characteristics a) Width of the parking slot should be within a predefined range b) The vertical lines in the two V-H pairs should be parallel. c) Supplementary angle property to validate the corner pair. The confidence score is calculated as shown in Eq. 3a, 3b, 3c and 3d. C_w, C_v, C_{hv} and C indicate individual scores of the candidate pair of corners forming the slot based on width characteristic, vertical line angle characteristic, angle relation between the V-H pair and overall confidence score respectively. W_R and W_A indicate reference slot width and the actual distance between two corner points. ϕ_L and ϕ_R indicate the angle of vertical lines forming the left corner and right corner respectively. θ_L and θ_R represent the angle between the V-H pair of left and right corners respectively, which is calculated as shown in Eq. 2.

$$C_w = 1 - (abs(W_R - W_A)/W_R) \quad (3a)$$

$$C_v = 1 - (abs(\phi_L - \phi_R)/90) \quad (3b)$$

$$C_{hv} = 1 - (abs((\theta_L + \theta_R) - 180)/180) \quad (3c)$$

$$C = C_w \times C_v \times C_{hv} \quad (3d)$$

Results of proposed slot detection method are depicted in Fig. 7. Red lines indicate the nearest horizontal bound along with left and right vertical bounds of the slot. Figure 8 depicts the flow for the proposed parking slot detection.

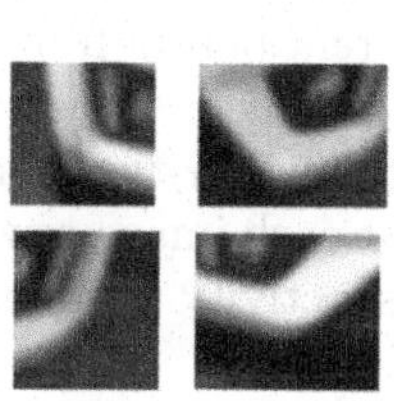

Fig. 6. Samples of image patches forming false V-H pattern

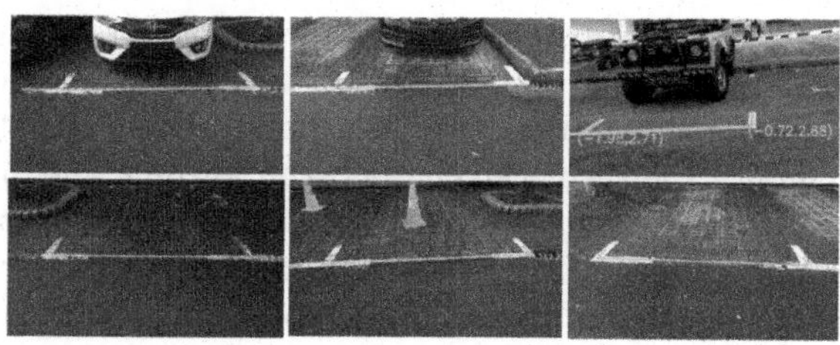

Fig. 7. Results of slot detection method (Color figure online)

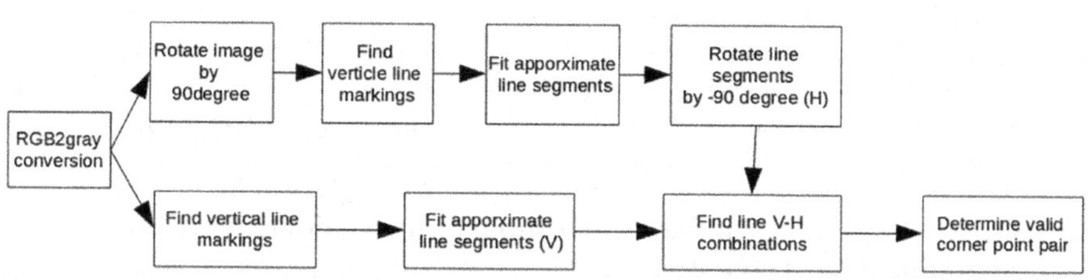

Fig. 8. Flow diagram for parking slot detection

4 Occupancy Check

After determining a parking slot region, it is processed further to check the occupancy status. Wan et al. [17] propose a moving object segmentation by motion analysis. As they consider rigid objects such as parked cars as background, such techniques are not suitable for occupancy check. We propose a novel method based on motion flow segmentation with reference to camera view to determine the presence of obstacles in the parking slot.

4.1 Motion Calculation

Optical flow is a technique to calculate the motion of all image pixels (dense flow) [18] or selected key pixels (sparse flow) [19] between two images captured with a small time delay. Optical flow operates on two constraints: a) color constancy b) small motion of corresponding pixels between two frames. Here we use the dense optical flow method [18] to produce a smooth motion field across pixels of the image. The motion flow u is computed between the current and previous frame in the parking slot detected by the process discussed in Sect. 3.

4.2 Homography Guided Reference Motion Estimation

To extract the obstacles, first, we compute a reference ground plane motion (ug). ug represents the motion flow of the ground plane for the current pair of frames. This is computed as explained below. Based on the current vehicle speed, we compute the displacement between current and previous frames in the world coordinate system. Then the equivalent pixel displacement at each image row is computed based on homography matrix h and reference perspectivity ratio map PR calculated as part of the calibration process.

To address the scenarios where the vehicle speed is not available, we propose an alternative method to use dense motion computed in the previous step. Mean motion at a seed row s, u_s, is computed as shown in Eq. 4. Typically, seed row s is a row indicating the ground plane. We use slot marking pixel value as a reference to select s. Then, motion at each image row j of width N pixels is computed using u_s and perspectivity ratio map (PR) as shown in Eq. 5.

$$u_s = 1/(N) \times \sum_{i=0}^{N-1} u(i) \qquad (4)$$

$$ug_j = u_s \times PR_j/PR_s \qquad (5)$$

4.3 Obstacle Detection Using Homography Guided Motion Segmentation (HGMS)

The reference motion is compensated by subtracting ug from dense flow map u to compute the obstacle motion uo. To handle any noise in the flow computation, we further apply a homography guided adaptive threshold A_j to produce binary masks of potential obstacle regions as shown in Eq. 6a, 6b and 6c. Here T is the threshold for a minimum motion for the seed row s. A_j is defined with perspectivity in view and gradually increasing with row number. These binary masks are further post-processed with binary morphology closing operation to eliminate breaks due to the smooth texture of any obstacle. Finally, a filter is applied based on the pixel area to suppress noise blobs of small size and retaining masks of the obstacles in the selected parking region in the current frame.

$$uo_{i,j} = u_{i,j} - ug_j \qquad (6a) \qquad\qquad A_j = T \times PR_j \qquad (6b)$$

$$ObstacleMap_{i,j} = \begin{cases} 1, & \text{if } uo_{i,j} \geq A_j \\ 0, & \text{otherwise} \end{cases} \qquad (6c)$$

Figure 9 represents output of each step followed for obstacle detection using HGMS. Here dense motion u (Fig. 9c) is computed from two frames shown in Fig. 9a and Fig. 9b. Computed reference ground motion ug is shown in Fig. 9d. After subtracting the reference motion and applying threshold, the final obstacle masks are shown in Fig. 9f. It can be observed from this example that the proposed algorithm is able to detect both car and tree present in the input image. Flow diagram of the occupancy check step is as shown in Fig. 10.

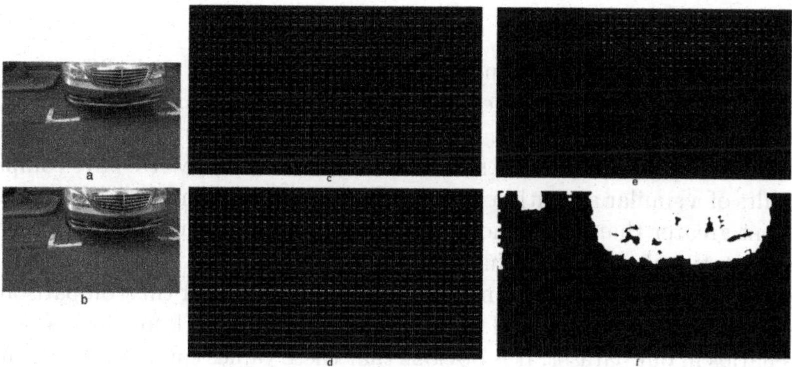

Fig. 9. HGMS a. Current frame b. Previous frame c. Motion detection using dense optical flow d. Homography guided reference motion e. Motion after reference compensation f. obstacle masks (better viewed in color) (Color figure online)

5 Results

The well-articulated problem of free parking slot detection is addressed by the proposed algorithm. The complete system of the algorithm has been depicted as a flow diagram in Fig. 11. As per our knowledge, there is no standard public dataset available for the problem of interest. So we have collected a dataset of 623 different parking slots, across different locations and at different times of the day. In the dataset, we have 402 free slots and 221 occupied slots. Among these, 65% are from the outdoors and around 10% of the slots have wet floors. Each slot data is a set of two successive frames recorded at 20fps and containing both markings of a parking slot. The comparison tests are performed on a computer with a CPU configuration of Intel®Core^{TM} i7-7700HQ CPU @ 2.80 GHz, 8 core processor.

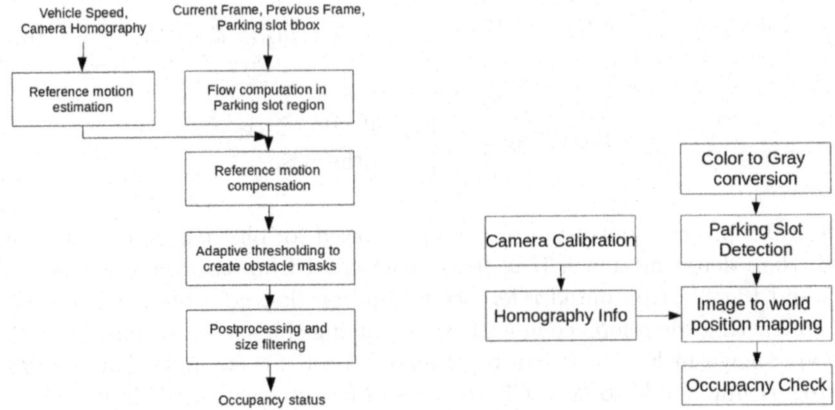

Fig. 10. Flow diagram for occupancy check using HGMS

Fig. 11. Flow diagram of proposed method

The performance of HGMS method has been compared with different state-of-art algorithms such as gradient intensity based occupancy check and deep learning based object detection. Wang et al. [5] proposed to compare the pixel gradient in the region of parking slots to check for occupancy. We have compared the results of a similar algorithm which checks for the total number of pixels with a gradient greater than a threshold value. Though the gradient method requires low computational power, the challenge is to determine the optimal threshold for gradient threshold and pixel count to decide as occupied. For this comparison, we have experimentally determined these thresholds which work for the majority of the scenarios in our dataset. It is obvious that these values can not be generalized for real-world variations in the parking slot data.

As several researchers highlight the advantage of deep learning in free slot detection using static cameras, we have considered a generic object detection algorithm [9] as part of our comparison. YOLO (You Only Look Once) is a state-of-art network for generic object detection which has support for several objects including vehicles, motorcycles, bicycles and pedestrians. When we used off-the-shelf models, the performance is poor and this is due to the unusual view angle of the parking camera and including objects such as construction cones. So we custom trained the YOLO network using transfer learning and included a set of 400 images for our problem. These images are not part of our test dataset. While inference, we use an input resolution of 160×160 which takes around 120 ms per frame.

For evaluating single-frame based methods such as gradient intensity and deep learning, we use the first frame of each parking slot frame sequence. Whereas for the proposed motion-based method, we use two successive frames of the dataset of each slot. Table 1 shows the comparison of different occupancy check methods for a set of real parking slot images shown in the first column. We considered practical scenarios including vehicles of different colors (rows 1 and

2), shadows (row 3) and obstacles such as traffic cones (row 4). The masks of obstacles detected using a gradient intensity based method similar to [5] are depicted in the second column. The third column shows object bounding boxes in blue rectangles detected using general object detection [9] and the last column presents masks of obstacles computed by the proposed method. The gradient-based method could detect the vehicles but failed to detect an empty slot. Shadows and floor gradient, affect this method as it is entirely based on gradient variations. And gradient intensity methods fail to detect obstacles other than vehicles. The default deep learning model fails to detect unknown objects such as cones but after custom training, the deep learning model detects well for different objects and works fine with shadows. But support for any new type of obstacle requires data collection, annotation and custom training.

Results from the proposed method show that it can handle the challenging scenarios of parking slots very well. This method is not sensitive to the color or shape of the obstacles and shows superior occupancy detection for different textures and shadows in the parking slots. It is able to detect objects of different sizes such as cars, trees, traffic cones etc. This is primarily due to the underlying principles of motion estimation which are immune to these variations. With an F1 score of 97%, the performance of our method is at par with the deep learning method in handling known obstacles, shadows, dirt, wet surfaces. In addition, our method does not require any prior knowledge of the obstacles and can handle any kind of obstacles. HGMS takes around 45 ms time to process a frame on a test computer with near real-time performance.

The proposed method performs well in a wide range of real-world scenarios with good to moderate quality. It has shown poor performance in detecting slot markings when occluded by other objects or low illumination conditions. These are mainly caused due to the limitations of primary sensors, i.e. cameras, used for the application.

To summarize our experiments, we evaluated these algorithms to detect free parking slots. Table 2 shows the performance of different methods. The performance indicators Precision (P), Recall (R) and F1 Score ($F1$) are computed. From the well designed comparative analysis using a real dataset, it is observed that the gradient method is simple and fast but has limitations in handling scenes with varying intensities. Custom deep learning method shows robust behaviour in varying scene intensities with known object types. But the performance is poor when unknown obstacles are present in the scene and slowest among the methods compared. The learning-based methods are also highly dependent on the quality of and variations in the dataset used for training. Proposed motion-based method handles the problems of intensity variations, real-time and has robust performance for any type of obstacles without prior knowledge.

Table 1. Comparison of gradient threshold, YOLO-160 and proposed methods

input	Gradient based	YOLO-160 custom	Proposed Algorithm

Table 2. Precession and recall for gradient threshold, YOLO-160 and proposed method

Method	Precision	Recall	F1 Score
Gradient	0.91	0.75	0.82
YOLO-160 default	0.81	1.0	0.89
YOLO-160 custom	0.96	1.0	0.98
HGMS (proposed)	0.98	0.95	**0.97**

6 Conclusions

Safe parking under challenging scenarios is a crucial requirement for an autonomous parking solution. The proposed free parking slot detection method shows commendable results under various real-world scenarios and stands out to be a generic solution. This method detects and validates candidate parking slot markers to eliminate noise or false patterns. Usage of the motion flow makes the proposed method insensitive to shadows and illumination variations and can detect obstacles of different sizes such as cones, trees or any other obstacle without any prior knowledge. As this method is developed based on computer vision techniques, it requires low computational power and is suitable for a low-cost parking solution. This makes our algorithm the right choice for unknown environments and suitable for both AD and ADAS. Currently, we are working on determining free space dimensions from the motion map to handle scenarios with partial or no visible parking lanes. The said work will be reported in near future.

References

1. Lee, B., Wei, Y., Guo, I.Y.: Automatic parking of self-driving car based on Lidar. Int. Arch. Photogramm. Remote Sens. Spat. Inf. Sci. **42**, 241–246 (2017)
2. Gupta, A., Divekar, R.: Autonomous parallel parking methodology for Ackerman configured vehicles. ACEEE Int. J. Control Syst. Instrum. **2**(2), 34–39 (2011)
3. Suhr, J.K., Jung, H.G.: A universal vacant parking slot recognition system using sensors mounted on off-the-shelf vehicles. Sensors **18**, 1213 (2018)
4. Razinkova, A., Chan, C.H., Hong, T.J.: An intelligent auto parking system for vehicles. Int. J. Fuzzy Logic Intell. Syst. **12**, 226–231 (2012). https://doi.org/10.5391/ijfis.2012.12.3.226
5. Wang, C., Zhang, H., Yang, M., Wang, X., Ye, L., Guo, C.: Automatic parking based on a bird's eye view vision system. Adv. Mech. Eng. **6**, 1–13 (2014)

6. Houben, S., Komar, M., Hohm, A., Lüke, S., Neuhausen, M., Schlipsing, M.: On-vehicle video-based parking lot recognition with fisheye optics. In: Proceedings of the IEEE Annual Conference on Intelligent Transportation Systems (2013)
7. Ma, S., Jiang, H., Han, M., Xie, J., Li, C.: Research on automatic parking systems based on parking scene recognition. IEEE Access **5**, 21901–21917 (2017)
8. Rathour, S., John, V., Nithilan, M.K., Mita, S.: Vision and dead reckoning-based end-to-end parking for autonomous vehicles. In: IEEE Intelligent Vehicles Symposium (IV), pp. 2182–2187 (2018)
9. Redmon, J., Farhadi, A.: Yolov3: an incremental improvement. arXiv preprint arXiv:1804.02767 (2018)
10. Krizhevsky, A., Sutskever, I., Hinton, G.: ImageNet classification with deep convolutional neural networks. In: NIPS (2012)
11. Jensen, T.H.P., Schmidt, H.T., Bodin, N.D., Nasrollahi, K., Moeslund, T.B.: Parking space verification: improving robustness using a convolutional neural network. In: Proceedings of the 12th International Joint Conference on Computer Vision, Imaging and Computer Graphics Theory and Applications, vol. 5, pp. 311–318 (2012)
12. Amato, G., Carrara, F., Falchi, F., Gennaro, C., Meghini, C., Vairo, C.: Deep learning for decentralized parking lot occupancy detection. Exp. Syst. Appl. **72**, 327–334 (2017)
13. Acharya, D., Yan, W., Khoshelham, K.: Real-time image-based parking occupancy detection using deep learning. In: Proceedings of the 5th Annual Conference of Research@Locate, vol. 2087, pp. 33–40 (2018)
14. Suddamalla, U., Kundu, S., Farkade, S., Das, A: A novel algorithm of lane detection addressing varied scenarios of curved and dashed lanemarks. In: Proceedings of the International Conference on Image Processing Theory, Tools and Applications, Orleans, France, 10–13 November 2015, pp. 87–92 (2015)
15. Das, A., Srinivasa Murthy, S., Suddamalla, U.: Enhanced algorithm of automated ground truth generation and validation for lane detection system by M2BMT. IEEE Trans. Intell. Transp. Syst. **18**(99), 996–1005 (2017)
16. Furukawa, Y., Shinagawa, Y.: Accurate and robust line segment extraction by analyzing distribution around peaks in Hough space. Comput. Vis. Image Underst. **92**(1), 1–25 (2003)
17. Wan, Y., Wang, X., Hu, H.: Automatic moving object segmentation for freely moving cameras. In: Math. Probl. Eng. 1–11 (2014). https://doi.org/10.1155/2014/574041
18. Farnebäck, G.: Two-frame motion estimation based on polynomial expansion. In: Bigun, J., Gustavsson, T. (eds.) SCIA 2003. LNCS, vol. 2749, pp. 363–370. Springer, Heidelberg (2003). https://doi.org/10.1007/3-540-45103-X_50
19. Lucas, B., Kanade, T.: An iterative image registration technique with applications to stereo vision. In: Proceedings Darpa IU Workshop, pp. 121–130 (1981)
20. Suhr, J.K., Jung, H.G.: Automatic parking space detection and tracking for underground and indoor environments. IEEE Trans. Ind. Electron. **63**(9), 5687–5698 (2016). https://doi.org/10.1109/TIE.2016.2558480
21. Zong, W., Chen, Q.: A robust method for detecting parking areas in both indoor and outdoor environments. Sensors **18**, 1903 (2018)

Hard-Mining Loss Based Convolutional Neural Network for Face Recognition

Yash Srivastava, Vaishnav Murali, and Shiv Ram Dubey(✉)

Computer Vision Group, Indian Institute of Information Technology, Sri City, Chittoor, Andhra Pradesh, India
{srivastava.y15,murali.v15,srdubey}@iiits.in

Abstract. Face Recognition is one of the prominent problems in the computer vision domain. Witnessing advances in deep learning, significant work has been observed in face recognition, which touched upon various parts of the recognition framework like Convolutional Neural Network (CNN), Layers, Loss functions, etc. Various loss functions such as Cross-Entropy, Angular-Softmax and ArcFace have been introduced to learn the weights of network for face recognition. However, these loss functions do not give high priority to the hard samples as compared to the easy samples. Moreover, their learning process is biased due to a number of easy examples compared to hard examples. In this paper, we address this issue by considering hard examples with more priority. In order to do so, We propose a Hard-Mining loss by increasing the loss for harder examples and decreasing the loss for easy examples. The proposed concept is generic and can be used with any existing loss function. We test the Hard-Mining loss with different losses such as Cross-Entropy, Angular-Softmax and ArcFace. The proposed Hard-Mining loss is tested over widely used Labeled Faces in the Wild (LFW) and YouTube Faces (YTF) datasets. The training is performed over CASIA-WebFace and MS-Celeb-1M datasets. We use the residual network (i.e., ResNet18) for the experimental analysis. The experimental results suggest that the performance of existing loss functions is boosted when used in the framework of the proposed Hard-Mining loss.

Keywords: Face Recognition · Deep learning · Loss functions · Sigmoid function · Hard-Mining loss

1 Introduction

In the past few years, the face recognition task has seen a tremendous growth in terms of the robust recognition and applications in various spheres of human lives. Face Recognition has been seen with a significant usage in multiple domains like biometric-based security tools and criminal identification system among many others. Such applications of the face recognition has lead to researchers and developers to work and design face recognition systems strongly built to work in

S. K. Singh et al. (Eds.): CVIP 2020, CCIS 1378, pp. 70–80, 2021.
https://doi.org/10.1007/978-981-16-1103-2_7

an unconstrained environment as its usage is expected to grow exponentially in the forthcoming years [35].

The advancements in deep learning have significantly accelerated the growth and performance of face recognition. AlexNet [14], proposed by Krizhevsky et al., is marked as the birth of the Convolutional Neural Networks (CNNs) which became a revolutionary architecture developed for the task of image classification and won the ImageNet Large Scale Challenge in 2012 [19]. Since then, many CNN based approaches have been introduced for face recognition such as, DeepFace [26], DeepID2 [24], FaceNet [20], SphereFace [17], and ArcFace [3]. The CNN based approaches [5,10,11,14,29] have shown a tremendous growth in the performance as compared to the hand-crafted features [1,6–8,13,22]. The above growth was accompanied by the development of large-scale face datasets for training and testing the CNN based models, which majorly include CASIA-Webface [33], MS-Celeb-1M [9], Labeled Faces in the Wild (LFW) [12] and YouTube Faces (YTF) [31] among other face datasets. In this work, the CASIA-Webface and MS-Celeb-1M face datasets are used for training. However, the LFW and YTF face datasets are used for the testing.

The trend of CNN over time shows that the deep CNN architectures perform better as compared to the shallow networks. It was the motivation for the deeper architectures like GoogleNet [25] and ResNet [10]. The residual network shows that the performance of the deeper plain model is not improved because it is hard to optimize such model [10]. Thus, researchers also started exploring the relevance of loss functions in optimizing the deep networks. The Cross-Entropy (i.e., Softmax) loss is very widely used for optimizing the deep learning models. Recently, the work in loss functions has been quite significant with functions like SphereFace (i.e., Angular-Softmax) [17] and ArcFace [3], specially designed for the face recognition task and have shown very promising gain in the performance. Some other existing loss functions are Marginal loss [4], Soft-margin softmax loss [15], Large-margin softmax loss [18], Additive margin softmax [27], Minimum margin loss [30], Cosface: Large margin cosine loss [28], and AdaptiveFace: Adaptive margin loss [16]. Moreover, in another work, we have conducted a performance analysis of different loss functions and found that the ArcFace outperforms other losses [23].

A few attempts are also made to utilize the complexity of data in training such as the hardest positive pairs and hardest negative pairs are computed using margin sample mining loss by Xiao et al. [32]; an adaptive hard sample mining strategy it used by Chen et al. [2] to pick the hard examples in the training pair images; and an auxiliary embedding is used by Smirnov et al. [21] to pick the hard examples in mini-batches. Note that these methods try to find out the hard examples first and then use it for training. Whereas, the proposed method gives the high priority to hard examples inherently during training based on the performance of model in that iteration.

The main drawback of above mentioned loss functions is associated with its inefficiency while modelling the hard examples which lead to mis-classification. The loss due to the more number of easy examples dominates over the loss due to the less number of hard examples. This is because while training is in progress, the number of hard examples decreases while the number of easy examples increases as network learns over iterations. In this paper, we address the above mentioned problem by giving more importance to hard examples through loss function in each iteration. We propose the Hard-Mining loss which increases the loss for the hard samples leading to high loss and decreases the loss for the easy samples leading to low loss. As a result, the average loss contains the significant contributions from the hard examples.

This paper is structured as follows: Sect. 2 proposes the Hard-Mining loss and existing losses in the Hard-Mining framework; Sect. 3 describes the experimental setup and details about the architecture and training and testing face datasets used. Section 4 presents the experimental results and comparisons; and finally, Sect. 5 concludes the paper with summarizing remarks.

2 Proposed Hard-Mining Loss

The loss functions are used in deep learning to judge the goodness of any model under given parameters. The stochastic gradient descent (SGD) optimization is widely adapted to train the Convolutional Neural Networks (CNNs). The SGD computes the gradient of loss function w.r.t. to the parameters which is used to update that parameter such that in the next iteration, the loss should decrease. Thus, the loss functions judge the performance of the designed architecture as well as guide the learning process. It is shown in introduction that most of the existing losses are not able to penalize the mis-classification efficiently caused by harder examples. In this paper, we propose the concept of Hard-Mining loss which increases the loss for harder examples and decreases the loss for easier examples such that the average loss should have the better representation of hard examples. A comparison between the Cross-Entropy loss and proposed Hard-Mining loss is presented in Fig. 1 as a function of probability of being classified in the correct class. In this section, first we present the Cross-Entropy loss, then we propose the idea of Hard-Mining loss, and finally we extend the existing losses such as Cross-Entropy, Angular-Softmax, and ArcFace in the proposed Hard-Mining framework.

2.1 Cross-Entropy Loss

The Cross-Entropy (or softmax) loss has been majorly used to judge the performance of CNN models for image classification task [10,14]. Mathematically, the Cross-Entropy loss can be given as

$$\mathcal{L}_{CE} = -\frac{1}{N}\sum_{i=1}^{N}\log\frac{e^{W_{y_i}^T x_i + b_{y_i}}}{\sum_{j=1}^{n} e^{W_j^T x_i + b_j}}, \tag{1}$$

where W is the weight matrix, b is the bias term, x_i is the ith training sample, y_i is the class label for i^{th} training sample, N is the number of samples, W_j and

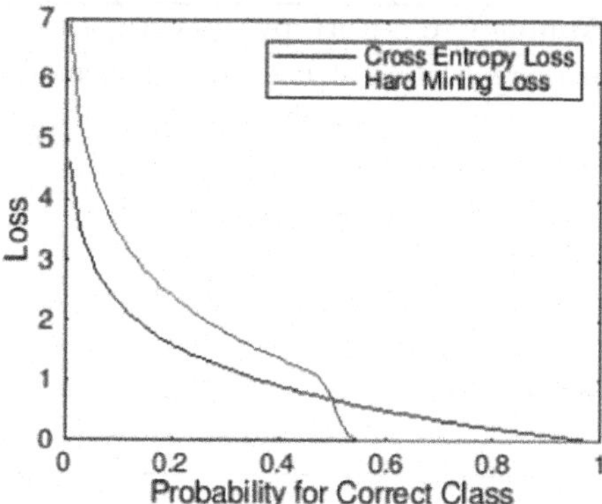

Fig. 1. Loss value vs Likelihood (i.e., probability for correct class) plot for the Cross-Entropy loss and Hard-Mining loss functions. Note that the Hard-Mining loss is computed on the output of Cross-Entropy loss.

W_{y_i} are the jth and y_i^{th} columns of W, respectively. The Cross-Entropy loss is used as the baseline by the recent loss functions such as Angular-Softmax and ArcFace over the face recognition problem. Hence, we also use the Cross-Entropy loss as the baseline along with Angular-Softmax and ArcFace losses.

The behavior of the Cross-Entropy loss w.r.t. the probability of being classified in the correct class for an example is plotted in Fig. 1. It can be observed from this analysis that the Cross-Entropy loss gradually follows a downward slope and there is no big difference between easy and hard examples. We believe that if the probability is more than 0.5 then the loss should be minimum. Whereas, if the probability is less than 0.5 then the loss should be on higher side. This is our intution to propose the Hard Mining Loss described next.

2.2 Hard-Mining Loss

Motivated from the fact that the loss for harder examples should be more, we propose the idea of Hard-Mining loss. The proposed Hard-Mining loss increases the loss if the probability is less than roughly 0.5, while at the same time it also decreases the loss if probability is more than 0.5 roughly. The Hard-Mining loss is defined as

$$\mathcal{L}_{HM} = \alpha \times \mathcal{L} \times \sigma(\beta \times \mathcal{L}) \tag{2}$$

where $\mathcal{L}$ is the loss generated by any other loss function such as Cross-Entropy, Angular-Softmax, etc., α and β are the hyperparameters and σ is the sigmoid function given as:

$$\sigma(x) = \frac{1}{1 + e^{-A(x-B)}} \tag{3}$$

where A and B are the hyperparameters.

Note that the Hard-Mining operation is generic in nature, i.e., it can be used along with any existing loss function. In this paper, we use the Hard-Mining operation along with Cross-Entropy, Angular-Softmax, and ArcFace losses.

Algorithm 1. Hard-Mining Cross-Entropy Loss Algorithm

Input: Predicted class scores, Ground-truth class label, and hyper-parameters α, β, A and B.
Output: Loss generated.

1. $\mathcal{L}_{CE} \leftarrow CrossEntropy(input, target, W)$
2. $x \leftarrow \beta \times \mathcal{L}_{CE}$
3. $y \leftarrow A \times (x - B)$
4. $z \leftarrow Sigmoid(y)$
5. $\mathcal{L}_{HM\_CE} \leftarrow \alpha \times x \times z$
6. return $\mathcal{L}_{HM\_CE}$

2.3 Hard-Mining Cross-Entropy Loss

As mentioned previously, the Hard-Mining concept is generic and can be used with existing losses. Primarily, we define the Hard-Mining loss with Cross-Entropy loss. The Hard-Mining Cross-Entropy loss ($\mathcal{L}_{HM\_CE}$) is defined as

$$\mathcal{L}_{HM\_CE} = \alpha * \mathcal{L}_{CE} * \sigma(\beta * \mathcal{L}_{CE}) \tag{4}$$

where α and β are the hyperparameters, σ is defined in (1), and $\mathcal{L}_{CE}$ is the Cross-Entropy loss given in (1). Algorithm 1 shows the step-by-step instructions for the proposed Hard-Mining Cross-Entropy loss ($\mathcal{L}_{HM\_CE}$).

The behavior of Hard-Mining operation on Cross-Entropy loss is depicted in Fig. 1. Note that the values of hyper-parameters α, β, A, and B are set to 1.5, 1.1, 35, and 0.75, respectively. It can be seen that the Hard-Mining operation increases the loss for hard examples (i.e., with less than half probability) while it decreases the loss for easy examples (i.e., with more than half probability). Our definition of hard/easy examples is relative to the probability of being classified in the correct class in a given iteration. Thus, the hard examples at the start of the training might become easy examples after training of some iterations.

Since, the Cross-Entropy is a very widely used loss function in various machine learning problems, it is paramount that we study the performance of Hard-Mining operation with loss functions specially designed for the face recognition problem. We consider two loss functions (i.e., Angular-Softmax [17] and ArcFace [3]) designed for the face recognition problem in the proposed Hard-Mining loss framework.

2.4 Hard-Mining Angular-Softmax Loss

The Hard-Mining Angular-Softmax loss ($\mathcal{L}_{HM\_AS}$) is defined as follows:

$$\mathcal{L}_{HM\_AS} = \alpha \times \mathcal{L}_{AS} \times \sigma(\beta \times \mathcal{L}_{AS}) \tag{5}$$

where α and β are the hyper-parameters, σ is given in (3), and $\mathcal{L}_{AS}$ is the Angular-Softmax loss defined in the SphereFace model [17] and given as

$$\mathcal{L}_{AS} = -\frac{1}{N}\sum_{i=1}^{N} \log\Big(\frac{e^{\|\boldsymbol{x}_i\|\psi(\theta_{y_i,i})}}{e^{\|\boldsymbol{x}_i\|\psi(\theta_{y_i,i})} + \sum_{j\neq y_i} e^{\|\boldsymbol{x}_i\|\cos(\theta_{j,i})}}\Big) \tag{6}$$

where x_i is the ith training sample, $\psi(\theta_{y_i,i})=(-1)^k \cos(m\theta_{y_i,i})-2k$ for $\theta_{y_i,i} \in [\frac{k\pi}{m}, \frac{(k+1)\pi}{m}]$, $k\in[0, m-1]$ and $m\geq 1$ is an integer controlling the size of angular margin.

2.5 Hard-Mining ArcFace Loss

ArcFace loss has been used in the recently developed ArcFace model for face recognition [3]. In a recent performance comparison study, ArcFace has been figured as the outstanding loss for face recognition [23]. The Hard-Mining ArcFace loss ($\mathcal{L}_{HM\_AF}$) is defined as

$$\mathcal{L}_{HM\_AF} = \alpha \times \mathcal{L}_{AF} \times \sigma(\beta \times \mathcal{L}_{AF}) \tag{7}$$

where α and β are the hyper-parameters, σ is given in (3), and $\mathcal{L}_{AF}$ is the ArcFace loss [3] and given as

$$\mathcal{L}_{AF} = -\frac{1}{N}\sum_{i=1}^{N} \log \frac{e^{s\cdot(\cos(\theta_{y_i}+m))}}{e^{s\cdot(\cos(\theta_{y_i}+m))} + \sum_{j=1,j\neq y_i}^{n} e^{s\cdot\cos\theta_j}}, \tag{8}$$

where s is the radius of the hypersphere, m is the additive angular margin penalty between x_i and W_{y_i}, and $\cos(\theta + m)$ is the margin which makes the class-separations more stringent.

3 Experimental Setup

In this section, we discuss the CNN architectures, training and testing datasets used for the experiments along with other settings like optimizers, learning rate, epochs, etc.

3.1 CNN Architectures

Several CNN architectures have been developed for different computer vision tasks. The recent trend is to utilize the power of residual learning. The ResNet model uses the residual blocks [10] which is very commonly used nowadays. In this paper, we consider ResNet architecture with 18 depth (i.e., ResNet18) for all the experiments.

3.2 Training Datasets

In our experiments, we primarily use two publicly available datasets such as CASIA-Webface [33] and MS-Celeb-1M [9] as the training datasets. The CASIA-Webface is one of the most widely adapted and available dataset used for the face recognition task. It contains 4,94,414 colored face images belonging to 10,575 different individuals. Second dataset used in our experiments is the MS-Celeb-1M dataset which consists of 1,00,000 face identities with each class containing 100 images leading to about 10M images, which are scraped from public sources. Being a humongous dataset, it contains a lot of noise and variations which impact the performance of the trained model. Hence, we use a cleaned and refined subset of the dataset as per the cleaned list provided by the ArcFace [10] authors.

3.3 Testing Datasets

We use the Labeled Faces in the Wild (LFW) [12] and Youtube Faces (YTF) [31] as the testing datasets in this paper. The LFW dataset contains 13,233 images of 5749 identities. The YTF dataset consists of 3,425 videos of 1,595 different people with images available in frame-by-frame format and retrieved through the provided meta data. Both the datasets use the standard LFW benchmark for face verification, which provide the verification accuracies over the testing dataset. These accuracies are used as the performance measure in the state-of-the-art face recognition works. Hence, we also use the accuracy as the performance measure in this paper.

3.4 Input Data and Network Settings

Following the recent trend [3,17], we use the MTCNN [34] to align the face images. The images are normalized by subtracting 127.5 from each pixel and then being divided by 128. The batch-size is kept at 64 with the initial learning rate as 0.01. The learning rate is multiplied by 0.1 at 8th, 12th and 16th epochs.

Table 1. Verification accuracies (%) using ResNet18 model over LFW and YTF face recognition testing datasets under different loss functions. The training is performed over CASIA-WebFace dataset.

Loss function	Accuracy on LFW dataset	Accuracy on YTF dataset
Cross-Entropy loss ($\mathcal{L}_{CE}$)	95.35	91.8
Hard-Mining Cross-Entropy loss ($\mathcal{L}_{HM\_CE}$)	96.75	93.1
Angular-Sofmax loss ($\mathcal{L}_{AS}$)	97.12	93.9
Hard-Mining Angular-Sofmax loss ($\mathcal{L}_{HM\_AS}$)	97.3	94.1
ArcFace loss ($\mathcal{L}_{AF}$)	97.79	94.54
Hard-Mining ArcFace loss ($\mathcal{L}_{HM\_AF}$)	97.9	94.67

The model is trained up to 20 epochs. The Stochastic Gradient Descent with Momentum (SGDM) is used as the optimizer to train the network. The values of hyper-parameters α, β, A, and B are empirically set to 1.5, 1.1, 35, and 0.75, respectively, in this paper.

4 Experimental Results and Observations

In order to show the effect of the proposed Hard-Mining loss, the face recognition experiments are conducted in this paper with ResNet18 model. Three existing loss functions, namely Cross-Entropy, Angular-Softmax and ArcFace, are used in the framework of the proposed Hard-Mining loss. The training is performed over the CASIA-WebFace and MS-Celeb-1M datasets and testing is performed over the LFW and YTF datasets.

The results in terms of the verification accuracies are reported in Table 1 using ResNet18 model for the CASIA-WebFace training dataset over the LFW and YTF testing datasets. It can be seen that an improvement is obtained by the Hard-Mining Cross-Entropy loss, Hard-Mining Angular-Softmax loss, and Hard-Mining ArcFace loss as compared to the Cross-Entropy loss, Angular-Softmax loss, and ArcFace loss, respectively, over both the LFW and YTF datasets.

The results in terms of the verification accuracies are reported in Table 2 using ResNet18 model for the MS-Celeb-1M training dataset over the LFW and YTF testing datasets. It is noticed from this result that the performance of Hard-Mining operation based losses is either better or comparable over LFW dataset w.r.t. the losses without Hard-Mining operation. Moreover, Hard-Mining operation is also suited with Cross-Entropy loss over YTF dataset when training is performed over MS-Celeb-1M datasets.

The experimental results suggest that increasing the loss for harder examples and decreasing the loss for easy examples in each iteration enforce the network to learn the characteristics of hard-examples as well. Overall, the proposed Hard-Mining loss is well suited for the face recognition problem along with the existing loss functions.

Table 2. Verification accuracies (%) using ResNet18 model over LFW and YTF face recognition testing datasets under different loss functions. The training is performed over MS-Celeb-1M dataset.

Loss function	Accuracy on LFW dataset	Accuracy on YTF dataset
Cross-Entropy loss ($\mathcal{L}_{CE}$)	95.1	92.45
Hard-Mining Cross-Entropy loss ($\mathcal{L}_{HM\_CE}$)	95.1	92.5
Angular-Softmax loss ($\mathcal{L}_{AS}$)	96.9	94.1
Hard-Mining Angular-Softmax loss ($\mathcal{L}_{HM\_AS}$)	97.05	93.8
ArcFace loss ($\mathcal{L}_{AF}$)	97.6	95.1
Hard-Mining ArcFace loss ($\mathcal{L}_{HM\_AF}$)	98	94.9

5 Conclusion

In this paper, a concept of Hard-Mining loss is proposed which increases the loss for hard examples being mis-classified and decreases the loss for easy examples. By doing so, we enforce the network to learn the characteristics of hard examples. The proposed concept is generic in nature and can be used with any existing loss function. We have tested the proposed Hard-Mining loss with Cross-Entropy, Angular-Softmax and ArcFace losses. The experiments are performed over CASIA-WebFace and MS-Celeb-1M training datasets and LFW and YTF testing datasets using ResNet18 model. It is observed from the experiments that the proposed Hard-Mining loss boosts the performance of existing losses in most of the cases.

References

1. Chakraborti, T., McCane, B., Mills, S., Pal, U.: Loop descriptor: local optimal-oriented pattern. IEEE Signal Process. Lett. **25**(5), 635–639 (2018)
2. Chen, K., Chen, Y., Han, C., Sang, N., Gao, C., Wang, R.: Improving person re-identification by adaptive hard sample mining. In: 2018 25th IEEE International Conference on Image Processing (ICIP), pp. 1638–1642. IEEE (2018)
3. Deng, J., Guo, J., Xue, N., Zafeiriou, S.: Arcface: additive angular margin loss for deep face recognition. arXiv preprint arXiv:1801.07698 (2018)
4. Deng, J., Zhou, Y., Zafeiriou, S.: Marginal loss for deep face recognition. In: Proceedings of the IEEE Conference on Computer Vision and Pattern Recognition Workshops, pp. 60–68 (2017)
5. Dubey, S.R., Roy, S.K., Chakraborty, S., Mukherjee, S., Chaudhuri, B.B.: Local bit-plane decoded convolutional neural network features for biomedical image retrieval. Neural Comput. Appl. **32**(11), 7539–7551 (2019). https://doi.org/10.1007/s00521-019-04279-6
6. Dubey, S.R., Singh, S.K., Singh, R.K.: Rotation and illumination invariant interleaved intensity order-based local descriptor. IEEE Trans. Image Process. **23**(12), 5323–5333 (2014)
7. Dubey, S.R., Singh, S.K., Singh, R.K.: Local wavelet pattern: a new feature descriptor for image retrieval in medical CT databases. IEEE Trans. Image Process. **24**(12), 5892–5903 (2015)
8. Dubey, S.R., Singh, S.K., Singh, R.K.: Multichannel decoded local binary patterns for content-based image retrieval. IEEE Trans. Image Process. **25**(9), 4018–4032 (2016)
9. Guo, Y., Zhang, L., Hu, Y., He, X., Gao, J.: MS-Celeb-1M: a dataset and benchmark for large-scale face recognition. In: Leibe, B., Matas, J., Sebe, N., Welling, M. (eds.) ECCV 2016. LNCS, vol. 9907, pp. 87–102. Springer, Cham (2016). https://doi.org/10.1007/978-3-319-46487-9_6
10. He, K., Zhang, X., Ren, S., Sun, J.: Deep residual learning for image recognition. In: Proceedings of the IEEE Conference on Computer Vision and Pattern Recognition, pp. 770–778 (2016)
11. Hu, J., Shen, L., Sun, G.: Squeeze-and-excitation networks. In: Proceedings of the IEEE Conference on Computer Vision and Pattern Recognition, pp. 7132–7141 (2018)

12. Huang, G.B., Ramesh, M., Berg, T., Learned-Miller, E.: Labeled faces in the wild: a database for studying face recognition in unconstrained environments. Technical report, 07–49, University of Massachusetts, Amherst, October 2007
13. Kou, Q., Cheng, D., Zhuang, H., Gao, R.: Cross-complementary local binary pattern for robust texture classification. IEEE Signal Process. Lett. **26**(1), 129–133 (2018)
14. Krizhevsky, A., Sutskever, I., Hinton, G.E.: ImageNet classification with deep convolutional neural networks. In: Advances in Neural Information Processing Systems, pp. 1097–1105 (2012)
15. Liang, X., Wang, X., Lei, Z., Liao, S., Li, S.Z.: Soft-margin softmax for deep classification. In: Liu, D., Xie, S., Li, Y., Zhao, D., El-Alfy, E.S. (eds.) ICONIP 2017. LNCS, vol. 10635, pp. 413–421. Springer, Cham (2017). https://doi.org/10.1007/978-3-319-70096-0_43
16. Liu, H., Zhu, X., Lei, Z., Li, S.Z.: AdaptiveFace: adaptive margin and sampling for face recognition. In: Proceedings of the IEEE Conference on Computer Vision and Pattern Recognition, pp. 11947–11956 (2019)
17. Liu, W., Wen, Y., Yu, Z., Li, M., Raj, B., Song, L.: SphereFace: deep hypersphere embedding for face recognition. In: Proceedings of the IEEE Conference on Computer Vision and Pattern Recognition, pp. 212–220 (2017)
18. Liu, W., Wen, Y., Yu, Z., Yang, M.: Large-margin softmax loss for convolutional neural networks. In: ICML, p. 7 (2016)
19. Russakovsky, O., et al.: ImageNet large scale visual recognition challenge. Int. J. Comput. Vis. **115**(3), 211–252 (2015)
20. Schroff, F., Kalenichenko, D., Philbin, J.: FaceNet: a unified embedding for face recognition and clustering. In: Proceedings of the IEEE Conference on Computer Vision and Pattern Recognition, pp. 815–823 (2015)
21. Smirnov, E., Melnikov, A., Oleinik, A., Ivanova, E., Kalinovskiy, I., Luckyanets, E.: Hard example mining with auxiliary embeddings. In: Proceedings of the IEEE Conference on Computer Vision and Pattern Recognition Workshops, pp. 37–46 (2018)
22. Song, T., Xin, L., Gao, C., Zhang, G., Zhang, T.: Grayscale-inversion and rotation invariant texture description using sorted local gradient pattern. IEEE Signal Process. Lett. **25**(5), 625–629 (2018)
23. Srivastava, Y., Murali, V., Dubey, S.R.: A performance comparison of loss functions for deep face recognition. arXiv preprint arXiv:1901.05903 (2019)
24. Sun, Y., Chen, Y., Wang, X., Tang, X.: Deep learning face representation by joint identification-verification. In: Advances in Neural Information Processing Systems, pp. 1988–1996 (2014)
25. Szegedy, C., et al.: Going deeper with convolutions. In: Proceedings of the IEEE Conference on Computer Vision and Pattern Recognition, pp. 1–9 (2015)
26. Taigman, Y., Yang, M., Ranzato, M., Wolf, L.: DeepFace: closing the gap to human-level performance in face verification. In: Proceedings of the IEEE Conference on Computer Vision and Pattern Recognition, pp. 1701–1708 (2014)
27. Wang, F., Cheng, J., Liu, W., Liu, H.: Additive margin softmax for face verification. IEEE Signal Process. Lett. **25**(7), 926–930 (2018)
28. Wang, H., et al.: CosFace: large margin cosine loss for deep face recognition. In: Proceedings of the IEEE Conference on Computer Vision and Pattern Recognition, pp. 5265–5274 (2018)
29. Wang, Y., Ward, R.K., Wang, Z.J.: Coarse-to-fine image dehashing using deep pyramidal residual learning. IEEE Signal Process. Lett. **26**, 1295–1299 (2019)

30. Wei, X., Wang, H., Scotney, B., Wan, H.: Minimum margin loss for deep face recognition. arXiv preprint arXiv:1805.06741 (2018)
31. Wolf, L., Hassner, T., Maoz, I.: Face recognition in unconstrained videos with matched background similarity. IEEE (2011)
32. Xiao, Q., Luo, H., Zhang, C.: Margin sample mining loss: a deep learning based method for person re-identification. arXiv preprint arXiv:1710.00478 (2017)
33. Yi, D., Lei, Z., Liao, S., Li, S.Z.: Learning face representation from scratch. arXiv preprint arXiv:1411.7923 (2014)
34. Zhang, K., Zhang, Z., Li, Z., Qiao, Y.: Joint face detection and alignment using multitask cascaded convolutional networks. IEEE Signal Process. Lett. **23**(10), 1499–1503 (2016)
35. Zhou, Y., Liu, D., Huang, T.: Survey of face detection on low-quality images. In: 2018 13th IEEE International Conference on Automatic Face & Gesture Recognition (FG 2018), pp. 769–773. IEEE (2018)

Domain Adaptive Egocentric Person Re-identification

Ankit Choudhary[1(✉)], Deepak Mishra[1], and Arnab Karmakar[1,2]

[1] Indian Institute of Space Science and Technology, Thiruvananthapuram, Thiruvananthapuram 695547, India
deepak.mishra@iist.ac.in

[2] Human Space Flight Center, ISRO, Bengaluru 560054, India
arnabk-hsfc@isro.gov.in

Abstract. Person re-identification (re-ID) in first-person (egocentric) vision is a fairly new and unexplored problem. With the increase of wearable video recording devices, egocentric data becomes readily available, and person re-identification has the potential to benefit greatly from this. However, there is a significant lack of large scale structured egocentric datasets for person re-identification, due to the poor video quality and lack of individuals in most of the recorded content. Although a lot of research has been done in person re-identification based on fixed surveillance cameras, these do not directly benefit egocentric re-ID. Machine learning models trained on the publicly available large scale re-ID datasets cannot be applied to egocentric re-ID due to the dataset bias problem. The proposed algorithm makes use of neural style transfer (NST) that incorporates a variant of Convolutional Neural Network (CNN) to utilize the benefits of both fixed camera vision and first-person vision. NST generates images having features from both egocentric datasets and fixed camera datasets, that are fed through a VGG-16 network trained on a fixed-camera dataset for feature extraction. These extracted features are then used to re-identify individuals. The fixed camera dataset Market-1501 [20] and the first-person dataset EGO Re-ID [3] are applied for this work and the results are on par with the present re-identification models in the egocentric domain.

Keywords: Egocentric · Person re-identification · Neural style transfer · Deep learning · Domain adaptation

1 Introduction

With the introduction of wearable cameras in the 1990s by Steve Mann, a new field of egocentric vision has opened up in the computer vision community. Due to the affordability of these first-person recording devices, huge data is being generated almost every day. However, the currently available structured datasets for egocentric vision are quite small, due to the inherent challenges of first-person vision such as blurriness due to motion of the camera, illumination

S. K. Singh et al. (Eds.): CVIP 2020, CCIS 1378, pp. 81–92, 2021.
https://doi.org/10.1007/978-981-16-1103-2_8

change, and poor video quality. Also, most of these data cannot be used for person re-identification tasks due to a lack of individuals in these videos, creating a lack of dedicated egocentric videos that can be used for the task of egocentric re-ID.

Ample research has been carried out in the field of fixed-camera based re-ID, but their applicability is limited for egocentric re-ID. A re-ID model trained on a third person re-ID dataset tends to learn the intricate features of that specific dataset only, but it becomes obsolete when re-identifying individuals in an egocentric dataset. The existing literature for first-person re-ID i.e. body parts based [3] and multiple views based [2] methods also suffer from dataset bias.

To overcome these challenges, we propose a neural style transfer (NST) based domain adaptation technique for egocentric person re-identification, which make use of present fixed camera re-ID datasets to improve the performance of egocentric re-ID. The application of domain adaptation to fixed camera datasets has been widely studied in literature [14,18]. But the idea of using domain adaptation to bridge the gap between fixed camera datasets and first-person datasets have never been studied before to the best of our knowledge.

In this work, the following contributions are made to the research on first-person re-identification: (1) we use style-transferred images generated by NST to develop a re-ID model which can accurately re-identify individuals from first-person vision dataset even when trained on a fixed-camera dataset (i.e., domain adaptation), thus decreasing/eliminating dataset bias; (2) we compare and contrast the accuracies of our re-ID model on the generated (or style-transferred) images as well as normal first-person images.

2 Related Work

2.1 Classic Person Re-ID

The initial developments in person re-ID make use of handcrafted features such as texture and color. Gray et al. [5] used color channels along with texture filters to re-identify pedestrian images partitioned into six horizontal stripes. Color histograms and moments are extracted followed by dimension reduction using PCA and LFDA in Pedagadi et al. [8]. With the onset of deep learning, CNNs have found wide applications in person re-ID. In [17], long short-term memory (LSTM) modules are utilized through a Siamese network. Gating functions after each convolutional layer are used in [16] to capture discriminative patterns in re-ID.

2.2 Egocentric Person Re-ID

Person re-ID in first-person videos have gained popularity with the widespread use of first-person recording devices. Visual and sensor metadata were used in [1] to successfully perform re-ID. Local features are extracted followed by the application of 3D convolution to encode temporal information. In [2], facial features were extracted and similarities were computed between a pair of cameras to yield optimal and consistent re-ID results. People are identified by dividing their images into meaningful body parts in [3]. Furthermore, the contribution of different body parts is calculated by taking into account human gaze information.

Our work utilizes an egocentric dataset shot through a single camera in [3]. Rather than depending on different body parts, we take into account the complete image of a person while re-identifying him.

2.3 Domain Adaptation in Image-to-Image Translation and Person Re-ID

Domain adaptation has led to significant success in image-to-image translation through GANs [19] and CNNs [7]. pix2pix framework for image-to-image translation was proposed in [6]. A conditional GAN was used to learn mappings between two different sets of images, i.e., source images and target images. Adapting simulation data to real-world data was done through domain confusion loss and pairwise loss in [15]. Gatys et al. [4] computed the differences between the style and content of the source and target images. This allowed the target images to be viewed as source images without the loss of content. A deep generative correlation alignment network (DGCAN) was proposed in [9] to bridge domain discrepancy between real and synthetic images. This was done by applying the content loss to several different layers.

Person re-ID intrinsically requires domain adaption, since, a model trained on a labeled dataset consisting of groups of individuals is required to perform well on unlabelled datasets without supervised fine-tuning. Self-supervised domain adaptation was used in [14] for person re-ID. The source data was pre-processed using GAN and a baseline was trained in a supervised manner using the pre-processed data. The authors then assigned pseudo labels to target data using the trained model and this constructed dataset was trained in a supervised learning manner. Xiao et al. [18] proposed the domain guided dropout algorithm that discards ineffective neurons while re-identifying individuals on several datasets. In [10], style based mapping from target domain to source domain was learned between different camera views. An effective and generalized re-ID model was proposed in [21] by investigating the intra-domain variations of the target domain.

Our work uses the state-of-the-art image-to-image translation model proposed by Gatys et al. in [4] for transferring styles between first-person and fixed camera dataset.

3 Approach

The schematic of the proposed egocentric re-ID model is shown in Fig. 1. The first step in our model is the generation of images which has combined features of fixed camera dataset (Market-1501 [20]) and first-person vision dataset (EGO Re-ID [3]). Our model makes use of a VGG-16 [12] based Neural Style Transfer (NST) model to produce high-quality images in a manner that helps in bringing

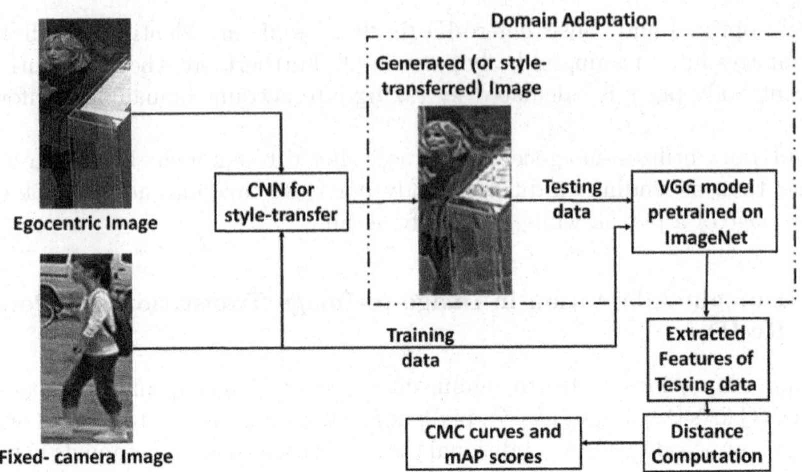

Fig. 1. Flow Diagram of our proposed egocentric re-ID model showing various blocks including style transfer and domain adaptation.

the qualities of Market-1501 [20] into EGO Re-ID [3] while preserving the content of EGO Re-ID [3]. This is achieved by formulating image generation problem as an optimization one that minimizes the following losses: **(1)** Content Loss, **(2)** Style Loss and **(3)** Total Loss.

The content difference between the generated and the EGO Re-ID [3] images are captured through the content loss using a CNN. The input image is transformed along the processing hierarchy of the CNN such that the image representations are oblivious to the precise appearance of the image but are aware of the image's actual content. Thus, a network's higher layers do not worry about the exact pixel values. To capture the content information we make use of these image representations which are present at higher layers as shown in Block C of Fig. 2.

The style loss captures the difference between the generated and the Market-1501 [20] images. The feature space responsible for capturing texture information is used for the computation of style loss. By computing the feature correlations between different filter responses, we obtain the style representation of the image. This style representation can thus be used to compute the style loss. Unlike content loss, the style loss is computed across all the layers as shown in Block A of Fig. 2.

After computing the content and style loss, the total loss is calculated as a linear relationship between content and style loss. After the images are generated by minimizing the total loss, a pre-trained VGG model is fine-tuned using images from Market-1501 [20] and image features are calculated for these generated images after passing them through this fine-tuned model employing domain adaptation as shown in the flow diagram of Fig. 1. Furthermore, average pooling

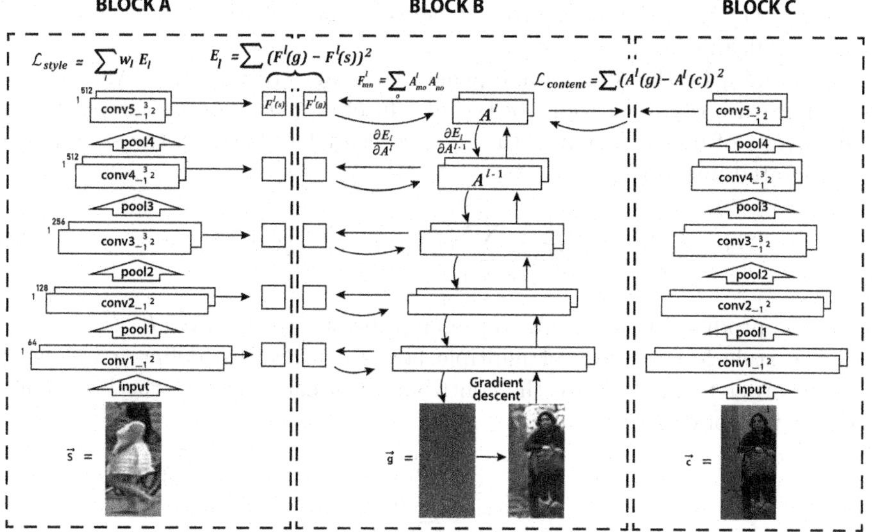

Fig. 2. Detailed illustration of Style Transfer Algorithm [4]. Blocks A and B are used for computing style loss between style image and the generated image, Blocks B and C are used for computing content loss between content image and the generated image.

operation is adopted for the image synthesis task. According to [4], replacing the max pooling with an average pooling offer somewhat better results.

3.1 Content Loss

Block C in Fig. 2 shows the computation of content loss. Let $\boldsymbol{g}$ and $\boldsymbol{c}$ be the generated and content image respectively. And $A^l_{mn}(I)$ be the feature representations of the mth feature map at position n in layer l of image I. Hence, the squared error loss between the content image and the generated image is:

$$\mathcal{L}_{\text{content}} = \frac{1}{2}\sum_{m,n}\left(A^l_{mn}(g) - A^l_{mn}(c)\right)^2 \quad (1)$$

The loss is back-propagated by taking its derivative with the activations present in layer l as shown in Block B in Fig. 2. And the initial white noise image $\boldsymbol{g}$ keeps on changing until we get the same response as the content image $\boldsymbol{c}$.

3.2 Style Loss

Block A in Fig. 2 shows the computation of style loss. The feature map correlations are given by Gram matrix:

$$F^l_{mn}(I) = \sum_{o} A^l_{mo}(I)A^l_{no}(I) \quad (2)$$

where, $F^l_{mn}(I)$ gives the inner product between the feature maps (in vectorised form) m and n at layer l of image I.

Let $\boldsymbol{s}$ and $\boldsymbol{g}$ be the original and generated images respectively. And $F^l_{mn}(I)$ be their feature representations of the mth filter which is located at position n in the layer l of image I. Hence, the squared error loss between the style image and generated image is:

$$E_l = \frac{1}{4N_l^2M_l^2}\sum_{m,n}\left(F^l_{mn}(g) - F^l_{mn}(s)\right)^2 \tag{3}$$

where, the product of N_l and M_l represents the size of the layer l.

Since, style loss consists of multiple layers, we need to define a weighting factor in order to incorporate the contribution of each layer to the loss. Thus, giving us the total style loss as:

$$\mathcal{L}_{\text{style}} = \sum_{l=0}^{L} w_l E_l \tag{4}$$

The derivatives of E_l with respect to the activations of layer l can be computed and backpropagated as shown in Block B in Fig. 2.

3.3 Total Loss

We intend to jointly minimize the content loss between the white noise image and the content from the first-person image at one layer and the style loss between the white noise image and the style from the fixed camera image on several layers. The loss function to be minimized is:

$$\mathcal{L}_{\text{total}} = \alpha\mathcal{L}_{\text{content}} + \beta\mathcal{L}_{\text{style}} \tag{5}$$

where α is the weight factor for content reconstruction while β is the weight factor for style reconstruction.

There is a trade-off between content and style being represented in a generated image. If the generated image has learned better content then its style will be bad and vice-versa. To balance both content and style, weighting factors are included in the final loss expression.

3.4 Style Transfer Based Person Re-ID

The style transferred images generated by the NST algorithm are used to re-identify individuals. VGG-16 [12] is used to extract the image descriptors. The overfit reduction techniques used were weight decay and dropout. To merge the EGO Re-ID dataset [3] (2343 images of 24 persons) with a fixed camera dataset, we used an equal number of images from the fixed camera dataset (Market-1501 [20]). The 'Training Set 1' consists of 2343 images from Market-1501 dataset [20] which were used as style images with the EGO Re-ID [3] content images. The

'Training Set 2' consists of arbitrary 2343 images from the Market-1501 dataset [20]. These images were not used for style transferring the EGO Re-ID dataset [3]. The 'Training Set 3' consists of images from both Training Set 1 and Training Set 2. Thus, comprising a total of 4686 images from Market-1501 dataset [20].

These three sets of images were used to finetune a VGG-16 model pre-trained on ImageNet. The three separate trained models were then used to predict the classes for the style transferred images from the EGO Re-ID dataset [3]. The results obtained through various evaluation methods are presented in Table 1.

For predicting the classes of the individuals from the first-person dataset, some changes were made to the trained model. The final softmax layer of the models trained on Training Set 1, Training Set 2, and Training Set 3 image sets were removed. So, after passing the images through the trained model, a 4096 length vector was extracted from the fifteenth layer of the network. This vector comprises all the features present in the style transferred images and is referred to as the image descriptor. The distance between these image descriptors was calculated using the Euclidean metric. Also, CMC curves are generated based on the Euclidean distance between these extracted feature vectors. Since there are multiple ground truths for a single query image, mAP scores were also computed.

4 Experiments and Results

4.1 Datasets

The experiment was conducted using two datasets to evaluate our model, (1) Market-1501 [20] as style dataset, and (2) EGO Re-ID [3] as content dataset.

The Market-1501 dataset [20] consists of over 32,000 annotated bboxes with over 1500 identities, plus a distractor set of over 500K images

EGO Re-ID dataset [3] is recorded in 3 different locations through a frontal camera of an eye-tracking device. Each location consists of 8 persons with 100 images of each under different viewpoints. There are a total of 2343 images across 24 identities.

4.2 Evaluation Methodologies

Cumulative matching characteristic (CMC) curves are most commonly used for evaluating person re-ID algorithms. They are accurate for evaluating re-ID methodology when only one ground truth for each query exists. In this work, a query can have multiple ground truths, so using only CMC curves does not fully reflect the true ranking results as well as the accuracy of the model. To tackle this issue we use both CMC and mAP (mean Average Precision) scores as the evaluation metric.

4.3 Implementation Details

TensorFlow was used to build our model. Style loss is calculated across layers 1_1, 2_1, 3_1, 4_1 and 5_1 of VGG-16 as shown in Block A of Fig. 2. For content loss, layer 5_2 was used as shown in Block C of Fig. 2. Each layer contributed equally to the style loss, hence the value of w_l for all the layers was set at 0.2. The ratio of α and β was set to 1×10^{-3} in the final loss function. The L2 regularization was set to a value of 5×10^{-4} in VGG to reduce overfitting of data. Also, the dropout rate was set to 0.5. 100 epochs were performed to generate style transferred images using NST. The learning rate was set to 1×10^{-3}. Each image took 3–4 min to generate. During training Adam optimizer was used with its default parameter values, i.e., $\beta_1 = 0.9$ and $\beta_2 = 0.999$.

4.4 Results

Given a content and style image, NST generated flawless images which incorporates both style and content images. A large number of generated images were successful in blending content and style (Fig. 3) whereas only a few images were unsuccessful in blending the styles (Fig. 4). These failure cases can be attributed to the lack of proper transfer of content or style features from the content and style images respectively.

(a) (b) (c)

Fig. 3. Success Case of image generated by NST: (a) Content image (EGO Re-ID dataset [3]); (b) Style image (Market-1501 dataset [20]); (c) Style transferred image. The incorporation of style into the content is very well.

The training data for our work was divided into three sets as mentioned earlier. The details of the nomenclature used are provided below:

- Basic Model is the VGG model trained on the ImageNet dataset. No other fine-tuning was done on this model.
- Training Set 1, 2, and 3 were used to fine-tune the Basic Model to obtain Model 1, 2, and 3 respectively.
- Style transferred images are the images generated by the NST algorithm.

– Normal images are the images from EGO Re-ID dataset [3] without undergoing style transfer.

The details mentioned above about different models will be helpful in understanding the contents of Table 1.

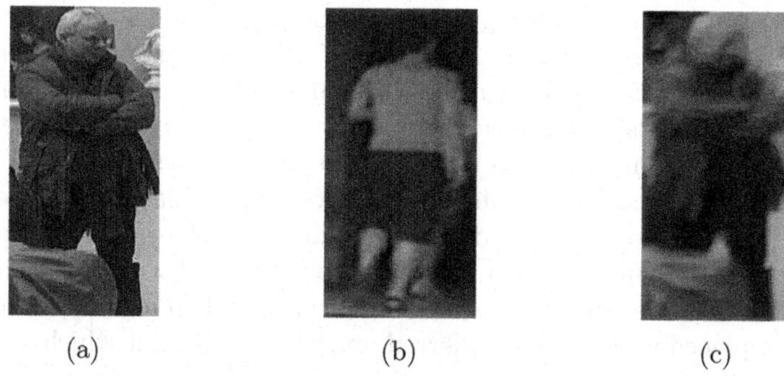

Fig. 4. Failure Case of image generated by NST: (a) Content image (EGO Re-ID dataset [3]); (b) Style image (Market-1501 dataset [20]); (c) Style transferred image. The content and generated images are similar except for the blur due to similarity in content and style images. Major reason for the loss of perceptual quality can be attributed to the fact that the style images are of low quality, hence the quality of all the generated images is degraded to an extent.

From Table 1, we can observe that the style transferred images whose features were extracted through Model 1 has the highest mAP score and the highest recognition rate across all ranks. We can also observe that the recognition rate of normal images across all the training models when compared with their style-transferred counterparts are the lowest.

Table 1. Column 1 lists the training sets which were used. Recognition percentage (%) at r-1, r-5 and r-10 are provided for different training sets. The mean Average Precision (mAP) scores of model trained under different training sets are provided in the last column.

Training model	Style transferred	Rank 1	Rank 5	Rank 10	mAP
Model 1	Yes	57.66	75.07	81.63	65.88
	No	19.60	43.74	59.32	31.79
Model 2	Yes	34.47	55.12	66.23	44.32
	No	26.60	45.67	56.26	36.35
Model 3	Yes	44.53	65.70	75.33	55.22
	No	18.98	44.27	59.23	31.61
Basic Model	Yes	33.42	62.12	75.15	47.30
	No	29.22	47.94	59.32	38.85

The high values of recognition rate obtained after computing the distance between the features of style transferred images extracted from Model 1 implies that individuals in first-person domain can be re-identified through domain adaptive techniques. For rank-1, the recognition percentage has jumped from 18.98% when using Model 3 and non-style transferred images to 57.66% when Model 1 and style transferred images are utilised. This is a 203.8% increment in the recognition rate. Even when considering the same model, i.e., Model 1, the recognition rate for rank-1 has jumped from 19.6% to 57.66% when non-style transferred images were replaced by style transferred images, which is a 194.2% increment in recognition percentage. Similar trends can be observed across all the ranks.

The main aim of this work was to present a egocentric person re-ID algorithm with good accuracy and a technique to eliminate dataset bias so that the models trained on third-person dataset does not become obsolete while testing on a first-person dataset. From Table 1 it is clear that this re-ID algorithm has good accuracy and the increment in recognition percentage when non-style transferred images are replaced with style transferred images is significant which shows that even though the model is trained on a third-person dataset, it's quite accurate when tested on a first-person dataset. The first-person dataset used in this work has been used for a different re-ID algorithm as well [3]. The comparison of the mAP scores of both the models has been provided in Table 2.

Table 2. Comparison of mean Average Precision (mAP) scores between [3] and our approach

Approach	mAP scores
Using Torso description	53.1
Using Face description	60.3
Using Full body (with uniform weights)	67.5
Using Full body (with gaze weights)	70.3
Ours	**65.88**

From Table 2 we can infer that our approach has better mAP scores when a few body parts of the individuals are used for re-ID in [3]. But when the full body of the individual is considered for re-ID in [3], our approach falls behind, but not by a large margin. Even though, our mAP score is lower than the approach in [3] when considering full body of the individual, our approach utilizes style transfer, which can give consistent results irrespective of the dataset it is trained on. The approach in [3] will fall behind in mAP scores when it is tested on a different dataset due to the issue of dataset bias. Our work can thus perform superior irrespective of datasets it will be trained on.

There has been other works on egocentric person re-ID using a different ego re-ID dataset. The comparison of the results of all those work with ours are provided in Table 3. The datasets used in the state-of-the-art approaches mentioned

Table 3. Recognition percentage (%) at r-1 and r-5 are provided to compare our approach with different state-of-the-arts approaches. The mean Average Precision (mAP) scores of our approach and different state-of-the-arts approaches are provided in the last column.

Approach	Rank-1	Rank-5	mAP scores
PSE+ECN [11]	15.17	25.79	8.58
MGCAM [13]	18.48	29.79	14.60
EgoRe-ID [1]	53.02	63.52	44.79
Ours	**57.66**	**75.07**	**65.88**

in Table 3 are different from our dataset. EgoRe-ID dataset is much bigger than EGO Re-ID dataset [3]. The difference in our results can be attributed to the differences in sizes of the dataset. Overall our approach performed well as can be seen from Table 2 and 3.

5 Conclusion

We have proposed a novel egocentric person re-ID approach by transferring styles of fixed camera datasets into first-person datasets. Fixed camera approaches cannot be used for re-identifying when the dataset changes due to dataset bias. Extensive experimentation by using different sets of training data has shown that our approach of re-identifying individuals through domain adaptation is acceptable. Increment in recognition rate as high as 203.8% was observed when style-transferred images were used. The best model came out to be Model 1, which was trained on the same images from Market-1501 [20] which were used for style transferring the EGO Re-ID dataset [3]. NST algorithm learns the style features from the Market-1501 dataset [20] in a really good way with some exceptions. The computation time required to generate these images is the bottleneck. Although our model performs well, some of the images generated by NST are not incorporating elements of the fixed camera dataset as discussed in failure cases. This problem can be solved by using GAN based image translation algorithms.

References

1. Basaran, E., Tesfaye, Y.T., Shah, M.: EgoReID dataset: person re-identification in videos acquired by mobile devices with first-person point-of-view. arXiv preprint arXiv:1812.09570 (2018)
2. Chakraborty, A., Mandal, B., Yuan, J.: Person reidentification using multiple egocentric views. IEEE Trans. Circuits Syst. Video Technol. **27**(3), 484–498 (2017)
3. Fergnani, F., Alletto, S., Serra, G., Mira, J.D., Cucchiara, R.: Body part based re-identification from an egocentric perspective. In: 2016 IEEE Conference on Computer Vision and Pattern Recognition Workshops (CVPRW), pp. 355–360 (2016)

4. Gatys, L.A., Ecker, A.S., Bethge, M.: Image style transfer using convolutional neural networks. In: Proceedings of the IEEE Conference on Computer Vision and Pattern Recognition (CVPR), pp. 2414–2423 (2016)
5. Gray, D., Tao, H.: Viewpoint invariant pedestrian recognition with an ensemble of localized features. In: Forsyth, D., Torr, P., Zisserman, A. (eds.) ECCV 2008. LNCS, vol. 5302, pp. 262–275. Springer, Heidelberg (2008). https://doi.org/10.1007/978-3-540-88682-2_21
6. Isola, P., Zhu, J.Y., Zhou, T., Efros, A.A.: Image-to-image translation with conditional adversarial networks. arXiv preprint arXiv:1611.07004 (2016)
7. Jing, Y., Yang, Y., Feng, Z., Ye, J., Yu, Y., Song, M.: Neural style transfer: a review. IEEE Trans. Vis. Comput. Graph. **26**, 3365–3385 (2019)
8. Pedagadi, S., Orwell, J., Velastin, S., Boghossian, B.: Local fisher discriminant analysis for pedestrian re-identification. In: Proceedings of the IEEE Conference on Computer Vision and Pattern Recognition (CVPR), pp. 3318–3325 (2013)
9. Peng, X., Saenko, K.: Synthetic to real adaptation with deep generative correlation alignment networks. arXiv preprint arXiv:1701.05524 (2017)
10. Ren, C., Liang, B., Ge, P., Zhai, Y., Lei, Z.: Domain adaptive person re-identification via camera style generation and label propagation. IEEE Trans. Inf. Forensics Secur. **15**, 1290–1302 (2020)
11. Sarfraz, M.S., Schumann, A., Eberle, A., Stiefelhagen, R.: A pose-sensitive embedding for person re-identification with expanded cross neighborhood re-ranking. In: IEEE Conference on Computer Vision and Pattern Recognition (CVPR), pp. 420–429 (2018)
12. Simonyan, K., Zisserman, A.: Very deep convolutional networks for large-scale image recognition. arXiv preprint arXiv:1409.1556 (2014)
13. Song, C., Huang, Y., Ouyang, W., Wang, L.: Mask-guided contrastive attention model for person re-identification. In: IEEE Conference on Computer Vision and Pattern Recognition (CVPR), pp. 1179–1188 (2018)
14. Tang, H., Zhao, Y., Lu, H.: Unsupervised person re-identification with iterative self-supervised domain adaptation. In: The IEEE Conference on Computer Vision and Pattern Recognition (CVPR) Workshops (2019)
15. Tzeng, E., et al.: Adapting deep visuomotor representations with weak pairwise constraints. CoRR (2015)
16. Varior, R.R., Haloi, M., Wang, G.: Gated Siamese convolutional neural network architecture for human re-identification. In: Leibe, B., Matas, J., Sebe, N., Welling, M. (eds.) ECCV 2016. LNCS, vol. 9912, pp. 791–808. Springer, Cham (2016). https://doi.org/10.1007/978-3-319-46484-8_48
17. Varior, R.R., Shuai, B., Lu, J., Xu, D., Wang, G.: A Siamese long short-term memory architecture for human re-identification. In: Leibe, B., Matas, J., Sebe, N., Welling, M. (eds.) ECCV 2016. LNCS, vol. 9911, pp. 135–153. Springer, Cham (2016). https://doi.org/10.1007/978-3-319-46478-7_9
18. Xiao, T., Li, H., Ouyang, W., Wang, X.: Learning deep feature representations with domain guided dropout for person re-identification. In: Proceedings of the IEEE Conference on Computer Vision and Pattern Recognition, pp. 1249–1258 (2016)
19. Yongxin, Z.: A survey of image to image translation with GANs (2020)
20. Zheng, L., Shen, L., Tian, L., Wang, S., Wang, J., Tian, Q.: Scalable person re-identification: a benchmark (2015)
21. Zhong, Z., Zheng, L., Luo, Z., Li, S., Yang, Y.: Invariance matters: Exemplar memory for domain adaptive person re-identification. In: Computer Vision and Pattern Recognition (CVPR) (2019)

Scene Text Recognition in the Wild with Motion Deblurring Using Deep Networks

Sukhad Anand(✉), Seba Susan, Shreshtha Aggarwal, Shubham Aggarwal, and Rajat Singla

Delhi Technological University, Bawana Road, New Delhi, India
sukhad_bt2k15@dtu.ac.in, sebasusan@dce.ac.in

Abstract. In this paper, the problem of text detection and recognition in videos has been addressed. We address two major issues that make it difficult to extract information in a video captured by a moving vehicle. Video captured by a moving vehicle contains a lot of blurs caused by motion which is one of the major issues preventing accurate recognition of text. The second major issue is the orientation of the text being detected, which may not be in the same plane. We propose a novel end-to-end pipeline consisting of deep networks. Our pipeline consists of a fully convolution network to detect text, Generative Adversarial Network to remove motion blur, a rectification network which makes use of Thin Spline Transformations and a Spatial Transform network to handle text which is not straight i.e. perspective and curved, and a recognition network to recognize the text. We only deblur the region around text boxes instead of complete images. We also track the text boxes in each frame to avoid re-recognition of text in consecutive frames. This significantly improves the performance of the system, as proved by higher classification scores achieved as compared to state of the art.

Keywords: Scene understanding · Motion blur · Optical character recognition · Fully Convolution network · Text recognition · Text detection · Deblurring

1 Introduction

Text can be used to understand images and videos. There are various fields where textual information can be useful. Navigation in autonomous vehicles, automating industrial processes, understanding complex scenes are some of the various applications.

A lot of text detection and recognition methods have been proposed. These methods proposed in literature [1–5] provide considerable accuracy in images, but they fail to perform well on videos. Some challenges in static images include extremely complex backgrounds, irregular illumination around the text, different varieties of text. Videos introduce some other challenges like motion blur and

S. K. Singh et al. (Eds.): CVIP 2020, CCIS 1378, pp. 93–103, 2021.
https://doi.org/10.1007/978-981-16-1103-2_9

focus change issues. Video compression also introduces some blocking occlusions. Blocking artifacts may be created by video compression. To extract temporal information from the videos, text tracking may be required that might be affected due to occlusions.

Therefore, an accurate pipeline is needed for robust text reading from videos. In the past few years, a lot of work has been done in the area of text detection and extraction from natural scenes, and scene text recognition has also attracted great interest from the industry in recent years due to its significance in a large number of applications. But natural scene videos are usually blurred due to motion, causing the loss of finer texture details, that results in low accuracy for scene text recognition and detection. The deblurring network we have used preserves these lost finer texture details in images and generates solutions that look convincing and are close to the real image. Detection of text boxes is done in natural scenes. Conventionally, text detection involves feature extraction and matching with some form of image contrast enhancement to highlight the text [6]. Text detection is a prerequisite and hence works as an important part in the procedure of extraction of textual information from backgrounds. Early approaches for text detection prove to be inefficient when dealing with perspective or curved text.

The specific contributions of this work are:

- An end-to-end system consisting of deep networks which is able to successfully detect and recognize text in real time, making it usable for automatic navigation in autonomous vehicles.
- To remove motion blur, we propose to use a Generative Adversarial Network because it achieves state-of-the-art performance and is 5 times faster than its closest competitor.
- To handle perspective text and curved text, we use an end-to-end trainable rectification network. We also handle in-plane rotated text by considering all positions 90° apart.
- The proposed pipeline significantly outperforms state-of-the-art methods in accuracy.
- We make sure that the pipeline runs in real time by deblurring only patches around the text boxes and not the complete image.

2 Related Work

In the past few years, there has been a lot of research in the domain of scene text recognition. Many methods have been proposed for this task [1–5]. Text recognition from videos along with text detection and localization has garnered huge interest in the industry. Various region based and connected component based methods were developed before the arrival of deep learning methods. Local image regions have been used in region based methods for the detection and recognition of text. In connected components based methods, the text is divided into connected components and then detection and recognition is performed on these connected components [3,4]. In [8], a novel image operator is presented that calculates the value of stroke width for every image pixel for the task of text detection in natural scenes.

In [3], maximally stable extreme regions are extracted as character candidates that are further grouped into text candidates using a single link clustering algorithm. For text recognition, various methods like [9] use part-based tree-structured character detection that models each type of character instead of using multi-scale sliding window approach to detect and recognize characters at the same time. It makes use of character specific structure information. Jon Almazan [10] uses an approach where both text strings and word images are embedded in a common vectorial subspace(label embedding) followed by learning of attributes and a common subspace regression. An example of document based text segmentation is [6] in which text is identified as a texture after application of adaptive contrast enhancement.

An integrated or end-to-end system is proposed by Wang et al. [2] in which two systems are built, where the first component is a two stage pipeline performing text detection followed by an OCR engine and the second is a system for generic object recognition. The methods used for text retrieval from images before deep learning methods were introduced, included extraction of low-level or mid level image features from the scene, which demanded repetitive pre-processing and post-processing steps. These methods cannot handle occlusions well, and hence with the appearance of deep learning methods having higher performance and efficiency, the shortcomings of traditional methods were overcome.

With the development of Convolution Neural Networks based methods [11,12], we can see that better performances are achieved in text detection and recognition. Various end-to-end systems for text detection and recognition, merged with text tracking techniques, where candidate text regions are detected by using stroke-map and morphological operations. Antani et al. divided scene text extraction into four simpler tasks: detection, localization, segmentation, and recognition [13], presenting a unified framework for video text detection, tracking and recognition.

In this paper, we have proposed an end-to-end system for scene text recognition consisting of simple pipeline that predicts arbitrary oriented words or text lines followed by motion deblurring of videos and finally a recognition network that predicts a sequence of characters from the rectified image. We use the DeblurGAN architecture proposed by [14] for motion deblurring. This method has higher recall and F1 score than its competitors and hence is significantly more efficient and helps in detection from blurred images and videos. Existing methods in the field of scene text recognition do not include deblurring of motion videos, neither is speed taken into account for the end-to-end system. Our system consists of four simpler tasks: text detection, video motion deblurring, text rectification and text recognition, and is a lot quicker than the earlier systems built for the same task and also removes blur caused in the scene due to motion. The previous work done on text recognition along with text tracking techniques have not used any temporal information of the videos, rather all the work is done on frames.

3 The Proposed Methodology

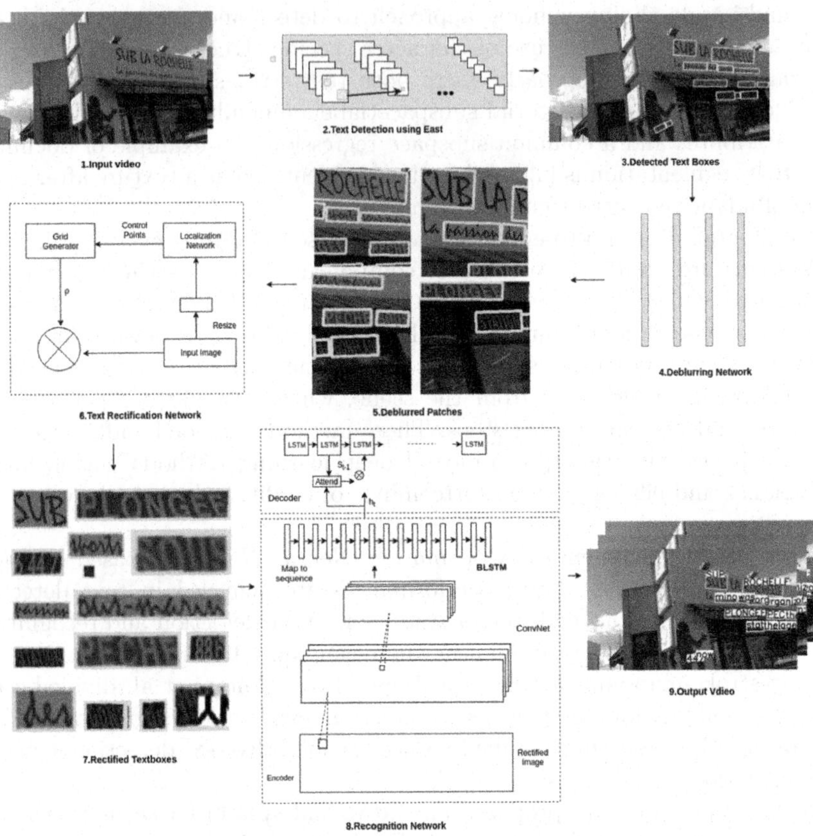

Fig. 1. Proposed end-to-end pipeline for scene text recognition from videos with motion deblurring

Our proposed architecture shown in Fig. 1 consists of a network that is an end-to-end learning method for a single pipeline that detects arbitrary oriented words or text lines of quadrilateral shapes in natural scenes from a video using a single neural network followed by motion deblurring of these detected shapes. We extract a 256×256 patch centered around the detected text boxes which is fed into the deblurring network. This not only helps to deblur the regions containing text but also provides a computational advantage as we don't have to deblur the complete image which saves a lot of time. After detecting and deblurring the text boxes in scenes, a recognition network predicts the stream of characters from a rectified image the details of which are described in next. Some challenging issues in scene text recognition include handling distorted or irregular text. So we first add a rectification network that transforms the image by rectifying the text in it and uses a flexible Thin-Plate Spline transformation to handle text irregularities. This is followed by a recognition network which uses attention mechanism to predict the text as found in the text boxes. We track the text boxes in the frames using Dlib's [28] implementation of [29]. We take a threshold of 7.0 for peak to side lobe ratio. If this ratio is below this value then we again perform recognition else we use the text recognised in previous frames. We achieve state-of-the art accuracy with processing speed of 20 FPS. We next describe each module in our end-to-end pipeline for text recognition from videos.

3.1 Textbox Detection

The first stage of the process flow is a neural network model used for text detection that generates word or text-line level predictions directly, without any redundant or slow intermediate steps, and produces the final text boxes detected. This pipeline can produce both word level or line level predictions, that can be of any geometric shape like a rotated box or a quadrangle. The model used here is a fully convolution neural network used for text detection and it outputs dense per-pixel predictions of words or text lines. This eliminates redundant or intermediate steps like text region formation, candidate proposal and word partition. The post-processing steps include only thresholding and Non Maximum Supression on the predicted geometric shapes. The detector is called EAST, an Efficient and Accurate Scene Text detection pipeline [7].

3.2 Deblurring

We then use the DeblurGAN(Generative Adversarial Network) introduced in [14] that is an approach based on conditional generative adversarial networks and a multi-component loss function. Here, a Wasserstein GAN with the gradient penalty and perceptual loss is used that is better than traditional MSE or MAE and hence helps in restoring finer texture details, which further works as a better input for the text recognition network. This model is trained on blurred outside-scene videos and hence works best for our experiments. We find that the formulation used in this model makes training faster and the resulting model generalizes better. The loss function is computed as a combination of content and adversarial loss.

$$L = \underbrace{\underbrace{L_{GAN}}_{\text{advloss}} + \underbrace{\lambda . L_X}_{\text{content loss}}}_{\text{total loss}} \tag{1}$$

where λ equals to 100 in all experiments; adversarial and content loss are defined as in [14].

3.3 Text Recognition

The proposed model in [15] comprises of two parts, a text rectification network and a text recognition network. A rectification network transforms the image by rectifying the text in it and uses a flexible Thin-Plate Spline (TPS) [19] transformation to handle irregularities in the text. It is much more flexible than other 2D transformations. TPS handles a vast variety of deformation on images and performs a non-rigid deformation. TPS is able to rectify both perspective and curved text that are the most common and typical types of irregular text.

A text recognition network is a trainable network which is trained with images and their ground truth text annotations. Connectionist Temporal Classification (CTC) method [20] gives a loss function which is differentiable and hence insensitive about horizontal placement of characters and spacing which makes the recognition network trainable end-to-end. Even though CTC is efficient, it fails to provide a mechanism which could model the dependencies among the output characters. Hence, [37] is based on an external language model, like a lexicon, to include language information prior to the recognition process. The recognition problem is tackled using a sequence-to sequence model with extensions to a bidirectional decoder. This network captures the character dependencies, and hence incorporates language modeling into the recognition process. The dependencies among the characters are captured by the bidirectional decoder in both directions. The model is trained end-to-end under a multi-task setting, whose objective is

$$L = \frac{-1}{2}\Sigma_{t=1}^{T}(\log p_{ltr}\frac{y_t}{I} + \log p_{rtl}\frac{y_t}{I}) \tag{2}$$

where y1,..., yt,..., yT constitutes the groundtruth text represented by a character sequence. The objective is the average of the losses on the left-to-right decoder and the right-to-left decoder, whose predicted distributions are denoted by p_{ltr} and p_{rtl}, respectively. I denotes the actual text.

4 Experiments

We train separate networks on different datasets and use them in a single system to perform end-to-end text detection and recognition. The end-to-end recognition accuracy on different datasets is calculated. The testing is also performed on some videos we collected using mobile phone camera for speed and accuracy.

4.1 Datasets

A single system is created which is able to perform text recognition in videos in real time. The deep networks are trained on different datasets and are then combined to boost the accuracy. We use GoPro dataset to train DeblurGAN. GoPro dataset [21] consists of 2103 pairs of blurred and sharp images in 720p quality, taken from various scenes.

For training the text detection network, we combine both ICDAR 2013 [22] and ICDAR 2015 [23] dataset and combine them to create trainset. ICDAR 2013 dataset contains most of the images from ICDAR 2003 [25] dataset. The dataset contains 1015 images. It contains no lexicon. ICDAR 2015 [23] is the baseline dataset for end-to-end scene text recognition. These are taken by a pair of Google Glasses without careful positioning and focusing. The dataset contains a lot of images containing irregular text including perspective text and curved text. This dataset helps to train a robust text detector which is able to detect perspective, curved and rotated text which may be found in videos.

We train recognition and rectification network on a dataset created by combining Street View Text [26] and ICDAR 2015 [23] dataset. Street View Text (SVT) is collected from the Google Street View. The test set contains 647 images of cropped words. Many images in SVT are severely corrupted by noise, blur, and low resolution. Each image is associated with a 50-word lexicon. Training on these datasets makes the model capable of detecting text in complicated scene images which are blurred and contain perspective and curved text.

All the trained models are combined into one system to work on videos. Our system performs better detection as shown by results of our approach on ICDAR 2013 test set.

To compare our system with other recognition systems, we have also performed experiments on the test sets of SVT and IIIT5K dataset [39]

4.2 Training Details

We use OpenCV [27] and Dlib [28] image processing for text boxes tracking and processing videos. All the experiments have been conducted on Google Compute Engine [30] with 1.2 GHz CPU, 64 GB RAM, Tesla K80 GPU and running Ubuntu 16.04. We use tensorflow for the networks implementation. We follow the training procedure for each of the deep networks as follows:

Detection Network. The network is trained on 512×512 corpus from images of ICDAR 2013 dataset with 24 as the batch size. The network is trained end-to-end using ADAM [31] optimizer. Initially learning rate is 1e-3 and is decayed to one-tenth with every 27000 mini-batches and is stopped at 1e-5. The network stops training when the performance stops improving.

DeblurGAN. The model was trained on a random corpus of number of images of size 256×256 extracted from 1000 Gopro dataset training images. The learning rate is fixed initially with the value 10-4 till 150 epochs. After this, the learning rate is decayed to zero over the next 150 epochs. The model is trained with batch size $= 1$, as cited by the authors in their research paper. The network is trained end-to-end using ADAM optimizer. The training phase took 6 days for training the DeblurGAN network.

Rectification and Recognition Network. The rectification and recognition network is trained on all the images in the SVT dataset [26]. The dataset contains 9 million images generated from a set of 90k common English words. Words are rendered onto natural images with random transformations and effects.

4.3 Results

We have tested our end-to-end text recognition method on the test of ICDAR 2013 scene image dataset to evaluate the performance of our method.

Table 1. Text recognition results on ICDAR 2013 scene image dataset (end-to-end)

Method	Precision	Recall	F score
Our method	0.94	0.80	0.88
Multi Frame Tracking	0.93	0.81	0.87
VGGMaxBBNet [5]	0.89	0.82	0.86
TextProposals [33]	–	–	0.81
Stradvision-1	0.88	0.75	0.81
TextSpotter [4]	0.85	0.69	0.77

Table 1 shows the results for end-to-end text recognition of our end-to-end system and various other state of the art methods. In this table, TextSpotter network is the baseline in the end-to-end text recognition task of ICDAR 2015 RRC Challenge 3 [24]. Multi Frame tracking network is a superior method than these methods for end-to-end text recognition because of higher tracking accuracy. Our method has better performance in terms of precision and F-score percentages than all of the state-of-the-art methods given in the table and hence it outperforms the best methods for the text recognition task.

Table 2 compares the recognition accuracies across a number of methods. Our method achieves best results out of all the previous approaches. Particularly, on IIIT5k [39] and SVT, our method significantly reduces recognition errors comparing to the previous bests. Considering that the tested datasets have covered an extremely wide range of real-world scenarios, it is clear that our method generally works better.

We also test the speed of our complete system on various videos captured. We achieve state-of-the art accuracy with processing speed of **20FPS**. Table 3 compares the recognition speed of our system as compared to others. The speed and accuracy of our system make it suitable for various autonomous systems.

Table 2. Recognition results comparison on SVT and IIIT5K dataset (accuracy)

Method	SVT	IIIT5K
Our method	0.9831	0.9917
Cheng et al. [34]	0.971	0.992
Yang et al. [18]	0.952	0.977
Lee et al. [35]	0.963	0.979
Shi et al. [36]	0.955	0.983
Shi et al. [37]	0.975	0.987
Jaderberg et al. [38]	0.932	0.978

Table 3. Recognition speeds per image

Method	Processing time (milliseconds)
Our method	17
Cheng et al. [34]	60
Yang et al. [18]	64
Lee et al. [35]	83
Shi et al. [36]	104
Shi et al. [37]	121
Jaderberg et al. [38]	243

5 Conclusion and Future Work

In this paper, we have proposed a pipeline of networks for an end-to-end scene text recognition from natural scene videos after blind motion deblurring. Our system consists of four simpler tasks: text detection, video motion deblurring, text rectification and text recognition, and is lot quicker than the earlier systems built for the same task and also removes blur caused in scene due to motion. The proposed pipeline performs better than other state-of-the-art methods in terms of accuracy, with a processing speed of 20 FPS. The system can be used in various autonomous systems and self driving cars. There can be further improvements in the processing speed by using tracking between the frames.

References

1. Chen, X., Yuille, A.L.: Detecting and reading text in natural scenes. In: CVPR (2), pp. 366–373 (2004)
2. Wang, T., et al.: End-to-end text recognition with convolutional neural networks. In: ICPR, pp. 3304–3308. IEEE Computer Society (2012)
3. Yin, X.-C., et al.: Robust Text Detection in Natural Scene Images. CoRR. abs/1301.2628 (2013)

4. Neumann, L., Matas, J.: Real-time lexicon-free scene text localization and recognition. IEEE Trans. Pattern Anal. Mach. Intell. **38**(9), 1872–1885 (2016)
5. Jaderberg, M., et al.: Reading text in the wild with convolutional neural networks. Int. J. Comput. Vis. **116**(1), 1–20 (2016)
6. Susan, S., Devi, K.M.R.: Text area segmentation from document images by novel adaptive thresholding and template matching using texture cues. Pattern Anal. Appl. **23**(2), 869–881 (2020)
7. Zhou, X., et al.: EAST: an efficient and accurate scene text detector. In: CVPR, pp. 2642–2651. IEEE Computer Society (2017)
8. Epshtein, B., et al.: Detecting text in natural scenes with stroke width transform. In: CVPR, pp. 2963–2970. IEEE (2010)
9. Shi, C., et al.: Scene text recognition using part-based tree-structured character detection. In: CVPR, pp. 2961–2968. IEEE Computer Society (2013)
10. Almazán, J., et al.: Word spotting and recognition with embedded attributes. IEEE Trans. Pattern Anal. Mach. Intell. **36**(12), 2552–2566 (2014)
11. Ciresan, D.C., et al.: Multi-column deep neural network for traffic sign classification. Neural Netw. **32**, 333–338 (2012)
12. Krizhevsky, A., et al.: ImageNet classification with deep convolutional neural networks. In: Advances in Neural Information Processing Systems, pp. 1097–1105 (2012)
13. Antani, S.K., et al.: Robust extraction of text in video. In: ICPR, pp. 1831–1834. IEEE Computer Society (2000)
14. Kupyn, O., et al.: DeblurGAN: Blind Motion Deblurring Using Conditional Adversarial Networks. CoRR. abs/1711.07064 (2017)
15. Shi, B., et al.: ASTER: an attentional scene text recognizer with flexible rectification. IEEE Trans. Pattern Anal. Mach. Intell. **41**(9), 2035–2048 (2019)
16. Mishra, A., et al.: Top-down and bottom-up cues for scene text recognition. In: CVPR, pp. 2687–2694. IEEE Computer Society (2012)
17. Jaderberg, M., Vedaldi, A., Zisserman, A.: Deep features for text spotting. In: Fleet, D., Pajdla, T., Schiele, B., Tuytelaars, T. (eds.) ECCV 2014. LNCS, vol. 8692, pp. 512–528. Springer, Cham (2014). https://doi.org/10.1007/978-3-319-10593-2_34
18. Yang, X., et al.: Learning to read irregular text with attention mechanisms. In: Sierra, C. (ed.) IJCAI, pp. 3280–3286. ijcai.org (2017)
19. Bookstein, F.L.: Principal warps: thin-plate splines and the decomposition of deformations. IEEE Trans. Pattern Anal. Mach. Intell. **11**(6), 567–585 (1989)
20. Graves, A., et al.: Connectionist temporal classification: labelling unsegmented sequence data with recurrent neural nets. In: Proceedings of the International Conference on Machine Learning, ICML 2006 (2006)
21. Nah, S., et al.: Deep multi-scale convolutional neural network for dynamic scene deblurring. In: CVPR, pp. 257–265. IEEE Computer Society (2017)
22. Karatzas, D., et al.: ICDAR 2013 robust reading competition. In: ICDAR, pp. 1484–1493. IEEE Computer Society (2013)
23. Karatzas, D., et al.: ICDAR 2015 competition on robust reading. In: ICDAR, pp. 1156–1160. IEEE Computer Society (2015)
24. Yao, C., et al.: Incidental Scene Text Understanding: Recent Progresses on ICDAR 2015 Robust Reading Competition Challenge 4. CoRR. abs/1511.09207 (2015)
25. Lucas, S.M., et al.: ICDAR 2003 robust reading competitions. In: ICDAR, pp. 682–687. IEEE Computer Society (2003)
26. Goodfellow, I.J., et al.: Multi-digit Number Recognition from Street View Imagery using Deep Convolutional Neural Networks (2013)

27. https://opencv.org/
28. http://dlib.net/
29. Danelljan, M., et al.: Accurate scale estimation for robust visual tracking. In: Valstar, M.F., et al. (eds.) BMVC. BMVA Press (2014)
30. https://cloud.google.com/
31. Kingma, D.P., Ba, J.: Adam: A Method for Stochastic Optimization. http://arxiv.org/abs/1412.6980 (2014)
32. Jaderberg, M., et al.: Synthetic Data and Artificial Neural Networks for Natural Scene Text Recognition. CoRR. abs/1406.2227 (2014)
33. i Bigorda, L.G., Karatzas, D.: TextProposals: a text-specific selective search algorithm for word spotting in the wild. Pattern Recogn. **70**, 60–74 (2017)
34. Cheng, Z., et al.: Focusing attention: towards accurate text recognition in natural images. In: ICCV. pp. 5086–5094. IEEE Computer Society (2017)
35. Lee, C.-Y., Osindero, S.: Recursive recurrent nets with attention modeling for OCR in the wild. In: CVPR, pp. 2231–2239. IEEE Computer Society (2016)
36. Shi, B., et al.: Robust Scene Text Recognition with Automatic Rectification. CoRR. abs/1603.03915 (2016)
37. Shi, B., et al.: An End-to-End Trainable Neural Network for Image-based Sequence Recognition and Its Application to Scene Text Recognition. CoRR. abs/1507.05717 (2015)
38. Jaderberg, M., et al.: Deep structured output learning for unconstrained text recognition. In: Bengio, Y., LeCun, Y. (eds.) ICLR (2015)
39. Mishra, A., et al.: Scene text recognition using higher order language priors. In: Bowden, R., et al. (eds.) BMVC, pp. 1–11. BMVA Press (2012)

Vision Based Autonomous Drone Navigation Through Enclosed Spaces

Sumit Veerawal[1(✉)], Shashank Bhushan[1], Mohak Raja Mansharamani[2], and Bishwajit Sharma[1]

[1] Centre for Artificial Intelligence and Robotics, DRDO Complex, C.V. Raman Nagar, Bangalore 560093, Karnataka, India
{sumitveerawal,bhushan,b_sharma}@cair.drdo.in

[2] Ramaiah Institute of Technology, MSRIT Post, MSR Nagar, Bengaluru 560054, Karnataka, India

Abstract. In this work, we present our approach to enable an autonomous drone to navigate in the absence of Global Positioning System (GPS) and traverse through opening of an enclosed space. To achieve this task, we have incorporated a) fusion of stereo visual odometry and Inertial Measurement Unit (IMU) readings to localise the drone for navigation; b) a novel method of point cloud processing to characterise the opening of enclosed space & compute trajectory and c) navigation module to traverse its way through the identified trajectory in autonomous mode. Our main contribution is an algorithm which computes entry point and its trajectory, and runs on-board in real time. The trajectory computation relies on point cloud data obtained from a stereo camera and the navigation uses fused position from the stereo camera and an IMU. Several innovations are made to ensure real-time performance of the algorithm. We study the accuracy of localization before and after fusion. We also vary the opening size in our experiments to evaluate the accuracy of our trajectory computation. The drone equipped with our algorithms was successful in autonomously traversing through the opening of an enclosed space.

Keywords: Autonomous drone · Visual odometry · Localisation · Point cloud processing · Real-time · Trajectory computation · Stereo · Opening

1 Introduction

Small drones are deployed for variety of tasks such as inspection, mapping and exploration and are ubiquitous in surveillance and reconnaissance tasks [1–3]. Drones are being used in lot of interesting applications like building 3D map of areas, tracking, aerial photography, package delivery etc. [4]. With modern computer vision techniques, capability of drones has increased vastly and they have been shown to perform even complex maneuvers [5].

Autonomous drones require accurate state estimation, localisation and navigation. Navigation of autonomous drones has been achieved through the use of

S. K. Singh et al. (Eds.): CVIP 2020, CCIS 1378, pp. 104–115, 2021.
https://doi.org/10.1007/978-981-16-1103-2_10

Global Navigation Satellite Systems (GNSS) such as Global Positioning System (GPS), GLObal NAvigation Satellite System (GLONASS) etc. and is well documented in [4,6]. One major drawback is accuracy of typical GPS positioning which is around 5 m [7]. This makes it impractical for tasks that require precise navigation of the drone system. GNSS signal also degrades in indoor environment. Drone can be localised through the use of motion capture systems or using vision based methods such as Simultaneous Localization and Mapping (SLAM) for indoor operation [8,9]. Experimentation and realization of an autonomous indoor drone navigation system is done by the use of monocular camera & Inertial Measurement Unit (IMU) [8,10–12]. It has also been attempted by use of stereo camera [13,14]. The current state of the art work in this field given by Oleynikova et al. explains in detail about full system architecture for global and local planning for an autonomous drone in cluttered environment using C-blox and Voxblox [15]. They have used a Visual Inertial (VI) sensor for visual inertial odometry (VIO) based localisation and RGB-D sensor for depth perception. Krajník et. has attempted similar work in ground vehicles in [16] and extended for aerial vehicles in [17].

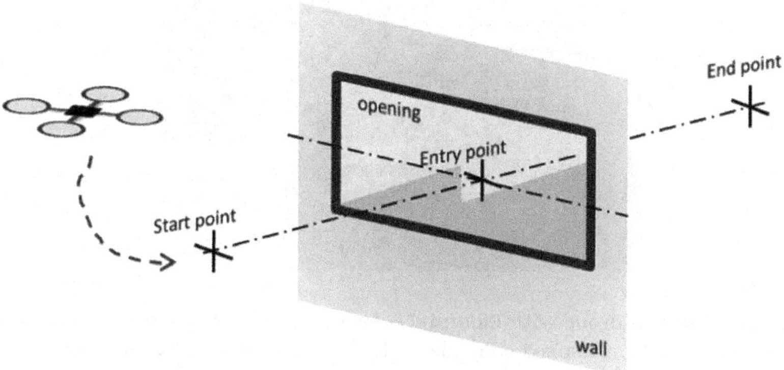

Fig. 1. Drone finding normal direction of the opening, safe entry point & navigating autonomously through an opening

In this work, vision based autonomous navigation of drones through opening of an enclosed space is demonstrated. For this purpose, we focused on stereo vision based localisation and depth perception. Our full system includes sensor fusion for drone localisation, characterisation of opening of enclosed space, trajectory generation and autonomous navigation. Sensors used are stereo camera and an IMU sensor. We propose a novel technique for entry point detection and trajectory generation by processing stereo vision based 3D point cloud which is used for mapping the enclosed space and characterising the navigable path. Navigation of drone is achieved through closed loop control. This approach has been tested by flying it through an open window located indoors. An example of this problem that we solve is shown in Fig. 1.

2 Overview

2.1 Hardware Setup

As shown in Fig. 2, the experimental setup consists of an assembled hexacopter drone using commercially available components which are mounted on DJI F550 frame. It has six brush-less motors(A), Pixhawk controller with PX4 flight stack(B) and Simonk 30A Electronic Speed Controller (ESC)(C). Nvidia Jetson TX2(D) module is mounted for on-board computation purpose and it is required to run stereo based 3D point cloud computation. A ZED stereo camera(E) is attached as a stereo vision sensor pointing in forward direction. External GPS module, Here 2(F) is mounted on the top. A Garmin LIDAR-Lite V3 LIDAR module provides height stabilisation. Drone is powered by 6500 milliamp-hour LiPo battery. We use a laptop with Intel i5, 2.3 GHz, 4 core processor and 16 GB RAM as our ground control station (GCS) which communicates to the drone through a telemetry module (433 MHz). Additionally, in-built WiFi (2.2 GHz) in Nvidia Jetson is also used to communicate sensor data to GCS.

Fig. 2. Experimental drone with mounted sensors; (A) Brushless motors, (B) Pixhawk controller, (C) Electronic speed controller, (D) Nvidia Jetson TX2, (E) Stereo camera, (F) GPS module

2.2 Software Setup

Data flow diagram is given in Fig. 3. Ground control station and Nvidia Jetson TX2 on the drone are using Robot Operating System (ROS) framework on Ubuntu Linux 16.04. ROS is an open-source, meta-operating system used for tasks such as hardware abstraction, low-level device control, message-passing between processes and also provides tools and libraries for building, writing, and running code across various computers [18]. Pixhawk controller is running on an open source PX4 firmware version 1.9 [19]. PX4 is an open source flight control software for drones and other unmanned vehicles. PX4 supports various sensors (e.g. IMU, GPS, Visual positioning) in order to control drone state which is needed for stabilization and autonomous control.

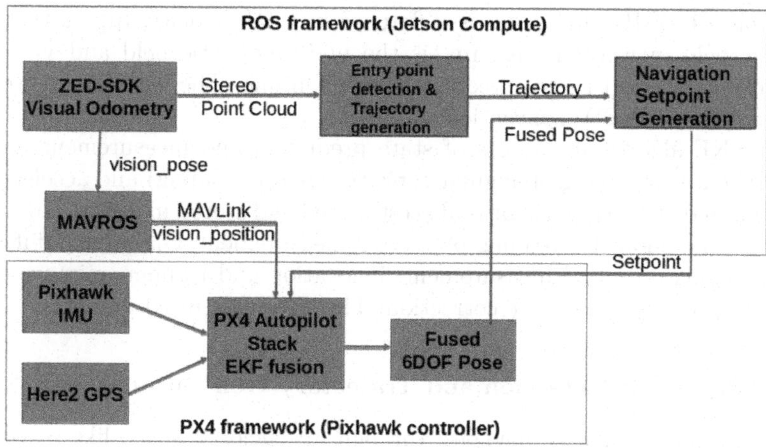

Fig. 3. Data flow diagram

In order to send visual odometry data to PX4 controller for fusion, we need to convert it to MAVLink protocol. MAVLink protocol is lightweight message controlling protocol optimized for small air vehicles like drones. MAVROS is used to convert vision pose data to MAVLink format. Major algorithm components are localisation, entry point detection & trajectory generation and navigation.

3 Our Approach

3.1 Localisation

Localisation module estimates six degrees-of-freedom (6DOF) pose of an object containing position and orientation relative to a particular coordinate system. Localisation module is very critical for a stable flight therefore Pixhawk controller requires a minimum of gyroscope, accelerometer, magnetometer (compass) and barometer. An external positioning system like GPS or vision based positioning is needed to enable autonomous mode [19]. For our set up, we have utilized Visual Odometry (VO) which is the process of estimating the state (pose and velocity) of an agent by using only the input of one or more cameras [20].

As shown in Fig. 3, we have used Extended Kalman Filter (EKF) formulation for pose estimation, which is a technique for filtering and prediction in linear systems [21]. EKF will fuse VO positioning and IMU data to give us a fused odometry. EKF based filtering is supported in PX4 stack, however we need to set parameters as per the sensors being used [22].
State of the system used in PX4:

$$\mathbf{x} = [\mathbf{q}\ \mathbf{v^w}\ \mathbf{p^w}\ \mathbf{\Delta a}\ \mathbf{\Delta v}\ \mathbf{m_e^w}\ \mathbf{m_b}\ \mathbf{v_i^w}]$$

where $\mathbf{q}$ is the quaternion representing the orientation of the body, $\mathbf{v^w}$ is the velocity of body in world frame, $\mathbf{p^w}$ is the position of body in world frame, $\mathbf{\Delta a}$

is difference in IMU angle, $\mathbf{\Delta v}$ is difference in IMU velocity, $\mathbf{m_e^w}$ is the earth magnetic field in world frame, $\mathbf{m_b}$ is the body magnetic field and $\mathbf{v_i^w}$ is the wind velocity in north-east direction in world frame. The world frame follows north-east-down (NED) convention.

The EKF algorithm consists of state prediction and measurement update. The IMU data consisting of angular rates (gyroscope reading) and accelerations is used in prediction step. Error is also estimated and stored in a state covariance matrix. Visual odometry reading provides a measurement. On basis of difference between observation and measurement, innovation and Kalman gain are calculated which are used for state correction. This give us a fused pose.

3.2 Entry Point Detection and Trajectory Generation

In order to autonomously navigate through an enclosed space like a window, drone needs to characterise the 3D space. Stereo camera mounted on it provides 3D point cloud with respect to its body frame at a certain frame rate. This point cloud is processed on-board to find out if path is navigable. Point cloud processing is carried out using the framework from point cloud library [23]. If path is navigable, trajectory through that space is calculated. Currently, our algorithm is tailored for planar surfaces, however it can be generalized for curved surfaces. Flow chart of the algorithm is given in Fig. 4. Following steps are part of our proposed algorithm:

- **Pre-processing:** Point cloud obtained from stereo camera is passed through a voxel filter to down-sample the data. It is further filtered by a pass through filter, which extracts specified 3D volume of data and discards points outside the volume. This pre-processing step firstly reduces the amount of data to be processed, and more importantly, discards faraway points which could distract the wall extraction algorithm.
- **Wall-extraction:** To find the opening, the wall plane must be extracted. We innovate a random sample consensus method (RANSAC) based approach, and incorporate physical constraints to segment a vertical wall. The wall is usually vertical, but there can be a relative deviation as measured in the drone's body frame. Expecting this deviation to be bound in a range $[\pm\theta]$, the normal of extracted dominant plane is compared to the x-axis of the body frame. If the dominant plane is verified to be in the permissible range angles, it is retained as a wall.
- **3D volume search:** A KD-Tree representation is built for dominant planar points. Now, a 3D volume search is performed with a 3D kernel of spherical shape and radius equal to drone's maximum span times a safety margin (parameter). This returns number of neighbouring points at center of the kernel. Number of neighbours is mapped to a 2D binary image with axes as two directions along the plane. We now traverse along the grid, go to its 3D location and find number of neighbours. If we get a zero response (which corresponds to free space), image pixel is assigned black intensity. For non-zero neighbours, pixel is assigned white intensity. This yields a binary image as

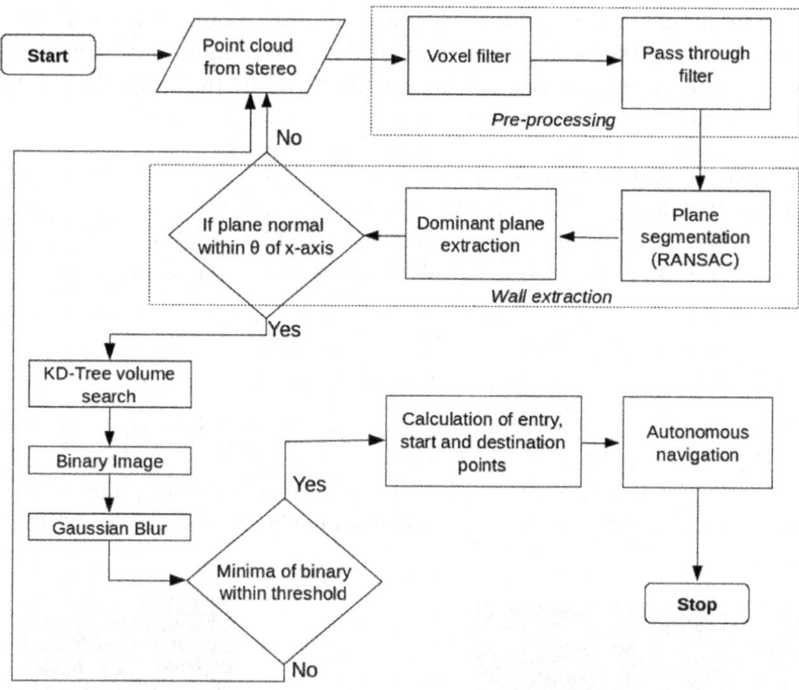

Fig. 4. Flow diagram of trajectory computation algorithm

shown in Fig. 5. Effectively, problem is now projected from 3D to 2D space which ensures faster data processing.

- **Entry point calculation:** The drone can ideally traverse through any point in the black region of the binary image. We, however, endeavor to find the optimal point which is safest for traversal, considering drift due to errors or wind. If distances from the surrounding edges are considered, we are looking for a maxima. The usual way to find this is using a distance transform [24]. However, computing the distance transform results in higher code and time complexity. Since we are aware of the maximum size of opening required, we optimize the maxima search by using a Gaussian kernel of dimensions larger than the desired opening size to blur the binary image, and then find the minima in the resulting image. In practice, spurious free spaces can distract the algorithm and hence, if this minima is located far from center of frame, the computation is discarded and we wait for a new point cloud. The innovation in this step ensures faster computations for a safe entry point detection.
- **Trajectory computation:** Approaching the entry point computed in the previous step directly from the current location can lead to collision if the drone is close to the wall. The safest direction to travel to the entry point is along the normal to the wall, as depicted in Fig. 6. We, therefore, compute a trajectory consisting of three points: (i) the start point positioned a safe

distance outside the window, λ_{out}, (ii) the entry point within the window plane, and (iii) the destination point inside the window, λ_{in}. These points are computed in Eqs. 1 and 2. This ensures that the platform always travels along the normal to the window.

The 3D plane equation is $ax + by + cz + d = 0$. This can be also be written as $\mathbf{n} \cdot \mathbf{p} + d = 0$, where $\mathbf{p} = (x, y, z)$ and $\mathbf{n}$ is the plane normal such that $\|\mathbf{n}\| = 1$. The computed entry point, $\mathbf{p_{entry}} = (e_x, e_y, e_z)$. The equations for computing 3D points for start point, $\mathbf{p_{start}}$ and destination point, $\mathbf{p_{dest}}$, are given below:

$$\mathbf{p_{start}} = -(\lambda_{out})\,\mathbf{n} + \mathbf{p_{entry}} \tag{1}$$

$$\mathbf{p_{dest}} = (\lambda_{in})\,\mathbf{n} + \mathbf{p_{entry}} \tag{2}$$

Refer to Fig. 5 for sample output of our algorithm. Note that the original point cloud contains planes in different orientations. Our method filters and segments the wall containing the opening. The computed entry point and finally the trajectory is passed on to the autonomous navigation stack of the drone.

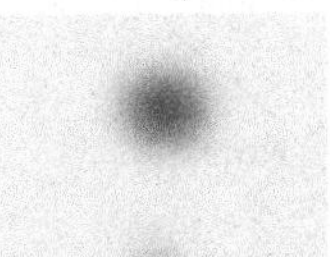

Gaussian blurred binary image (obtained after projecting nearest neighbours

Fig. 5. Trajectory computation of corridor (actual picture and point cloud output)

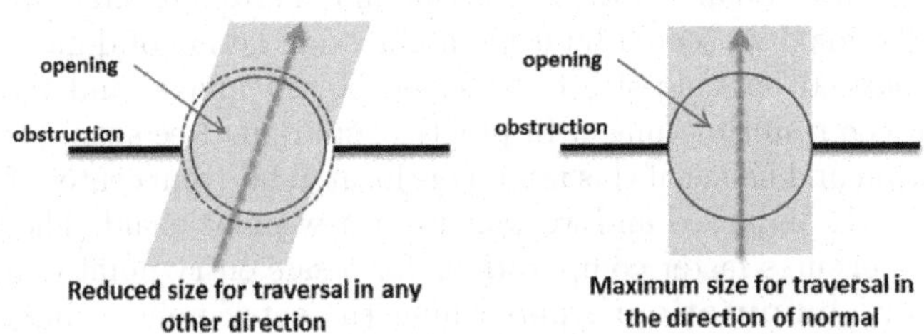

Fig. 6. Choice of normal direction

3.3 Autonomous Navigation

The objective of this module is to maneuver the platform through the computed trajectory autonomously. The trajectory contains start, entry and destination points along with a quaternion in the direction of window plane's normal. These points are first transformed to drone's navigation frame (North-East-Down for PX4). The navigation starts with orienting yaw of the platform with the quaternion and points are fed to fight controller sequentially. The drone starts flying to these points. After it reaches with in a tolerance of τ cm of start point, it considers itself to have attained this point. It repeats this for entry point and destination point. After reaching the destination point, which is inside the window at a pre-defined distance, it will now start tracing the same points backward without turning around i.e. with the same yaw as previous. It sequentially traces the points in reverse order. It terminates at the start point and controller switches to position hold.

4 Experimentation and Results

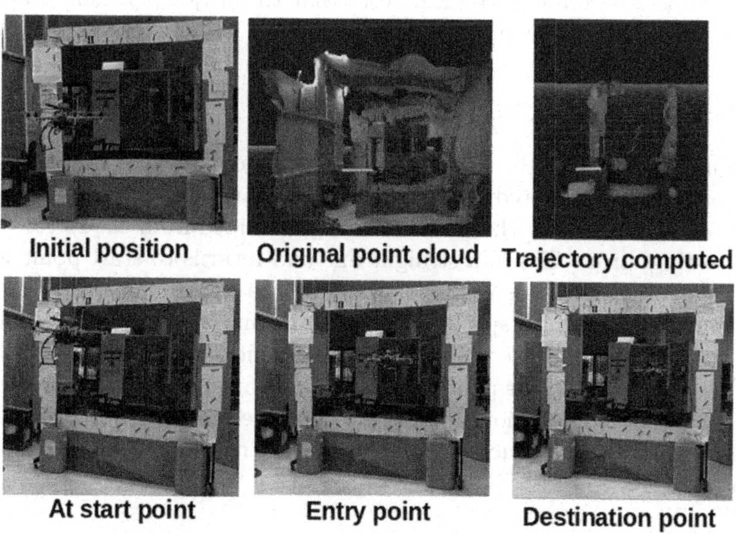

Fig. 7. Complete workflow demonstration for our drone

We tested our complete workflow with the drone system for an indoor scenario using a window frame of dimensions 1.7 m (width) by 1.6 m (height). For a stable flight indoors, extensive parameter tuning was required. PX4 flight stack allows a parameter viz. EKF2_AID_MASK, to select how the measurement update and data fusion will take place in the Pixhawk controller. We tuned parameters of EKF fusion (PX4) related to EKF2_AID_MASK setting which are

IMU noise & bias values (for both accelorometer & gyroscope) and vision sensor position. After this tuning, drone was able to take off and sustain position hold mode indoors without using GPS signal. Similarly, entry point detection required parameter tuning for plane threshold, voxel filter size, distance thresholds etc. A combined list of parameters is shown in Table 1. The lateral dimensions of the drone including propellers is 0.60 m. Horizontal field of view of ZED stereo camera is 90°. The minimum window size we can traverse for a safety margin of 2× is 1.2 m and λ_{out} for lateral coverage of window is 0.6 m. However for additional safety, we used larger window sizes for experimentation.

For this experiment, the drone is initiated in position mode at a safe distance in front of the window. Once the platform detects an open window of appropriate size and is able to successfully generate trajectory (visible on GCS), user switches the drone in autonomous mode (called off-board control in PX4) for window traversal. Autonomous navigation module subscribes to this trajectory and traverses through the points in trajectory as explained earlier. Refer to Fig. 7, to see the complete workflow in action. Finally, our algorithm pipeline was successful in computing trajectory and navigating the flying drone through the trajectory autonomously. We observed that input point cloud from stereo camera was generated 5 Hz using ZED-SDK while our trajectory computation algorithm runs 1 Hz on Jetson TX2. Note that the trajectory computation did not utilise any GPU processing on Jetson TX2.

4.1 Accuracy of Localisation Module

As explained in Sect. 3.1, the system fuses visual odometry and IMU data to get a fused position. We collected data in different scenarios to measure the accuracy of fusion and compare it with visual odometry obtained from the stereo camera. For this testing, drone flies in a straight line and returns to start point without changing its yaw angle. This is similar to our traversal strategy. The test results are shown in Table 2 which specifies the total distance travelled and Root Mean Square Error (RMSE) of the system at return point of trajectory. RMSE is calculated by using mean of squared differences between 3D observed positions, (x_i^o, y_i^o, z_i^o) and actual positions, (x_i^a, y_i^a, z_i^a) obtained for multiple runs of experiment. Observed RMSE values are lower for fused trajectory which validates the use of fusion.

4.2 Accuracy for Entry Point Detection

To evaluate performance of our entry point computation, we recorded data in two different scenarios where opening size was varied from 1 m^2 to 1.7 m^2. We compared observed center of opening and actual center. We have taken at least 10 runs for each scenarios and computed average RMSE values. RMSE was found to be less than 0.10 m for both scenarios, which shows that the algorithm is accurate enough for our navigation where we keep a tolerance of 0.10 m. One of the sample trajectory is shown in Fig. 5.

Table 1. Parameter tuning

Module	Parameter	Parameter description	Value	Units
Localisation (PX4)	EKF2_GYR_NOISE	Gyroscope Noise	0.01	rad/s
	EKF2_GYR_B_NOISE	Gyroscope Bias Noise	0.1	rad/s^2
	EKF2_ACC_NOISE	Accelerometer Noise	1.0	m/s^2
	EKF2_ACC_B_NOISE	Accelerometer Bias Noise	0.01	m/s^3
	EKF2_EV_POS_X/Y/Z	X, Y, Z position of vision sensor	0.16, 0.06, 0.05	m, m, m
Entry point and trajectory computation (Proposed algorithm)	Leaf size	Voxel filter size	0.02	m
	Plane Threshold	Inlier threshold for fitting	0.1	m
	Angle θ	Threshold on plane's normal with x-axis	30	Degrees
	(xmin, xmax)	X-direction limit for Pass-through Filter (PF)	(0, 3)	m
	(ymin, ymax)	Y-direction limit for PF	(−1.5, 1.5)	m
	(zmin, zmax)	Z-direction limit for PF	(−1.5, 1.5)	m
	Kernel Size	Gaussian Filter Kernel	32	Pixels
	Safety margin	Factor for drone size	2	None
	Distance, λ_{out}	Start point distance outside	1.5	m
	Distance, λ_{in}	Destination point distance inside	1.5	m
Navigation	Tolerance τ	Tolerance to reach a point	0.1	m

Table 2. Analysis of accuracy of localisation module

Scenarios	Travelled distance (m)	RMSE of ZED odometry (m) [%]	RMSE of fused odometry (m) [%]
Workshop	20	0.972 [4.86%]	**0.847 [4.23%]**
Corridor	16	0.582 [3.63%]	**0.575 [3.59%]**
Portico	30	1.095 [3.65%]	**0.782 [2.60%]**

5 Conclusion

We have demonstrated that using fusion of visual odometry and IMU, a drone can be navigated through an opening of enclosed spaces with the aid of trajectory planning in the absence of GPS. The proposed algorithm is specifically useful in formulating a safe straight line trajectory through an opening of an enclosed space. In contrast, local planners like Voxblox [15] end up with a non-linear trajectory which might be better suited for point-to-point navigation. The proposed algorithm can serve as an additional module to be used only when transitioning through openings. Performance achieved in this work can be improved by using more accurate localisation like (i) integrating visual inertial odometry (VIO) with PX4 and (ii) by incorporating faster and more accurate stereo computation methods on-board. Our approach can also be extended for curved surfaces by using appropriate parametrization during point cloud segmentation.

Acknowledgment. The authors would like to thank Director, Center for Artificial Intelligence and Robotics, DRDO (Ministry of Defence, India) for supporting this research work.

References

1. Delmerico, J., Mintchev, S., Giusti, A., et al.: The current state and future outlook of rescue robotics. J. Field Robot. **36**(7), 1171–1191 (2019). https://doi.org/10.1002/rob.21887
2. Panigrahi, N., Sankalp Panigrahi, S.: Processing data acquired by a drone using a GIS: designing a size-, weight-, and power-constrained system. IEEE Consumer Electron. Mag. **7**(2), 50–54 (2018). https://doi.org/10.1109/MCE.2017.2714718
3. Eschmann, C., Kuo, C.M., Kuo, C.H., Boller, C.: Unmanned aircraft systems for remote building inspection and monitoring. In: Proceedings of the 6th European Workshop on Structural Health Monitoring, Dresden, Germany, vol. 36, p. 13 (2012)
4. Patrik, A., et al.: GNSS-based navigation systems of autonomous drone for delivering items. J. Big Data **6**(1), 1–14 (2019). https://doi.org/10.1186/s40537-019-0214-3
5. Loianno, G., Brunner, C., McGrath, G., Kumar, V.: Estimation, control, and planning for aggressive flight with a small quadrotor with a single camera and IMU. IEEE Robot. Autom. Lett. **2**(2), 404–411 (2016)
6. Kan, M., Okamoto, S., Lee, J.H.: Development of drone capable of autonomous flight using GPS. In: Proceedings of the International Multi Conference of Engineers and Computer Scientists, vol. 2 (2018)
7. Van Diggelen, F., Enge, P.: The worlds first GPS MOOC and worldwide laboratory using smartphones. In: Proceedings of the 28th International Technical Meeting of the Satellite Division of the Institute of Navigation (ION GNSS+ 2015), pp. 361–369 (2015)
8. Loianno, G., Thomas, J., Kumar, V.: Cooperative localization of MAVs using RGB-D sensors. In: 2015 IEEE International Conference on Robotics and Automation (ICRA), pp. 4021–4028 (2015)
9. López, E., et al.: Indoor SLAM for micro aerial vehicles using visual and laser sensor fusion. Robot 2015: Second Iberian Robotics Conference. AISC, vol. 417, pp. 531–542. Springer, Cham (2016). https://doi.org/10.1007/978-3-319-27146-0_41
10. Achtelik, M., Achtelik, M., Weiss, S., Siegwart, R.: Onboard IMU and monocular vision based control for MAVs in unknown in-and outdoor environments. In: 2011 IEEE International Conference on Robotics and Automation, pp. 3056–3063 (2011)
11. Weiss, S., Scaramuzza, D., Siegwart, R.: Monocular-SLAM-based navigation for autonomous micro helicopters in GPS-denied environments. J. Field Robot. **28**(6), 854–874 (2011)
12. Shen, S., Michael, N., Kumar, V.: Tightly-coupled monocular visual-inertial fusion for autonomous flight of rotorcraft MAVs. In: 2015 IEEE International Conference on Robotics and Automation (ICRA), pp. 5303–5310 (2015)

13. Shen, S., Mulgaonkar, Y., Michael, N., Kumar, V.: Vision-based state estimation and trajectory control towards high-speed flight with a quadrotor. Robot.: Sci. Syst. **1**, 32 (2013)
14. Achtelik, M., Bachrach, A., He, R., Prentice, S., Roy, N.: Stereo vision and laser odometry for autonomous helicopters in GPS-denied indoor environments. Unmanned Syst. Technol. XI Int. Soc. Opt. Photonics **7332**, 733219 (2009)
15. Oleynikova, H., et al.: An open-source system for vision-based micro-aerial vehicle mapping, planning, and flight in cluttered environments. J. Field Robot. **37**(4), 642–666 (2020)
16. Krajník, T., Faigl, J., Vonásek, V., Košnar, K., Kulich, M., Přeučil, L.: Simple yet stable bearing-only navigation. J. Field Robot. **27**(5), 511–533 (2010)
17. Krajník, T., Nitsche, M., Pedre, S., Přeučil, L., Mejail, M.E.: A simple visual navigation system for an UAV. In: International Multi-Conference on Systems, Signals & Devices, pp. 1–6. IEEE (2012)
18. Documentation- ROS Wiki. http://wiki.ros.org/Documentation. Accessed 20 July 2020
19. PX4 Autopilot User Guide (master). https://docs.px4.io/master/en/index.html. Accessed 20 July 2020
20. Scaramuzza, D., Fraundorfer, F.: Visual odometry [tutorial]. IEEE Robot. Autom. Mag. **18**(4), 80–92 (2011)
21. Sorenson, H.W. (ed.): Kalman Filtering: Theory and Application. Piscataway, IEEE (1985)
22. PX4 Autopilot guide: Using Vision or Motion Capture Systems for Position Estimation. https://dev.px4.io/v1.9.0/en/ros/external_position_estimation.html. Accessed 20 July 2020
23. Rusu, R.B., Cousins, S.: 3D is here: Point cloud library (pcl). In: 2011 IEEE International Conference on Robotics and Automation, pp. 1–4 (2011)
24. Sironi, A., Lepetit, V., Fua, P.: Multiscale centerline detection by learning a scale-space distance transform. In: Proceedings of the IEEE Conference on Computer Vision and Pattern Recognition, pp. 2697–2704 (2014)

Deep Learning-Based Smart Parking Management System and Business Model

Yatharth Kher[1(✉)], Aditya Saxena[2], P. S. Tamizharasan[1,2], and Amit D. Joshi[1,2]

[1] Department of Computer Science, Birla Institute of Technology and Science (BITS), Pilani, Dubai Campus, Dubai, UAE
f20170253@dubai.bits-pilani.ac.in

[2] Department of Computer Engineering and IT College of Engineering Pune, Pune, MS, India

Abstract. In this fast-developing world, the increase in the number of vehicles demands a smart parking system in smart cities. The issue of spending a lot of time finding parking slots needs to be addressed. The increase of smartphones provides the space to develop smart applications enabled with AI and deep learning. This paper proposes an AI-based smart parking management system and a business model to provide a solution for both user and the owner of the parking space. Owners of the parking slots can opt for fixed or variable timeslots to make use of their parking spaces. Registered users can check the availability of the parking spaces at the destination in real-time and details of the users such as the time and vehicle details can be detected and updated automatically. Billing for the parking space usage will also be done automatically as per the regulated guidelines. Raspberry Pi and deep learning tools are used for the implementation. The proposed system is cost-effective and reduces time and energy.

Keywords: Smart parking · AI · Deep learning · Android · Raspberry Pi

1 Introduction

A smart city uses information and communication technologies to improve the efficiency of the public, helps in improvement towards the quality of life for citizens. Blockchain and IoT are emerging technologies that are changing the present world towards a technologically driven world. Any city can be considered for smart city initiative, by introducing system like, smart parking system uses a mobile app to manage parking system. As it will efficiently control the management of parking, people will not park in no-parking zones as they will find parking slots using this App. Also, it will be easy for the government to keep a check on the parking system so that everything is smooth and easy for citizens. The Fig. 1 shows strategic component to develop smart city mission improvement, smart innovation, energy, smart transportation, smart traffic light, automatic streetlight, smart parking, smart innovation on thinking, etc.

S. K. Singh et al. (Eds.): CVIP 2020, CCIS 1378, pp. 116–127, 2021.
https://doi.org/10.1007/978-981-16-1103-2_11

Taking the example of a person who works on a 9 to 5 job and leaves his parking slot vacant for the hours he goes to work. The person can rent out the parking space for those limited hours through which he vans get some profit and also help the society. Using technology to integrate this win-win situation for both a person who has space and for a person who is tired of finding a parking spot [1].

Recently, various techniques relying on the use of video cameras have been proposed to monitor the occupancy of parking lots [7–9]. Smart Application using TensorFlow API and raspberry pi can be said to be using AI and making the model learn more and more and get better. In our model, the TensorFlow API will detect car plates with the help of raspberry pi and webcam. This approach would reduce manpower and cost. Such systems can also be used on roads to detect speeding vehicles, drivers not driving properly, etc.

The main purpose of a smart parking system is to get people parking where they can park when the normal government parking slots are over hence it reduces time wastage, fuel consumption. Raspberry Pi and a webcam will be deployed in parking slots for owners who want to rent out their parking spaces. Owners can also earn by giving there free and available parking slots on rent and also the government can earn by monitoring it and earning a commission. Users can book online and can pay online as well.

Countries like India, face problems with large free parking space management. Conventional parking management systems use sensors and other communications modules but they always count the parking for disabled people and also does not address solution for free private parking spaces of individuals.

Our solution solves the problem of the modern megacities which have the major problem of increasing vehicles day by day. Also, we solve the problem of people who have parking spaces empty near to a public attraction and can earn some bounty for the same. On the other hand, the tourists and visitors can use the parking spaces which will lead to the sustainable development of a smart city.

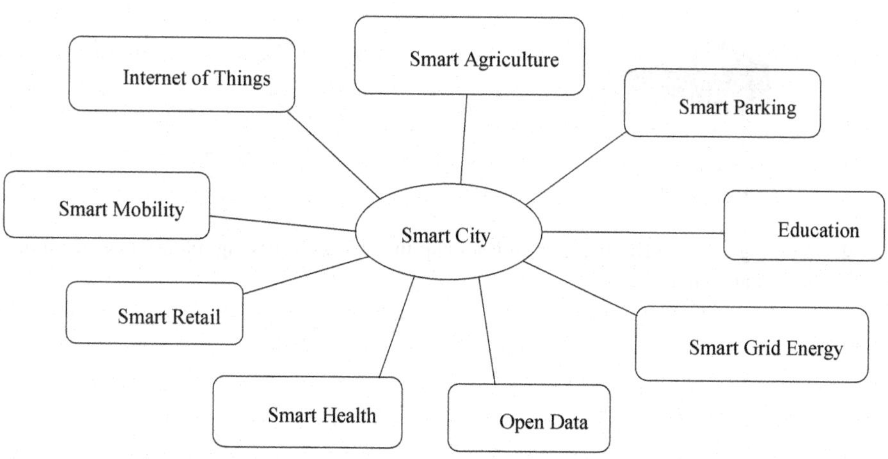

Fig. 1. Smart city smart amenities

Figure 1 explains what all a city should have to call itself a smart city and what all amenities it should have. Smart Parking is one of the best examples and a major step to turn a city into a smart city. As seen in [2] and [3] it is improved that by comprising this idea into an android app which will be easy to use and handy for users. Where even a common citizen will be able to use it.

2 System Model

2.1 System Architecture

In metropolitan areas, people prefer a cab or car as convenient to go for work, shopping, theatres, etc. Finding a place to park their vehicle in a densely populated city is too difficult in the present situation as all the parking slots provided by the Government get over. But parking lots in private societies or buildings are empty as people go to work in the morning and get back in the evening. So, the whole day their parking space is vacant. There is a need for an assistive application that can allow people to find car parking for private parking owners [4]. In this way, people with private parking can rent it to people finding parking and earn money through their free vacant parking space. Figure 2 clearly explains the working of our idea how it looks on the user end.

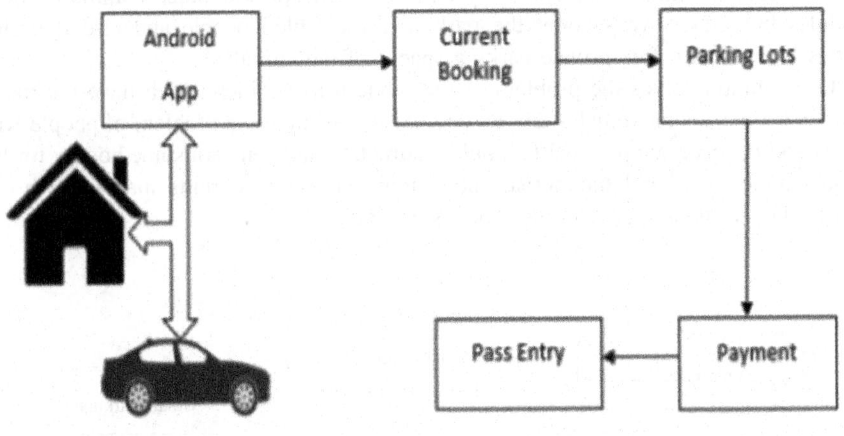

Fig. 2. Working on our idea, the user android app then books a parking lot and pays for it and enters and gets authenticated.

3 Proposed System

The proposed system consists of two phases explained below:

1. Development of Android Application
2. Free Space Identification
3. Authenticating User Vehicle
4. Notifying the owner of the parking

To enable a user to use the Smart Parking system, the user needs to register with a vehicle number. Users can set up a payment system in their account settings. The android app is made for booking parking slots and payments. The application is used to find the free parking slot and mention arrival and departing time. Also, the owner has to mention the time parking will be made available. The database will check and tell if the parking slot is empty or not. Also, this can be done later with sensors and can be improved more. All these four phases comprise of different steps for making up this model making up from development of the app, then detecting free space which is rented out by the owner, then authenticating if the legit user has parked car in the designated slot, and lastly informing the owner about his asset. The proposed system is better than the previous systems which does not record the details of car owners in the database and which does not allow users to interact with a user-friendly interface to book parking slots. It is a bit ahead of the sensor approach for allocating parking as deep learning and IoT take things to a next level.

An algorithm is formulated so that a user can give parking for rent and also the customer can book the parking slot.

1. Both customers and users sign up on our platform (Mobile Application).
2. The user gives details about its parking slot's location and free timings.
3. The customer chooses whenever he wants the parking and offers a 30 min buffer for the convenience of the customer.
4. Customer selects Parking slot and books for the timing he wants and pays for the same.
5. Comprises of a friendly rating system where both customer and user give a rating to each other.

3.1 OCR

The main and the most important software for the proposed algorithm is the detection of vehicle number plate. This is done with the help of Optical Character Recognition, which is categorized into three categories-

- Capture and locate the image of the car number plate.
- Feature extraction from the number plate
- Recognize the numbers from the extracted features.

The first step in capturing the image of the vehicle by the Pi Camera interfaced with the Raspberry Pi. The image is captured in RGB format so it can be further processed for the number plate extraction.

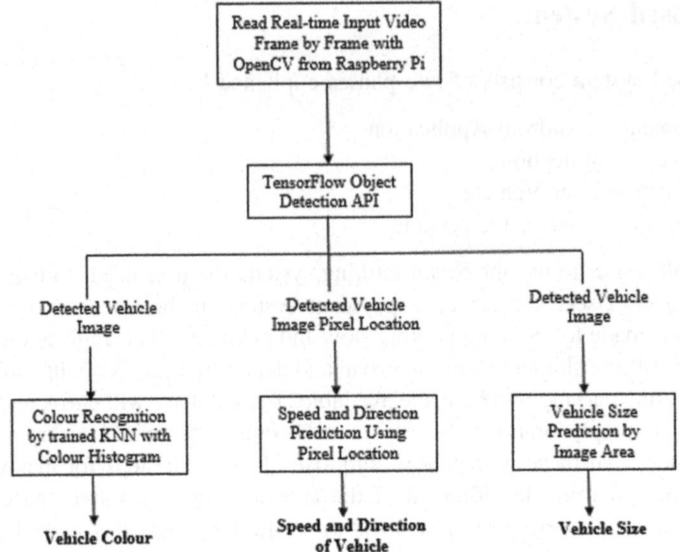

Fig. 3. Working of OpenCV and Raspberry Pi

3.2 Localization and Segmentation

The OCR algorithm searches for the number plate text on the captured image. Segmentation determines the constituents of an image, necessary to locate the regions where the data is printed and differentiate it from background figures and graphics. As the Vehicle number plates are a combination of black and white text and numbers, with Alphanumeric characters written in black, it is easy for the algorithm to localize the coordinates of the number plate. The captured image is searched for the black color pixels or something closer to black in value. If the pixel value is black the pixel is set to 1 or else the value is set to 0. After each pixel value of the captured image is set, the image is filtered by removing all the white patches connected to any borders by connecting them to a pixel value of 0.

3.3 Pre-processing and Feature Extraction

The main aim of feature extraction is to capture and filter the essential characteristics of the symbols, in this case, the alphanumeric characters. The captured image may contain a certain amount of noise or disturbance due to some systematic error or background disturbance depending on the resolution of the camera. This may lead to poor recognition rates. Feature Extraction helps the model to extract the most significant symbols leaving out the unimportant attributes, helping the algorithm to classify and predict more accurately.

3.4 Recognition of Alphanumeric

Once the characters are separated, each character is stored as separate variables. The OCR algorithm now compares each separate individual character against the complete alphanumeric database. The OCR algorithm uses the correlation method to match the individual character and the number identified is stored in string format in a variable. The string is then compared with the stored database for the vehicle authorization.

3.5 TensorFlow Lite

TensorFlow Lite provides the framework for a trained TensorFlow model to be compressed and deployed to a mobile or embedded application. Interfacing with the TensorFlow lite Interpreter, the application can then utilize the inference-making potential of the pre-trained model for its purposes [6] (Fig. 4).

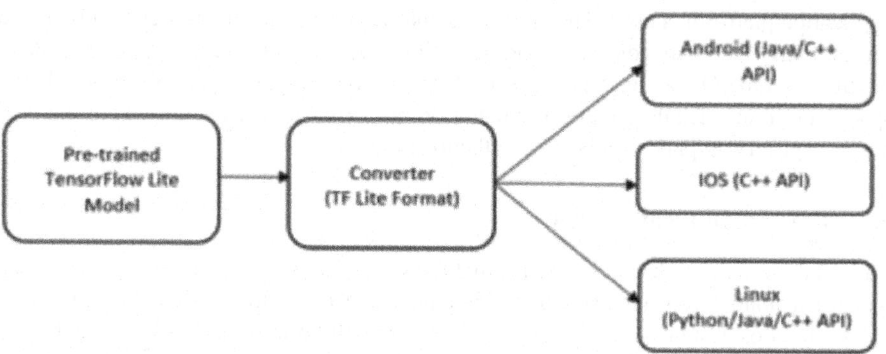

Fig. 4. Working on TensorFlow API with our android app

3.6 Hardware

3.6.1 Raspberry Pi

The main hardware component used to develop the parking management system is the Raspberry Pi 4+ and NoirV2 Pi camera. The Raspberry Pi 4+ Model B is the 4th generation of Raspberry Pi. Whilst maintaining its affordability, it has Quad Core GPU which is four times better than the first-generation models. The core of Model 4 B+ is Cortex-A72 (ARM v8) 64-bit as compared to ARM 1176JZF-S and Cortex-A53 64- bit core found in first- and second-generation models respectively. This significantly reduces the computational power and electricity consumption for the working device, thereby reducing net heat output. The board has inbuild wireless LAN and Bluetooth connectivity making it the ideal solution for powerful connected designs.

3.6.2 Noir V2 Pi Camera

The Raspberry Pi NoIR Camera Module v2 is a high-quality 8-megapixel Sony IMX219 image sensor custom designed add-on board for Raspberry Pi, featuring a fixed focus lens. It's capable of 3280 × 2464-pixel static images, and also supports 1080p30, 720p60 and 640 × 480p60/90 video. It attaches to Pi by way of one of the small sockets on the board upper surface and uses the dedicated CSi interface, designed especially for interfacing to cameras.

The board itself is tiny, at around 25 mm × 23 mm × 9 mm. It also weighs just over 3 g, making it perfect for mobile or other applications where size and weight are important. It connects to Raspberry Pi by way of a short ribbon cable.

The NoIR Camera has a No InfraRed (NoIR) filter on the lens which makes it perfect for doing Infrared photography and taking pictures in low light (twilight) environments.

4 Implementation

4.1 Mobile Application

The mobile application is developed using the Android Bundle and the Android Studio application platform is used. The application has two ends one the user end and one the owner end. User end consists of Registration, log in. Selection of time and date, payment setup. Owner end consists of Registration, Login, Available time of free space, and Bank details. Figure 3 registration page for our application where the user has to register his plate number for authentication.

4.2 Free Space Identification

The database will be checked if it says that the spot is not empty and also the owner has made it available then it means that it is empty and ready to use. So, this way other users can book it and avail the parking. The user will be informed of how much time the parking is available to be rented hence after deciding the correct parking for the vehicle, the user can book the parking and setup his payment option for the same. In the future, this app will also be identifying that the parking slot available can park what size of the vehicle. Figure 5 shows that TensorFlow API can predict vehicle size using image area which will allow heavy vehicle users to use this app and find parking for their vehicles.

4.3 Authenticating User Vehicle

Raspberry Pi, webcam, and TensorFlow API will help to detect the user vehicle by detecting the car number plate. TensorFlow Object Detection API will be used to detect the car number plate and authenticate if the correct user is using the parking, if it does not match then our system will notify the owner about this. For such purposes, a monitoring authority is needed that is the reason Government will be the perfect monitoring authority for this application which will lead to a more secure environment for both user and owner. Also, will be another source of revenue for the Government and will give more data to Government in the form of car plates and parking trends, leading to the removal of the burden from the Government to build more and more parking slots and shrinking the roads.

4.4 Notifying the User

Once the parking is booked by a User, the parking owner is notified about it and the time for the parking is booked is also notified to the Owner. User cannot book for the time more than the Owner has specified so that whenever Owner reaches home back has his parking ready for Owner's vehicle. This way he will be helping society as well as getting a bit of profit out of it as a bonus of being a helpful citizen.

5 Business Model

The government can control this application and get revenue for extra parking. This application can cut commission for every time a booking is made which can in return increase more to the government treasury. So, this is how AI can help the government to create a new kind of parking business and control it efficiently. We have added a business model to our project to make it a win-win situation for everyone. We take this as an advantage that we are giving a technological solution with a business opportunity. Take an example of vacant parking and a parking owner rents it and the user rents it for $5 per hour and out of which the owner gets $4 per hour and the Government earns $1 per hour.

A remotely monitoring authority is required for the smooth use of this application and no one can be better than the Government in taking up this charge and hence making it run smoothly and making up a safe environment for both user and owner of parking slots. Also, it can add up a bit for Government's revenue for monitoring this application and by controlling it they will need necessary data of users which can be used for making new policies.

6 Experimental Results

In the Experiment, a parking spot of a private owner is chosen who uses our algorithm to rent his empty parking while the owner is away on work. RaspberryPi and TensorFlow integrated with our mobile application for the user and customer [5]. The limitation is that the proposed algorithm does not allocate the parking for the customer. A person has to choose themselves concerning the location.

- Profit- When the owner rents parking using our algorithm.
- Loss- When the owner's parking is left empty as our algorithm is not used.
- Net – Profit-Loss.

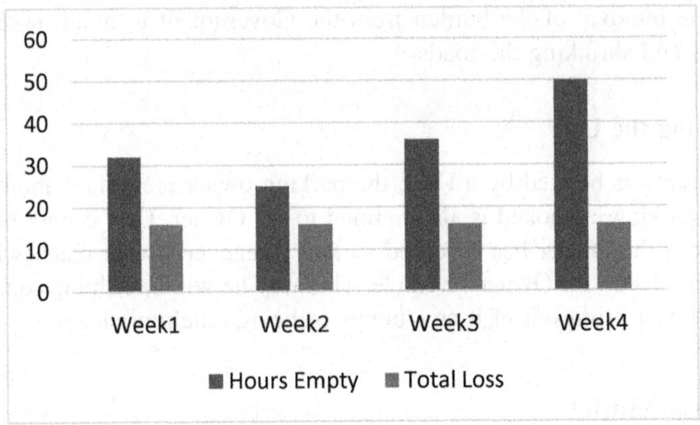

Fig. 5. Number of empty hours and loss vs time

Figure 5 clearly shows hours for which parking is empty and the loss is the cost which he pays weekly for his parking.

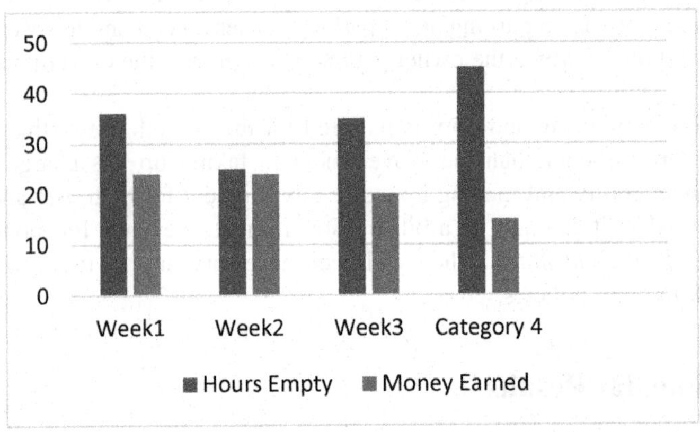

Fig. 6. Number of empty hours and profit vs time

Whereas Fig. 6 clearly shows that when a user is using our algorithm to rent his parking and how much profit he is making out of which.

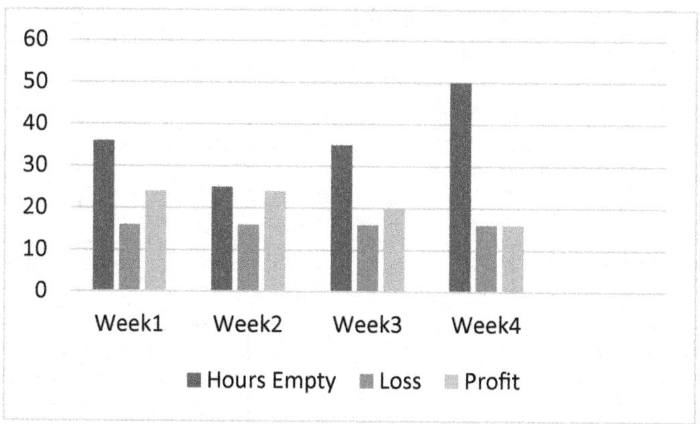

Fig. 7. The number of empty hours, loss, profit vs time. Which depicts that the owner is in net profit as profit > loss.

In Fig. 7 comparison of Fig. 6 and Fig. 5 and the result came out that 4 weeks the user's Net Amount was in Profit.

Net Amount = Profit – loss. The user was easily covering up his cost which he was paying for the parking space.

In this work, Computer Vision (AI) based smart parking system has been proposed which integrates Deep Learning and Android Development. The user can book their parking slot and owners can rent out their available parking spaces and Government can control this app and can earn revenue by taking commission per booking by which they can control as well as making the parking business profitable.

Figure 8 shows the working of our app and how the full proposed idea moves step by step for a user. This app is a more user-friendly app for any user to simply understand the concept and book parking. Thus, reducing time wastage and costs of fuel also a lot of stress. This also benefits Government and Parking Owners as they can earn money from their free parking lots which are not in use. With better control over parking management, a city can take its first steps towards a smart city initiative.

This paper has a few points which make it unique like covering up the parking system in just an android app with a MySQL database and use of AI to detect number plates and authenticate the vehicle. The algorithm worked on specific private parking lots of owners whose parking lots are left empty for most of the time in the day. The same idea can be implemented on the government public parking and it will serve as good as it serves for a private ownership parking. A business model has been made for both owners and government to make money from their dead assets. Also, taking up a case study of a highly populated tourist spot like Burj Khalifa, usually, parking slots are occupied in the dedicated parking lot. But, in contrary there are many offices which get empty after the employees leave for home thus, it makes parking slots in those office building empty. So, those office owners can give their parking lots for rent on this application and earn revenue even while not working. This way, this application is the first step for a city to be smart, and helping out everyone using this application from users, owners to the Government makes this application easily adaptable and highly user friendly. The dataset used for car plate detection was from UCSD. Also, a raw dataset was taken to test the model.

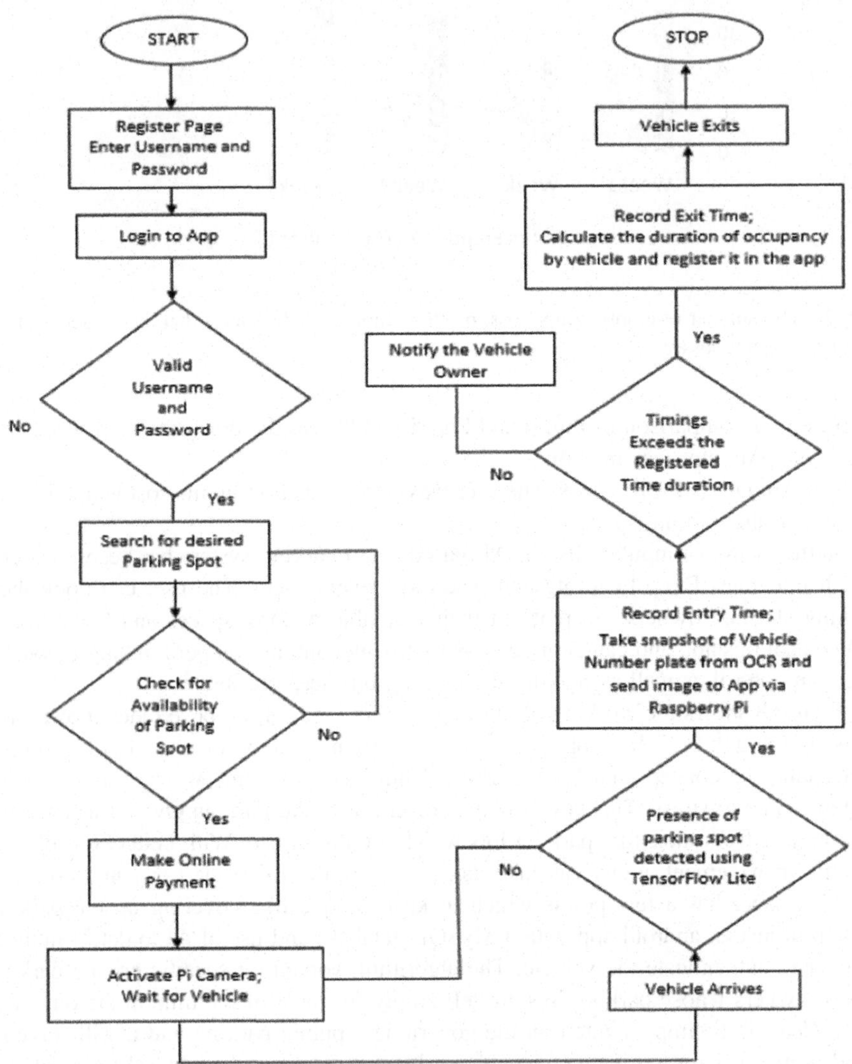

Fig. 8. Working on the proposed idea

7 Conclusion

In this work, Computer Vision-based smart parking system has been proposed which integrates Deep Learning and Android App Development. The user can book their parking slot and owners can rent out their available parking spaces and Government can control this app and can earn revenue by taking commission per booking by which they can control as well as making the parking business profitable. This app is a more user-friendly app for any user to simply understand the concept and book parking. Thus, reducing time wastage and costs of fuel also a lot of stress. This also benefits Government and Parking Owners as they can earn money from their free parking lots which are not in use. With better control over parking management, a city can take its first steps towards a smart city initiative. This idea can be further taken ahead with more and more additional work done on adding more security and also Government will get more information as they will have an eye on every number plate and hence they can easily have a control on people who do not fill up their fines and also, on theft.

8 Limitations

The biggest limitation to be faced is that in today's world the number of vehicles is too high and to register all the vehicles on our database will be a big task. Also, we are not improving the method to improve the accuracy of the detection of number plates. If the Government allows and takes it as a smart city initiative then it can be linked to annual insurance as your car will only be insured if you sign up for this smart city initiative.

References

1. Acharya, D., Yan, W., Khoshelham, K.: Real-time image-based parking occupancy detection using deep learning (2018)
2. Xiang, X., Lv, N., Zhai, M., El Saddik, A.: Real-time parking occupancy detection for gas stations based on haar-AdaBoosting and CNN. IEEE Sens. J. 1 (2017). https://doi.org/10.1109/jsen.2017.2741722
3. Valipour, S., Siam, M., Stroulia, E., Jagersand, M.: Parking-stall vacancy indicator system, based on deep convolutional neural networks, pp. 655–660 (2016). https://doi.org/10.1109/wf-iot.2016.7845408
4. Geng, Y., Cassandras, C.G.: New "smart parking" system based on resource allocation and reservations. IEEE Trans. Intell. Transp. Syst. **14** (2011). https://doi.org/10.1109/tits.2013.2252428
5. Hodel, T., Cong, S.: Parking space optimization services, a uniformed web application architecture (2020)
6. Alsing, O.: Mobile object detection using TensorFlow lite and transfer learning. Dissertation (2018)
7. Dan, N.: Parking management system and method. US PatentApp. 10/066,215, January 2002
8. Wu, Q., Huang, C., Wang, S.-Y., Chiu, W.-C., Chen, T.: Robust parking space detection considering inter-space correlation. In: IEEE International Conference on Multimedia and Expo, pp. 659–662. IEEE (2007)
9. del Postigo, C.G., Torres, J., Menéndez, J.M.: Vacant parking area estimation through background subtraction and transience map analysis. IET Intell. Transp. Syst. **9**, 835–841 (2015)

Design and Implementation of Motion Envelope for a Moving Object Using Kinect for Windows

Jhansi V. Setty[1(✉)] and Subarna Chatterjee[2(✉)]

[1] CSN, Department of CSE, M. S. Ramaiah University of Applied Sciences, Bengaluru, India

[2] Department of CSE, M. S. Ramaiah University of Applied Sciences, Bengaluru, India

subarna.cs.et@msruas.ac.in

Abstract. Everything we see around us is three-dimensional (3D) in nature. The traditional cameras throw light on two-dimensional (2D) behavior of the objects without considering the third dimension or the depth information. This poses a restriction on understanding the complete behavior of any object in space. Thus, this work aims at enlarging the scope of studying and analyzing the 3D behavior of an object through depth imaging. It has its application across the field of robotics and Ergonomics [2]. Ergonomics deals with designing the workspaces and components based on the requirement of the users. The 3D volume occupied by an object moving in space is one of the key focus of ergonomics. This volume representation of an object is known as Motion Envelope (ME). This paper proposes a unique approach to extract the ME of an object moving in space. Techniques like feature extraction is used to detect the required object followed by homography [3] to estimate its pose with motion in space. The 3D position of the object is tracked to reproduce the path followed by the object and a 3D object model is aligned to the detected path to reconstruct the ME. Kinect [6] V1 with colour and depth imaging capabilities is used as the depth sensing device. The results shown in this paper include the object detection and tracking for objects of different shapes and surfaces. The object tracking results are processed to construct ME using the proposed algorithm. This approach emerges to be cheaper and accurate due to the low cost associated with the Kinect sensor compared to the traditional laser-based depth sensors. Thus, we can conclude that this work leads us one-step further in analyzing and understanding the complexity of real-world 3D objects.

Keywords: Kinect · Motion envelope · Computer vision · Object detection · Feature matching · Homography

1 Introduction

Tremendous amount of research has been going on in the field of 3D surface imaging technologies from several decades. With the introduction of high speed and high-resolution electronic sensors and increased computational power, there is an increased demand for 3D surface imaging technologies across various segments of the market.

S. K. Singh et al. (Eds.): CVIP 2020, CCIS 1378, pp. 128–140, 2021.
https://doi.org/10.1007/978-981-16-1103-2_12

In this paper, one such 3D surface imaging technologies known as structured light sensing is used to identify the total space occupied by an object moving in space also known as the envelope of motion. This is based on the concept of protecting the space of a moving object where the space occupied by the object is identified to prevent any unwanted interference into its space. Ergonomics is one such field where space protection plays an important role. It is also used to design the workspace and the workspace components such that it fits the people who use them and is highly used in designing the interiors or office workspaces, manufacturing units, vehicle interiors, etc.

In this work, the ME of an object is constructed using Kinect V1. The process includes identifying the object of focus and capturing its position in 3D space continuously. The recorded data is processed to identify the total volume occupied by the moving object in 3D. The Kinect provides a colour stream that is used to identify the object and depth stream is used to estimate the 3D pose of the object and to obtain its 3D reconstruction.

ME, an application of ergonomics, can be obtained by simulation of the 3D object and replicating its motion. However, generation of ME based on the real time movement is challenging. Thus, the work aims at capturing the real-time movements of the 3D objects in space.

Generally, Time of Flight cameras and Laser cameras are used for motion capture of 3D objects. But, they are expensive. Thus, a cheaper alternative is the Kinect, originally designed for gaming and can generate 3D representation of the space in real time. The accuracy of the Kinect is like that of time-of-flight (ToF) cameras and for smaller distances, is similar to laser-based devices. Thus, Kinect can be used to obtain the 3D reconstruction of the objects and track them to obtain their ME.

The paper is organized as follows: Sect. 2 gives an overview of the concepts behind the design of the work. The Sect. 3 is about the design and implementation of the proposed algorithm. Section 4 presents the results and discussions and Sect. 5 provides the conclusion.

2 Background

2.1 Motion Envelope

"A motion envelope is a mechanism to represent a virtual volume by taking all positions, and linkages, which is achieved during the complete range of motion of an object". ME can be better demonstrated using a simulation. Figure 1 shows the snapshots of the simulated movements of an object using the PTC Creo Parametric where the 3D motion of the object is captured, and ME is developed.

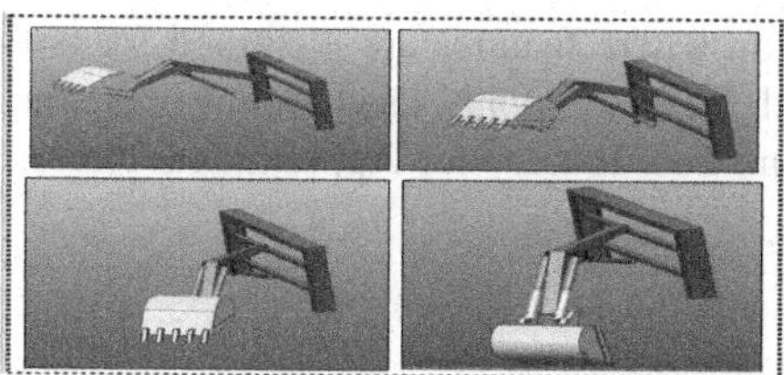

Fig. 1. Motion envelope of an object moving in space

ME identifies the 6° of motion of an object in focus including their translation and rotation. ME has several applications in the field of robotics, automobile design, ergonomics, etc. For example, Gauthier, S., et al. [7] develops a ME using Kinect to analyze the movements of a person's arms and legs during an exercise. This approach can help trainers to remotely train their students and analyze their performance or doctors to analyze the movements of the patient and asses their progress. P. Horejsi et al. [6], uses the Kinect device to analyze the movements of a person in a work environment with the help of simple case studies.

2.2 Kinect Sensor

Kinect is a motion capture device shown in Fig. 2. The Kinect consists of an RGB camera, Infrared projector, Infrared camera and a microphone array at the bottom for audio support. A tilt motor is present at the base to adjust the angle of the camera with a range of ±27°.

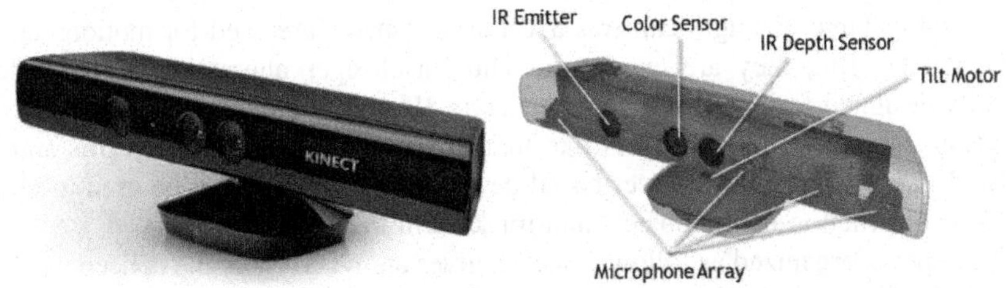

Fig. 2. Kinect for Windows sensor and Kinect hardware composition

Kinect is available in two versions, V1 and V2. V1 is based on structured light technique whereas the V2 is based on ToF measurements. As measurements using structured light are accurate compared to ToF cameras, Kinect V1 is chosen for the study.

2.3 Feature Based Object Detection

Feature Detection [10] deal with identifying those parts of the image where there are maximum changes. Some of the well-known feature detection algorithms are Harris Corner Detector, Scale Invariant Feature Transform (SIFT), Speeded-up Robust Features (SURF), etc.

Feature Matching is used for object detection where features are identified for both the reference and target images and matched. The commonly used feature matching algorithms are Brute Force Matching (BF) and Fast Library for Approximate Nearest Neighbors (FLANN) Matching [4].

2.4 Object Localisation Using Homography

To draw a boundary around the detected object, the result of feature matching algorithm is sent to homography [3] to identify the perspective transform. The perspective transform is a matrix, which represents the translation, rotation and scaling which the boundaries of the reference image should undergo to represent the object in the target image. To overcome the errors in matching, algorithms RANSAC [3] and LEAST_-MEDIAN [3] are used. The good matches that give correct estimations are inliers and others are outliers.

3 Design and Implementation

Figure 3 shows the approach followed to solve the problem in the form of block diagram. The left side of the block diagram represents the processes that take place at real time (Algorithm 1) and the right side of the flow chart represents the steps involved in post processing (Algorithm 2).

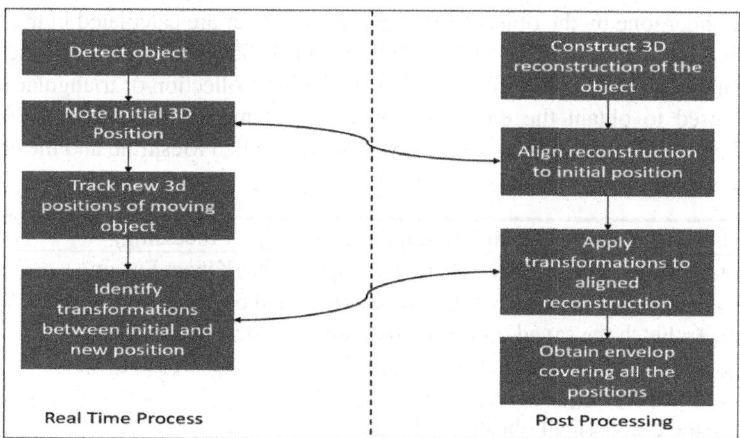

Fig. 3. Block diagram describing the process of constructing motion envelope

At real time (Algorithm 1), the RGB and depth video is obtained from the Kinect at the rate of 30 frames/sec. Object is tracked through feature detection and feature matching for every successive video frame with the help of reference image. Homography is used to estimate the initial pose and the pose change of the object from one frame to other. The initial position and pose changes of the object are recorded in the form of point cloud (3D points) and a text file respectively. They are used later during the post processing.

Algorithm 1: To track the moving object (Real time Process)

1. F_{ref} ← Extract features from the reference image (Object of focus).
2. $f_1 \ldots f_n$ ← Extract frames from the video.
3. F_{frame} ← Extract features from each frame f_x.
4. M ← Matching features between F_{ref} and F_{frame}.
5. N ← Minimum no. of matching features required for object detection.
6. $object_{Detected}$ = True ← If M > N, else go to step 4.
7. $O_{p1} \ldots O_{pn}$ ← Capture object points from the current video frame and save it.
8. Repeat step 4 to step 8 for successive video frames.

In the post processing (Algorithm 2), the complete 3D mesh of the object is derived using Kinect Fusion and is aligned to the initial pose of the object captured from the 1st video frame where the object was detected. It uses the object points saved by the algorithm 1 for each frame and recreates the trace of the object in 3D. Initially a complete 3D mesh of the object is obtained. Later the recorded data is used to identify the pose of the object in successive frame. The transformations (Tf) are then applied on the 3D mesh to obtain the view of all the positions that the object would have occupied in 3D. Tf undergone by the object from one frame to other are calculated in the form of rotation(R) and translation(T) matrix. The R and T obtained for each pose Tf are applied on the initial 3D mesh of the object to obtain a collection of triangular meshes, which is used to obtain the envelope. Once all the meshes are obtained, they are imported onto a 3D mesh processing software system called MeshLab and the envelope of the collection of 3D meshes is obtained.

Algorithm 2: To construct the motion envelope (Post Processing)

1. Obtain the complete 3D reconstructed object using Kinect Fusion.
2. O_{init} ← Fetch point cloud of the 3D reconstructed object.
3. D_{curr} ← Fetch the saved object points of the first detected frame O_{p1}.
4. R_{curr} , T_{curr} ← Compute Rotation and Translation from O_{init} to D_{curr}.
5. O_{curr} ← Apply R_{curr} and T_{curr} on O_{init}.
6. Save the transformed object points (O_{curr}) as a polygonal model.
7. D_{next}←Fetch the saved object points from the 2nd detected frame onwards ($O_{p2\ldots}$ $\ldots O_{pn}$).
8. Repeat the process from step 4 to step 6 using O_{curr} and D_{next} instead of O_{init} and D_{curr} respectively.

3.1 Object Detection and Tracking

Object detection is implemented using python and OpenCV library. Here two images are used, one as template(reference) and other as target in which the object will be detected as shown in block A of Fig. 4 (obtained from Kinect video streams). In Fig. 4A, down one is the target image and upper one is the reference image of the object. The template image contains only the object.

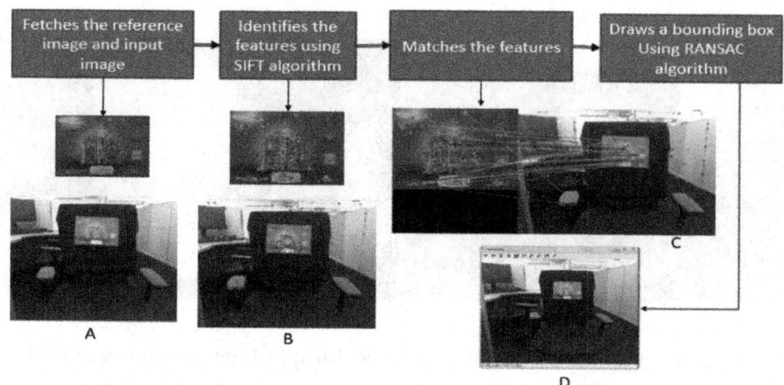

Fig. 4. Block diagram for object detection using feature matching

Colour and **depth** streams are fetched from Kinect to detect the object and capture the 3D points. Kinect Library is applied to develop a complete 3D model of the object using Kinect Fusion. Python wrapper class is used to access the depth and colour data.

Features are identified using method SIFT [5] algorithm, which takes the target and template as parameters and returns the key points and computes the descriptors for both the template and the target image. The features identified are drawn on the image as shown in the B block of Fig. 4.

FLANN based matcher is used to match the features between two images. The block C of Fig. 4 shows the matched features between the target and reference image. They are represented using lines joining the corresponding features. This matcher trains on a train descriptor collection and calls its nearest search method to find the best matches. Thus, it is faster than the brute force matcher for a large train collection. Here the FLANN based matcher takes the reference and the target image as input and uses k-nearest neighbor (kNN) [1] method with k = 2 to find the matches.

Homography takes the feature points from reference and target images that are obtained from the object detection process as an input and returns the perspective transform of the object. Random Sample Consensus RANSAC is used as it is observed that all the features are not matched properly. Here, 4 random good matches are considered and homography is computed. The good matches that are consistent with the homography are known as inliers and those that are not consistent are known as outliers. Finally, the homography for which the number of outliers is minimum is considered as the result. A mask is calculated using the inlier and outlier points. The blue colour-bounding box for the detected object in the block D of Fig. 4 represents the result of the perspective transform.

The bounding box drawn on the object after applying homography gives 4 corners of the object in a 2D format (x, y). But in order to capture the location of the object in 3D space, 3D coordinates x, y, z are required for all the 4 points. As x and y for the 4 points are already available, the 3D is obtained with the help of a depth map. The depth map gives the information about the distance of each pixel from the camera. Thus, for every pixel represented by (x, y) the corresponding depth is obtained from the depth image.

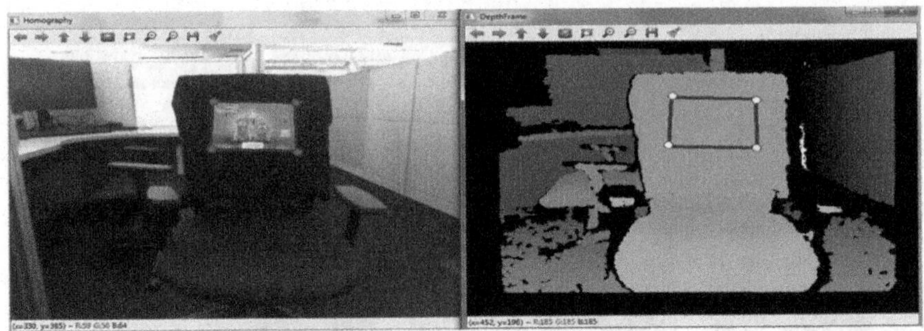

Fig. 5. Object detected in the colour image (left) and mapped onto depth image (right) (Color figure online)

Figure 5 shows the mapping of the object points from colour image (L) to the depth image (R), that are represented by red and yellow circles respectively. The process is repeated for each frame. These 3D points are stored in a text file for each frame of the video.

3.2 Post Processing

Here, a chair is considered for studying its envelope of motion. As the colour and the features of the chair are not many, a card containing a greater number of features are attached to the chair. This helps in identifying the pose of the chair while it is moving. Thus, the aim of the post processing is to identify the ME of the chair in 3D space. The steps in post processing include creating the complete 3D mesh of the object, aligning the mesh with the initial position of the object, identifying the transformations undergone by the object and applying the transformation to the 3D mesh and representing the object trace in 3D using MeshLab.

First, Kinect Fusion library is used to obtain the 3D reconstruction of the object is shown in Fig. 6. The 3D scan is stored. In this case, a 3D mesh of the chair is obtained by using Kinect. The object is kept stagnant and the Kinect is moved around the chair to capture the 3D points of the chair from all the angles.

Fig. 6. 3D scan of the chair

Fig. 7. 3D mesh of the initial position of the chair

The 1st frame where the object is detected is used to obtain a 3D point cloud of the scene captured by the frame by extracting the distance of each pixel in the frame from the camera using the depth stream. This point cloud (x, y, z points) is converted into a 3D mesh using mesh lab. Figure 7 shows the 3D mesh of the chair formed from the front view of the scene as soon as the object is detected. This process is carried out to obtain the initial pose of the object in 3D space. The x, y, z coordinates of the 4 corners of the box bounding the detected object of the block D of Fig. 4 is saved in a text file and is shown in Fig. 8. For n frames in the video stream from Kinect, n such values are recorded.

```
[-266.73695247571334, 102.53482729304082, 770.4568677637391]
[-263.65392092129514, 15.995659480401855, 767.49291947398]
[-172.42002226228732, 21.38272884887641, 768.6083684526958]
[-174.66339328170432, 107.43739034318088, 767.4418443095849]
```

Fig. 8. Corner points of the object

Aligning Complete 3D Mesh to Initial Mesh: The complete mesh shown in Fig. 6 and the initial mesh shown in Fig. 7 are constructed separately with different camera poses and thus they do not occupy the same position within the camera coordinate space. In order to overcome this challenge, the complete mesh is aligned to the Initial mesh so that the resulting aligned complete mesh represents the position of the chair in the first frame where the object was detected. The Iterative Closest Point (ICP) [11] algorithm is used for aligning the two meshes. Figure 9 shows the components being aligned and the resulting mesh.

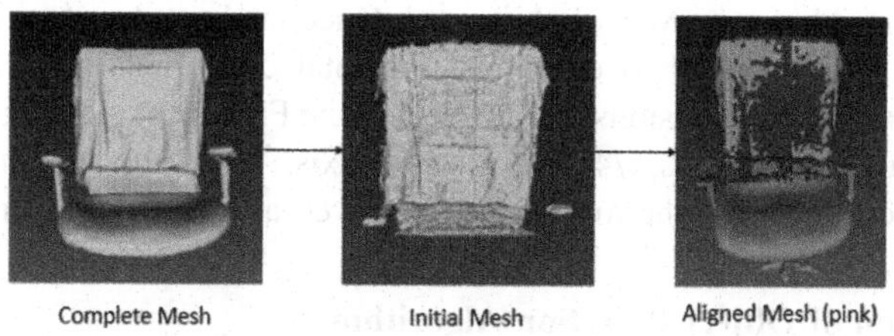

Fig. 9. Complete 3D mesh aligned to initial mesh

Transformation of the Aligned Mesh: Once all the data is ready, the last step is to recreate the positions of the object. The aligned mesh (Fig. 9) and recorded object corner points (Fig. 5) are used for this purpose. The process includes, determining the rotation and translation between every successive set of points and applying the transformation to the aligned mesh.

Figure 10 shows the two sets of points, one representing the initial position of the chair (a) and the other representing the next position of the chair (b). The corresponding points are represented using same colours. Once the initial points and the next set of 3D points are obtained, the rotation R and translation t that the points (a) should undergo to occupy points (b) are determined. The resulting R and t are applied on the 3D mesh and is shown in Fig. 10(c). The mesh obtained because of transformation is shown in Fig. 10 (d). This process is repeated to obtain a collection of meshes as shown in Fig. 10(e).

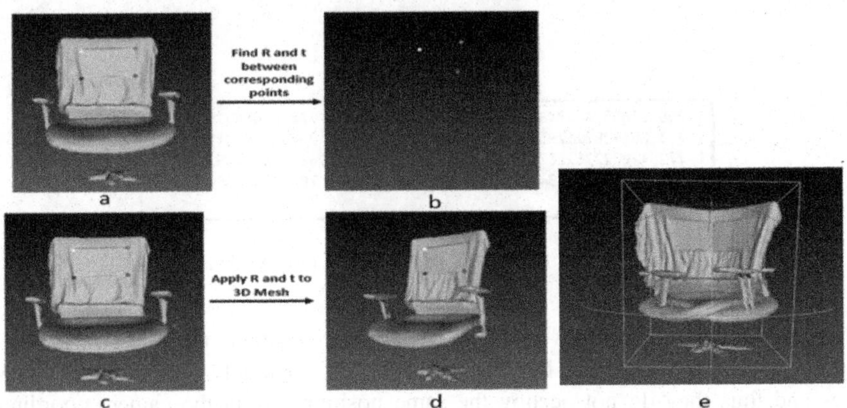

Fig. 10. Generation of collection of meshes

4 Results and Discussion

4.1 Determine Motion Envelope

In this work, a bounding box containing all the transformed meshes are identified. For this purpose, a tool know as Mesh Lab is used. Once the bounding box is constructed, its dimensions are measured to determine the total cubic volume occupied by the object. In this case, the dimensions with respect to the Fig. 10(e) include: 693 cm along X axis, 934 cm along y axis, 747 cm along z axis. Thus, the volume of the cube containing the collection of the meshes can be given as 483,504,714 cm^3.

4.2 Evaluation of Object Detection Algorithm

The object detection technique based on feature extraction and homography is expected to detect the objects of different shapes and surface properties including their translation and rotation or both. Below are some detection experiments using diverse objects.

Case 1: Handheld Card, the reference object is planar in nature and circular in shape as shown in Fig. 11(A).

Observations: The object detection works well with different angles of rotation, tilts and translation as shown in Fig. 11(a) up to (h). But, the object detection fails when the object is rotated and tilted by large angles as shown in Fig. 11(e).

Analogy: The object detection works at its best for planar objects. The influence of the shape of the object on localisation is lesser and the detection is successful for circular objects.

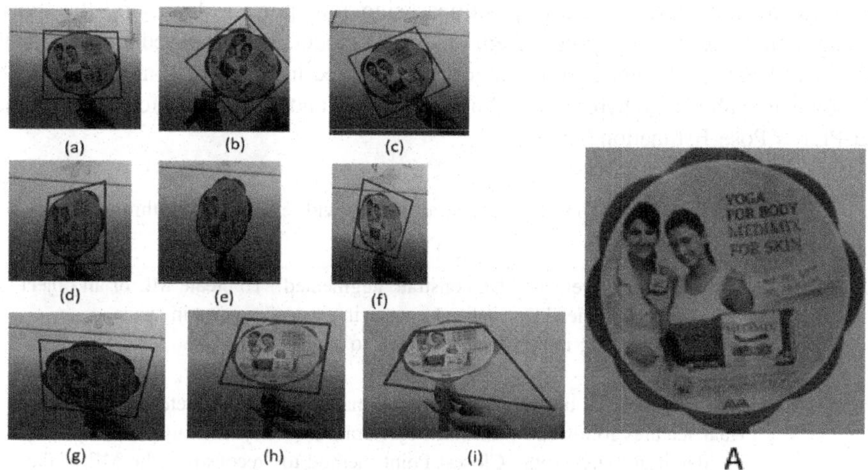

Fig. 11. Handheld card detection with translation and rotation

Case 2: Pillow, the object is non planar in nature and rectangular in shape.

Observations: The object detection and localisation is successful for object in stable position and it is stable with rotation and translation of object as shown in Fig. 12(b), (c), (d) and (f). But, it fails with larger angles (beyond 40°) of deviation like in Fig. 12 (e) and (g). Thus we can conclude that the object detection algorithm works well for non planar objects, provided it has more number of features.

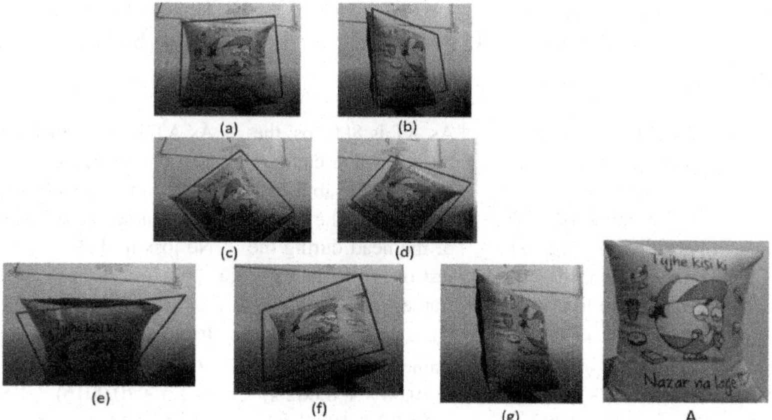

Fig. 12. Pillow detection with translation and rotation

4.3 Evaluation of the Designed Algorithm

The algorithm proposed in the Sect. 3 focuses on recreating the position of the object in 3D space to determine the envelope of motion. The algorithm shows how a single 3D model of the object can be used to represent all the positions occupied by the object in 3D space by capturing the object positions using four points, identifying the transformation undergone and applying them on the 3D model. The proposed algorithm has number of benefits in comparison to algorithms defined in Paper 1 [8] and Paper 2 [9] as shown in Table 1. Where, AT = Alignment time and TT = Transformation Time and PET = Pose Estimation Time.

Table 1. Comparison of proposed algorithm with existing algorithms.

	Paper 1	Paper 2	Our work
Aim	To study the movement of the occupants head in the vehicle during rapid manoeuvres	Demonstrate augmented reality by applying Kinect Fusion to faces	To create ME of an object moving in space
Algorithm	2D face detection using Haar features followed by identifying the depth points and fitting a 3D head to it using Iterative Closest Point method	Head pose estimation followed by Iterative Closest Point method to reconstruct the subsequent head poses	Object detection followed by tracking in 3D space to reconstruct the ME of the object
Memory required	Very less memory close to few kbs is required as only the centre point of the aligned 3D head is saved	No memory required as no data is stored	500 kb to 10 Mb is required to save the real-time data. 10 to 500 Mb is required for post processing based on the number of positions captured
Cost	Costlier due to multiple cameras and infrared sensors	Cheaper as it uses only Kinect	Cheaper as it uses only Kinect
System configuration	Intel i7 3.6 GHz processor, 32 GB RAM	Intel i7, 3.5 GHz, 8 GB RAM	Xenon CPU, E31505M, 35 GB RAM
Alignment time (AT)	570 ms	80 ms	1.56 s
Data loss	As AT is 570 ms, the head position can be recorded only once or twice per second. The position of the head during the rest of the 28 frames are lost	As AT is 800 ms, the head position can be recorded for about 12–13 frames. The position of the head during the rest of the 17 to 18 frames are lost	As AT is performed during post processing, the position of the reference object in each frame can be captured. No loss in data.
Processing time for n frames (n = 100)	PT = (AT + 3D TT) * n frames = (0.57 s + 0.002 s) * n = 0.572 * 100 = 57.2 s	PT = (AT + 3D TT) * n frames = (0.08 s + 0.002 s) * n = 0.082 * 100 = 8.2 s	PT = AT + (PET + 3D TT) *(n-1) = 1.5 + (0.0016) * 100 = 1.5 + 1.6 = 2.1 s

From the below tables, we can infer that the proposed algorithm provides multiple benefits over the existing algorithms like:

i. The algorithm keeps a memory of all the positions occupied by the object in space.
ii. The algorithm is designed in the way that the data of each frame is captured, and it is not lost while processing one frame.
iii. The time taken for processing n frames is 1/18 of the algorithm mentioned in paper 1 and ¼ of the algorithm proposed in paper 2. The time taken in our work is less compared to the Paper 1 and Paper 2 as 3D ICP alignment is performed only once between the complete 3D reconstruction and the object points of the first frame. This also reduces the space complexity, as the entire 3D point cloud (N points) will not be used further in the processing. Only detected object points (n points) will be used where n is almost 1/100 of N.

Thus, we can conclude that the algorithm is more accurate, efficient and fast.

5 Conclusion and Future Work

This work revolves around determining the motion envelope of real-world objects moving in space. It provides better understanding of behavior of the objects in 3D. This concept has many applications in the field of ergonomics and robotics. Example: Designing the interiors of a car by studying the human movements inside it during different maneuvers. The approach applied in the work is a low-cost way to implement the idea as Kinect device is used to capture the depth image, which is quite cheap compared to the 3D laser scanners. The soft wares and tools used for capturing the data from the Kinect and post processing are open source and easy to use. The algorithm used to align the meshes gives accurate results with a maximum variation up to 1 cm which is acceptable. Thus, we can conclude that the concepts of computer vision and the output of the depth sensing devices like Kinect can be utilized to recreate, analyze and understand the complexity of the real-world 3D objects.

Though the alignment algorithms are accurate enough, the results may be affected by the errors associated with the object detection method used. As feature extraction and homography are one of the primitive methods of object detection and pose estimation, the outcomes are less accurate. Thus, more robust results can be obtained by using neural networks to determine the 6° of freedom of the object motion based on the trained model. Further, additional visualization techniques can be used to demonstrate the object transition in an animated manner.

References

1. Yang, L., Jin, R.: Distance metric learning: a comprehensive survey. Technical report, Department of Computer Science and Engineering, Michigan State University (2006)
2. Bridger, R.: Introduction to Ergonomics. 3rd edn. CRC Press (2008)

3. Dubrofsky, E.: Homography estimation. Diplomová práce. Univerzita Britsk´e Kolumbie, Vancouver (2009)
4. Muja, M., Lowe, D.G.: Fast approximate nearest neighbors with automatic algorithm configuration. In: International Conference on Computer Vision Theory and Applications (VISAPP 2009) (2009)
5. Pavel, F.A., Wang, Z., Feng, D.D.: Reliable object recognition using sift features. In: International Workshop on Multimedia Signal Processing, pp. 1–6. IEEE (2009)
6. Horejsi, P., Gorner, T., Kurkin, O., Polasek, P., Januska, M.: Using Kinect technology equipment for ergonomics. MM Sci. J. **389**, 388–392 (2013)
7. Gauthier, S. and Cretu, A.M.: Human movement quantification using Kinect for in-home physical exercise monitoring. In: International Conference on Computational Intelligence and Virtual Environments for Measurement Systems and Applications (CIVEMSA), pp. 6–11. IEEE (2014)
8. Park, B.K.D., Jones, M., Miller, C., Hallman, J., Sherony, R., Reed, M.: In-vehicle occupant head tracking using a low-cost depth camera. SAE Technical Paper 2018(1)(1172), pp. 1–7 (2018)
9. Macedo, M.C., Apolinário Jr., A.L., Souza, A.C.: Kinect Fusion for faces: real-time 3D face tracking and modeling using a kinect camera for a marker less AR system. SBC **4**(2), 2–7 (2013)
10. Cheng, G., Han, J.: A survey on object detection in optical remote sensing images. ISPRS J. Photogr. Remote Sens. **117**, 11–28 (2016)
11. He, Y., Liang, B., Yang, J., Li, S., He, J.: An iterative closest points algorithm for registration of 3D laser scanner point clouds with geometric features. Sensors **17**(8), 1862 (2017)

Software Auto Trigger Recording for Super Slow Motion Videos Using Statistical Change Detection

Rakshit Shukla(✉), Ishu Jain, and S. K. Pradeep Kumar

Samsung R&D Institute Bangalore, Bagmane Tech Park, Doddanekundi, Bangalore 560037, India
{rl.shukla, ishu.jain, pradeep.sk}@samsung.com

Abstract. Handheld devices like smartphones have an inherent disadvantage in recording high frame rate (greater than 480 fps) videos because of limited RAM, limited CPU and GPU capabilities and memory. Almost all handheld devices cannot record such videos indefinitely and have a time limit (usually around 1 s) to keep the system from straining and crashing. In this time limit, anywhere around 480 or 960 or more full HD (resolution 1920 × 1080) frames are recorded per second (around 1 GB data per second is encoded and stored). Most handheld devices that have the capability to record high frame-rate videos and are designed for the common user, use hardware sensor trigger to automatically detect events and record slow motion videos. High framer-rate videos are generally used to record high speed events, the user cannot be expected to press/start the recording manually by timing the event. Therefore the need arises for a method to automatically detect events and trigger the recording. Hardware sensor triggers are basically a camera sensor with an attached circuit board that detects events in the scene. However hardware triggers are expensive, have limited peripheral memory, supports fixed frame rate, cannot overcome global motion, are incompatible with heterogeneous architecture, supports fixed sensor type and inefficient in low lighting conditions. Such limitations are efficiently overcome with the proposed method without compromising on performance and accuracy. Proposed method uses statistical inference along with global motion vectors to detect event in the scene (video frames) for Super Slow Motion (SSM) video capture. The qualitative performance prior to testing on device is elucidated along with quantitative analysis with leaderboard motion detection methods.

Keywords: SSM (Super Slow Motion) · ROI (Region of Interest) · Motion detection · Event detection

1 Introduction

Recent developments in video acquisition hardware and increased capability of CMOS camera sensor along with addition of DRAM (faster RAM associated directly with the sensor instead of the CPU), have enabled handheld devices or smartphones to record extremely high frame rate videos (greater than 1000 fps). These videos capture high

S. K. Singh et al. (Eds.): CVIP 2020, CCIS 1378, pp. 141–150, 2021.
https://doi.org/10.1007/978-981-16-1103-2_13

quality frames every millisecond or less and when played at 30 fps, portray real life events in slow motion. This allows for a lot of creative content from a user's perspective. However, unlike professional grade video cameras, the smartphone sensors cannot keep recording in this mode for long periods of time due to limitations on DRAM and CPU/GPU capabilities of the system. This essentially means that the user has to manually trigger a small time frame recording exactly when the event that is to be captured, happens. Therefore, to allow for more accurate event recordings and to provide convenience to the user, there is a need for a method which can automatically detect and record videos when a change is detected in the scene. The use of a camera sensor with a logic circuit that can detect events is utilized in a lot of smartphones but these hardware sensors have inherent disadvantages like poor quality of detection in low light scenes, need for better hand stability from the user due to absence of a global motion compensation method, support for a fixed frame rate which cannot be changed once the logic circuit is fabricated and they're more expensive than similar sensors without the detection logic. These disadvantages hinder a widespread deployment of this feature to different devices. A software based approach can overcome these disadvantages easily and be deployed with similar ease to existing video capture architecture in most handheld devices today.

A lot of research and patents in computer vision pander to motion detection problem with different assumptions and circumstances. [1] discusses the challenges and the current progress along with the future directions of background subtraction based models for motion detection. Statistical models discussed within [1], like the Gaussian Mixture Model, are highly complex and require dedicated hardware if they are to run in real time at high frame-rate videos. The requirement for the auto trigger feature is a computationally inexpensive method that can accurately trigger recording in case of an event while taking care of factors like dynamic background, hand jitters and camera movement, and noise in low light conditions. Methods discussed in [2] and [3] employ probability computation and a complex model for the background that will not be able to run on high frame rates. However, [2] and [3] both discuss solutions that work not only for static videos but are focused on motion detection in moving videos. These solutions are more robust for a handheld use-case since biologically human hands have certain movements which cannot be prevented. These methods, even though suitable on accounts of accuracy, fail on performance for slow-motion use-case in real time for frame-rates greater than 120 fps. Table 3 discusses some of the learning based methods that extract features from the frame and then perform motion detection on a pixel level. Each pixel is separately classified as a motion/non-motion pixel. These learning based models are highly accurate and are capable of classifying the category of the event to some extent. Shadows, trees and running water will not be considered in motion and only moving objects such as humans, cars etc. are capable of reflecting motion in the frames. As it is evident from the table and complexity knowledge of such models, they can only run up to 40 fps on high end hardware like Intel i5 and i3 processors. Other simpler and popular methods like [4], are designed for static camera cases and have multiple filtering on the frames to reduce error on a pixel level making them unsuitable for SSM use-case. Therefore, the authors proposed a simple yet robust statistical model that can accurately trigger recording and detect event whilst taking care of cumbersome factors like noise, global motion of camera, and dynamic/moving background. The proposed statistical method performs motion detection on block level. A simple global motion engine that can classify blocks as global motion/local motion blocks is also proposed. The proposed method can stream input up to 480 fps, taking around 2 ms per HD frame on Qualcomm Snapdragon 855 with an accuracy of 94% (based on around 200 videos).

The major contributions of this paper are a super-fast statistical inference based event detection method, a method to differentiate global motion and local motion to account for camera jitters, and robustness to work in different lighting conditions with similar accuracy and results.

2 Method

2.1 Proposed Method

Flowchart. The method works on a stream of frames received at high frame rate. Figure 1 depicts the flow of logic for the method. The inputs to the method are 2 frames, the current frame to check for motion and the previous frame to differentiate between global and local motion. Global motion is movement of the camera or the entire frame. Local motion is motion in a small part of the frame and is considered as an event candidate to trigger recording. A few frames are used to model the background before detection can take place. The ROI is divided into blocks. During background modeling, statistics of blocks within the ROI are computed and stored to be referenced later on during detection. During detection, blocks in the ROI are compared with block information stored during modeling and against the same block in the previous frame. If a block difference in pixel value crosses a certain threshold, it is stored to be further checked for global motion. The global motion engine takes all such blocks and compares them to shifted co-ordinates in the previous frame if there is any kind of global motion in the frame. If the blocks are local motion blocks and the total number of such blocks crosses an event threshold, then SSM recording is triggered.

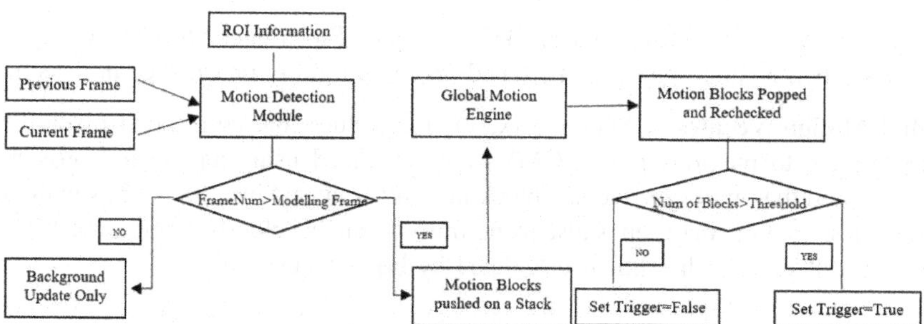

Fig. 1. Flowchart for the proposed algorithm.

Background Modeling. In this method divide the ROI into small blocks of size k * k each. Tuning is done on k to maximize accuracy.

$$\hat{Y}_n(i,j) = \frac{1}{k^2} \sum_{k*kblock} Y(x,y) \tag{1}$$

In (1), $Y(x,y)$ stands for luminance value of pixel (x, y) in (i, j) block, $\hat{Y}_n(i,j)$ stands for the mean of individual pixel luminance values for (i, j) block. For the first few seconds of the video the background is modelled statistically by maintaining mean and variance of all blocks within the ROI.

$$\mu(\mathrm{i,j}) = \frac{1}{\mathrm{N}} \sum_{\mathrm{N\ frames}} \hat{Y}_{\mathrm{n}}(\mathrm{i,j}) \tag{2}$$

In (2) $\mu(\mathrm{i,j})$ stands for mean of (i, j) block over N modelling frames. Similarly a variance measure is also maintained. The variance helps with in dynamic background.

$$\sigma^2(i,j) = \frac{1}{N} \sum_{N\ rames} \{\hat{Y}_n(i,j) - \mu(\mathrm{i,j})\}^2 \tag{3}$$

The variance, $\sigma^2(i,j)$, for (i, j) block in image is maintained as (3) shows. The variance takes into account non SSM triggering actions such as flowing water. Events not significant enough to trigger motion detection need to be occasionally included in the background.

Motion Detection. Every block that exceeds its mean value and the previous frame value by a multiple of the standard deviation is considered for motion. Assuming a Gaussian distribution any value outside ~3.5 * σ(x, y) is an outlier and is a part of the foreground. The thresholding is done by (4).

$$\left|\hat{Y}_n(i,j) - \mu(\mathrm{i,j})\right| > Max\{M * \sigma(i,j),\ Offset\} \tag{4}$$

A minimum of No foreground blocks are required to trigger SSM recording. The parameters No, M and Offset can be tuned for extra rigidity or lenience in detection.

Global Motion Vectors. GMVs are (x, y) shift values that correspond pixels from current frame to previous frame. GMVs are calculated using an Integral projection based method that works on average block intensity values. Since SSM deals with high frame rates, motion between subsequent frames can be closely approximated with linear shift of pixels. The shift is calculated by Eqs. (5) and (6).

$$S_n(i) = \sum_{All\ Columns} Y(i,y) \tag{5}$$

$S_n(i)$ represents the sum of all Luma values in ith row of the nth frame. A list of all $S_n(i)$ values is maintained and similarly another list of all $S_n(j)$ values (Sum of all luma values in a column) is also maintained.

$$|S_n(i) - S_{n-1}(i+k)| \tag{6}$$

The value of "k" for which the SAD (Sum of Absolute Difference) in Eq. (6) is minimum is considered the global shift in x coordinate. Similarly another shift in y coordinate is also computed. Once the global motion vectors are known, Foreground motion blocks are verified against shifted values to differentiate between local and global motion events.

Adjustment of Model μ and σ. Mean and Variance values for blocks needs to be updated to account for new movements/objects in scene. An average of the luma value of the scene is used as the separator between Low-Light and Day-Light, since low light scenes are more prone to noise. Mean and Variance update frequency & thresholding parameters (M, Offset) are different for both scenes. Low light scenes are updated more frequently to accommodate for noise and illumination changes in the scene.

Product Development. The method was implemented and commercialized in Samsung Galaxy S20 Ultra where HD frames are streamed at greater than 100 fps. The first 0.5 s are used for modeling the background. Tuning was performed on an internal dataset with multiple scenarios to obtain optimal thresholding parameters (M, Offset) for Daylight (3.605, 18.708) and Lowlight (3.741, 21.213). Proposed method analyses an HD frame in less than 2 ms.

3 Experiments and Results

3.1 Qualitative Analysis

Figure 2 and Fig. 3 portray the frames at which SSM is triggered on an internal dataset and Galaxy S20 ultra respectively. Further Quality verifications were done as part of commercialization activities for Samsung Galaxy S20 Ultra. Since the proposed method is a statistical method that runs in real time, shadows or other changes within the ROI are also considered as events.

Figure 2-(a), (b) shows lowlight scenarios where proposed method outperforms the hardware Trigger (Samsung Galaxy S20+) which fails to detect motion after a distance of approx. 5ft. in lowlight. An in depth comparison with the hardware circuit based auto trigger in S20+ and other third party competitors reveals that the proposed software auto trigger is much better at handling lowlight scenarios, global motion, and in most cases smaller objects that can trigger SSM. Small, fast moving objects are the most difficult to accurately trigger recording with. However, with the ability to tune the method so intimately on a dataset of varied videos and scenarios, proposed method is

Fig. 2. From left-Proposed method detects pen-drop at a distance of (a) 12 ft. (b)15 ft., (c) Basketball, (d) a little bird within the ROI is detected. (a) and (b) are low-light experiments.

able to detect pen drops at a distance of 15 feet in low light conditions and around 18 feet in daylight conditions. On the internal dataset, the hardware trigger fails to detect motion in most lowlight scenarios however the software trigger is successful. True Positive and an accurate result is when the solution triggers SSM recording within 3 frames of the beginning of the event/motion inside the ROI.

The calculation of variance and thresholding based on the variance, elucidated in Eqs. (3) and (4) allows the solution to work with dynamic conditions such as wind and moving leaves and tree branches in the background. The variance threshold ensures that a previously encountered block value will not trigger recording unnecessarily. Table 1 elucidates the difference in accuracy between the hardware trigger in Galaxy S20+ and the software trigger in Galaxy S20 Ultra. 85 of the 130 videos were handheld recordings. Due to the presence of a global motion compensation method in the software trigger, it achieves greater accuracy in highly textured backgrounds where small camera movement also triggers recording in the hardware trigger. The false positives are reduced by around 50% in the case of the software trigger. However rotation of the smartphone still triggers recording in both the cases almost always.

Figure 3 shows frame dumps taken from Galaxy S20 Ultra. The frame data was dumped when software trigger indicated motion. These frames are first motion frames from the video. The small ball was thrown from the right hand side with the background that is very similar in YUV. The input stream to the method is 120 fps. The software trigger indicated motion when the ball has just entered the right hand boundary which is a criterion for accuracy. An accurate detection is indication of motion within 3 frames of motion in the scene.

Table 1. Comparison of accuracy on an internal dataset of ~130 videos consisting of different scenarios with varying object size, distance from camera, speed and location (within or outside the ROI). Along with the variation most (~85) of the videos are recorded on hand held devices to check for global motion accuracy.

Solution	Accuracy (detection within 3 frames of motion)
Hardware solution (Galaxy S20+)	~85%
Software solution (Galaxy S20 ultra)	~94%

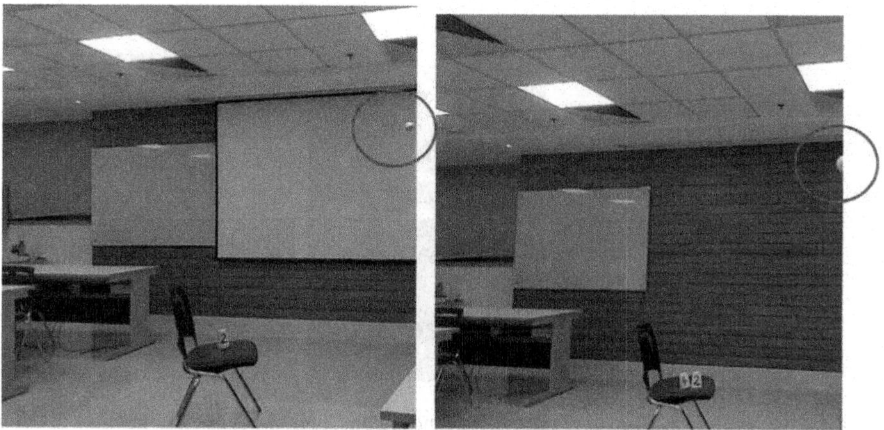

Fig. 3. First Frame of motion at 120 fps of a high speed ball (small fast moving object) thrown from the right (marked by a red circle). The ball has just entered the frame when the algorithm has indicated motion and triggered SSM video recording. (Color figure online)

3.2 Quantitative Analysis

Since the proposed method deals with a very specific requirement, it is difficult to compare it with any other existing method fairly. However, the authors have compared it with existing motion detection methods by shifting proposed method to a pixel level paradigm where the output is a motion map for each frame. The method was tested on a relevant dataset taken from [5]. The dataset has various categories with varying fps and resolutions, upon which all motion detection methods are tested [5] to evaluate accuracy parameters and rankings. The block size of the proposed method is shifted from 8 × 8 to 1 × 1 which is pixel level. Doing this allows the solution to output motion maps at a pixel level to be compared with leaderboard methods that perform motion detection instead of event/change detection. Figure 4 represents motion maps generated by proposed method from the universal dataset taken from [5]. In the first image comparison from the left, it can be seen that the static pathway is also shown to be under motion since the proposed method is not designed/tuned to work on pixel level.

Table 2. Comparison against best values achieved by leaderboard methods from [5]. TP: True Positive, FP: False Positive, FN: False Negative, TN: True Negative, Re (Recall): TP/(TP + FN), Sp (Specificity): TN/(TN + FP), FPR (False Positive Rate): FP/(FP + TN), FNR (False Negative Rate): FN/(TP + FN), PWC (Percentage of Wrong Classifications): 100 * (FN + FP)/(TP + FN + FP + TN), F-Measure: (2 * Precision * Recall)/(Precision + Recall), Precision: TP/(TP + FP); These parameters are used to analyze motion detection methods.

Method	Recall	Specificity	FPR	FNR	PWC	Precision	F-measure
Proposed	0.854	0.985	0.014	0.145	1.93	0.683	0.745
Best scores	0.973	0.999	0.001	0.027	0.357	0.965	0.950

Fig. 4. A qualitative show of moving objects and output motion map of the method (motion pixels are marked white).

Table 3. Comparison of hardware requirements of leaderboard methods from [5] and their performance. State of the art methods are highly complex.

Method	Processor	Performance
SOBS-CF	Intel i3-2.15 GHz	43.5 ms (~23fps)
SubSENSE	Intel i5-3200-2.8 GHz	22.2 ms (~45 fps)
Cdet	Intel i5-3200-2.8GH	25 ms (~40 fps)
SC-SOBS	Intel i3-2.15 GHz	43.5 ms (~23fps)
PAWCS	Intel i5-3200-2.8GH	37 ms (~27 fps)
Proposed	Qualcomm Snapdragon 855	2 ms (>240 fps)

As Table 2 shows, Best scores in the leaderboard methods are better than proposed solution in the case of motion maps. However, the dataset from [5] is such that shadows, trees, wind and clouds are not considered for motion in the ground truth. SOTA (State of the art) techniques are always better than proposed technique in motion maps, however these methods have limited FPS (15 fps–43 fps) even on high end hardware like the Intel i3 and i5 processors. Due to higher rendering these techniques aren't suitable for the use-case targeted by the proposed algorithm. The proposed method, if tuned for a pixel level analysis and statistics, could improve in performance.

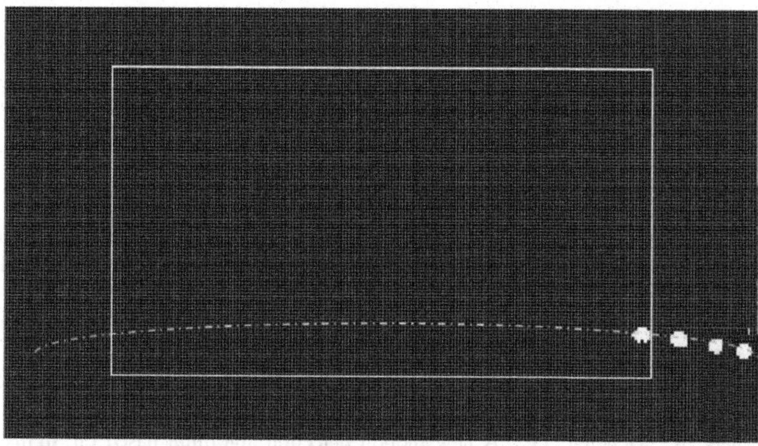

Fig. 5. Object tracking using a combination of motion maps using proposed algorithm and clustering algorithm. The predicted path of the object is shown by white-dashed curve.

Figure 5 shows an extended use-case of the proposed method. Motion maps generated by running the proposed method on pixel level are passed as input to a clustering method. K-Means clustering applied on motion maps along with tracking the centroid of the cluster over a few frames is used to predict the path of an object. The path is computed by solving the parabolic equations using the centroid coordinates obtained over at least 6 frames. This method however has not been productized and requires modifications for robustness. It is presented only as an example of the versatility of the proposed algorithm to be used as a low computation high speed object tracking method. This use-case if designed and tuned appropriately can also be used to keep the camera centered at an object during video recording. Even at high zoom levels, a computationally light method that can detect and track objects in real time can be used to keep the focus on the object automatically to avoid user's inconvenience.

4 Conclusion

Proposed method works extremely well for slow-motion auto trigger requirement of a simple yet accurate method to detect fast events. A software solution for SSM is easily portable to multitude of handheld devices with limited hardware capabilities. The pixel level comparison shows the robustness in motion detection as well as the vast difference in performance times with the leaderboard methods on lower processing power. The flexibility to be easily tunable for different sensors and needs, applications in multiple use-cases such as high speed photography, high speed object tracking and motion detection make proposed method especially innovative, simple and unique. The method has scope for improvement in the areas of accuracy enhancements. Proposed method works well indoors against the hardware trigger and can be improved. Proposed method can also be used in combination with inertial sensor values, or rotational global motion to better handle camera shake scenarios. Used together with AI scene analysis and the object detection and tracking method described in experiments section, the proposed algorithm can be used for event prediction within the ROI and improved quality of trigger.

References

1. García García, B., Bouwmans, T., Rosales-Silva, A.J.: Background sub traction in real applications: challenges, current models and future directions. Comput. Sci. Rev. **35**, 100204 (2020)
2. Chapel, M.-N., Bouwmans, T.: Moving objects detection with a moving camera: a comprehensive review. CoRR abs/2001.05238 (2020)
3. Aach, T., Kaup, A., Mester, R.: Statistical model-based change detection in moving video. Signal Process. **31**(2), 165–180 (1993)
4. Manzanera, A., Richefeu, J.C.: A new motion detection algorithm based on Sigma -Delta background estimation. Pattern Recognit. Lett. **28**(3), 320–328 (2007)
5. Change-Detection Homepage. http://changedetection.net/

Using Class Activations to Investigate Semantic Segmentation

Manas Satish Bedmutha(✉) and Shanmuganathan Raman

Indian Institute of Technology Gandhinagar, Gandhinagar 382355, Gujarat, India
{bedmutha.manas,shanmuga}@iitgn.ac.in
https://people.iitgn.ac.in/~shanmuga/

Abstract. Semantic segmentation is one of the most popular tasks in computer vision. Its applications span from medical image analysis to self driving cars and beyond. For a given image, in semantic segmentation, we generate masks of image segments corresponding to each type or class. However, these segmented maps may either segment a region properly but assign it to a different class or they may have a possibly poor segmented region identification. Hence there is a need to visualize the regions of importance in an image for a given class. Class Activation Maps (CAMs) are popularly used in the classification task to understand the correlation of a class and the regions in an image that correspond to it. We propose a new framework to model the semantic segmentation task as an end to end classification task. This can be used with any deep learning based segmentation network. Using this, we visualize the gradient based CAMs (GradCAM) for the task of semantic segmentation. We also validate our results by using sanity checks for saliency maps and correlate them to those found for the classification task.

Keywords: Class activation maps · Semantic segmentation · Saliency maps · GradCAM

1 Introduction

Image segmentation has been a long standing problem in computer vision. In the recent past, we have achieved immense progress in terms of segmenting the regions of similarity as well as identifying the physical connotation they represent. This task involves multiple sub-tasks such as object detection and localization, edge detection, semantic segmentation as well as instance segmentation. Object detection and localization only requires a bounding box around the objects of interest. Recent solutions to the ILSVRC [5] challenge have even outranked human annotators in terms of error rate for object detection and localization. The task however, becomes a little more difficult when an exact mask corresponding the object/class of interest is needed. This is sought under the semantic segmentation task.

In semantic segmentation, we wish to generate a mapping of a given image to the corresponding feature mask map. These masks are the regions in the

S. K. Singh et al. (Eds.): CVIP 2020, CCIS 1378, pp. 151–161, 2021.
https://doi.org/10.1007/978-981-16-1103-2_14

image where an object of that class is present. The mask may at times even be completely empty, showing absence of segments corresponding to a given class. This task has been approached using multiple methods. Popular works such as [1] and [13] use classical methods while [4,10,11] and the more recent [15] and [17] are few of the most famous end to end deep learning based networks for semantic segmentation.

1.1 Our Contribution

In this work, we propose a new framework to understand the saliency (regions of importance) in the network for an image for the segmentation task. Since segmentation depends on masks while saliency depends on target label of the classification, there is no way (to the best of our knowledge) to use saliency visualization methods for segmentation. We propose a new framework that enables us to visualize saliency in segmentation networks. We demonstrate this by masking the original image in order to build a classification sub-network beyond the segmentation network. This framework thus creates an end to end network to visualize the saliency maps in the image, thus converting the segmentation task into classification task as well.

Our major contribution is creating and explaining the existence of such a framework that can be used for any semantic segmentation network. For training, inputs to the system are the image and its masks for each label. For each label, a masked image is generated for the classification section. For visualization, we need only the image and we can check for salient regions for every label class in the dataset.

For an example, we demonstrate the framework using gradient based Class Activation Maps (GradCAM). To explain if the framework is learning the correct saliency maps, we validate the sanity checks for saliency maps as proposed in [2].

2 Background Formulation

2.1 Semantic Segmentation

For an image X in the z-channelled colour space say, $w \times h \times z$; our goal is to generate a mask map (Y) for N classes. That is, Y has dimensions $w \times h \times N$. We wish to learn a function f such that

$$f : R^{w \times h \times z} \rightarrow R^{w \times h \times N} \text{ and } f(X) = Y \tag{1}$$

The aim of the segmentation neural network here is to approximate as closely as possible to the function f from the training data provided to it. Although the above equation holds for two dimensional images, it can easily be expanded to higher dimensional data.

2.2 Class Activation Maps

A Class Activation Map or CAM [18] is a technique to study the regions of importance in the image firing up with respect to some class. CAM generates a saliency heatmap corresponding to a given image which is basically the relation between the output prediction with respect to the input. It is mathematically expressed as $\frac{\partial output}{\partial input}$ for each pixel in the input image.

A positive class activation means the feature is positively contributing to classification to that label while the negative implies reducing importance of feature for classifying that label.

This is done with the means of a global average pooling (GAP) layer added after the last convolutional layer. This can be thought as each slice of the feature map representing a particular heatmap and the weighted mean of these maps generates the final saliency map for the image. The coefficients to weigh these slices are found by processing the output of the global average pooling layer. Following notation with respect to [12], let the second-last layer produce K feature maps. The output score for each class c will be Y^c when the feature map is spatially pooled across the GAP layer. Therefore we get,

$$Y^c = \sum_k w_k^c \frac{1}{Z} \sum_i \sum_j A_{i_j}^k \tag{2}$$

where, the summation $\sum_i \sum_j 1 = Z$ and w_k^c represents the weights of the Class Activations and A^k corresponds to the kth feature map of the GAP output A.

2.3 GradCAM

In addition to the regular class activation mapping, we can enhance the saliency by calculating the gradients of the values obtained after the pooling layer. For GradCAM, we find the gradient of a w × h image for a class c. It is found by taking the derivative of the output value y_c, just before the softmax with respect to each feature map of the convolutional layer. For the kth map, this gradient is given by $\frac{\partial y_c}{\partial A^k}$. These gradients are pooled instead of directly pooling the values to obtain the neuron importance weights α.

$$\alpha_k^c = 1/Z \sum_i \sum_j \frac{\partial y_c}{\partial A^k} \tag{3}$$

This weight α_k^c represents the importance to be assigned to each individual feature map for a class c. The final localization heatmap is thus a linear combination of all A^k's weighed by α_k^c. It is given as:

$$L_c = ReLU\left(\sum_k \alpha_k^c A^k\right) \tag{4}$$

where,

$$ReLU(x) = \begin{cases} 0 \text{ if} \mathrm{x} \leq 0, \\ x\ if x \geq 0 \end{cases} \tag{5}$$

2.4 Guided GradCAM

In another variation, the GradCAM can be guided to not choose values that are negative in the previous layer. This is done based on the belief that a negative value, either absolute or its gradient, contributes negatively to that class.

There are basically two modifiers that can be altered to supposedly improve the GradCAM visualization, namely (1) gradient and (2) backpropagation. In the gradient, we may first find gradient then ReLU (referred in future as ReLU grad) or find ReLU and then take its gradient (referred in future as Guided grad). Similarly we may first do the backpropagation then ReLU (referred in future as ReLU back) or do the ReLU to guide the backpropagation (referred in future as Guided back). We can execute each independently as well as combine the two together for visualizations. A numerical example for the same came be found in the Fig. 1.

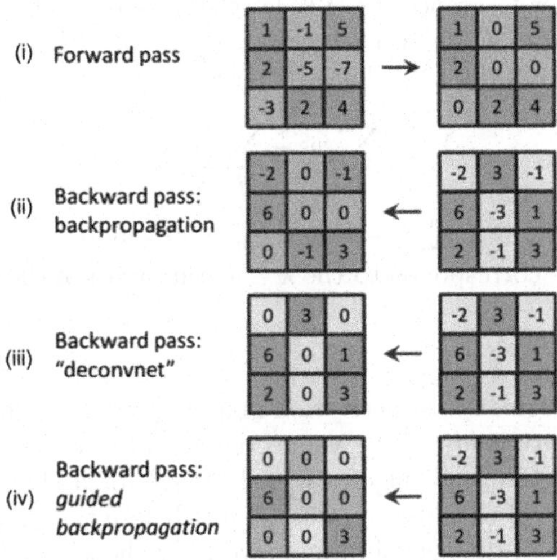

Fig. 1. Possible variants of modifiers used in GradCAM. The subfigures (i)–(iv) represent ReLU forward pass, guided ReLU, gradient ReLU and guided backpropagation respectively in our paradigm. (*Image Courtesy:* [7])

In the guided ReLU the negative values of the forward pass are not allowed to propagate further, while in gradient ReLU, it is the negative values of gradient that a discarded during backpropagation. Also, the initial negative values can be made zero in addition to making the negative values obtained in the gradient. This is called as a guided backpropagation.

3 Proposed Framework

Despite the tremendous success of the idea of CAMs, we have never applied them to visualize a segmentation task. We propose an end to framework to convert the purely segmentational task to a segmentation and classification task. This enables us to utilize CAM based frameworks for segmentation.

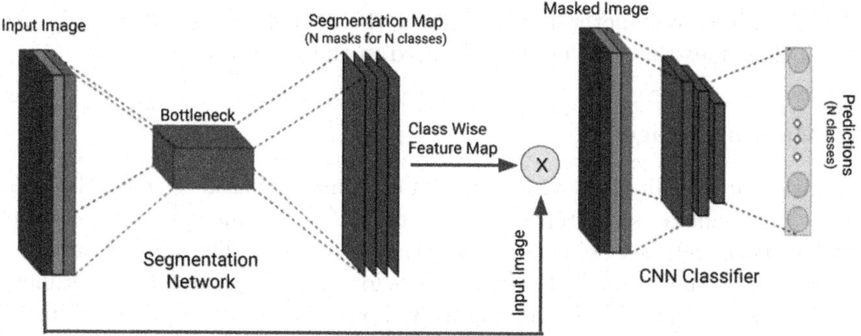

Fig. 2. The figure shows the proposed framework. The image masked with class-wise feature masks is classified by the classification network. Any saliency visualization technique can now be tested on the segmentation network.

The segmentation network can be any network that the user wishes to visualize. The masks generated as outputs from that subnetwork are split in a classwise fashion. Thus, we will have N masks. Every image is masked with these masks one by one. Finally a classifier network is added to the network to classify this masked image. Figure 2 provides an overall summary of the pipeline to create our framework. The network consists of two subparts. For training, the only data needed is what the segmentation network will need.

3.1 Key Features

1. The use of masked images enables as very fast learning curve with very less parameters for the classification network. This ensures that the number of parameters are almost the same as that of the segmentation sub network.
2. Due to training by only already extracted and meaningful regions of the image, the classifier network has a very high accuracy of learning.
3. When the end to end model is trained together, the addition of the classification loss improves the training metrics for segmentation too.

3.2 Segmentation Subnetwork

Our framework is independent of the segmentation network used. It is a general observation that most networks use a feature extractor to extract important features and a deconvolution based subnetwork to map those features into corresponding masks. The feature extractors usually have a backbone, predominantly a pretrained model of a popular network like [5] or [9]. Common models for pretrained networks are VGG [14], Residual Nets (ResNet) [6] or Inception Net [16].

However any segmentation methods that may not even follow the above pattern can be safely used in our paradigm. We are only concerned with the output of the network. Although a small restriction is that this sub-network should be end-to-end connected. This is just to ensure a smooth flow of gradients.

On the whole, our method only requires the network to satisfy Eq. (1). Any network that does that can be directly used in the framework.

3.3 Masking Images

The mask map is split class-wise and then each mask is used to mask the image with it. This generates the representative regions of an image that the segmentation network believes belongs to the class of interest. The main intuition to further extract the network belief features for a class so that the classifier is trained with minimum learning. Figure 3 shows the results after masking the image with a known mask.

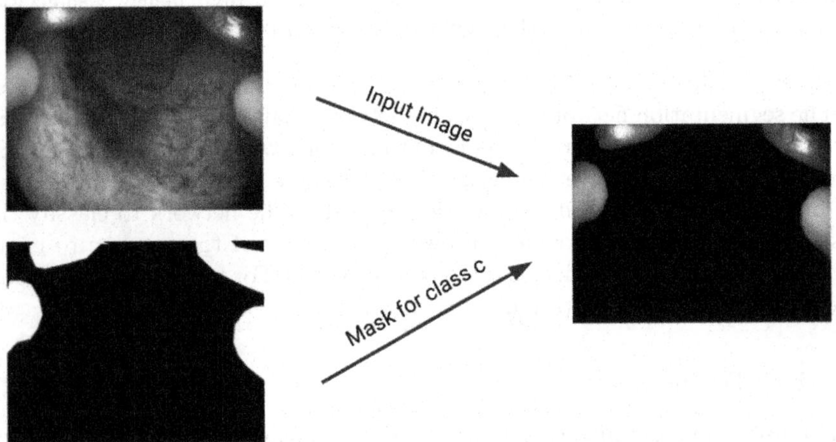

Fig. 3. The figure shows masking of an image with a feature map mask for a given class

We propose that upon masking the image, we are essentially highlighting only the region of the image that the previous subnetwork believes has elements from the required class. Sometimes there may not be any object corresponding to the given class in the image. This will ideally give us a completely black mask. In order to ensure small dots or noise might creep in as a mask, we will check for the average of pixels over the entire mask. If it is smaller than a fixed ϵ, then we will discard that image from training the classification network. For regions with size smaller than ϵ, such missed entries will be recorded and used during the fine-tuning of weights by feeding such segments.

3.4 Classifier

The classifier can be any CNN based classifier that takes in the masked image from obtained from Sect. 3.3 and classifies it as probabilities y which will be an N dimensional vector. We necessarily require the final activation to be softmax to ensure we get probabilities of each class. This will be complemented by taking the loss function as categorical crossentropy to make sure each wrong classification is penalized equally. It is given by,

$$Crossentropy\, Loss = \sum_{i=1}^{N} -y_{true}\, log(y_{pred}) \tag{6}$$

where y_{true} is the ground truth value while y_{pred} is the predicted class value. This is summed over all the classes N.

To increase the range of the network, we can replace the activation of the network with linear or a tangent. This will create the need to probably fine-tune a network but might provide a larger range for the saliency map to operate. This tweak is a suitable method for post training or when recreating and testing an old training scenario after certain number of epochs using saved weights.

We remove any masked image that has all values zero or less than a set ϵ. This is because the mask has predicted no region corresponding to the class of interest and we wish to save network training time. Also, learning a mapping of all zeros to each class will only end up negatively distorting the weights of the classifier.

Based on the above template for the framework, we propose that any deep learning based network can be visualized and tested for its saliency relations.

4 Sanity Checks for Saliency Maps

In a recent work by [2] it was shown that saliency methods may not be truly visualizing the salient regions beyond the gradient shifts. The authors propose two tests to check if the saliency map is not acting as a simple edge detector but actually learning useful representations from the network. This is demonstrated by two tests.

1. **Model Parameter Test:** The weights of the network are changed to random values, one layer at a time. If the map is learning the saliency, then there must be a change in the feature map.
2. **Data Randomization Test:** The labels for an image are permuted and the saliency is visualized. If the map is learning the saliency, then there must be a change in the feature map for each input-label pair.

It was found that guided methods fail to show any variation with respect to class labels with respect to the masked images. This means that the intuition of discarding negative values even before processing did not give the true intended results. We test our framework on this test setup to investigate if similar behaviour is observed for segmentation too.

We do not consider the Model Parameter Test in the ambit of the current work as we are concerned more with the labels being correctly assigned than about the learning parameters.

5 Experiments

The network is built on Keras while the implementation of saliency maps is used from Keras-Vis [8]. Each subnetwork is created as Model object. The larger framework only requires these objects and their corresponding weight files to compile. The framework is built using Lambda layers to split each mask separately. We use the EAD dataset [3] for our study. It consists of images with 5 labels annotated for presence of endoscopic artifacts.

The larger network can be trained in two ways - (1) separately training each subnetwork and fine-tuning it together or (2) using the joint network to train from scratch. In the former, the convergence is attained easily and hence we prefer that. However, in case the network is not performing as expected and debugging is needed, then we choose the latter to understand the proceedings at each step.

5.1 Segmentation Subnetwork

For our testing and analysis, we assume a U-Net [11] styled deep network with base weights and backbone from VGG [14]. Due to computational constraints and small size of dataset, we only downscale the features after pooling once. These layers are then upsampled and deconvolved using transposed convolutions. For the purpose of the experiments, we first fine tune the segmentation network with the training data from the EAD dataset [3]. The segmentation network is trained over a loss function of the mean squared error and an Adam optimizer as a default setup. Upon attaining convergence, the weights from the segmentation sub-network are added to the bigger framework of the network.

5.2 Masked Image Classifier

We generate masked images of all images and classes and train the classifier. As mentioned above, any training samples for the classifier with all values zero or less than ϵ are discarded as the image does not have any region corresponding to the class of interest. We take the value of $\epsilon = 12.75$ with the assumption that no mask is less than 5% of image size and that all pixel values will either be fully white (255) in the worst case. All these assumptions can be changed as per availability of data samples in the dataset. The loss function taken is the categorical cross-entropy loss and the optimizer is kept to be the standard Adam.

5.3 Overall Analysis

Upon convergence of both smaller sub networks, we take their weights into the larger network. After this, we may or may-not fine tune our network. We may even choose to analyze by loading weights from previous checkpoints. Since we are majorly concerned with classifying incorrectly, as explained in Sect. 4, we majorly consider results only from the Data Randomization test. For our framework we vary the parameters for backpropagation and gradients to validate the claims made by [2] for classification on segmentation.

For testing the images, we randomly permute the classes of these masked images. We set the mask corresponding to one of the labels as the base and permute the labels for the classifier network. Each time, for the same image, the network is told it belongs to a different class. For each case GradCAM is modified.

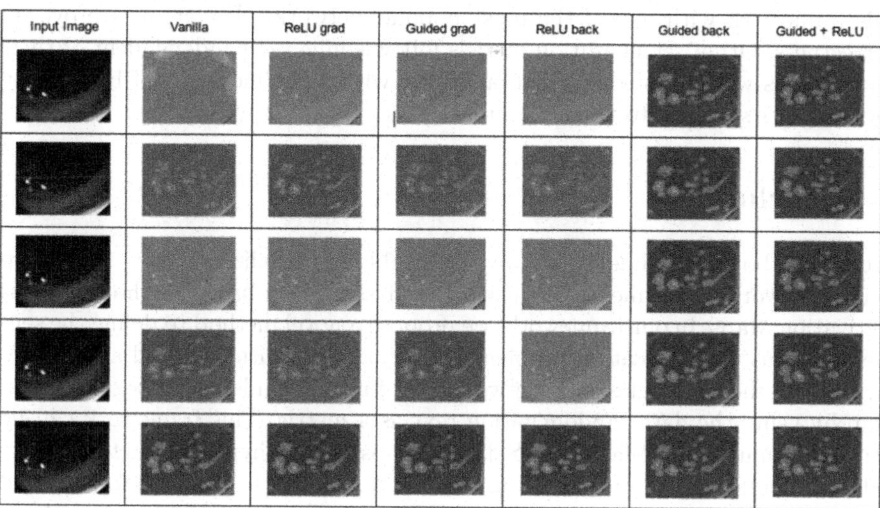

Fig. 4. The figure shows the results of our mapping for GradCAM. The columns represent the variation in the modifiers. At any instant, for the given image, it is masked with one (last) class, for each of the five classes. The saliency maps shown are obtained for that masked image with assigning a different label for it each time. The *grad* modified terms have their gradient calculations modified, while *back* refers to modifications in backpropagation. As evident, the guided backpropagation fails to capture classwise different information and may simply be behaving as an edge detector.

6 Results and Discussions

Figure 4 explains a comprehensive summary of our framework on the GradCAM saliency map for one image. The last row represents the correct label class for the image. The saliency maps shown are obtained by assigning a different label for the image each time. The *grad* modified terms have their gradient calculations modified, while *back* refers to modifications in backpropagation.

Vanilla refers GradCAM without modifiers. In others, every column change refers to a change in modifier as explained above. The change in saliency is observed clearly for each class. As evident, the guided backpropagation fails to capture classwise different information and may simply be behaving as an edge detector. Hence, as [2] claimed for classification, the guided methods fail for segmentation too. Since the testing is fairly subjective, we sample random images to check for saliency maps across different variants. The framework held true for majority of the sample-label pairs that we checked.

It can also be seen that the other labels are learning different things as can be observed based on the gradation of the saliency map. The change in output for classes with no region corresponding to the image is seen as lighter shades with no enhanced visible features.

Note that this is a general framework, we demonstrate the application of this framework with one of the most popular networks (U-Net) and prove its correctness. Other segmentation models follow similar suit independent of their structure as we are not disturbing anything within the model itself but simply forwarding its output to the next subnetwork.

7 Conclusion

From the above experiments we have been able to visualize saliency for a deep neural network for segmentation using the classification based method of Class Activation Maps. In our framework, we propose a novel method to define the segmentation as a classification problem and explain the intuition and advantages for adding the small classifier network. We further validate our segmentation map by using the data randomization text as a metric. This framework can be utilized in multiple applications. Saliency maps help in hyperparameter tuning, network debugging as well as using the CAMs as inputs for the segmentation network. Based on its utility it can also be explored over other recent methods of visualization.

8 Future Work

The primary goal of our project was to enable classification based analysis methods to be applied to segmentation networks. While current demonstrative examples explain the correctness of such a network, we would like to assess the quantitative impact of this framework. In the future we plan to vary the dataset, segmentation networks and visualization methods to gain deeper insights about saliency models and semantic segmentation.

References

1. Achanta, R., Shaji, A., Smith, K., Lucchi, A., Fua, P., Süsstrunk, S.: Slic superpixels. Technical report (2010)
2. Adebayo, J., Gilmer, J., Muelly, M., Goodfellow, I., Hardt, M., Kim, B.: Sanity checks for saliency maps. In: Advances in Neural Information Processing Systems, pp. 9505–9515 (2018)
3. Ali, S., et al.: Endoscopy artifact detection (EAD 2019) challenge dataset. arXiv preprint arXiv:1905.03209 (2019)
4. Chen, L.C., Papandreou, G., Kokkinos, I., Murphy, K., Yuille, A.L.: DeepLab: semantic image segmentation with deep convolutional nets, atrous convolution, and fully connected CRFs. IEEE Trans. Pattern Anal. Mach. Intell. **40**(4), 834–848 (2017)
5. Deng, J., Dong, W., Socher, R., Li, L.J., Li, K., Fei-Fei, L.: ImageNet: a large-scale hierarchical image database. In: 2009 IEEE Conference on Computer Vision and Pattern Recognition, pp. 248–255. IEEE (2009)
6. He, K., Zhang, X., Ren, S., Sun, J.: Deep residual learning for image recognition. In: Proceedings of the IEEE Conference on Computer Vision and Pattern Recognition, pp. 770–778 (2016)
7. Kim, D.: Guided prop (2019). https://donghwa-kim.github.io/guidedprop.html
8. Kotikalapudi, R.: Keras vis (2019). https://github.com/raghakot/keras-vis
9. Lin, T.-Y., et al.: Microsoft COCO: common objects in context. In: Fleet, D., Pajdla, T., Schiele, B., Tuytelaars, T. (eds.) ECCV 2014. LNCS, vol. 8693, pp. 740–755. Springer, Cham (2014). https://doi.org/10.1007/978-3-319-10602-1_48
10. Long, J., Shelhamer, E., Darrell, T.: Fully convolutional networks for semantic segmentation. In: Proceedings of the IEEE Conference on Computer Vision and Pattern Recognition, pp. 3431–3440 (2015)
11. Ronneberger, O., Fischer, P., Brox, T.: U-net: convolutional networks for biomedical image segmentation. In: Navab, N., Hornegger, J., Wells, W.M., Frangi, A.F. (eds.) MICCAI 2015. LNCS, vol. 9351, pp. 234–241. Springer, Cham (2015). https://doi.org/10.1007/978-3-319-24574-4_28
12. Selvaraju, R.R., Cogswell, M., Das, A., Vedantam, R., Parikh, D., Batra, D.: Grad-CAM: visual explanations from deep networks via gradient-based localization. In: Proceedings of the IEEE International Conference on Computer Vision, pp. 618–626 (2017)
13. Shi, J., Malik, J.: Normalized cuts and image segmentation. Departmental Papers (CIS), p. 107 (2000)
14. Simonyan, K., Zisserman, A.: Very deep convolutional networks for large-scale image recognition. arXiv preprint arXiv:1409.1556 (2014)
15. Sun, K., et al.: High-resolution representations for labeling pixels and regions. arXiv preprint arXiv:1904.04514 (2019)
16. Szegedy, C., et al.: Going deeper with convolutions. In: Proceedings of the IEEE Conference on Computer Vision and Pattern Recognition, pp. 1–9 (2015)
17. Zhang, H., et al.: ResNeSt: split-attention networks. arXiv preprint arXiv:2004.08955 (2020)
18. Zhou, B., Khosla, A., Lapedriza, A., Oliva, A., Torralba, A.: Learning deep features for discriminative localization. In: Proceedings of the IEEE Conference on Computer Vision and Pattern Recognition, pp. 2921–2929 (2016)

Few Shots Learning: Caricature to Image Recognition Using Improved Relation Network

Rashi Agrawal, Upendra Pratap Singh(✉), and Krishna Pratap Singh

Machine Learning and Optimization Lab, Indian Institute of Information Technology Allahabad, Prayagraj, India
{mit2018033,rsi2017001,kpsingh}@iiita.ac.in

Abstract. Inspired by the human ability to learn instance-label associations given only a handful of examples, few-shots learning is gaining increased attention from the researchers. In this direction, we have proposed a modified relation network to perform few shots caricature to image recognition. Since caricature and real images come from different modalities, we have extended the relation network to contain separate feature extracting networks for the two modalities in the embedding module. This extension was necessitated by the fact that since caricature and real images come from different modalities and hence different distributions, a single feature extracting network in the embedding module may not learn cross-modal features. Experiment results on caricature recognition dataset and subsequent comparison of our proposed network against the baseline model quantitatively substantiates our hypothesis. While comparing the performance of our modified network against the baseline, we were able to improve the recognition accuracy by 26.3% for $5-way, 1-shot$ setting and by 25.5% for $5-way, 5-shot$ setting.

Keywords: Few-shots learning · Meta-learning · Relation network · Caricature recognition · Embedding · Relation score · Modality

1 Introduction and Related Work

Deep Learning is capable of learning unstructured data using neural networks and has attempted to mimic human brain and perform decision making just like humans. It has been applied in various domains such as speech recognition [13], computer vision [3], audio recognition [15], natural language processing [14] etc. and has achieved great success. In the real world, it is not always easy to collect large amount of data especially in the field of medical sciences and security. This could be due to high cost of data acquisition or absence of relevant data altogether. Deep Learning fails here as it simply over-fits the data resulting in poor generalization [5]. On the other hand, humans are very good at working with few examples and able to transfer knowledge from one domain/task to other. For example, given an image of a dog and a cat, humans can easily distinguish

S. K. Singh et al. (Eds.): CVIP 2020, CCIS 1378, pp. 162–173, 2021.
https://doi.org/10.1007/978-981-16-1103-2_15

between the two; this shows that humans can generalize well even with few examples. Inspired by this ability, few-shots learning has been gaining attention of researchers lately with many researchers trying to get an elegant solution to this problem to get human like abilities.

Caricature refers to the drawing or a sketch where some features of the image are oversimplified while other are exaggerated [22]. Identifying caricature is an easy task for humans but not for machines. Caricatures generally do not contain actual facial features and they are different in terms of point of view or expressions as designed by the artist. Recognition of caricatures are very difficult task. Few data set for caricatures of individuals are available, so it becomes difficult even deep learning models to work directly on these small data set. Few shots learning, a concept of transfer learning, is a plausible solution for such problem. In real life it will be helpful to a police personnel, which have only one sketch of the thief and he intends to compare it with all culprits record.

Many different approaches have been proposed to solve few-shots learning problem; among all these, mix of deep learning and meta-learning based approaches have achieved near human performances [16,19,21]. Meta-learning, better known as *learning to learn* is a science of systematically observing and exploiting the way various machine learning algorithms perform on a wide range of learning tasks, and then using this acquired knowledge to complete the target task. Easier said than done, meta-learning approaches come with its own set of challenges - firstly, we need to collect relevant meta-data such as exact algorithmic configuration, hyper-parameter settings, network architecture, network parameters etc. and then ensure that this meta-data is correctly incorporated in the target model. The knowledge acquired in this step compensates for limited number of training examples.

Memory-reinforcement based approaches for few-shots learning [16] use a recurrent neural network with a memory to store information contained in the hidden layers; this information is then used at a later stage. The major challenge associated with the above approaches is the management of memory itself. Meta-learning based approach, Meta-SGD [10], optimize adopt and initialize any learner. It is capable of meta-learning the direction, learner initialization and learning rate using gradients. Meta-metric learning [1] is used by learners for identifying labels whereas good parameters are identified by meta learners. It is known as "learning optimizer" as the learner learns to update its parameters on its own. Such models works well in generating task-specific learners and in handling unbalanced classes. Multi-scale relation network [2] is developed to solve few-shots learning problems. It is combination of metric learning with meta learning to make the best use of the prior knowledge.

Feature embedding along with metric learning [9], to solve few shot learning problem, network work well both on training data and unseen data. Such embedding network gives similar feature embedding for similar samples and vice-versa. A deep K-tuplet Network helps in comparing K samples. Another, metric-learning based architecture, Prototypical networks [17] uses embedding for each class around which all the points of that class cluster. It works with episodic based meta learning training and uses a metric space formed by computing distances between prototypical representations of corresponding classes for classification.

Matching Network [20] uses an embedding network to learn representations and a similarity function to calculate distances between these representations. Prototypical networks and matching networks have good generalization capability, however, these metric based methods are constant in nature and believe that element-wise comparison can be performed on features as they are linearly separable. As a result, quality of extracted features limit the performance of these methods. Few-shots based caricature face recognition proposed in [9] uses idea proposed in [11] with additional hand crafted features. However, challenge in the work is to get hand crafted features for better accuracy. To handle this issue We have modified relation network by using an additional convolution neural network (CNN) based feature extractor in the embedding module. One CNN is used to act as a feature extractor for support data set and other act as a feature extractor for query data set. Moreover the original implementsation of relation network assumes that support and query datasets come from the same modality; we argue that this assumption is quite practical. Accordingly, we modify the original relation net so that instead of similar feature extractors for the two sets, we have different feature extractors for different modalities (in case query and support sets have same modality). This would ensure that the different data distributions contained in multi-modal datasets are learnt independently. We have tested our modified model on Omniglot Digit Recognition dataset [8], MiniImageNet dataset [20] and caricature recognition (IIIT-CFW) dataset [12].

The rest of the paper is organized as follows - In Sect. 2, we describe our proposed methodology, Experiment Results and consequent discussion has been put in Sect. 3. We conclude our work in Sect. 4 while also suggesting future works associated with our work.

2 Methodology

2.1 Problem Formulation

We divide our data set into three subsets namely training, support and test sets [18]. Support and test sets have the same label space while training set have a label space disjoint from the support set, as described in Fig. 1). Though in theory, it is quite possible to build our few-shots learning model from support set alone, it has been found to given sub-optimal results. These sub-optimal results indicate that the model fails to learn an effective mapping from limited samples in the instance space to the label space. So, in order to compensate for this ineffective learning from instance to label space, our model uses training data to extract transferable knowledge to fine tune the learning taking place on the support set.

In short, our model *meta-learns* on the training data and uses this knowledge while learning in the support set. Depending upon the number of samples from

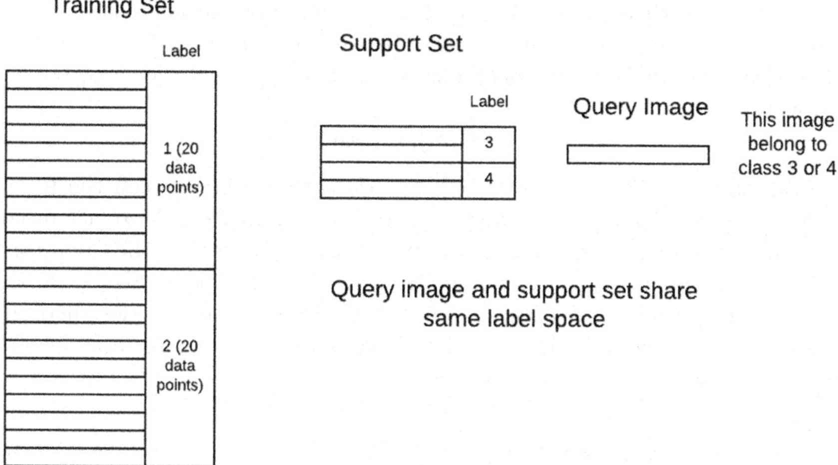

Fig. 1. Few shots learning model exploits ample labeled instances present in the training dataset to extract transferable knowledge; this knowledge can then be used to fine tune the learning taking place in the support set. Support and query sets have the same label space while training and support sets have disjoint label spaces.

each class, K and the number of classes, C that participate from the support set, we have corresponding C-way K shot learning configuration.

We perform an episode based training where in each iteration, an episode is created by randomly selecting K samples per class from C classes present in the training set; this forms our sample set i.e. $S = \{(x_i, y_i)\}_{i=1}^{m}$ where $m = K \times C$. A fraction of samples from the remaining classes form our query dataset $Q = \{(x_j, y_j)\}_{j=1}^{n}$. The sample and query sets simply mimic the support and test sets respectively. In our experiments with learning caricatures from corresponding real images, real and caricature images form our support and query sets respectively.

2.2 Proposed Model

Real and caricature images belong to different modalities: as such, caricatures fail to preserve facial structures/features which the real faces have. Hence, we require two separate feature extraction modules to learn feature representations in both the modalities. In contrast to the original implementation [18] where a single feature extracting network was used, our model uses two feature extraction modules for support and query sets respectively. The motivation behind using two separate modules is to preserve the features belonging to different modalities.

In our notation, x_i represents a support set (real) image while x_j represents a query (caricature) image; both these images are fed to their corresponding feature extracting networks $h_{\psi(.)}$ and $g_\theta(.)$ that give $h_\psi(x_i)$ and $g_\theta(x_j)$ respectively as feature representations (see Fig. 2). These feature representations are then concatenated together $C(h_\psi(x_i), g_\theta(x_j))$ and eventually passed to the relation network t_ϕ that learns the relation scores between the image pairs (see Fig. 3).

The relation score for the concatenated feature representation can be computed as:

$$r_{i,j} = t_\phi(C(h_\psi(x_i), g_\theta(x_j))) \tag{1}$$

where the operator C is a simple concatenation operation between the feature vectors $h_\psi(x_i)$ and $g_\theta(x_j)$ where $h_\psi(x_i)$ is followed by $g_\theta(x_j)$; the relation score $r_{i,j}$ captures the degree of similarity between them. Note that the operator C used in the above equation is different from C that appears in C-way K shot learning. The optimization function for the relation network is designed such that same class image-pairs have a relation score close to 1 while different class image-pairs have relation scores close to 0.

$$\psi, \theta, \phi \leftarrow argmin_{\psi,\theta,\phi} \sum_{i=1}^{m} \sum_{j=1}^{n} (r_{i,j} - 1(y_i == y_j))^2 \tag{2}$$

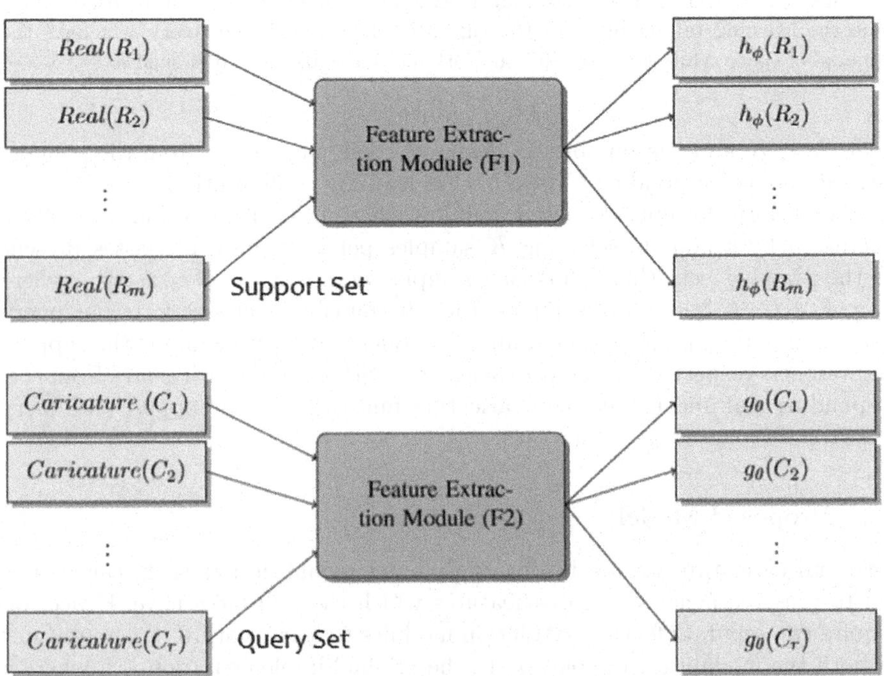

Fig. 2. In our experiments, real images (K samples per class from C classes) are taken to form our support set while some fraction of caricature images from the remaining classes constitutes our query set. Since real and caricature images come from different modalities, separate feature extraction modules are used to learn their corresponding embedding.

where m, n are the number of images in support and query set respectively; y_i and y_j are the ground-truths for i^{th} support and j^{th} query set image in the same order. While previous approaches to few-shots learning involved fixed distance metrics, our proposed methodology is based on learning a deep non-linear metric in a data-driven fashion [21].

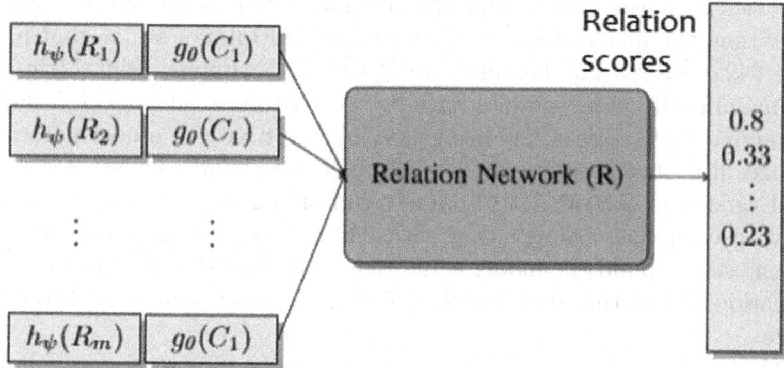

Fig. 3. The feature embeddings of real and caricature images are concatenated and pair-wise passed to the relation network ($\mathcal{R}$). This relation network learns the similarity between the image pairs using their true labels (aka ground truth).

2.3 Testing

Class-wise feature representations in the support set are computed by averaging the image-level representations obtained using $h_\psi(.)$. Given a test caricature x_{test}, we extract its embedding $g_\theta(x_{test})$ and pair-wise concatenate it with class-level representations in the support set. The concatenated vector pairs are then passed to the relation network to give a relation score. The class corresponding to highest relation score is assigned to x_{test}.

2.4 Network Architecture

- **Feature Embedding module:** Convolutional Neural Network is used to extract the image features. The network contains 4 convolution blocks or layers each containing 64 filters with a filter size 3×3, a batch normalization layer and a rectified linear unit (non-linear). Max-pooling operation is also performed on first two layers with the pool size equal to 2×2.
- **Relation module:** It houses two convolutional layers with two fully connected layers each. Each convolutional layer contains 64 filters of filter size 3×3, a batch normalization layer followed by ReLU non-linearity unit and a Max Pooling layer with a pool size 2×2.

3 Experiments and Results

3.1 Dataset Description

Firstly, we build our modified relation network on two image recognition datasets namely Omniglot Digit Recognition [8] and MiniImageNet dataset [20]. Omniglot dataset is made up of 1623 characters (or classes) from 50 different languages or alphabet sets with each class containing 20 handwritten image samples. For data augmentation, the images have been rotated in multiples of 90° so that in total we have 6492 classes. For training, we have taken samples from 4219 classes while remaining 973 class samples have been used to test our model. Validation set containing 1300 classes has been used to fine tune the model parameters. The images have been resized to 28 × 28 pixel size. MiniImageNet dataset is a modified version of ILSVRC-2012 dataset containing images from 100 different classes with each class contributing with 600 images. Samples from 64 classes have been used to build the model while 16 and 20 class samples have been used for validation and testing respectively. The images have been resized to 84 × 84 pixel size.

We then use our network to implement image-to-caricature recognition on IIIT-CFW dataset [12]. This dataset contains real and cartoon (caricature) images of 100 public figures extracted from Google Image search results. The images collected contain 8928 cartoon faces and 1000 real faces spanning across 100 public figures. For training, we take 7142 cartoon images and 750 real images coming from 75 public figures while for testing, we have 1786 cartoon images and 250 real images from the remaining 25 personalities. As a part of image pre-processing, the images have been resized to 256 × 256 × 3.

3.2 Experimental Settings

We have conducted our experiments on a workstation powered by a Xeon CPU E5-2650 v4 processor, 128 GB RAM and GeForce GTX 1080Ti graphics card with 3584 CUDA cores. Relevant Python libraries like Numpy, Pytorch, Keras etc. have been used as and when required.

For optimizing our loss function, we have used Adam optimizer with an initial learning rate set to 10^{-3}. The model has been incrementally trained and fine tuned on 10000 episodes.

3.3 Results and Discussion

Analysis on Omniglot Digit Recognition and MiniImageNet Datasets Table 1 shows the performance of the proposed model on Omniglot Digit Recognition dataset using accuracy (in %) as an evaluation metric. Accuracy of the model is computed for different values of C and K i.e. for different $C - way$,

Table 1. Accuracy (in %) computed on Omniglot dataset using Modified Relation Network

Episodes	5-way, 1-shot (in %)	5-way, 5-shot (in %)	10-way, 1-shot (in %)	10-way, 10-shot (in %)
50	16.89	17.64	15.67	17.32
100	16.71	17.93	16.42	17.24
300	18.46	19.49	17.83	19.36
500	19.84	20.57	18.94	20.37
1000	22.47	21.73	20.38	22.64
5000	46.38	40.41	44.67	48.31
10000	63.48	70.57	67.29	72.62

Table 2. Accuracy (in %) obtained on MiniImageNet dataset using Modified Relation Network

Episodes	5-way, 1-shot (in %)	5-way, 5-shot (in %)	10-way, 1-shot (in %)	10-way, 10-shot (in %)
50	8.35	10.48	7.23	12.52
100	12.77	13.28	10.61	15.38
300	13.49	14.22	12.53	17.26
500	14.21	17.37	12.44	19.32
1000	16.64	20.35	18.38	23.41
5000	20.37	26.17	25.39	27.14
10000	40.17	46.26	39.61	48.53

Table 3. Performance of our proposed model on IIIT-CFW dataset using accuracy (in %) as an evaluation metrics

Episodes	5-way, 1-shot (in %)	5-way, 5-shot (in %)	10-way, 1-shot (in %)	10-way, 10-shot (in %)
50	5.24	7.56	5.45	10.40
100	7.32	10.21	6.31	12.63
300	10.46	12.72	9.44	15.35
500	15.61	17.33	13.57	20.32
1000	29.13	34.76	30.14	35.47
5000	43.51	49.24	46.12	49.78
10000	56.73	59.15	50.41	59.37

$K-shot$ configurations. Further, for a fixed C, K value pair, we have also evaluated the performance as a function of episodes. We see a general trend where for a given $C-way$, $K-shot$ configuration, the performance of the model improves with increasing episodes. For example, in 5-way, 1-shot configuration, we see that the model performance increases from 16.89% to 63.48% when learning episodes are increased from 50 to 10000. This behavior can be explained as follows - with increased number of episodes, the model gets trained on more number of related tasks and hence is able to generalize well across many tasks.

Also, for a fixed episode and C value, the model accuracy improves with increased K value; for instance, with a fixed episode value say 50, the accuracy of the model for 10-way,1-shot configuration is 15.67% as against 17.32% for 10-way, 10-shot configuration. This is because with increased K i.e. the number of image samples per class in the support set, the model gets to learn a more generic representation for that class.

Similarly, Table 2 shows the model performance on the MiniImageNet dataset. We infer that the accuracy of the recognition model generally increases with increased K value. For example, for 10-way, 1-shot configuration, the model accuracy is 39.61% as against 48.53% for 10-way, 10-shot configuration when the models have been trained on 10000 episodes. This can be justified by the fact that with an increased feature representations available per class, we get a better representation for that class and consequently a better performance.

In our experiments with Omniglot and MiniImageNet datasets, the two feature extracting networks in the embedding module are identical as the training, support and test sets follow the same modality for aforementioned datasets.

Analysis on IIIT-CFW (Caricature Dataset)

Table 3 shows performance of the proposed model for caricature to image recognition task on IIIT-CFW dataset. The performance of the model has been evaluated for different C, K and episode values. We can infer that the performance of the model increases with increasing episodes, for example, in 10-way, 10-shot setting, the performance increases from 10.40% to 59.37% when number of episodes are increased from 50 to 10000. It means more episodic training is giving better accuracy. Similarly, in columns 2 and 3 (5-way, 1-shot and 5-way, 5-shot), we observe that with increasing K value (number of instances in each class), the performance of the model increases. That could be attributed to the fact that with increased number of samples per class, the model is able to learn better representations and so its accuracy increases. Similar trends could be observed for columns 3 and 4 (10-way, 1-shot and 10-way, 10-shot) where the model performance improves with increased K values.

Similarly, for a fixed (C, K) values, the model performance improves when it is trained on more number of episodes. The increase in the model performance with increased episodes may be attributed to learning of the model that generalizes well across multiple related tasks.

For the baseline, we have chosen the original implementation of relation network [18] where the same feature extracting network has been used for extracting support and query set features. We hypothesized that since support and query sets follow different modalities, there ought to be two independent feature extraction networks instead of just one. In order to test our hypothesis, we built our proposed relation network using two separate feature extraction networks for the two sets. Table 5 compares the performance of the baseline model against our modified network for caricature to image recognition task. It can be clearly seen that our proposed approach outperforms the baseline model by 26.3% for 5-way, 1-shot setting and by 25.5% for the 5-way, 5-shot setting. This improvement in the model performance validates our hypothesis for the need of separate feature extracting networks for different modalities (Table 4).

Table 4. Performance comparison between the baseline model and our proposed model for caricature recognition task on IIIT-CFW dataset. The results are obtained on 10000 episodes using accuracy as an evaluation metric

Model	5-way, 1-shot (in %)	5-way, 5-shot accuracy (in %)
Baseline model [18]	30.53%	33.61%
Proposed model	**56.73%**	**59.15%**

Table 5. Comparison: Matching network based works on caricature to image recognition

Serial No.	Work	Datasets	Performance (accuracy)
1	Relation Network using prior features [22]	WebCaricature, Caricature-207, IIIT-CFW	92.5%, 94.4% 93.7% respectively
2	Automated Caricature Recognition [6]	Caricature images from artists and Web resources	61.9%
3	Web Caricature [4]	Caricature images from artists and Web resources	61.57%
4	Our Work	IIIT-CFW	59.15%

4 Conclusion

We have implemented a modified relation network to perform caricature to image recognition task. The proposed network is a meta-learning based architecture to perform few-shots recognition. The modification comes in the form of an additional convolutional neural network based feature extracting network in the embedding module. The underlying rationale is that since real face images and caricature images come from two different modalities, there ought to be a separate feature extraction module for the two sets of images. The network is trained in an episodic end-to-end manner where it learns to fine-tune the embedding and the distance metrics. The proposed approach was tested on three benchmark datasets; experiment results using the modified network and its subsequent comparison with an appropriate baseline supports the use of separate feature extracting networks for different data modalities.

In future, we plan to extend our proposed few-shots learning architecture i.e. our modified relation network to perform zero shot recognition in conventional as well as generalized settings.

References

1. Cheng, Y., Yu, M., Guo, X., Zhou, B.: Few-shot learning with meta metric learners. arXiv preprint arXiv:1901.09890 (2019)
2. Ding, Y., et al.: Multi-scale relation network for few-shot learning based on meta-learning. In: Tzovaras, D., Giakoumis, D., Vincze, M., Argyros, A. (eds.) ICVS 2019. LNCS, vol. 11754, pp. 343–352. Springer, Cham (2019). https://doi.org/10.1007/978-3-030-34995-0_31
3. Guo, J., et al.: GluonCV and GluonNLP: deep learning in computer vision and natural language processing. J. Mach. Learn. Res. **21**(23), 1–7 (2020)
4. Huo, J., Li, W., Shi, Y., Gao, Y., Yin, H.: WebCaricature: a benchmark for caricature recognition. arXiv preprint arXiv:1703.03230 (2017)
5. Kadam, S., Vaidya, V.: Review and analysis of zero, one and few shot learning approaches. In: Abraham, A., Cherukuri, A.K., Melin, P., Gandhi, N. (eds.) ISDA 2018 2018. AISC, vol. 940, pp. 100–112. Springer, Cham (2020). https://doi.org/10.1007/978-3-030-16657-1_10
6. Klare, B.F., Bucak, S.S., Jain, A.K., Akgul, T.: Towards automated caricature recognition. In: 2012 5th IAPR International Conference on Biometrics (ICB), pp. 139–146. IEEE (2012)
7. Koch, G., Zemel, R., Salakhutdinov, R.: Siamese neural networks for one-shot image recognition. In: ICML Deep Learning Workshop, vol. 2. Lille (2015)
8. Lake, B.M., Salakhutdinov, R., Tenenbaum, J.B.: Human-level concept learning through probabilistic program induction. Science **350**(6266), 1332–1338 (2015)
9. Li, X., Yu, L., Fu, C.W., Fang, M., Heng, P.A.: Revisiting metric learning for few-shot image classification. Neurocomputing **406**, 49–58 (2020)
10. Li, Z., Zhou, F., Chen, F., Li, H.: Meta-SGD: learning to learn quickly for few-shot learning. arXiv preprint arXiv:1707.09835 (2017)
11. Mai, S., Hu, H., Xu, J.: Attentive matching network for few-shot learning. Comput. Vis. Image Underst. **187**, 102781 (2019)
12. Mishra, A., Rai, S.N., Mishra, A., Jawahar, C.V.: IIIT-CFW: a benchmark database of cartoon faces in the wild. In: Hua, G., Jégou, H. (eds.) ECCV 2016. LNCS, vol. 9913, pp. 35–47. Springer, Cham (2016). https://doi.org/10.1007/978-3-319-46604-0_3
13. Nassif, A.B., Shahin, I., Attili, I., Azzeh, M., Shaalan, K.: Speech recognition using deep neural networks: a systematic review. IEEE Access **7**, 19143–19165 (2019)
14. Otter, D.W., Medina, J.R., Kalita, J.K.: A survey of the usages of deep learning for natural language processing. IEEE Trans. Neural Netw. Learn. Syst. (2020)
15. Purwins, H., Li, B., Virtanen, T., Schlüter, J., Chang, S.Y., Sainath, T.: Deep learning for audio signal processing. IEEE J. Sel. Top. Signal Process. **13**(2), 206–219 (2019)
16. Santoro, A., Bartunov, S., Botvinick, M., Wierstra, D., Lillicrap, T.: One-shot learning with memory-augmented neural networks. arXiv preprint arXiv:1605.06065 (2016)
17. Snell, J., Swersky, K., Zemel, R.: Prototypical networks for few-shot learning. In: Advances in neural information processing systems, pp. 4077–4087 (2017)
18. Sung, F., Yang, Y., Zhang, L., Xiang, T., Torr, P.H., Hospedales, T.M.: Learning to compare: relation network for few-shot learning. In: Proceedings of the IEEE Conference on Computer Vision and Pattern Recognition, pp. 1199–1208 (2018)
19. Vanschoren, J.: Meta-learning: a survey. arXiv preprint arXiv:1810.03548 (2018)

20. Vinyals, O., Blundell, C., Lillicrap, T., Wierstra, D., et al.: Matching networks for one shot learning. In: Advances in Neural Information Processing Systems, pp. 3630–3638 (2016)
21. Wang, Y., Yao, Q., Kwok, J., Ni, L.: Few-shot learning: a survey. arXiv preprint arXiv:1904.05046 (2019)
22. Zheng, W., Yan, L., Gou, C., Zhang, W., Wang, F.Y.: A relation network embedded with prior features for few-shot caricature recognition. In: 2019 IEEE International Conference on Multimedia and Expo (ICME), pp. 1510–1515. IEEE (2019)

Recognition of *Adavus* in *Bharatanatyam* Dance

Himadri Bhuyan(✉) and Partha Pratim Das

Indian Institute of Technology Kharagpur, Kharagpur 721302, West Bengal, India
ppd@cse.iitkgp.ac.in

Abstract. Digital heritage has been a challenging problem to preserve the cultural heritage like a dance. Digitization of dance requires systematic analyses and understanding the semantics. However, while several work has been reported in non-Indian Classical Dance (ICD); only few has been done in the ICD because of its complexity. *Bharatanatyam* is an important ICD form, and *Adavus* constitute the primary collections of postures and movements in *Bharatanatyam*. There are 15 classes of *Adavus* having 52 sub-classes between them. *Adavus* are the critical building blocks for *Bharatanatyam* and critical for understanding its artefacts and semantics. Hence, this paper attempts to recognize *Adavus* based on the sequence of Key Postures (KPs) that define and constitute them. Kinect captures dance performances. The videos are then manually segmented into sequences of Key Frames (KFs) corresponding to the expected KPs. For recognizing KP, we follow two approaches; a) skeleton videos and angles of skeleton bones as features, b) The HOG features from the RGB frames. In both approaches, we train SVMs and recognize the KPs using them. The classifier generated by SVM predicts the sequence of KPs involved in a given *Adavu*. Since KPs are the string-like encoding symbols of an *Adavu*, we use the predicted sequence and master sequence of KPs in Edit Distance to recognize the matching *Adavu*. We use a pre-existing annotated data set of *Natta* (with eight variants) and *Mettu* (with four variants) *Adavus* to achieve over 99% accuracy.

Keywords: *Adavu* · *Bharatanatyam* · Key posture · SVM

1 Introduction

The dance performance includes audio, video, temporal and spatial informations. Hence, understanding its underlying semantics is a challenging task. Analysis and interpretation of dance forms and moves are critical for the various applications; preservation of cultural heritage, build tutoring systems etc. While there have been some studies with dance forms like Ballet, Samba, Salsa [3,14,17,19] and the like; systematic analyses of Indian Classical Dance (ICD) forms have been far and few.

S. K. Singh et al. (Eds.): CVIP 2020, CCIS 1378, pp. 174–185, 2021.
https://doi.org/10.1007/978-981-16-1103-2_16

Bharatanatyam is an important ICD form which has a complex combination of visual and auditory information. *Adavus*[1] constitute the basic collections of postures and movements in *Bharatanatyam.* There are 15 classes of *Adavus* having 52 sub-classes (variants) between them. *Adavus* are the key building blocks for *Bharatanatyam* and are critical for the understanding of its artifacts and semantics. In an *Adavu* the visual information is associated with the *Key Postures*[2] (KP), motion and trajectory. The audio information deals with the *Sollukattu*[3], *Bols*[4], beat[5] and tempo[6]. In this paper we only deal with visual information of *Adavus*.

In this paper we build a system to recognize the *Adavus* on the basis of the key postures. So we first survey the major subproblems in the task and the existing work on those in Sect. 2. Naturally, such work depend critically on good annotated data set. We use the data set created by Mallick [12] as described in Sect. 3. For the data set, a dance performance is first captured in RGB, Depth and Skeleton videos using Kinect Xbox 360 [15]. The videos are then manually segmented into sequences of Key Frames (KF) corresponding to the expected KPs. To recognize the KPs in the segmented Key frames we develop two approaches as outlined in Sect. 4 and detailed in terms of features, recognizers, and results in Sect. 5. In the first approach, we use the skeleton videos and angles of skeleton bones as features. In the second, we use HOG features from the RGB frames. In both approaches, we train linear Multi-class *Support Vector Machine* (SVM) and recognize the KPs using them. The classifier generated by SVM predicts the sequence of KPs involved in a given *Adavu.* KPs are used as symbols in a string-like encoding of an *Adavu.* Then, we use the predicted sequence and master sequence of KPs in Edit Distance algorithm [5] to recognize the matching *Adavu.* We use 8 joint angles of Kinect skeleton (Fig. 1) out of 20 joints and RGB HOG which has 9576 bins as feature set after resizing the RGB image ($480 \times 640 \Rightarrow 120 \times 160$). We train and test with of *Natta* (with 8 variants) and *Mettu* (with 4 variants) *Adavus* to achieve over 99% accuracy. We compare with earlier works and show improvements in the result of recognition of KPs as well as *Adavus* on the same data set. We conclude in Sect. 6.

2 Related Work

For recognizing *Adavus*, we intend to use Key Postures occurring in Key Frames. This involves solutions for three sub-problems as: (a) Segmentation of video and Extraction of *Key Frames* (b) Recognition of Key Postures in *Key Frames* (c) Recognition of *Adavus* as sequences of *Key Postures*. Hence, we survey the recent

[1] An *Adavu* is a basic unit of *Bharatanatyam* performance which is used to train the dancers.

[2] Momentarily stationary well-defined postures occurs within the *Adavu.*

[3] Accompanying Sound Track of an *Adavu.*

[4] An utterance, a mnemonic syllable in *Sollukattu.*

[5] Basic unit of time in music.

[6] Pace or speed at which a section of music is played.

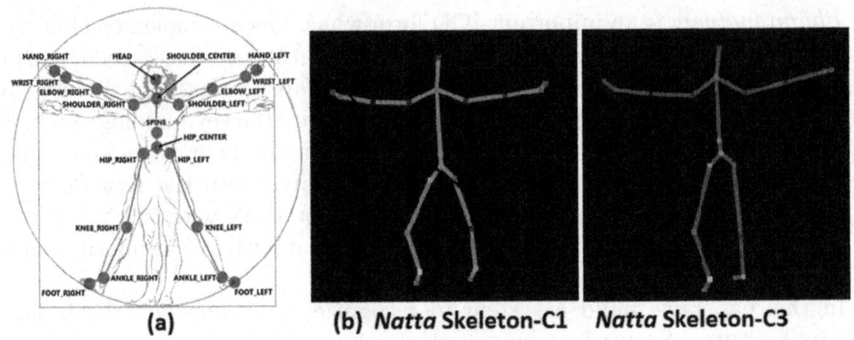

Fig. 1. (a) Kinect skeletal joints for Understanding [15] (b) Skeleton joints as Recorded

literature for work on these problems. On the way, we also contextualize our work in this paper to compare and contrast the approaches for every problem as discussed.

2.1 Key Frame Extraction

A set of *Key Frames* (KFs) in a video is the range of frames containing a particular *Key Postures* (KPs) in an *Adavu* video. During a KP, the dance remains momentarily stationary. KPs are assumed to be synced with the audio beats. Hence, an *Adavu* is an alternating sequence of KPs and transitions (where the dancer changes from one KP to the next – both in sync with the beat). KPs give rise to a set of KFs while transitions give rise to a set of non-KFs. A given video therefore needs to be segmented in terms of KFs and non-KFs. For posture and sequence recognition, it is critical. Several researchers [7,16,22] worked on posture and gesture recognition without worrying about the segmentation. They assume that the video is already segmented. While deep learning based *Convolution Neural Network* (CNN) algorithms are proposed by Mohanty et al. in [16] to identify hand gestures and body postures in order to express the semantics of the ICD performances. A methodology is porposed in [22] by Samanta et al. to classify the different ICDs using Pose descriptor of each frame of an ICD video. In [7] Guo et al. develop a system to recognize 3D dance postures.

In contrast to the above, Kahol et al. in [9] successfully detected gesture boundaries with an accuracy 93%. Similarly In [24,25], musical information is used for motion segmentation and its structural analysis. Mallick [12] also extracts the KFs containing KPs from a video using audio information and frame differencing technique. In this paper, we do not attempt the segmentation problem and assume that videos are available with manually pre-segmented KFs and non-KFs.

2.2 Recognition of Key Postures

There are several works that have been reported on pose recognition and estimation in [6,8,18,26]. Mohanty et al. [16] explore the recognition of body postures (or KPs) in ICD. The authors identifies that CNN [11] performs better than SVM (Support Vector Machine) while using HOG (*Histogram of Oriented Gradient*) features.

Further, Mallick [12] used three different classifiers; namely *Gaussian Mixture Model* (GMM) [21], SVM and CNN with different input features (Skeleton-Angle and RGB-HOG) to recognize the key postures in 8 variants of *Natta Adavus* in *Bharatanatyam*. She reports the best recognition rate (99.12%) using CNN with RGB data for 15 classes only, whereas SVM with RGB-HOG features does commendably well (97.95%) for 23 classes. An accuracy of 83.04% is claimed using GMM on (Kinect) skeleton angle as feature.

In this paper, we use the data set captured by Mallick [12] and use SVM on skeleton angle as well as RGB-HOG to show improvements on her results for *Natta Adavus*. We also report results on *Mettu Adavu* which is new.

2.3 Recognition of Dance Sequence or *Adavu*

During an *Adavu* performance, dancers follows a predefined postures in a particular order by following the musical beats. The rules which are adapted to change from one KP to another is critical and challenging as well. The classifier needs to follow those rules to recognize an unknown *Adavu*.

First work on *Adavu* recognition was reported by Sharma [23] on the basis of the posture sequence without considering the temporal information. Whereas, [23] uses *Hidden Markov Model* (HMM) [20] retain temporal information while recognising *Adavu*. The authors in [10] use RGB-D data captured by Kinect to recognise *Adavu* and achieve an accuracy 73%. Mallick [12] has improved on Sharma's results by applying HMM on RGB-HOG data (in stead of simple histogram of postures) to recognize 8 *Adavus* with an accuracy of 94.64% – nearly 15% improvement compared to [23].

In this paper, we use the data set captured by Mallick [12], encode the sequence of KPs recognized by SVM as KP ID strings, and recognize the *Adavu* by matching the encoded strings against master sequence definitions by Edit Distance. Again we report better results for *Natta Adavus* and new results for *Mettu Adavus*.

3 Data Set

Mallick et al. [13] recorded a data set for 8 different *Bharatanatyam Adavus* performed by *Bharatanatyam* dancers – learners as well as experts. They used Kinect to capture RGB, depth and skeleton videos which are synchronized at a rate of 30 fps. The details of the studio set-up, sensors, and tools for data recording are available in [1] and [12]. A part of the data set (*Natta Adavus*) is available at [13].

We use 8 variations in *Natta* and 4 variations in *Mettu Adavus* from this set for our work here. Each set was performed by 3 dancers as shown in the Table 1. Every *Adavu* was performed by each dancer for a number of times. The number of *Natta Adavu* and *Mettu Adavu* videos are 24 and 12 respectively. In the same time, the number of sequences associated with *Natta* and *Mettu Adavus* are 254 and 72 respectively. For the notion of *Sequence*, check Sect. 3.1

Table 1. Data set for *Natta* & *Mettu Adavus*

(a) *Natta* & *Mettu Adavu* Data Set			(b) Sample KP Annotation of *Natta Adavu*		
Adavu names	Dancer	# of *Adavus* Recorded	Start frame	End frame	Key posture ID
Natta:1–8	Dancer 1	8	101	134	C1
Natta:1–8	Dancer 2	8	144	174	C3
Natta:1–8	Dancer 3	8	189	218	C2
Mettu:1–4	Dancer 1	4	231	261	C1
Mettu:1–4	Dancer 2	4	...	...	...
Mettu:1–4	Dancer 3	4	...	...	...

Every video in the recorded data set is first annotated by experts to mark the *Key Frames* (KFs) occurrence. *Key Frames* where the dancer remains momentarily stationary. The annotation is marked in the RGB video and the corresponding depth and skeleton frames are extracted from the respective videos using the sync information. A sample of annotated data for a *Natta Adavu* is shown in the Table 1(b).

Across 8 variations of *Natta Adavus*, there are 23 distinct KPs. Similarly, there are 32 KPs for 4 variations of *Mettu Adavus*. A subset of these KPs are shown in Fig. 2 and Fig. 3 respectively for *Natta* and *Mettu Adavus*. Two KPs are common between the *Adavus* (C1 & C6 KPs of *Natta* matches with C1 & C9 of *Mettu*). Hence, we have 53 (= 23 + 32 – 2) distinct KPs in total.

After frame-based segmentation of videos into KFs, each KF is further annotated with the KPs it represents. The annotated data set is then used either for training or for validation during tests.

Fig. 2. Sample KPs of *Natta Adavus*

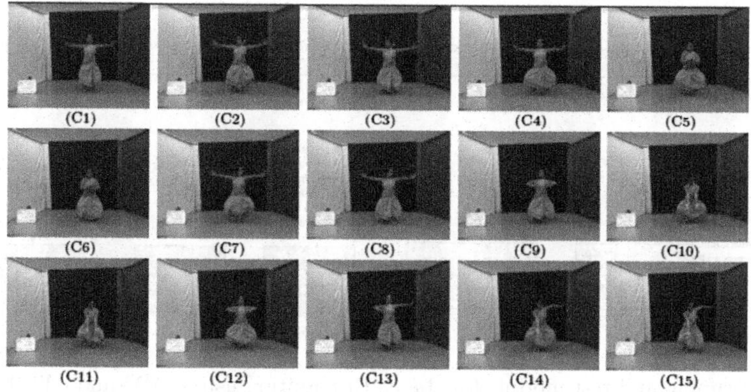

Fig. 3. Sample KPs of *Mettu Adavus*

3.1 Data Set Extension – Video Sub-Sequences

Dance videos are very data intensive. So it is really difficult to annotate very large number of videos for the purpose of training and test. Hence, we make a simple sampling strategy here to extend and enhance the data set.

We note that every KP has a number of corresponding KFs in the video (as segmented in Table 1(b)). Hence, there indeed are a number of candidate sub-sequences of KFs that can actually define any *Adavu* (where a KF is chosen from the set of KFs for a specific KP).

Let us take an example to construct such candidate sub-sequences. Consider Table 1(b) where the *Adavu* is a sequence of, say, 4 KPs – namely C1-C3-C2-C1 (then it repeats) and the KFs corresponding to each KP is given. So 101–144–189–231, 102–145–190–232, etc. can be valid sub-sequences[7]. The number of such candidates will, naturally, be limited by the shortest KF set for a KP (29 in this case, see the Table 1(b)). Hence, there can be 29 such sub-sequences. The 29th sequence is: 129–172–218–259 that is C01–C03–C02–C01. In general, if the minimum size of KF set in a video is M, then M sub-sequences can be generated from the video. Using this extension strategy we have created a number of sequences from videos in the data set (Table 1(a)) that can be used as separate inputs[8] for *Adavu* recognition.

4 System Architecture

The architectures of our training (learning) as well as test (recognition) systems are shown in the Fig. 4, where components marked in peach color are being

[7] To preserve the periodicity of the KPs, which must align with the beats, we need to proceed in an order and cannot arbitrarily associate any member KFs on the sub-sequence. That is, while 101–144–189–231 (first KF of each) is a valid sub-sequence, 125–146–195–259 is an invalid one as it would violate the beat periodicity.

[8] These sequences, however, are highly correlated and cannot be used where strict independent inputs are needed.

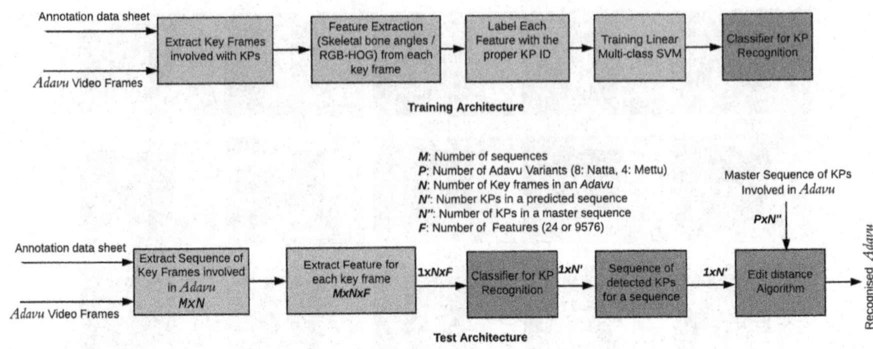

Fig. 4. Training and test module for *Adavu* Recognition using SVM and edit distance

reused from [12] while components marked in green are our contributions in this paper. We assume that each video is already segmented in terms of KFs by manual annotation as described above. For any *Adavu* video, therefore, the sequence of such groups of KFs is given as the input to the system.

Features are then extracted and labeled for each Key Frame as discussed in Sect. 5.1. The labeled features are fed to a linear multi-class SVM for training and generating a set of classifiers to recognize the KPs (Sect. 5.2). The resultant SVM classifiers for KPs are used to recognize the KPs in an *Adavu*. The sequence of recognized KPs are matched against the sequence definitions of *Adavus* using the Edit distance algorithm to recognize the *Adavu*. This is explained in Sect. 5.3.

5 Feature Extraction and Recognizers

5.1 Feature Extraction

Since our objective is to recognize *Adavus* based on the KPs, our system needs to be first trained to recognize the KPs. Hence, the characterize the KPs we design two sets of features: (a) Skeleton Joint Angle feature (b) RGB-HOG feature.

Skeleton Joint Angle Feature. The position of the limbs (two legs and two arms) dominates the postures in a dance sequence. We restrict our focus to the 8 limb bones – 4 each from the left and right sides of the body (Fig. 1(a)) respectively. As the skeleton provides estimates for body joints, the bones are defined as connectors between specified joints as, **Upper Arm:** SHOULDER_LEFT – ELBOW_LEFT & SHOULDER_RIGHT – ELBOW_RIGHT, **Lower Arm:** ELBOW_LEFT – WRIST_LEFT & ELBOW_RIGHT – WRIST_RIGHT, **Upper Leg:** HIP_LEFT – KNEE_LEFT & HIP_RIGHT – KNEE_RIGHT, and **Lower Leg:** KNEE_LEFT – ANKLE_LEFT & KNEE_RIGHT – ANKLE_RIGHT.

We describe every bone's angular orientation by its angles associated with X-, Y-, and Z-axes. Hence for 8 bones the total feature vector is $8 \times 3 = 24$ dimensional.

RGB-HOG Feature. While skeleton descriptors are very suitable for postures, the ill-formed skeleton due to the noise may affect our KP recognition result. Hence, we alternately use RGB frame features for posture recognition. A binary mask [12] that identifies a *player* (or human) in a depth frame is used to mark out the human figure in the RGB image. The resultant image is then to converted to gray-scale. We compute the HOG [4] descriptors for each such frame. For this we scale the image from 480×640 to 120×160 and then compute the histogram. This feature, in our case, has 9576 dimensions.

5.2 Recognition of KP Using SVM

We use linear multi-class Support Vector Machines for Key Posture recognition. SVM [2]. Out of two approaches of multi-class SVM (*One vs. Rest* and *One vs. One*), we use *One vs. One*, where

- *For Training*: SVM learns for every pair of KP classes[9]. So, the number of classifiers required = ${}^nC_2$ For n classes.
- *For Testing*: The test data uses ${}^nC_2$ SVMs to vote for a class and label the KP accordingly.

We divide our entire data set in: 60% for Training, 20% for Cross Validation, and 20% for Test. We choose the model which performs best on cross validation to be applied on 20% test cases. The result shows the recognition accuracy on test data in the Table 2.

Table 2. Key posture recognition results

Adavu	# of frames in training set	# of frames in test set	Features	Recognizer	# of KP classes	Accuracy (%)
Natta	7456	1865	Angle	SVM	23	97.10
Mettu	3663	908	Angle	SVM	32	87.66
Natta+Mettu	11119	2773	Angle	SVM	53	93.36
Natta	7456	1865	HOG	SVM	23	97.90
Mettu	3663	908	HOG	SVM	32	98.54
Natta+Mettu	11119	2773	HOG	SVM	53	94.15
Earlier results						
Natta	7381	1854	HOG	SVM	23	97.84 [12]
Natta	7381	1854	Angle	GMM	23	83.04 [12]

Analysis of KP Recognition Results. The KP recognition results for *Natta* & *Mettu Adavus* are shown in the Table 2. When skeleton joint angle features are used, we observe that significant miss classifications in case of *Natta Adavu*

[9] *Natta*=23 classes, *Mettu*=32 classes.

happens between C3 and C1 (Fig. 1(b)). Though these postures are quite different, the skeletons data often are ill-formed (even over a number of consecutive frames) and make the postures look similar in skeletons (Fig. 1(b)).

In case of *Mettu Adavu* significant miss classifications are observed as (<Expected Posture> → <Detected Posture>): C4→C3, C12→C9, C14→C15 (Fig. 3). The only difference in each of these pairs is in the feet support – in one, for example C4, the dancer stands on her tows, while in the other (C3), the dancer stands on flat feet. In skeleton these need to get captured between the FOOT and ANKLE joints. Typically, these are ill-formed in the skeleton and cannot be reliably used (the reason we are using only limb bones). Hence, these differences are non-existent in our features.

When we use RGB-HOG features, most of the above issues do not arise. Hence these pairs of postures get rightly classified leading to better accuracy over the angle-based method. Especially, in case of *Mettu Adavu* we get over 10% improvement (Table 2). Overall, thus, RGB-HOG features outperform the skeleton angle in KP recognition. We compare our improved result with [12] on the *Natta Adavu* data set. Results on *Mettu* or on the mixed data set could not be compared as there is no earlier report.

5.3 *Adavu* Recognition using SVM and Edit Distance

Once KPs have been recognized in a video, our next task is to recognize the *Adavu* of the video. Without loss of generalization, we treat an *Adavu* Sequence (Sect. 3.1) as a video. If there are N KPs ($N = 4$ in Table 1(b)) in an *Adavu* and an F ($= 24$ for angles, and $= 9576$ for HOG) dimensional feature is used, then the such a video (sequence) can be represented by an $N \times F$ dimensional feature. Once this is given as input to the SVM classifiers for KPs we get a $1 \times N'$ vector of recognized KP IDs as output.

Next we note that every *Adavu* is uniquely characterized by a fixed ordered sequence of KPs (Table 4 lists the KP sequences for variants of *Mettu Adavus*). Hence the *Adavu* recognition problem reduces to a sequence matching problem for KFs that have already been recognized to represent certain KPs. If there are P (for *Natta* $= 8$ & *Mettu* $= 4$) *Adavus* in consideration, each represented by a master sequence of KPs (as in Table 4), then we need to match the $1 \times N'$ recognized KP ID vector with the master sequences ($P \times N''$, N'': Length of the master sequence) and find the *best* match. We use Edit Distance (ED) for this purpose and pick the one having the minimum distance as the recognized *Adavu*. Note that a master sequence may have a length N'' which is different from N', and ED takes care of it through insert and delete operations.

Analysis of *Adavu* Recognirion Results. We use the sequences from our data set (Table 1 and Sect. 3.1) for recognition of *Adavus*. The summary of the results are shown in Table 3. We get good results with both feature sets and perform better than the earlier results by [12,23]. Sharma [23] used HMM on RGB-D features for 12 *Adavus* (from a different closed data set) and achived

80.55% accuracy. Mallick [12] used HMM on RGB-HOG feature for 8 *Natta Adavus* and reported an accuracy of 94.64% for 56 test sequences whereas we obtain 99.21% for 254 test sequences. Results on *Mettu Adavu* are not reported in [12] and could not be compared.

Table 3. *Adavu* Recognition results

Method	Features	*Adavu*	# of *Adavus*	# of test sequences	# of correct recognition	Accuracy (%)
SVM & ED	Angle	*Natta*	8	254	253	99.61
SVM & ED	Angle	*Mettu*	4	72	72	100.0
SVM & ED	Angle	*Natta* + *Mettu*	8 + 4	326	325	99.69
SVM & ED	HOG	*Natta*	8	254	252	99.21
SVM & ED	HOG	*Mettu*	4	72	72	100.00
SVM & ED	HOG	*Natta* + *Mettu*	8 + 4	326	324	99.38
Earlier results						
HMM [23]	RGB-D	–	12	–	–	80.55
HMM [12]	HOG	*Natta*	8	56	54	94.64

We observe that, though *Mettu Adavu* has a weaker result in KP recognition by angle (87.66%), the *Adavu* recognition gives 100%. To understand this apparent contradiction, consider the master KP sequences for *Mettu* in Table 4. It may be noted that except for C9 & C12 none of the KPs are repeated in the 4 variations of *Mettu Adavu*. Moreover, C9 & C12 are present in *Mettu*-2 & *Mettu*-4 and are mutually misclassified (Table 2). Edit Distance matching is robust up to this misclassification.

Table 4. Sequences of KPs in *Mettu Adavus*

Mettu	KPs
1	C2–C3–C4–C1–C5–C6–C4–C1–C7–C8–C4–C1–C5–C6–C4–C1
2	C10–C11–C12–C9–C10–C11–C12–C9–C10–C11–C12–C9–C10–C11–C12–C9
3	C14–C15–C16–C13–C14–C15–C16–C13–C18–C19–C20–C17–C18–C19–C20–C17
4	C21–C22–C12–C9–C23–C24–C12–C9–C25–C26–C27–C28–C29–C30–C31–C32

Further, let us consider a sequence of KPs, predicted by SVM for a *Mettu*-1 *Adavu* input (KP recognition errors are marked in red with underline):

C2–C1–C4–C1–C5–C6–C4–C1–C7–C8–C4–C8–C5–C6–C4–C3

When this is compared with master sequences (Table 4) using Edit Distance, the computed distances with *Mettu*-1, 2, 3 & 4 are 3, 16, 16 & 16 respectively. The least value = 3 (due to 3 replacements), imply the given sequence of KPs is matching with *Mettu-1*. Similar robustness of matching is observed in other cases as well.

6 Conclusions

The Key Postures are identified from videos of *Adavus* segmented manually into Key frames. The sequence of postures are used to recognize the *Adavu*. Two sets of features – bone angles in skeleton frames and HOG in RGB frames. The system has been tested with a pre-existing and annotated data set of *Natta* and *Mettu Adavus*. We extend the data set with further resampling. Our approach outperform earlier reports on KP and *Adavu* recognition [23] and [12]. Our approach is simpler and effective as we just use linear SVM in place of complex sequence models like HMM as in [23] and deep learning in [16]. However, The different variants of SVM, deep learning technique and random forest for classification are to be explored.

There are several issues that need to be explored and developed in future. First, manual segmentation into Key Frame needs to be automated. An audio-guided approach is given in [12]. We would like to integrate that and also develop independent motion-based approaches. Second, we need to improve on the SVM classifiers from One vs. One to One vs. Rest. That will reduce the time complexity of our classifiers. Third, we need to explore the criticality and challenges, when multiple dancers appear in a single scene. Finally, we need to train and test the system with more *Adavu* and more videos.

References

1. Aich, A., Mallick, T., Bhuyan, H.B.G.S., Das, P.P., Majumdar, A.K.: NrityaGuru: a dance tutoring system for Bharatanatyam using kinect. In: Rameshan, R., Arora, C., Dutta Roy, S. (eds.) NCVPRIPG 2017. CCIS, vol. 841, pp. 481–493. Springer, Singapore (2018). https://doi.org/10.1007/978-981-13-0020-2_42
2. Allwein, E.L., Schapire, R.E., Singer, Y.: Reducing multiclass to binary: a unifying approach for margin classifiers. J. Mach. Learn. Res. **1**(Dec), 113–141 (2000)
3. Boukir, S., Cheneviere, F.: Compression and recognition of dance gestures using a deformable model. Pattern Anal. Appl. **7**(3), 308–316 (2004)
4. Dalal, N., Triggs, B.: Histograms of oriented gradients for human detection. In: IEEE Computer Society Conference on Computer Vision and Pattern Recognition, CVPR 2005, vol. 1, pp. 886–893. IEEE (2005)
5. Damerau, F.J.: A technique for computer detection and correction of spelling errors. Commun. ACM **7**(3), 171–176 (1964)
6. Dantone, M., Gall, J., Leistner, C., Van Gool, L.: Human pose estimation using body parts dependent joint regressors. In: Proceedings of the IEEE Conference on Computer Vision and Pattern Recognition, pp. 3041–3048 (2013)
7. Guo, F., Qian, G.: Dance posture recognition using wide-baseline orthogonal stereo cameras. In: 7th International Conference on Automatic Face and Gesture Recognition (FGR06), pp. 481–486. IEEE (2006)
8. Johnson, S., Everingham, M.: Learning effective human pose estimation from inaccurate annotation. In: 2011 IEEE conference on Computer vision and pattern recognition (CVPR), pp. 1465–1472. IEEE (2011)
9. Kahol, K., Tripathi, P., Panchanathan, S.: Automated gesture segmentation from dance sequences. In: 2004 Proceedings of Sixth IEEE International Conference on Automatic Face and Gesture Recognition, pp. 883–888. IEEE (2004)

10. Kale, G., Patil, V.: Bharatnatyam adavu recognition from depth data. In: 2015 Third International Conference on Image Information Processing (ICIIP), pp. 246–251. IEEE (2015)
11. LeCun, Y., Bengio, Y., et al.: Convolutional networks for images, speech, and time series. Handb. Brain Theory Neural Netw. **3361**(10), 1995 (1995)
12. Mallick, T.: A framework for modeling, analysis and transcription of bharatanatyam dance performances. Ph.D. thesis, CSE, IIT Kharagpur, India (2017)
13. Mallick, T., Bhuyan, H., Das, P.P., Majumdar, A.K.: Annotated bharatanatyam data set, May 2017. http://hci.cse.iitkgp.ac.in
14. Masurelle, A., Essid, S., Richard, G.: Multimodal classification of dance movements using body joint trajectories and step sounds. In: 2013 14th International Workshop on Image Analysis for Multimedia Interactive Services (WIAMIS), pp. 1–4. IEEE (2013)
15. Microsoft: Tracking users, with kinect skeletal tracking, November 2010. https://msdn.microsoft.com/en-us/library/hh438998.aspx
16. Mohanty, A., et al.: Nrityabodha: towards understanding Indian classical dance using a deep learning approach. Signal Process.: Image Commun. **47**, 529–548 (2016)
17. Naveda, L.A., Leman, M.: Representation of samba dance gestures, using a multimodal analysis approach. In: Enactive 2008, pp. 68–74. Edizione ETS (2008)
18. Ning, H., Xu, W., Gong, Y., Huang, T.: Discriminative learning of visual words for 3D human pose estimation. In: IEEE Conference on Computer Vision and Pattern Recognition, CVPR 2008, pp. 1–8. Citeseer (2008)
19. Pohl, H., Hadjakos, A.: Dance pattern recognition using dynamic time warping. Sound Music Comput. **2010** (2010)
20. Rabiner, L.R.: A tutorial on hidden Markov models and selected applications in speech recognition. Proc. IEEE **77**(2), 257–286 (1989)
21. Reynolds, D.: Gaussian mixture models. Encycl. Biometr. 827–832 (2015)
22. Samanta, S., Purkait, P., Chanda, B.: Indian classical dance classification by learning dance pose bases. In: 2012 IEEE Workshop on the Applications of Computer Vision (WACV), pp. 265–270. IEEE (2012)
23. Sharma, A.: Recognising bharatanatyam dance sequences using RGB-D data. Ph.D. thesis, IIT Kanpur, India (2013)
24. Shiratori, T., Nakazawa, A., Ikeuchi, K.: Rhythmic motion analysis using motion capture and musical information. In: Proceedings of IEEE International Conference on Multisensor Fusion and Integration for Intelligent Systems, MFI2003, pp. 89–94. IEEE (2003)
25. Shiratori, T., Nakazawa, A., Ikeuchi, K.: Detecting dance motion structure through music analysis. In: 2004 Proceedings of Sixth IEEE International Conference on Automatic Face and Gesture Recognition, pp. 857–862. IEEE (2004)
26. Tian, Y., Zitnick, C.L., Narasimhan, S.G.: Exploring the spatial hierarchy of mixture models for human pose estimation. In: Fitzgibbon, A., Lazebnik, S., Perona, P., Sato, Y., Schmid, C. (eds.) ECCV 2012. LNCS, vol. 7576, pp. 256–269. Springer, Heidelberg (2012). https://doi.org/10.1007/978-3-642-33715-4_19

Digital Borders: Design of an Animal Intrusion Detection System Based on Deep Learning

Prashanth C. Ravoor[1](✉), T. S. B. Sudarshan[1], and Krishnan Rangarajan[2]

[1] Department of CSE, PES University, Bengaluru, India
[2] Department of CSE, Dayananda Sagar College of Engineering, Bengaluru, India

Abstract. Animals straying into human settlements in search for food cause conflicts, resulting in injury to humans, animals, or both. Application of technology can help reduce human–animal conflicts, and one such solution is the use of a fully automated monitoring system to detect animal transgressions. This paper describes a novel, end to end design of a Computer Vision and Deep Learning based, distributed, cost-effective, scalable, and robust cross-camera tracking system for animal intrusion detection, proposed to be installed along the borders of vulnerable areas (hence the name, *Digital Borders*). In this context, a unique application of animal re-identification to track an individual across multiple cameras is also discussed. A prototype of the design is constructed using Raspberry Pi devices connected to a laptop computer, with Raspberry Pi devices running object detection. The MobileNetv2-SSD model is used to detect presence of animals, and the ResNet50 model, trained using Triplet Loss, is used for animal re-identification. The prototype is tested using three animal species, and achieves detection accuracy of 80%, 89.47% and 92.56%, and re-identification accuracy of 99.6%, 86.2% and 61.7% respectively for tigers, jaguars and elephants. The integrated prototype operates at 2–3 frames per second, which is sufficient for near real time function.

Keywords: Animal intrusion detection · Animal re-identification · Computer vision · Cross-camera tracking · Deep learning · Human-animal conflict · Internet of things · Object detection

1 Introduction

Animal transgression into human settlements is an unfortunate, yet common, occurrence in India, especially in villages and towns bordering forest regions. Reported causes for such conflict include dwindling forest cover and expanding human population, resulting in displacement of animals from their natural habitat and forcing them to stray close to human settlements in search of food.

S. K. Singh et al. (Eds.): CVIP 2020, CCIS 1378, pp. 186–200, 2021.
https://doi.org/10.1007/978-981-16-1103-2_17

Although intruding animals typically attack and carry away cattle or raid crops, there are instances where humans fall prey as well. According to official Government of India reports, there have been at least 1,606 reported human causalities due to tiger and elephant attacks alone between 2013–2017 [15]. A separate, nation-wide study on human animal conflict in vulnerable areas conducted by the Centre for Wildlife Studies (CWS), Bengaluru found that 71% of the households surveyed had suffered crop loss, and 17% had suffered livestock loss [5]. A recent report published by the CWS estimates that there are approximately 80,000 recorded human-wildlife conflicts every year in India, with elephant, tiger, leopard and rhesus macaque being the top conflict prone species [19]. The problem is acute as well as widespread, and an effective solution can potentially alleviate difficulties of the affected populace. This is the key motivation behind the work presented here.

This paper proposes a system that uses deep learning and computer vision to reduce animal human conflicts by automatically detecting animal intrusions. After a detailed discussion with Dept. of Forestry officials[1] from the Bannerughatta National Park, Bengaluru, a few desirable characteristics of an animal intrusion detection system are formulated, including round the clock automatic monitoring, accurate animal detection, identification of the type of animal, the system's ability to scale to large deployments, and a fail-safe mode of user alerts. Several existing intrusion detection systems surveyed fail to meet most of these requirements. Specific shortcomings are highlighted in the following section.

The main contributions of the paper are as follows:

1. The architecture of an automatic, distributed, low cost and scalable animal intrusion detection system is presented
2. A novel method of tracking animal movement across multiple cameras using re-identification is described

Section 2 reviews recent publications of animal intrusion detection systems. The design of the system is elucidated in Sect. 3. Section 4 describes the datasets used for testing, Sect. 5 presents the results obtained, and the conclusion is provided in Sect. 6.

2 Related Work

A few recent publications regarding detection of animal intrusion and animal re-identification are reviewed here, and their shortcomings highlighted. A summary of the animal intrusion detection publications reviewed is presented in Table 1.

2.1 Animal Intrusion Detection Systems

Suganthi et al. [24] and Sailesh et al. [4] both describe systems to detect intrusion by elephants to reduce agricultural losses. Suganthi et al. use multiple vibration sensors, and based on the number of triggered sensors, a camera trap acquires

[1] Mr. Prashanth Shankinamatha, Deputy Conservator of Forests.

Table 1. Summary of animal intrusion detection systems surveyed

Reference (year)	Detection method	Identify species	Automated deterrance	Species specific
[24] (2018)	Vibration sensors	Yes	No	Yes
[4] (2019)	Image compare	Yes	Yes	Yes
[16] (2016)	PIR sensors	Yes	Yes	No
[17] (2018)	Image compare	Yes	Yes	Yes
[1] (2019)	CNN	Yes	No	No
[25] (2017)	IR UWB	No	No	No
[7] –	PIR sensors	No	Yes	No

a photo, and Google Vision API is used to detect if an elephant is close by. Sailesh et al. use a camera connected to a Raspberry Pi device that continuously captures images and checks if the images contain an elephant. Both methods contain deterrance mechanisms, such as playing of sounds and switching on some powerful lights to drive away the approaching elephants.

Pooja et al. [16] and Prajna et al. [17] both use multiple Passive Infrared (PIR) sensors to detect presence of wild animals. Pooja et al. use the number of motion sensors triggered as an indicator to the size of the animal, and hence its type, whereas Prajna et al. use motion detection as part of a camera trap, and compares the captured images to a pre-populated database to identify the type of animal. Both systems have capabilities of taking different actions based on the type of animal detected. This includes playing different types of sounds, flashing lights and even spraying aerosol solutions to deter animals from moving further into farmlands.

Angadi et al. [1] present an intrusion detection system that is the closest in design to the method described in this paper. Camera traps to acquire images on detection of movement, and use object detection Convolutional Neural Networks (CNNs) to detect animals. The Single Shot Multi-box Detection model [13] is used for object detection, and if any wild animals are found in the image, then an alert message is sent to the owner to take appropriate action. All processing is carried on a Raspberry Pi device, installed at the same location of the camera trap.

Xue et al. [25] describe a unique method of animal intrusion detection through use of IR Ultra-Wide-Band (UWB) signals. Multiple wireless IR-UWB sensors are mounted at strategic locations, and the captured signals are classified using CNNs to detect animals. A major drawback of this approach is the inability of the system to identify species of the animal.

Animal Intrusion and Detection System (ANIDERS) [7] is a commercially available solution to help farmers prevent crop loss by detecting and preventing animal intrusions using a combination of AIR (Active Infrared) and PIR sensors. On detection, an alarms are triggered to repel intruders. The pilot study conducted by WWF-India[2] notes that out of 539 captures recorded to be within the

[2] https://www.wwfindia.org/news_facts/feature_stories/lessons_from_makhanthpur_uttarakhand/.

range of the ANIDERS, the system detected the animal 368 times, which implies an accuracy of around 68%. There is room for improvement in this regard.

Several challenges exist with all the surveyed methods. Most notably, the systems built for animal intrusion detection have to ensure correct species identification. Animals react differently to stimulus – loud sounds may scare away wild boar, but might startle an elephant causing it to go on a rampage. Apart from detecting the animal, it is also necessary to ascertain its intentions before creating alerts to ensure fewer false positives. Additionally, the rate of false alarms for these systems is not known. After an alarm goes off, it is also not clear if the systems can alert the user as to whether deterring the animal is successful. It would also be useful to find the last known location of the animal and its direction of movement, apart from counting the number of animals, in case there were multiple detected. All of this needs to be performed in real or near-real time. Since the solution also needs to be cost-effective, small compute devices such as embedded systems would need to be used, which can be deployed on site. The solution proposed in this paper attempts to address all of these challenges, and an overview of the design is presented in the next section.

2.2 Animal Re-identification

Re-identification is the ability of a system to distinguish two individuals of the same type, be it persons, vehicles, animals etc. Re-identification systems extract feature vectors from images, and compare their similarity using standard measures such as Euclidean distance. Several animal re-identification systems exist today, but nearly all are specific to a particular species. Ravoor et al. [18] provide a comprehensive survey of existing animal re-identification systems that use deep learning. The article further highlights the suitability of Triplet Loss [3] and the ResNet50 model [2] for re-identification systems. In furtherance of the conclusions drawn from the article, the system implemented here makes use of the ResNet50 model, trained using Triplet loss to identify individuals in cross-camera setups.

3 Proposed Methodology

There are multiple facets to the method proposed in this paper, and each is described in detail in this section.

3.1 Animal Detection

Object Detection is a method commonly employed to automatically find objects of interest in images. It consists of two steps: finding portion(s) of the image that are of interest, and then classifying these locations into one of the known categories. Popular object detection models include Faster R-CNN [21], YOLO [20] and SSD [13].

Table 2. Training parameters for (a) Object Detection models, and (b) animal re-identification model

Parameter	**YOLOv3**	**MobileNetv2-SSD**
# classes	3	3
Framework	DarkNet	TensorFlow
Pretrained Weights	MS COCO [11]	Open Images [6]
Objective Function	Multi-part Loss [20]	Weighted Sigmoid
Batch Size	32	4
Optimizer	SGD	Adam
Base Learning Rate	10^{-3}	10^{-5}
Quantization	—	8-bit

(a)

Parameter	**Value**
Backbone Model	ResNet50 (2 dropout layers)
Input Image Dimensions	$256 \times 256 \times 3$
Objective Function	Triplet Loss and Center Loss [14]
Optimizer	Adam
Batch Size	16
Base Learning Rate	10^{-4}
Batch Hard Mining	3 ids, 8 samples per id
Label Smoothing	Off

(b)

A key requirement of the intrusion detection system is real time operation; the object detection network is required to be both fast and accurate. Faster R-CNN is not suitable for real time operation, since it is relatively slow. A variation of YOLO – tiny-YOLO is a light weight object detection model that can perform up to 155 fps on a GPU [20]. Similarly, a combination of the SSD detector with the MobileNetv2 [22] backbone is a lightweight network, optimized for embedded systems and mobile devices. In this paper, performance of both the tiny-YOLO and the MobileNetv2-SSD models are compared for animal detection.

Since off-the-shelf pre-trained models do not perform well for specialized applications, both models are *fine-tuned* for better performance. Fine-tuning refers to altering the final classifier layer of a trained neural network to predict a different number of classes (in this case three) and re-training the model to update its weights to attain better performance for the new set of classes. Data used for fine tuning the models is described in Sect. 4. A summary of the parameters used during fine tuning are illustrated in Table 2a.

3.2 Animal Re-identification Network

The approach described in this paper implements a novel application of animal re-identification, where the extracted features are used by the system to determine if an animal spotted in two cameras is the same individual. It is therefore possible to track the animal across cameras, and additionally, in cases of overlapping cameras, accurately count the number of detected animals.

Training the network for re-identification of animals closely follows the method described by Luo et al. [14], who combine several successful procedures from past research to create a formidable person re-identification system. The ResNet50 model [2] is the backbone network used, with a combination of triplet-loss [3] and center loss as the objective function. Triplet loss takes as input three images: *anchor*, the image being trained upon, *positive*, a sample image of the same identity as the anchor, and *negative*, a sample which belongs to a separate identity. The triplet loss function maximises the distance between the *anchor* and

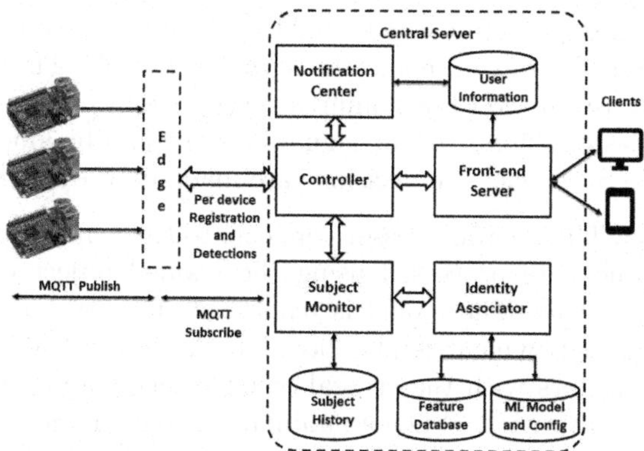

Fig. 1. Architecture of the proposed system

the *negative*, while reducing the distance between the *anchor* and the *positive*, effectively minimising intra-class distance and maximising inter-class distance. Since Luo et al. use the system for person re-identification, a few minor changes are made to adapt the procedure to the datasets used here, but otherwise the overall mechanism for training the network remains the same. A summary of a few important parameters used for training the model is summarized in Table 2b. Different models are trained for different species, and the trained models are used at inference time to extract features from animal images and associate identities using feature comparison methods. This is different from the more typical classification like approach, and allows for open set identification.

The integration of animal re-identification and object detection for cross-camera tracking is described through the system design.

3.3 System Design

The design of the proposed system for animal intrusion detection and deterrance is illustrated in Fig. 1. The distributed architecture consists of the end points – the camera and processing devices, an optional edge server and the central server. The end points are deployed on site, at carefully selected locations to maximize coverage of the vulnerable areas. The communication between devices and sensors is wired, but the communication with the edge or central servers is through a wireless medium, such as WLAN, WiFi or a cellular network.

Sensors: Sensors include cameras and associated hardware, such as a PIR based motion sensor, which together can act similar to a camera trap. The cameras are activated only when movement is detected, thereby saving energy. There could be several such devices at every site, depending on the area to be covered. It is therefore essential for these devices to be inexpensive and readily available in the market. The PiCamera[3] is used in the prototype for image acquisition.

[3] https://www.raspberrypi.org/products/camera-module-v2/.

In addition to cameras, there could be lighting or sound systems installed that could be used to scare away animals (the *deterrance unit*). The deterrance unit performs actions customized to each animal species – for example, tigers could be scared away by flashing lights, or for jaguars there could be loud sounds played through speakers. Such selective decisions are made by the central server.

Microprocessor: The microprocessor connects to the camera and receives raw image frames, which are processed using the trained object detection model loaded on to the device. The model is *quantized*[4] for low inference time. Per site custom model deployment is also possible. As soon as it is activated, the microprocessor registers with the central or edge server and sets up a channel for all future communication. When an animal is detected, an on board Message Queue Telemetry Transport (MQTT) publisher (client) dispatches a message to the server containing the type of animal detected, the location of animal within the image, and corresponding portions of the image. Every device deployed on-site performs the same set of actions independently and communicates only with the edge/central server. This increases the system resilience and scale out, since adding new devices or replacing a malfunctioning device needs no change to the rest of the system. The Raspberry Pi[5] device is used in the prototype, since it is powerful enough to run object detection and also supports a variety of communication interfaces.

Central and Edge Servers: The central server operates by communicating with all registered devices, and monitors them for health and active detections. Edge server functions are identical to central server but are used only to scale to large deployments, when the number of local devices is far too many or far too distributed for a single central server. The trained re-identification model for each type of animal is stored on these servers. The server also has access to persistent storage, such as a NoSQL database for quick retrieval of feature vectors and per device animal detection history. The *subject monitor* stores information about animal movements and the current number of active detections in each registered device. The *notification center* has access to the user information and is responsible for sending alerts and user messages through proper channels.

Identity Association and Tracking: If an animal moves in between the range of two cameras, it could falsely be detected as two animals. It is therefore necessary to determine if two animals (of the same species) are in fact the same *individual* – doing so will enable the system to both count the number of detected animals and track them efficiently. Tracking within a single camera uses Intersection over Union (IOU) based matching to track individuals, and feature extraction using the re-identification model is only used when animals move between cameras. Post detection, the portion of the image that contains the animal (the bounding box) is passed through the re-identification network and the resultant feature vector is compared to feature vectors stored in the database. If there are no records in the database, then the animal is being spotted for the first time,

[4] https://www.tensorflow.org/lite/performance/model_optimization#quantization.
[5] https://www.raspberrypi.org/products/raspberry-pi-3-model-b-plus/.

and a new identity is generated. If the database is not empty, then a new identity is assigned if

$$d(q, g_x) > (d_\mu + 2 \times d_\sigma), \quad x = 1 \cdots |D| \tag{1}$$

where $d(x, y)$ is the Euclidean distance between feature vectors of two images x and y, q is the feature vector of the image under consideration, $g_x \in D$, the database of feature vectors. d_μ and d_σ are mean value of the inter-class Euclidean distance and standard deviation respectively calculated separately for each species over the training set. d_μ is calculated by measuring the distance between each individual and every other individual in the training set and taking the average of these distances. Essentially, the algorithm assigns a new identity when the Euclidean distance between the current image and closest matching image in the DB exceeds two standard deviations from the mean inter-class distance calculated over the training set. In other cases, the identity of the closest matching animal is assigned. In either case, the DB is updated with the feature vector and the corresponding identity, which will be used for subsequent feature matching. This algorithm to determine new identities can be replaced by any different dynamic approach, such as using an Open-Set SVM [23].

Using the associated identities, the animal's movement with respect to the device (left, right or inwards) is ascertained. Inward movement detection is critical to create timely alerts and notifications. The inward movement for frame i, m_i is calculated as per Eq. 2.

$$m_i = \begin{cases} inward & \text{if } A_{i-1}/A_i > T_a \\ outward & \text{if } A_{i-1}/A_i < 1/T_a \end{cases} \tag{2}$$

where A_i is the area of the bounding box for frame i and T_a is a threshold. So a bounding box growing progressively larger is considered to be moving inwards if the difference is greater than some threshold T_a. This procedure is independent of animal size, and can track small or large animals. A similar threshold, T_l is used to determine direction of lateral movement. The device alerts the central server if it finds that the animal is moving inward (towards the device), which may decide to activate the deterrance unit (play sounds or flash lights for example). If activated, the system monitors the reaction of the animal and finds if it moved away. The central server collates information from all sources and issues user notifications as necessary, alerting users of possible danger. The alert contains the animal's approximate location, recently detected animals, their types, the time each animal was last seen and an estimate of their direction of movement. Such information is critical for swift and decisive action.

In summary, object detection and re-identification are effectively used to build a solution for animal intrusion detection and subsequent monitoring. The datasets used for measuring the effectiveness of the prototype for these two parameters are described in Sect. 4. The results from the prototype of the proposed system for detection and re-identification are presented in Sect. 5.

Table 3. Details of the datasets used

Dataset	Source	Total size	Detection	Re-identification		
			# images	# identities	# images	# images per id Mean/Median
Tiger	[10]	3649	1200	107	1887	17.91/13.0
Elephant	[8]	2078	1500	276	2078	7.6/7.0
Jaguar	On Req.[a]	1083	700	49	1077	22.1/6.0

[a] Prof. Marcella Kelly: http://www.mjkelly.info/

Table 4. Detection accuracy results. FPR stands for False Positive Rate

Dataset	Type	MobileNetv2-SSD		tiny-YOLO	
		Acc. (%)	FPR (%)	Acc. (%)	FPR (%)
Tiger	Detection	80.00	4.76	**89.00**	**0.00**
	Re-Id	**99.79**	**0.21**	85.00	0.08
Elephant	Detection/Re-Id	92.56	0.1	**97.0**	**0.09**
Jaguar	Detection	**89.47**	**4.06**	74.00	0.00
	Re-Id	**97.05**	**3.04**	72.00	0.00

4 Datasets

Three species are included as part of this study – tigers, jaguars and elephants. For training and evaluation, randomized, overlapping subsets for object detection and animal re-identification are generated for each dataset based on availability of annotation data. Annotations (labels) for the detection dataset are bounding box coordinates, and for re-identification a unique identifier (an integer) for each individual in the dataset. For elephants and jaguars, bounding box annotations are manually created using the LabelImg tool[6]. For re-identification, the full body of tigers and jaguars are used, whereas the head and trunk is used for elephants, as per the procedure followed in [9]. A summary of the size of each dataset is presented in Table 3. The mean and median number of samples per each identity is indicated, which provides an overview of the skew or bias in the dataset.

5 Results and Discussion

The accuracy of animal detection over each dataset for both the MobileNetv2-SSD [13] and tiny-YOLO [20] is provided in Table 4. Boldface indicates better results. The table also indicates the rate of false positives i.e., where an animal is either mislabelled or bounding box placement is incorrect. The model is trained over the detection dataset, and evaluated over both the re-identification and the detection sets. The parameters used for model training are illustrated in Table 2a.

[6] https://github.com/tzutalin/labelImg.

Fig. 2. A few results of the object detection model (MobileNetv2-SSD). Images with a green outline indicate a successful detection. The images in the last column, containing red outlines indicate misclassification

Although YOLO performs better than SSD for the detection datasets, the SSD model generalizes better as observed from its higher accuracy over the re-identification set. This could be due to the training parameters used, rather than being a characteristic of the models themselves. Table 6 illustrates the object detection inference times, and tiny-YOLO is much slower than SSD on Raspberry Pi. The difference is due to use of *quantization training* of the SSD model, and use of the TensorFlow Lite[7] runtime. The tiny-YOLO model is not quantized, and has scope for optimization. For the prototype, the MobileNetv2-SSD model is used for object detection.

Qualitative results of running detection using the MobileNetv2-SSD model is illustrated in Fig. 2. The figures contain bounding boxes around the animals, with the confidence score and the label appearing on the top left of the rectangle. A green outline indicates success. The SSD model appears to be biased towards the Tigers dataset, with several images being mislabelled as a tiger. The *false positive rate* is 4.76% for tigers, which is significantly high. Large false positive rates increase the likelihood of the system erroneously reporting a harmless animal, such as a dog or pig, instead of ignoring it, which is the expected behavior. To reduce false positives, training needs to be improved with use of more diverse *distractor images* (nearly 2500 distractors are currently used). It is also optimal to train the model on larger datasets to achieve better quality. For the prototype used here, the current detection rates are sufficient.

To evaluate the animal re-identification model, the available *identities* (and not images directly) in each dataset are split into two disjoint sub-sets with an

[7] https://www.tensorflow.org/lite/.

Table 5. Test set accuracy for re-identification using the proposed method compared to known state-of-the-art

Dataset	State-of-the-art			Proposed method	
	Ref.	Top-1 (%)	Top-5 (%)	Top-1 (%)	Top-5 (%)
Tiger	[12]	97.7	99.1	99.6±0.5	100.0 ± 0.0
Elephant	[9]	56.0	71.6	61.7±3.9	81.1 ± 1.4
Jaguar	–	–	–	86.2±9.0	97.0 ± 4.1

Table 6. Time taken for various steps. Average time represents amortized cost, considering SSD for object detection

Step	Platform	Operation frequency	Time (ms)
Obj. Det. (SSD)	Raspberry Pi	Always	**280–350**
Obj. Det. (YOLO)	Raspberry Pi	Always	1400–1550
Feature extraction	Laptop	Intermittent	350–400
Id association	Laptop	Always	5–10
Communication time	Network	Intermittent	50–75
Average per frame			**400**

80:20 ratio forming the train and test identities respectively; all corresponding images of the train identities form the *train set* (used for model training), and the remainder form the *test set* (for evaluation). The metric typically used for evaluating re-identification models is the *top-k* rank. The top-1 and top-5 ranks are reported here. The results of the re-identification network appear in Table 5. The accuracy reported is the mean value calculated through three random trails over the test set and the corresponding standard deviation. A few qualitative results of animal re-identification is illustrated in Fig. 3 for jaguars and elephants. The identity of each individual (an integer) appears directly above the image. The results show the working of the re-identification model in correctly identifying the individual in the *query* image (first column), and successful identifications are marked with a green outline, whereas incorrect identities are marked with red. The full integrated system operation is illustrated using images of tigers.

The comparison against known state-of-the-art methods for each dataset illustrates that the model used here is performing quite well. It is to be noted that for the Amur Tiger dataset, the accuracy is calculated differently – the accuracy reported by Liu et al. [12] is over a separate test set of the Amur Re-Identification challenge[8], as evaluated by the workshop rules. The Jaguars dataset is not publicly available, and hence no existing performance measure could be found. The elephants dataset is far more challenging compared to Jaguars and Tigers since images are captured across a period spanning nearly two decades. Although not designed specifically for any species, the proposed method performs close to the best known methods for each species. It is however, to be noted that the data lacks labels for camera identification, and hence no distinction is made in this regard. Typically re-identification evaluation excludes images from the same camera while measuring accuracy, so that the effect of image *sequences* – images taken only a few seconds apart, are minimized. For the system described in this paper however, the results obtained are sufficient for seamless operation.

[8] https://cvwc2019.github.io/leaderboard.html.

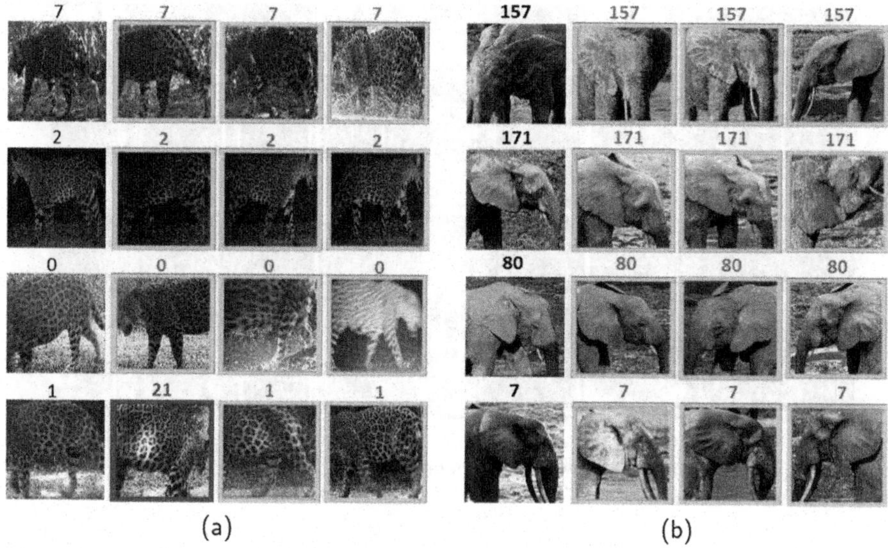

Fig. 3. Illustration of the trained re-identification model on (a) Jaguars, and (b) Elephants. The first column is the query image. The top-3 ranked results returned by the system are shown alongside the query. Green outline indicates a success, and red indicates failure. (Color figure online)

The integration of object detection and re-identification models for cross camera tracking is visualized in Fig. 4, which shows a sequence of images of two tigers moving across from each other, with one tiger completely obstructing the other for a few frames. The tracking system correctly associates identities to the individuals before and after they cross, using the feature vectors extracted from each tiger. The same technique is used to track the movement of the individual between two cameras. The identities are associated as described previously in Sect. 3.3.

The time taken by each step in the tracking system is summarized in Table 6. The amortized inference time for entire system operation, including network transfer latency is around 400 ms per frame. The dominant cost is from the object detector which uses up to 300 ms per image (for MobileNetv2-SSD). The feature extraction network is run on a Laptop computer (CPU only) and takes approximately 300–400 ms per image. Since it is intermittent, it does not affect amortized running time. Although use of TensorFlow Lite significantly improved detection performance, the slowest operation in the entire pipeline is still object detection – which operates at roughly 2–3 frames per second. Edge TPUs, such as Intel's Movidius Neural Compute stick and Google Coral USB accelerator boost performance up to a factor of 4, and are to be considered for actual deployments.

The proposed system allows for a scale-out architecture due to use of independent device operation, off-site feature extraction, centralized identity association, and split-responsibility between edge and central servers. Off-site fea-

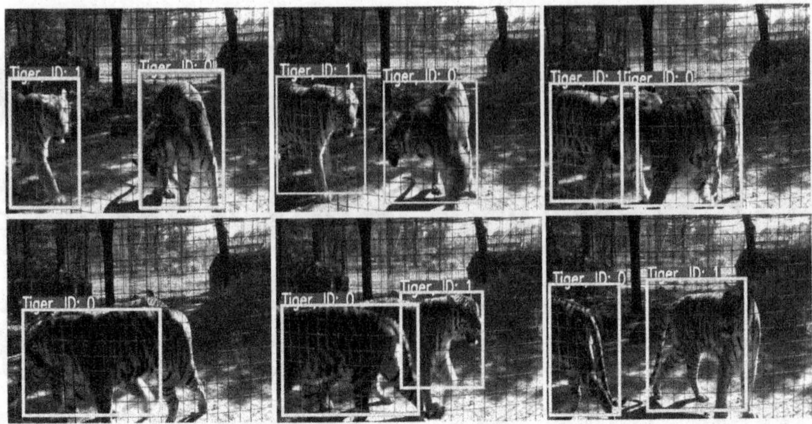

Fig. 4. Sequence of images show two tigers crossing each other. Identities are retained before and after cross-over

ture extraction and identity association are critical to break any relationships between devices, and reduce inter-device communication. A new device can be easily added to the system with minimum configuration. MQTT offers QoS based services, so edge and central servers are notified when a device fails. The system is fully distributed, and can easily be deployed even for very large sites. The central server and the MQTT broker (usually the edge server) need redundancy to prevent unexpected failures, but since they are off-site, adding high availability is only limited by resource constraints.

6 Future Work and Conclusion

The proposed system allows for a scale-out architecture due to independent end-point device operation, off-site feature extraction, centralized identity association, and split-responsibility between edge and central servers. The system is fully distributed, and can easily be deployed even for very large sites. Further improvements include use of IR cameras and wide-angle cameras to increase system versatility. In addition, better algorithms for in-camera tracking such as the use of Recurrent Neural Networks like LSTM can be leveraged. There is also scope to improve object detection performance with the use of TPUs at the edge server. In addition, there are several operational challenges that are to be considered for wide adoption of such systems. Notably, animals tend to get accustomed to alarm sounds and subsequently ignore them. Another such challenge is the physical safety of the units deployed in the field, which are susceptible to theft or damage due to animal movement.

This paper describes an end-to-end system for animal intrusion detection, tracking, deterrence and alert notification. Each individual component in this pipeline is extensively studied and optimized for deployment on embedded systems. The result is a design of an accurate, distributed, robust, efficient and scalable system. While re-identification has so far been a human-in-the-loop approach, a novel application is proposed here which leverages it for effective cross-camera tracking of individual animals. The prototype is tested using three animal species, and achieves animal detection accuracy of 80%, 89.47% and 92.56%, and re-identification accuracy of 99.6%, 86.2% and 61.7% respectively for tigers, jaguars and elephants. The integrated prototype built using Raspberry Pi devices is capable of achieving a frame rate of 2–3 fps, and is proof-of-concept for real time operation of the system. The methods proposed in this paper could be leveraged to build a robust animal intrusion detection system for vulnerable areas prone to animal attacks, and could go a long way in reducing causalities due to wild animal transgressions by not only detecting the presence of animals, but also assessing current risks posed by the wild animal and create a situation specific alert that serves as an early warning, thereby offering timely information to prevent further conflict.

Acknowledgment. The authors thank Dr. Marcella Kelly, Professor, Dept. of Fish and Wildlife Conservation, Virgina Tech, Mr. Peter Wrege, Director, Elephant Listening Project and Mr. Matthias Körschens, Friedrich Schiller University, Jena, for graciously sharing the datasets of jaguar and elephant images. Many thanks to Mr. Prashanth Shankinamatha, Deputy Conservator of Forests, Bannerughatta National Park. Whose valuable inputs have helped better the design of the system.

References

1. Angadi, S., Katagall, R.: Agrivigilance: a security system for intrusion detection in agriculture using raspberry pi and openCV. Int. J. Sci. Technol. Res. **8**(11), 1260–1267 (2019)
2. He, K., Zhang, X., Ren, S., Sun, J.: Deep residual learning for image recognition. In: 2016 IEEE Conference on Computer Vision and Pattern Recognition (CVPR), pp. 770–778, June 2016. https://doi.org/10.1109/CVPR.2016.90
3. Hermans, A., Beyer, L., Leibe, B.: In defense of the triplet loss for person re-identification. arXiv preprint arXiv:1703.07737 (2017)
4. Sailesh, K., Balina, H.V., Sivakumar, T., Vijaya Poojitha, P.: Detection of wild elephants using image processing on raspberry pi3. Int. J. Comput. Sci. Mob. Comput. **8**(2), 104–115 (2019)
5. Karanth, K.K., Kudalkar, S.: History, location, and species matter: insights for human-wildlife conflict mitigation from India. Hum. Dimens. Wildl. **22**(4), 331–346 (2017). https://doi.org/10.1080/10871209.2017.1334106
6. Kuznetsova, A., et al.: The open images dataset V4. Int. J. Comput. Vis. **128**(7), 1956–1981 (2020)
7. Kyari - The Nursery of Innovations: Animal intrusion detection and repellent system (2020). http://aniders.com/
8. Körschens, M., Denzler, J.: Elpephants: a fine-grained dataset for elephant re-identification. In: 2019 IEEE/CVF International Conference on Computer Vision Workshop (ICCVW), pp. 263–270, October 2019. https://doi.org/10.1109/ICCVW.2019.00035
9. Körschens, M., Barz, B., Denzler, J.: Towards automatic identification of elephants in the wild. arXiv preprint arXiv:1812.04418 (2018)

10. Li, S., Li, J., Lin, W., Tang, H.: Amur tiger re-identification in the wild. arXiv preprint arXiv:1906.05586 (2019)
11. Lin, T.-Y., et al.: Microsoft COCO: common objects in context. In: Fleet, D., Pajdla, T., Schiele, B., Tuytelaars, T. (eds.) ECCV 2014. LNCS, vol. 8693, pp. 740–755. Springer, Cham (2014). https://doi.org/10.1007/978-3-319-10602-1_48
12. Liu, C., Zhang, R., Guo, L.: Part-pose guided amur tiger re-identification. In: 2019 IEEE/CVF International Conference on Computer Vision Workshop (ICCVW), pp. 315–322 (2019). https://doi.org/10.1109/ICCVW.2019.00042
13. Liu, W., et al.: SSD: single shot multibox detector. In: Leibe, B., Matas, J., Sebe, N., Welling, M. (eds.) ECCV 2016. LNCS, vol. 9905, pp. 21–37. Springer, Cham (2016). https://doi.org/10.1007/978-3-319-46448-0_2
14. Luo, H., Gu, Y., Liao, X., Lai, S., Jiang, W.: Bag of tricks and a strong baseline for deep person re-identification. In: The IEEE Conference on Computer Vision and Pattern Recognition (CVPR) Workshops, June 2019
15. Ministry of Environment Forest and Climate Change: Human animal conflict, rajya sabha unstarred question no-222, February 2018. https://pqars.nic.in/annex/245/Au222.pdf
16. Pooja, G., Bagal, M.U.: A smart farmland using raspberry pi crop vandalization prevention & intrusion detection system. Int. J. Adv. Res. Innov. Ideas Educ. **1**(S), 62–68 (2016)
17. Prajna, P., Soujanya, B.S., Divya: IoT-based wild animal intrusion detection system. Int. J. Eng. Res. Technol. (IJERT) **6**(15) (2018). https://www.ijert.org/iot-based-wild-animal-intrusion-detection-system
18. Ravoor, P.C., Sudarshan, T.S.B.: Deep learning methods for multi-species animal re-identification and tracking - a survey. Comput. Sci. Rev. **38**, 100289 (2020). https://doi.org/10.1016/j.cosrev.2020.100289
19. Reddy, A., Vanamamalai, A., Gupta, S., Karanth, K.: Human-wildlife conflict in Karnataka (2020)
20. Redmon, J., Divvala, S., Girshick, R., Farhadi, A.: You only look once: unified, real-time object detection. In: 2016 IEEE Conference on Computer Vision and Pattern Recognition (CVPR), pp. 779–788 (2016). https://doi.org/10.1109/CVPR.2016.91
21. Ren, S., He, K., Girshick, R., Sun, J.: Faster R-CNN: towards real-time object detection with region proposal networks. IEEE Trans. Pattern Anal. Mach. Intell. **39**(6), 1137–1149 (2017)
22. Sandler, M., Howard, A., Zhu, M., Zhmoginov, A., Chen, L.: MobileNetV 2: inverted residuals and linear bottlenecks. In: 2018 IEEE/CVF Conference on Computer Vision and Pattern Recognition, pp. 4510–4520 (2018). https://doi.org/10.1109/CVPR.2018.00474
23. Scheirer, W.J., de Rezende Rocha, A., Sapkota, A., Boult, T.E.: Toward open set recognition. IEEE Trans. Pattern Anal. Mach. Intell. **35**(7), 1757–1772 (2013). https://doi.org/10.1109/TPAMI.2012.256
24. Suganthi, N., Rajathi, N., Inzamam, M.F.: Elephant intrusion detection and repulsive system. Int. J. Recent Technol. Eng. **7**(4S), 307–310 (2018)
25. Xue, W., Jiang, T., Shi, J.: Animal intrusion detection based on convolutional neural network. In: 2017 17th International Symposium on Communications and Information Technologies (ISCIT), pp. 1–5 (2017). https://doi.org/10.1109/ISCIT.2017.8261234

Automatic On-Road Object Detection in LiDAR-Point Cloud Data Using Modified VoxelNet Architecture

G. N. Nikhil(✉), Md. Meraz, and Mohd. Javed

Indian Institute of Information Technology, Allahabad, Prayagraj 211015, India
{irm2015501,pro2016001,javed}@iiita.ac.in

Abstract. Automatic detection of objects play an important and key role in developing real time applications related to robotics and autonomous driving vehicles. The latest research trend in computer vision is to detect objects in the 3D point cloud data produced by LiDAR (Light Detection and Ranging) sensors mounted on the self driving cars. This research paper aims at proposing modifications to the existing VoxelNet architecture for object detection. The proposed models perform direct 3D convolution on the point cloud data. Firstly, the point cloud is encoded into a suitable format in the detection pipeline, and next, the feature maps are extracted from the encoded output of the encoder, and lastly, object detection is done using this learnt feature maps in the final stage. Experimental results on the benchmark KITTI dataset show that the proposed modifications outperform the existing VoxelNet based models and other fusion based methods in terms of accuracy as well as time.

Keywords: Object detection · Point cloud data · 3D convolution neural networks · VoxelNet

1 Introduction

Autonomous driving vehicles basically in the field of computer vision, involve three types of challenges like object detection, tracking and segmentation [1]. Object classification implies identifying which class of objects are present in the point cloud data, and further object detection helps in locating the specific objects. Object detection is generally considered as tough problem due to high number of classes and overlapping of objects [1]. In autonomous driving, object detection is very crucial because the vehicle needs to know its surroundings, and it has to create a path to the destination such that it will not hit any obstacles during navigation. Object detection technology in self driving cars is aimed at detecting all the obstacles/objects such as pedestrians, cars, trucks, bicycles, etc., which should take place in real time and has to be very accurate, because a small mistake may incur a very huge damage of life and property.

S. K. Singh et al. (Eds.): CVIP 2020, CCIS 1378, pp. 201–213, 2021.
https://doi.org/10.1007/978-981-16-1103-2_18

In autonomous vehicles, LiDAR (Light Detection and Ranging) sensors are responsible for providing better understanding of objects around, and maintaining geometric information. A LiDAR instrument generally has a laser, GPS and scanner [2]. The laser is radiated in all directions, and whenever there is an obstacle, they hit the object and bounce back to the source, thereby giving three dimensional information about the objects and its shape, surface details. The difference between the transmitted time and received time divided by the speed at which laser is being transmitted gives the distance of the object. This can be used to create a 3D map(point cloud) of the surroundings.

In the literature, there are many 3D representations for an object which include- Euclidean structured data (Descriptors, Projections, RGB-D, Voxel, Octree) and Non-Euclidean structured data (Point Cloud, Graphs, Meshes) [3]. Point cloud is one way of representing any object in 3- dimension. In this research paper, we choose to work with point cloud data i.e., we will be doing object detection directly in the Point cloud data. Point cloud data is mainly used because it is very close to raw sensor data and it gives good results irrespective of weather conditions [4]. In many applications like autonomous navigation and robotic systems, automatic detection of objects with high accuracy in 3D point clouds is the key issue. In case of RGB Colour images, accuracy depends on image quality, lighting in the surroundings and camera pose. Camera is susceptible to noise and occlusion, and image quality is not good in rainy and dark conditions. Hence point cloud is more suitable for autonomous driving vehicles.

The 3D object detection directly in point cloud is a difficult problem [5] mainly because of highly sparsity and irregularities in the data. There are different state-of-the-art approaches to solve this problem. The first approach among 3D detection methods is to first extract features from the 3D point cloud space and then project them onto 2D space, where the standard 2D detection architectures can be directly applied [5]. The second approach is to work on the fusion of RGB and LiDAR data. The third approach is to work directly with the 3D point cloud data using 3D techniques, and the VoxelNet [6] architecture is one of the popular techniques.

2 Literature Review

In the literature, object detection in point cloud is basically carried out in four different ways- Bird Eye View (BEV) based, image based, fusion based, and 3D based. The models are briefly described below.

2.1 Bird's Eye View Based Method

MV3D [7] was the first model to use BEV representation which used Multi view 3D networks for 3D based object detection in autonomous driving. It is a fusion method which uses both RGB images and LIDAR data. There are two sub networks in the main network; the first part does region proposal for 3D objects, and the other sub network fuses the features obtained from multi views.

The proposal sub network is used to generate the 3D bounding boxes from the BEV. A deep fusion scheme is used here which combines the local features from the multiple views. There are only limited models which use the multiple views of the data to solve the object detection problem in autonomous driving.

2.2 Front-View and Image-Based Method

These can be further classified based on front view, BEV and direct image based methods [8]. In image based methods, CNN is used or handcrafted methods are used to extract the feature maps. They use the RGB-D representation of the 3D data in Frustum PointNets [9]. They used data from both indoor and outdoor. Region proposals and localisation of the objects in the point clouds of large scenes efficiently was the main problem to be solved here. These methods perform poorly compared to the other methods.

2.3 Fusion-Based Methods

A Novel 3D object detection architecture is proposed in Cont-Fuse [10]. This is also a fusion method which uses RGB and LIDAR data to perform end to end 3D object detection. The feature maps extracted from point cloud and RGB images are fused at various resolutions from low to high using convolution operations. The proposed end to end architecture can be used for multiple sensors because both the features of the image and the information of geometry is encoded using the continuous fusion layers. Fusion methods perform better than the previous methods but take much time because it needs to process the images as well as point clouds.

2.4 3D-Based Methods

In 3D based methods, raw point clouds are used directly for object detection. In PointNet [4], point cloud data is used to represent the 3D space. Point cloud is not generally used because of its highly irregular format. Generally, 3D space is transformed to 3D voxels, however many issues are caused by this transformation, and converting to voxels will not be suitable for all types of applications. A novel architecture is proposed in PointNet [4] which directly takes the point cloud as the input. In point cloud there is no permutation variance of input points. In the work by [6], a novel architecture called VoxelNet is proposed in which the input point cloud data is partitioned into voxels. The need for manual feature extraction is replaced by the architecture being proposed. An end to end network for 3D object detection where in a single stage feature extraction and predicting bounding boxes takes place. In VoxelNet, point cloud is divided into partitions which are equally spaced and called 3D voxels. There are three parts in the VoxelNet architecture. The first part is Voxel Feature Encoder (VFE) which extracts features from each voxel and then features are encoded and transformed. Each voxel is then represented by one encoded feature which represents the volumetric description of the objects. These features are then passed to the middle convolution layers where the convolution operations takes place and the feature maps are extracted. These feature maps are then passed to the Region Proposal Networks (RPN), then the RPN does region proposal and gives the final bounding boxes for the objects. This method shows that high accuracy can be attained by working on Point cloud directly.

3 Background for the Proposed Architecture

Object detection in raw point cloud is a 3 Dimensional problem as point cloud is 3D representation of 3D point space.

In this paper, we propose to use a 3-stage network as in voxelNet [6] as shown Fig. 1. The first stage is feature encoder that encodes the features and projects them onto a pseudo image. The second stage is about semantic segmentation (Backbone Network) which extracts features from the pseudo image and converts into high-level representation. The third stage is object detection head in point cloud that takes feature maps generated by Backbone network and then performs convolution operation for object detection and prediction of 3D bounding boxes.

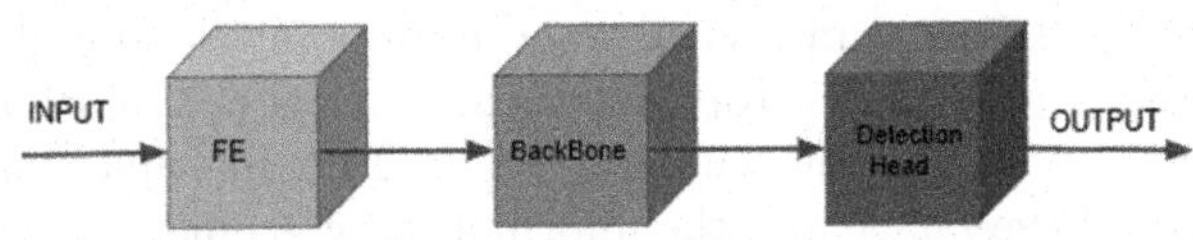

Fig. 1. Generic model

3.1 Feature Encoder in Point Cloud

Feature Encoder is the first stage in the proposed 3-stage pipeline. Point cloud has a very large number of points, and most of them are sparse and empty. Hence, feature encoder extracts the necessary features which can represent the whole information in the point cloud and passes those features to the next stage. Feature encoder saves a lot of memory and makes the computation faster for the next stages. In this paper Voxel Feature Encoder (VFE) [6] is used as feature Encoders in the proposed models.

Voxel Feature Encoder (VFE). Each point in point cloud is represented by 4 coordinates $[x, y, z, r]$, where x, y, z are the 3D coordinates in the space for each point and r is the reflectance. In VFE [6], the entire point cloud is divided into voxels which are equally spaced. Point cloud has W, H, D dimensions along X, Y, Z axes. Then the size of each voxel will be $D^{'} = D/v_D, W^{'} = W/v_H, H^{'} = H/v_W$ where v_D, v_H and v_W are the size of voxels. A Point cloud contains more than 100K points. Considering all the points for computation will highly increase the complexity and the computational dependencies. The variable density will also affect the classification. Since the voxels are equally spaced and fixed in size, each voxel will have different number of points. Some voxels have higher density of points while some have less density and some voxels can be empty. This is because of variable density of points in the point cloud space and the point cloud itself is highly sparse. Hence, We choose or sample T random points from each voxel. If there are less than T points then the minimum of T and number of points present in the voxel is taken as the sample points. This helps in highly reducing the computational complexity and reducing the biasness in detection.

VFE Architecture Details. In this architecture stacked feature encoding is used. Voxel Feature Encoder (VFE) [6] layers are connected in hierarchy, where a single VFE layer each Point P in voxel is described by $P_i = \{x_i, y_i, z_i, r_i\}$, where x, y, z are the co-ordinates of point in 3D space and r represents reflectance. A voxel in point cloud is represented by V. Each V is a set of T points. A voxel can be described as $V = P_i = \{x_i, y_i, z_i, r_i\}_{i=1,2,3...t}$. The local mean for each voxel is calculated as the centroid of all points in a voxel which is represented by (v_x, v_y, v_z). Then the relative offset of each point with its mean in a voxel is taken and augmented to each point P_i. Then each V_i is $V_i = P_i = \{x_i, y_i, z_i, r_i, x_i - v_x, y_i - v_y, z_i - v_z\}_{i=1,2,3...t}$. Then each P_i is transformed when it is passed through a Fully Connected Network (FCN) into a feature space of higher dimensions.

The ouptut of VFE layer is then sent to the next layer as input where it is transformed into a higher dimension. Finally when the input is passed through all the layers, the feature space is finally transformed to 128 dimesnions. The FCN consists of a BatchNorm Layer, a Linear layer and a Rectified Unit layer. Information is aggregated in the feature space domain to encode details like shape, structure etc. of the surfaces within the voxel. This encoding is local to the voxel, therefore, point wise input is passed through FCN which produces point wise feature in a voxel. Then, element wise max pooling is done which gives locally aggregated features. This local aggregated features are local to some voxels. This locally represented voxel can constitute the overall information present in voxels. The output feature is a result of encoding of point wise feature as well as locally aggregated feature, which gives the interaction between points in a voxel and within voxels too, that overall describe the shape information of the objects. This locally aggregated feature is concatenated to the point wise feature. All Voxels are encoded in the same manner.

3.2 The Backbone Network

Middle convolution layers does the job of convolution network (CNN). It learns the features and helps in classifying and detecting the objects. Middle convolution layers take the pseudo image and the feature map outputs from the feature encoders as input to this layer. It extracts the useful features from the input and generates the feature maps which are passed to the next segment where RPN does the object detection using these feature maps. Here, in this paper, 3D U-Net and BackBone Network [6] used in voxelNet are used as Middle Convolution Layers.

3D UNet Architecture. In the proposed models of this paper, 3D Unet architecture [15] will be used. This architecture is the 3D version of the UNet architecture. All the 2D convolution operations and the 2D feature maps are replaced by the 3D convolution operations and the 3D feature maps. Each layer in the analysis block consists of two 3D convolutions followed by BatchNorm and ReLU, and then 3D max pooling takes place. Each layer in the synthesis block consists of a 3D up convolution followed by two 3D convolutions and then BatchNorm and ReLU takes place. The bottom most layer transfers the features from the synthesis block to the analysis block.

MiddleConvLayer. The MiddleConvLayer [6] is used in VoxelNet. The Convolutional operation where the operator is represented as Conv $(C_{in}, C_{out}, k, s, p)$, where C_{in} represents the number of input channels, C_{out} represents the number of output channels, p is padding size, s is stride size, k is kernel size. Each middle convolutional layer applies 3D convolution, BatchNorm layer followed by Rectified Linear Unit layer. The MiddleConvolution layers aggregate the features voxel-wise in a expansion field, giving more fine texture to the description of the shape. The architecture of this network is similar to that of U-Net architecture. The architecture is shown in Fig. 2.

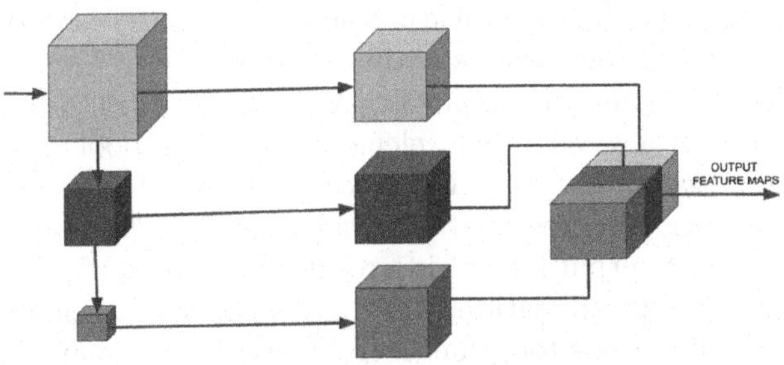

Fig. 2. MiddleConvLayer [6]

3.3 Object Detection in Point Cloud

Detection head takes the learned features from the backbone and predicts the 3D bounding boxes for the objects. It does both the regression and classification. In our proposed models, we have used both RPN [16] and Single Short Detector (SSD) [17] as detection heads.

Region Proposal Network. For object detection, Region Proposal networks [16] are an important part of all the latest detection models. Some changes are made to the RPN architecture, and it is combined with the feature encoder and MiddleConvolution layers which form a pipeline so that it can be trained easily. The architecture is shown in Fig. 3. RPN is the backbone of the entire architecture and is very efficient in object detection. The main purpose of RPN is to propose regions where the targeted object has higher probability to be found and then detecting the objects. Regression and classification both are used in the RPN. Regression for Proposal of regions and then Classification for Object Detection.

Feature maps from previous MiddleConvLayers are provided as input to the RPN. RPN is made up of three blocks of fully convolutional layers. In each block, in the first layer, features are down sampled by half by means of convolution with stride length of 2, the on the output features obtained, Rectified Linear Unit and Batch Normalization operations are applied. Each block's output is upsampled to constant size. All these features are then concatenated to build a higher feature map of higher resolutuion. Then regression is applied on feature maps for learning the desired objects. Regression map and Probability score map are used if more than one object have similar structures.

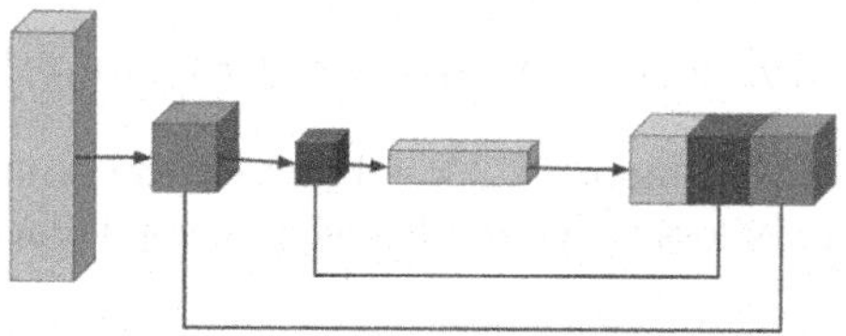

Fig. 3. RPN architecture [16]

RPN generates proposals for the objects. To generate the proposals for the region where the object might lie, a small network is slid over the feature maps. The feature maps are the output of the input block. Multi scale anchors helps in more regions of proposals. It is also cost efficient computationally and in terms of time complexity too. Here RPN is translational invariant. In each sliding window, the central point is called the anchor of the window. Classifier determines the probability of a region proposal having the required object which is target. Regression is required for the location of the proposals. Number of anchors in and image is $Width \times Height \times k(boundingbox)$. Generally for an anchor, that is for a pixel, 9 proposal regions are used.

The Intersection over union (IoU) between the ground truth boxes and the anchors should be greater than 0.7 and they should have the highest overlap. Then these anchors are given labels. The Loss function [16] for RPN is:

$$L(p_i, t_i) = (1/N_{cls}) X \Sigma L_{cls}(p_i, p_i^*) + (\lambda/N_{reg}) X \Sigma p_i^* L_{reg}(t_i, t_i^*).$$

In this loss function, we optimise both the regression cost L_{reg} and the classification cost L_{cls}. If and only if the object is likely to be there,then the regression cost optimisation happens, otherwise regression cost is zero in the above equation. λ value is 10 by default. N_{cls} and N_{reg} are the normalization costs.

Single Shot Detector (SSD). Single Shot Detector (SSD) [17] also does 3D object detection. It is similar to RPN but twice as fast as RPN. The feature maps from previous layer are passed as input to the SSD. Similar to RPN, does both the regression and classification. RPN requires two passes but SSD requires only one pass, hence called Single Shot. MultiBox Detector is just a part of SSD. In multibox detector also, there are anchors. For each anchor, there are k bounding boxes. The K bounding boxes have different aspect ratios and sizes instead of all having the same size.This helps in identifying objects of different sizes as all objects will not have the same apsect ratio. For each bounding box, 4 more bounding boxes are calculated w.r.t to the original bounding box and C class scores are also computed.

The feature map is of size m × n at layer K. 3 × 3 conv is applied at each layer. There are 4 bounding boxes in each layer with C + 4 outputs. Therefore, outputs at each layer will be $m \times n \times 4x(C+4)$. SSD loss function [17] is similar to that of RPN. It consists of confidence loss and Localisation loss.

$$L(x, c, l, g) = (1/N)X(L_{conf}(x, c) + \alpha L_{loc}(x, l, g)).$$

Localization loss is the smooth L1 loss between the ground truth boxes and predicted boxes. Softmax loss is over multiple class confidences is the Confidence loss.

4 Proposed Models

The following section will discuss in detail the three proposed modifications to VoxelNet Model.

4.1 Method-1

In method 1, VoxelFeatureEncoder (VFE) [6] is used as the feature encoder. The Feature Encoder (FE) is replaced by VFE in the method-1 proposed. VFE is used here because VFE encodes features in the 3 dimensions where as the most of the feature encoders used in the standard models encodes the features and projects them into 2D pseudo image. Projecting 3D data onto 2D plane will result in loss of some information. Hence, VFE is used which works in 3 dimensions directly.

The MidConvLayer described in the previous section is used for semantic segmentation in the second stage. MidConvLayer is used as the backbone network in the proposed method-1 which performs 3D convolutions on the encoded features generated by the VFE. The backbone used in the standard architectures is different from the back bone used in method-1. The back bone used in the standard architectures performs 2D convolutions on 2D pseudo images generated by the feature encoders whereas the back bone used in method-1 performs 3D convolutions in 3D space. There will be loss of some information when the 3D data is projected onto 2D Plane. Hence, 3D convolutions are used in the back-bone network to preserve the information without loss. The SingleShotDetector (SSD) [17] described in the previous section is used as the detection head for predicting the bounding boxes in the third stage (Fig. 4).

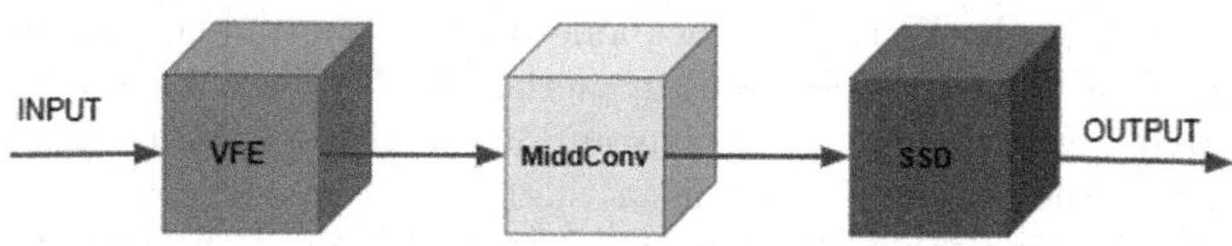

Fig. 4. Proposed method-1

4.2 Method-2

In method-2, VoxelFeatureEncoder is used as the feature encoder. VFE is used here because VFE encodes features in the 3D space where as the most of the feature encoders used in the standard models encodes the features and projects them into 2D pseudo image. Projecting 3D data onto 2D plane will result in loss of some information. Hence, VFE is used which works in 3 dimensions directly.

The 3D UNet is used here for semantic segmentation in the second stage. 3D UNet which is a modification of 2D UNet is used as the backbone network in the proposed method-2 which performs 3D convolutions on the encoded features generated by the VFE. The backbone used in the standard architectures is different from the back bone used in method-2. The back bone used in the standard architectures performs 2D convolutions on 2D pseudo images generated by FE whereas the back bone used in method-2 performs 3D convolutions in 3 dimensions. The Region Proposal Network (RPN) is used here as the detection head for predicting the bounding boxes in the third stage (Fig. 5).

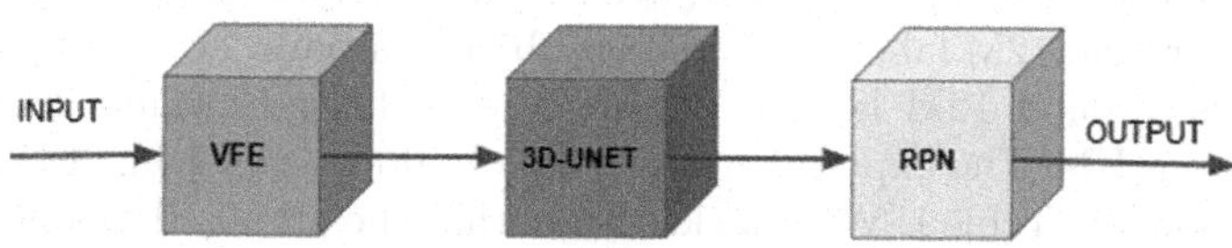

Fig. 5. Proposed method-2

4.3 Method-3

In method-3, VoxelFeatureEncoder is used as the feature encoder. VFE is used here because VFE encodes features in the 3D space where as the most of the feature encoders used in the standard models encodes the features and projects them into 2D pseudo image. Projecting 3D data onto 2D plane will result in loss of some imformation. Hence, VFE is used which works in 3D space directly. The 3D UNet is used here for semantic segmentation in the second stage. 3D UNet which is a modification of 2D UNet is used as the backbone network in the proposed method-3 which performs 3D convolutions on the encoded features generated by the VFE. The backbone used in the standard architectures is different from the back bone used in method-3. The back bone used in the standard architectures performs 2D convolutions on 2D pseudo images generated by FE whereas the back bone used in method-3 performs 3D convolutions in 3 dimensions. The SingleShotDetector (SSD) is used here as the detection head for predicting the bounding boxes in the third stage (Fig. 6).

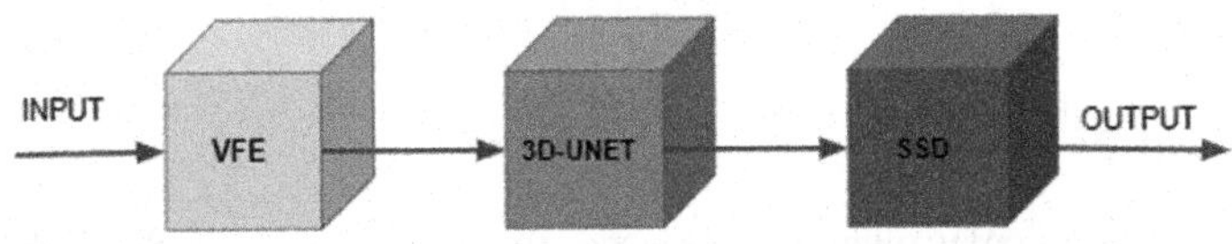

Fig. 6. Proposed method-3

5 Experimental Results

This section reports the datasets used, and performance obtained with the three methods proposed in the previous section. This research work uses two popular datasets- KITTI and WAYMO dataset by Google. The KITTI object detection benchmark dataset [18], has both the images and LiDAR point clouds. There are 15K samples in the dataset. They are split into 7481 training and 7518 testing samples. KITTI benchmark requires detections of cars, cyclists and the pedestrians. The WAYMO Dataset [19] is similar to KITTI. It has the images and lidar point clouds. There are car, cyclists, pedestrians and sign classes. The dataset has around 12M labeled 3D LiDAR objects, around 113K unique LiDAR tracking IDs, around 12M labeled 2D image objects and around 254k unique image tracking IDs. The experimental results obtained from KITTI benchmark dataset is shown in Table 1. We can clearly see that the proposed models perform much better the voxelNet architecture both in terms of accuracy and inference time. The difference between method-1 and state-of-the-art is the difference in the back bone network and the detection head. In voxelnet, RPN is used as detection head whereas in the proposed method-1, SSD is used as detection head. SSD is twice as fast as RPN. Both SSD and RPN do the same work of

Table 1. Performance comparison of proposed models in 3D Object detection: average precision (in %) on KITTI validation set.

Method	Modality	Car			Pedestrian			Cyclist			Speed (in sec.)
		Easy	Moderate	Hard	Easy	Moderate	Hard	Easy	Moderate	Hard	
VoxelNet [6]	LiDAR	77.47	65.11	57.73	39.48	33.69	31.5	61.22	48.36	44.37	0.22
Method 1 (VFE + MidConv + SSD)	LiDAR	78.03	67.19	59.78	38.47	34.12	32.31	63.37	49.21	45.9	**0.15**
Method 2 (VFE + 3D-UNet + RPN)	LiDAR	77.35	68.39	**60.27**	43.05	35.79	33.59	65.82	51.52	46.22	0.26
Method 3 (VFE + 3D-UNet + SSD)	LiDAR	**78.29**	**70.43**	61.62	**45.67**	**38.28**	**36.17**	**67.41**	**54.7**	**47.63**	0.18

predicting the boxes but SSD requires only one pass to do the work whereas RPN needs two passes. Hence SSD is twice as fast as the RPN. Also, SSD is good at predicting boxes than RPN, hence a slight increase in accuracy. Because of SSD, we can see that accuracy and speed of method-1 is better than state of the art Voxelnet. Method-1 also has the highest speed among all the methods because of Single Shot Detector (SSD).

The difference between method-2 and state-of-the-art is the difference in the back bone network. In voxelNet, MiddleConvLayer is used whereas in the proposed method-2, 3D UNet architecture is used as middle convolution layers for feature extraction. UNet architecture is very well known for object detection, object classification, semantic segmentation. Hence, using UNet we got better accuracy than the standard Voxelnet. In terms of speed, UNet architecture is deep, goes until 28 × 28 and has more layers and neurons and hence more computation, therefore it takes more time than the MiddleConvLayer used in the VoxelNet but also produces more accuracy. Hence, method-2 has more accuracy because of UNet and less speed than voxelNet also because of UNet. It is now clear that both SSD and UNet help in increasing the accuracy and speed. Hence, in method-3 both the SSD and UNet are used in the method-3 and they replace the back bone and RPN in the VoxelNet. In method-3, VFE is used as the feature encoder and 3D-UNet as middle convolution layers and SSD as detection head. According to the validation and testing done on KITTI Benchmark dataset, this method has better results than all the other methods and standard VoxelNet after training the network. As it is known that Unet works better than MiddleConvlayer and SSD works better than RPN. So on using these two stages together, the results should be better than the other methods and the state of the art VoxelNet according to the above mentioned reasons. The theory justifies the results. Because of UNET and SSD, there is an improvement in accuracy. But due to high computations required in UNet, the speed of this method is less than the method-1 in which there are less computations and SSD to increase

Table 2. Comparison with the state-of-the-art in 3D Object detection: average precision (in %) on KITTI validation set.

Method	Modality	Car			Pedestrian			Cyclist			Speed (in sec.)
		Easy	Moderate	Hard	Easy	Moderate	Hard	Easy	Moderate	Hard	
MV3D [7]	Lidar & Img	71.09	62.35	55.12	N/A	N/A	N/A	N/A	N/A	N/A	N/A
Cont-Fuse [10]	Lidar & Img	72.54	66.22	64.04	N/A	N/A	N/A	N/A	N/A	N/A	N/A
VoxelNet [6]	LiDAR	77.47	65.11	57.73	39.48	33.69	31.5	61.22	48.36	44.37	0.22
Method 1 (VFE + MidConv + SSD)	LiDAR	78.03	67.19	59.78	38.47	34.12	32.31	63.37	49.21	45.9	0.15
Method 3 (VFE + 3D-UNet + SSD)	LiDAR	78.29	70.43	61.62	45.67	38.28	36.17	67.41	54.7	47.63	0.18
PointRCNN [12]	LiDAR	**85.94**	**75.76**	**68.32**	**49.43**	**41.78**	**38.63**	**73.93**	**59.60**	**53.59**	0.1
FastPointRCNN [13]	LiDAR	84.28	75.73	67.39	N/A	N/A	N/A	N/A	N/A	N/A	**0.065**

the speed in method-1. SSD in method-3 also increases the speed and accuracy in method-3. Hence increase of speed due to SSD is balanced by decrease of speed because of UNET. Hence finally method-3 has better speed than the method-2 but less speed than method-1. The performance comparison with the state-of-the-art models and the best proposed model are shown in Table 2. We can observe that, though our proposed model boosted the performance of voxelNet, however it could not beat the state-of-the-art result when compared with other latest methods. Table 3 shows the results when trained and tested on the WAYMO dataset. The results are low because it was trained only on 1/8th of the total dataset. These results can be further improved by training on the whole dataset.

Table 3. Comparison with the state-of-the-art in 3D Object detection on WAYMO dataset: average precision (in %) for Pedestrian Class.

Method	Range (in meters.)		
	[0,30)	[30,50)	[50,inf)
SPA[20]	0.5835	0.4647	0.3242
Method 3 (VFE + 3D-UNet + SSD)	0.152	0.187	0.114

6 Conclusion

This paper proposed modifications to existing VoxelNet model for object detection in point cloud data. Three models were proposed and experimented with

KITTI and WAYMO datasets. The performance result for the modified network was much better than the VoxelNet model both in terms of accuracy and speed. However, the model could not beat the current state-of-the-art models like PoinRCNN [12] and FastPointRCNN [13] models. There is still scope to improve the proposed models for accomplishing much better performance which can be take as future work.

References

1. Liu, L., Ouyang, W., Wang, X.: Deep learning for generic object detection: a survey. Int. J. Comput. Vis. **128**, 261–318 (2020)
2. https://oceanservice.noaa.gov/facts/lidar.html
3. Ahmed, E., Das, R.: A survey on deep learning advances on different 3D data representations (2019)
4. Qi, C.R., Su, H., Mo, K., Guibas, L.J.: PointNet: deep learning on point sets for 3D classification and segmentation. In: CVPR (2017)
5. Guo, Y., Wang, H., Hu, Q., Liu, H., Liu, L.: Deep learning for 3D point clouds: a survey (2019)
6. Zhou, Y., Tuzel, O.: VoxelNet: end-to-end learning for point cloud based 3D object detection. In: CVPR (2018)
7. Chen, X., Ma, H., Wan, J., Li, B., Xia, T.: Multi-view 3D object detection network for autonomous driving (MV3D). In: CVPR (2017)
8. Chen, X., Kundu, K., Zhang, Z., Ma, H., Fidler, S., Urtasun, R:. Monocular 3D object detection for autonomous driving. In: CVPR (2016)
9. Qi, C.R., Liu, W., Wu, C., Su, H., Guibas, L.J.: Frustum PointNets for 3D object detection from RGB-D data. In: CVPR (2018)
10. Liang, M., Yang, B., Wang, S., Urtasun, R.: Deep continuous fusion for multi-sensor 3D object detection. In: Ferrari, V., Hebert, M., Sminchisescu, C., Weiss, Y. (eds.) ECCV 2018. LNCS, vol. 11220, pp. 663–678. Springer, Cham (2018). https://doi.org/10.1007/978-3-030-01270-0_39
11. Yan, Y., Mao, Y., Li, B.: Sparsely embedded convolutional detection. MDPI Sens. **18**(10), 3337 (2018)
12. Shi, S., Wang, X., Li, H.: PointRCNN: 3D object proposal generation and detection from point cloud. In: CVPR (2019)
13. Chen, Y., Liu, S., Shen, X., Jia, J.: Fast point R-CNN (2019)
14. Ronneberger, O., Fischer, P., Brox, T.: U-net: convolutional networks for biomedical image segmentation. In: CVPR (2015)
15. Çiçek, Ö., Abdulkadir, A., Lienkamp, S.S., Brox, T., Ronneberger, O.: 3D U-net: learning dense volumetric segmentation from sparse annotation. In: Ourselin, S., Joskowicz, L., Sabuncu, M.R., Unal, G., Wells, W. (eds.) MICCAI 2016. LNCS, vol. 9901, pp. 424–432. Springer, Cham (2016). https://doi.org/10.1007/978-3-319-46723-8_49
16. Ren, S., He, K., Girshick, R., Sun, J.: Faster R-CNN: towards real-time object detection with region proposal networks. In: ICCV (2015)
17. Liu, W., et al.: SSD: single shot multibox detector. In: Leibe, B., Matas, J., Sebe, N., Welling, M. (eds.) ECCV 2016. LNCS, vol. 9905, pp. 21–37. Springer, Cham (2016). https://doi.org/10.1007/978-3-319-46448-0_2
18. KITTI 3D detection benchmark dataset. http://www.cvlibs.net/datasets/kitti/eval_object.php
19. WAYMO Open Dataset. https://waymo.com/open/

On the Performance of Convolutional Neural Networks Under High and Low Frequency Information

Roshan Reddy Yedla and Shiv Ram Dubey(✉)

Computer Vision Group, Indian Institute of Information Technology, Sri City, Chittoor, Andhra Pradesh, India
{roshanreddy.y17,srdubey}@iiits.in

Abstract. Convolutional neural networks (CNNs) have shown very promising performance in recent years for different problems, including object recognition, face recognition, medical image analysis, etc. However, generally the trained CNN models are tested over the test set which is very similar to the trained set. The generalizability and robustness of the CNN models are very important aspects to make it to work for the unseen data. In this letter, we study the performance of CNN models over the high and low frequency information of the images. We observe that the trained CNN fails to generalize over the high and low frequency images. In order to make the CNN robust against high and low frequency images, we propose the stochastic filtering based data augmentation during training. A satisfactory performance improvement has been observed in terms of the high and low frequency generalization and robustness with the proposed stochastic filtering based data augmentation approach. The experimentations are performed using ResNet50 model over the CIFAR-10 dataset and ResNet101 model over Tiny-ImageNet dataset.

Keywords: Convolutional neural networks · Robustness · High and low frequency information · Residual network · Image classification

1 Introduction

The emergence of deep learning has changed the way data was being handled in the early days. The existence of the large scale data sets and high end computational resources is the key to its success [15]. Deep learning based models learn the important features from the data automatically in a hierarchical manner through the combination of linear and non-linear functions [23]. Convolutional neural network (CNN) is a special form of deep learning architecture designed to deal with the image data [16]. It consists of several layers including convolution, non-linearity, pooling, batch normalization, dropout, etc.

The AlexNet [13] was the revolutionary CNN model that became a state-of-the-art after winning the ImageNet Large-Scale Object Recognition Challenge in 2012 [21] with a great margin w.r.t. the hand-designed approaches. Motivated

S. K. Singh et al. (Eds.): CVIP 2020, CCIS 1378, pp. 214–224, 2021.
https://doi.org/10.1007/978-981-16-1103-2_19

from the success of the AlexNet CNN model, various CNN models have been investigated for the object recognition such as VGGNet [25], GoogleNet [30], and ResNet [9], etc. The CNNs have been also used for many other applications such as image classification [3,5], object localization [19], image segmentation [8], image super-resolution [32], image retrieval [6,34], face recognition [24,28], medical image analysis [4,6], hyperspectral image classification [20], image to image translation [2] and many more.

Though several CNN models have been investigated, the generalization and robustness of the trained model over unseen data are still a concern. Generally, the datasets are divided into two sets including a train set for the training of the CNN models and a test set to judge the performance of trained model. Various attempts have been made to generalize the CNN models by introducing the regularization layers like batch normalization [10], dropout [27], data augmentation [18,22], ensemble generalization loss [4], etc. The effect of different aspects of CNN is also analyzed by different researchers in the recent past, such as kernel size and number of filters of convolution layer [1], fully connected layers [3], activation functions [7], loss functions [29], etc.

In the usual dataset setup, the test set is very similar to the train and validation sets. Thus, the generalization and robustness of the trained CNN models are not tested effectively. Very limited work has been done so far where CNN meets with filtering. The median filtering based attack on images is dealt with residual dense neural network [31]. Deep learning is also explored for median filtering forensics in the discrete cosine transform domain [33]. The correlation filters are also utilized with CNNs for visual tracking problem [17]. The high-frequency refinement is applied in the CNN framework for sharper video super-resolution [26]. However, the effect of filtering over data is not well analyzed over the performance of CNNs.

In this letter, we study the performance of CNN models over the high and low frequency images. The basic idea originates from the thought process that if humans can identify the objects from the high and low frequency components, then the CNN models should be also able to do. We also propose a stochastic filtering based data augmentation technique to cope with the generalization and robustness issues of CNN models for high and low frequency information. The application of this work is under scenario, where low and high frequency images are generated, including medical and hyperspectral images.

The rest of this letter is organized in following manner: Sect. 2 presents the datasets used along with the low and high frequency image datasets created; Sect. 3 presents the CNN model and training settings used in this work; Sect. 4 illustrates the experimental results and analysis including stochastic filtering based data augmentation; and finally, Sect. 5 concludes the letter with summarizing remarks of this study.

2 High and Low Pass Image Dataset Preparation

In order to show the effect of high and low frequency components over the performance of CNN, we use two widely adapted image classification datasets,

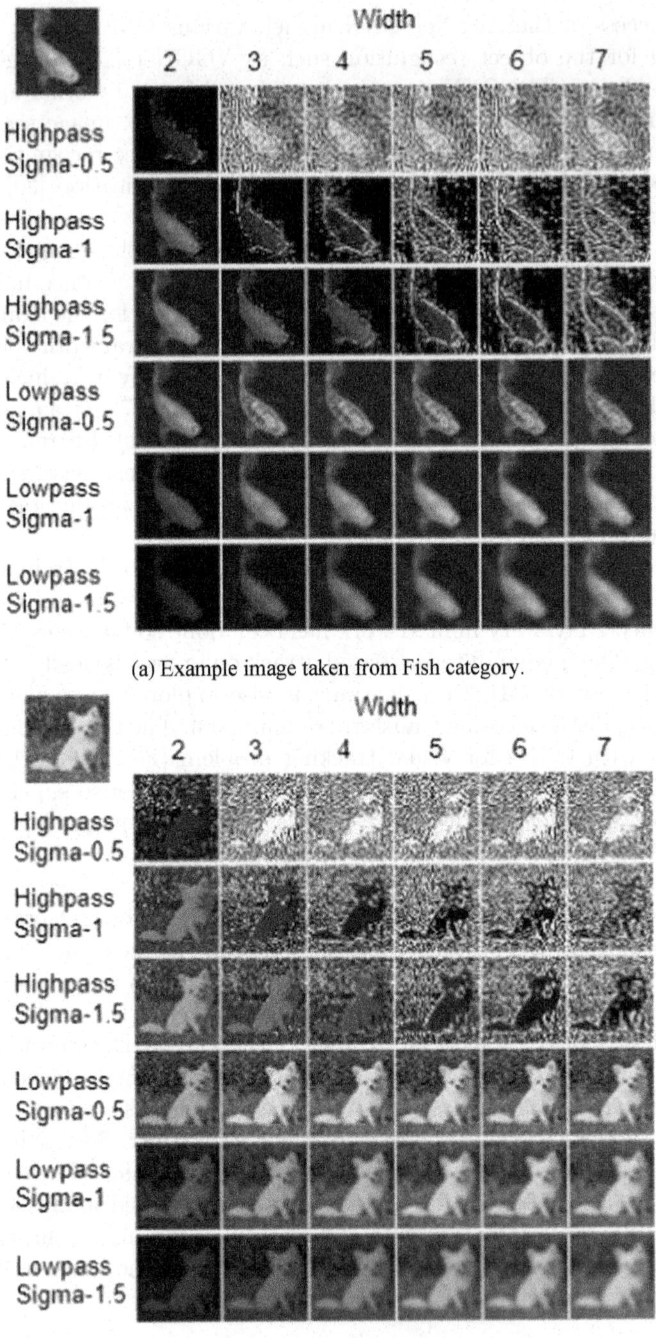

Fig. 1. The example high and low frequency generated images by varying the standard deviation (Sigma) and width of the kernel for filtering.

namely, CIFAR10 [12] and TinyImageNet [14]. The CIFAR10 dataset[1] consists of 50,000 images for training and 10,000 images for testing equally contributed from 10 categories. The TinyImageNet dataset[2] contains 1,00,000 images for training and 10,000 images from testing equally distributed in 200 categories.

2.1 New Test Sets Generation Using High and Low Pass Filtering

We generate the multiple test sets using the original test set of both datasets in high and low frequency domain to judge the robustness of CNN models. The Gaussian filtering of the images is performed in both highpass and lowpass domains under different settings. Basically, we generate multiple high and low frequency images by varying the standard deviation (σ) and kernel width (k) of the filter.

A high pass filter tends to retain the high frequency information in the image while reducing the low frequency information. The high frequency information of an image lies in its edges. Thus, the high pass filtering of an image produces the resultant image with only the edge information, or with the edges as more prominent. The lack of low frequency information makes the object recognition, challenging for the trained CNN models. A low pass filter tends to retain the low frequency information in the image while reducing the high frequency information. The low frequency information of an image lies in the smoother regions. Thus, the low pass filtering enforces the image to become blurry by smoothing the edge information. Due to the this loss of information the trained CNN model might find it hard to classify the image.

For both high and low pass filtering over the test set, we use three different sigma values (standard deviation) for the kernel, i.e., 0.5, 1 and 1.5 and six different kernel widths including 2, 3, 4, 5, 6 and 7. Basically, we generate 36 new test sets for a dataset from the original test set that includes 18 having high frequency information and another 18 having low frequency information. The number of samples in any generated test set is same as the original test set. The example generated images for two examples under different settings are illustrated in Fig. 1. It can be noticed that the high frequency images consists of mostly edge information, whereas the low frequency images consists of the blurry ambiance information.

2.2 Training Set Augmentation Using Stochastic Filtering

To demonstrate the robustness problem of the CNN models against high and low pass filtered images, first we train the CNN model on the actual training sets of different datasets. However, we test the performance of the trained CNN model using the original test sets as well as the generated test sets having the transformed images.

---

[1] https://www.cs.toronto.edu/~kriz/cifar.html.
[2] https://www.kaggle.com/c/tiny-imagenet.

Further, in order to improve the robustness of CNN models against the high and low frequency information of the image, we propose to augment the dataset with stochastic filtering. It is performed by transforming each image in the training set with either high pass filter or a low pass filter (selected randomly), with a random standard deviation chosen in the range of [0.25, 1.75] and random kernel size taken from the set {2, 3, 4, 5, 6, 7}. Basically, the training set gets doubled by including the stochastic filtering based transformed images with the original images.

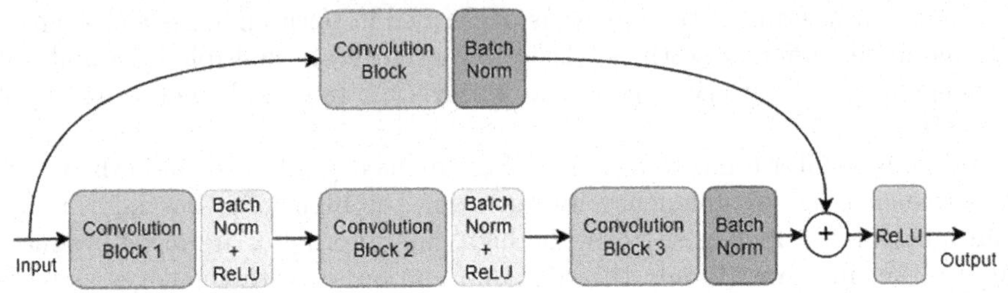

Fig. 2. A bottleneck residual block of ResNet50 and ResNet101 architectures [9]. Batch Norm refers to the batch normalization regularizer [10] and ReLU refers to the rectified linear unit [21] based activation function.

3 Network Architecture and Training Settings

This section is devoted to the description of the network architecture and training settings used for the experiments.

3.1 Residual Network

The ResNet architectures [9] have been widely used for various applications including object recognition, image synthesis, image segmentation, action prediction, etc. with state-of-the-art performance [11]. In this letter, we also opt for the ResNet architectures. We train the ResNet50 from scratch for the CIFAR-10 dataset and fine-tune the ResNet101 for the TinyImagenet dataset. The TinyImagenet dataset is having more training images and more number of classes (i.e., wider) than CIFAR10 dataset, thus, we choose the deeper ResNet for the TinyImageNet dataset. Both ResNet50 and ResNet101 use the bottleneck based residual module as illustrated in Fig. 2. A residual block consists of the two paths, one having three convolution layers while the other one having a bottleneck convolution layer. The batch normalization [10] is used for increasing the generalization of the network. The rectified linear unit (ReLU) is used as the activation function. The plain deeper networks are difficult to converge during training due to vanishing/exploding gradient problem. The residual connection of ResNet architectures helps in the gradient descent optimization by flowing the gradient during backpropagation.

Table 1. Testing accuracy in % using high and low pass test sets of CIFAR-10 with actual train set. The accuracy over the original test set is 94.95%.

Filter	Kernel sigma	Kernel width					
		2	3	4	5	6	7
High pass	0.5	58.13	17.59	17.77	17.94	17.94	17.94
	1	90.64	45.72	29.88	17.13	16.02	14.04
	1.5	93.63	85.45	62.77	33.15	26.63	22.01
Low pass	0.5	93.89	91.00	90.87	90.95	90.95	90.95
	1	63.42	40.79	33.22	25.85	25.99	25.95
	1.5	25.48	23.71	20.07	16.86	16.34	16.14

3.2 Training Settings

We have carried out all our experiments using the GPU service provided in the free tier of Google Colab. The PyTorch deep learning library is used to run the experiments. The stochastic gradient descent (SGD) optimizer is used to train the ResNet models with softmax based cross-entropy loss function with a batch size of 128. The multi-step learning rate scheduler is used with initial learning rate set at 0.1. The ResNet50 model is trained from scratch over the CIFAR10 dataset for 200 epochs with learning rate drops by a factor of 0.1 at the 100th and 150th epoch. The dimension of CIFAR10 images is $32 \times 32 \times 3$. The pre-trained ResNet101 model is fine-tuned over the TinyImageNet dataset for 20 epochs with learning rate drops by a factor of 0.1 on every 5th epoch. The first 7 layers of ResNet101 are frozen. The TinyImageNet images are resized to $224 \times 224 \times 3$ using bicubic interpolation to make it fit with the pretrained ResNet101. Based on the training dataset, four experiments are performed, including 1) original CIFAR10 train set, 2) original TinyImageNet train set, 3) original + stochastic filtering transformed CIFAR10 train set, and 4) original + stochastic filtering transformed TinyImageNet train set. However, the original test set as well as 36 low and high pass transformed test sets for each dataset are used to evaluate the performance in each experiment.

4 Experimental Results and Discussion

We illustrate the classification results under different experimental settings to present the insight about the CNN robustness against high and low pass filtering.

4.1 Experiment-1

The original CIFAR-10 train set is used to train the ResNet50 in this experiment. The most commonly used data augmentations on the training data are used, including random cropping, horizontal flipping and normalization. The

Table 2. Testing accuracy in % using high and low pass test sets of TinyImageNet with actual train set. The accuracy over the original test set is 71.41%.

Filter	Kernel sigma	Kernel width					
		2	3	4	5	6	7
High pass	0.5	6.36	1.99	2.00	2.05	2.05	2.05
	1	32.05	5.31	3.74	1.94	1.71	1.42
	1.5	47.13	22.20	10.97	5.18	4.05	2.72
Low pass	0.5	65.69	59.42	59.60	59.14	59.13	59.13
	1	40.66	46.36	45.54	43.57	43.78	43.62
	1.5	23.99	32.19	31.95	28.95	27.29	25.51

Table 3. Testing accuracy in % using high and low pass test sets of CIFAR10 with stochastic filtering based augmented train set. The accuracy over the original test set is 93.94%.

Filter	Kernel sigma	Kernel width					
		2	3	4	5	6	7
High pass	0.5	90.82	75.87	62.22	77.14	77.14	63.33
	1	92.98	89.90	87.98	86.28	85.76	84.87
	1.5	93.27	92.43	90.99	87.48	87.24	84.41
Low pass	0.5	93.11	92.60	92.60	92.65	92.65	92.65
	1	92.18	90.75	90.34	90.00	90.01	89.86
	1.5	91.56	90.25	89.02	85.35	84.44	82.91

testing is conducted using original test set and the generated test sets with transformed images. The classification accuracy over **original test set** is observed as **94.95%**. The results of the transformed test sets are summarized in Table 1. As expected, the performance degrades for higher values of kernel width in both the cases of high and low frequency images. The higher values of kernel width lead to the blurring in the low frequency and finer edges in high frequency. Moreover, it is also noticed that the performance of ResNet50 degrades more for smaller kernel standard deviation (i.e., Sigma) for high frequency. However, the same is also observed for low frequency, but using higher kernel standard deviation. Basically, the higher kernel width and smaller kernel sigma based high frequency fools CNN more. Similarly, the higher kernel width and higher kernel sigma based low frequency generates more confusing images for CNN.

4.2 Experiment-2

This experiment is performed by fine-tuning the pretrained ResNet101 on the original TinyImagenet train set and testing over original and generated test sets. Minor data augmentation such as horizontal flipping and normalization is

Table 4. Testing accuracy in % using high and low pass test sets of TinyImageNet with stochastic filtering based augmented train set. The accuracy over the original test set is 70.00%.

Filter	Kernel sigma	Kernel width					
		2	3	4	5	6	7
High pass	0.5	29.62	21.05	21.38	21.33	21.33	21.33
	1	52.37	35.37	33.42	27.45	26.13	23.73
	1.5	58.59	47.30	40.13	34.59	32.49	28.78
Low pass	0.5	66.38	63.67	64.14	63.65	63.65	63.66
	1	56.85	61.22	60.95	59.99	60.30	59.99
	1.5	47.23	54.03	54.52	52.76	51.29	49.71

applied to the training data. An accuracy of **71.41%** is achieved on the **original validation set**. The results using the high and low pass filtering based transformed test sets are presented in Table 2. A similar trend of CNN robustness is followed over TinyImageNet dataset also. The performance of ResNet101 degrades heavily with higher kernel width and lower kernel sigma based high frequency images. Similarly, its performance also gets deteriorated with higher kernel width and higher kernel sigma based low frequency images.

4.3 Experiment-3

In order to improve the robustness of the trained CNN model for the high and low frequency information of the image, this experiment is conducted to double the CIFAR10 training set with stochastic filtering process. For each image of training set, a new image is generated by applying the high or low pass filtering (decided randomly) with random kernel width and kernel standard deviation. Note that after stochastic filtering based training data augmentation, the performance of ResNet50 over **original test set** is observed as **93.94%** which is marginally reduced than the without augmentation. However, great performance improvement has been reported over the high and low frequency test sets as summarized in Table 3. It shows the increased robustness of trained model w.r.t. the high and low pass images.

4.4 Experiment-4

In this experiment, the stochastic filtering based data augmentation is performed over the training set of TinyImageNet dataset. Thus, doubling the number of images for training. The ResNet101 is fine-tuned over the transformed TinyImageNet dataset and tested over original and high and low frequency test sets. We observe an accuracy of **70.00%** on the **original test set** which is marginally lower than the accuracy without stochastic filtering augmentation. However, a significantly improved performance is portrayed over high and low frequency test sets as described in Table 4.

5 Conclusion

In this letter, we posed the robustness problem of trained CNN models for high and low frequency images. We observed that the CNN models trained over normal dataset are robust for individual low and high frequency components. It is revealed that CNN faces high difficulty to recognize the (a) high frequency images generated using higher kernel width and lower kernel standard deviation based filtering, and (b) low frequency images generated using higher kernel width and higher kernel standard deviation based filtering. In order to improve the performance of CNNs over high and low frequency components, a stochastic filtering based data augmentation approach is very useful. Very promising results are observed using the proposed stochastic filtering based data augmentation in terms of the CNN's robustness against low and high frequency components without degrading much the performance over normal images.

References

1. Agrawal, A., Mittal, N.: Using CNN for facial expression recognition: a study of the effects of kernel size and number of filters on accuracy. Vis. Comput. **36**(2), 405–412 (2020)
2. Babu, K.K., Dubey, S.R.: PCSGAN: perceptual cyclic-synthesized generative adversarial networks for thermal and NIR to visible image transformation. arXiv preprint arXiv:2002.07082 (2020)
3. Basha, S.S., Dubey, S.R., Pulabaigari, V., Mukherjee, S.: Impact of fully connected layers on performance of convolutional neural networks for image classification. Neurocomputing **378**, 112–119 (2020)
4. Choi, J.Y., Lee, B.: Combining of multiple deep networks via ensemble generalization loss, based on MRI images, for Alzheimer's disease classification. IEEE Signal Process. Lett. **27**, 206–210 (2020)
5. Dubey, S.R., Chakraborty, S., Roy, S.K., Mukherjee, S., Singh, S.K., Chaudhuri, B.B.: DiffGrad: an optimization method for convolutional neural networks. IEEE Trans. Neural Netw. Learn. Syst. **31**, 4500–4511 (2019)
6. Dubey, S.R., Roy, S.K., Chakraborty, S., Mukherjee, S., Chaudhuri, B.B.: Local bit-plane decoded convolutional neural network features for biomedical image retrieval. Neural Comput. Appl. **32**, 7539–7551 (2020)
7. Hayou, S., Doucet, A., Rousseau, J.: On the selection of initialization and activation function for deep neural networks. arXiv preprint arXiv:1805.08266 (2018)
8. He, K., Gkioxari, G., Dollár, P., Girshick, R.: Mask R-CNN. In: Proceedings of the IEEE International Conference on Computer Vision, pp. 2961–2969 (2017)
9. He, K., Zhang, X., Ren, S., Sun, J.: Deep residual learning for image recognition. In: Proceedings of the IEEE Conference on Computer Vision and Pattern Recognition, pp. 770–778 (2016)
10. Ioffe, S., Szegedy, C.: Batch normalization: accelerating deep network training by reducing internal covariate shift. arXiv preprint arXiv:1502.03167 (2015)
11. Khan, A., Sohail, A., Zahoora, U., Qureshi, A.S.: A survey of the recent architectures of deep convolutional neural networks. Artif. Intell. Rev. **53**(8), 5455–5516 (2020). https://doi.org/10.1007/s10462-020-09825-6

12. Krizhevsky, A.: Learning multiple layers of features from tiny images. Master's thesis, University of Tront (2009)
13. Krizhevsky, A., Sutskever, I., Hinton, G.E.: ImageNet classification with deep convolutional neural networks. In: Advances in Neural Information Processing Systems, pp. 1097–1105 (2012)
14. Le, Y., Yang, X.: Tiny ImageNet visual recognition challenge. CS 231N **7**, 7 (2015)
15. LeCun, Y., Bengio, Y., Hinton, G.: Deep learning. Nature **521**(7553), 436–444 (2015)
16. Liu, W., Wang, Z., Liu, X., Zeng, N., Liu, Y., Alsaadi, F.E.: A survey of deep neural network architectures and their applications. Neurocomputing **234**, 11–26 (2017)
17. Ma, C., Xu, Y., Ni, B., Yang, X.: When correlation filters meet convolutional neural networks for visual tracking. IEEE Signal Process. Lett. **23**(10), 1454–1458 (2016)
18. Perez, L., Wang, J.: The effectiveness of data augmentation in image classification using deep learning. arXiv preprint arXiv:1712.04621 (2017)
19. Ren, S., He, K., Girshick, R., Sun, J.: Faster R-CNN: towards real-time object detection with region proposal networks. In: Advances in Neural Information Processing Systems, pp. 91–99 (2015)
20. Roy, S.K., Krishna, G., Dubey, S.R., Chaudhuri, B.B.: HybridSN: exploring 3-D-2-D CNN feature hierarchy for hyperspectral image classification. IEEE Geosci. Remote Sens. Lett. **17**, 277–281 (2019)
21. Russakovsky, O., et al.: ImageNet large scale visual recognition challenge. Int. J. Comput. Vis. **115**(3), 211–252 (2015)
22. Salamon, J., Bello, J.P.: Deep convolutional neural networks and data augmentation for environmental sound classification. IEEE Signal Process. Lett. **24**(3), 279–283 (2017)
23. Schmidhuber, J.: Deep learning in neural networks: an overview. Neural Netw. **61**, 85–117 (2015)
24. Schroff, F., Kalenichenko, D., Philbin, J.: FaceNet: a unified embedding for face recognition and clustering. In: Proceedings of the IEEE Conference on Computer Vision and Pattern Recognition, pp. 815–823 (2015)
25. Simonyan, K., Zisserman, A.: Very deep convolutional networks for large-scale image recognition. arXiv preprint arXiv:1409.1556 (2014)
26. Singh, V., Sharma, A., Devanathan, S., Mittal, A.: High-frequency refinement for sharper video super-resolution. In: The IEEE Winter Conference on Applications of Computer Vision, pp. 3299–3308 (2020)
27. Srivastava, N., Hinton, G., Krizhevsky, A., Sutskever, I., Salakhutdinov, R.: Dropout: a simple way to prevent neural networks from overfitting. J. Mach. Learn. Res. **15**(1), 1929–1958 (2014)
28. Srivastava, Y., Murali, V., Dubey, S.R.: Hard-mining loss based convolutional neural network for face recognition. arXiv preprint arXiv:1908.09747 (2019)
29. Srivastava, Y., Murali, V., Dubey, S.R.: A performance evaluation of loss functions for deep face recognition. In: Babu, R.V., Prasanna, M., Namboodiri, V.P. (eds.) NCVPRIPG 2019. CCIS, vol. 1249, pp. 322–332. Springer, Singapore (2020). https://doi.org/10.1007/978-981-15-8697-2_30
30. Szegedy, C., et al.: Going deeper with convolutions. In: Proceedings of the IEEE Conference on Computer Vision and Pattern Recognition, pp. 1–9 (2015)
31. Tariang, D.B., Chakraborty, R.S., Naskar, R.: A robust residual dense neural network for countering antiforensic attack on median filtered images. IEEE Signal Process. Lett. **26**(8), 1132–1136 (2019)

32. Tirer, T., Giryes, R.: Super-resolution via image-adapted denoising CNNs: incorporating external and internal learning. IEEE Signal Process. Lett. **26**(7), 1080–1084 (2019)
33. Zhang, J., Liao, Y., Zhu, X., Wang, H., Ding, J.: A deep learning approach in the discrete cosine transform domain to median filtering forensics. IEEE Signal Process. Lett. **27**, 276–280 (2020)
34. Zhu, Y., Li, Y., Wang, S.: Unsupervised deep hashing with adaptive feature learning for image retrieval. IEEE Signal Process. Lett. **26**(3), 395–399 (2019)

A Lightweight Multi-label Image Classification Model Based on Inception Module

Shreya Jain(✉), Poornima S. Thakur, Kusum Bharti, Pritee Khanna, and Aparajita Ojha

PDPM Indian Institute of Information Technology, Design and Manufacturing, Jabalpur 482001, India
{1811017,poornima,kusum,pkhanna,aojha}@iiitdmj.ac.in

Abstract. Convolutional Neural Networks (CNNs) have shown enormous potential for solving multi-label image classification problems. In recent years, a lot of experimentation is done with various state-of-the-art CNN architectures. The CNN architectures have evolved to become deeper and more complex in these years. These architectures are big due to a greater number of layers and trainable parameters. However, there are many real-time applications which demand fast and accurate classification. Keeping this in consideration, a simple model inspired by Inception V7 is proposed for multi-label image classification in this work. The proposed model consists of six convolution layers including three inception blocks with one million parameters approximately, which are very few as compared to many state-of-the-art CNN models. This makes the model deployable in lightweight devices for some real-time applications. The comparison experiments with other deep state-of-the-art CNNs were carried out on image datasets from multiple domains including general benchmark datasets, medical datasets, and agricultural datasets. The model exhibits better performance on many datasets making it feasible to use in various domains for multi-label image classification.

Keywords: Multi-label image classification · Deep learning · Convolution neural network · Inception V7

1 Introduction

Machine learning has many applications; image classification is one of those. In the process of image classification, the image is classified into one or more of the pre-defined categories of objects. Multi-class image classification refers to the classification where each image is assigned to one and only one label. Multi-label image classification refers to the classification where each image may be assigned many labels according to the presence of different class objects in the image. Most of the real-world images contain objects of more than one category which makes multi-label image classification an important research area. Multi-label image

S. K. Singh et al. (Eds.): CVIP 2020, CCIS 1378, pp. 225–236, 2021.
https://doi.org/10.1007/978-981-16-1103-2_20

classification can be used for applications such as scene understanding, visual object recognition, image annotation, content-based image retrieval, and plant and medical diagnosis [4].

The main challenges in achieving multi-label image classification include mutually inclusive object classes and ambiguity in the number of classes of objects present in an image. State-of-the-art methods in the literature lag because of the complex structure of the models, which makes difficult to deploy these models on real-time identification devices or lightweight devices. Since most of the applications involving image classification are real-time, the objective of this work is to reduce the complexity of the model in such a way that comparable or better performance can be attained using fewer parameters. The aim is to reduce average classification time to perform multi-label classification. Inspired by the Inception architecture, a CNN model is proposed in this work for multi-label image classification. It consists of three convolution layers followed by three inception-like blocks. The model performs classification based on the spatial features of the image and has very few parameters as compared with the state-of-the-art architectures like VGG16 [18], Inception [20], ResNet [6], DenseNet [8] and MobileNet [16]. The overall contribution of the work is a lightweight convolutional neural netowrk (CNN) with lesser number of trainable parameters that can be deployed for real-time multi-label classification tasks.

The work is organized into five sections. Section 2 gives an introduction of the previous works done in this area and their limitations in the context of real-time applications. It also outlines the motivation for the proposed approach. The proposed approach is described in Sect. 3 along with its implementation details. Experimental analysis is performed in Sect. 4 and finally, Sect. 5 concludes the work.

2 Related Work

Multi-label image classification is handled through three categories of approaches namely, conventional methods, machine learning methods and deep learning methods. Conventionally multi-label classification problem is transformed into multiple sub-problems which are then tackled using the single-label approach. For example, the label powerset [21] method assumes each label combination set as one class, which makes the problem as a single label classification problem. This method sometimes faces an explosion of classes and thus has extremely complex computations. Binary relevance [23] breaks the multi-label problem into multiple independent binary classification problems. Boutell et al. [1] solved the multi-label scene classification problem by building an individual classifier for each label. The labels of a new sample are determined by the outputs of these individual classifiers. The drawback of this method is that it completely ignores the label correlations. To overcome this drawback, classifier chains were introduced [15]. Several ensemble methods are proposed to boost the performance of multi-label classification [10,22,27].

Wei et al. [24] gave a deep learning solution and introduced the concept of CNNs for multi-label image classification. They reused existing CNNs that were initially used in classifying single-labelled images in a multi-label dataset. Zhu et al. [28] suggested a deep neural network (DNN) that utilizes spatial and semantic both types of relations between labels having just image-level supervision. Spatial regularization network (SRN) suggested by them produces attention maps for every label from a multi-label image and records the underlying relations amongst them. Park et al. [13] proposed MarsNet in which they used the dilated residual network (DRN) to produce high-resolution feature maps to make the network flexible for images of varying size.

Guan et al. [5] worked on chest X-ray images for multi-label thorax disease classification. They used ResNet-50 and DenseNet-121 for feature extraction. A residual model-based attention module is added to the network for classification. Both ResNet-50 and DenseNet-121 are very deep architectures. Li et al. [11] came up with a CNN-RNN based architecture for multi-label classification. CNN is used for feature extraction and RNN is used for label correlation management. CNN structure consists of channel-wise attention mechanism to focus on the object in the image and then RNN module is added to relate the labels in image semantic space. Wen et al. [25] extracted images feature using ResNet-101 architecture. In the network, 1×1 convolution filters are applied and the output is used for feature and label mapping. Output of ResNet-101 is flattened and combined with 1×1 filters with channel-wise pooling to co-project to the input for label mapping. They experimented with MS-COCO and PASCAL VOC datasets. In the work by Hua et al. [7], an attention-based approach was used for multi-label aerial image classification. They used VGG-16, ResNet50, and InceptionV3 architectures for image feature extraction. Feature-learning is performed with the help of the attention mechanism before the output layer. As per their results ResNet50 with the attention mechanism shows the best performance.

In most of the works available in the literature, deep CNN models are used for image feature extraction and multi–label classification [5,7,11,25]. Deep CNN models are computationally complex and time-consuming. For real-time applications these may not be suitable, specially when deployed on lightweight devices. The objective of the present work is to devise a lightweight CNN for image feature extraction. The idea is to perform multi-label image classification with fewer parameters and reduced computation time without compromising the quality of the model. The proposed CNN model with around 1 million parameters performs better than other state-of-the-art methods on various datasets from different domains.

3 The Proposed Method

Many state-of-the-art CNN models such as VGG, ResNet, Inception, DenseNet etc. have been adopted in recent years for various classification problems. Among these models, VGG is the simplest but the heaviest model with more than 138 million parameters. Another model is Inception that uses varying size filters in the same layer for better feature extraction. Inception model is composed of multiple small inception blocks. Each block has a complex structure that consists of filters of different sizes within the same layer. The basic idea to use filters of different sizes is to capture and integrate features of multiple levels simultaneously. Different versions of Inception models are proposed with minor modifications in inception blocks for improving the feature extraction capability as well as for reducing the computational complexity. For instance, in Inception V7, 3×3 filters are replaced by $3 \times 1 + 1 \times 3$ filters to reduce the number of multiplications [19]. The lightweight CNN model for multi-label image classification introduced in this work is inspired by Inception V7 [19] to achieve comparatively good results with a smaller number of parameters.

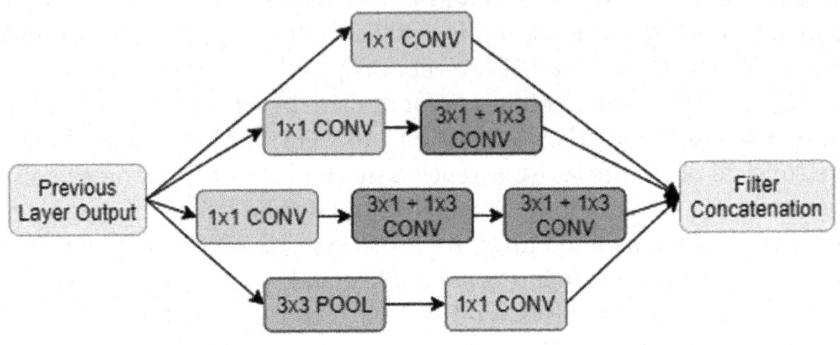

Fig. 1. Inception V7 block

Inception V7 block used in the proposed model is shown in Fig. 1. A unit of Inception V7 block has a succession of convolutions carried out at various scales and eventually the results are obtained. For every cell, the model learns a set of 1×1, 3×3, and a combination of '3×1 and 1×3' kernels, thus the model learns to extract features from the input image at various scales. For reducing the input channel depth, 1×1 convolution is used to save computations. Max pooling is also used, along with "valid" padding to save the dimensions to concatenate the output properly.

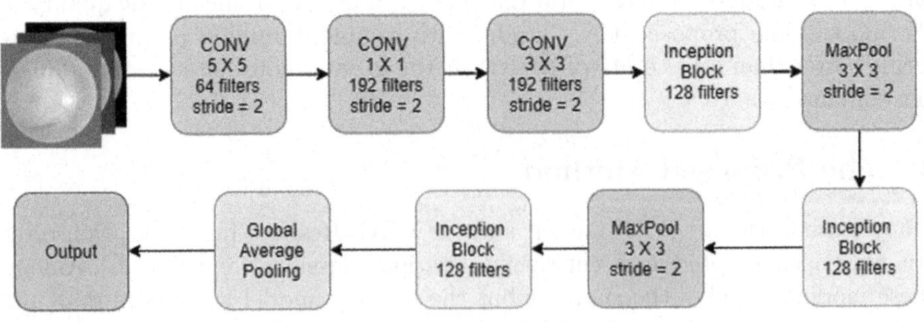

Fig. 2. Block diagram of the proposed model

Table 1. Model description.

Layer	Filter size	# Filters	Stride	# Parameters
Convolutional	5 × 5	64	2	4,864
Convolutional	1 × 1	192	2	12,480
Convolutional	3 × 3	192	2	331,968
Inception v7 block	–	256	–	137,296
Max Pooling	3 × 3	–	2	0
Inception v7 block	–	256	–	367,712
Max pooling	3 × 3	–	2	0
Inception v7 block	–	256	–	446,530
Global average pooling	1 × 1	–	–	0
Dense	–	4	–	12025
Total number of parameters				**1,312,905**

The model shown in Fig. 2 consists of three convolution layers. The first convolution layer is having 64 filters of size 5×5, padding 'valid', and stride 2×2. The second convolution layer has 192 filters of size 1 × 1, padding 'valid', and stride 2 × 2. Third convolution layer has 192 filters of size 3 × 3, padding 'valid', and stride 2 × 2. Convolution layers are followed by three units of "Inception V7 block" having max-pooling layers of 3 × 3 in between. The last inception block is followed by a global average pooling layer (GAP). The final sigmoid output layer uses a dropout rate of 0.4.

Three Conv layers are added as initial layers which extract features in the form of horizontal lines, vertical lines, and curves. As the depth of CNN increases, the complex features of images are extracted, hence Inception V7 blocks are added at the end. The model is trained with Adam optimizer, setting the learning rate as 0.001 for 30 epochs. With this model, it is supposed to achieve a comparable accuracy on most of the datasets with around 1 million trainable parameters as shown in Table 1, which are very less when compared to standard architectures like VGG16, ResNet, Inception, MobileNet, and DenseNet with millions of parameters.

4 Results and Discussion

4.1 Datasets Used in the Experiment

Image data needs to be annotated properly with precise metadata to make objects recognizable to machines for computer vision. Six standard multi-label image datasets from three different domains are used in this work for the evaluation of the proposed method. The three domains considered in this work are general benchmark images, medical images, and agricultural images. Figure 3 depicted some sample images from each of the dataset.

General Benchmark Image Datasets
DOTA is a large-scale dataset for object classification and detection in aerial images [26]. It could be used to implement and evaluate object detectors in aerial images. DOTA contains 2806 aerial images taken from different sensors and various platforms. Each image has the size in the range from about 800×800 to 4000×4000 pixels. Every image contains objects exhibiting a wide variety of shapes, orientations, and scales. These DOTA images have been annotated by aerial image interpretation experts using fifteen object categories.

Movie Genre from its Poster dataset consists of movie poster images obtained from the IMDB website [3]. It contains 7320 images of movie posters of varying sizes along with their genres in an XML file. These images belong to twenty-five categories.

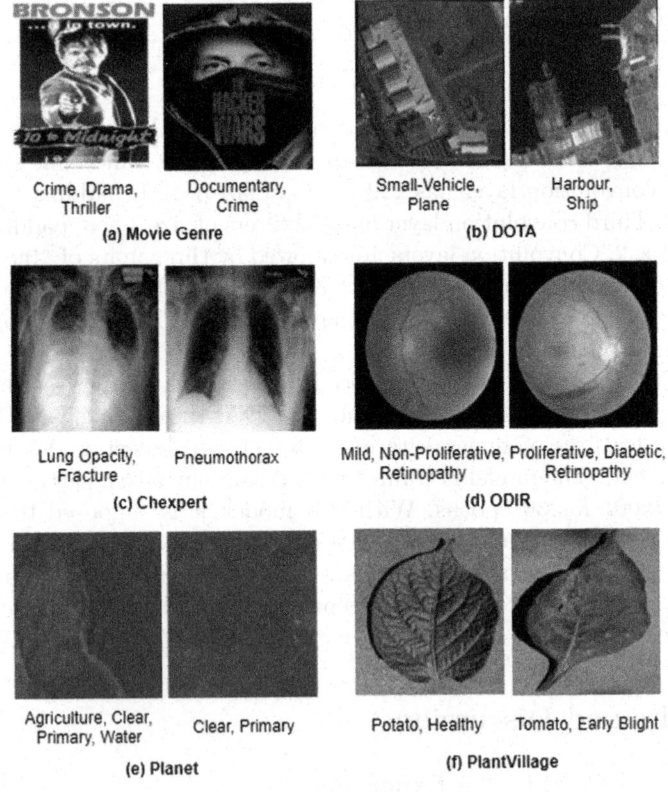

Fig. 3. Sample images from datasets along with their respective labels

Medical Image Datasets

CheXpert is a large public dataset consisting of chest radiograph interpretation, having 224,316 chest radiograph images from 65,240 patients. Images are labelled for the presence of 14 observations as positive, negative, or uncertain [9]. It is a very big dataset, from a major US hospital (Stanford Medical Center). It contains chest X-rays obtained over 15 years from 2002–2017.

ODIR (Ocular Disease Intelligent Recognition) is a well-structured ophthalmic dataset [2]. The dataset contains 10,000 colored fundus images of the left and right eye belonging to 5000 patients. Each image is having a size of 224×224 pixels. Along with fundus images, patient's age and diagnostic keywords from doctors are also provided. The images belong to eight categories of diseases.

Agricultural Image Datasets

PlantVillage Dataset [12] consists of healthy and unhealthy plant leaf images divided into categories by species and disease. It is a standard dataset for plant disease classification. It contains 54,306 images with 26 diseases for 14 crops like potato, tomato, pepper bell. The size of each image is 64×64 pixels.

Planet: Understanding the Amazon from Space dataset was introduced in a competition [14] which took place in Kaggle in the year 2017. The dataset contains a set of satellite images capturing the Amazon rainforest, Brazil. It has 17 categories belonging to atmospheric conditions. It has 40,000 training images in both TIFF and JPEG format with a size of 256×256 pixels.

4.2 Performance Metrics

The classification results are evaluated using performance metrics [17] defined in this section. A good performance metric provides the results that measure clearly defines classes and characterizes how strong the model is depending on the dataset. Confusion matrix-based performance measures are used in this work. Accuracy, precision, recall, and F1-score are the most commonly used metrics for classification. Accuracy (Eq. 1) refers to the fraction of correct predictions to the total number of predictions. Precision (Eq. 2) is the fraction of correctly allocated outcomes to the total retrieved outcomes. Recall (Eq. 3) is the fraction of correctly retrieved outcomes to the total relevant outcomes that should have been retrieved. F1-score (Eq. 4) considers the weighted average of precision and recall.

$$Accuracy = \frac{TruePositive + TrueNegative}{TotalExamples} \tag{1}$$

$$Precision = \frac{TruePositive}{TruePositive + FalsePositive} \tag{2}$$

$$Recall = \frac{TruePositive}{TruePositive + FalseNegative} \tag{3}$$

$$F1 - Score = 2 * \frac{Precision * Recall}{Precision + Recall} \tag{4}$$

4.3 Experimental Results and Comparative Study

Various state-of-the-art architectures like VGG, ResNet, Inception, MobileNet, DenseNet along with the proposed model are initially trained on ImageNet weights over Movie Genre and DOTA datasets, which are general benchmark datasets. The parameters selected through this training are used to train all the architectures on the other datasets. This section discusses the results obtained based on the performance metrics discussed in the previous subsection. The number of parameters involved in each experiment is also compared along with the testing time required by each experiment over the randomly selected test images. There is a change in number of parameters in output layer based on the number of classes in the datasets. Results obtained with the proposed model and the other best performing model are highlighted. Time reported in the result section is the time taken by the test dataset which depends on the number of images in the test dataset.

Performance of General Benchmark Dataset. The first set of experiments is performed on the general benchmark image dataset, i.e., Movie Genre dataset which has movie poster images along with genres as annotations. Adam optimizer was used during training with a learning rate of 0.0001. Model is trained for 200 epochs and results on test datasets are shown in Table 2. From the results given below, it is clear that the proposed 3 Layer Inception module-based architecture achieved a comparable performance as other heavy weighted state-of-the-art architectures with quite a smaller number of parameters and reduced testing time over 720 test images out of 7320 total images.

In the DOTA dataset, adam optimizer was used during training with a learning rate of 0.0001 and it was executed for 200 epochs as shown in Table 3. For this dataset, the proposed architecture and MobileNet V2 are performing better than other architectures in terms of accuracy. The proposed architecture has taken fewer parameters and reduced testing time over 230 test images randomly selected from 2806 total images.

The standard architectures are performing well in all the datasets. However, it can be seen in the above tables, the performance of the proposed architecture on general benchmark image datasets is good enough with the merit of having a smaller number of parameters and reduced testing time.

Table 2. Results on movie genre dataset.

Model	Parameters (M)	Time (sec.)	Accuracy	Precision	Recall	F1 score
3 layer inception	**1.31**	**129.00**	**0.9147**	**0.9574**	**0.5016**	**0.6583**
VGG 16	201.47	411.00	0.9135	0.7166	0.6609	0.6876
VGG 19	206.78	419.00	0.9113	0.7059	0.6452	0.6482
ResNet 50	28.71	132.00	0.9160	0.7268	0.5849	0.6481
DenseNet 121	9.11	137.40	0.9157	0.7241	0.6099	0.6621
Inception V5	**5.99**	**298.00**	**0.9182**	**0.7476**	**0.5858**	**0.6569**
MobileNet V2	5.46	259.80	0.9137	0.7159	0.6469	0.6796

Table 3. Results on DOTA dataset.

Model	Parameters (M)	Time (sec.)	Accuracy	Precision	Recall	F1 score
3 layer inception	**1.06**	**0.21**	**0.8795**	**0.5590**	**0.7132**	**0.6268**
VGG 16	165.78	5.00	0.8559	0.7662	0.7131	0.7386
VGG 19	171.03	5.30	0.8480	0.7479	0.7134	0.7302
ResNet 50	158.87	0.78	0.8698	0.7886	0.7550	0.7714
DenseNet 121	75.21	0.76	0.8624	0.7729	0.7522	0.7624
Inception V5	5.99	0.31	0.8594	0.7717	0.7256	0.7479
MobileNet V2	**3.57**	**0.39**	**0.8829**	**0.8204**	**0.7619**	**0.7901**

Performance on Medical Image Datasets. Better performing architectures from the above datasets are selected and implemented on two popular medical image datasets having very different set of images as compared to general benchmark image datasets. Adam optimizer was used during training with a learning rate of 0.0001 and it was executed for 30 epochs. The results of the implementations can be seen in Table 4 and Table 5 given below.

Table 4. Results on CheXpert dataset.

Model	Parameters (M)	Time (sec.)	Accuracy	Precision	Recall	F1 score
3 layer inception	**0.94**	**23.4**	**0.8130**	**0.6878**	**0.3876**	**0.4958**
ResNet 50	**23.60**	**60.84**	**0.7970**	**0.5711**	**0.5818**	**0.5764**
Inception V5	1.07	18.72	0.7924	0.6151	0.3652	0.4583
MobileNet V2	2.27	53.82	0.7751	0.6262	0.4505	0.5204

In both of the above datasets, it can be seen that the proposed architecture is performing better than the other standard architectures for the given datasets. Also, it is giving higher performance than the other architectures with a smaller number of parameters and less testing time taken over 2234 test images out of 224,316 total images in CheXpert dataset and 3000 test images randomly obtained from 1000 total images of ODIR dataset.

Table 5. Results on ODIR dataset.

Model	Parameters (M)	Time (sec.)	Accuracy	Precision	Recall	F1 score
3 layer inception	**0.95**	**26.67**	**0.8067**	**0.4940**	**0.4959**	**0.4949**
ResNet 50	**25.78**	**176.0**	**0.7988**	**0.4889**	**0.4905**	**0.4897**
VGG 19	146.67	222.0	0.7851	0.4866	0.4981	0.4923
MobileNet V2	4.54	89.4	0.7663	0.4940	0.4955	0.4947

Performance on Agricultural Image Datasets. Similar architectures are used for two popular agricultural image datasets having very different types of images then the general benchmark image datasets. Adam optimizer was used during training with a learning rate of 0.0001 and it was executed for 30 epochs. The results of the implementations can be seen in Table 6 and Table 7 given below.

Table 6. Results on planet dataset.

Model	Parameters (M)	Time (sec.)	Accuracy	Precision	Recall	F1 score
3 layer inception	**1.19**	**23.87**	**0.9562**	**0.9349**	**0.9050**	**0.9197**
VGG 16	165.79	35.81	0.9578	0.9245	0.9251	0.9248
VGG 19	**171.09**	**41.00**	**0.9635**	**0.9422**	**0.9255**	**0.9338**
ResNet 50	23.62	75.60	0.9561	0.9317	0.9083	0.9199
MobileNet V2	2.28	55.71	0.9623	0.9492	0.9131	0.9308

Table 7. Results on PlantVillage dataset.

Model	Parameters (M)	Time (sec.)	Accuracy	Precision	Recall	F1 score
3 layer inception	**1.31**	**0.80**	**0.9424**	**0.9551**	**0.9484**	**0.9517**
VGG 16	33.66	1.68	0.9702	0.9709	0.9695	0.9702
ResNet 50	24.13	3.22	0.9729	0.9749	0.9730	0.9739
DenseNet 121	**7.31**	**4.10**	**0.9826**	**0.9837**	**0.9825**	**0.9831**
MobileNet V2	2.59	1.96	0.8411	0.8564	0.8446	0.8505

In both of the above datasets, it can see that the proposed model has the least number of parameters as well as testing time over 10,876 test images from 54,303 images of PlantVillage dataset and 3979 test images randomly selected from 40,479 total images of Planet dataset. Also, it is giving a comparable performance as those of other architectures in the agricultural image domain. This shows that the proposed lightweight model can be used in this domain as well.

By analysing the performance of different architectures as compared to the proposed architecture, it can be inferred that the proposed architecture is giving comparable or better performance over datasets belonging to three different domains. Therefore, the proposed architecture can be used to replace such heavy models for multi-label classification of images based on spatial features.

5 Conclusion and Future Work

Deep Convolutional Neural Networks have been effectively applied to image classification in recent years. Many standard architectures have been explored to achieve greater accuracy in multi-label image classification. We have focused on classifying images based on spatial features. As real-time applications require a quick response which can be achieved with lightweight models. Therefore, the work is aimed to achieve a comparable or better classification performance with reduced model complexity. The proposed lightweight model is based on InceptionV7 architecture. The model is implemented and analyzed by comparing its performance with other architectures on six datasets belonging to three different categories. It is observed that the proposed lightweight model can be used to replace the CNN module for performing the multi-label classification of images in various domains like medical and agricultural images. Further, the proposed custom CNN can be implemented as a CNN module in multi-label image classification algorithms to work on extracting spatial features along with a semantic module to find label-correlation. It can also be used with some object detection algorithms as a pre-processing module.

References

1. Boutell, M.R., Luo, J., Shen, X., Brown, C.M.: Learning multi-label scene classification. Pattern Recogn. **37**(9), 1757–1771 (2004)
2. Challenge, G.: Ocular disease intelligent recognition (ODIR-2019) (2019). https://odir2019.grand-challenge.org/. Accessed 19 Feb 2020
3. Chu, W.T., Guo, H.J.: Movie genre classification based on poster images with deep neural networks. In: Proceedings of the Workshop on Multimodal Understanding of Social, Affective and Subjective Attributes, pp. 39–45 (2017)
4. Devkar, R., Shiravale, S.: A survey on multi-label classification for images. Int. J. Comput. Appl. **162**(8), 39–42 (2017)
5. Guan, Q., Huang, Y.: Multi-label chest x-ray image classification via category-wise residual attention learning. Pattern Recogn. Lett. **130**, 259–266 (2020)
6. He, K., Zhang, X., Ren, S., Sun, J.: Deep residual learning for image recognition. In: Proceedings of the IEEE Conference on Computer Vision and Pattern Recognition, pp. 770–778 (2016)
7. Hua, Y., Mou, L., Zhu, X.X.: Relation network for multilabel aerial image classification. IEEE Trans. Geosci. Remote Sens. **58**, 4558–4572 (2020)
8. Huang, G., Liu, Z., Van Der Maaten, L., Weinberger, K.Q.: Densely connected convolutional networks. In: Proceedings of the IEEE Conference on Computer Vision and Pattern Recognition, pp. 4700–4708 (2017)
9. Irvin, J., et al.: CheXpert: a large chest radiograph dataset with uncertainty labels and expert comparison. Proceedings of the AAAI Conference on Artificial Intelligence, vol. 33, pp. 590–597 (2019)
10. Jia, D., et al.: An ensemble neural network for multi-label classification of electrocardiogram. In: Liao, H., et al. (eds.) MLMECH/CVII-STENT -2019. LNCS, vol. 11794, pp. 20–27. Springer, Cham (2019). https://doi.org/10.1007/978-3-030-33327-0_3

11. Li, P., Chen, P., Xie, Y., Zhang, D.: Bi-modal learning with channel-wise attention for multi-label image classification. IEEE Access **8**, 9965–9977 (2020)
12. Mohanty, S.P., Hughes, D.P., Salathé, M.: Using deep learning for image-based plant disease detection. Front. Plant Sci. **7**, 1419 (2016)
13. Park, J.Y., Hwang, Y., Lee, D., Kim, J.H.: MarsNet: multi-label classification network for images of various sizes. IEEE Access **8**, 21832–21846 (2020)
14. Planet: Planet: Understanding the Amazon from Space (2017). https://www.kaggle.com/c/planet-understanding-the-amazon-from-space/data. Accessed 10 Feb 2020
15. Read, J., Pfahringer, B., Holmes, G., Frank, E.: Classifier chains for multi-label classification. Mach. Learn. **85**(3), 333 (2011)
16. Sandler, M., Howard, A., Zhu, M., Zhmoginov, A., Chen, L.C.: MobileNetV 2: Inverted residuals and linear bottlenecks. In: Proceedings of the IEEE Conference on Computer Vision and Pattern Recognition, pp. 4510–4520 (2018)
17. Shung, K.P.: Performance metrics (2018). https://towardsdatascience.com/accuracy-precision-recall-or-f1-331fb37c5cb9. Accessed 10 Mar 2019
18. Simonyan, K., Zisserman, A.: Very deep convolutional networks for large-scale image recognition. arXiv preprint arXiv:1409.1556 (2014)
19. Szegedy, C., Ibarz, J.: Scene classification with inception-7. In: Large-Scale Scene Understanding Challenge Workshop (lSUN), p. 5. CVPR, Boston (2015)
20. Szegedy, C., et al.: Going deeper with convolutions. In: Proceedings of the IEEE Conference on Computer Vision and Pattern Recognition, pp. 1–9 (2015)
21. Szymański, P., Kajdanowicz, T.: A scikit-based Python environment for performing multi-label classification. ArXiv e-prints, February 2017
22. Tahir, M.A., Kittler, J., Bouridane, A.: Multilabel classification using heterogeneous ensemble of multi-label classifiers. Pattern Recogn. Lett. **33**(5), 513–523 (2012)
23. Tsoumakas, G., Katakis, I.: Multi-label classification: an overview. Int. J. Data Warehous. Min. (IJDWM) **3**(3), 1–13 (2007)
24. Wei, Y., et al.: HCP: a flexible CNN framework for multi-label image classification. IEEE Trans. Pattern Anal. Mach. Intell. **38**(9), 1901–1907 (2015)
25. Wen, S., et al.: Multilabel image classification via feature/label co-projection. IEEE Trans. Syst. Man Cybern.: Syst. (2020)
26. Xia, G.S., et al.: DOTA: a large-scale dataset for object detection in aerial images. In: Proceedings of the IEEE Conference on Computer Vision and Pattern Recognition, pp. 3974–3983 (2018)
27. Zhang, L., Shah, S.K., Kakadiaris, I.A.: Hierarchical multi-label classification using fully associative ensemble learning. Pattern Recogn. **70**, 89–103 (2017)
28. Zhu, F., Li, H., Ouyang, W., Yu, N., Wang, X.: Learning spatial regularization with image-level supervisions for multi-label image classification. In: Proceedings of the IEEE Conference on Computer Vision and Pattern Recognition, pp. 5513–5522 (2017)

Computer Vision based Animal Collision Avoidance Framework for Autonomous Vehicles

Savyasachi Gupta(✉), Dhananjai Chand, and Ilaiah Kavati

National Institute of Technology Warangal, Warangal 506004, India

Abstract. Animals have been a common sighting on roads in India which leads to several accidents between them and vehicles every year. This makes it vital to develop a support system for driverless vehicles that assists in preventing these forms of accidents. In this paper, we propose a neoteric framework for avoiding vehicle-to-animal collisions by developing an efficient approach for the detection of animals on highways using deep learning and computer vision techniques on dashcam video. Our approach leverages the Mask R-CNN model for detecting and identifying various commonly found animals. Then, we perform lane detection to deduce whether a detected animal is on the vehicle's lane or not and track its location and direction of movement using a centroid based object tracking algorithm. This approach ensures that the framework is effective at determining whether an animal is obstructing the path or not of an autonomous vehicle in addition to predicting its movement and giving feedback accordingly. This system was tested under various lighting and weather conditions and was observed to perform relatively well, which leads the way for prominent driverless vehicle's support systems for avoiding vehicular collisions with animals on Indian roads in real-time.

Keywords: Computer Vision · Object Tracking · Vehicle-to-Animal Collision Avoidance · Mask R-CNN · Lane Detection

1 Introduction

Animal detection has been an area of interest for wildlife photographers for finding animals in wildlife. However, it has found recent use for the development of autonomous vehicles because it has been observed that in countries such as India, animals are seen to be roaming freely on the roads, which leads to unwanted accidents [1]. As a result, it becomes vital to have an effective method for detecting animals on the roads.

Additionally, such a method can be used for the development of a support system that can help reduce the number of accidents caused due to vehicle-to-animal collision in autonomous vehicles. This support system may even perform

S. K. Singh et al. (Eds.): CVIP 2020, CCIS 1378, pp. 237–248, 2021.
https://doi.org/10.1007/978-981-16-1103-2_21

better than the standard human reaction time to stop the manually controlled vehicle in the presence of an obstructing animal on the road and thus make riding an autonomous vehicle safer than manually driven vehicles [2].

Currently, some existing methods provide animal detection already. For instance, Sharma and Shah [3] use Cascade Classifiers and Histograms of Oriented Gradients (HOG) for animal detection. However, this approach is limited by a few factors. Firstly, it only provides an accuracy of 82.5% and secondly, it is limited to just cow detection, which is one of the many animals found on Indian roads. Burghardt and Calic [4] have introduced a methodology that depends on animals taking a pose and facing the camera for detection (i.e. similar to face detection for humans). The drawback of this approach is that animals are detected using facial recognition which may not always be the case by the video capturing device as the animals may not always be facing directly towards it.

Furthermore, Mammeri *et al.* [5] introduced a method that uses a two-stage approach: utilization of the LBP-Adaboost algorithm in the first stage and an adaptation of HOG-SVM classifier in the second stage for detection of animals. However, there are two major drawbacks of this system: it only considers moose for detection and that too only its side-view. This indicates that other animals that are found on Indian roads such as cows and dogs are not detected by this system. Additionally, this approach can detect only on side-views of the animals and not their front or rear views, thus severely restricting the practical utility of the approach.

Ramanan *et al.* [6] proposed a different method for animal detection and tracking based on SIFT, which utilizes a texture descriptor that matches it with a predeveloped library of animal textures. The drawback of this approach is that it is limited to footages containing a single animal only and requires the background to be clutter-free. Lastly, Atri Saxena *et al.* [7] has proposed their models based on SSD and faster R-CNN for the detection of animals. The authors have compared the two approaches, however, apart from object detection, no method has been devised that precisely track or pinpoint the presence of the animals on the car's lane. Hence, we determined that an efficient approach was needed which detects a variety of animals found in the Indian roads, overcomes some of the drawbacks in the former approaches, and provides a better detection accuracy for the same.

2 Methodology

Stray animals have been a common sighting on Indian roads for a long time. They are commonly sighted on highways, rural roads, and sometimes even in urban cities. These animals are mostly cattle and dogs, but occasionally animals such as elephants and deer can also be observed. Hence, it becomes essential for an autonomous vehicle designed for Indian roads to be able to detect these animals to prevent unwanted accidents and resultant damage to both the vehicle and the animal. The following methodology has been proposed to achieve vehicular collision avoidance with animals based on the input video from a dashboard camera.

2.1 Animal Detection

In the first stage, we use the state-of-the-art Mask R-CNN (Region-based Convolutional Neural Networks) model, which is proposed by He *et al.* [8], as the primary object detection model for detecting and identifying animals in the following categories: cat, dog, horse, sheep, cow, elephant, bear, zebra, and giraffe. One of the key reasons for using Mask R-CNN as the object detection model is that it has been trained on the MS COCO dataset [9], which contains 91 common object categories with 82 of them having more than 5,000 labeled instances. This ensures that the aforementioned animal classes have been trained extensively on several thousands of images per class. Since the objective of this support system is to identify animals on Indian roads, we evaluated the ability of the model by primarily testing on frequently found animals such as cows and dogs.

Our Mask R-CNN network has been constructed using a ResNet-101 backbone (bottom-up pathway) through which the input image is passed. Multiple layers are grouped and convolution stages pass through 1×1, 3×3, and 1×1 sized kernels in that order. Each convolution layer is followed by a batch normalization layer and a ReLU activation unit. The layers in the bottom-up pathway are passed through a 1×1 convolution layer so that depth can be downsampled to the corresponding depth of the top-down layer to perform in-place addition. Each feature map is passed through a 3×3 convolution to generate pyramid feature maps. Feature maps are fed to box detection and objectness subnets to generate region proposals. Thereafter, FPN-RoI mapping is performed followed by RoI Align which results in 1024 length vectors for all RoIs from which classification and box regression is performed. The outputs are fed to box regression, classification, and mask branch where regression is performed on each.

Additionally, we use Mask R-CNN as it improves Faster R-CNN [10] by using Region of Interest (RoI) Align instead of RoI Pooling. The key feature of RoI Align is that it rectifies the location misalignment issue present in RoI Pooling when it takes the input proposals from the Region Proposal Network (RPN) by dividing them into 'bins' using bilinear interpolation. Hence, Mask R-CNN improves upon the core accuracy of Faster R-CNN and is therefore used over it. The architecture for Mask R-CNN is illustrated in Fig. 1. This stage outputs a dictionary, which contains the class IDs, bounding boxes, detection scores, and the generated masks for a video frame.

2.2 Lane Detection

In this stage, we use an efficient lane detection system, proposed by Aggarwal [12], to identify lane demarcations on the road. This is used to provide feedback to the autonomous vehicle about the animals which are in the path or near to it. For example, in the countryside areas, it is common to see animals in fields on either side of the road in India. These animals do not pose a threat to the vehicle and hence need to be distinguished from those that are of concern, i.e., animals on roads. Hence, we use the lane detection system to deduce whether an animal is in the autonomous vehicle's lane or not. The location of each animal

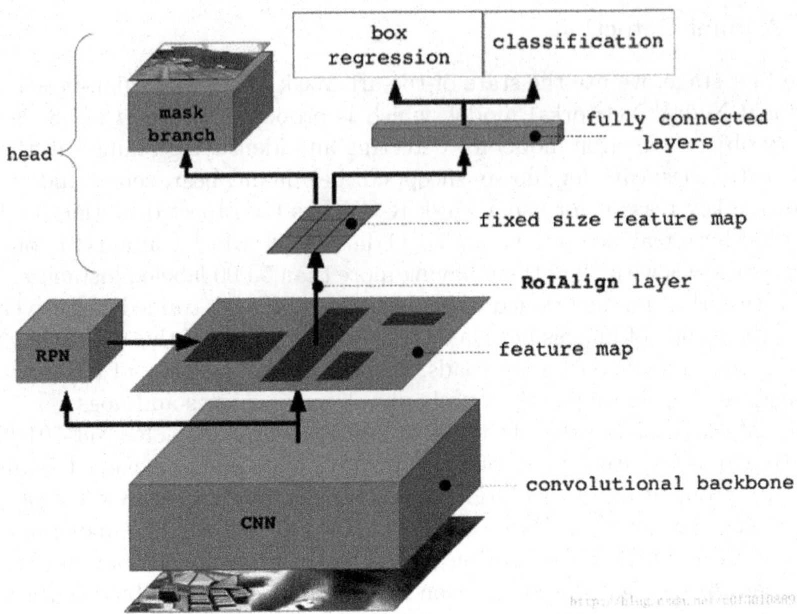

Fig. 1. Mask R-CNN architecture [11]

can either be within the lane of the road or outside it. If it's within the lane, we notify the vehicle to stop. Otherwise, we perform animal direction analysis and vicinity tracking to provide predictive feedback informing us if an animal outside the lane is about to enter it and possibly collide with the autonomous vehicle. The process of detecting the lane on the highway is shown in Fig. 2.

2.3 Animal Direction and Vicinity Tracking

In this stage, we track the location of the detected animals and their direction of movement using a centroid tracking algorithm [13]. If an animal is outside a lane but moving towards it, and is in the vicinity of the lane, then we alert the autonomous vehicle even before the animal enters the lane, leading to improved safety. In this step, two criteria need to be met for the animal to be considered as a threat for a possible collision:

i. The animal is outside the detected lanes and is moving towards the lane
ii. The animal is in the vicinity of the vehicle

Animal Direction Tracking. After performing object detection, correctly detected animals are retained based on their class IDs and scores by filtering from all detected objects. This paves the way for the next task which is animal tracking over the future time frames of the recording. This is accomplished by utilizing a straightforward yet productive object tracking algorithm called

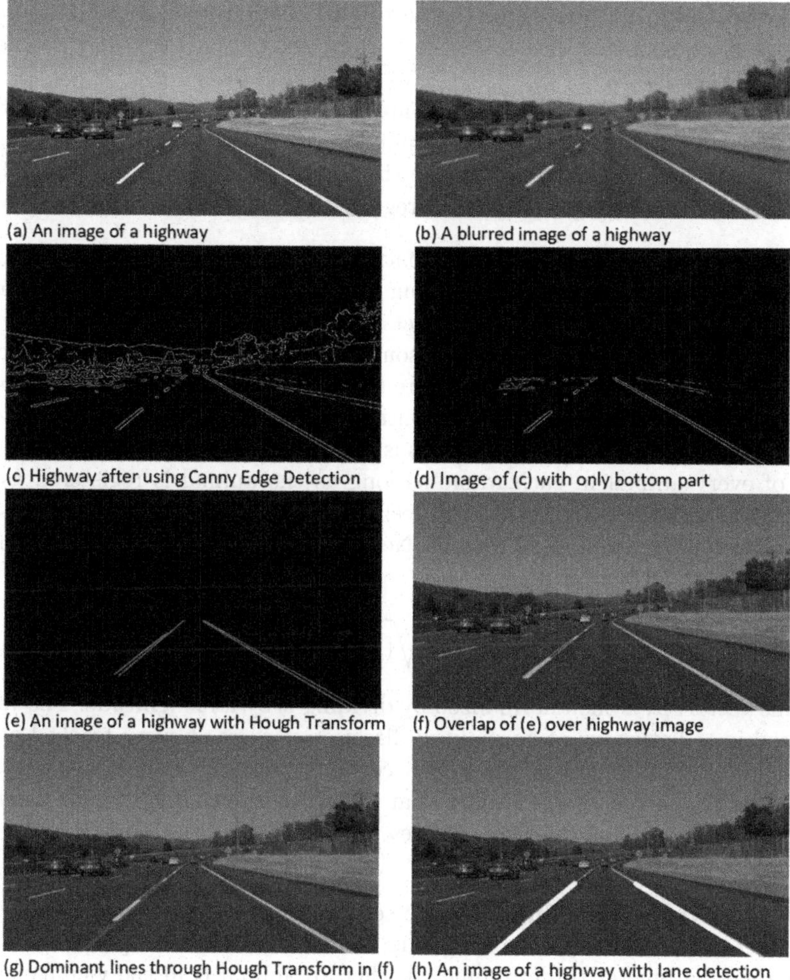

Fig. 2. Lane detection procedure applied on a highway [12]

centroid tracking [13]. This calculation works by taking the Euclidean distance between the centroids of identified animals over successive frames as clarified further ahead. The centroid tracking algorithm used in this framework can be described as a multiple-step technique which is explained in the following steps:

i. The object centroid for all objects is determined by taking the midpoint of the meeting lines from the middle of the bounding boxes for each distinguished animal.
ii. The Euclidean distance is determined between the centroids of the newly recognized objects and the current objects.

iii. The centroid coordinates for the new items are refreshed depending on the least Euclidean distance from the current set of centroids and the newly stored centroid.
iv. New objects in the field of view are registered by storing their centroid coordinates in a dictionary and appointing fresh IDs.
v. Objects which are not noticeable in the current field of view for a predefined set of frames in progression are deregistered from the dictionary.

An important presumption of the centroid tracking algorithm is that, though an object will move between the resulting frames of the recording, the separation between the centroid of the same object between successive frames will be less than the separation to the centroid of some other object identified in the frame. The next task in the system is to acquire the trajectories of the tracked animals. These are calculated by finding the contrasts between the centroids of tracked animals for five sequential frames. This is made conceivable by keeping the centroid of every animal in each frame as long as the animal is registered as per the centroid tracking algorithm. The result is a 2D vector, $\boldsymbol{\mu}$, which represents the direction of the animal movement. Next, we determine the magnitude of the vector, $\boldsymbol{\mu}$, as described in Eq. 1.

$$\text{magnitude} = \sqrt{(\boldsymbol{\mu}.i)^2 + (\boldsymbol{\mu}.j)^2} \tag{1}$$

This vector, $\boldsymbol{\mu}$, is then normalized by dividing it by its magnitude. The vector is stored in a dictionary of normalized direction vectors of every tracked object only if its original magnitude is over a certain threshold. If not, this vector is discarded. This is done to guarantee that minor variations in centroids for static objects do not result in false trajectories.

Animal Vicinity Tracking. For the second criterion, we use the horizontal midpoints of the lane and the bounding box of the animal respectively as the comparison parameter to determine whether an animal is in the vicinity of the autonomous vehicle. If the horizontal midpoint of the animal's bounding box lies between the midpoints of the lane, then we consider that the animal is effectively in the vicinity of the vehicle. The reason is that most of the time, the lane of a road inclines towards the horizon of the road and hence has a gradient which may miss intersecting the bounding box of the animal. This serves as a measure of providing predictive feedback on the possibility of an animal entering the lane of the road.

Combining Animal Direction and Vicinity Tracking. Once we track the direction and vicinity of the detected animals, we are able to alert the autonomous vehicle before an animal enters the lane which is moving towards it as shown in Fig. 3.

(a) Animal detected at the beginning of the feed

(b) Predictive feedback before animal enters lane

Fig. 3. A sequence of steps for predictive feedback of animals outside the lanes

2.4 Overall Pipeline

We construct an overall pipeline by combining the Mask R-CNN model results and lane detection output to get the relevant animal detection alert for the autonomous vehicle. If the animal is within the detected lane, then the support system directly sends a 'STOP' alert to the autonomous vehicle. Otherwise, the animals are tracked continuously to determine the direction of their movements. Additionally, the location of the animals' bounding boxes is compared with the midpoints of the lane to check whether the animals are in the vicinity of the path of the autonomous vehicle or not. If an animal is found to be both in the vicinity of the lane and moving towards it, then the support system can send a 'STOP' alert to the autonomous vehicle based on a predictive analysis mechanism. Essentially, the objective of this support system is to provide a robust method for preventing potentially unwanted vehicle-to-animal collisions by timely detecting relevant animals on the autonomous vehicle's path.

The proposed framework was tested under various lighting and weather conditions and was observed to perform relatively well for the same as illustrated in Fig. 4. In this work, we have focused primarily on two most commonly found animals on Indian roads, which are stray cows and stray dogs, for the purpose of evaluation, while at the same time retained the detection of other animals.

3 Experimental Results

3.1 Datasets

The following datasets have been used for testing the Vehicle-to-Animal Accident Detection framework:

i. MS COCO Dataset: The Microsoft Common Objects in Context (MS COCO) dataset [9] is a well-known dataset that has annotations for instance segmentation and ground truth bounding boxes, which are used to evaluate how well object detection and image segmentation models perform. It contains 91 common objects as classes. Out of the total classes, 82 have 5,000 annotations or more. There are overall 328,000 images with more than 2,500,000 annotated

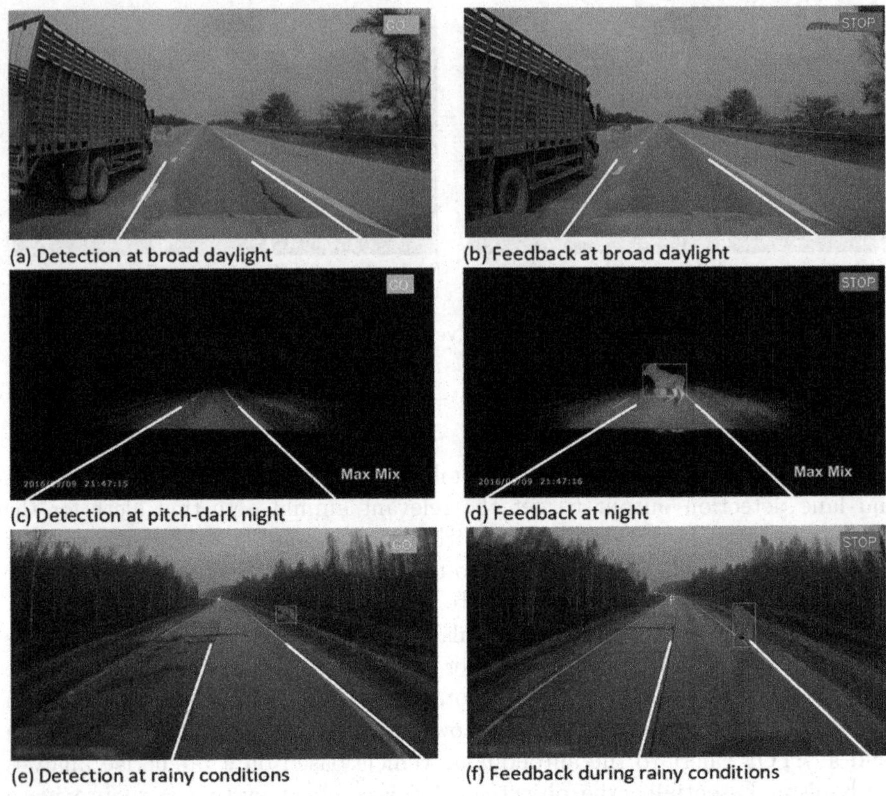

(a) Detection at broad daylight (b) Feedback at broad daylight (c) Detection at pitch-dark night (d) Feedback at night (e) Detection at rainy conditions (f) Feedback during rainy conditions

Fig. 4. Animal detection system under various lighting and weather conditions

objects. The MS COCO dataset has been used for training the Mask R-CNN framework on multiple object classes including a multitude of animal species.

ii. Custom animals sighted on roads dataset: Accuracy of Mask R-CNN and the overall framework has been evaluated on dashcam footage of animals crossing the lanes in front. These videos have been compiled from YouTube. The dashcam videos have been taken at 30 frames per second and consist of footage from various countries around the world, including India, the USA, and Australia. A handful of dataset images are shown in Fig. 5.

3.2 Results

Our framework for Vehicle-to-Animal collision avoidance is evaluated in two stages. Firstly, we evaluate how well the Mask R-CNN model identifies the two animal classes on which we based our analysis, i.e. cows and dogs. The evaluation is done using two parameters: precision (Eq. 2) and recall (Eq. 3). If the model detects the animals correctly, then we achieve a high recall. If the model distinguishes animals from non-animals, then we get high precision. Generally,

Fig. 5. Screenshots taken from test videos of animals sighted on roads dataset

precision and recall experience an inverse relationship, where if one increases, the other decreases. The interpolated precision is denoted as r, which is computed at each recall level. This is accomplished by selecting the greatest precision measured as shown in Eq. 4. We then generate precision-recall and interpolated precision-recall curves from these values to calculate average precision (Eq. 5).

$$Precision = TP/(TP + FP) \tag{2}$$

$$Recall = TP/(TP + FN) \tag{3}$$

$$p_{interp}(r) = \max_{r' \geq r} p(r') \tag{4}$$

$$AP = \sum_{i=1}^{n-1} (r_{i+1} - r_i) p_{interp}(r_{i+1}) \tag{5}$$

We compute the precision and recall by checking if our model detected the number of animals in the image correctly, as well as the accuracy of the masks. This is done by checking for the degree of the overlap of the predicted bounding boxes (by the Mask R-CNN model) with the actual bounding boxes (of animals). Intersection over Union (IoU) parameter is used to check the extent to which the predicted bounding box corresponds with the actual bounding box. The IoU is calculated by dividing the intersectional area by the area of the union of predicted and actual bounding boxes respectively.

We arrange the predicted bounding boxes which match the actual bounding box based on the descending order of their IoU scores. In the case where there isn't a single match, we label this ground truth box as unmatched and move on to evaluate the next set of bounding boxes. This process is repeated. The results were collected for cows and dogs separately. The results for testing on cows are shown in Fig. 6 and Table 1. It can be seen that the proposed model predicted the cows with a precision of 86.95% and a recall of 83.33%. It can also be observed that the model predicts the dogs with a precision of 84.12% and recall of 85.58% (Fig. 7 and Table 1).

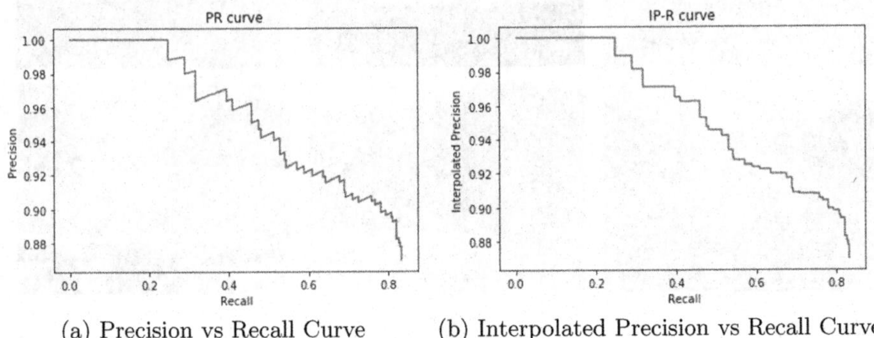

(a) Precision vs Recall Curve (b) Interpolated Precision vs Recall Curve

Fig. 6. a) Precision vs Recall curve plotted on the output of Mask R-CNN framework tested on the test set consisting of cows on roads at IoU of 0.5 b) Plotting precision-recall curve after interpolating precision values from the curve a)

Table 1. Evaluation metrics for Mask R-CNN tested on test set consisting of cows on roads, IOU = 0.5

Animal	Precision	Recall	Average Precision (AP)
Cow	0.8695	0.8333	79.47%
Dog	0.8412	0.8558	81.09%

The second stage of the framework deals with predicting whether the detected animal may be on the path of the vehicle based on the predictive feedback mechanism (explained in Sect. 2.3). We evaluate this mechanism based on Potential Accident Detection Ratio (PADR) (Eq. 6) and False Alarm Rate (FAR) (Eq. 7).

$$\text{PADR} = \frac{\text{Detected potential accident cases}}{\text{Total positive cases in the dataset}} \times 100\% \tag{6}$$

where 'Detected potential accident cases' refers to animals near lane which were detected by the predictive feedback mechanism and 'Total positive cases in the dataset' refers to the number of instances where animals outside the lane entered the lane eventually.

$$\text{FAR} = \frac{\text{Patterns where false alarm occurs}}{\text{Total number of patterns}} \times 100\% \tag{7}$$

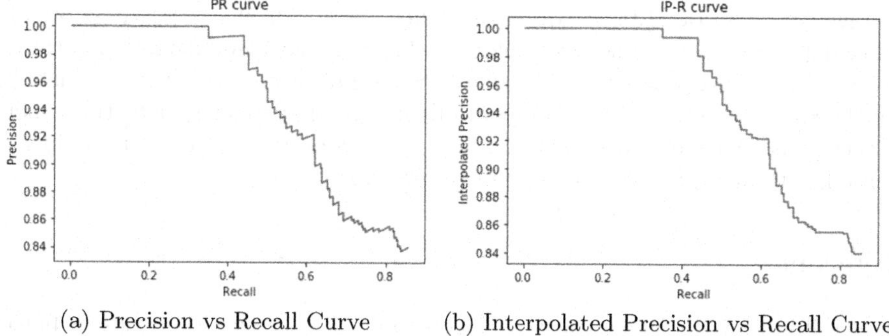

(a) Precision vs Recall Curve (b) Interpolated Precision vs Recall Curve

Fig. 7. a) Precision vs Recall curve plotted on output of Mask R-CNN framework tested on test set consisting of dogs on roads at IoU of 0.5 b) Plotting precision-recall curve after interpolating precision values from curve a)

The results are compared with other studies that have worked in the same domain of detecting animals and have been tabulated as shown in Table 2.

Table 2. Evaluating results of proposed framework in comparison to other frameworks for Potential Vehicle-to-Animal Accident Detection

Approach	PADR %	FAR %
S. U. Sharma *et al.* [3]	80.40	0.08
Mammeri *et al.* [5]	82.19	0.088
Our Framework	84.18	0.026

Hence, we observed that our framework performs superiorly when evaluated using the Detection Rate and exhibits a lesser False Alarm Rate than similar works. This is achieved by utilizing Mask R-CNN for object detection model and using lane detection to develop a predictive feedback mechanism which helps in detecting animals even before they enter the lanes.

4 Conclusions and Future Scope

A novel neural network based framework has been proposed for the avoidance of collision with animals. It uses a multitude of techniques including object detection, lane detection, and object tracking with the help of CNNs and computer vision based techniques to ensure an accurate response. The proposed framework can detect animals that are either in the path of the vehicle or are potentially going to be using a predictive feedback mechanism. It was determined that the system can detect cows with an average precision of 79.47% and dogs with an average precision of 81.09%. Moreover, when tested for the correctness of collision detection, our model was able to achieve an accident detection ratio of 84.18% and a false alarm rate of 0.026%. Some limitations of this work include are the size of test samples and deviations in lane demarcation detection when the actual lanes haven't been marked or in cases of blurry/low-resolution videos. These limitations can be addressed in future works.

References

1. TT Editor: With humans locked indoors, animals take over the roads in India, Times of India (2020). https://timesofindia.indiatimes.com/travel/destinations/with-humans-locked-indoors-animals-take-over-the-roads-in-india/as74851938.cms
2. Bagrecha, D., Rathoure, A.K.: Biodiversity assessment for asian highway 48 (near jaldapara national park) from bhutan to bangladesh passing through India: Case study. In: Current State and Future Impacts of Climate Change on Biodiversity, pp. 179–209. IGI Global (2020)
3. Sharma, S.U., Shah, D.J.: A practical animal detection and collision avoidance system using computer vision technique. IEEE Access **5**, 347–358 (2017)
4. Burghardt, T., Calic, J.: Analysing animal behaviour in wildlife videos using face detection and tracking. In: IEE Proceedings - Vision, Image and Signal Processing, vol. 153, no. 3, pp. 305–312 (2006)
5. Mammeri, A., Zhou, D., Boukerche, A., Almulla, M.: An efficient animal detection system for smart cars using cascaded classifiers. In: 2014 IEEE International Conference on Communications (ICC), pp. 1854–1859. IEEE (2014)
6. Ramanan, D., Forsyth, D.A., Barnard, K.: Building models of animals from video. IEEE Trans. Pattern Anal. Mach. Intell. **28**(8), 1319–1334 (2006)
7. Saxena, A., Gupta, D.K., Singh, S.: An animal detection and collision avoidance system using deep learning. In: Hura, G.S., Singh, A.K., Siong Hoe, L. (eds.) Advances in Communication and Computational Technology. LNEE, vol. 668, pp. 1069–1084. Springer, Singapore (2021). https://doi.org/10.1007/978-981-15-5341-7_81
8. He, K., Gkioxari, G., Dollár, P., Girshick, R.: Mask R-CNN. In: IEEE International Conference on Computer Vision (ICCV) 2017, pp. 2980–2988 (2017)
9. Lin, T.-Y., et al.: Microsoft COCO: common objects in context. In: Fleet, D., Pajdla, T., Schiele, B., Tuytelaars, T. (eds.) ECCV 2014. LNCS, vol. 8693, pp. 740–755. Springer, Cham (2014). https://doi.org/10.1007/978-3-319-10602-1_48
10. Ren, S., He, K., Girshick, R., Sun, J.: Faster R-CNN: towards real-time object detection with region proposal networks. IEEE Trans. Pattern Anal. Mach. Intell. **39**(6), 1137–1149 (2017)
11. Jiang, R.: Understanding-mask R-CNN. (2018). https://ronjian.github.io/blog/2018/05/16/Understand-Mask-RCNN. Accessed 30 May 2020
12. Aggarwal, P.: Detecting lanes with opencv and testing on Indian roads, Medium (2016)
13. Nascimento, J.C., Abrantes, A.J., Marques, J.S.: An algorithm for centroid-based tracking of moving objects. In: Proceedings of IEEE International Conference on Acoustics, Speech, and Signal Processing (ICASSP), vol. 6, pp. 3305–3308 (1999)

L2PF - Learning to Prune Faster

Manoj-Rohit Vemparala[1(✉)], Nael Fasfous[2], Alexander Frickenstein[1], Mhd Ali Moraly[1], Aquib Jamal[1], Lukas Frickenstein[1], Christian Unger[1], Naveen-Shankar Nagaraja[1], and Walter Stechele[2]

[1] BMW Autonomous Driving, Munich, Germany
{manoj-rohit.vemparala,alexander.frickenstein, mhd.moraly,aquib.jamal,lukas.frickenstein, christian.unger,naveen-shankar.nagaraja}@bmw.de
[2] Technical University of Munich, Munich, Germany
{nael.fasfous,walter.stechele}@tum.de

Abstract. Various applications in the field of autonomous driving are based on convolutional neural networks (CNNs), especially for processing camera data. The optimization of such CNNs is a major challenge in continuous development. Newly learned features must be brought into vehicles as quickly as possible, and as such, it is not feasible to spend redundant GPU hours during compression. In this context, we present Learning to Prune Faster which details a multi-task, try-and-learn method, discretely learning redundant filters of the CNN and a continuous action of how long the layers have to be fine-tuned. This allows us to significantly speed up the convergence process of learning how to find an embedded-friendly filter-wise pruned CNN. For ResNet20, we have achieved a compression ratio of 3.84× with minimal accuracy degradation. Compared to the state-of-the-art pruning method, we reduced the GPU hours by 1.71×.

1 Introduction

With the advent of scalable training hardware and frameworks, the trend towards training larger deep neural networks (DNNs) or ensembles of networks has become more prevalent than ever [8]. As a result, compression of DNNs has become an increasingly popular field of research in recent years. This is particularly the case for convolutional neural networks (CNNs), which have become the state-of-the-art solution for most computer vision problems, and often find applications in embedded scenarios, necessitating a reduction in their storage requirements and computational costs for inference. In the field of autonomous driving [4], embedded hardware [2,18] is highly constrained and short development cycles are key for being first to market.

Many standard techniques exist in literature to reduce the number of network parameters and the complexity of the computations involved in CNNs [8,11]. Due

M.-R. Vemparala, N. Fasfous, A. Frickenstein and M.A. Moraly—Indicates equal contributions.

S. K. Singh et al. (Eds.): CVIP 2020, CCIS 1378, pp. 249–261, 2021.
https://doi.org/10.1007/978-981-16-1103-2_22

to their inherent complexity and redundancy, CNNs can sustain many forms of structural and algorithmic approximation while still delivering adequate functional accuracy w.r.t. the given task, e.g. image classification. With the help of fine-tuning iterations, CNNs can recover the lost accuracy after a compression method has been applied, with negligible degradation.

Network compression can be viewed as a standard optimization problem. The search space composes of the possible combinations to compress neurons, kernels or layers. Exploring this design space is a difficult task when considering its size and the computational overhead required to sufficiently evaluate each potential configuration in it. Referring back to the healing effect of network fine-tuning after pruning, efficiently traversing this search space necessitates a fair balance between the number of epochs the fine-tuning is done for and the computational overhead required by those fine-tuning epochs. This ultimately leads to shorter product and time-to-market cycles and facilitates continuous development.

As with many other optimization problems, existing literature covers various forms of design space exploration w.r.t. pruning [9,12,20]. Automated pruning was an inevitable step in the evolution of this compression technique due to its complex nature. Automated pruning makes tools usable for researchers and product developers with little to no background in CNN optimization.

In this work, we build upon a learning-based pruning approach [12] to tackle the challenge of choosing the optimal number of fine-tuning epochs[1] for a potential pruning solution. The decisions of our RL-based pruning agent are based not only on the features embedded in the CNNs kernels, but also on the fine-tuning potential of the individual layers. This results in feature-conscious decisions and reduced overall time required by the pruning technique. The contributions of this paper can be summarized as follows:

- A multi-task learning approach involving a reinforcement learning agent, which learns a layer's features and adequate fine-tuning time concurrently.
- Formalizing the design space exploration problem w.r.t. pruning effectiveness and time-effort.
- A study on the sequence of layer-wise pruning of a convolutional neural network.

2 Related Work

In the following sections, we classify works which use pruning techniques into heuristic-based, in-train and learning-based strategies.

Heuristic-Based Pruning: Heuristic-based compression techniques consider static or pseudo-static rules that define the compression strategy, when pruning an underlying CNN. The pruning method proposed by [6] utilizes the magnitude of weights, where values below a threshold identify expendable connections. Such pruning of individual weights, as presented in [6], leads to inefficient

[1] An epoch describes a complete cycle of a data set, *i.e.* training data set.

memory accesses, rendering irregular pruning techniques impractical for most general purpose computing platforms. Regularity in pruning is a key factor in accelerator-aware optimization. Frickenstein et al. [5] identifies redundant kernels in the weight matrix based on magnitude based heuristic. He et al. [10] prune redundant filters based on the geometric median heuristic of the filters. In [11], He et al. introduce an iterative two-step algorithm to effectively prune layers in a given CNN. First, redundant feature maps are selected by LASSO regression followed by minimizing the output errors of the remaining feature maps by solving least squared minimization.

In-Train Pruning: Integrating the pruning process into the training phase of CNNs is characterized as in-train pruning. The auto-encoder-based low-rank filter-sharing technique (ALF) proposed by Frickenstein et al. [3] utilizes sparse auto-encoders that extract the most salient features of convolutional layers, pruning redundant filters. Zhang et al. [22] propose ADAM-ADMM, a unified, systematic framework of structured weight pruning of DNNs, that can be employed to induce different types of structured sparsity based on ADMM.

Learning-Based Pruning: Defining the pruning process as an optimization problem and exposing it to an RL-agent has been done in a variety of works [9,12]. He et al. [9] demonstrate a channel pruning framework leveraging a Deep Deterministic Policy Gradient (DDPG) agent. Their framework first learns the sparsity ratio to prune a layer, while actual channel selection is performed using $\ell 1$ criteria. The appealing higher compression ratio, better preservation of accuracy as well as faster, coarse and learnable exploration of the design space with few GPU hours, highlight the strong points of the AMC framework. However, this leaves room for improvement in search-awareness, as AMC is unaware of the exact features it is pruning. Huang et al. [12] demonstrated a 'try-and-learn' RL-based filter-pruning method to learn both sparsity ratio and the exact position of redundant filters, but it leaves out the number of fine-tuning epochs as a hyper-parameter. Here, the optimal value can change, depending on the model's architecture and the data set at hand. We extend the work of Huang et al. [12] incorporating GPU hour awareness by proposing an iterative method with a learned minimum number of iterations for fine-tuning, hyper-parameter free method.

3 Method

In this chapter, we propose a multi-task learning approach, namely *Leaning to Prune Faster* (L2PF) involving a RL-agent, which learns a layer's features and adequate fine-tuning time concurrently. In this regard, the pruning problem in the context of a RL framework is formulated in Sect. 3.1. The environment and state space is defined in Sect. 3.2. We discuss the discrete and continuous action spaces in Sect. 3.3, and the reward formulation in Sect. 3.4. Lastly, the agent's objective function is formulated in Sect. 3.5.

3.1 Problem Formulation

The structured filter-pruning task within an RL framework can be expressed as a 'try-and-learn' problem, similar to the work from Huang et al. [12]. We aim to find the best combination of filters that achieve the highest compression ratio (CR) while incurring a minimum loss of accuracy (Acc) and requiring a minimum number of fine-tuning epochs during the exploration episodes. Figure 1 demonstrates the interplay between the proposed pruning agent and CNN environment. The proposed method is able to learn three aspects: First, the minimum number of epochs required to explore each pruning strategy. Second, the degree of sparsity of each layer in the model. Third, the exact position of the least important filters to be pruned.

Formally, let B be a fully-trained model with L layers and the input of the ℓth convolutional layer has a shape $[c^\ell \times w^\ell \times h^\ell]$, where c^ℓ, h^ℓ and w^ℓ represents number of input channels, height and width. The ℓth layer is convolved with the weight tensor $\mathbf{W}^\ell$, *i.e.* 2D convolutional layer's trainable parameters, with shape $\left[N^\ell \times c^\ell \times k^\ell \times k^\ell\right]$, where k^ℓ represents the kernel size and N^ℓ is number of filters. After pruning n^ℓ filters, the weight tensor is of shape $\left[(N^\ell - n^\ell) \times c^\ell \times k^\ell \times k^\ell\right]$. To enable a direct comparison with the work of He et al. [9], the layer compression ratio is defined as $\frac{c^\ell - n^{\ell-1}}{c^\ell}$. Additionally, we define model compression ratio to be the total number of weights divided by the number of non-zero weights.

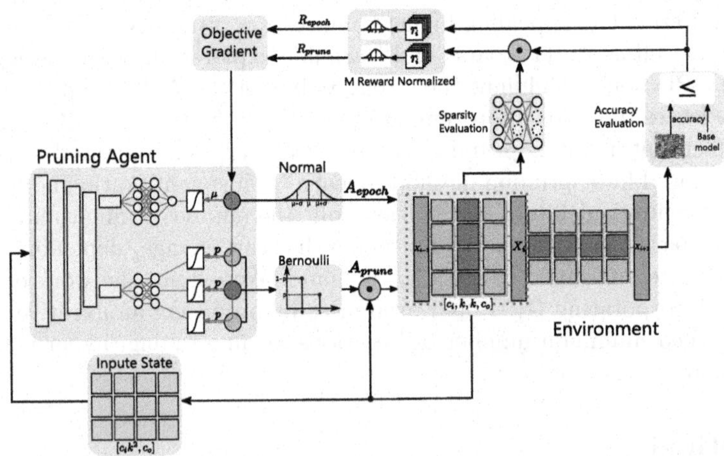

Fig. 1. Agent receives rewards and weights as input state, whereas environment receives both prune and epoch actions. In each prune episode, M = 5 Monte-Carlo set of actions are sampled ($\mathbf{A}_{\text{prune}}$ and A_{retrain}). The corresponding M rewards (R_{prune} and R_{retrain}) are normalized to zero mean and unit variance [12].

3.2 Environment

The environment is the pre-trained CNN model B to be pruned. The `state space` is the fully trained weight tensor $\mathbf{W}^{\ell}$ of the layer to be pruned, which is used as an input for the agent, similar to Huang et al. [12]. For each layer (or residual block), a new agent is trained from scratch. The environment receives two actions from the agent: pruning action $\mathbf{A}_{\text{prune}}$ and fine-tuning epoch action A_{retrain}. Subsequently, it generates a reward $R = R_{\text{prune}} + R_{\text{retrain}}$. For each filter there is a binary mask $\mathbf{m}_i^{\ell} \in \{0,1\}^{c^{\ell} \times k^{\ell} \times k^{\ell}}$. Pruning the ith filter $\mathbf{W}_i^{\ell}$ in layer ℓ is performed by element-wise multiplication between the filter $\mathbf{W}_i^{\ell}$ and its corresponding mask $\mathbf{m}_i^{\ell}$. When pruning $\mathbf{W}_i^{\ell}$, the ith kernel of all filters in the $(\ell+1)^{th}$ layer are also pruned. At each pruning step, masks are updated according to $\mathbf{A}_{\text{prune}}$ and the environment is fine-tuned for a few epochs e_{retrain}.

3.3 Distinct Action Space for Pruning and Epoch-Learning

The action space of the proposed RL-framework is split into two distinct spaces to satisfy the discrete and continuous requirements of actions for pruning and epoch learning respectively.

Discrete Pruning Action Space: The discrete pruning action space is the combination of all possible prune actions $\mathbf{A}_{\text{prune}}$. It is clear that action space dimension grows exponentially as $\mathcal{O}(2^N)$, where N is the number of filters in a layer. Discrete actions are sampled from N independent stochastic Bernoulli units [19]. Each unit has one learnable parameter p that represents the probability of keeping the filter.

Continuous Epoch-Learning Action Space: The continuous epoch-learning is used to determine the number of fine-tuning epochs e_{retrain}. Like the discrete action, the continuous action A_{retrain} must also be sampled from some distribution. Practically, e_{retrain} takes values within a bounded range $\in \mathbb{Q}^{+}$. A continuous action A_{retrain} is sampled from a Normal distribution which has two learn-able parameters μ and σ. Since e_{retrain} is bounded while Normal distribution has unbounded support, it must be truncated. Truncating a Normal distribution might cause the estimated policy to get biased into the direction of the truncation boundary where the reward peaks (boundary effect) [1]. To circumvent the boundary effect, we employ the approach from Chou et al. [1]. The sampled action A_{retrain} is sent to the environment with no alteration. To calculate e_{retrain}, the action value is truncated within $[0,1]$. However, for gradient calculations, non-truncated action values are used.

3.4 Multi-objective Reward Function

The quality of agent action is conveyed back to the agent by the reward signal, R_{prune} and R_{retrain} for $\boldsymbol{A}_{prune}$ and $A_{retrain}$ respectively.

Prune Reward: The prune reward R_{prune} is a measure for sparsity level and model accuracy acc_{pruned}. It promotes actions that remove filters with minimum accuracy loss of the pruned model w.r.t. the validation set. Following the work of Huang et al. [12], we define the prune reward as a product of two terms, *i.e.* acc_{term} and eff_{term}, as stated in Eq. 1.

$$R_{\text{prune}}\left(\mathbf{A}^{\ell}_{\text{prune}}, acc_{\text{pruned}}\right) = acc_{\text{term}} \cdot eff_{\text{term}} \tag{1}$$

Accuracy Term: Similar to Huang et al. [12], acc_{term} is defined in Eq. 2. The bound b is a hyper-parameter introduced in the reward function to allow control over the trade-off between model compression and tolerable accuracy drop. When the accuracy drop is greater than b, acc_{term} is negative, otherwise it lies in the range $[0, 1]$ respectively 0 and 100%.

$$acc_{\text{term}} = \frac{b - \max\left[0, acc_{\text{base}} - acc_{\text{pruned}}\right]}{b} \tag{2}$$

Efficiency Term: To prevent the agent from changing the model depth, the efficiency term eff_{term} proposed by Huang et al. [12] is extended as shown in Eq. 3. If the prune action is aggressive, the accuracy drop will be less than the bound b resulting in a negative reward. If layer sparsity ratio is low, eff_{term} will drive reward to zero.

$$eff_{\text{term}} = \begin{cases} \log \dfrac{N}{(N-n)} & \text{if } \ (N-n) \leq N \\ -1 & \text{if } \ (N-n) = 0 \end{cases} \tag{3}$$

Fine-Tuning Epoch Reward: The fine-tuning epoch reward R_{retrain} is responsible for promoting a lower number of fine-tuning epochs. The reward is expressed in Eq. 4. An action is considered *good* when $|A_{\text{retrain}}|$ is low without causing an intolerable accuracy drop. If the environment incurs no accuracy loss then $R_{\text{retrain}} = 0$, when loss is incurred then it will be a negative value scaled by the absolute value of A_{retrain}.

$$R_{\text{retrain}}\left(A_{\text{retrain}}, acc_{\text{pruned}}\right) = |A_{\text{retrain}}| \times \left(acc_{\text{pruned}} - acc_{\text{base}}\right) \tag{4}$$

In each prune episode, M Monte-Carlo set of actions are sampled again resulting in M corresponding rewards R_{prune} and R_{retrain}. The reward values are normalized to zero mean and unit variance for both set of rewards [7,14].

3.5 Agent Design

The agent is a non-linear stochastic functional approximator parameterized by θ. It is composed of four convolutional layers, two classifiers each with two feed-forward layers [12], and two types of stochastic output units, *i.e.* Bernoulli and Normal. The agent parameters are $\theta = \{\mathbf{w}, \mu, \mathbf{P}\}$, where parameters $\mathbf{w}$ are the agent weights, μ is a learnable parameter to sample the fine-tuning action A_{retrain}, and $\mathbf{P}$ is the set of probabilities for Bernoulli units. The agent outputs two actions: discrete action $\mathbf{A}_{\text{prune}}$ for pruning, and continuous action A_{retrain} for fine-tuning epochs.

The `pruning action` $\mathbf{A}_{\text{prune}}$ is a set $\{a_1^\ell, a_2^\ell, ..., a_{N^l}^\ell\}$, where $a_i^\ell \in \{0,1\}$ is equivalent to $\{prune, keep\}$ and N^ℓ is the number of filters in the ℓth layer [12]. Using this scheme, the agent is able to explore both sparsity ratio and to select the exact position of filters to prune.

The `fine-tuning action` A_{retrain} is a continuous action sampled from a normal distribution with two parameters - μ, σ. The mean μ is a learnable parameter, while σ is chosen to be non-learnable and set to be proportional to $|R_{\text{retrain}}|$ [17,19]. The value of σ controls how far a sample can be from the mean. When reward signal R_{retrain} is low indicating bad actions, then σ takes higher value which allows the agent to explore actions further away from μ. Actions $A_{\text{retrain}} \notin [0,1]$ are considered *bad* and give negative reward. The environment fine-tunes for the number of epochs given in Eq. 5, where β is an upper limit for e_{retrain}.

$$e_{\text{retrain}} = \min[\max[0, A_{\text{retrain}}], 1] \times \beta \tag{5}$$

We leverage the stochastic policy gradient (SPG) method to find an optimal policy π^*. SPG is guaranteed to converge at least to a local optimum without requiring the state space distribution [16]. Our objective function $J(\theta)$ is the expected sum of all rewards over one episode. The objective gradient w.r.t. the policy parameters is given in Eq. 6. Both terms in Eq. 6 can be solved approximately using the policy gradient theorem. Specifically, we implement a variant of SPG called REINFORCE [12,19]. The agent parameters θ are updated with gradient ascent so that actions with higher rewards are more probable to be sampled [19].

$$\nabla_\theta J(\theta) = \nabla_\theta \mathbb{E}\left[r_{\text{prune}}\right] + \nabla_\theta \mathbb{E}\left[r_{\text{retrain}}\right] \tag{6}$$

The first term in Eq. 6 has the Bernoulli policy $\pi_B\left(\mathbf{A}_{\text{prune}}|\mathbf{W}^\ell, \mathbf{P}, \mathbf{w}\right)$, while the second has the Normal policy $\pi_N\left(\mathbf{A}_{\text{retrain}}|\mathbf{W}^\ell, \mu, \mathbf{w}\right)$, where $\mathbf{W}^\ell$ are weights for layer to prune. Finding a closed-form solution for the expectation is not feasible, so it is approximated using M samples of a Monte-Carlo gradient estimator with score function [14,16]. The gradient of our objective function is given by Eq. 7.

$$\nabla_\theta J(\theta) \approx \sum_{j=1}^{M}\left[(R_{\text{prune}})_j \cdot \sum_{i=1}^{n} \frac{a_{ij} - p_{ij}}{p_{ij}(1-p_{ij})} \cdot \frac{\partial p_{ij}}{\partial \mathbf{w}} + (R_{\text{retrain}})_j \cdot \frac{a_j - \mu_j}{\sigma_j^2} \cdot \frac{\partial \mu_j}{\partial \mathbf{w}}\right] \tag{7}$$

4 Experimental Results

Our experiments are conducted on the CIFAR-10 [13] data set. One-time random splitting of the 50k images into 45k training and 5k evaluation is performed.

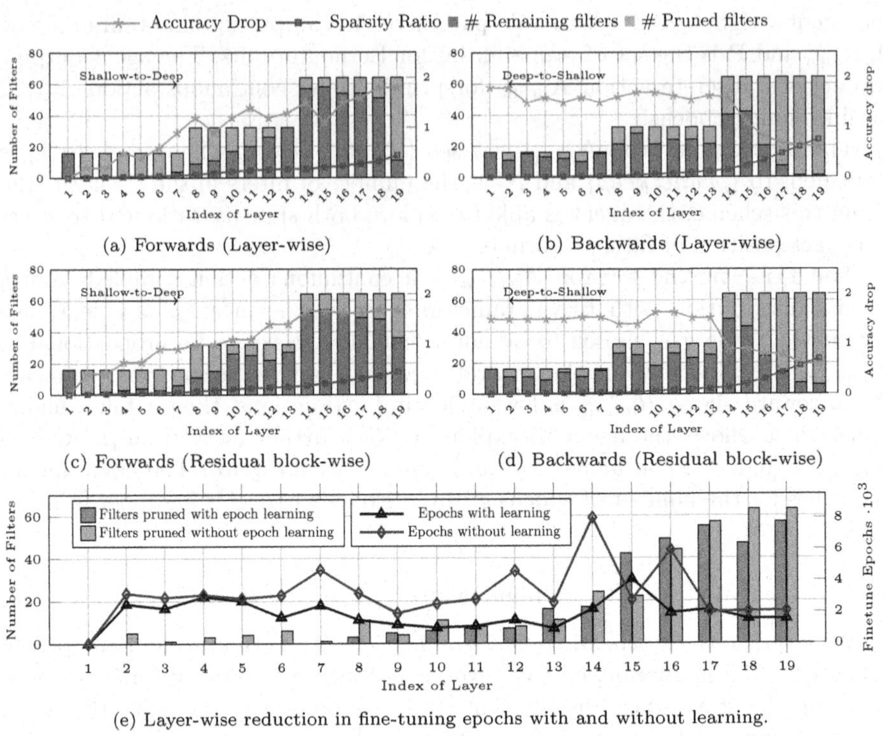

(a) Forwards (Layer-wise)

(b) Backwards (Layer-wise)

(c) Forwards (Residual block-wise)

(d) Backwards (Residual block-wise)

(e) Layer-wise reduction in fine-tuning epochs with and without learning.

Fig. 2. Exploration of filter pruning order and epoch-learning effect.

Agent reward is evaluated on 5k images. To ensure that our pruning method generalizes, the 10k images in the test data set are held separate and only used after the agent learns to prune a layer, to report actual model accuracy. No training or reward evaluation is performed using the test data set. As a baseline, ResNet-20 is trained from scratch as described in [8] until convergence with validation accuracy 92.0%, and test accuracy of 90.8%. After each pruning episode, the environment is retrained for a few epochs (8 w/o epochs learning) using mini-batch momentum SGD [15] with learning rate of 0.001, gamma 0.5, step size of 1900, batch size of 128, and $l2$ regularization. After learning to prune a layer, the model is fine-tuned for 150 epochs before moving to the next layer. The agent is also trained using mini-batch momentum SGD with fixed learning rate of 0.005 and batch size equal to the number of Monte-Carlo samples $M = 5$.

4.1 Design Space Exploration

Exploration of Efficient Pruning Order: We investigate four different strategies based on the pruning order and the agent's capability to prune layers simultaneously (layerwise or blockwise). We exclude the first convolutional layer since pruning it offers insignificant compression benefits, while damaging the

Table 1. Evaluating various configurations for L2PF to analyze the influence of exploration granularity, pruning order, accuracy bound w.r.t. prediction accuracy and compression ratio.

Configuration	Pruning Order	Bound [%]	Learnable Epochs	Acc [%]	CR [×]
ResNet-20 [8]	–	–	–	90.8	1.00
L2PF (Block-wise)	Forwards	2.0	✗	89.9 (−0.9)	1.84
L2PF (Layer-wise)	Forwards	2.0	✗	89.6 (−1.2)	1.79
L2PF (Block-wise)	Backwards	2.0	✗	89.5 (−1.3)	3.38
L2PF (**Layer-wise**)	**Backwards**	2.0	✗	**89.9** (−0.9)	**3.90**
L2PF (Layer-wise)	Backwards	1.0	✗	90.2 (−0.6)	2.52
L2PF (**Layer-wise**)	**Backwards**	**2.0**	✗	**89.9** (−0.9)	**3.90**
L2PF (Layer-wise)	Backwards	3.0	✗	89.2 (−1.0)	4.53
L2PF (Layer-wise)	Backwards	4.0	✗	88.5 (−2.3)	7.23
L2PF (Layer-wise)	Backwards	2.0	✗	89.9 (−0.9)	3.90
L2PF (Layer-wise)	**Backwards**	**2.0**	✓	**89.9** (−0.9)	**3.84**

learning ability of the model. When pruning a full residual block, we preserve the element-wise summation by zero-padding the output channels of the second layer in a residual block to restore the original number of output channels, such that the order of pruned channels is preserved. Figure 2 shows results of pruning ResNet-20 with loss bound b of 2%. In Fig. 2a, we perform layer-wise pruning following the forward pruning order (`conv2_1_1` → `conv4_3_2`). The agent starts pruning initial layers aggressively and struggles to find redundant filters in the deep layers (indicated by large blue bars). In Fig. 2b, we perform a similar layer wise pruning analysis for the backward pruning order (`conv2_1_1` ← `conv4_3_2`). From Table 1, we observe that the backward pruning order results in higher CR with lower accuracy degradation (0.9%). In Fig. 2c and d, we perform block wise pruning allowing the agent to prune the entire residual block simultaneously. Similar to layer-wise pruning, we prune the residual blocks both in forward and backward orders. Lower compression ratio is observed when compared to layer-wise pruning, see also Table 1. Thus, we prune layer-wise in backward order as it results in lower accuracy degradation and high CR for the subsequent experiments.

Effect of Accuracy Bound on Compression Ratio: In Table 1, we also evaluate the impact of the prediction accuracy and compression ratio by varying the agent's loss bound b. As we increase b, we obtain higher CR with lower prediction accuracy after fine-tuning. We choose b as 2% to maintain a trade-off between accuracy degradation and CR.

Effect of Accuracy and Pruning Rate on Exploration Time: Previous experiments were conducted with fine-tuning epochs set manually to 8 at each exploration step. We allow the agent to decide the amount of fine-tuning time required to evaluate the pruning strategy based on the retrain epoch reward presented in Eq. 4. Figure 2e shows a comparison of number of fine-tuning epochs required to decide the pruning strategy for each layer. Pruning with epochs learning achieves 1.71× speedup in search time with a slight reduction in compression ratio, see Table 1.

4.2 Class Activation Maps

The discrete action space proposed by Huang et al. [12] and applied in L2PF (described in Sect. 3.3) allows the integration of class activation mapping (CAM) [23] into the design process. CAM allows the visualization of regions of interest (RoI) in an input image to identify the corresponding prediction label. Regions with red color denote the part with higher interest for CNN model and blue denotes regions with less importance w.r.t. the target label. Table 2 shows three exemplary CAMs for the learned features of vanilla ResNet-20 and the influence of L2PF pruning (backwards) on the learned features and thus the RoIs. The progression of discriminative regions of classes can be compared across pruning steps.

Table 2. CAM visualization for three examples images from the validation dataset. Each column shows the CAM output after pruning, using backwards pruning order before model fine-tuning.

Input image	ResNet-20 unpruned	Learning to Prune Faster (Backwards) conv4_3_2 →	conv3_3_2 →	conv2_3_2 →	conv2_1_2
raw	*deer*(0.53)	*car*(0.99) →	*car*(0.99) →	*car*(0.99) →	*car*(0.88)
raw	*ship*(0.99)	*ship*(0.51) →	*ship*(0.98) →	*ship*(0.81) →	*ship*(0.99)
raw	*truck*(0.99)	*truck*(0.98) →	*truck*(0.77) →	*truck*(0.62) →	*truck*(0.67)

In the first row, the vanilla ResNet-20 predicts the wrong class, *i.e. deer*. After pruning layer conv3_3_2, the RoI shifts towards the *trunk* of the *car* indicating the correct class. In the second row, the vanilla ResNet-20 predicts the *ship* class. The agent tries to retain the prediction across different stages of pruning with high confidence. In the third row, the vanilla ResNet-20 predicts the *truck* class. Accordingly, the pruned model at different stages also predict a *truck*. However, we can observe that the RoI becomes narrower indicating that the pruned model requires only few concentrated regions due to lower model capacity. We consider potential directions of our future work as follows: (1) Considering the CAM output as a state embedding instead of a weight matrix, making the pruning more feature-aware and interpretable. This would not possible with threshold based approaches like AMC [9], (2) Understanding, the impact of feature-aware pruning on model robustness [21].

4.3 Comparison with the State-of-the-Art

In this section, we compare the proposed L2PF with other RL-based state-of-the-art filter pruning works proposed in literature. In Fig. 3, we compare our pruning configuration using layer-wise CR and final prediction accuracy with AMC [9], L2P [12], ALF [3]. We reimplemented L2P using forward pruning order with an accuracy bound b=2% to obtain pruning results for ResNet-20. Compared to L2P, we obtain 0.3% better prediction accuracy, 2.11× higher CR and 1.71× less fine-tune epochs. ALF and AMC do not require fine-tuning during the pruning process. Compared to AMC's pruning implementation for Plain-20, we obtain 2.08× higher CR with 0.3% lower prediction accuracy. Compared to ALF, we achieve 0.5% better accuracy with comparable CR.

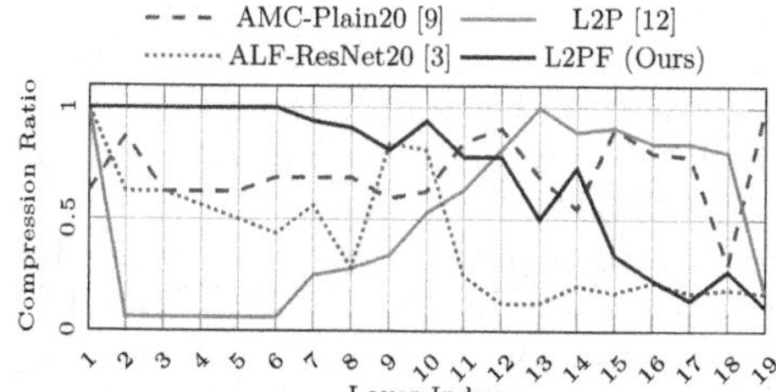

Configuration	Pruning Type	Acc [%]	CR [×]	Fine-tune [epochs]
ResNet-20 [8]	-	90.8	1.00	-
AMC-Plain20 [9]	RL-agent	90.2	1.84	-
ALF [8]	In-train	89.4	3.99	-
L2P [12]	RL-agent	89.6	1.79	60.3K
L2PF (Ours)	**RL-agent**	**89.9**	**3.84**	**35.2K**

Fig. 3. Comparing L2PF pruning statistics on ResNet-20 with State-of-the-Art.

5 Conclusion

In this work, we demonstrated an RL-based filter-wise pruning method which is both feature and time-aware. Our multi-task approach achieved high compression ratios, while minimizing the required GPU-hours and the accuracy degradation. The analysis on the sequence of layer-wise pruning led to the conclusion that backward (deep-to-shallow) pruning can surpass the existing state-of-the-art compression ratios, with minimal degradation in task accuracy. Finally, we visually analyzed the effect of our pruning technique with the help of class activation maps to build a better understanding of our agent's pruning decisions. GPU-hours for CNN compression can have many negative consequences on development cycles, profitability and fast exploration. The GPU-hour-aware approach presented can help mitigate this impediment and achieve a competitive advantage in active research fields such as autonomous driving.

References

1. Chou, P., Maturana, D., Scherer, S.: Improving stochastic policy gradients in continuous control with deep reinforcement learning using the beta distribution. In: ICML (2017)
2. Fasfous, N., Vemparala, M.R., Frickenstein, A., Stechele, W.: OrthrusPE: runtime reconfigurable processing elements for binary neural networks. In: DATE, Grenoble, France (2020)
3. Frickenstein, A., et al.: ALF: Autoencoder-based low-rank filter-sharing for efficient convolutional neural networks. In: ICML (2020)
4. Frickenstein, A., et al.: Binary DAD-Net: binarized driveable area detection network for autonomous driving. In: ICRA (2020)
5. Frickenstein, A., Vemparala, M.R., Unger, C., Ayar, F., Stechele, W.: DSC: dense-sparse convolution for vectorized inference of convolutional neural networks. In: CVPR-W (2019)
6. Han, S., Pool, J., Tran, J., Dally, W.: Learning both weights and connections for efficient neural network. In: NIPS (2015)
7. Hasselt, H.V., Guez, A., Hessel, M., Mnih, V., Silver, D.: Learning values across many orders of magnitude. In: NeurIPS (2016)
8. He, K., Zhang, X., Ren, S., Sun, J.: Deep residual learning for image recognition. In: CVPR (2016)
9. He, Y., Lin, J., Liu, Z., Wang, H., Li, L.-J., Han, S.: AMC: AutoML for model compression and acceleration on mobile devices. In: Ferrari, V., Hebert, M., Sminchisescu, C., Weiss, Y. (eds.) ECCV 2018. LNCS, vol. 11211, pp. 815–832. Springer, Cham (2018). https://doi.org/10.1007/978-3-030-01234-2_48
10. He, Y., Liu, P., Wang, Z., Hu, Z., Yang, Y.: Filter pruning via geometric median for deep convolutional neural networks acceleration. In: Proceedings of the IEEE Conference on Computer Vision and Pattern Recognition (CVPR) (2019)
11. He, Y., Zhang, X., Sun, J.: Channel pruning for accelerating very deep neural networks. In: ICCV (2017)
12. Huang, Q., Zhou, S.K., You, S., Neumann, U.: Learning to prune filters in convolutional neural networks. In: WACV (2018)
13. Krizhevsky, A., Nair, V., Hinton, G.: Cifar-10 (Canadian institute for advanced research). http://www.cs.toronto.edu/~kriz/cifar.html
14. Mohamed, S., Rosca, M., Figurnov, M., Mnih, A.: Monte Carlo gradient estimation in machine learning. CoRR abs/1906.10652 (2019)
15. Ning, Q.: On the momentum term in gradient descent learning algorithms. Neural Netw. **12**(1), 145–151 (1999)
16. Sutton, R.S., Barto, A.-G.: Reinforcement Learning: An Introduction. Adaptive Computation and Machine Learning Series. MIT Press, Cambridge (2018)

17. Sutton, R., McAllester, D., Singh, S., Mansour, Y.: Policy gradient methods for reinforcement learning with function approximation. In: NIPS (1999)
18. Vemparala, M.R., Frickenstein, A., Stechele, W.: An efficient FPGA accelerator design for optimized CNNs using OpenCL. In: Schoeberl, M., Hochberger, C., Uhrig, S., Brehm, J., Pionteck, T. (eds.) ARCS 2019. LNCS, vol. 11479, pp. 236–249. Springer, Cham (2019). https://doi.org/10.1007/978-3-030-18656-2_18
19. Williams, R.J.: Simple statistical gradient-following algorithms for connectionist reinforcement learning. Mach. Learn. **8**(3–4), 229–256 (1992). https://doi.org/10.1007/BF00992696
20. Yang, T.-J., et al.: NetAdapt: platform-aware neural network adaptation for mobile applications. In: Ferrari, V., Hebert, M., Sminchisescu, C., Weiss, Y. (eds.) ECCV 2018. LNCS, vol. 11214, pp. 289–304. Springer, Cham (2018). https://doi.org/10.1007/978-3-030-01249-6_18
21. Ye, S., et al.: Adversarial robustness vs. model compression, or both? In: ICCV (2019)
22. Zhang, T., et al.: ADAM-ADMM: a unified, systematic framework of structured weight pruning for DNNs. CoRR abs/1807.11091 (2018)
23. Zhou, B., Khosla, A., Lapedriza, A., Oliva, A., Torralba, A.: Learning deep features for discriminative localization (2015)

Efficient Ensemble Sparse Convolutional Neural Networks with Dynamic Batch Size

Shen Zheng, Liwei Wang, and Gaurav Gupta(✉)

College of Science and Technology, Wenzhou-Kean University, Wenzhou, China
{zhengsh,wangli,ggupta}@kean.edu

Abstract. In this paper, an efficient ensemble sparse Convolutional Neural Networks (CNNs) with dynamic batch size is proposed. We addressed two issues at the heart of deep learning—speed and accuracy. Firstly, we presented ensemble CNNs with weighted average stacking which significantly increases the testing accuracy. Secondly, we combine network pruning and Winograd-ReLU convolution to accelerate computational speed. Motivated by electron movement in electrical fields, we finally propose a novel, dynamic batch size algorithm. We repeatedly increase the learning rate and the momentum coefficient until validation accuracy falls, while scaling the batch size. With no data augmentation and little hyperparameter tuning, our method speeds up models on FASHION-MINST, CIFAR-10, and CIFAR-100 to 1.55x, 2.86x, and 4.15x with a testing accuracy improvement of 2.66%, 1.37%, and 4.48%, respectively. We also visually demonstrate that our approach retains the most distinct image classification features during exhaustive pruning.

1 Introduction

In the past few decades, Convolutional Neural Networks (CNN) have achieved state-of-art results on a variety of machine learning applications such as visual recognition, speech recognition, and natural language processing. LeCun et al. [1] proposed a simple CNN model with only two convolutional neural networks and three fully-connected layers. Later, Krizhevsky et al. [2] introduced AlexNet, being the first one to adopt ReLU as the activation function and to use drop-out technique to reduce overfitting. After that, Simonyan et al. [3] designed VGG, which improves AlexNet by decreasing kernel filter sizes to 3×3. Most recently, He et al. [4] developed ResNet, which popularized connections skipping to design deeper CNN without compromising its generalization ability.

Despite excellent classification accuracy, CNN is slow for computation. In deep learning, two accessible research directions have been explored to address this problem. One is to combine network pruning and convolutional accelerator for matrix compression and computations. The other is to investigate various activation functions. Details of them are in Sect. 2. Unfortunately, prior efforts in CNN fails to consider ensemble methods, which leads to diminishing margin return on

S. K. Singh et al. (Eds.): CVIP 2020, CCIS 1378, pp. 262–277, 2021.
https://doi.org/10.1007/978-981-16-1103-2_23

the testing accuracy. Besides, previous studies tend to use small, fixed batch size. However, our analysis show that small batch size result in noisy gradient descent steps and low optimal learning rates. Therefore, the convergence rate is slow. To overcome these challenges, we design an efficient stacked convolutional neural network structure. First, we use a weighted average stacking algorithm with three base CNNs. Next, we conduct network pruning to exploit model sparsity. Simultaneously, we perform the Winograd convolution with ReLU as the activation function. To address the accuracy loss from sparsity and to further increase computational speed, we finally propose a novel framework with dynamic batch size.

2 Related Work

2.1 Convolutional Accelerator

Various convolution algorithms have been introduced to reduce arithmetic complexity and thus to enhance the computational speed. Mathieu et al. [5] has incorporated Fast Fourier Transform convolution algorithms to accelerate the computation process of convolution neural network. However, it fails to work well with small filters. To address this issue, Lavin & Gray [6] have applied Winograd convolution [7], which has fast computation on minimal complexity convolution over small filters and batch sizes. Ioffe & Szegedy [8] presented a novel mechanism for dramatically accelerating the training of deep networks which is based on the premise that covariate shift, which is known to complicate the training of machine learning systems, applies to sub-networks and layers, and removing it from internal activations of the network may aid in training. Liu & Liang [9] further speeds up Winograd Convolution by rearranging the filter layout and by implementing dynamic programming algorithms to balance the computation among different processing components. However, Winograd Convolution is inconsistent with network pruning [8], which removes weak predictors to lower complexity by the reduction of overfitting. To address this problem, Liu & Turakhia [10] uses pruning in the first epoch to create sparse data, with subsequent retraining to help retain accuracy. Sheng et al. [11]) demonstrates that introducing Winograd layer in place of a standard convolution layer could achieve minimal accuracy loss with high sparsity. Liu et al. [12] provides a novel approach that moves ReLU activation into the Winograd domain to exploit weight sparsity and to reduce the computational complexity.

2.2 Activation Function

Activation Function helps the network learn complex patterns in the data. An activation function must be computationally efficient because it is calculated across thousands or even millions of neurons for each data sample. The need for speed has led to the development of new activation functions. Nair and Hinton [13] introduced rectified linear units (ReLU), a non-linear activation function that prevents gradients from being progressively small by having a gradient slope of 1. ReLU is also computationally efficient. However, ReLU can trigger the dying neuron problem, where small inputs value mute the backpropagation. Recent researches have therefore introduced variants of ReLU such as Leaky ReLU [14] and Parametric ReLU [15]. They address the dying neurons by having a slight positive slope in the negative zones but do not demonstrate a robust noise control. Clevert et al. [16] later propose exponential linear unit (ELU). ELU uses mean shifts toward zero to reduce bias and variance in the forward propagation, leading to faster learning and generalization performance.

2.3 Batch Size

Early works in neural networks have shown that larger batch size results in degradation of the model accuracy. Krizhevsky [17] demonstrates that large batch size has resulted in "Generalization Gap", namely worse generalization abilities. Keskar et al. [18] shows that this is because large batch methods tend to converge to sharp minima. In contrast, Hoffer et al. [19] provide numerical evidence at the initial high learning rate region to demonstrate that "Generalization Gap" arise from the insufficient number of updates. Hoffer [19] is supported by Balles et al. [20] and McCandlish et al. [21], who both show that increasing batch size to reduce the gradient variance can also remove the 'Generalization Gap' increasing batch size. Later, Smith and Le [22] offers a Bayesian perspective on the generalization behaviour of neural nets. Smith et al. [22] further his claim by maintaining that one can encounter the accuracy loss of large batch methods with no additional updates by increasing the learning rate and the momentum coefficient while scaling the batch size. However, a large learning rate after scaling can result in divergence behaviour when the loss surface around the starting points is not smooth. To address this problem, Goyal et al. [23] propose a procedure for learning rate warmup, which ensures model stability at the initial phases.

3 Proposed Method

3.1 Stacking

Stacking is an ensemble learning technique that combines the predictions of multiple models. The reason we use stacking is that stacking combines the advantages of various heterogeneous models. By exploiting the predictive power of different models, stacking usually yields better accuracy than any single one of the trained models. Here we propose a weighted average stacking model which train the base models on the entire training set and then takes the best-weighted average of them to form an ensemble CNN. Following is the architecture for our weighted average stacking neural networks, where W1, W2 and W3 are weights for CNN1, CNN2 and CNN3, respectively.

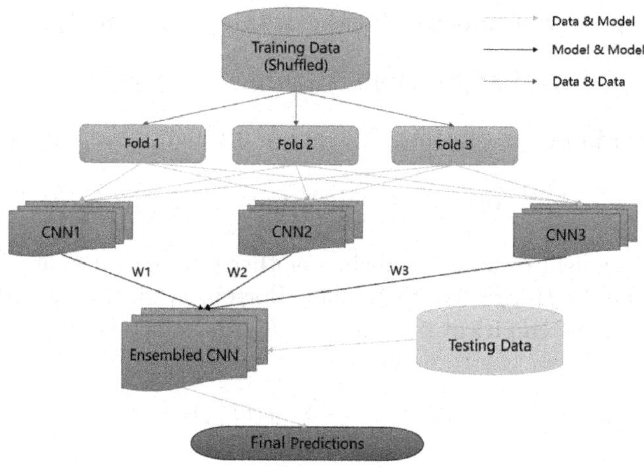

Fig. 1. Architecture for our weighted average stacking neural networks

3.2 Winograd-ReLU CNN

In deep learning, pruning is a model compression and acceleration technique to reduce the dimensions of the neural network by removing unnecessary weights connections. Lavin and Gray [6] has implemented the Winograd Minimal Filtering Algorithm [7].

$$Y = A^T\left[\left(GgG^T\right) \odot \left(B^T dB\right)\right] A \tag{1}$$

where G, B^T, A^T are filter, data and inverse transform, respectively, d, g represent input tile and filter, and Y represents output tile. However, Liu et al.'s [11]) study show that Winograd minimal filtering algorithm will occupy the sparse space and eliminate the gain from pruning. Liu et al. [11] then introduce the Winograd-ReLU CNN, which move ReLU into the Winograd Domain to eliminate the spatial-domain kernel. We will be implementing their framework, which obeys the following pruning schedule for creating model sparsity.

$$Y = A^T\left[\left[\text{Prune}\left(\text{Gg}G^\top\right)\right] \odot \left[\text{ReLU}\left(\text{B}^\top\text{dB}\right)\right]\right] \text{A} \tag{2}$$

Where ReLU is an activation function and Prune means network pruning action.

3.3 Strategies for Better Convergence

Firstly, we examine the convergence performance of stochastic gradient descent. Suppose θ is a deterministic variable and $f(\theta)$ is the corresponding loss function. To ensure convergence for gradient descent algorithms, we must satisfy the condition that the gradient $\nabla_\theta f(\theta)$ is 'stable':

$$\nabla_\theta f(\theta) \approx \nabla_\theta f(\theta + \Delta\theta), \text{ where } \|\Delta\theta\| < \epsilon \cong 0 \tag{3}$$

From the perspective of Lipschitz Continuous Gradient hypothesis:

$$\|\nabla_\theta f(\theta + \Delta\theta) - \nabla_\theta f(\theta)\| \leq L\|\Delta\theta\|_2 \tag{4}$$

Where L is the Lipschitz constant. The above inequality has an important conclusion:

$$f(\theta + \Delta\theta) - f(\theta) \leq \frac{1}{2}L||\Delta\theta||_2^2 + \nabla_\theta f(\theta)^T \Delta\theta \tag{5}$$

In stochastic gradient descent, we define another random variable φ and rewrite the loss function as $f(\theta, \varphi)$. We then follow Bottous et al. [24]'s footstep, replacing $f(\theta, \varphi)$ with the empirical risk function $R_N(\theta)$, which is measured as

$$R_N(\theta) = \frac{1}{N}\sum_{i=1}^{N} f(\theta, \varphi_i) \tag{6}$$

Where N is the total numbers of data points. We keep $R_N(\theta)$ out of summation form for readability. When optimizing $R_N(\theta)$, the updates at the tth step is $\Delta\theta_t = -\eta * g(\theta_t, \varphi_t)$, where η is the learning rate. Substituting it into (5):

$$R_N(\theta_{t+1}) - R_N(\theta_t) \leq \frac{1}{2}\eta^2 L|\,|g(\theta_t, \varphi_t)|\,|_2^2 - \eta\nabla_\theta R_N(\theta_t)^T g(\theta_t, \varphi_t) \tag{7}$$

Where $g(\theta_t, \varphi_t)$ is the gradient estimate at t. To eliminate the randomness for each update, we apply mathematical expectations to both sides of the inequality and get:

$$E[R_N(\theta_{t+1})] - E[R_N(\theta_t)] \leq \frac{1}{2}\eta^2 LE\left[||g(\theta_t, \varphi_t)||_2^2\right] - \eta\nabla_\theta R_N(\theta_t)^T E[g(\theta_t, \varphi_t)] \tag{8}$$

To make sure that $R_N(\theta)$ keeps decreasing, that is, the left side of (8) always less than 0, we try to let the right side less than 0:

$$\frac{1}{2}\eta^2 LE\left[||g(\theta_t, \varphi_t)||_2^2\right] - \eta\nabla_\theta R_N(\theta_t)^T E[g(\theta_t, \varphi_t)] \leq 0 \tag{9}$$

Since $\eta > 0$, the above inequality can be written as:

$$\frac{1}{2}\eta LE\left[||g(\theta_t, \varphi_t)||_2^2\right] - \nabla_\theta R_N(\theta_t)^T E[g(\theta_t, \varphi_t)] \leq 0 \tag{10}$$

Now we have two options:

- to minimize $\frac{1}{2}\eta LE\left[||g(\theta_t, \varphi_t)||_2^2\right]$
- to maximize $\nabla_\theta R_N(\theta_t)^T E[g(\theta_t, \varphi_t)]$

To minimize $\frac{1}{2}\eta LE\left[||g(\theta_t, \varphi_t)||_2^2\right]$, we first repeatedly reduce the learning rate when the validation accuracy stops improving. Since the variance of the gradient estimate is calculates as

$$\mathrm{Var}[g(\theta_t, \varphi_t)] = E\left[|\,|g(\theta_t, \varphi_t)|\,|_2^2\right] - \|E[g(\theta_t, \varphi_t)]\|_2^2 \tag{11}$$

According to the central limit theorem, when the sample size (in this case, batch size m) is large, the distribution is approximate normal. Then we can compute variance from sample variance$\mathrm{Var}_s\left[g\left(\theta_t,\varphi_t\right)\right]$:

$$\mathrm{Var}\left[g\left(\theta_t\varphi_t\right)\right]=\frac{\mathrm{Var}_s\left[g\left(\theta_t,\varphi_t\right)\right]}{\sqrt{m}} \tag{12}$$

Here we can increase the batch size m to reduce variance and thereby minimizing $\frac{1}{2}\eta LE\left[\|g\left(\theta_t,\varphi_t\right)\|_2^2\right]$. To maximize $\nabla_\theta R_N\left(\theta_t\right)^T E\left[g\left(\theta_t,\varphi_t\right)\right]$, we shuffle the training data to ensure independent and identical distribution of the sample data. This makes sure $E\left[g\left(\theta_t,\varphi_t\right)\right]\cong\nabla_\theta R_N\left(\theta_t\right)$. In this case, we obtain the minimum angle between the estimated gradient from SGD and the true gradient with full batch.

Secondly, we decrease the Lipschitz constant by batch normalization and skip connection (for residual network). This reduce 'sharp minima' and allow larger learning rate to operate. Consider the following equation:

$$\|\nabla_\theta f(\theta+\Delta\theta)-\nabla_\theta f(\theta)\|\leq L\|\Delta\theta\|_2 \tag{13}$$

This is equivalent to

$$\nabla_\theta\left(\nabla_\theta f(\theta)\right)=\frac{\|\nabla_\theta f(\theta+\Delta\theta)-\nabla_\theta f(\theta)\|}{\|\Delta\theta\|_2}\leq L \tag{14}$$

When the Lipschitz constant is large, the upper bound for the rate of change of the gradient $\nabla_\theta f(\theta)$ is large. Therefore, the loss surface is less smooth and the effective gradient estimation range is narrow, where small input change can result in huge output alternations. Prior studies have attempted to improve the smoothness of the loss surface. Li et al. [25] visually display that skip-connection can smooth the loss surface. Santurkar et al. [26] demonstrates that batch normalization achieves the similar effect with reparameterization, making model training less sensitive to parameter initialization.

Finally, we adopt the learning rate warmup technique by Goyal et al. [23], who demonstrate that linear scaling rule will not hold when the neural network is changing rapidly (i.e. during the initial training phase). Goyal then proposes the gradual warmup strategy, in which he accumulate the learning rate by a constant amount such that it reaches reasonable condition after 5 epochs. This learning rate warmup strategy avoid model to stuck at local minimum at the start of training so that it is less sensitive to initial points selection on the loss surface.

3.4 Dynamic Batch Size

Smith and Le [21] analysis the noise scale for SGD with momentum

$$\text{noise }=\frac{\eta}{1-m}\left(\frac{N}{B}-1\right) \tag{15}$$

where m is the momentum coefficient, η is the learning rate, N is the data size, and B is the batch size. If $B \ll N$, the noise is approximated as

$$\text{noise} \approx \frac{\eta N}{B(1-m)} \tag{16}$$

Smith & Le [21] propose that we should increase the batch size by a factor of 3 and then scale the learning rate and the momentum coefficient to keep the noise scale. However, their empirical result shows that increasing momentum coefficient leads to significantly worse testing accuracy. To address this issue, we increase the learning rate and the momentum coefficient and then scale the batch size. We borrow the idea from the motion of electrons in the electric field to stabilize the growing process. In Electromagnetic, a positive electron receives repulsive force when it approaches an electrode plate with evenly distributed positive electrical charges. The magnitude of that force is proportional to the reciprocal of the distance between the electron and the plate. We can transfer this idea for increasing the momentum coefficients:

$$y''(n) = \frac{k}{y(n)} \tag{17}$$

Simplification gets us:

$$y''(n) * y(n) - k = 0 \tag{18}$$

Where y is the distance between the data points and the line $m = 1, n$ is the numbers of epochs and k is a constant that decides how violently momentum coefficient slow down when m approaches 1. We apply numerical methods and we will list the best value selection in Sect. 5.

Based on the previous discussion, we finally propose our algorithm for dynamic batch size.

- Warm Up the Learning Rate gradually from 0.01 to 0.02, for the beginning 10% of the total epochs.
- Increase the learning rate by a multiplier of 2 every n epoch until validation accuracy falls, keeping momentum coefficient fixed. Linearly Scale the batch size to the learning rate.
- Increase the momentum coefficient, keeping learning rate fixed. Scale the batch size to momentum coefficient.
- Stop the above action until reaching maximum batch size, which is determined by three restrictions: GPU memory limits, non-decreasing validation accuracy and linear scaling rule constraints ($B \ll N/10$)
- If validation accuracy does not improve for five consecutive epochs, decrease the learning rate by a multiplier of 0.1.

Following is the pseudo-code for in-epoch learning during the scaling period. The Round and the Clip function ensure the batch size be an integer between the minimum and the maximum batch size. The Stepwise function ensures the batch size will be a multiple of 32.

Algorithm 1. Mini-Batch SGDM with Dynamic Batch Size.

Require: Learning rate η, batch size B, momentum coefficient m, numbers of steps T, number of data points N, loss function $f(\theta)$.

for $t \in [1, T]$ **do**
  $B_{min} = B_0$
  $B = \text{Round\_\&\_Clip}\left(\frac{\eta(1-m_0)}{\eta_0(1-m)} B_0, B_{\min}, B_{\max}\right)$
  $B = Stepwise(B)$
  $g_t = \frac{1}{B}\sum_{i=1}^{B} \nabla f(\theta_i)$
  $v_t = m v_{t-1} + \eta g_t$
  $\theta_t = \theta_{t-1} - v_t$
end for
return B, θ_t

4 Experiments

For this experiment, we will use different convolutional neural networks on different datasets. All models will use ReLU as the activation function. One is that ReLU perform fast derivative operations on the gradient. The other is that ReLU mutes all negative values, resulting in higher network sparsity. We select image classification datasets including FASHION MNIST [27], CIFAR-10 [28] and CIFAR-100 [28]. For network architectures, we choose AlexNet [2], VGG-16 ch233 and ResNet-32 [4] respectively on the three datasets above. Using the TensorFlow framework and Nvidia RTX 2080 TI GPU, we train the Conventional CNN (C-CNN), Stacked Conventional CNN (SC-CNN), Stacked Winograd-ReLU CNN (SWR-CNN) and Stacked Winograd-ReLU CNN + Dynamic Batch Size (SWR-CNN + DBS). The stacked model takes a weighted average of the original model, ConvPool and AllCNN [29]. All models are iteratively pruned and retrained. Besides, batch normalization is applied. For a specific dataset, we will list the computational speed and visualize the testing accuracy. If not else specified, 'Time' in the table refers to training time per epoch in the unit of second.

4.1 FASHION MNIST (AlexNet)

We first examine the performance of AlexNet on Fashion MNIST. A baseline AlexNet without pruning takes 17 s per epoch to train on our GPU. We compute the relative computational speed to this number. A dropout [30] rate of 0.2 and an l2 regularization rate of 0.01 is used in convolutional layers for Conventional CNN. In contrast, the convolutional layers for all stacked models use no dropout and an l2 regularization rate of 0.001. Table 1 shows the computational speed for different AlexNet models at different sparsity. Pruning C-CNN speed up training to 1.49x, whereas SC-CNN slow down to 0.46x. Pruning SWR-CNN and SWR-CNN + DBS speed up training to 1.03x and 1.61x, respectively.

Table 2 shows the computational speed for different batch sizes at 30% sparsity where all models have the best or the second-best testing accuracy. Our

Table 1. Computational speed for different AlexNet models on FASHION-MNIST at Different sparsity

Sparsity	C-CNN		SC-CNN		SWR-CNN		SWR-CNN + DBS (ours)	
	Time	Speed	Time	Speed	Time	Speed	Time	Speed
20%	12	1.42x	37	0.46	17	1.00x	11	1.55x
30%	12	1.42x	37	0.46	17	1.00x	11	1.55x
40%	12	1.42x	36	0.47	16	1.06x	11	1.55x
50%	11	1.55x	37	0.46	17	1.00x	11	1.55x
60%	11	1.55x	37	0.46	16	1.06x	10	1.7x
70%	11	1.55x	36	0.47	16	1.06x	10	1.7x
80%	11	1.55x	37	0.46	16	1.06x	10	1.7x
Overall	11.42	1.49x	36.71	0.46x	16.43	1.03x	10.57	1.61x

dynamic batch size speeds up C-CNN, SC-CNN, SWR-CNN + DBS from 0.85x to 2.83x, 0.32x to 0.71x and 0.71x to 1.55x, respectively.

Table 2. Computational speed for different AlexNet models on FASHION-MNIST with different batch sizes

Batch size	C-CNN		SC-CNN		SWR-CNN	
	Time	Speed	Time	Speed	Time	Speed
64	20	0.85x	53	0.32x	24	0.71x
128	12	1.42x	37	0.46x	17	1.00x
256	7	2.43x	28	0.61x	13	1.31x
512	5	3.4x	22	0.77x	10	1.70x
1024	3	5.67x	21	0.81x	8	2.13x
DBS(Ours)	6	2.83x	24	0.71x	11	1.55x

Figure 2(a) shows the testing accuracy for different AlexNet models at different sparsity. Our SWR-CNN + DBS has the best testing accuracy at most sparsity. At 30% sparsity, SC-CNN, SWR-CNN and SWR-CNN + DBS has the testing accuracy of 92.29%, 92.45% and 93.49% respectively, whereas C-CNN only of 90.83%. When we prune the model to 60% sparsity, the C-CNN outperforms other models with an accuracy of 89.49%. If we prune the network to 80% sparsity, SWR-CNN + DBS outperforms others with a 90.94% accuracy. Figure 2(b) shows the testing accuracy for different models at 30% sparsity. Batch Size is the legend. Increasing batch size from 64 to 1024 reduce the testing accuracy for C-CNN, SC-CNN, SWR-CNN from 90.62% to 89.51%, 90.87% to 88.02%, 90.95% to 88.34%, respectively. Our dynamic batch size enhance the accuracy for three models, from left to right, to 90.97%, 93.35% and 93.49%.

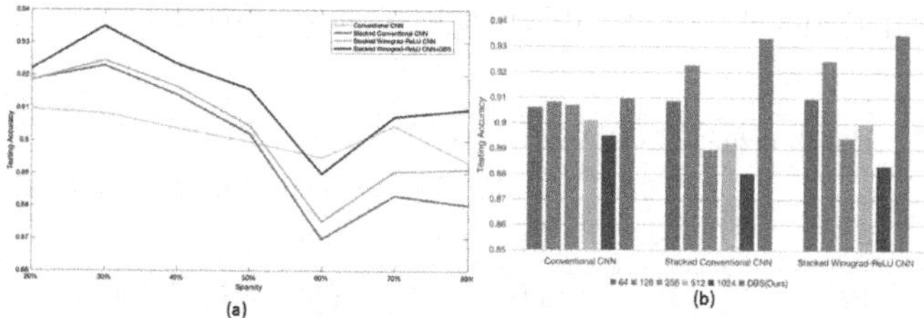

Fig. 2. (a) Testing accuracy for different AlexNet models on FASHION-MNIST with different batch sizes (b) Testing accuracy for different AlexNet models on FASHION-MNIST with different batch sizes

4.2 CIFAR-10 (VGG-16)

We then examine the performance of VGG-16 on CIFAR-10. A baseline VGG-16 without pruning takes 26 s per epoch to train on our GPU. The relative computational speed bases on this number. A dropout rate of 0.2 and an l2 regularization rate of 0.01 is applied to convolutional layers for Conventional CNN. In contrast, convolutional layers for all stacked models use no dropout and an l2 regularization rate of 0.001.

Table 3 shows the computational speed for different VGG-16 models at different sparsity. Pruning C-CNN speed up training to 1.42x, whereas SC-CNN slow down the model to 0.65x. Pruning SWR-CNN and SWR-CNN + DBS speed up training to 1.47x and 1.92x, respectively.

Table 3. Computational speed for different VGG models on CIFAR-10 at different sparsity

Sparsity	C-CNN		SC-CNN		SWR-CNN		SWR-CNN +DBS (ours)	
	Time	Speed	Time	Speed	Time	Speed	Time	Speed
20%	19	1.37x	41	0.63x	18	1.44x	15	1.73x
30%	19	1.37x	41	0.63x	18	1.44x	14	1.86x
40%	18	1.44x	40	0.65x	18	1.44x	14	1.86x
50%	18	1.44x	40	0.65x	18	1.44x	14	1.86x
60%	18	1.44x	40	0.65x	18	1.44x	13	2.00x
70%	18	1.44x	39	0.67x	17	1.53x	13	2.00x
80%	18	1.44x	39	0.67x	17	1.53x	12	2.17x
Overall	18.3	1.42x	40.0	0.65x	17.71	1.47x	13.57	1.92x

Table 4 shows the computational speed for different batch sizes at 40% sparsity where all models have the best or the third-best testing accuracy. Our dynamic batch size speeds up C-CNN, SC-CNN, SWR-CNN from 0.93x to 2.00x, 0.42x to 0.90x and 0.93x to 1.86x, respectively.

Table 4. Computational speed for different VGG models on CIFAR-10 with different batch sizes

Batch size	C-CNN		SC-CNN		SWR-CNN	
	Time	Speed	Time	Speed	Time	Speed
64	28	0.93x	62	0.42x	28	0.93x
128	18	1.44x	40	0.65x	18	1.44x
256	13	2.00x	32	0.81x	15	1.73x
512	11	2.36x	28	0.93x	13	2.00x
1024	9	2.89x	27	0.96x	12	2.17x
DBS(Ours)	13	2.00x	29	0.90x	14	1.86x

Figure 3(a) shows the testing accuracy for different VGG-16 models at different sparsity. Our SWR-CNN + DBS has the best testing accuracy when sparsity is at 20%, 40% and 50% At 40% sparsity, SC-CNN, SWR-CNN and SWR-CNN + DBS has testing accuracy of 88.34%, 89.02% and 89.73% respectively, whereas C-CNN of 88.36%. When we prune the model to 60% sparsity, C-CNN outperforms other models with an accuracy of 88.42%. If we prune the model to 80% sparsity, C-CNN CNN significantly outperforms other models with an accuracy of 83.65%.

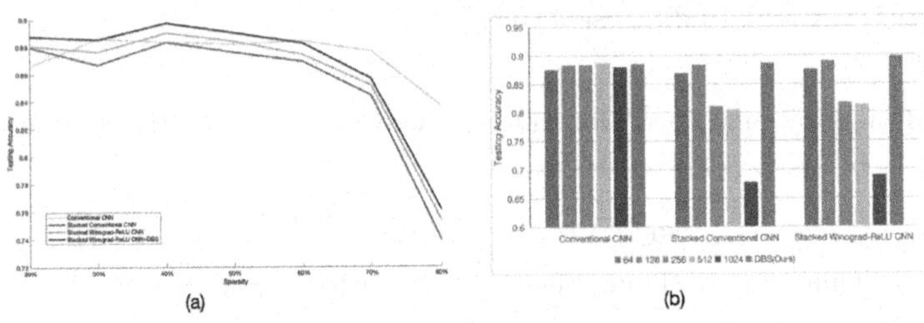

Fig. 3. (a) Testing accuracy for different VGG models on CIFAR-10 at different sparsity (b) Testing accuracy for different VGG models on CIFAR-10 with different batch sizes

Figure 3(b) shows the testing accuracy for different models at 40% sparsity. Batch Size is used as the legend. Increasing batch size from 64 to 1024 change the testing accuracy for C-CNN, SC-CNN, SWR-CNN from 87.54% to 87.99 86.87% to 67.73%, 87.50% to 68.91%, respectively. Our dynamic batch size enhance the accuracy for three models, from left to right, to 88.54%, 88.67% and 89.73%

4.3 CIFAR-100 (ResNet-32)

We last examine the performance of ResNet-32 on CIFAR-100. A baseline ResNet-32 without pruning takes 54 s per epoch to train on our GPU. Our relative computational speed grounds on this number. A dropout rate of 0.1 and an l2 regularization rate of 0.001 is used at convolutional layers for Conventional CNN. In contrast, convolutional layers in all stacked models use the same dropout and an l2 regularization rate of 0.01.

Table 5. Computational speed for different ResNet models on CIFAR-100 at different sparsity

Sparsity	C-CNN		SC-CNN		SWR-CNN		SWR-CNN +DBS (ours)	
	Time	Speed	Time	Speed	Time	Speed	Time	Speed
20%	28	1.93x	51	1.06x	25	2.16x	21	2.57x
30%	28	1.93x	51	1.06x	25	2.16x	21	2.57x
40%	29	1.86x	49	1.10x	24	2.25x	20	2.7x
50%	28	1.93x	53	1.02x	26	2.08x	22	2.45x
60%	29	1.86x	53	1.02x	26	2.08x	22	2.45x
70%	30	1.8x	51	1.06x	25	2.16x	21	2.57x
80%	28	1.93x	49	1.1x	24	2.25x	20	2.7x
Overall	28.57	1.89x	51	1.06x	25	2.16x	21	2.57x

Table 5 shows the computational speed for different ResNet-32 models at different sparsity. Pruning C-CNN and the SC-CNN speed up training to 1.89x and 1.06x, respectively. Pruning SWR-CNN and SWR-CNN + DBS speed up training to 2.16x and 2.57x, respectively.

Table 6. Computational speed for different ResNet models on CIFAR-100 with different batch sizes

Batch size	C-CNN		SC-CNN		SWR-CNN	
	Time	Speed	Time	Speed	Time	Speed
64	49	1.10x	90	0.60x	53	1.02x
128	29	1.86x	49	1.10x	20	2.70x
256	20	2.70x	34	1.59x	14	3.86x
512	14	3.86x	25	2.16x	11	4.91x
1024	12	4.50x	22	2.45x	10	5.40x
DBS(Ours)	18	3.00x	29	1.86x	13	4.15x

Table 6 shows the computational speed for different batch sizes at 40% sparsity where all models have the best or the second-best testing accuracy. Our dynamic batch size speeds up C-CNN, SC-CNN, SWR-CNN from 1.10x to 3.30x, 0.60x to 1.86x and 1.02x to 4.15x, respectively.

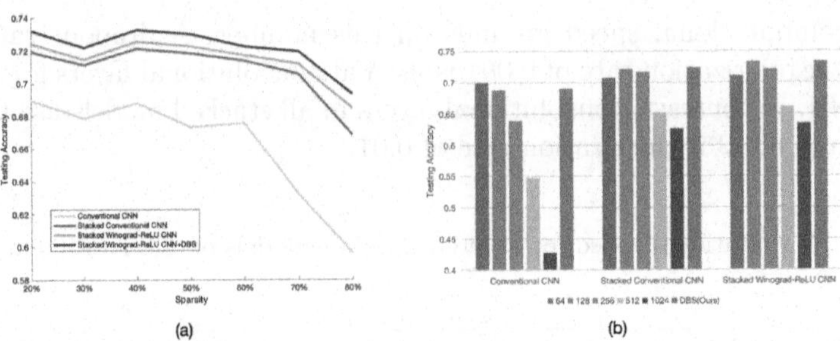

Fig. 4. (a) Testing accuracy for different ResNet models on CIFAR-100 at different sparsity (b) Testing accuracy for different ResNet models on CIFAR-100 with different batch sizes

Figure 4(a) shows the testing accuracy for different ResNet-32 models at different sparsity. Our SWR-CNN + DBS has the best testing accuracy for all sparsity. At 40% sparsity, the Stacked Conventional CNN, SWR-CNN and SWR-CNN + DBS have testing accuracy of 72.12%, 72.56% and 73.26% respectively, whereas C-CNN of 68.81%. If we prune the model to 80% sparsity, C-CNN significantly underperforms other models with an accuracy of 59.62%.

Figure 4(b) shows the testing accuracy for different models at 40% sparsity. Batch Size is the legend. Increasing batch size from 64 to 1024 reduce the testing accuracy for C-CNN, SC-CNN, SWR-CNN from 70.00% to 42.71%, 70.72% to 62.64%, 71.04% to 63.49%, respectively. Using our dynamic batch size change the accuracy for three models, from left to right, to 68.98%, 72.33% and 73.29%

5 Discussion

5.1 Result Interpretation

For Alexnet on Fashion-MNIST, we note that C-CNN has the least accuracy reduction when we increase sparsity. Recall that pruning reduces the model size by removing connections that have little classification power. In this way, pruning reduces the model complexity and prevent overfitting. In C-CNN architecture, a single model learns more from the data patterns and is more overfitted than stacked ones. Therefore, increasing sparsity save some accuracy loss by reducing C-CNN's overfitting, whereas less-overfitted stacked model loss more accuracy along the pruning process. This phenomenon is more evident for VGG on CIFAR-10, where we can prune the C-CNN from 20% to 80% sparsity with only 1.64% of accuracy loss.

Conversely, the Stacked VGG models experience massive accuracy loss of 13.98%, 12.78% and 12.66% respectively. This is reasonable since VGG-16 is much more complex and therefore suffers more from overfitting. Note that Stacked ResNet models do not exhibit this behaviour. This is because ResNet adopts multiple 'skip-connection' to reduce the model complexity. When sparsity is less than 60%, both SC-CNN and C-CNN displays similar accuracy loss from pruning. However, C-CNN and SC-CNN drop accuracy massively from 60% and 70 % sparsity, respectively. We believe that they lost essential connections and begin to underfitting at that strong sparsity.

We also find that weighted stacking methods will generally increase the testing accuracy but will significantly reduce the computational speed. However, this negative effect can be mostly encountered by Winograd-ReLU methods, where we move the ReLU layer after Winograd Transformation. For VGG on CIFAR-10 and ResNet on CIFAR-100, SWR-CNN have faster speed then C-CNN. For AlexNet, however, the SWR-CNN is still significantly slower than the C-CNN. The reason is that we use ConvPool and AllCNN to stack the models. They are considerably less complicated than VGG and ResNet but have similar perplexity as AlexNet. Therefore, Stacked AlexNet with these two models will almost triple the computational time, whereas Stacked VGG and ResNet with them will not.

In contrast to Smith et al. [31]'s findings that increasing momentum coefficient will reduce the testing accuracy, we find that increasing momentum coefficient within our dynamic batch size framework will insteadincreasethe testing accuracy. For almost all experiments, our SWR-CNN + DBS outperforms other models, although in VGG and AlexNet it loses the match at high sparsity. Besides, our dynamic batch size method achieves similarly accurate result as the smaller batch size of 64 and 128 with faster training speed between that of a batch size of 256 and 512. In short, it allows the model to enjoy high accuracy and fast computational speed.

5.2 Kernel Sparsity Visualization

We visualize the kernels of the proposed Stacked Winograd-ReLU + DBS model. Figure 5(a) show we chose the first 6 inputs and output channels of layer 2 of ResNet-32 at three different pruning densities. During pruning, we find that the values tend to be kept in the shape of 2*2 blocks in each 4*4 patch. Note that 2*2 blocks are the only element that is linearly transformed with only addition, which is computational efficient than multiplication. Besides, our algorithm keeps distinct value and average the weak values (because of weighted average stacking) during aggressive pruning. It helps the model focus on the most crucial features and helps Winograd-ReLU operation retain more classification accuracy from pruning.

5.3 Optimizing Momentum Increase

We start with $m = 0.90$ and $= 0.50$ so that momentum coefficient should rise to 1.00 when proportion of total epochs reach 0.20, if k value for is zero. To choose the best k value for increasing momentum coefficient, we interpolate and plot the momentum coefficient to the proportion of total epochs with k values ranging from 1.30 to 1.75. We want the k value that achieves the faster increase subject to the best convergence when the portion of total epochs is 0.30. Figure 5(b) shows the optimal k value is approximate 1.60.

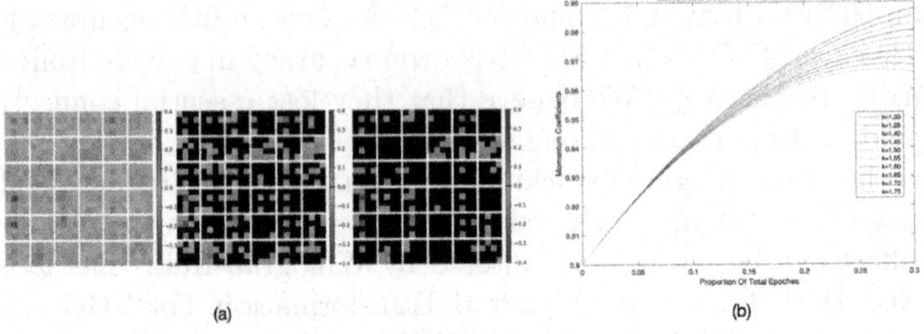

Fig. 5. (a) Kernels of Layer 2 from Winograd-ReLU ResNet-32 Model with dynamic batch size at different pruning sparsity (Left 0, Middle 60%, Right 80%) (b) Increase of momentum coefficient with different k values.

6 Conclusion

In this paper, we have shown that we can construct an efficient CNN with ensemble methods, convolutional accelerator and dynamic batch size. We first ensemble three CNNs and take a weighted average of their predictions. This stacking approach increases accuracy but slows down model training. Therefore, we iteratively prune and retrain the model, while performing Winograd convolution with ReLU as the activation function to accelerate computational speed. We also demonstrate that Winograd-ReLU operation will restore more accuracy loss when model sparsity is high. Finally, we further speed up model learning by sequentially increasing the learning rate and momentum coefficient and scale the batch size. With little hyperparameter tuning and no data augmentation, we speed up AlexNet on Fashion-MNIST, VGG on CIFAR-10 and ResNet on CIFAR-100 to 1.55x, 2.86x, and 4.15x with a testing accuracy increase of 2.66%, 1.37% and 4.48%, respectively.

References

1. Lecun, Y., Bottou, L., Bengio, Y., Haffner, P.: Gradient-based learning applied to document recognition. Proc. IEEE **86**(11), 2278–2324 (1998)
2. Krizhevsky, A., Sutskever, I., Hinton, G.E.: Imagenet classification with deep convolutional neural networks. Commun. ACM **60**(6), 84–90 (2017)
3. Simonyan, K., Zisserman, A.: Very deep convolutional networks for large-scale image recognition (2014)
4. He, K., Zhang, X., Ren, S., Sun, J.: Deep residual learning for image recognition (2015)
5. Mathieu, M., Henaff, M., LeCun, Y.: Fast training of convolutional networks through FFTs (2013)
6. Lavin, A., Gray, S.: Fast algorithms for convolutional neural networks (2015)
7. Winograd, S.: Arithmetic Complexity of Computations. Society for Industrial and Applied Mathematics (1980)
8. Ioffe, S., Szegedy, C.: Batch normalization: accelerating deep network training by reducing internal covariate shift (2015)

9. Lu, L., Liang, Y.: SpWA: an efficient sparse winograd convolutional neural networks accelerator on FPGAs. In: 2018 55th ACM/ESDA/IEEE Design Automation Conference (DAC), pp. 1–6 (2018)
10. Liu, X.: Pruning of winograd and FFT based convolution algorithm (2016)
11. Li, S., Park, J., Tang, P.T.P.: Enabling sparse winograd convolution by native pruning (2017)
12. Liu, X., Pool, J., Han, S., Dally, W.J.: Efficient sparse-winograd convolutional neural networks (2018)
13. Nair, V., Hinton, G.E.: Rectified linear units improve restricted Boltzmann machines. In: Proceedings of the 27th International Conference on International Conference on Machine Learning, ICML 2010, Madison, WI, USA, pp. 807–814. Omnipress (2010)
14. Maas, A.L.: Rectifier nonlinearities improve neural network acoustic models (2013)
15. He, K., Zhang, X., Ren, S., Sun, J.: Delving deep into rectifiers: surpassing human-level performance on ImageNet classification (2015)
16. Clevert, D.A., Unterthiner, T., Hochreiter, S.: Fast and accurate deep network learning by exponential linear units (ELUs) (2015)
17. Krizhevsky, A.: One weird trick for parallelizing convolutional neural networks (2014)
18. Keskar, N.S., Mudigere, D., Nocedal, J., Smelyanskiy, M., Tang, P.T.P.: On large-batch training for deep learning: generalization gap and sharp minima (2016)
19. Hoffer, E., Hubara, I., Soudry, D.: Train longer, generalize better: closing the generalization gap in large batch training of neural networks (2017)
20. Balles, L., Romero, J., Hennig, P.: Coupling adaptive batch sizes with learning rates (2016)
21. McCandlish, S., Kaplan, J., Amodei, D., OpenAI Dota Team: An empirical model of large-batch training (2018)
22. Smith, S.L., Le, Q.V.: A Bayesian perspective on generalization and stochastic gradient descent (2017)
23. Goyal, P., et al.: Accurate, large minibatch SGD: training ImageNet in 1 hour (2017)
24. LeCun, Y., Cortes, C., Burges, C.J.: MNIST handwritten digit database. ATT Labs, 2 (2010). http://yann.lecun.com/exdb/mnist
25. Li, H., Xu, Z., Taylor, G., Studer, C., Goldstein, T.: Visualizing the loss landscape of neural nets (2017)
26. Santurkar, S., Tsipras, D., Ilyas, A., Madry, A.: How does batch normalization help optimization? (2018)
27. Xiao, H., Rasul, K., Vollgraf, R.: Fashion-MNIST: a novel image dataset for benchmarking machine learning algorithms (2017)
28. Krizhevsky, A., Hinton, G.: Learning multiple layers of features from tiny images (2009)
29. Springenberg, J.T., Dosovitskiy, A., Brox, T., Riedmiller, M.: Striving for simplicity: the all convolutional net (2014)
30. Srivastava, N., Hinton, G., Krizhevsky, A., Sutskever, I., Salakhutdinov, R.: Dropout: a simple way to prevent neural networks from overfitting. J. Mach. Learn. Res. **15**(1), 1929–1958 (2014)
31. Smith, S.L., Kindermans, P.J., Ying, C., Le, Q.V.: Don't decay the learning rate, increase the batch size (2017)

Inferring Semantic Object Affordances from Videos

Rupam Bhattacharyya[1(✉)], Zubin Bhuyan[2], and Shyamanta M. Hazarika[3]

[1] Indian Institute of Information Technology Bhagalpur, Bhagalpur, India
rbhattacharyya.cse@iiitbh.ac.in

[2] University of Massachusetts, Lowell, USA
Zubin_Bhuyan@student.uml.edu

[3] Indian Institute of Technology Guwahati, Guwahati, Assam, India
s.m.hazarika@iitg.ac.in

Abstract. Lately there has been an increasing interest in learning object affordances. This is particularly to address human activity understanding and intention recognition for household robots. However, most existing approaches do not concentrate on imbibing new perceptual models of inferring affordances from visual input. Such models are key for object usage by household robots. Towards this goal, this paper introduces a knowledge based approach to inferring semantic object affordances. This is achieved by integrating ontology and qualitative reasoning within a statistical relational learning scheme. Encouraging results are obtained for the CAD-120 dataset consisting of indoor household activity videos involving human-object interactions.

Keywords: Object affordance · Ontology · Qualitative reasoning · Markov logic network · Cognitive human computer interaction

1 Introduction

Vision capabilities of most robots are often limited to identification of a particular object or its parts. This does not suffice in addressing the question: What can I do with the object? [14]. Consider Fig. 1. Apart from appearance based features of the scene, human can quickly gather non-trivial information about object properties (such as weight) along with the abstract information about human object interactions. It might enable humans to effortlessly comprehend the possible actions. Replicating this human reasoning process is complex and may not be feasible at times. The work reported in this paper concerns a fundamental concept underlying such human object interactions i.e., the concept of object affordances. The term object affordance is best understood as "properties of an object that determine what actions a human can perform on them" [6].

Finding possible activities with objects detected in a scene requires combination of contextual information from various sources. Retrieval of such information in terms of object affordances can impact the acceptance of household robots

S. K. Singh et al. (Eds.): CVIP 2020, CCIS 1378, pp. 278–290, 2021.
https://doi.org/10.1007/978-981-16-1103-2_24

Fig. 1. Common household environment involving multiple objects (video frame source: CAD-120 [10])

[15]. Categorization of object affordances based on *source of activation* helps to locate the source of such contextual information [7]. Sources of activation are usually grouped into three major categories: a. geometry and morphology of the object, b. spatio-temporal dynamics of the object and c. physical attributes of the object (e.g. weight).

Existing computational models [10] proposed for learning semantic object affordance from video: a. fail to consider different kinds of object properties; b. do not provide generalized solution which exploits everyday human reasoning in handling various objects; and c. do not employ useful background knowledge within the computation model. To address all of the above, the proposed solution combines a knowledge structure for object properties and qualitative spatial reasoning within Markov Logic Network (MLN) for inferring semantic object affordances from video. O-PrO and Qualitative Distance Calculus(QDC) [3] is used. Use of O-PrO in conjunction with an MLN has enabled accurate mapping of objects to object properties. We assume that objects involved in the input source video can be detected and tracked over the video frames. Ground truth temporal segmentation of the sub-activities corresponding to the high level activities are assumed to be available. Performance of the proposed method is validated through experiments on the standard CAD-120 dataset.

2 Background

Research in learning object affordance from video data involving human-object interactions has been resurrected by [10]. Object properties, for example, a

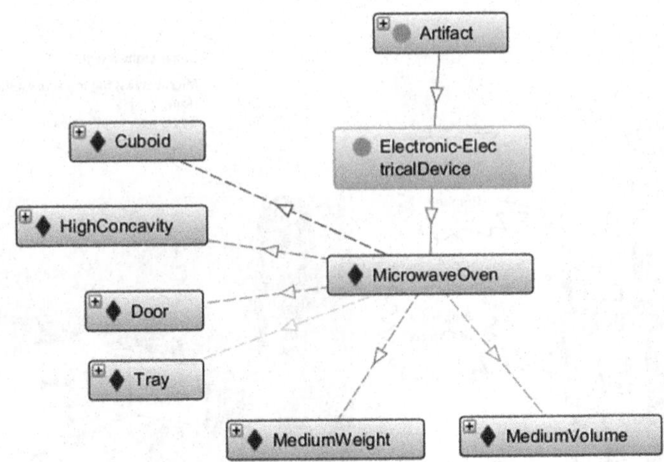

Fig. 2. Various attributes of microwave oven within O-PrO

microwave oven's overall structure or its constituent parts, activate its affordances like *openable* and *closeable.* Metric spatial relations like *nearby*, *on top of* alone do not enable object affordance inference. However, [10] uses only such metric spatial relations, making their technique of inferring semantic object affordance very much different from the human visual reasoning process.

An affordance-based ontology is presented in [8]. Their approach have rough idea about object affordances; which are used later to complete certain actions. AfNet is an affordance network which furnishes affordance knowledge ontologies for household articles [1]. AfRob, Affordance Network for Robots has been proposed in [13] which is an extension to AfNet [1]. AfRob offers inference mechanisms to recognize semantic affordance features from visual scene.

Deep Learning (DL) techniques mostly require large datasets to produce effective results. For, video based semantic object affordance detection, such publicly available large datasets are scarce. A *generalized solution* should ensure that the semantic object affordance inference mechanism utilize minimal training data. To the best of our knowledge, no solution focusing on *one shot learning* has been provided in inferring object affordance from videos. Work reported in [14] is based on static RGB images which further refines the main functionality of the object into finer possible actions such as an object can be *open*ed with *spherical grasp.* It utilizes ontology along with convolutional neural networks(CNN) for visual object recognition. In [4], DL techniques has been demonstrated to simultaneously detect objects as well as their affordances. Neglecting the implication of visual features such as shape along with physical properties such as weight in identifying possible object affordance looks lame. We detect object affordances from human-object interactions present in the indoor household videos.

Ontology for Knowledge Representation: Substantial efforts have been made towards creating knowledge structures for object affordance [13,15].

Ontology in [13] is not suitable for the kind of reasoning depicted in Fig. 1. [13] do not consider physical and categorical attributes. Major issues in knowledge structure for inferring affordance from images [15] is discussed in [2].

Qualitative Distance Calculus: QDC is qualitative relational calculi which abstracts Euclidean distance between two points depending on defined region boundaries [3]. Set of QDC relations between human-object and object-object can represent a scene; and any change used to explain relative motion.

Markov Logic Network: MLN can be conceptualized as a log-linear model with one node per ground atom and one feature per ground formula [15]. The joint distribution over possible worlds x is given by

$$P(X = x) = \frac{1}{Z} exp(\sum_{i=1}^{n} w_i f_i(x_{\{i\}})) \tag{1}$$

where Z is the partition function; $F = \{F_i\}$ is the set of first-order formulae in MLN and n is the number of formulae in F; $x_{\{i\}}$ is a state of ground atoms appearing in the formula F_i and the feature function $f_i(x_{\{i\}}) = 1$ if $x_{\{i\}}$ has a particular value and 0 otherwise. The weights w indicate the likelihood of the formulae being true.

3 Knowledge Driven Inference of Object Affordances

Framework to infer semantic object affordance from video is shown in Fig. 3.

Features: Features used in the proposed approach are listed in Table 1. These features are derived automatically by the video processing module and the ontology processing module. Within a sub-activity, three categories of features - a. object features, b. sub-activity features and c. object-sub-activity features can be captured. Ontology processing module deals with the calculation of object features. Upon observing the video frame shown in Fig. 1, the robot finds out that Jessica deals with a. *microwave oven* and b. *box*. It finds out all the three features (A1, A2 and A3 in Table 1) for each object. The robot interprets Jessica's skeletal posture through the video processing module. Four joints (B1 in Table 1) have been considered as we are dealing with table top scene understanding scenarios. A4 and A5 are two object specific features calculated by this module. Rest of the features i.e. B2 and C1 are deduced for identifying various human-object and object-object relations from the observed sub-activity.

Phase 1: Video Processing

Skeleton: We have considered only four joints namely Head, Torso, Left_Hand, Right_Hand. The robot extracts features B1 and B2 w.r.t Jessica's above joints.

Objects: This module is related to capturing the object labels and their positions w.r.t the world frame. Various open source algorithms for object recognition and tracking are available. However, we have used the annotations provided in

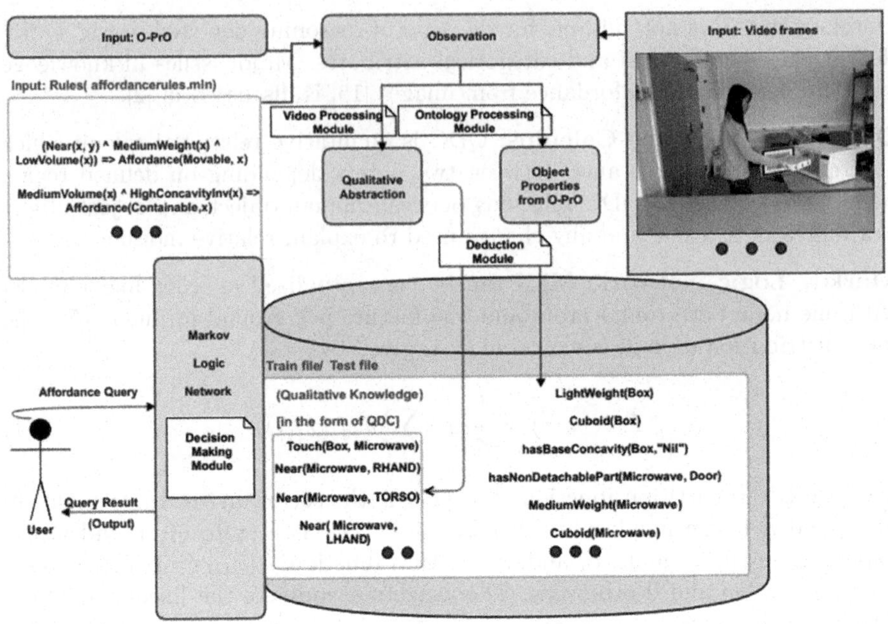

Fig. 3. Knowledge driven framework for inferring object affordances from videos (video frame source CAD-120 [10]).

Table 1. Summary of the features used in our approach

Description	Count
Object Features	**8**
A1. Geometric shape	1
A2. Structural attribute (Sub-component, hasConcavity) of objects	2
A3. Physical attribute (weight and volume)	2
A4. Centroid Location	2
A5. Distance moved by the centroid	1
Sub-activity Features	**12**
B1. Location of each joint (4 Joint: Head, Torso, Left Hand, Right Hand)	8
B2. Distance moved by each, joint	4
Object–sub-activity Features	**4**
C1. Distance between object centroid and each joint location	4

the video dataset. There can be multiple objects in a particular frame. The 2D centroid of all the objects present in a RGBD frame corresponding to particular sub-activity are computed. The robot extracts features A4 and A5 (of Table 1) for the *box* as well as for the *microwave oven*. Thereafter, we calculate feature C1 of Table 1. This module facilitates abstraction of the scenes through computation of QDC relations.

Phase 2: Ontology Processing

O-PrO: O-PrO [2] is an ontology for computing semantic and cognitive object affordances. O-Pro considers three types of object properties namely, physical, categorical and structural. Any household robot should be able to extract various features envisioned in Fig. 2. The object affordance detection scheme is expected to easily extract various non trivial object properties in similar household environments. O-PrO allows one to obtain various non-trivial object properties from the object detected in the video frame. O-PrO is considered in our proposed framework as another input along with the videos.

Features such as A1, A2 and A3 (mentioned in Table 1) is extracted. Previous phase provide us the object names that appeared in each video frame. Description logic[1] query need be formulated for retrieving various object properties from O-PrO. Seven such queries are formulated for identifying various information about the objects such as volume, weight, geometric shape, concavity along with information about various parts of the object. The module has been implemented in Java using OWL API 3.4.3 and Hermit 1.3.8.1 (reasoner). It extracts object properties from the ontology, O-PrO.

Phase 3: Deduction

Primitive Entity Generation: Information obtained from interactions and object properties are to be represented in first order logic predicates. Two types of primitive entities are introduced: a. Direct Primitive Entity (DPE) and b. Indirect Primitive Entity (IPE). DPE corresponds to the object properties extracted from O-PrO. IPE corresponds to the QDC relations computed between human-object and object-object in a RGBD frame.

Video processing module enables our approach to extract feature such as B2 and C1 (from Table 1). This sub-module utilizes those features to conceptualize four QDC relations. These relations are namely 1. 'touch', 2. 'near', 3. 'medium', and 4. 'far'. The thresholds for these relations are defined as: 'touch' [0, 200], 'near' (200, 800], 'medium' (800, 1200], 'far' (>1200). One may consider these user defined thresholds as a drawback of the proposed approach. However, our approach requires less training data which might be an indication towards better generalizing capability of our solution.

Ground Formula Generation: This sub-module works closely with the video processing and the ontology processing modules and the previous sub-module entitled as "primitive entity generation". This phase prepares one to utilize MLN properly. Algorithm 1 iterates over the stored content generated by the previous modules/sub-modules to generate ground formulas. Few grounded DPE are shown below:

[1] http://dl.kr.org/.

Algorithm 1. Pseudo-code for *Primitive Entity Generation*

Input: *countObj*, number objects in the frame; *countJoints*, number skeletal joints in the frame;

Output: *F_train*, train file containing the ground formulas; *F_test*, test file containing ground formulas

Begin procedure: Generate_IPE_DPE(*countObj*, *countJoints*)

```
Extract stored information from objArr[6] and jointArr_ik[1]
Calculate QDC relations between objects and write the corresponding predicate to F_train/F_test.
Calculate QDC relations between object and
human joints and write the corresponding predicate to F_train/F_test.
Save the extracted object property predicates into F_train/F_test.
return the F_train/F_test file.
```

End procedure

$LightWeight\ (Box)$
$Cuboid\ (Box)$
$hasDetachablePart\ (Microwave, Tray)$
$hasNonDetachablePart\ (Microwave, Door)$

The robot (from a scenario as in Fig. 1) stores the perceptual information about the current interactions in terms of grounded IPEs. Few grounded IPE are shown below:

$Near\ (Microwave, LHAND)$
$Touch\ (Microwave, RHAND)$
$Touch\ (Box, Microwave)$

Construction and Training of MLN

Our approach takes three inputs: a. Video data b. O-PrO and c. MLN Rules. MLN is closely associated with deduction and decision making. Rules in the framework influence both modules. Previous modules/sub-modules stores perceptual information of the video frames in the form of grounded DPEs or IPEs.

Let us consider a FOL (First Order Logic) rule, r^1 given below:

$$hasBaseConcavity\ (x, \text{“}Nil\text{”}) \wedge LightWeight\ (x) \wedge$$
$$LowVolume\ (x) \rightarrow Affordance\ (Placeable, x)$$

Above rule is for “placeable” affordance. Human perform similar kind of reasoning before executing “placing” sub-activity. The sub-module tells us how to prioritize this rule so that we can discriminate improbable affordances.

The representation schema is a 4-tuple, $\mathcal{M} = <\mathcal{V}, \mathcal{O}, \mathcal{H}, \mathcal{C}>$ where $\mathcal{V}$ = finite set of observable predicates corresponding to RGBD video frames, $\mathcal{O}$ = finite set of observable predicates obtained from O-PrO, $\mathcal{H}$ = *Affordances*, which are treated as a finite set of hidden predicates, $\mathcal{C}$ = finite set of *constants*. An MLN is a set of pairs $\{F_i, w_i\}$, $1 \leq i \leq n$, where each F_i is built from $\mathcal{V} \cup \mathcal{O} \cup \mathcal{H}$ and each $w_i \in \mathbb{R}$ is the weight of the formula F_i.

For the rule, r^1 mentioned above, there are two objects namely a. *microwave oven* and b. *box* present in the video frame (demonstrated in the Fig. 3). These two serves as the constants, $\mathcal{C}$ to be replaced for 'x'; the variable in the rule. Each FOL rule like r^1 or formulae corresponds to a clique in the Markov network. Weight learning of the grounded formulas is accomplished using discriminative weight learning algorithm provided by Alchemy [9]. This leads to grounded markov networks with various weights associated with different rules.

Phase 4: Decision Making
Any RGBD frame will automatically generate a set of grounded predicates, and these will be used by the MLN to compute the relevance score (weight) of each affordance for each object present in the frame.

Inference Routine: Our approach performs semantic object affordance detection by executing *Maximum-A-Posterior* (MAP) query over Markov network using Eq. 1. MAP query outputs the semantic object affordance labels of objects present in the RGBD frame (w.r.t a particular sub-activity) along with the probabilities attached with the labels. The label with the highest probability value would be considered as the inferred affordance label.

4 Evaluation of Proposed Approach

4.1 Experimental Method

Experiments were conducted on the CAD-120 dataset [10]. This benchmark dataset is publicly available and commonly used for the analysis of semantic object affordance from video.

Dependent Measures: Performance evaluation is based on *accuracy*.

Accuracy: Considering new sequence of frames present in a sub-activity of CAD-120 dataset, *accuracy* measure how perfectly does the given computational system provide semantic object affordance labels on those frames.

Hypotheses:Based on the dependent measure described above, in this experiment three main hypotheses were raised:

$\mathbf{H_1^0}$: Inferring semantic object affordance from video with a knowledge structure does not lead to an improved recognition accuracy compared to state-of-the-art results for affordance labels with source of affordance activation in geometrical and physical attributes of the object.

$\mathbf{H_2^0}$: Inferring semantic object affordance from video with a knowledge structure does not lead to an improved recognition accuracy compared to state-of-the-art results for affordance labels with source of affordance activation in geometrical, physical attributes and spatio-temporal pattern of the object.

$\mathbf{H_3^0}$: Inferring semantic object affordance from video with a knowledge structure does not lead to an improved recognition accuracy compared to state-of-the-art results for affordance labels with source of affordance activation in spatio-temporal pattern of the object.

4.2 Results

Assessment: Based on Precision, Recall and F-Score. CAD 120 data set is divided into four folds where each fold represents one subject's demonstrations. Here *one shot learning* could be defined as "training the proposed approach with one person while keeping the rest of the data (involving 3 persons) present in the dataset as unlabeled". Reported results in Table 2 are obtained by averaging performance across the folds. Figure 4 shows the confusion matrix for labeling semantic object affordances with the proposed approach[2].

Assessment: Based on Accuracy. Table 3 presents accuracy results of the proposed approach. State-of-the-art accuracies from [10] is recorded in the third column. Accuracy in recognition of "placeable" is lower than that reported by [10]. Our accuracy[3] in recognizing "drinkable" and "pourable" is 0%. Except for these two specific affordance labels, encouraging results have been obtained for the remaining affordance labels. Without using more features, more training data and precise metric information as compared to the state-of-the-art results [10]; our performance in predicting affordance labels is better than [10].

Table 2. Result in terms of precision, recall and F-Score

Semantic object affordance labels	Precision	Recall	F-Score
Movable	1.0	0.9615	0.9804
Reachable	1.0	0.7407	0.8511
Pourable	0.0	0.0	0.0
Pourto	1.0	1.0	1.0
Containable	1.0	1.0	1.0
Drinkable	0.0	0.0	0.0
Openable	1.0	0.9167	0.9565
Placeable	1.0	0.5385	0.7
Closable	1.0	1.0	1.0
Scrubbable	1.0	1.0	1.0
Scrubber	1.0	1.0	1.0
Performance averages	**0.82**	**0.742**	**0.77**

Table 3. Performance comparison

Serial Number	Affordance Labels	Koppula et al. [10] (% accuracy)	Our method (% accuracy)
A1	Reachable	75	74
C1	Containable	58	100
B1	Movable	94	96
B2	Drinkable	100	0
B3	Scrubbable	58	100
C2	Openable	67	92
B4	Pourable	84	0
C3	Pourto	84	100
B5	Placeable	87	54
C4	Scrubber	58	100
C5	Closable	50	100

[2] Code of our proposed approach can be found at https://git.io/vDdcA.

[3] See Sect. 5 for probable reasons of this outcome.

	movable	reachable	pourable	pourto	containable	drinkable	openable	placeable	closable	scrubbable	scrubber
movable	0.96	0	0	0.03	0	0	0	0	0	0	0
reachable	0	0.71	0	0.11	0.03	0.03	0	0	0.03	0.03	0
pourable	0	0	0	0.66	0	0	0.33	0	0	0	0
pourto	0	0	0	1	0	0	0	0	0	0	0
containable	0	0	0	0	1	0	0	0	0	0	0
drinkable	0	0.83	0	0	0	0	0	0	0	0	0.16
openable	0	0	0	0	0	0	0.92	0	0	0	0.08
placeable	0	0	0	0.07	0.03	0.03	0	0.54	0.12	0	0.2
closable	0	0	0	0	0	0	0	0	1	0	0
scrubbable	0	0	0	0	0	0	0	0	0	1	0
scrubber	0	0	0	0	0	0	0	0	0	0	1

Fig. 4. Confusion matrix for affordance labelling of test videos from CAD-120.

To test H_1^0, we have conducted t-test. Affordance labels pertaining to C1, C2, C3, C4 and C5 rows from Table 3 are activated due to geometrical and physical properties of the object. Obtained p-value for the t-test is 0.005732. So the null hypothesis H_1^0 is rejected. Alternative hypothesis, H_1^a is accepted.

Alternative Hypothesis ($\mathbf{H_1^a}$): Inferring semantic object affordance from video with a knowledge structure lead to an improved recognition accuracy compared to the state-of-the-art results for affordance labels with source of affordance activation in geometrical and physical attributes of the object.

To test H_2^0, we have conducted t-test. Affordance labels activated due to geometrical, physical properties of the object and spatio-temporal pattern of the object pertain to B1, B2, B3, B4 and B5 rows from Table 3. Obtained p-value for this t-test is 0.130001. So the null hypothesis H_2^0 was accepted.

Null Hypothesis ($\mathbf{H_2^0}$): Inferring semantic object affordance from video with a knowledge structure does not lead to an improved recognition accuracy compared to state-of-the-art results for affordance labels with source of activation in geometrical, physical attributes and spatio-temporal pattern of the object.

Although QDC have a role to play, the incorporation of QDC and O-PrO within MLN is not able to produce statistically significant result whenever spatio-temporal dynamics is involved as a part of *source of activation.*

In CAD-120 *reachable* is the only affordance due to spatio-temporal dynamics. A conclusive t-test could not be performed for H_3^0 due to small sample size.

5 Discussion

A knowledge based approach to inferring semantic object affordances is achieved through integrating ontology and qualitative reasoning within a statistical relational learning scheme. In particular, we presented an architecture which uses

O-PrO, an object ontology to infer semantic object affordance exploiting QDC, a qualitative representation formalism within MLN. We have defined operation of a set of modules to implement the proposed architecture. Experiments on the CAD-120 data set have yielded promising results.

1. How important is O-PrO for inferring object affordance?
Object properties are essential in conceptualizing activities. Alternative hypothesis, H_1^a was accepted. For a 95% confidence interval, we conclude that inferring semantic object affordance from video with a knowledge structure lead to an improved recognition accuracy. This is for affordance labels with source of affordance activation in geometrical and physical attributes of the object; and O-PrO as the knowledge structure. This indicates the advantage of using O-PrO.

2. How does QR influence inference of object affordance from video?
Qualitative knowledge abstracted through QDC is used. Accuracies from Table 3 support the intuition that QR through a set of QDC relations help to overcome the limitation of less training data. We have assumed ground truth temporal segmentation ; we argue that the set of QDC relations help to discriminate the temporal segmentation of input videos. QSR based approach [11] achieves automatic temporal segmentation in videos. Incorporation of QDC and O-PrO within MLN is not able to produce statistically significant result whenever spatio-temporal dynamics is involved as a part of *source of activation*. The null hypothesis H_2^0 was accepted.

3. How is the list of grounded primitive entities related to a generalized solution for inferring semantic object affordance?
First, the proposed approach do not claim that the list of DPEs and IPEs are exhaustive enough for object affordance reasoning. The list of DPEs are directly related to types of object attributes represented in O-PrO. These two lists might work in domains similar to indoor household environments. The variability in handling the objects by different persons could be addressed by the proposed solution. This claim is reasonable as the proposed approach utilizes less training data for inferring object affordances. We are striving to provide a generalized solution for inferring semantic object affordances from video data. However, the proposed solution cannot be termed as a generalized solution. This is because the list of DPEs and IPEs will change whenever different objects (not within O-PrO) and multiple human beings are present in the scene. It may also require one to provide new rules if one wants to access new affordances. Nevertheless, the list of grounded predicates allows our inference mechanism to work with less training data. The grounded predicates definitely allows us to handle noise as well as capture abstract "causal" structures. Our approach for object affordance detection is a first positive step towards generalized solution.

4. Why poor performance over two categories of object affordance?
Our accuracy in recognizing "drinkable" and "pourable" is 0%. Less training data is used in our approach as compared to [10]. Missing data and outlier values within the training data may have led to incorrect inferences in these two categories of affordances.

6 Conclusion

O-PrO together with QDC emulate the abstractions underlying sensory and cognitive aspects of human visual reasoning. A novel framework for inferring object affordance from video is discussed. Experimental evaluation on CAD-120 dataset yield encouraging results. In the future, the methodology would be verified over video dataset [5,12] which not only predicts affordance but also interaction regions. The proposed approach is an attempt to bridge the gap between sensor readings and high level reasoning. Handcrafted rules in MLN is a hindrance in automating affordance inference. It may be possible to learn such rules automatically. Augmenting the framework through addition of a rule learning scheme is part of on-going research.

References

1. : Afnet 2.0: The affordance network (2014). http://affordances.info/workshops
2. Bhattacharyya, R., Bhuyan, Z., Hazarika, S.M.: O-PrO: an ontology for object affordance reasoning. In: Basu, A., Das, S., Horain, P., Bhattacharya, S. (eds.) IHCI 2016. LNCS, vol. 10127, pp. 39–50. Springer, Cham (2017). https://doi.org/10.1007/978-3-319-52503-7_4
3. Clementini, E., Di Felice, P., Hernández, D.: Qualitative representation of positional information. Artif. Intell. **95**(2), 317–356 (1997)
4. Do, T.T., Nguyen, A., Reid, I.D., Caldwell, D.G., Tsagarakis, N.G.: AffordanceNet: an end-to-end deep learning approach for object affordance detection. CoRR abs/1709.07326 (2017)
5. Fang, K., Wu, T.L., Yang, D., Savarese, S., Lim, J.J.: Demo2vec: reasoning object affordances from online videos. In: Proceedings of the IEEE Conference on Computer Vision and Pattern Recognition, pp. 2139–2147 (2018)
6. Gibson, J.J.: The ecological approach to the visual perception of pictures. Leonardo **11**(3), 227–235 (1978)
7. Hassanin, M., Khan, S., Tahtali, M.: Visual affordance and function understanding: a survey. arXiv preprint arXiv:1807.06775 (2018)
8. Hidayat, S.S., Kim, B.K., Ohba, K.: Learning affordance for semantic robots using ontology approach. In: IEEE/RSJ International Conference on Intelligent Robots and Systems, IROS 2008, pp. 2630–2636. IEEE (2008)
9. Kok, S., Sumner, M., Richardson, M., Singla, P., Poon, H., Domingos, P.: The alchemy system for statistical relational AI (Technical report). Department of Computer Science and Engineering. University of Washington, Seattle, Washington (2006)
10. Koppula, H.S., Gupta, R., Saxena, A.: Learning human activities and object affordances from RGB-D videos. Int. J. Robot. Res. **32**(8), 951–970 (2013)
11. Tayyub, J., Tavanai, A., Gatsoulis, Y., Cohn, A.G., Hogg, D.C.: Qualitative and quantitative spatio-temporal relations in daily living activity recognition. In: Cremers, D., Reid, I., Saito, H., Yang, M.-H. (eds.) ACCV 2014. LNCS, vol. 9007, pp. 115–130. Springer, Cham (2015). https://doi.org/10.1007/978-3-319-16814-2_8
12. Thermos, S., Daras, P., Potamianos, G.: A deep learning approach to object affordance segmentation. In: International Conference on Acoustics, Speech and Signal Processing (ICASSP), pp. 2358–2362. IEEE (2020)

13. Varadarajan, K.M., Vincze, M.: Afrob: the affordance network ontology for robots. In: International Conference on Intelligent Robots and Systems, pp. 1343–1350 (2012)
14. Ye, C., Yang, Y., Mao, R., Fermüller, C., Aloimonos, Y.: What can i do around here? Deep functional scene understanding for cognitive robots. In: 2017 IEEE International Conference on Robotics and Automation, pp. 4604–4611 (2017)
15. Zhu, Y., Fathi, A., Fei-Fei, L.: Reasoning about object affordances in a knowledge base representation. In: Fleet, D., Pajdla, T., Schiele, B., Tuytelaars, T. (eds.) ECCV 2014. LNCS, vol. 8690, pp. 408–424. Springer, Cham (2014). https://doi.org/10.1007/978-3-319-10605-2_27

An Unsupervised Approach for Estimating Depth of Outdoor Scenes from Monocular Image

Shankhanil Mitra[1], H. Pallab Jyoti Dutta[2(✉)], and M. K. Bhuyan[2]

[1] Department of Electrical and Communication Engineering, IISc, Bengaluru 560012, India
shankhanilm@iisc.ac.in

[2] Department of Electronics and Electrical Engineering, IIT Guwahati, Guwahati 781039, India
{h18,mkb}@iitg.ac.in

Abstract. Majority of the existing deep learning based depth estimation approaches employed for finding depth from monocular image need very accurate ground truth depth information to train a supervised decision framework. However, it is not always possible to get an accurate depth information particularly for diverse outdoor scenes. To address this, a convolutional network architecture is proposed, which comprises of two encoder-decoders for utilizing stereo matching criterion for training. The image reconstruction error measure is employed for optimization of network parameters instead of ground truth depth information. To estimate an accurate disparity map in low textured and occluded regions, a cross based cost-aggregation loss term is proposed along with a novel occlusion detection and filling method in the post-processing stage. The proposed method achieves an improvement of 6.219% RMS error for a depth cap of 80m and 6.15% RMS error for a depth cap of 50 m among the unsupervised approaches on KITTI 2015 dataset. The importance of channel-wise descriptor for training a deep neural network is also established through the performance measure.

Keywords: Stereo matching · Disparity map · Occlusion · Fully Convolutional Network (FCN)

1 Introduction

Depth estimation is a challenging and fundamental research problem in computer vision, and the problem is even more complicated when the target is to estimate depth from single image instead of multiple images. Reconstructing shape of a scene from monocular or multiple images is a rudimentary problem in various fields, such as medicine, film industry, robotics, autonomous driving vehicles, etc.

Various methods, such as synthesizing scene from different lighting conditions [1], stereo [2] or multiview [3] depth estimation or from temporal sequence

S. K. Singh et al. (Eds.): CVIP 2020, CCIS 1378, pp. 291–304, 2021.
https://doi.org/10.1007/978-981-16-1103-2_25

[4] involves multiple images for processing depth information. Saxena et al. [5] segmented a single image into small homogeneous patches, and used Markov Random field to learn the plane parameter to estimate location and orientation of the patches.

With the advent of convolutional neural networks (CNN), depth can be estimated from raw pixels as shown by the multi-scale network of [6]. Laina et al. [7] proposed an auto-encoder type architecture to produce dense depth map from RGBD indoor images. However, these methods require accurate ground truth depth for supervision. Garg et al. [8] suggested an encoder-decoder setup to generate depth from stereo image pair during training using photometric reconstruction loss and without the need of ground truth depth. Godard et al. [9] further improved this method by introducing consistency loss, similarity index etc. Depth estimation in an semi-supervised [10] manner has also been proposed, where both unsupervised loss criteria and ground truth supervision is being used to train the network. Other works involve depth estimation by self-supervised learning [11–13], or generating depth from monocular video [14–16] using visual odometry. In this work, the unsupervised approach is followed, where stereo image pair is used during training, and during the testing phase depth is generated from single image. This work proposes a fully convolutional deep network inspired by the works of [9,14]. Two encoder-decoder CNN model is proposed, which gives a trade off between a deeper model and a shallow network with channel-wise excitation and dilated convolution filters. To accurately predict depth in specular region, a cost aggregation similarity measure in utilized. A post-processing step is incorporated for occluded pixel detection and filling as shown in [22]. The block diagram for the proposed work is shown in Fig. 1.

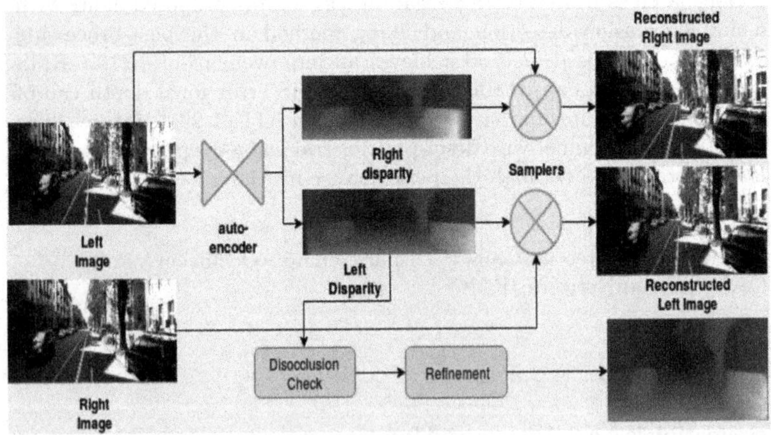

Fig. 1. The block diagram of the proposed method.

2 Proposed Method

The proposed method is based on developing a fully convolutional network (FCN).

2.1 Warping Based Depth Synthesis

The purpose of the CNN network is to learn a non-linear mapping function which estimates per-pixel depth value d. Every training sample is a rectified [4] image pair $\{I_l, I_r\}$ taken from pre-calibrated stereo cameras having a focal length f and a baseline distance between the cameras B. The stereo correspondence between the images, also known as left disparity map d_{lr} and right disparity map d_{rl} is estimated by the network. Using the left disparity map, the left image is reconstructed by sampling from right source image or vice-versa as follows:

$$\hat{I}_l(x) = I_r(x + d_{lr}(x)) \tag{1}$$

$$\hat{I}_r(x) = I_l(x + d_{rl}(x)) \tag{2}$$

If the scalar disparity value of the stereo pair is d, then estimated depth of the pixel is given by $f \times B/d$.

2.2 Network Architecture

An encoder-decoder fashioned CNN is design with long skip connection for pixel-wise disparity estimation. The left image is fed as an input to the network, while the output being both left-to-right and right-to-left image disparity map. Two networks have been proposed with distinct encoder architecture but similar decoder structure.

Encoder Version 1: The encoder section resembles an aggregated residual transformation network *viz.* ResNeXT-101 [17]. The proposed network is fully convolutional without any fully connected layer which enables the encoder to produce feature map directly. The encoder has 5 stages of residual convolution block or max pooling with downsampling by a factor of 2 after each stage.

Encoder Version 2: Another variant of encoder based on ResNeXT-50 [17] without fully connected layers is presented. In the final two stages of convolution block, instead of downsampling the spatial dimension by 2, dilated convolution filter is preferred to enlarge the field of view of filters. Dilation rate of the filter kernel for pre-final and final stage being 2 and 4 respectively. For exploiting channel-wise dependencies of feature map layers, squeeze and excitation block as given in [18] is implemented in parallel with the residual connection in the encoder. The governing equation of the block as stated by Squeeze and Excitation Network [18] is given by:

$$z_c = \frac{1}{H \times W} \sum_{i=1}^{H} \sum_{j=1}^{W} u_c(i,j) \tag{3}$$

where, c being the channel. The above equation is known as squeezing operation. Global information in each spatial dimension $H \times W$ is compressed into channels descriptors z_c. To exploits the channel dependencies, a channel-wise non-linear function is learnt given by:

$$s = \sigma(W_2\delta(W_1 z)) \tag{4}$$

$$x_c = s_c * u_c \qquad \forall \text{ channels c} \tag{5}$$

where, δ is ReLU and σ is sigmoid activation function, $W_1 \in R^{\frac{C}{r}\times C}$ and $W_2 \in R^{C\times\frac{C}{r}}$. r is the dimentionality reduction factor. Equation 5 defines the scaling of the input residual channel u_c with the channel dependency factor s_c.

Skip Connection: Long skip connection between encoder and decoder blocks are used to obtain finer feature map as stated in [8]. Rather than directly adding the output of the encoder layers to the up-scaled feature map, the encoder output is convolved with $3 \times 3 \times C$ separable convolutional filter. Unlike normal convolutional filter, separable filter performs spatial convolution followed by channel wise convolution. Thus, the network can learn the proportion of the finer feature channels required to produce a refined feature map at higher resolution.

For C output channels there are C number of 3×3 filter kernel which individually operate on all the input channels like:

$$\delta(x_i) = (f * x_i) \tag{6}$$

where, x_i is the ith channels of the input feature map x and f is 3×3 filter. This is followed by point wise convolution *i.e.*, linear combination as follows:

$$L\ (x) = \sum_{j=1}^{N} w_i * \delta(x_i) \tag{7}$$

where, w_i is convolution weights. Thus, the network learns the proportion of the input channels to be concatenated with the decoder layers.

Decoder: The decoder up projects the feature map produced in the final layer of the encoder non-linearly. Unlike the general approach [8,9], an up-projection block is designed with residual link instead of up-convolutional.

The configuration of the up-projection block is depicted as follows:

- The input map is scaled to twice its resolution by nearest neighbour upsampling.
- Next the upscaled map is splitted into $output\_channels/(width = 4)$ number of paths known as cardinality. $Output\_channels$ is the number of channels of the block output.
- In each path, a 3×3 dilated convolution filter is implemented producing feature layers with channel width 4.
- This is followed by a 3×3 convolutional filter with both input and output channels being 4.

- Grouping the above residual paths as in $\sum_{i=1}^{C} \tau(x)$. $\tau(x)$ is the above residual transformation on input feature map x.
- Applying a 3×3 dilated convolution operation on the input map to serve as a projection branch between the lower resolution input and higher resolution output.
- The above up-projection block can be summed up as $f * x + \sum_{i=1}^{C} \tau(x)$, where f is a 3×3 dilated filter kernel.

The block output is then convolved with the skip layer input to get the disparity map. 6 such block are used to get the disparity map at the same resolution as the input image. In this architecture, 3×3 dilated convolution filter with dilation rate of 2 is used instead of 5×5 filter to reduce the network parameters.

2.3 Error Terms

The network produces both left and right disparity map at four different scales. Therefore, the loss term $\mathcal{L}$ is defined as:

$$\mathcal{L}_s = \psi_{ph}(\mathcal{L}^l_{ph} + \mathcal{L}^r_{ph}) + \psi_{con}(\mathcal{L}^l_{con} + \mathcal{L}^r_{con}) + \psi_{spec}(\mathcal{L}^l_{spec} + \mathcal{L}^l_{spec}) + \psi_{ds}(\mathcal{L}^l_{ds} + \mathcal{L}^r_{ds}) \quad (8)$$

where, $\mathcal{L}_{ph}$ is the photometric loss, $\mathcal{L}_{con}$ denotes the left-right consistency between the estimated disparity map pair, $\mathcal{L}_{spec}$ refers to the disparity map aggregation term, and finally $\mathcal{L}_{ds}$ indicates the semi-global smoothness term. The total loss being $\mathcal{L} = \sum_s \mathcal{L}_s$.

Photometric Reconstruction Loss. Inspired by [11], for minimising the contrariety between original and reconstructed input image pair, $L1$ penalty is applied to image and image gradient as follows:

$$\mathcal{B} = ||\hat{\mathcal{I}} - \mathcal{I}|| + ||\nabla\hat{\mathcal{I}} - \nabla\mathcal{I}|| \quad (9)$$

where, $\hat{I}$ and I are the reconstructed and original image respectively.

As image reconstruction itself is an ill-posed problem, similarity measure between the original and reconstructed image is taken into consideration. Structural Similarity (SSIM) measures correlation between two images in terms of perception, by treating image degradation as a change in structural information. SSIM term basically involves both luminance and contrast mask rather than intensity of the pixel. For two image patches x and y, SSIM term is defined as:

$$SSIM(x, y) = \frac{(2\mu_x\mu_y + c_1)(2\sigma_{xy} + c_2)}{(\mu_x^2 + \mu_y^2 + c_1)(\sigma_x^2 + \sigma_y^2 + c_2)} \quad (10)$$

where, μ and σ are mean and variance parameter of the patches, and c_1, c_2 are constants in the order of 10^{-4}. To minimize the dissimilarity between original and reconstructed patches, a combination of structural dissimilarity and reconstruction loss term is used, which is as follow:

$$\mathcal{L}_{ph} = \frac{1}{N}\sum_{i,j}\alpha_{ssim}\frac{(1 - SSIM(I_{ij}, \hat{I}_{ij}))}{2} + \alpha_{rec}\mathcal{B}_{ij} \tag{11}$$

where, N being the total number of image pixel. During optimization, $\alpha_{ssim} = 0.85$ and $\alpha_{rec} = 0.45$ for encoder-1 and 0.15 for encoder 2, which are experimentally determined.

Consistency Loss. The proposed network outputs both left to right d_{LR} and right to left d_{RL} disparity maps. The stereo property of the images suggests that the disparity maps generated are inverse of each other. If this property fails then the pixel (x, y) is termed as occluded pixels. Therefore, for unoccluded pixels L-R check [20] gives:

$$d_{lr}(x, y) = -d_{rl}(x + d_{lr}(x, y), y) \tag{12}$$

Similar to Eq. 12, to ensure soundness between the disparity maps, the discrepancy between projected right disparity map and left disparity map is calculated as follows:

$$\mathcal{L}_{con} = \frac{1}{N}\sum_{x,y}||d_{LR}(x, y) + d_{RL}(x + d_{LR}(x, y), y)|| \tag{13}$$

Consistency error is computed for both left and right view disparity map at all output scales.

Cost Aggregation Term. Image synthesis by photometric loss can be done by various warping functions, indicating specular or low textured surface will produce inconsistent depth. Like Kuwahara filter window [21], a $(2m+1)$ square window centred around the pixel (x, y) is constructed for both the disparity map and input image. The window is divided into four sub-region P_1, P_2, P_3, P_4 as given below:

$$P_i = \begin{cases} [x, x-m] \times [y, y-m] & for \quad i = 1 \\ [x, x-m] \times [y, y+m] & for \quad i = 2 \\ [x, x+m] \times [y, y-m] & for \quad i = 3 \\ [x, x+m] \times [y, y+m] & for \quad i = 4 \end{cases} \tag{14}$$

This window is employed to the disparity map for computing $\mu_i(x, y)$ *i.e.*, the mean intensity of each sub-region of the disparity map is given by:

$$\mu_i(x, y) = \frac{1}{n}\sum_{a,b} d(a, b) \quad for \quad i = 1, 2, 3, 4 \tag{15}$$

where, n is the number of pixel and d is the estimated disparity value within the sub-region.

Similarly, applying the same filter on the input image to calculate $\sigma_i(x, y)$, the standard deviation of the sub-regions as follows:

$$\sigma_i(x,y) = \frac{1}{n}(\sum_{a,b}\{\hat{I}(a,b)\}^2 - \{\sum_{a,b}\hat{I}(a,b)\}^2) \quad , for \quad i = 1,2,3,4 \quad (16)$$

where, I^2 corresponds to the variance of pixel intensity.

Therefore, the disparity value at pixel (x, y) is considered as the mean disparity value of the sub-region which has the minimum variation in pixel intensity in input image. The filtered disparity at (x, y) is defined as :

$$\delta(x,y) = \mu_i(x,y) \quad (17)$$

where,

$$i = \arg\min_i \sigma_i(x,y) \quad (18)$$

Specular loss term is taken by enforcing a $L1$ penalty between the filtered disparity and the estimated disparity as stated below:

$$\mathcal{L}_{spec} = \frac{1}{N}\sum_{x,y}||\delta(x,y) - d(x,y)|| \quad (19)$$

Regularization Term. Finally, a semi-global regularization term is integrated to make the disparity locally smooth. To do so, a $L1$ norm is exercised on the gradient of the estimated disparity both horizontally and vertically. Since disparity change can occur at object boundaries, the image gradient is weighted by an edge-aware term. Overall regularizer term for smoothness correction is defined as:

$$\mathcal{L}_{ds} = \frac{1}{N}\sum_{x,y}(|\partial_x d(x,y)|e^{-|\partial_x I(x,y)|} + |\partial_y d(x,y)|e^{-|\partial_y I(x,y)|}) \quad (20)$$

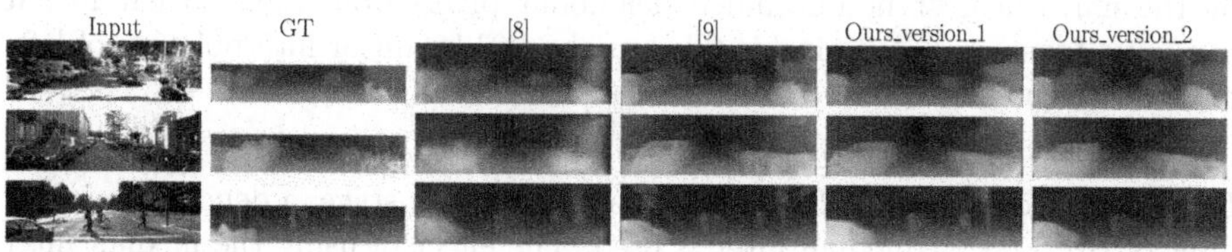

Fig. 2. Qualitative comparison with other unsupervised methods on KITTI 2015 using Eigen split [6]. For visualization, the ground truth data (sparse) is interpolated. The proposed method produce detailed views of cars, posts and pedestrians.

2.4 Post Processing

Stereo Dis-Occlusion Check. Since, the network is trained with stereo image pair, the problem of dis-occlusion appear as noted by [9]. Firstly, during testing disparity map of the input image d_l and its warped version $d_l^{'}$ is estimated [9]. Thereafter, the disparity map is computed as the mean of the original disparity map d_l and the flipped version of the wrapped disparity map $d_l^{'}$ *i.e.*, $d_l^{''}$. However, this step also does not remove artifacts at occluded object boundaries. Hence, an occlusion detection and filling method is proposed which takes care of occluded object disparity ramp. This procedure also checks wrongly calculated disparity value in occluded region as discussed below.

Similar to [22], the occlusion detection problem in this work is based on the fundamental property of stereo matching *i.e.*, continuity, ordering and uniqueness constraints. For an image pixel (x, y) in the left image having disparity value $d_{lr}(x, y)$, the corresponding right image pixel $F_r(x, y)$ is given by:

$$F_r(x, y) = x - d_{lr}(x, y) \tag{21}$$

where, x is the horizontal index of the left image pixel. This mapping function F_r necessarily follows a linear curve; thus can be estimated by a linear function. If the disparity value breaks any one of the constraints, the linearity condition will fail. Dis-occlusion occurs on the left image boundary and on the occluded object boundary, which can be identified by the failure of linearity in L_r. First, a linear curve is fitted through the observed value of F_r for all the image pixels as follows:

$$\hat{F}_r = A \times F_r + \epsilon \tag{22}$$

where, A and ϵ being the regression matrix and error constant. Now for every disparity value, if the estimated disparity is outside a certain threshold of $\hat{F}_r$, it is marked as occluded one.

$$F \in [\hat{F} - Th, \hat{F} + Th] \tag{23}$$

where, $Th = c \times g$, c is a constant and g is the weighted gradient of the disparity map defined as:

$$g = exp(-[(\delta_x d_l)^2 + (\delta_y d_l)^2)]) \tag{24}$$

So, the occluded pixels are identified, and filled the boundary occluded pixels by the naive nearest non-occluded neighbour pixels from right to left in left disparity. Inner occluded pixel is filled or checked by linear interpolation of left-most and right-most non-occluded pixels of it.

Disparity Refinement: In the final post-processing stage, a denoising median filter of size 11 × 11 median filter is used. The effect of using the median filter in shown in Table 1.

Table 1. Comparison of different variant of our model as well as other methods using [9] split for training. For testing 200 high quality disparity map provides as KITTI 2015 dataset [23] is used. Here, **SC**: Specularity check, **OC**: Dis-occlusion check, **MF**: Median filter, **K**: KITTI, **CS**: Cityscapes.

Method	Dataset	Abs Rel	Sq Rel	RMSE	RMSE log	*D1-all*	$\delta < 1.25$	$\delta < 1.25^2$	$\delta < 1.25^3$
[9]	K	0.124	1.388	6.125	0.217	30.272	0.841	0.936	0.975
[12]	K	0.117	1.202	5.953	0.210	**29.612**	0.845	0.938	0.976
Ours_v1(w/o SC & OC)	K	0.119	1.279	5.983	0.218	29.871	0.849	0.944	0.978
Ours_v1(with SC & w/o OC)	K	0.114	1.161	5.819	0.212	29.810	0.850	0.946	0.979
Ours_v1(with SC & OC)	K	0.1137	1.095	5.696	0.199	29.859	0.850	0.946	0.980
Ours_v1(with SC & OC + MF)	K	**0.1136**	**1.089**	**5.687**	**0.199**	29.770	**0.850**	**0.946**	**0.980**
[9]	CS	0.699	10.060	14.445	0.542	94.757	0.053	0.326	0.862
Ours_v1	CS	0.667	7.496	10.718	0.528	93.667	0.056	0.401	0.878
Ours_v2	CS	0.688	7.967	11.217	0.536	93.711	0.057	0.381	0.872

Table 2. Comparison of our model with various approaches using [6] split on KITTI 2015 [23] dataset. All the methods except [6] uses the crop provided by [8]. With the exception of [6], all the methods are unsupervised. The results for 80 m depth cap, and 50m depth are shown as done in [8].

Method	Supervised	Abs Rel	Sq Rel	RMSE	RMSE log	$\delta < 1.25$	$\delta < 1.25^2$	$\delta < 1.25^3$
Depth Cap: 80 m								
[6]	Yes	0.203	1.548	6.307	0.282	0.702	0.890	0.958
[9]	No	0.148	1.344	5.927	0.247	0.803	0.922	0.964
[14]	No	0.208	1.768	6.856	0.283	0.678	0.885	0.957
[10]	No	0.214	1.932	7.157	0.295	0.665	0.882	0.950
[15]	No	0.163	**1.240**	6.220	0.250	0.762	0.916	0.968
[19] (Temporal)	No	0.144	1.391	5.869	0.241	0.803	0.922	**0.969**
Our_v1	No	0.146	1.287	5.510	**0.228**	0.809	0.927	**0.969**
Ours_v2	No	**0.143**	1.242	**5.504**	0.232	**0.810**	**0.929**	**0.969**
Depth Cap: 50 m								
[8]	No	0.169	1.080	5.104	0.273	0.740	0.904	0.962
[9]	No	0.140	0.976	4.471	0.232	0.818	0.931	0.969
[14]	No	0.201	1.391	5.181	0.264	0.696	0.900	0.966
Ours_v1	No	0.139	0.973	**4.196**	**0.215**	**0.824**	0.935	0.972
Ours_v2	No	**0.137**	**0.928**	4.223	0.219	**0.824**	**0.936**	**0.973**

3 Experimental Results and Discussion

The performance of the proposed model is evaluated on KITTI 2015 [23] outdoor scene data. For generalization, the network performance is also tested on Cityscapes and Make3D dataset. Experimental results are shown in Fig. 2, 3, and 4, and all these results show the efficacy of the proposed methods. The network is mainly trained using KITTI 2015 [23] dataset using Godard split [9] and

Eigen Split [6]. The KITTI raw dataset contains 42,382 rectified stereo image pairs of 61 outdoor scenes of various German cities.

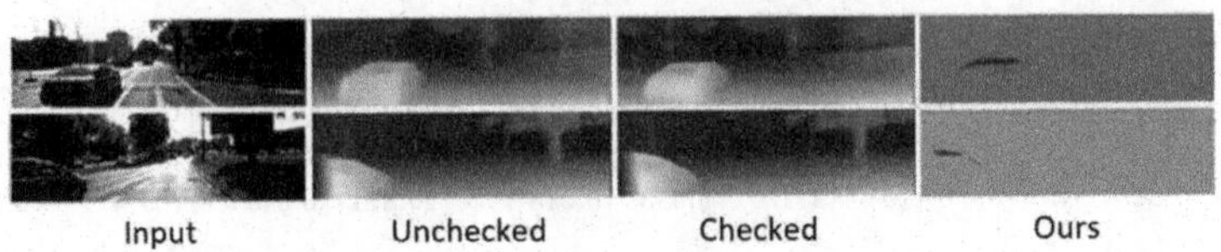

Fig. 3. Analysis of the importance of cost-aggregation loss term. **First column**: Input Image, **Second column**: Without Cost-Aggregation loss, **Third column**: With Cost-Aggregation loss, **Forth column**: Specularity Correction.

Godard Split: The same data split is used as indicated by [9] on the KITTI raw dataset. Out of the 61 scenes, 33 scenes containing 30,159 image pairs are used for training and the rest for validation. While 29,000 images are used for training and the rest 1,159 are kept as validation set for tuning the hyper-parameters. For evaluation, 200 disparity maps covering 28 scenes given as a part of KITTI official train data is utilized. These disparity images are better in quality than projected from velodyne laser, as they employed a CAD model which was inserted instead of moving cars.

Eigen Split: For fair comparison with the existing methods, the model is tested on 697 images covering 29 scenes of KITTI raw dataset proposed by [6]. The remaining 32 scenes comprises of 23,488 image pairs of which 22,600 is used for training and the remaining for validation. To obtain the ground truth depth for the 697 test images, 3D points taken by the velodyne laser is projected onto the left camera. Reconstructing ground truth depth this way gives only 5% of the pixels values. Error are also introduced due to motion of the velodyne laser, camera and vehicle.

The two proposed networks contain approximately 110 and 57 million parameters, and it takes nearly 52 mins and 35 mins, respectively for training on a batch size of 4 image pairs for 1k epochs on a Tesla K20 GPU. The input images of resolution 375×1275 are rescaled using bi-cubic interpolation to 256×512.

To introduce non-linearity in the network, exponential linear unit instead of RELU is preferred as proposed by [9]. After each convolutional layer, batch-normalization layer is introduced. However, it is not done for the final output layer. The system is also tested without using batch-normalization, but the results were not good. For optimization, Adam optimizer is used with $\beta_1 = 0.9$, $\beta_2 = 0.999$ and $\epsilon = 10^{-8}$. The learning rate is 10^{-4} and it is decreased by a factor of 10 depending upon validation set error. During optimization, loss co-coefficients ψ_{ph} and ψ_{con} are kept at 1, while ψ_{spec} and ψ_{ds} are kept at 0.1. The specularity and smoothness loss coefficients are weighted by their scale factor as the disparity between neighbouring pixels generally differs by scale factor of 2 per scale. The output disparity map is processed through the post-processing block, and the map is rescaled to original input image size.

To counter overfitting of the model, colour augmentation is used by randomly multiplying image intensity by a value $i \in [0.8, 1.3]$ and also randomly flip the input with a probability of 0.5 on training dataset.

In context of comparison to other unsupervised methods, firstly, the proposed model was evaluated using Godard split [9] and shown the relevance of different components of the model. The method achieves state-of-the-art performance among the methods that used Godard split [9] in all metrics. The model is further tested using the most generalized Eigen split [6], and compare with other unsupervised methods of depth estimation from monocular image. The method achieves state-of-the-art results in 6 out of 7 metrics using a depth cap of 80m, as indicated in Table 2. Performance measure for a depth cap of 50m in accordance with [8] is also shown.

Make3D [5] is one of the earliest dataset used for evaluating various supervised depth estimation methods. To demonstrate the robustness of the method, a comparison is drawn between the proposed method and other supervised and unsupervised models tested with Make3D test set [5]. Since Make3D contains only RGB/Depth image pairs and no stereo pairs, the proposed model was trained on KITTI for evaluation. It is evident from the results shown in Table 3 that it achieved reasonable results with other supervised methods and unsupervised methods.

Next, the diversity of the proposed network on Cityscapes dataset [24] is tested. For training, the data split provided in [9] (containing 22,973 urban stereo images) is followed. For comparison, this model is tested on 200 disparity maps of KITTI dataset, similar to [9] as shown in Table 1.

In this work, encoder-decoder type fully convolutional network with two variant of encoders for extracting depth information from a RGB image is also presented. The first variant of the model is similar to ResNeXt-101 [17] without fully connected layers. The next encoder setup comprises of a ResNeXT-50 [17] architecture along with squeeze and excitation block which exploits channel dependencies. In Table 2, a comparative study on KITTI 2015 dataset using Eigen split [6] is illustrated. The exposition of the proposed models are also given on Cityscapes [24] dataset in Table 1 and Make3D [5] dataset in Table 3. In Table 3, though with ground truth supervision, the evaluation metrics show better results (for [7]), it still performed better than some of the other methods ([25,26]). However, for methods without ground truth supervision, it has the upper hand. The second model achieves similar performance and even beats the first variant on many metrics, taking into account that it has half the number of layers. Therefore, a network which exploits channel-dependencies, and with dilated convolution filters (to increase the field of view) gives comparable performance to that of a much deeper network.

Table 3. Results on the Make3D dataset [5]. Evaluation metric given by [9] is followed, and depth is evaluated for less than 70 m. In this, * denotes ground truth supervision.

Method	Sq Rel	Abs Rel	RMSE	$\log_{10}$
[25]*	4.894	0.417	8.172	0.144
[26]*	6.625	0.462	9.972	0.161
[7]*	**1.665**	**0.198**	**5.461**	**0.082**
[9] pp	7.112	0.443	8.860	0.142
[10]	12.341	0.647	11.567	NA
Ours_v1	6.810	0.344	6.951	0.155
Ours_v2	7.255	0.337	6.736	0.150

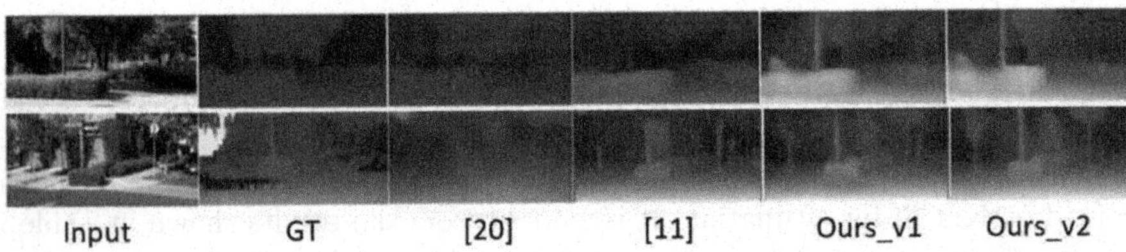

Fig. 4. Make3D [5] results trained on KITTI dataset. Qualitative comparison is showed with an unsupervised [9] and a supervised [7] learning method.

4 Conclusion

In this work, an unsupervised framework for estimating depth from monocular images is presented which doesn't need any ground truth depth for supervision. To take care of inconsistent depths of specular regions and dis-occlusion ramps, a novel cost-aggregation term along with asymmetric occlusion detection and filling post-processor are introduced. It is also shown that use of channel-wise characteristics and other network modifications produce state-of-the-art results with much less network complexity. An up-project network is depicted which produces high quality depth map with better accuracy.

For future work, monocular videos would be used instead of images. Moreover, the claim of equivalent accuracy through the use of channel dependencies would be dealt with by performing on other set of computer vision problems, like image semantic segmentation, visual odometry, etc.

References

1. Abrams, A., Hawley, C., Pless, R.: Heliometric stereo: shape from sun position. In: Fitzgibbon, A., Lazebnik, S., Perona, P., Sato, Y., Schmid, C. (eds.) ECCV 2012. LNCS, pp. 357–370. Springer, Heidelberg (2012). https://doi.org/10.1007/978-3-642-33709-3_26
2. Scharstein, D., Szeliski, R., Zabih, R.: A taxonomy and evaluation of dense two-frame stereo correspondence algorithms. In: Proceedings IEEE Workshop on Stereo and Multi-Baseline Vision, SMBV, Kauai, HI, USA, pp. 131–140 (2001)
3. Furukawa, Y., Hernández, C.: Multi-view stereo: a tutorial, now (2015)
4. Hartley, R., Zisserman, A.: Multiple View Geometry in Computer Vision, 2nd edn. Cambridge University Press, Cambridge (2004)
5. Saxena, A., Sun, M., Ng, A.Y.: Make3D: learning 3D scene structure from a single still image. IEEE Trans. Pattern Anal. Mach. Intell. **31**(5), 824–840 (2009)
6. Eigen, D., Puhrsch, C., Fergus, R.: Depth map prediction from a single image using a multi-scale deep network. In: Proceedings of the 27th International Conference on Neural Information Processing Systems, (NIPS 2014), vol. 2, pp. 2366–2374. MIT Press, Cambridge (2014)
7. Laina, I., Rupprecht, C., Belagiannis, V., Tombari, F., Navab, N.: Deeper depth prediction with fully convolutional residual networks. In: 2016 Fourth International Conference on 3D Vision (3DV), Stanford, CA, pp. 239–248 (2016)
8. Garg, R., B.G., V.K., Carneiro, G., Reid, I.: Unsupervised CNN for single view depth estimation: geometry to the rescue. In: Leibe, B., Matas, J., Sebe, N., Welling, M. (eds.) ECCV 2016. LNCS, vol. 9912, pp. 740–756. Springer, Cham (2016). https://doi.org/10.1007/978-3-319-46484-8_45
9. Godard, C., Mac Aodha, O., Brostow, G.J.: Unsupervised monocular depth estimation with left-right consistency. In: 2017 IEEE Conference on Computer Vision and Pattern Recognition (CVPR), Honolulu, HI, pp. 6602–6611 (2017)
10. Kundu, J.N., Uppala, P.K., Pahuja, A., Babu, R.V.: AdaDepth: unsupervised content congruent adaptation for depth estimation. In: 2018 IEEE/CVF Conference on Computer Vision and Pattern Recognition, Salt Lake City, UT, pp. 2656–2665 (2018)
11. Zhong, Y., Dai, Y., Li, H.: Self-supervised learning for stereo matching with self-improving ability. CoRR abs/1709.00930 (2017)
12. Chen, L., Tang, W., John, N.W.: Self-supervised monocular image depth learning and confidence estimation. CoRR abs/1803.05530 (2018)
13. Johnston, A., Carneiro, G.: Self-supervised monocular trained depth estimation using self-attention and discrete disparity volume. In: 2020 IEEE/CVF Conference on Computer Vision and Pattern Recognition (CVPR), Seattle, WA, USA, pp. 4755–4764 (2020)
14. Zhou, T., Brown, M., Snavely, N., Lowe, D.G.: Unsupervised learning of depth and ego-motion from video. In: 2017 IEEE Conference on Computer Vision and Pattern Recognition (CVPR), Honolulu, HI, pp. 6612–6619 (2017)
15. Mahjourian, R., Wicke, M., Angelova, A.: Unsupervised learning of depth and ego-motion from monocular video using 3D geometric constraints. In: 2018 IEEE/CVF Conference on Computer Vision and Pattern Recognition, Salt Lake City, UT, pp. 5667–5675 (2018)
16. Andraghetti, L., et al.: Enhancing self-supervised monocular depth estimation with traditional visual odometry. In: 2019 International Conference on 3D Vision (3DV), Québec City, QC, Canada, pp. 424–433 (2019). https://doi.org/10.1109/3DV.2019.00054

17. Xie, S., Girshick, R., Dollár, P., Tu, Z., He, K.: Aggregated residual transformations for deep neural networks. In: 2017 IEEE Conference on Computer Vision and Pattern Recognition (CVPR), Honolulu, HI, pp. 5987–5995 (2017)
18. Hu, J., Shen, L., Albanie, S., Sun, G., Wu, E.: Squeeze-and-excitation networks. IEEE Trans. Pattern Anal. Mach. Intell. **42**(8), 2011–2023 (2020)
19. Zhan, H., Garg, R., Weerasekera, C.S., Li, K., Agarwal, H., Reid, I.: Unsupervised learning of monocular depth estimation and visual odometry with deep feature reconstruction. arXiv preprint arXiv:1803.03893 (2018)
20. Scharstein, D., Szeliski, R.: High-accuracy stereo depth maps using structured light. In: 2003 IEEE Computer Society Conference on Computer Vision and Pattern Recognition, Proceedings, Madison, WI, USA, pp. I-I (2003)
21. Kuwahara, M., Hachimura, K., Eiho, S., Kinoshita, M.: Processing of RI-angiocardiographic images. In: Preston, K., Onoe, M. (eds.) Digital Processing of Biomedical Images, pp. 187–202. Springer, Boston (1976). https://doi.org/10.1007/978-1-4684-0769-3_13
22. Malathi, T., Bhuyan, M.K.: Asymmetric occlusion detection using linear regression and weight-based filling for stereo disparity map estimation. IET Comput. Vis. **10**(7), 679–688 (2016)
23. Geiger, A., Lenz, P., Stiller, C., Urtasun, R.: Vision meets robotics: the KITTI dataset. Int. J. Robot. Res. **32**(11), 1231–1237 (2013)
24. Cordts, M., et al.: The cityscapes dataset for semantic urban scene understanding. In: Proceedings of the IEEE Conference on Computer Vision and Pattern Recognition (CVPR) (2016)
25. Karsch, K., Liu, C., Kang, S.B.: Depth transfer: depth extraction from video using non-parametric sampling. IEEE Trans. Pattern Anal. Mach. Intell. **36**(11), 2144–2158 (2014)
26. Liu, M., Salzmann, M., He, X.: Discrete-continuous depth estimation from a single image. In: 2014 IEEE Conference on Computer Vision and Pattern Recognition, Columbus, OH, pp. 716–723 (2014)

One Shot Learning Based Human Tracking in Multiple Surveillance Cameras

A. Arulprakash, Md. Meraz(✉), and Mohd. Javed(✉)

Indian Institute of Information Technology Allahabad, Allahabad 211015, India
{iim2015002,pro2016001,javed}@iiita.ac.in

Abstract. Video surveillance based human tracking is rapidly developing field in the Computer Vision domain, which is basically aimed at automatically detecting of abnormal activities and securing high alert areas like airports, frontiers, public places, banks, etc. Through this research work, we propose an unsupervised method of human tracking in multiple surveillance cameras using one shot learning. Facial feature extraction and detection is carried out using Histogram of Oriented Gradients (HOG) and Support Vector Machine (SVM), and further Siamese Network combined with GoogleNet is used for learning, differentiating and tracking. The proposed model is computationally efficient because the training phase requires less GPU time and avoids re-training whenever new individual is added into the system, and also very useful when only few images of a person are available. The experimental results show that the accuracy of tracking is not compromised even in case variable illumination and partial facial occlusion.

Keywords: Human tracking · Multiple surveillance camera · Deep learning · Siamese networks · HoG · SVM

1 Introduction

Video surveillance systems play an important role in keeping our society safe and secure from any untoward incidents, and basically they are used in high alert areas. Manual tracking of individuals in a video surveillance system is totally a strain full and tedious task. Moreover, in the last decade, though there were huge demands and subsequent technology advancements in video based surveillance systems, but still they lacked automation and intelligence in solving many real life problems. Once such significant problem that requires attention is automatic human tracking in surveillance videos [4]. Most of the research attempts in the literature are focused on single camera based tracking [8,14,16], where the tracking is lost once the person disappears from the camera frame. The problem of human tracking becomes much more complex when multiple cameras are involved [7]. This research paper aims to work towards developing an intelligent and efficient human monitoring system based on face detection

S. K. Singh et al. (Eds.): CVIP 2020, CCIS 1378, pp. 305–317, 2021.
https://doi.org/10.1007/978-981-16-1103-2_26

and tracking in multiple surveillance cameras [2] taking into account the cases of disappearance and reappearance of the person being tracked by the system.

The conventional techniques for object recognition include making use of block-wise orientation histogram (SIFT [26] or HOG [15]) feature which were not capable of achieving high levels of precision in customary datasets like PASCAL VOC [27]. These techniques encode less discriminatory attributes of the objects, and as a result they are not able to differentiate well amidst varied labels. Deep learning, specifically Convolutional Neural networks (CNN) [8] based techniques have become the latest and modern approaches to object detection in images and videos. They build a depiction in a stratified manner with ascending order of abstraction from lower to higher degrees of neural network. There are Deep Learning architectures, that utilize various techniques inside, to carry out the task of object detection. The most well known variations being Single Shot Detector (SSD) [6], You Only Look Once (YOLO) [24] and R-FCN networks [25]. Model size and accuracy of final result are heavily influenced by base classifier of each model. While picking an object detection algorithm, there is constants trade off between speed, accuracy and size.

Face detection in human tracking system is the most tedious job, and thus plethora of research work has been done on face detection to increase speed and produce more accurate results [2,4,9,14]. In paper [9], authors have discussed about various techniques and their shortcomings related to image classification application. The work of [4], also gives a detailed comparisons of various techniques in identifying and classifying moving human beings i.e., background subtraction, optical flow and spatio-temporal filtering. On the other hand, need for unsupervised surveillance system is highly essential. Observing an object's movement in an unsupervised surveillance video thereby detects abnormal activities. The work by [14], reports about the approaches for single and multiple person's unsupervised classification of videos. There are two steps in human detection and tracking. First, the human face need to be recognized, then the recognized face needs to be tracked. The research work of [2], proposes an interesting new method for human tracking and face detection using Gaussian mixture model (GMM). Every 3rd, 5th and 10th frame of the first 100 frames of video footage are taken into consideration. Rest of the frames are taken for testing using SVM classifier. The experimental results show that as the dataset complexity increases, the performance metrics decreases [2].

In this paper, we propose deep learning based end-to-end framework for human tracking in multiple cameras using one shot learning. Using one shot detection reduces re-training cost, and also requires only few images. Experimental results show better performance in presence of illumination and occlusion. Given a set of n cameras, we need to track the person in the given cameras. The output of this system is to log the details of the person if found in one of the cameras. The output is of the form [$< TimeStamp >$, $< PersonName >$, $< CameraNumber >$, $< Frame >$]. In the deep learning framework, objective is to map two given images to a single distance measure. We take suitable thresholds to predict whether two images are similar or not. The data logged is used to track the person and predict the path traversed by the person. We will merge the benefits of both detection and tracking in one single pipeline in this paper. Every frame detects approximate articulations of every person based on face and its features. The paper is sorted in the following manner - Sect. 2 bears description of the proposed model and different stages involved, Sect. 3 reports experimental results, and Sect. 4 encapsulates the research work.

2 Proposed Model

For human tracking in surveillance videos we have presented the proposed model in this section and the different stages involved in the model are shown in Fig. 1, and they are discussed in detail one by one.

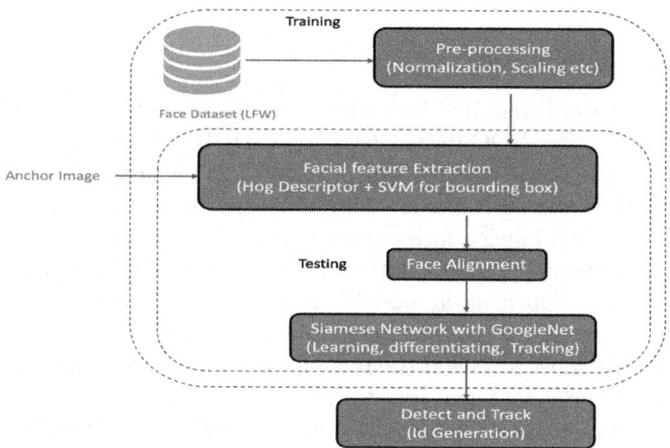

Fig. 1. Flow chart of proposed model

2.1 Problem Background

For any tracker to track objects we need to have a bounding box around the object. Tracker cannot track objects without detector, so let's assume we have detector available. We have bounding box information of an object in frame and thus, an ID is assigned to it. We need to track and maintain the same ID in future frames. In centroid based ID assignment (see Fig. 2), we can relegate IDs by looking at the bounding box centroids. To do this, centroids of every bounding box is measured in frame 1. Moving on to frame 2, new centroids are considered and based on the distance from past centroids we can appoint IDs by considering relative distances. The essential supposition is that frame-to-frame centroids would just move a tad. This straightforward method works fine till centroids are placed apart from one another. But this methodology fails when individuals are near one another since it might switch IDs at that point.

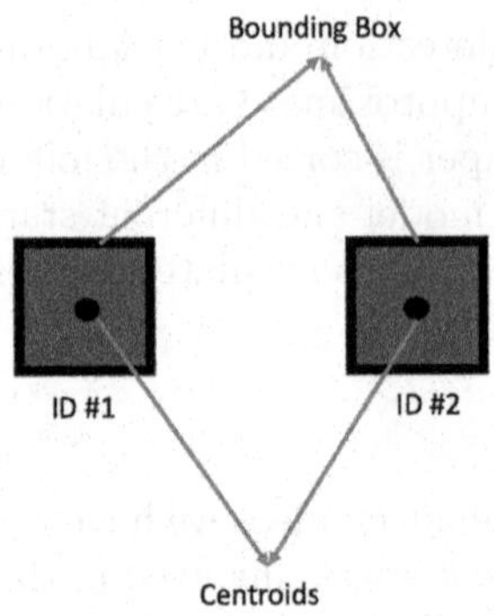

Fig. 2. Centroid based ID assignment

2.2 Dataset Description

Facial image dataset is required for training proposed model. Different databases like Coco Dataset [28], VOC Pascal 2007 [27], FDDB data set [29], LFW dataset [1]. We found LFW dataset (consisting of total 13,233 images, with 5,749 individuals, and 1,680 people with two or more images) more suitable for our problem which has around 6K labeled face images with different scales, poses, and occlusions for each person but other datasets do not have segregated people faces. Since our learning algorithm is modeled to learn to differentiate between faces [1], the normal procedure followed is face verification. Given a couple of images, a binary classifier must foresee if the two pictures are of the same individual. An alternate to this process, facial recognition or identification that can be undertaken is, given the image of the front profile of an obscure individual, recognizes the name of an individual by referring to a gallery of recently observed images of recognised faces.

2.3 Pre-processing Stage

Pre-processing is an important step that is necessary before solving any problem. Here, it basically means converting raw data to a clean dataset which is to achieve better results from the model designed. Techniques for pre-processing include normalisation, scaling of the data, binarizing the data and standardizing the data.

2.4 Facial Detection Stage

Face detection using deep learning is an essential and major problem in computer vision. Face Detection refers to determining whether image has faces or not, so if face is found in image then it returns the location with a bound box for each face in the image. Face detection is important and base part of face verification in various applications [11]. Face must be located in the image before recognizing it. To recognize faces in real time, here we are using HOG descriptor. It is a descriptor built on facial features which is utilised for object recognition[10]. Taking HOG of the picture, we figure out the weights that provide facial landmarks. Positive loads of highlights are pronounced fully to envision a face. This method consistently identifies the facial profile from +90 to −90° facial movements in any event, even if face is impeded. HOG does not only explains the attributes of facial contours, but also, it is immune to brightness and little offset. HOG creates human facial attributes by joining the features of all blocks in line.

The step by step process is given below.

1. Input a picture: which here is the video frame caught continually by the webcam.
2. Split the input picture into smaller cells (including 256×256 pixels) and join $4(2 \times 2)$ cells to make single block.
3. Choice of direction channel: divide $0 - 180°$ or $0 - 360°$ into n channels on an average. In our research, we have split +90 to −90° in 13 uniform halves, that is, 13 channels in totality. Hence, 4×13 equal to 52 features in every block are present.
4. Attainment of histogram: obtain the statistics of every pixel inside every cell of its HOG. The abscissa of histogram symbolizes the 13 direction channels taken in the step above, and the ordinate signifies the sum of the gradient, associated with a specific direction channel. This is how a vector set is obtained.
5. Normalization process: the vectors in blocks are normalized, wherein pixels compared to vectors. Block normalization adjusts neighbourhood contrast disparity along with normalizing histograms of the cells for every block.
6. Formation of HOG features: combining all the vectors calculated using above given equation, build vector sets. These vector sets make up the HOG features.

The other major steps involved in facial detection stage are discussed below in brief.

Gradient Computation. Calculating gradient values is the primary tread. Procedure includes putting one dimensional masks in both vertical and horizontal rules. The masks utilized here are 1×3 and 3×1 kernels. To be precise, this procedure needs masking the colour data of picture with the given masks:

$$D_x = [-1, 0, 1] \text{ and } D_y = [-1, 0, 1]^T$$

D_x : x-axis kernel mask while, D_y : y-axis kernel mask.

$$G_x(x, y) = H(x + 1, y) - H(x - 1, y) \tag{1}$$

$$G_y(x, y) = H(x, y + 1) - H(x, y - 1). \tag{2}$$

$$G(x, y) = \sqrt{G_x^2(x, y) + G_y^2(x, y)} \tag{3}$$

$$\alpha(x, y) = tan^{-1}(\frac{G_y(x, y)}{G_x(x, y)}) \tag{4}$$

Orientation Binning. Following the first tread to extricate HOG features, Orientation binning is the next tread. Guided by the values acquired in the previous step, every pixel in each cell projects a weighted vote for a histogram channel based on orientation. In light of whether the blocks have signed or unsigned gradient, the cells can take the shape of either radial or rectangle and then these channels spread over either $0 - 180°$ or $0 - 360°$. It is being recorded that 9 histogram channels utilised in addition to unsigned gradients showed finest results for face recognition. The donation of pixels can either be function of magnitude of gradient or the gradient itself. Gradient magnitude yields accurate results while testing. Another substitute for voted weight can be square of the gradient [10].

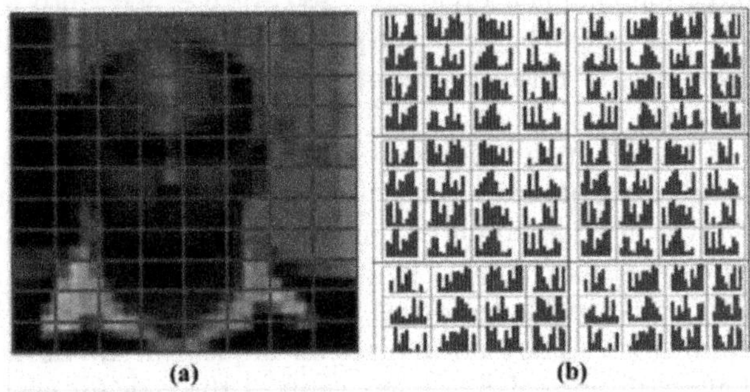

Fig. 3. (a) Facial photo split in cells (b) Histogram of every cell [2]

Descriptor Blocks. The normalized local weight of gradient must be taken into consideration for the variations in contrast and brightness. To compute this, we need to cluster cells into bigger and joined blocks. By chaining the cell components in histograms that have been normalized from all the blocks, we get HOG descriptor. These blocks overlap which means each cell's contribution is more than one to descriptors's final result as shown in Fig. 6. Block geometries are of two types: Rectangular HOG blocks i.e., R-HOG and Circular HOG blocks [3]. R-HOG blocks defined by 3 criteria: each block containing cells, each cell containing pixels and lastly, channels in every histogram; are either rectangular or square grids. In the human face detection experiments, the most accurate parameters are noticed that of 4 counts of 8×8 pixel cells in every block (16×16 pixels per block) comprising of 9 histogram channels.

Block Normalization. Block normalization factor (L2 Norm) is given as below:

$$f = \frac{v}{\sqrt{||v||^2 + e^2}} \tag{5}$$

Support Vector Machine for Bounding Box of Face and Classification. For using SVM [2] in our proposed model, we decided to use parameter σ between 0.8k and 1.6k for Gaussian kernel [10]. Here the range of colored pixels namely red, blue and green is 0 to 256. The value of σ is so picked with the end goal that it should be equitable with 3.125 and 6.250 respectively for values of pixels of input info that is normalized. Gaussian radial basis function as shown in Eq. 5, sometimes parametrized using $\gamma = 1/2\sigma^2$. The bound of weight C of σ_i was picked to be 10. Predictable with the past researches, SVM classifier worked best with σ_i values in the range of 1.2k and 1.6k (approximately in the range of 5 and 6.3 for normalized input data). During testing, highlights of the input image are acquired. These features and features of the reference are fed to SVM classifier. The classifier scans for perfect hyperplane to be used as decision boundary. The HOG features in the input picture and reference are picked up by SVM. From there, classifier scans for the nearest facial profile which matches the features from the reference with the input picture and provides that face as output. Figure 7 shows multiple faces being detected by the algorithm. Once these facial landmarks are extracted, these features are distinguished using any classification algorithm. We have used SVM classifier for this purpose. To the classifier, a chosen test photo is given for characterization [2].

2.5 Face Alignment

To make face alignment possible, we will attempt to warp each image with the goal that the eyes and lips are consistently in the sample place in the picture. This will make it much simpler for us to contrast faces in the subsequent stages. For this, we utilize an algorithm known as face landmark estimation designed in 2014 by Vahid Kazemi and Josephine Sullivan [12]. The fundamental thought is we will concoct 68 explicit focuses (called landmarks) that exist on each face, the top of the jaw, the outside edge of each eye, the inward edge of each eyebrow, and so forth. At that point, we will prepare an algorithm to have the option to locate these 68 explicit focuses on any face

2.6 Face Recognition and Siamese Neural Network

In Siamese network, we make use of an input image of an individual and then codings/features of that image are found. Subsequently, we take the same network without making any updates on weights or biases, and input an image of an alternate individual, and again foresee its encodings. Presently, we contrast these two encodings to check whether there is any matching between the two images. These two encodings go about as an inactive component portrayal of the images. Images with same individual have similar features/encodings. Utilizing this, we contrast and tell if the two images have a same individual or not.

$$L = max(d(a,p) - d(a,n) + margin, 0) \tag{6}$$

The Eq. (6) above represents the triplet loss function utilizing which gradients are determined. The variable a indicates the anchor image, p indicates a $+ve$

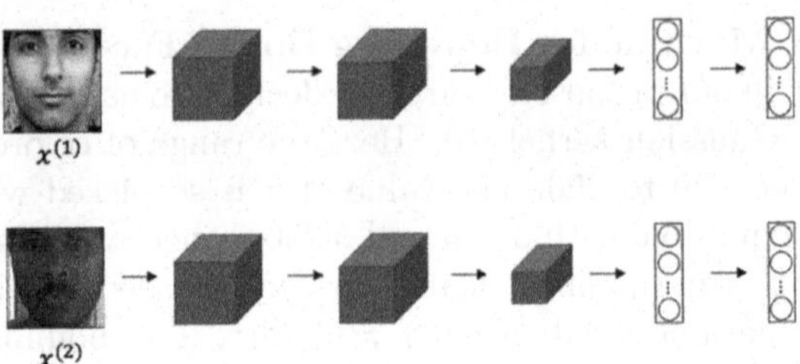

Fig. 4. Siamese model

image and n indicates a $-ve$ image. We realize that the difference between a and p has to be less than the difference between a and n. A hyper-parameter variable known as margin is brought into the loss function. Margin defines how distanced the difference can be i.e. in the event that $margin = 0.2$ and $d(a, p) = 0.5$ then $d(a, n)$ should at any rate be equivalent to 0.7. Margin aids in distinguishing the two images better. Therefore, gradients are calculated by utilizing the loss function obtained [5], biases and weights of the Siamese network are updated. An anchor image and arbitrarily test positive and negative images to train the Siamese network and figure its loss function and make changes in its gradients.

In this paper, we will be using a Siamese model with a GoogleNet CNN as the backbone (Siamese Network + GoogleNet). On high level, we can consider GoogleNet as a lightweight CNN that extract features from the image, and Siamese network as a method to train the CNN efficiently and HOG+SVM scales a set of default bounding boxes around the targets and ID them. After we have trained the model, the model has learnt to differentiate between two images. So we take two images i.e. anchor face and a facial profile in the image. We pass it through the network and we get two feature vectors of 128 dimensions each. The mean-square error between the two vectors is calculated. This serves as the distance factor. If the distance factor is below certain threshold, then both the images are similar else they are not. Detection and tracking will be limited by occlusion and illumination, may get limited for tiny faces. Problems may arise in crowded areas and detection is based on face not body parts and at last detecting people's face using machine learning training, so will need high GPU for tiny faces. Aligning the faces with dlib module increased the accuracy of the model. Manually setting the threshold score to 0.56 we can differentiate between two different person.

3 Experimental Results and Discussions

Here all the software libraries or packages used are open sourced that are licensed by the Open Source Initiative. We have trained the model using Nvidia M600 24 GB RAM on LFW dataset [17] for 100 epochs. The inference is done on MacBook Air 2015 model, 4 cores 1.7 GHz, 4 GB RAM. The dataset contains more than 13000 images. 5749 distinct people are present out of which 1,680 people having more than 2 distinct images.

It is extremely difficult to have a reasonable correlation among various object detectors. There is no direct indication to which one might surface out to be the best design. For genuine applications, we settle on decisions to adjust precision and speed.

Our model has entirely not worthy frame per seconds (FPS) utilizing lower resolution pictures at the expense of exactness. Other models used for comparison is purely based on face detection. All in all, Faster R-CNN is increasingly exact while R-FCN and Siamese Learnt are quicker. Faster R-CNN utilizing Inception Resnet with 300 recommendations gives the highest exactness at 1 FPS for all the tried cases. Siamese learnt on GoogleNet has the most elevated mean average precision(mAP) amidst the models made for live processing. In our model we have GoogleNet CNN combined with siamese network, since it takes lesser GPU (single core) time. A comparison is done by calculating average GPU time taken for each model with siamese network and by training it and running it on LFW dataset, chart of GPU time vs. the models are shown in Fig. 7.

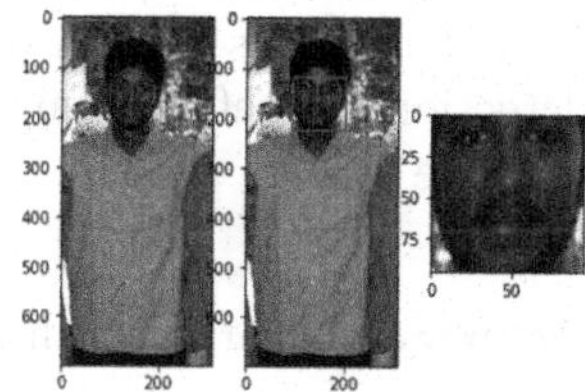

Fig. 5. Alignment with dlib

Out[20]: <matplotlib.image.AxesImage at 0x1260d2898>

Distance = 0.29

Out[35]: <matplotlib.image.AxesImage at 0x1248e99b0>

Distance = 1.68

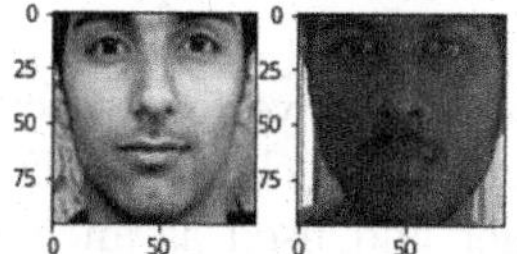

Fig. 6. Distance scores

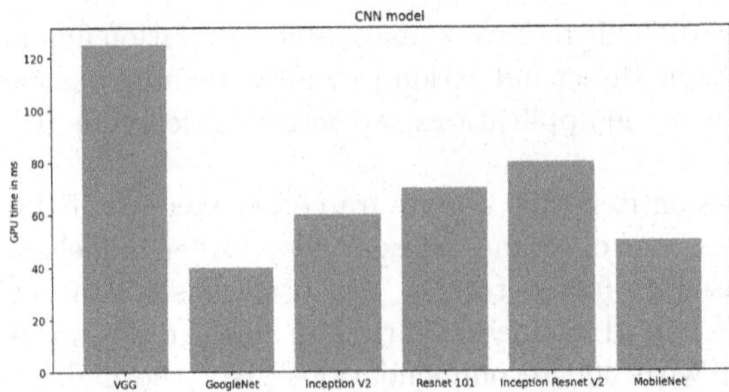

Fig. 7. GPU time (in millisecond) for different models

For enormous articles, Siamese Learnt network performs really well even with a straightforward extractor. It can even align with other detectors' exactness utilizing better extractor. Be that as it may, Siamese Learnt network performs a lot of much worse on little items contrasting with different techniques. Both MS-COCO and ImageNet dataset contains images of various objects. Here we are only interested in face detection, therefore a subset of images are used for our comparison are shown in Table 1.

Table 1. Accuracy comparison with CaffeNet

Datasets	Weights	Accuracy %
MSCOCO	CaffeNet	74
MSCOCO	**Proposed method**	77
ImageNet subset	CaffeNet	93
ImageNet subset	**Proposed method**	96

In practical situation the target might leave and re-enter in the camera, therefore an ideal tracker should be able to remember and locate the target for relatively longer period. However, most of the existing benchmarks have been centered around short term tracking in which the average length of sequence is under 600 frames (20 s with 30 fps) and the objective quite often shows up in the video outline. The assessment on these momentary benchmarks may not mirror the genuine efficiency of a tracker in real-world applications, and hence limit the deployment in practical scenario.

LaSOT dataset contains objects from various categories , where as we are only interested human. We have evaluated class containing people. Person's face is identified from training data set and used as anchor image and for testing dataset the person is tracked. our model achieves tracking using single anchor image (also unsupervised) in Table 2.

Table 2. Precision comparison with other models using LaSOT Dataset

Architecture	Precision
MDNet [18]	0.674
VITAL [19]	0.672
SINT [20]	0.599
CFNet [21]	0.565
Proposed method	0.541
DSST [23]	0.496

4 Future Work and Conclusion

We tried to achieve human tracking with single anchor image in this paper and we were able to do it using siamaese network with GoogleNet CNN. Though there are various methods to track a person in multi-cameras they are done using training a dataset of images of people in multiple angles and lighting conditions whereas our goal was to achieve tracking with single anchor image. Here difference appear in how the model is trained rather than accuracy and speed comparison between various models. Here we have tried to address limitations of training and alternative way to achieve goal. Huge dataset would not be available for training all the time. Therefore we need to have a model which should be able work with alternative methodology. In our paper we have modeled and trained a network to identify and track a person in multi-camera environment with one to few anchor image and it is achieved by training the network with available data, since there was no prior knowledge of the person under surveillance.

We also give some improvements to the proposed model as future work. A faster HOG descriptor can be used, which will improve the speed of face detection by few factors [13]. By making use of certain hardware features of our hosts (e.g. digital signal processor) and by making few modification, speed of HOG descriptor can be improved significantly. Face detection and tracking needs more datasets for training and testing especially in small faces with illumination and occlusion. Training and testing small and tiny faces in many scales template. Face detection can be combined with human body parts detection to make a hybrid model to improve the accuracy of detection in future.

References

1. Huang, G.B., Mattar, M., Berg, T., Learned-Miller, E.: Labeled faces in the wild: a database for studying face recognition in unconstrained environments (2007)
2. Dadi, H.S., Pillutla, G.K.M., Makkena, M.L.: Face recognition and human tracking using GMM, HOG and SVM in surveillance videos. Ann. Data. Sci. **5**, 157–179 (2018). https://doi.org/10.1007/s40745-017-0123-2

3. Sharma, S.U., Shah, D.J.: A practical animal detection and collision avoidance system using computer vision technique. IEEE Access **5**, 347–358 (2017). https://doi.org/10.1109/ACCESS.2016.2642981
4. Paul, M., Haque, S.M.E., Chakraborty, S.: Human detection in surveillance videos and its applications - a review. EURASIP J. Adv. Signal Process. **2013**, 176 (2013). https://doi.org/10.1186/1687-6180-2013-176
5. Serdouk, Y., Eglin, V., Bres, S., Pardoen, M.: KeyWord spotting using siamese triplet deep neural networks. In: 2019 International Conference on Document Analysis and Recognition (ICDAR), Sydney, Australia, pp. 1157–1162 (2019). https://doi.org/10.1109/ICDAR.2019.00187
6. Liu, W., et al.: SSD: single shot multibox detector. In: Leibe, Bastian, Matas, Jiri, Sebe, Nicu, Welling, Max (eds.) ECCV 2016. LNCS, vol. 9905, pp. 21–37. Springer, Cham (2016). https://doi.org/10.1007/978-3-319-46448-0_2
7. Yamashita, A., Ito, Y., Kaneko, T., Asama, H.: Human tracking with multiple cameras based on face detection and mean shift. In: 2011 IEEE International Conference on Robotics and Biomimetics, Karon Beach, Phuket, pp. 1664–1671 (2011). https://doi.org/10.1109/ROBIO.2011.6181528
8. Fan, J., Xu, W., Wu, Y., Gong, Y.: Human tracking using convolutional neural networks. IEEE Trans. Neural Netw. **21**(10), 1610–1623 (2010). https://doi.org/10.1109/TNN.2010.2066286
9. Zhou, X., Huang, T.: Relevance feedback in image retrieval: a comprehensive review. Multimed. Syst. **8**, 536–544 (2003). https://doi.org/10.1007/s00530-002-0070-3
10. Deniz, O., Bueno, G., Salido, J., Delatorre, F.: Face recognition using histograms of oriented gradients. Pattern Recognit. Lett. **32**, 1598–1603 (2011). https://doi.org/10.1016/j.patrec.2011.01.004
11. Rekha, N., Kurian, M.Z.: Face detection in real time based on HOG (2014)
12. Sherif, M., Azab, M., Emad, Y., Sameh, S., Menisy, F., Kandil, B.: Eyes in the sky: a free of charge infrastructure-less mobile ad-hoc cloud, pp. 131–137 (2017). https://doi.org/10.1145/3147234.3148122
13. Huang, C., Huang, J.: A fast HOG descriptor using lookup table and integral image (2017)
14. Gupta, S.: Intelligent video surveillance system-B, Doctoral dissertation. Indian Institute of Technology Delhi
15. Rekha, N., Kurian, M.Z.: Face detection in real time based on HOG. Int. J. Adv. Res. Comput. Eng. Technol. (IJARCET) **3**(4), 1345–1352 (2014)
16. Ghaemmaghami, M.P.: Tracking of humans in video stream using LSTM recurrent neural network (2017)
17. Kae, A., Sohn, K., Lee, H., Learned-Miller, E.: Augmenting CRFs with Boltzmann machine shape priors for image labeling. In: Computer Vision and Pattern Recognition (2013)
18. Jung, I., Son, J., Baek, M., Han, B.: Real-time MDNet. In: Ferrari, V., Hebert, M., Sminchisescu, C., Weiss, Y. (eds.) ECCV 2018. LNCS, vol. 11208, pp. 89–104. Springer, Cham (2018). https://doi.org/10.1007/978-3-030-01225-0_6
19. Song, Y.: Vital: visual tracking via adversarial learning. In: Proceedings of the IEEE Conference on Computer Vision and Pattern Recognition (2018)
20. Li, D., Yu, Y., Chen, X.: Object tracking framework with Siamese network and re-detection mechanism. J Wirel. Commun. Netw. **2019**, 261 (2019). https://doi.org/10.1186/s13638-019-1579-x

21. Zhao, J., Zhan, Y.: TA-CFNet: a new CFNet with target aware for object tracking. In: Zhao, Y., Barnes, N., Chen, B., Westermann, R., Kong, X., Lin, C. (eds.) ICIG 2019. LNCS, vol. 11901, pp. 618–630. Springer, Cham (2019). https://doi.org/10.1007/978-3-030-34120-6_50
22. Ou, W., Yuan, D., Liu, Q., Cao, Y.: Object tracking based on online representative sample selection via non-negative least square. Multimed. Tools Appl. **77**, 1–19 (2017). https://doi.org/10.1007/s11042-017-4672-3
23. tsyklon: (2019). From shutterstock, cctv-security-room-1047388429. https://www.shutterstock.com/image-photo/cctv-security-room-1047388429. Accessed 11 May 2020
24. Simon, M., et al.: Complexer-YOLO: real-time 3D object detection and tracking on semantic point clouds. In: 2019 IEEE/CVF Conference on Computer Vision and Pattern Recognition Workshops (CVPRW), pp. 1190–1199 (2019)
25. Dai, J., Li, Y., He, K., Sun, J.: R-FCN: object detection via region-based fully convolutional networks. In: NIPS (2016)
26. Tao, Y., Skubic, M., Han, T., Xia, Y., Chi, X.: Performance evaluation of SIFT-based descriptors for object recognition. Lecture Notes in Engineering and Computer Science, p. 2181 (2010)
27. Hoiem, D., Divvala, S.K., Hays, J.H.: Pascal VOC 2008 Challenge (2009)
28. Lin, T., et al.: Microsoft COCO: common objects in context (2014). arXiv preprint arXiv:1405.0312
29. Vidit, J., Erik, L.M.: FDDB: A benchmark for face detection in unconstrained settings. Technical Report UM-CS-2010-009, Dept. of Computer Science, University of Massachusetts, Amherst. (2010)

Fast Road Sign Detection and Recognition Using Colour-Based Thresholding

Farah Jamal Ansari(✉) and Sumeet Agarwal

Department of Electrical Engineering, IIT Delhi, Hauz Khas, New Delhi, India
sumeet@ee.iitd.ac.in

Abstract. Automation of road sign detection and recognition is an important task in the context of applications like self-driving cars. Current popular, state of the art detectors, employing Deep Neural Networks (DNN) are very accurate but at the same time, very complex and have a very high processing time which might not be desirable for real-time applications in autonomous vehicles. In this paper, we present a road sign detection cum recognition pipeline, which exhibits the potential to achieve a considerable speed-up over the DNN based detection algorithms with a relatively small reduction in accuracy. The purpose of the detector is to capture as many road signs as possible in the least possible time. We also propose several techniques at the recognition stage to improve the performance of the pipeline. Comparison has been made to various state-of-the-art DNN based detector pipelines. The proposed pipeline is the fastest amongst all the detection-cum-recognition pipelines with an average processing time of 0.103 secs. per frame. The best F-score achieved by the pipeline is 0.87377. In comparison to this Faster R-CNN achieved the best F-Score of 0.9474 but with an average processing time of 17.664 secs. per frame.

Keywords: Fine tuning · Advanced driver assistance system · Deep learning · Object detection · Feature extraction · Object recognition

1 Introduction

Road sign recognition is a very important module of an advanced driver assistance system. It informs the driver about the navigational details like prohibitions, dangers and warnings lying ahead on the road. It helps in reducing the cognitive control of the driver. Road sign detection is also used for inventory management and maintenance of road signs. The detection and recognition of road signs has to account for many factors like illumination and different weather conditions of fog, thunder, rain, or sunlight. Road signs are broadly classified into four categories: Mandatory, Prohibitory, Danger and Others. A few examples of these categories are shown in Fig. 1. The proposed pipeline is divided into three phases. 1) The segmentation phase in which region of interests

S. K. Singh et al. (Eds.): CVIP 2020, CCIS 1378, pp. 318–331, 2021.
https://doi.org/10.1007/978-981-16-1103-2_27

(ROIs) are extracted on the basis of colour thresholds in the RGB normalized colour space. 2) Confirmation of regions of interest as road signs using radial basis function (RBF) SVM. 3) The output of the detection phase is passed to a Convolutional Neural Network (CNN) for recognition as a specific type of road sign. Recognition also reduces the false positive considerably. Therefore road sign detection is a pre-processing step to recognition and the main aim is to capture as many road signs as possible in the least possible time. Finally similar pipelines have been created with the state-of-the-art detectors: You Only Look Once (YOLO)v2, YOLOv3, Faster R-CNN, Single Shot Detector (SSD) and Fast Feature Pyramids (FFP) to compare with the proposed detection cum recognition pipeline.

The rest of the paper is organised as follows: Sect. 2 presents an overview of the existing methods for road sign detection and classification. Section 3 narrates our proposed contribution. The detailed methodology of the proposed algorithm is explained in Sect. 4. An introduction to the FFP and the CNN based state-of-the-art detectors is given in Sect. 5. In Sect. 6 we present our experimental results followed by Discussions & Conclusion in Sect. 7.

Fig. 1. Examples of the Mandatory, Prohibitory, Danger and Other signs.

2 Related Work

A lot many different approaches have been proposed in this domain varying from segmentation to CNN based techniques. Work related to road sign detection is as follows: In [15], shape templates are matched to extract region of interests as road signs and finally classified into the right category using SVM. Maximally stable extremal regions (MSERs) are used in [10] to detect the road signs. Multi class traffic sign detection is proposed in [17] using Multi block normalization local binary pattern (MN-LBP) and tilted MN-LBP (TMN-LBP) along with ADABOOST algorithm. A coarse-to-fine approach is presented in [28]. LDA in the coarse step and SVM in the fine step along with Histogram of Gradient (HOG) [4] are used for detection using sliding windows. In [19], Integral channel features(ICF) is proposed to detect road signs using a sliding window approach. In [20], the performance of Aggregate Channel Features (ACF) is compared with ICF on US signs. The approaches in [30] and [2] are based on deep learning. In [30], detection and classification is based on the 'Overfeat' model on Chinese data set (Tsinghua-Tencent 100K). In [2], the state-of-the-art object-detection systems (YOLOv2, SSD, R-FCN, and Faster R-CNN) are evaluated combined with several different feature extractors for road sign detection.

Classification: Mathias *et al.* have used HOG features in [19] along with iterative nearest neighbors-based linear projection for the dimensionality reduction and an iterative nearest neighbors classifier for classification. A multi column deep neural network is proposed in [3] where several CNNs are trained on different pre-processed data. A new data set of Croatian signs along with single CNN for all data sets is presented in [14]. A multi-scale two-stage CNN architecture is developed in [23] for achieving a very high classification accuracy. In [1], a new data set of Arabian road signs has been created and a CNN has been designed for the recognition of the same.

In [29], Segmentation, Histograms of gradients along with SVM is used for detection and CNN is used for classification of road signs on Italian road signs. In [7], geometric moments are utilised for road sign detection. HOG along with local self similarity (LSS) is used for classification on the German Traffic sign detection benchmark (GTSDB) [11]. In [26] image processing techniques have been used for detection and an ensemble of CNN for recognition, giving very high recognition rates of 99% on circular road signs on German and Belgium road signs. [27] have discussed the techniques for implementing road sign detection, recognition and tracking and have also stated the trends and challenges involved.

Table 1. Results of other methods for road sign detection on GTSDB.

Method	AUC (Prohibitory)	AUC (Danger)	Avg. time
HOG+LDA+SVM [28]	100	99.1	NA
ICF [19]	100	100	0.4 secs. on GeForce GTX 470 GPU.
SVM+Shape matching [15]	100	98.85	NA
colSeg+HOG [29]	98.67	96.01	231 ms for Prohibitive signs & 234 ms for Danger signs

3 Contribution

In this paper a fast colour based detection-cum-recognition pipeline has been proposed which exhibits speed-up over the state-of-the-art. In the detection phase, a very simple colour based detector (CBD) has been introduced which detects the red coloured road signs in considerably lesser time. In the recognition, stage while training the CNN there is no separate class for non-road signs, instead a reject option is incorporated that reduces the false positives considerably. The CNN in the recognition phase has been trained on German Traffic sign recognition benchmark (GTSRB) [24] and tested on GTSDB. To overcome the data set bias problem, the CNN weights trained on GTSRB are fine tuned on GTSDB which results in significant improvement in the accuracy of the pipeline.

4 Proposed Method

The proposed method is divided onto three phases. The colour space conversion & segmentation phase extracts the desired ROIs to capture red coloured road signs. This is followed by road sign detection where ROIs are given to the RBF SVM classifier for confirmation as road signs. The final phase is the recognition phase where the road sign detected is given to a CNN to be assigned into the right class (Fig. 2).

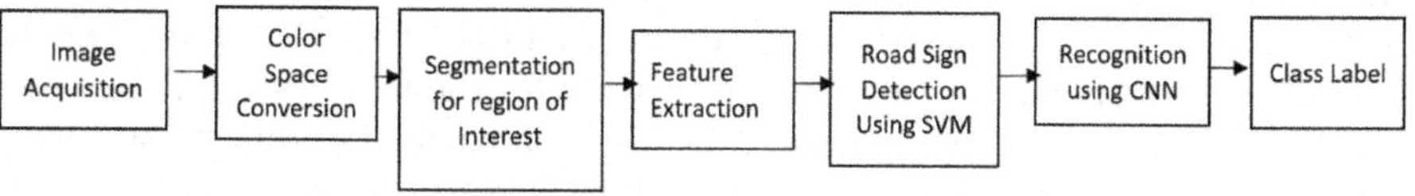

Fig. 2. Block diagram of the proposed pipeline.

4.1 Colour Space Conversion and Segmentation

Colour segmentation is computationally faster than the sliding window technique. Road Signs are captured on the basis of the border colour in the normalized RGB (NRGB) colour space as it is insensitive to lighting and illumination changes. A colour histogram showing the frequency of pixel intensity values of red coloured road signs in the training set of GTSDB as in Fig. 3 is used to calculate the threshold for capturing the road signs. As in the histogram, most pixels lie in the range of $NR > 0.3$ and $NG < 0.32$. Many combinations of NR and NG were tried and the ideal range was found to lie in $NR >= 0.39$ and $NG <= 0.32$. Based on this threshold, image binarization captures the red coloured pixels in the image. Contours are formed by connecting the pixels that demarcate an intensity change leading to the road signs. A bounding box or a blob is then fitted on the contour. Additional features like width and height (based on the size of the road signs found in the GTSDB) listed in Table 2 are used to reduce the number of candidates purported to be road signs.

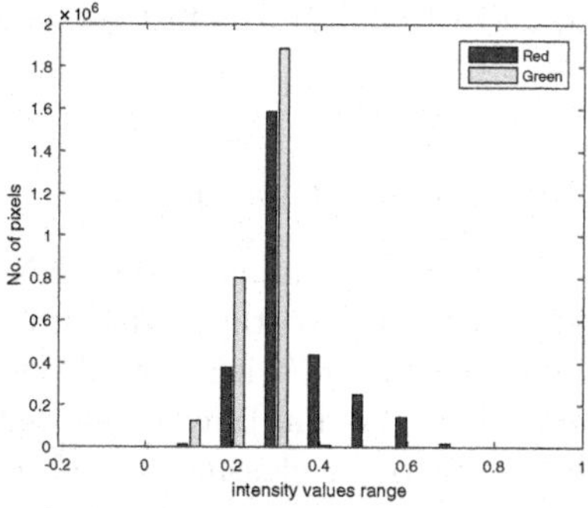

Fig. 3. Histogram distribution of red and green channels. (Color figure online)

Table 2. Limiting values for features used to filter out candidates.

Minimum height (pixels)	Maximum height (pixels)	Minimum width (pixels)	Maximum width (pixels)
9	100	9	100

4.2 Road Sign Detection Using SVM

The ROIs captured are further tested by an RBF SVM for road sign detection. In the baseline CBD, histograms of the normalized RGB (RGBN) values for each channel are concatenated to form colour features for the RBF SVM for road sign detection. There are 12 equal density bins for each channel leading to 36 colour features for each ROI. Concatenation of HOG features to the colour features reduce the false positives considerably. HOG features capture edge gradients along with intensity changes, hence are excellent for identifying road signs. For extracting HOG features, ROIs are resized to 32×32 and are presented in the RGB color space. The HOG features are calculated by selecting the channel with the highest gradient magnitude for each pixel. The ROIs are divided into cells of 8×8 pixels, and blocks of 2×2 cells. The number of orientations is taken to 9. This gives a feature vector of 324. The length of the combined feature vector for each ROI is 360. 10-fold cross validation yields the optimum values for the RBF SVM hyper parameters as $C = 1.25$ and $\gamma = 0.50625$. Non maximum suppression (NMS) reduces the false positives further by choosing the highest scored bounding box amongst bounding boxes overlapping more than 50% [9].

Training of SVM For Road Sign Detection: A total of 900 images in the GTSDB is divided into 600 for training and 300 for testing. We put the red signs in one class and the (non signs and non red road signs) in the other class. Prohibitory, Danger and Stop & Warning signs in the others category are red coloured road signs. There are 578 red-coloured road signs in the training set. This is increased to 1156 by applying jittering. Out of the 600 training images, 187 images have no red-coloured road sign. The negative set is created by applying colour thresholding on 187 images with no red-coloured road signs. The regions of interest, captured as probable road signs from 187 images comprises of the negative set and is equal to 15533. In the test set there are 238 red coloured road signs.

4.3 Detection-cum-Recognition Pipeline

Recognition is done using a two-stage multi-scale CNN described in [23]. The architecture as in Fig. 4 consists of two stages of learn-able layers, where each stage includes the convolutional layer (with 108 filters), a non-linearity layer (tanh), and a sub-sampling (Max Pooling) layer followed by local contrast normalization layer [23]. The input to the classifier is the combined output of both the stages. A two-layer fully connected soft-max classifier is used with 100 hidden

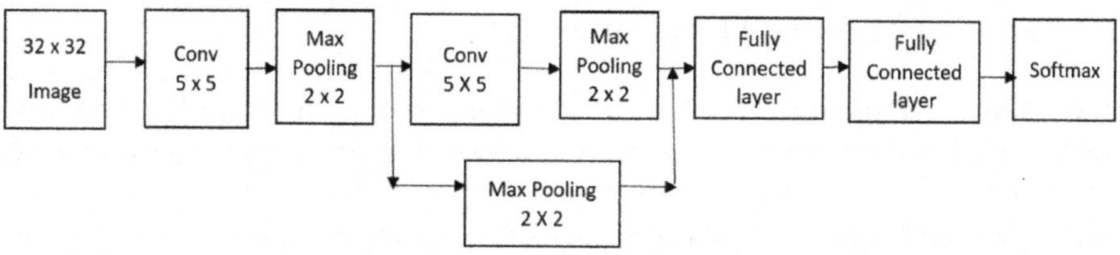

Fig. 4. CNN architecture.

nodes. ADAM optimizer has been used. Tensorflow 1.2 is used for both training and testing the CNN. All the images are resized to 32 × 32. The images are converted to YUV colour space. As suggested in [23], gray scale images give the best accuracy, therefore the U and V parts are discarded and the Y component is only used.

The CNN is trained on GTSRB. The GTSRB data set has 43 classes comprising of Mandatory, Danger, Prohibitory and Other signs. The total number of images in the data set is 39209. But since red-coloured signs have been considered, only 29 classes are used for training. 56 tracks in the training set of the GTSRB were overlapping with the road signs in the test set of the GTSDB data set and are therefore removed. 26490 images are used for training.

The trained CNN model is used to process the output of the detector. The ROIs detected as road signs are given to the CNN to be assigned the right class. The complete pipeline is tested on the GTSDB. Some of the ROIs detected are false positives. But there is no separate class for treating the false positives at the recognition phase. Instead there is a reject option where in a threshold is applied on the CNN score. If the probability score of a sign (for the most probably class) as per the CNN is below the threshold, we reject it as a non sign. Because of the reject option a lot of false positives captured at the detection phase are rejected at the final pipeline stage. The pipeline is evaluated on the basis of the best weighted F-Score where we are aggregating true positives and false positives over all the classes. The F-beta score is harmonic mean of precision and recall. In Table 5, we also show how the β parameter assigns weight to the recall in the F-Score. $\beta < 1$, tends to give more weight to precision, where as $\beta > 1$ is more towards the recall. While creating the detection-cum-recognition pipeline, a data set bias problem was noticed between the GTSRB and GTSDB (training on one data set and evaluating on another data set), due to which good results were not obtained. Therefore the weights of the CNN model, trained on GTSRB are fine tuned on the training set of the GTSDB data. This leads to better results for the proposed pipeline. The recognition model discussed above is also attached with the state of the art detectors to form detection cum recognition pipelines for comparison.

5 State-of-the-art Detectors

Fast Feature Pyramids: The idea that multi-resolution image features need not be calculated explicitly, but can be approximated from near by scales using extrapolation [6] lead to an accurate, and a much faster object detection algorithm than the state-of-the-art. In [19], as shown in Table 1, road sign detection has been performed using (ICF) with very good processing time. Proposed algorithm is compared with Fast Feature Pyramids (FFP) as they are the improved version of ICF.

Faster R-CNN: Faster R-CNN [22] introduces a Region Proposal Network (RPN) which shares the convolutional features of the entire image with the detection network. The RPN trained end-to-end, generates region proposals with high score, which are further used by the Fast R-CNN for detection.

Single Shot Detector: These detectors perform object detection in one shot. SSD [18] utilizes anchor boxes with varying aspect ratios. To handle objects of different scales, feature maps from different convolutional layers are considered.

You Only Look Once: YOLO [21], meant for real time detection, divides an input image into grids and each grid cell is responsible for predicting bounding boxes for an object.

6 Experimental Results

6.1 Road Sign Detection

Road sign detection in the proposed algorithm as explained in Sect. 4.2 has been implemented using Python 3.7.4 incorporating Numba 0.50.1 which is an open source, just in time compiler for Python. For comparison purposes, road sign detection has also been implemented using FFP and CNN based architectures like Faster R-CNN, SSD, YOLOv2 and YOLOv3 as described in [2]. Road sign detection using FFPs is implemented on MATLAB 15 using [5]. The main detection code for FFP is written in C which is called through a MEX interface. Faster R-CNN and SSD have been implemented using Tensorflow Object Detection API [12]. Inception Resnet v2 has been used for extracting features for Faster R-CNN. SSD has been implemented using two feature extractors: Inception v2 and, Mobilenet V1. Publicly available object detection models have been used for these frameworks, which are pre-trained on the Microsoft COCO data set [16] and fine tuned on GTSDB through transfer learning. YOLOv2 has been implemented using Darkflow [25] and YOLOv3 using Darknet [13]. All the detectors have been tested on a local machine having i5 processor with 8 GB RAM at 1.80 GHz. Models were trained on IIT Delhi HPC facility using GPU: NVIDIA V100 (32GB 5120 CUDA cores), CPU: 2x Intel Xeon G-6148 (20 cores 2.4 GHz) and RAM: 96 GB.

Detection has been performed on GTSDB. During testing for all detectors, a bounding box or window is considered as a true positive if it overlaps with the ground truth by at least 50%; otherwise it is a false positive [8]. As can be seen from Fig. 5, Faster R-CNN, YOLOv2 and YOLOv3 are the best detectors performance wise with the highest precision, recall, AUPR and best F-Score. SSD and FFP are very fast but not very accurate, as SSD is unable to detect small road signs and FFP generates a lot of false positives. SSD with mobilenet V1 is faster than the Inception V2 SSD but is less accurate. A trade off can be made with the speed and accuracy of YOLOv3 by just changing the model size with out retraining. That is why YOLOv3 with 608 × 608 model size performs better than the 416 × 416 model size with an increase in the processing time. The baseline CBD (RGBN) is the fastest (average processing time of 0.053 secs per frame) amongst all the detectors and is able to capture most of the road signs but at the cost of huge number of false positives. This results in low values for precision, best F-Score and AUPR but which is significantly boosted up after recognition. Our main concern at the detection phase was to capture as many road signs as possible in the least possible time as false negatives are more dangerous than false positives. In CBD (RGBN+HOG), the false positives are already less even at the detection stage giving rise to increased best F-Score, AUPR and Precision. This is because RGBN features captures the colour, and HOG captures the edge gradients and therefore ideal for road sign detection. In Table 3 CBD (RGBN+HOG) is ranked fourth in terms of accuracy after Faster R-CNN, YOLOv2 and YOLOv3. But Faster R-CNN and YOLO are too slow, with an average processing time of 17.663 and 1.5233 secs per frame respectively. CBD (RGBN+HOG) is vary fast with a best F-Score of 0.8577 and average processing time of 0.1 secs per frame. The false negatives in all the CBD's are mainly due to illumination problems and occurrence of multiple signs lying close to each other (Figs. 6 and 7).

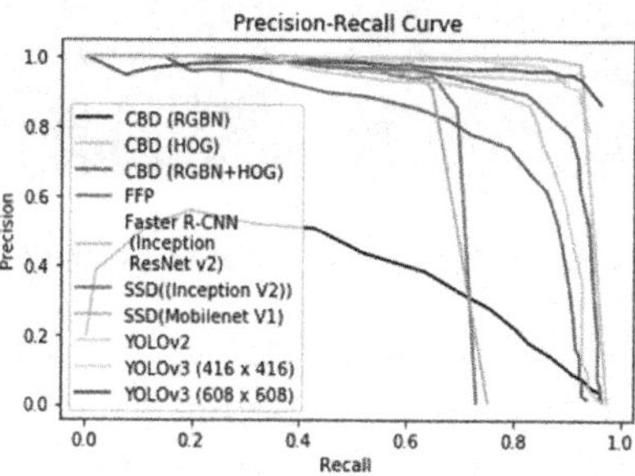

Fig. 5. Comparison of AUPR for different detectors.

Table 3. Comparison of the CBD with state-of-the-art detectors.

Method	AUPR	Max. recall	Best F-score	Avg. time per frame (in secs.)
CBD (RGBN)	0.374	0.966	0.4786	**0.053**
CBD (HOG)	0.8569	0.966	0.8455	0.09413
CBD (RGBN+HOG)	0.8955	0.966	0.8577	**0.1**
FFP	0.7816	0.9369	0.7657	0.14
Faster R-CNN (Inception ResNet v2)	**0.9406**	**0.9747**	**0.952**	17.663
SSD (Inception V2)	0.67712	0.7319	0.7715	1.103
SSD (Mobilenet V1)	0.67	0.7521	0.756	0.91
YOLOv2	0.9073	0.9412	91.44	1.6324
YOLOv3 (416 × 416)	0.8895	0.8992	0.9167	0.7488
YOLOv3 (608 × 608)	0.9309	0.9621	0.9322	1.5233

Fig. 6. Examples of German road signs missed by the CBD (RGBN+HOG).

Fig. 7. Examples of German road signs detected by the CBD (RGBN+HOG).

6.2 Detection-cum-Recognition Pipeline

5-fold cross-validation on the GTSRB yields training accuracy of 100% and validation accuracy of 98.321% at 25 epochs and at a regularization parameter value of 0.06. To deal with the data set bias problem, the recognition model (initially trained on GTSRB) is fine tuned on the GTSDB. This resulted in an increase in the best F-Score value of the baseline pipeline for CBD (RGBN) from 0.689 to 0.8348. Therefore this model was also adopted to form recognition cum detection pipelines with CBD (HOG), CBD (RGBN+HOG) detectors and the state of the art detectors mentioned in Sect. 5. ROIs or blobs captured by the respective detectors is given to the CNN for being recognized in the right class (Figs. 9, 10, 11 and 12). Detectors like CBD (RGBN), CBD(HOG), CBD (RGBN+HOG), FFP and SSD have shown an increase in the best F-Score value after the recognition phase. The best F-score for the CBD (RGBN) detector is 0.4786 which rose to 0.8348 after recognition as at the recognition stage, many false positives are eliminated because of the rejection threshold as seen in the confusion matrix in Fig. 8. But Faster R-CNN and YOLO (v2&v3) have shown a slight drop in their best F-Score values after recognition as the false positives at the detection phase were already less and after recognition, some of the road signs got wrongly classified. Also it is observed that the CBD (RGBN+HOG) has a higher processing time than the CBD (RGBN) at the detection phase. But the total processing time for the whole pipeline is lesser for the CBD (RGBN+HOG) as the number of false positives moving to the recognition phase from the detection phase is lesser in CBD (RGBN+HOG). CBD (RGBN+HOG) pipeline reported its best F-Score to be 0.8737 with an average processing time per frame of 0.103 secs. Faster RCNN, YOLOv3 and YOLOv2 pipelines have reported very high best F-Scores but their processing time is also very high as shown in Table 4. Also the state of the art CNN detectors are very heavy applications, having very high number of parameters and thus occupying a lot of memory space which might not be so easily available in automobiles.

Table 4. Comparison of the proposed pipeline with state-of-the-art detection-cum-recognition pipelines.

Detector	Best. F-score	Precision	Recall	Avg. time per frame (in secs.)
CBD (RGBN)	0.8348	0.864	0.806	0.138
CBD (RGBN without fine tuning)	0.6889	0.8	0.605	0.13
CBD (HOG)	0.8658	0.89285	0.8403	0.10723
CBD (RGBN + HOG)	0.87377	0.86122	0.8865	**0.10373**
FFP	0.7874	0.8421	0.7395	0.145
Faster R-CNN (Inception ResNet v2)	**0.9474**	**0.986**	**0.9118**	17.664
SSD (Inception V2)	0.795	0.964	0.6764	0.943
SSD (Mobilenet V1)	0.75288	0.954	0.6218	0.8826
YOLOv2	0.9127	0.97607	0.8571	1.63569
YOLOv3 (416 × 416)	0.9029	0.975	0.84033	0.7519
YOLOv3 (608 × 608)	0.92609	0.9594	0.895	1.5266

Table 5. Variation of F-Score metric based on β

Detector	$\beta = 0.75$			$\beta = 1.5$		
	F-Score	Precision	Recall	F-Score	Precision	Recall
CBD (RGBN)	0.8447	0.8820	0.7857	0.8237	0.8648	0.8237
CBD (HOG)	0.8827	0.9320	0.806	0.8679	0.829	0.8782
CBD (RGBN+HOG)	0.8775	0.9230	0.806	0.8809	0.8425	0.899
FFP	0.8124	0.9294	0.6639	0.7775	0.7686	0.7815
Faster R-CNN (Inception ResNet v2)	0.9557	0.9907	0.8991	0.9323	0.9812	0.9111
SSD(Inception V2)	0.8361	0.9641	0.6764	0.7448	0.9368	0.6848
SSD (Mobilenet V1)	0.74418	0.966	0.6050	0.6982	0.9430	0.6260
YOLOv2	0.9296	9.97607	0.8571	0.8961	0.8987	0.8950
YOLOv3 (416 × 416)	0.9247	0.9877	0.8192	0.8777	0.9751	0.8235
YOLOv3 (608 × 608)	0.9352	0.9595	0.8450	0.9250	0.8951	0.9328

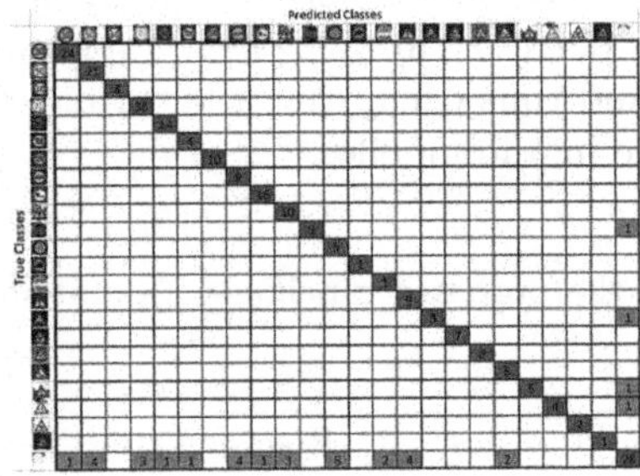

Fig. 8. Confusion matrix of the CBD (RGBN+HOG) recognition cum detection pipeline.

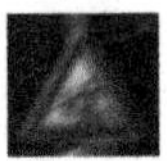

Fig. 9. Examples of road signs wrongly classified by the CBD (RGBN+HOG) recognition cum detection pipeline.

Fig. 10. Examples of false positives not rejected by the CBD (RGBN+HOG) recognition cum detection pipeline.

Fig. 11. Examples of road signs correctly classified by the CBD (RGBN+HOG) recognition cum detection pipeline.

Fig. 12. Examples of false positives rejected by the CBD (RGBN+HOG) recognition cum detection pipeline.

7 Discussions and Conclusions

A fast detection-cum-recognition pipeline is developed in this paper. RGB normalised colour space has been used to capture red coloured road signs on the basis of the RGB values of the pixels as it is insensitive to illumination changes. The ROIs captured are further filtered on the basis of size. RBF SVM along with simple features like histograms of normalized RGB values and HOG are utilised to select a subset of these ROIs as road signs. CNN has been used to recognise the road sign into its proper class (1 out of 29). The recognition phase employs a reject option through which it is able to reduce most of the false positives fetched at the detection phase. Fine tuning of CNN weights on the training set of GTSDB to remove the data set bias problem results in significant improvement in the performance of the pipeline. The proposed pipeline is compared with the various state-of-the-art detection-cum-recognition pipelines. The best F-Score for CBD (RGBN+HOG)-cum-recognition pipeline is 0.87377 with an average processing time of 0.103 secs per frame. Faster R-CNN and YOLOv3 (608×608) have very high accuracy with their best F-Scores being 0.946 and 0.92609 respectively but with higher average processing times of 17.664 secs. and 1.5266 secs per frame. The proposed pipeline is very fast but it is not as accurate as the other state of the art detectors. This is because manually set thresholds are utilised to capture the road signs leading to a large number of false positives. This kind of a pipeline boosts the performance of the detectors which are able to fetch the maximum road signs in the least possible time without caring about false positives. For evaluation on other data sets, the proposed pipeline and the FFP pipeline were implemented on the Data-Set of Italian Road Signs (DITS) [29] as well. DITS has more complex world images in the day, night and fog categories. The proposed pipeline is evaluated on red coloured road signs in the day category but a very low best F-Score of 0.46 was obtained. The best F-Score by FFP pipeline on DITS was found to be 0.654 which is also very low. The road signs in the Italian data-set are more complex with varying colour distributions and illuminating conditions, and some of the signs are very small and difficult to detect. Therefore in the future we plan to implement adaptive thresholding to capture the road signs. We also propose to implement tracking to improve the detection rate further by restricting the search space in the subsequent frame by acquiring spatial information from prior frames. Tracking will lead to a development of a robust and efficient real time road sign detection cum recognition pipeline.

References

1. Alghmgham, D.A., Latif, G., Alghazo, J., Alzubaidi, L.: Autonomous traffic sign (ATSR) detection and recognition using deep CNN. Procedia Comput. Sci. **163**, 266–274 (2019)
2. Arcos-Garcia, A., Alvarez-Garcia, J.A., Soria-Morillo, L.M.: Evaluation of deep neural networks for traffic sign detection systems. Neurocomputing **316**, 332–344 (2018)

3. CireşAn, D., Meier, U., Masci, J., Schmidhuber, J.: Multi-column deep neural network for traffic sign classification. Neural Netw. **32**, 333–338 (2012)
4. Dalal, N., Triggs, B.: Histograms of oriented gradients for human detection. In: 2005 IEEE Computer Society Conference on Computer Vision and Pattern Recognition (CVPR 2005), vol. 1, pp. 886–893. IEEE (2005)
5. Dollár, P.: Piotr's computer vision matlab toolbox (PMT) (2014)
6. Dollár, P., Appel, R., Belongie, S., Perona, P.: Fast feature pyramids for object detection. IEEE Trans. Pattern Anal. Mach. Intell. **36**(8), 1532–1545 (2014)
7. Ellahyani, A., El Ansari, M., El Jaafari, I.: Traffic sign detection and recognition based on random forests. Appl. Soft Comput. **46**, 805–815 (2016)
8. Everingham, M., Van Gool, L., Williams, C.K., Winn, J., Zisserman, A.: The pascal visual object classes (voc) challenge. Int. J. Comput. Vision **88**(2), 303–338 (2010)
9. Felzenszwalb, P.F., Girshick, R.B., McAllester, D., Ramanan, D.: Object detection with discriminatively trained part-based models. IEEE Trans. Pattern Anal. Mach. Intell. **32**(9), 1627–1645 (2010)
10. Greenhalgh, J., Mirmehdi, M.: Real-time detection and recognition of road traffic signs. IEEE Trans. Intell. Transp. Syst. **13**(4), 1498–1506 (2012)
11. Houben, S., Stallkamp, J., Salmen, J., Schlipsing, M., Igel, C.: Detection of traffic signs in real-world images: the German traffic sign detection benchmark. In: International Joint Conference On Neural Networks (2013)
12. Huang, J., et al.: Speed/accuracy trade-offs for modern convolutional object detectors. In: Proceedings of the IEEE Conference on Computer Vision and Pattern Recognition, pp. 7310–7311 (2017)
13. Joseph, R.: Darknet: open source neural networks in C. Pjreddie.com (2016)
14. Jurišić, F., Filković, I., Kalafatić, Z.: Multiple-dataset traffic sign classification with OneCNN. In: 2015 3rd IAPR Asian Conference on Pattern Recognition (ACPR), pp. 614–618. IEEE (2015)
15. Liang, M., Yuan, M., Hu, X., Li, J., Liu, H.: Traffic sign detection by ROI extraction and histogram features-based recognition. In: The 2013 International Joint Conference on Neural Networks (IJCNN), pp. 1–8. IEEE (2013)
16. Lin, T.-Y., et al.: Microsoft COCO: common objects in context. In: Fleet, D., Pajdla, T., Schiele, B., Tuytelaars, T. (eds.) ECCV 2014. LNCS, vol. 8693, pp. 740–755. Springer, Cham (2014). https://doi.org/10.1007/978-3-319-10602-1_48
17. Liu, C., Chang, F., Chen, Z.: Rapid multiclass traffic sign detection in high-resolution images. IEEE Trans. Intell. Transp. Syst. **15**(6), 2394–2403 (2014)
18. Liu, W., et al.: SSD: single shot multibox detector. In: Leibe, B., Matas, J., Sebe, N., Welling, M. (eds.) ECCV 2016. LNCS, vol. 9905, pp. 21–37. Springer, Cham (2016). https://doi.org/10.1007/978-3-319-46448-0_2
19. Mathias, M., Timofte, R., Benenson, R., Van Gool, L.: Traffic sign recognition–how far are we from the solution? In: The 2013 International Joint Conference on Neural Networks (IJCNN), pp. 1–8. IEEE (2013)
20. Møgelmose, A., Liu, D., Trivedi, M.M.: Detection of us traffic signs. IEEE Trans. Intell. Transp. Syst. **16**(6), 3116–3125 (2015)
21. Redmon, J., Divvala, S., Girshick, R., Farhadi, A.: You only look once: unified, real-time object detection. In: Proceedings of the IEEE Conference on Computer Vision and Pattern Recognition, pp. 779–788 (2016)
22. Ren, S., He, K., Girshick, R., Sun, J.: Faster R-CNN: towards real-time object detection with region proposal networks. In: Advances in Neural Information Processing Systems, pp. 91–99 (2015)

23. Sermanet, P., LeCun, Y.: Traffic sign recognition with multi-scale convolutional networks. In: The 2011 International Joint Conference on Neural Networks (IJCNN), pp. 2809–2813 (2011)
24. Stallkamp, J., Schlipsing, M., Salmen, J., Igel, C.: The German traffic sign recognition benchmark: a multi-class classification competition. In: The 2011 International Joint Conference on Neural Networks (IJCNN), pp. 1453–1460 (2011)
25. Trieu, T.H.: Darkflow. GitHub Repository (2018). https://github.com/thtrieu/darkflow. Accessed 14 Febr 2019
26. Vennelakanti, A., Shreya, S., Rajendran, R., Sarkar, D., Muddegowda, D., Hanagal, P.: Traffic sign detection and recognition using a CNN ensemble. In: 2019 IEEE International Conference on Consumer Electronics (ICCE), pp. 1–4. IEEE (2019)
27. Wali, S.B., et al.: Vision-based traffic sign detection and recognition systems: current trends and challenges. Sensors **19**(9), 2093 (2019)
28. Wang, G., Ren, G., Wu, Z., Zhao, Y., Jiang, L.: A robust, coarse-to-fine traffic sign detection method. In: The 2013 International Joint Conference on Neural Networks (IJCNN), pp. 1–5. IEEE (2013)
29. Youssef, A., Albani, D., Nardi, D., Bloisi, D.D.: Fast traffic sign recognition using color segmentation and deep convolutional networks. In: Blanc-Talon, J., Distante, C., Philips, W., Popescu, D., Scheunders, P. (eds.) ACIVS 2016. LNCS, vol. 10016, pp. 205–216. Springer, Cham (2016). https://doi.org/10.1007/978-3-319-48680-2_19
30. Zhu, Z., Liang, D., Zhang, S., Huang, X., Li, B., Hu, S.: Traffic-sign detection and classification in the wild. In: Proceedings of the IEEE Conference on Computer Vision and Pattern Recognition, pp. 2110–2118 (2016)

Dimensionality Reduction by Consolidated Sparse Representation and Fisher Criterion with Initialization for Recognition

Parita Chavda(✉), Srimanta Mandal, and Suman K. Mitra

Dhirubhai Ambani Institute of Information and Communication Technology, Gandhinagar, India
{srimanta_mandal,suman_mitra}@daiict.ac.in

Abstract. A sparse representation-based classifier has demonstrated potential results in face recognition but meets a small sample problem i.e. number of input images is less than an image dimension. To overcome this issue, dimensionality reduction methods can be employed in a sparse representation framework. Along this direction, sparse representation is often clubbed with the Fisher discriminant criterion. Most of these methods consider a random projection matrix to start with. The performance of dimensionality reduction procedure mostly depends on the projection matrix. In this paper, we show that a better-initialized projection matrix can perform much better than its random counterpart. Further, we are able to reduce the dimension of the projection matrix by half without losing much information. The experiments performed on the Extended Yale B, CMU-PIE and Coil-20 datasets demonstrate the efficacy of the proposed approach.

Keywords: Dimensionality reduction · Sparse Representation (SR) · Sparse Representation Classifier (SRC) · Initialization · Face recognition

1 Introduction

In the last several years, various DR techniques have been developed and have shown potential results in face recognition. Most popular DR methods are Principle Component Analysis (PCA) [2], Linear Discriminant Analysis (LDA) [2], kernel-based [3] and manifold learning methods [5,6]. PCA and LDA mainly focus on the scatter of input data to extract the most important features. However, they fails to discover manifold on which images may reside [3]. This leads to a decrease in the recognition rate for faces.

In non-linear DR methods, kernel- based techniques produce good results in face recognition, but they are computationally expensive and the mechanism for manifold structure preservation is not clear [1]. On the other hand, Laplacian Eigenmaps [6], locally linear embedding [5], isomap, locality preserving

S. K. Singh et al. (Eds.): CVIP 2020, CCIS 1378, pp. 332–343, 2021.
https://doi.org/10.1007/978-981-16-1103-2_28

projection (LPP) [7] and neighborhood preserving embedding (NPE) [8] are well known manifold learning methods. However for these methods, the projection of unseen testing data is not as natural as PCA.

In the last few years, sparse representation (SR) has gained greater attention from researchers by demonstrating potential results in face recognition due to advance research in L1 minimization and computer vision applications like image classification and clustering. Sparse representation-based classification(SRC) uses sparse reconstruction residual to classify different human subjects [9]. To get optimal sparsity coefficient, a fixed and over-complete dictionary i.e. more training images compare to the input image dimension is needed. In face recognition, the training dictionary is fixed but under-complete [16]. In this case, DR is compulsory before performing a classification task by SRC.

The most widely used DR techniques like PCA, LDA can be applied before applying SRC, but the extracted features often produce sub-optimal results [3]. To overcome this, various sparse representation based dimensionality techniques are developed and shown effective results even if input data is noisy and corrupted. Sparsity preserving projection (SPP) [1], SRC steered discriminative projection (SRC-DP) [10] and SRC integrated with Fisher discriminant criterion (SRC-FDC) [3] are few recently proposed SR based DR techniques. SPP and SRC-DP mainly focus on the reconstruction of the input data and hence identify only the local relationship and ignores the global relationship of the input data that affects the classification accuracy [1,10]. SRC-FDC solves this problem by using the Fisher criterion and sparse coding to extract the most suitable features for SRC.

Most of these approaches randomly initialize the projection matrix, which affects the performance of DR method as well as SRC. Random initialization tends to behave poorly for lower dimensional projection. To overcome this, in our method, an initialization technique is employed in sparse representation based DR technique with Fisher criterion. Further, the dimensionality is reduced to half by averaging every pair of eigenvectors without loosing much information.

The major contributions of this paper are: i) We propose an initialization technique in the fusion of sparse-representation, dimensionality reduction, and Fisher discriminant criterion for applications as face recognition; ii) We propose to reduce the dimension of projection matrix by averaging pairs of eigenvectors without losing much information; iii) We show that the proposed method works effectively on various datasets including facial and non-facial images without any bias.

The rest of the paper is organized as follows. Section 2 includes mathematical background and more details about LDA, SRC, SRC-DP, and SRC-FDC. In Sect. 3, the proposed method is discussed. Section 4 demonstrates the experimental results and analysis of performance of our proposed method with existing methods. The paper is summarized in Sect. 5.

2 Background

Let us consider, A be the number of input images and $\boldsymbol{C}$ represents the input data, $\boldsymbol{C} = [\boldsymbol{C}_1, \boldsymbol{C}_2, ..., \boldsymbol{C}_p, ..., \boldsymbol{C}_x]$, where $\boldsymbol{C}_p = [\boldsymbol{c}_1^p, \boldsymbol{c}_2^p, ...\boldsymbol{c}_q^p, ..., \boldsymbol{x}_{a_p}^p] \in R^{n \times a_p}$.

Here c_q^p represent one image arranged as a column vector in $\boldsymbol{C}$, $p = 1, 2, ..., x$ and it represents a class, q represents an image in that class and a_p represents the number of images in class-p. So overall, $\boldsymbol{C} = [\boldsymbol{c}_1^1, \boldsymbol{c}_2^1, ...\boldsymbol{c}_q^p, ..., \boldsymbol{c}_{a_x}^x] \in R^{n \times A}$ is a given data where $A = \sum_{i=1}^{x} a_p$.

2.1 Linear Discriminant Analysis(LDA)

The optimal projection matrix for LDA [2] is chosen in such a way that the ratio of between class scatter($\boldsymbol{S}_{bn}$) to the within class scatter($\boldsymbol{S}_{wn}$) is maximized. Scatters can be defined as

$$\boldsymbol{S}_{bn} = \sum_{p=1}^{x} a_p \left(\boldsymbol{m}_p - \boldsymbol{m}_a\right)\left(\boldsymbol{m}_p - \boldsymbol{m}_a\right)^T \tag{1}$$

$$\boldsymbol{S}_{wn} = \sum_{p=1}^{x} \sum_{q=1}^{a_p} \left(\boldsymbol{c}_q^p - \boldsymbol{m}_p\right)\left(\boldsymbol{c}_q^p - \boldsymbol{m}_p\right)^T \tag{2}$$

where $\boldsymbol{m}_p \in R^n$ is the mean of the input data related to class-p and $\boldsymbol{m}_a \in R^n$ is the total mean of input data.

The cost function to get the optimal projection matrix $\boldsymbol{M}_{opt}$ is defined as follows, provided $\boldsymbol{S}_{wn}$ is nonsingular:

$$\boldsymbol{M}_{opt} = \arg\max_{M} \frac{|\boldsymbol{M}^T \boldsymbol{S}_{bn} \boldsymbol{M}|}{|\boldsymbol{M}^T \boldsymbol{S}_{wn} \boldsymbol{M}|}, \tag{3}$$

2.2 Sparse Representation Classifier(SRC)

Sparse representation(SR) represents a new test image $\boldsymbol{t}$, as a weighted linear combination of the training samples, i.e. $\boldsymbol{t} = \boldsymbol{Cs}$ where $\boldsymbol{s} \in R^A$ is a sparse representation coefficient of $\boldsymbol{t}$ [9,20]. The optimal solution for below mentioned problem give the sparsest possible solution for $\boldsymbol{t}$ [11]:

$$\hat{\boldsymbol{s}_1} = \arg\min_{\boldsymbol{s}} \|\boldsymbol{s}\|_1 \quad s.t.\ \boldsymbol{t} = \boldsymbol{Cs} \tag{4}$$

After getting an optimal sparse solution, one can apply SRC for classification [9]. Let $\delta_p : R^A \rightarrow R^A$ is the function which extracts the entries from $\boldsymbol{s}$ that are related to the class-p only. Given $\boldsymbol{s} \in R^A$, $\delta_p(\boldsymbol{s})$ be a vector whose nonzero coefficients are related to class-p. One can reconstruct a given test image $\boldsymbol{t}$ as $\boldsymbol{t}_p = \boldsymbol{C}\delta_p(\boldsymbol{s})$. The sparse reconstruction error can be defined as the following:

$$r_p(\boldsymbol{t}) = \|\boldsymbol{t} - \boldsymbol{t}_p\|_2 = \|\boldsymbol{t} - \boldsymbol{C}\delta_p(\boldsymbol{s})\|_2 \tag{5}$$

Test sample $\boldsymbol{t}$ is classified to class-x if it has the minimum error. The following equation defines the decision rule of SRC.

$$r_x(\boldsymbol{t}) = \min_{p} r_p(\boldsymbol{t}) \tag{6}$$

2.3 Sparse Representation Classifier Steered Discriminative Projection(SRC-DP)

SRC-DP [10] is a SR based supervised DR technique that focuses on preservation of the class reconstruction relationship of the input data. It tries to maximize the ratio of between-class residual($\boldsymbol{E}_{bn}$) to the within-class residual($\boldsymbol{E}_{wn}$) that are defined below:

$$\boldsymbol{E}_{wn} = \frac{1}{A}\sum_{p=1}^{x}\sum_{q=1}^{a_p}(\boldsymbol{c}_q^p - \boldsymbol{C}\delta_p(\boldsymbol{s}_q^p))(\boldsymbol{c}_q^p - \boldsymbol{C}\delta_p(\boldsymbol{s}_q^p))^T \tag{7}$$

$$\boldsymbol{E}_{bn} = \frac{1}{A(x-1)}\sum_{p=1}^{x}\sum_{q=1}^{a_p}\sum_{b\neq p}(\boldsymbol{c}_q^p - \boldsymbol{C}\delta_b(\boldsymbol{s}_q^p))(\boldsymbol{c}_q^p - \boldsymbol{C}\delta_b(\boldsymbol{s}_q^p))^T \tag{8}$$

The cost function to get the optimal projection matrix $\boldsymbol{M}_{opt}$ of SRC-DP can be written as follow [10]:

$$\boldsymbol{M}_{opt} = \arg\max_{M}\frac{|\boldsymbol{M}^T\boldsymbol{E}_{bn}\boldsymbol{M}|}{|\boldsymbol{M}^T\boldsymbol{E}_{wn}\boldsymbol{M}|} \tag{9}$$

2.4 Sparse Representation Classifier Integrated with Fisher Criterion

Sparse Representation Classifier integrated with Fisher Discriminant Criterion (SRC-FDC) [3] is a supervised and a combined DR method using LDA and SRC-DP. It discovers the global discriminant structure of data by LDA and local reconstructive relationship of data via sparse representation. SRC-FDC tries to maximize the ratio of linear combination of between-class scatter and between-class reconstruction error to the within-class scatter and within-class reconstruction error. So, the cost function can be written as follows:

$$\boldsymbol{M}_{opt} = \arg\max_{M}\frac{|\boldsymbol{M}^T(\boldsymbol{E}_{bn}+\boldsymbol{S}_{bn})\boldsymbol{M}|}{|\boldsymbol{M}^T(\boldsymbol{E}_{wn}+\boldsymbol{S}_{wn})\boldsymbol{M}|}, \tag{10}$$

3 Proposed Approach

Here, we discuss the motivation followed by the proposed approach.

3.1 Motivation

Sparse Representation based Classifier(SRC) has been proven as a state of art for face recognition and recognized as a robust tool in pattern recognition by successfully classified face images with different facial expressions, variation in lighting conditions, and sometimes, noisy and corrupted as well [23]. SRC chooses a subset of input data which best represents new unseen test data as a linear combination of subset images and discovers sparsest coefficients to calculate reconstruction residual and classify test image to class which has lowest residual known [22]. Applications like face recognition faces small sample problem i.e. the training images are generally less compared to the dimension of input image. In this case, Sparse Representation(SR) contains non-zero coefficients that are not related to the class to which the input image belongs. Therefore, to obtain optimal SR, Dimensionality Reduction(DR) becomes a compulsory pre-processing step before applying SRC.

Famous DR methods like PCA, LDA, kernel based and manifold learning methods applied before SRC but it doesn't show impressive results for recognition. Later, sparse coding based techniques are suggested and shown robust results in face recognition. Some of the well known examples are SPP, SRC-DP and SRC-FDC. SPP and SRD-DP uses sparse reconstruction residual to obtain optimal projection matric for DR procedure while SRC-FDC additionally uses Fisher criterion with SRC to better differentiate human subjects [4]. Let denote the initial version of the projection matrix as $\boldsymbol{M}_0$. In [4,11], the initial projection matrix $\boldsymbol{M}_0$ is chosen as a random matrix of dimension $n \times m$ where n is the dimension of a vectorized image and m is a projection dimension. Therefore, the projection of the data $\boldsymbol{C}$ onto the projection matrix $\boldsymbol{M}_0$ is known as random projection. Since $\boldsymbol{M}_0$ plays an important role in both SR and DR, we need to devise a better method to initialize it. Moreover, a dimensionality reduction technique is also desired without loss of much information.

3.2 Proposed Initialization Technique

If sparsity is preserved after linear transformation in low dimension space, then sparse representation $\boldsymbol{s}_q^p$ of projected data $\boldsymbol{y}_q^p = \boldsymbol{M}^T \boldsymbol{c}_q^p$ is the same as it is obtained from input data [10]. Under this assumption, $\boldsymbol{s}_q^p$ is calculated for all input data directly using following equation:

$$\arg\min_{s} \left\|\boldsymbol{c}_q^p - \boldsymbol{C}\boldsymbol{s}_q^p\right\|_2^2 + \gamma \left\|\boldsymbol{s}_q^p\right\|_1 \tag{11}$$

Where γ is the regularization parameter. After getting sparsest representation, one can calculate scatter matrices ($\boldsymbol{S}_{bn}$ & $\boldsymbol{S}_{wn}$) and reconstruction error matrices ($\boldsymbol{E}_{bn}$ & $\boldsymbol{E}_{wn}$) in input space using Eq. (1), (2), (7), and (8). Here, scatter matrices provide better class separability while error matrices ensure the reconstruction of input image. We can get optimal initialization matrix($\boldsymbol{M}_0$) by solving following generalized eigen equation:

$$(\boldsymbol{E}_{bn} + \boldsymbol{S}_{bn})\boldsymbol{\alpha} = \lambda(\boldsymbol{E}_{wn} + \boldsymbol{S}_{wn})\boldsymbol{\alpha} \tag{12}$$

Generalized eigenvectors related to largest m eigenvalues of the above generalized eigenvalue equation constructs optimal initial projection matrix. The proposed initialization algorithm is described in Algorithm 1:

Algorithm 1: Proposed Initialization Technique for $\boldsymbol{M}_0$

Result: Optimal initial projection matrix $\boldsymbol{M}_0$

Given the training data: $\boldsymbol{C} = [\boldsymbol{c}_1^1, \boldsymbol{c}_2^1, ...\boldsymbol{c}_q^p, ..., \boldsymbol{c}_{a_x}^x] \epsilon R^{n \times A}$

Steps:

1:Calculate the sparse representation $\boldsymbol{s}_q^p$ for all training samples by solving,

$$\arg\min_{s} \left\|\boldsymbol{c}_q^p - \boldsymbol{C}\boldsymbol{s}_q^p\right\|_2^2 + \gamma \left\|\boldsymbol{s}_q^p\right\|_1$$

2:Calculate scatter and error matrices $\boldsymbol{S}_{bn}, \boldsymbol{S}_{wn}, \boldsymbol{E}_{bn}$ and $\boldsymbol{E}_{wn}$

3:Calculate generalized eigenvectors of following generalized eigen-equation,

$$(\boldsymbol{E}_{bn} + \boldsymbol{S}_{bn})\boldsymbol{\alpha} = \lambda(\boldsymbol{E}_{wn} + \boldsymbol{S}_{wn})\boldsymbol{\alpha}$$

4: $\boldsymbol{M}_0 = [\boldsymbol{\alpha}_1, \boldsymbol{\alpha}_2, ..., \boldsymbol{\alpha}_m]$

In reality, the assumption that sparsity preserved under linear mapping might not hold [10]. In this case, this algorithm may not help. The assumption makes the procedure of obtaining initial projection matrix $\boldsymbol{M}_0$ simpler. Obtained $\boldsymbol{M}_0$ may not be the optimal one but it can be viewed as a better initial solution. Here, the calculation for eigenvectors is expensive for original input data. To overcome this problem, we use PCA to reduce the dimension of the input images. Afterwards, the proposed initialization method is applied to initialize $\boldsymbol{M}_0$. This initialization technique behaves better than the random one in discriminating among faces.

3.3 Proposed Dimensionality Reduction Technique

After getting initialized projection matrix $\boldsymbol{M}_0$, PCA projected input data is projected onto a lower dimension as $\boldsymbol{y}_q^p = \boldsymbol{M}_0{}^T \boldsymbol{c}_q^p$. Later, we get sparse representation for each projected training sample $\boldsymbol{y}_q^p$ with the help of remaining training data samples by solving L_1 minimization problem. Next, between($\boldsymbol{S}_{bn}$ & $\boldsymbol{E}_{bn}$ and within ($\boldsymbol{S}_{wn}$ & $\boldsymbol{E}_{wn}$) class scatter and error matrices are constructed by using Eq. (1), (2), (7) and (8). To obtain next projection matrix, we solve generalized eigen equation given in Eq. (12). This way, we run iterative algorithm until algorithm converge. The following criterion function is used to decide convergence:

$$F(\boldsymbol{M}) = \frac{tr(\boldsymbol{M}^T(\boldsymbol{S}_{bn} + \boldsymbol{E}_{bn})\boldsymbol{M})}{tr(\boldsymbol{M}^T(\boldsymbol{S}_{wn} + \boldsymbol{E}_{wn})\boldsymbol{M})} \tag{13}$$

The projection matrix obtained after performing ($k - 1^{th}$) iteration, $\boldsymbol{M}_{k-1}$ is given as a input matrix in k^{th} iteration to map the input data in lower dimension. We repeat same steps discussed in above paragraph in each iteration and algorithm stops when value of criterion function doesn't change. Overall, the generalized eigenvectors of generalized eigen Eq. (12) contributes towards construction of the final projection matrix as shown in Algorithm 2.

Further, due to limited memory, it is difficult to store a huge training dictionary which is required to identify a person. Therefore, researchers always aim to build a face recognition framework with the lowest memory requirement without much compromising the classification accuracy.

Along with initialization technique, we propose to deal with such a memory problem while aiming to maintain as much as information possible. The optimal projection matrix($\in R^{n\times m/2}$) is constructed by taking the average of consecutive eigenvectors obtained by solving Eq. (12) to reduce the dimension by half i.e., $\frac{m}{2}$. Therefore, the optimal projection matrix is constructed as

$$\boldsymbol{M}_{opt} = \left[\frac{\boldsymbol{\alpha}_1 + \boldsymbol{\alpha}_2}{\mathbf{2}}, \frac{\boldsymbol{\alpha}_3 + \boldsymbol{\alpha}_4}{\mathbf{2}}, \ldots, \frac{\boldsymbol{\alpha}_{m-1} + \boldsymbol{\alpha}_m}{\mathbf{2}} \right]. \tag{14}$$

Algorithm 2: Proposed Dimensionality Reduction Technique for $\boldsymbol{M}_{opt}$

Result: Optimal projection matrix $\boldsymbol{M}_{opt}$
Take obtained $\boldsymbol{M}_0$ as the projection matrix i.e. $\boldsymbol{M} = \boldsymbol{M}_0$
Steps:
1: Transform all the input data in m-dimensional space i.e. $\boldsymbol{y}_q^p = \boldsymbol{M}^T \boldsymbol{c}_q^p$
2:Calculate the sparse representation $\boldsymbol{s}_q^p$ for all training samples by solving,
$$\arg\min_{s} \left\| \boldsymbol{c}_q^p - \boldsymbol{C}\boldsymbol{s}_q^p \right\|_2^2 + \gamma \left\| \boldsymbol{s}_q^p \right\|_1$$
3:Calculate scatter and error matrices $\boldsymbol{S}_{bn}, \boldsymbol{S}_{wn}, \boldsymbol{E}_{bn}$ and $\boldsymbol{E}_{wn}$
4:Calculate generalized eigenvectors of following generalized eigen-equation,
$$(\boldsymbol{E}_{bn} + \boldsymbol{S}_{bn})\boldsymbol{\alpha} = \lambda(\boldsymbol{E}_{wn} + \boldsymbol{S}_{wn})\boldsymbol{\alpha}$$
5:Construct $\boldsymbol{M}_k = [(\boldsymbol{\alpha}_1 + \boldsymbol{\alpha}_2)/\mathbf{2}, (\boldsymbol{\alpha}_3 + \boldsymbol{\alpha}_4)/\mathbf{2}, \ldots, (\boldsymbol{\alpha}_{m-1} + \boldsymbol{\alpha}_m)/\mathbf{2}$
6: Repeat step (1) to (5) while $F(\boldsymbol{M}_k) - F(\boldsymbol{M}_{k-1}) > \eta$ where η is error tolerance
7: The optimal projection matrix $\boldsymbol{M}_{out} = \boldsymbol{M}_k$

By this method, the dimension is reduced by half without much performance degradation. This is due to the fact that the average of a sequence of numbers can represent sufficient statistic of the individual numbers [17]. Sufficient statistic contains the summary of all the individual data points. Hence, the averages of consecutive eigenvectors contain important information that can provide discriminative ability.

4 Experimental Results

To check the effectiveness of the suggested method, several experiments are performed for image classification. The performance of proposed methods is measured on two face and one non-face popular databases i.e. Extended Yale B [13], CMU-PIE [14], and Coil-20 [15]. The experimental results are compared with two competitive approaches SRC-DP [10] and SRC-FDC [3]. To see the effectiveness of different components of our method, we also show the results (in Tables 1, 2, 3 and 4) of employing the initialization technique only (**Our**

Method1). Whereas the results of our dimensionality reduction technique is denoted by **Our Method2**, and the combination of these techniques are represented by **Our Combined Method**. To compute the sparse vector for the input image, the Lasso model [12] from the sklearn machine learning library is used in Python.

4.1 Experiments on Extended Yale B Database

The Extended Yale B dataset(cropped version) [13] contains total 2432 human subject images. It includes 38 persons images under 64 lightning situations. We resize each input image to 32×32 dimension. Few images of one human subject are given below in Fig. 1.

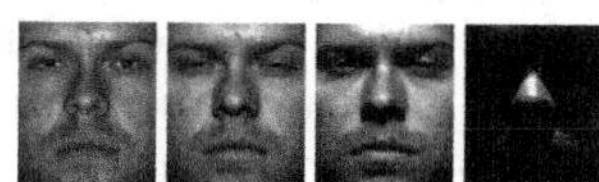

Fig. 1. Some samples from the Extended Yale B database

To train the lasso model, we randomly choose 32 images per person and the remaining images are used to measure classification accuracy of SRC from the Extended Yale B dataset. So, a total of 1216 images are used in training process and 1216 images are used for classification using SRC. As a preprocessing step, we use PCA to decrease the size of each input image to 200 pixels. Results are obtained by projecting data on different dimensions i.e. 20, 40, ..., 140. Table 1 represents the recognition rate for different approaches. One can observe that Our Method1 i.e., the initialization method performs better than SRC-FDC methods for most of the cases. However, the improvement in performance for higher dimensions is not as large as that for lower dimensions. The reason being that for lower-dimensional cases, the data is being projected onto only a few dimensions like 20, 40, etc. If we do not use the initialization technique, the data will be projected onto a few dimensions, which are randomly defined. However, this random projection may not lead to a good representation of the data, even after optimization. On the other hand, the initialization technique gives a better projection matrix, which is derived from the data. Hence, it can represent the data better for lower dimensions. However, for higher dimensions, the data is being projected onto a more number of dimensions. Hence, there is a possibility that even if we randomly initialize the projection matrix, after optimization the matrix gets refined and represents the data better as compared to the lower-dimensional case.

Further, our dimensionality reduction technique i.e., Our Method2 and Our Combined Method they both provide good results. Although the results are somewhat lagging behind the our initialization based method, but the dimension has been reduced by half. For fair comparison, the performance of the combined

Table 1. Classification results for different dimension on the Extended Yale B dataset

Dimension	SRC-DP	SRC-FDC	Our Method1	Our Method2	Our combined method
20	31.82	76.97	87.99	45.47	45.47
40	69.73	90.21	92.76	84.29	87.82
60	87.84	96.29	96.29	90.95	92.02
80	94.40	96.71	97.28	91.85	93.42
100	95.97	96.79	97.28	94.16	94.81
120	97.20	97.45	97.77	95.64	95.64
140	96.71	97.53	97.61	96.62	97.12

method for m^{th} dimension should be compared with the $m/2^{th}$ dimension of other methods as our dimension reduction technique has reduced the dimension by half. For example, our combined method provides 93.42% accuracy for dimension 80 which is equivalent to dimension 40 due to dimensional reduction. Hence, if we compare the results of other methods for 40 dimension, we find that our combined method is able to provide best result. This also proves that our dimension reduction technique is quite effective.

4.2 Experiments on the CMU-PIE Dataset

The CMU-PIE dataset [14] has 68 person's face data for 43 variable lightning scenarios along with 4 facial expressions. We choose total 2795 images as input data which contains 65 human subjects and 43 images per human subject. We resize all input images to 64 × 64 dimension. Few images of one human subject are given below in Fig. 2.

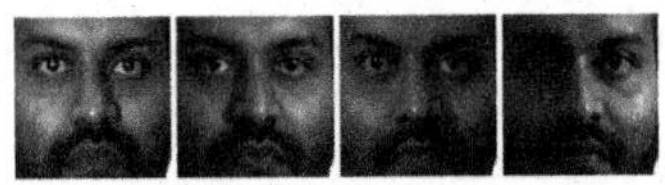

Fig. 2. Some samples from CMU-PIE dataset

To train the lasso model, we randomly choose 22 images per person and the remaining images are used to measure classification accuracy of SRC from the CMU-PIE dataset. Therefore, we choose total 1430 images for training process and 1365 images are used for classification task by SRC. As a pre-processing step, we use PCA to decrease the size of each input image to 200 pixels. Results are obtained by projecting data on different dimensions i.e. 10,20, ..., 70. Table 2 represents the recognition rate of different approaches for different dimensions. The Table shows that our methods outperform existing approaches. Our

Table 2. Recognition rate for different dimension on the CMU-PIE dataset

Dimension	SRC-DP	SRC-FDC	Our Method1	Our Method2	Our combined method
10	11.20	20.88	24.54	7.39	8.27
20	21.68	47.03	64.24	25.05	32.01
30	39.63	83.81	84.61	42.34	49.52
40	63.37	93.62	95.09	67.83	69.81
50	93.18	96.63	97.43	84.54	81.61
60	97.43	98.97	98.97	92.08	91.35
70	98.75	99.41	99.70	95.75	96.04

methods are able to consistently outmatch the existing approaches for different face datasets. Hence, it can be forwarded that our methods are not biased by any particular face dataset.

4.3 Experiments on Coil-20 Dataset

To see the efficacy of our approach on non-face dataset, we use Columbia Object Image Library (COIL-20) dataset [15]. It has 20 different objects and each object has 72 different images. The dimension of each image is 128 × 128 pixels. Few images of one object are given below in Fig. 3. To train the lasso model, we randomly choose 36 images per object and the remaining images are used to measure classification accuracy of SRC from the Coil-20 dataset. Therefore, we choose total 720 images are used for training process and 720 images are used for classification task by SRC. As a preprocessing step, we use PCA to decrease the size of each input image to 200 pixels. Results are obtained by projecting data on different dimensions i.e. 20,40, ..., 140. Table 3 represents the classification accuracy of various approaches for different dimensions. The table shows that our methods perform better than existing approaches. This points out the robustness of our methods even for non-face data. We further use this dataset for checking the performance of our method for different number of training samples. The results can be observed in Table 4 for different approaches. Observe that our methods are able to produce better results even for lesser training samples. The performance increases with increasing training samples.

Fig. 3. Some samples from Coil-20 dataset

Table 3. Classification accuracy of SRC for various dimensions on the Coil-20 dataset

Dimension	SRC-DP	SRC-FDC	Our Method1	Our Method2	Our combined method
20	20.55	61.66	95.13	31.11	85.83
40	64.02	87.50	95.97	83.47	93.61
60	86.66	94.16	96.80	90.27	95.00
80	91.94	93.88	97.91	90.41	97.22
100	93.75	94.86	97.22	92.91	95.55
120	96.38	96.80	97.63	94.16	96.52
140	96.94	97.50	98.19	95.83	97.91

Table 4. Classification accuracy for different size of training dictionary on the Coil-20 dataset

Images per class	SRC-DP	SRC-FDC	Our Method1	Our Method2	Our combined method
15	85.70	86.75	88.33	82.98	87.45
20	91.05	91.05	91.25	88.17	92.40
25	91.80	92.76	93.19	89.25	92.87
30	94.88	94.76	95.23	93.21	95.00
35	95.67	96.08	97.16	94.32	96.08

5 Conclusion

We have proposed an initialization technique and a dimensionality reduction method for the integrated sparse representation and Fisher criterion based classifier. In this kind of dimensionality reduction based classifiers, the projection matrix plays an important role. Our both contributions have focused on improving the projection matrix. The initialization technique has been proposed to derive one better and optimal projection matrix. Further, the averaging of the pair of consecutive eigenvectors has helped to reduce the dimension by half without losing much information. We have evaluated our techniques on facial as well as non-facial images. The results have demonstrated the efficacy of our methods as compared to the existing approaches.

References

1. Chen, S., Qiao, L., Tan, X.: Sparsity preserving projections with applications to face recognition. Pattern Recogn. **43**(1), 331–341 (2010)
2. Belhumeur, P.N., Hespanha, J.P., Kriegman, D.J.: Eigenfaces vs. fisher-faces: recognition using class specific linear projection. IEEE Trans. Pattern Anal. Mach. Intell. **19**(7), 711–720 (1997)

3. Gao, Q., Wang, Q., Huang, Y., Gao, X., Hong, X., Zhang, H.: Dimensionality reduction by integrating sparse representation and fisher criterion and its applications. IEEE Trans. Image Process. **24**(12), 5684–5695 (2015)
4. Tenenbaum, J.B.: Mapping a manifold of perceptual observations. In: Advances in Neural Information Processing Systems, pp. 682–688 (1998)
5. Roweis, S.T., Saul, L.K.: Nonlinear dimensionality reduction by locally linear embedding. Science **290**(5500), 2323–2326 (2000)
6. Belkin, M., Niyogi, P.: Laplacian eigenmaps for dimensionality reduction and data representation. Neural Comput. **15**(6), 1373–1396 (2003)
7. He, X., Niyogi, P.: Locality preserving projections. In: Advances in Neural Information Processing Systems, pp. 153–160 (2004)
8. Gui, J., Sun, Z., Jia, W., Rongxiang, H., Lei, Y., Ji, S.: Discriminant sparse neighborhood preserving embedding for face recognition. Pattern Recogn. **45**(8), 2884–2893 (2012)
9. Yang, M., Zhang, L., Yang, J., Zhang, D.: Robust sparse coding for face recognition. In: CVPR 2011, pp. 625–632. IEEE (2011)
10. Yang, J., Chu, D., Zhang, L., Xu, Y., Yang, J.: Sparse representation classifier steered discriminative projection with applications to face recognition. IEEE Trans. Neural Netw. Learn. Syst. **24**(7), 1023–1035 (2013)
11. Donoho, D.L., Tsaig, Y.: Fast solution of l1-norm minimization problems when the solution may be sparse. IEEE Trans. Inf. Theory **54**(11), 4789–4812 (2008)
12. Pedregosa, F., et al.: Scikit-learn: machine learning in Python. J. Mach. Learn. Res. **12**, 2825–2830 (2011)
13. Lee, K.-C., Ho, J., Kriegman, D.J.: Acquiring linear subspaces for face recognition under variable lighting. IEEE Trans. Pattern Anal. Mach. Intell. **27**(5), 684–698 (2005)
14. Sim, T., Baker, S., Bsat, M.: The CMU pose, illumination, and expression (PIE) database. In: Proceedings of Fifth IEEE International Conference on Automatic Face Gesture Recognition, pp. 53–58. IEEE (2002)
15. Nene, S.A., Nayar, S.K., Murase, H.: Columbia image object library (coil-20). Department of Computer Science, Columbia University, New York, NY, USA, Technical report CUCS-006-96 (1996)
16. Zhao, W., Chellappa, R., Jonathon Phillips, P., Rosenfeld, A.: Face recognition: a literature survey. ACM Comput. Surv. (CSUR) **35**(4), 399–458 (2003)
17. Kay, S.M.: Fundamentals of Statistical Signal Processing: Estimation Theory. Prentice-Hall Inc., Upper Saddle River (1993)
18. Shen, C., Chen, L., Dong, Y., Priebe, C.E.: Sparse representation classification beyond l1 minimization and the subspace assumption. IEEE Trans. Inf. Theory **66**(8), 5061–5071 (2020). https://doi.org/10.1109/TIT.2020.2981309
19. Xu, Y., Cheng, J.: Face recognition algorithm based on correlation coefficient and ensemble-augmented sparsity. IEEE Access **8**, 183972–183982 (2020). https://doi.org/10.1109/ACCESS.2020.3028905
20. Mandal, S., Thavalengal, S., Sao, A.K.: Explicit and implicit employment of edge-related information in super-resolving distant faces for recognition. Pattern Anal. Appl. **19**(3), 867–884 (2016). https://doi.org/10.1007/s10044-015-0512-0

Deep Learning and Density Based Clustering Methods for Road Traffic Prediction

D. N. Jagadish(✉), Lakshman Mahto, and Arun Chauhan

Indian Institute of Information Technology Dharwad, Dharwad, India

Abstract. Road traffic prediction is a necessary requirement for traffic management. Deep neural networks can perform multiple vehicle detection leading to traffic prediction. Neural networks trained on vehicles dataset detects multiple vehicles on road. Large area occlusion and vehicles that are there at far distances have lesser probability of detection. We propose a technique for improved estimate of traffic, despite presence of occlusion and poor detection probability in the video frame based on density based clustering. Grid averaged density estimated maps representing spatial-temporal traffic data are fed to a trained convolutional LSTM network to predict the road traffic. The output predictions are chosen from a 10 min horizon. The validation when done on 30 h of traffic video yielded a mean absolute percentage error equal to 4.55.

Keywords: Deep learning · Density based clustering · Road traffic prediction

1 Introduction

Prediction and management of road traffic and vehicles at parking lots necessarily rely on approximate count obtained via multiple object detection algorithms. Owing to computation capabilities and sophisticated deep learning models availability, vision based traffic estimation is feasible. Generally, a moderate to high resolution camera is fixed at an elevated point on the road or traffic signal to capture a good view of vehicles on the road. Primarily, a video of the traffic scene is recorded, which is a time series data. The video frame rate will be desirably low. The captured frames are fed to a trained deep neural network to detect vehicles in the scene. Convolutional neural network layers upfront in the neural network captures the spatial information of the scene [1]. Fully connected layers of the trained network will detect vehicles belonging to various categories with a probability score.

Baseline deep neural network models popular for multiple object detection are RetinaNet [2] and YOLOv3 [3]. They can detect diverse classes of objects. However, when these models are utilized specifically to detect vehicles that hit the road, such as, car, bus, truck and cycle, the outcome is inaccurate. The problem is attributed to the models' inability to cope with vehicle's diminished size at low resolution and distinguish between highly overlapped vehicles that are similar [4]. Additionally, illumination and shadow may cause loss of vehicle appearance information, which may cause omissions in the detection process [5]. Transfer learning is a viable approach to enhance accuracy of vehicle detection, wherein feature vectors are preserved and

S. K. Singh et al. (Eds.): CVIP 2020, CCIS 1378, pp. 344–355, 2021.
https://doi.org/10.1007/978-981-16-1103-2_29

output layers are trained to minimize loss function. A network trained with vehicles dataset performs better than baseline networks in detecting vehicles, however, quite not up to the mark due to vehicles at far distance captured under low resolution, occlusion, illumination and shadow effects. The network suffers from an overfit.

In this work, we feed in traffic video frames into a trained network for multiple vehicles detection and post process the model output to attain better estimate of the vehicle traffic. We introduce a density-based clustering technique to estimate traffic density in the frame. We compute inter cluster distances and try interpolating the density at regions of poor vehicle detection probability. On estimating the traffic density, to predict traffic of 10 min horizon, we feed in the spatial density and temporal information into a convolutional long-term short memory (convLSTM) recurrent neural network [6]. We test our algorithms for traffic prediction ability on a traffic video dataset.

The remainder of the paper is organized as follows: Related work is introduced in Sect. 2. Sect. 3 describes the proposed methods. In Sect. 4, performance of proposed techniques in predicting traffic on a recorded video dataset is discussed, and methods validated. Finally, the paper is concluded in Sect. 5.

2 Related Works

Several works have been carried out and they fall into two categories. They address the challenges in traffic estimation and prediction domains. To solve the difficulty of detecting small and weak objects with low resolution in complex large scenes, a dynamic region zoom-in network is proposed in [5]. The network down-samples the images of high-resolution large scenes while maintaining the detection accuracy of small and weak objects with low resolution in high resolution images through dynamic region zoom. The detection is performed in a coarse-to-fine manner. First, the down sampled version of the image is detected and then the areas identified as likely to improve the detection accuracy are sequentially enlarged to higher resolution versions and then detected. Detection based methods in [7, 8] try to identify and localize vehicles in each frame. They perform poorly in scenarios of low resolution and high occlusion. Methods in [9, 10] employ tracking to estimate traffic flow. These methods are unsuitable as the demand for high frame rate and motion information is intensive. Some of the speedy vehicle's trajectory cannot be well estimated. Several deep learning methods have been introduced for counting objects [11–15]. The architecture in [11] combines a linear model fitted using lasso regularization and a sequence of tanh layers. The paper shows that deep learning architectures can capture nonlinear spatial-temporal effects. The architecture in [12] fits a ridge regressor to perform final density estimation. However, the size of the estimated final density map is not of the same size of the input image. Based on a fully convolutional network, an output density map is achieved in [14], but the map is much smaller than the input image due to absence of deconvolutional layers. Work in [15] jointly learns density map and foreground mask for object counting, while it does not solve the large perspective and object scale variation problems. For a deeper understanding of traffic density, [16] explores both optimization and deep learning based methods. Both methods map the dense image feature into vehicle density, one based on rank constrained regression and the other on fully convolutional networks.

The primitive techniques for traffic flow prediction mainly included Kalman filter [17, 18], Markov chain model [19] and even support vector machine (SVM) [20], which is good at classification, was used for extracting temporal features. Though these prediction methods are simpler, these models do not completely capture the deep relationship between data. On the other hand, neural networks can do better in predicting the traffic flow as these models can mine big data and discover internal structure and potential characteristics. Recently, deep belief network [21, 22], long-term short memory (LSTM) neural network [23–25] and deep architecture based prediction methods [26, 27] have been widely used in traffic flow prediction. Recently, hybrid deep neural networks inheriting the benefits of convolutional neural network (CNN) and LSTM networks are explored. They can capture spatial temporal correlations in the traffic. In [28], the road is treated as a sequence of segments yielding vectors as inputs. CNN mines the spatial features, whereas LSTMs extract short-term temporal features and periodic features. A regressor at the output makes traffic predictions. Traffic network is converted to grid maps [29]. CNN and LSTM networks together learn spatial-temporal features. Many of the works try to predict traffic speed for a city by collecting GPS information of the vehicles. The disadvantage of GPS data is that the movements of one car do not contain information about the state of the surrounding traffic and in addition, the measurement error, which is up to several meters. In our work we perform density based road traffic estimation [30] and predict traffic at a single road segment.

3 Our Approach

We divide traffic prediction tasks in two parts. First, we do traffic estimation and second, we do traffic prediction from the estimations. We introduce a method to estimate traffic on a road segment. The method utilizes a trained deep learning model for multiple vehicle detection. We process the output of the detection model to identify clusters and their linear densities using a density-based clustering algorithm. Taking account of clusters and outliers data probability, we interpolate the inter cluster and cluster-noise areas to estimate traffic in our method. The technique of estimation outputs spatial traffic density data into an LSTM network, which can make traffic prediction. The block diagram of traffic prediction framework is put forward in Fig. 1.

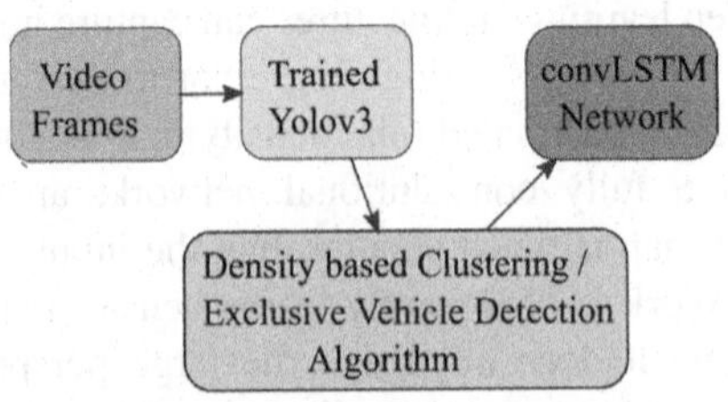

Fig. 1. Block diagram of traffic prediction framework.

The subsections will describe the deep learning model and proposed method.

3.1 Multiple Vehicle Detection Model

Yolov3 object detection model can detect 80 categories of objects. Since we focus over detecting road vehicles alone, we trained the network with vehicles images from a public dataset [31]. The dataset has as large as 0.472 million of vehicles, 3 images each, collected from multiple cameras, each annotated by a bounding box. With the trained network, the accuracy of vehicle detection saw an improvement of 9.3% over the baseline object detection model.

3.2 Traffic Estimation

A camera at certain elevation captures video of traffic on the road. A sample traffic video frame that is considered for illustration of proposed method is as shown in Fig. 2 (a). The frame is fed into the detection model. The model outputs a list of detected objects, bounding boxes and their class probabilities (refer Fig. 2(b)).

Density Based Estimation. For the post detection process, let us consider the number of objects detected be N and bounding boxes described by diagonal vertices (x1, y1) and (x2, y2) for each of these boxes. We compute centroid value (x, y) for each of these boxes. A plot of these data points is shown in Fig. 3(a).

The objects nearer to the camera are less dense and spread compared to objects at far. To have uniformity in spatial resemblance of objects, we apply normalization to the data points, given by (1) and (2).

$$x' = x\left\{1 + \left(\frac{x - X_{mid}}{X_{mid}}\right)\left(\frac{Y_{max} - y}{Y_{max}}\right)\right\} \tag{1}$$

$$y' = ye^{\left(1 - \frac{\beta y}{Y_{max}}\right)} \tag{2}$$

Fig. 2. Vehicle detection output by trained neural network. (a) Input sample video frame (b) Detected vehicles with spatial information.

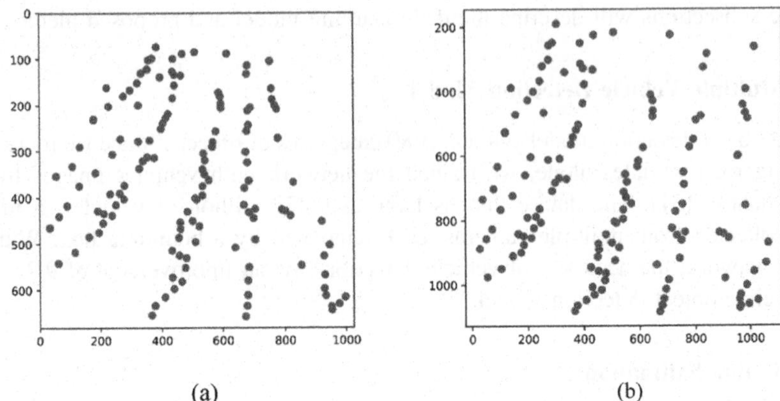

Fig. 3. Plots of data points describing spatial information. (a) before normalization and (b) after normalization.

Objects at far and middle of the horizon are stretched, while the space towards the corner of the horizon and near to the camera are compressed. β is a hyper parameter learnt in an initial phase of analysis, while emphasizing symmetry in variance for data points above and below Y_{mid} for high density traffic situations. A plot of the data points after normalization is shown in Fig. 3(b).

Given a data point p, we would like to find out other data points in its vicinity that are within the distance of ε, where ε > 0. The number of data points within the ε ball will provide the notion of neighborhood density [32]. A cluster could be formed by moving the ε ball in the neighborhood and observing at least minimum specified density. As an outcome of this process, we can classify data points in the categories of core, boundary and outlier. A data point p is a core point if Nbhd(p,ε) [ε neighborhood of p] contains at least minimum data points. A data point q is a border point if Nbhd(q, ε) contains less than minimum data points, but q is reachable from some core point p. A data point o is an outlier if it is neither a core point nor a border point. Unlike K-Means, which always form spherical clusters and require a number of cluster parameters beforehand, ε nearest neighborhood can discover clusters of arbitrary shape and infers the number of clusters based on data. Figure 4(a) shows the plot of cluster formation on normalized data points.

In the context of road traffic, where vehicles follow lane discipline, spherical density does not hold valuable information. Rather it is the linear density along the length of the cluster that turns out to be more useful. A 2-degree polynomial curve is fit for each of the clusters as shown in Fig. 4(b). Linear density d is expressed as a ratio of total data points in a cluster to its cluster length l.

We associate a probability score for boundary points in the clusters, essentially to capture the inability of off-the-shelf object detection models in detecting small and

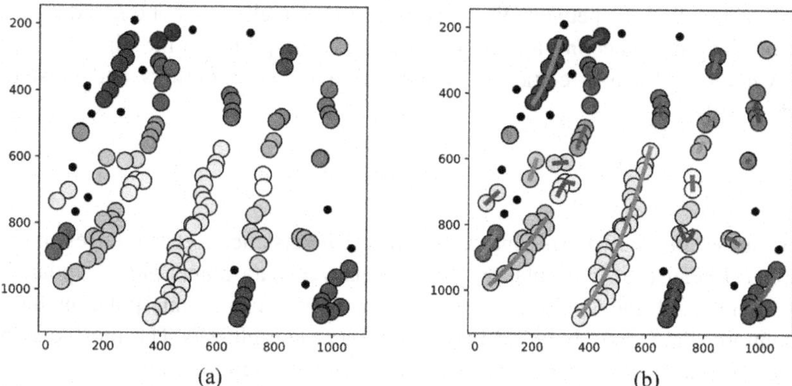

Fig. 4. Plots of clusters formation on (a) normalized data points and (b) normalized data points with 2-degree polynomial curves on clusters depicting cluster lengths.

weak objects under low resolution. For a boundary point belonging to the cluster k, the probability score P_k is given by (3).

$$P_k = \left\{1 - \left(\frac{y_k}{Y_{max}}\right)\right\}\left(\frac{C}{D}\right) \tag{3}$$

where C is the count of data points in all the clusters and D is the total of all data points. A cluster will have two boundary points, hence will have scores P_{k1} and P_{k2}.

We assume the regions of occlusion and poor detection probability always lower the cluster density and in the worst case introduce discontinuities leading to cluster segmenting. As a remedy, we interpolate data points in such void regions with the help of probability scores. The spatial closeness amongst clusters and outliers and clusters can be expressed well by Mahalanobis distance metric. We compute mean covariance of all the clusters. The distance between any boundary point of cluster k and data point j, which could be a boundary point of some other cluster or an outlier, is given by (4).

$$distance = (x,y)_k \, \Sigma^{-1} (x,y)_j \tag{4}$$

The minimum value so obtained will identify the clusters for pairing. The same is true for outlier and cluster pairing. The links in Fig. 5(a, b) shows the identified pairs.

The attributes of clusters and outliers obtained will help in interpolation of data points along the inter cluster and inter outlier-cluster gaps. Given boundary points belonging to paired clusters, k and j, with (P_k, l_k, d_k) and (P_j, l_j, d_j) as their respective boundary point probabilities, cluster lengths and linear density, the number of interpolated data points is found using (5).

$$c_{kj} = \left(\frac{P_k l_k d_k + P_j l_j d_j}{l_k + l_j}\right) l_{kj} e^{-\left(\frac{l_{kj}}{L_{max}}\right)} \tag{5}$$

where l_{kj} is the distance between the boundary points in clusters k and j, and L_{max} is the maximum length connecting any two normalized data points in the direction of maximum variance. When it comes to interpolation between outliers and clusters, (5) reduces to (6).

$$c_{kn} = P_k d_k l_{kn} e^{-\left(\frac{l_{kn}}{L_{max}}\right)} \tag{6}$$

Here subscript n in (6) is the index of outlier. The distance metric referred in (5, 6) is Euclidean. Because of interpolations, the normalized data points plot is updated with additional inferred points; circles in red are due to inter cluster interpolation and those in brown are due to interpolation between outliers and clusters The plot is shown in Fig. 4(c). Table 1 shows cluster representatives for the sample frame.

Table 1. Cluster representatives for the sample frame. (Objects detected by the detection model = 133, True count = 196).

k	P_{k1}	P_{k2}	d_k	l_k	j	l_{kj}	c_{kj}	n	l_{kn}	c_{kn}
0	0.699	0.691	0.036	54.4	3	214	4	1	72	1
1	0.679	0.545	0.04	199.8	0	99	2	0	60	1
2	0.648	0.628	0.046	43.4	6	210	5			
3	0.622	0.537	0.040	122.6	0	63	1	3	62	1
4	0.536	0.502	0.059	67.8	2	207	5	2	199	5
5	0.552	0.497	0.043	91.3	18	133	2			
6	0.479	0.492	0.087	22.8	8	105	3			
7	0.455	0.431	0.060	66.0	3	70	1			
8	0.415	0.424	0.073	27.4	6	60	2			
9	0.368	0.353	0.033	59.6	10	64	0	5, 8	146, 136	1, 1
10	0.363	0.392	0.048	41.1	7	60	1			
11	0.393	0.005	0.051	563.9	4	102	1			
12	0.326	0.329	0.053	37.5	8	80	1			
13	0.31	0.312	0.086	46.2	7	113	2			
14	0.282	0.291	0.039	51.1	19	178	1	7	70	0
15	0.24	0.139	0.041	168.9	12	61	0			
16	0.227	0.093	0.045	283.4	13	71	0			
17	0.163	0.192	0.079	37.9	20	244	2	11, 12	144, 126	1, 1
18	0.667	0.679	1.388	1.4	5	223	3			
19	0.436	0.461	0.709	2.8	1	128	2	4, 6	139, 65	–
20	0.371	0.4	1.260	2.3	5	121	2			
21	0.173	0.165	0.039	75.5	16	150	0	9	66	0
22	0.08	0.013	0.053	169.0	17	156	0	13	62	0
23	0.034	0.003	0.048	103.9	15	76	0	10	62	0
Interpolated Data points							***40***			***12***

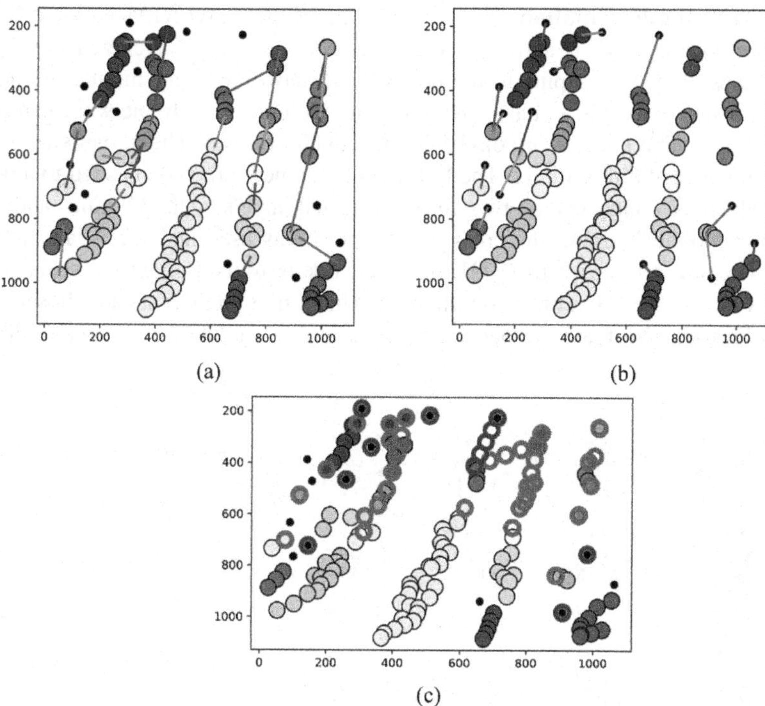

Fig. 5. Plots of (a) segregation of clusters (b) segregation of outliers to clusters and (c) normalized data points showing clusters and interpolated data points.

3.3 Traffic Prediction

The estimation method discussed will output a two dimensional image as shown in Fig. 5(c). The 2D image delivers spatial information of the road traffic. For the ease of computation, every traffic estimation image will be mapped on to a 12 × 11 grid forming a 2D array of 12 × 11. We collect 5 such 2D arrays of traffic estimation performed on consecutive video frames and take their average. In doing so, more or less the same number of vehicles are in the camera vision and we enhance the estimation accuracy suppressing noise and detection inability. The averaged 2D array is the input x at time instant t to the convLSTM network.

ConvLSTM. ConvLSTM is basically an extension of LSTM networks designed to specifically handle spatial-temporal data. All of the inputs x_t, cell outputs c_t, hidden states h_t and internal gates in a convLSTM network are 3D tensors whose last two dimensions are rows and columns. The ConvLSTM mines spatial features from any given 2D array while simultaneously learning temporal information. The received spatial density map, represents cluster conditions based on the current and historical data. The network is able to learn the distribution and therefore predicts future traffic clustering conditions.

ConvLSTM Implementation. The architecture of the convLSTM network that has been used in this work is shown in Fig. 6. The 12 × 11 grid averaged density estimated maps Φ_i are the inputs to the convLSTM network. Every minute the network receives a new map. T is equal to 10, implying the output of the network can predict 10 min traffic. The number of convLSTM layers chosen is 3. The kernel size is 3 X 3 and the number of filters are 32. The last layer in the network is connected to a pooling layer, which is connected to two fully-connected layers with 32 units and ReLU activations. While training the cross entropy loss was used and the Adam optimizer with a learning rate equal to 0.001. The network is trained against a scalar output, which is the number of vehicles on the road. The output predictions are chosen from a 10 min horizon. We fixed the batch size to 32 and the number of epochs to 30.

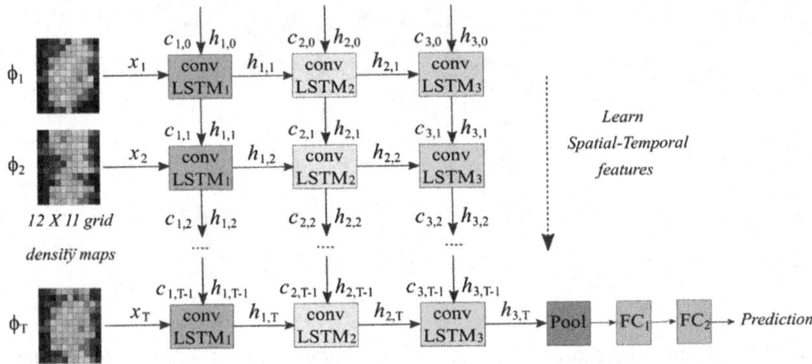

Fig. 6. Architecture of traffic prediction network using convLSTM [33].

4 Validation

4.1 Dataset

We use a dataset that contains traffic surveillance video in the area of Nevsky prospect, a central street of Saint Petersburg, between the Moika river and the street Bolshaya Konuyshennaya [34]. The scene captured in the video contains a street having a two-way road with dense vehicle movement. The resolution of each video is 960 × 720 pixels. The dataset was collected in the months of November, December in 2017 and January 2018. We sample the video at uniform rate to get 5 consecutive frames in the video for every minute. A collection of videos is made by shifting the sampling instant, to achieve 140 h duration, to get enough samples to train, test and validate the convLSTM network.

4.2 Results

We use a dataset that contains traffic surveillance video in the area of Nevsky prospect. The performance of the proposed technique is evaluated using the following metrics. The mean absolute error (MAE), mean absolute percentage error (MAPE) and mean square error (MSE) will highlight the benefits and drawbacks. Table 2 shows the records of the performance of the various techniques on the dataset for a 10 min horizon. The validation is done on 30 h of traffic video. Figure 7 shows the predicted errors in traffic for a 100 min video. Since the movement of vehicles is on a two-way road in the dataset, the traffic features such as occupancy ratio, vehicle flow rate and speed can be very different on each direction. Thus these features are not a direct indicator of traffic conditions like jams. However, the spatial density maps capture the requirement to predict such conditions.

Table 2. Performance comparison of methods.

Algorithms	Evaluation metrics		
	MAE	MAPE	MSE
Proposed	5.13	4.55	44.17
SVM	8.87	7.96	121.08
LSTM	7.92	7.53	92.2

Our proposed technique uses convLSTM for spatial temporal learning and prediction. The other methods for comparison, SVM [20] and LSTM [23], use trained Yolov3 for vehicle detection. Owing to the better estimation capability and spatial temporal feature processing, our proposed method shows a better performance when compared to others.

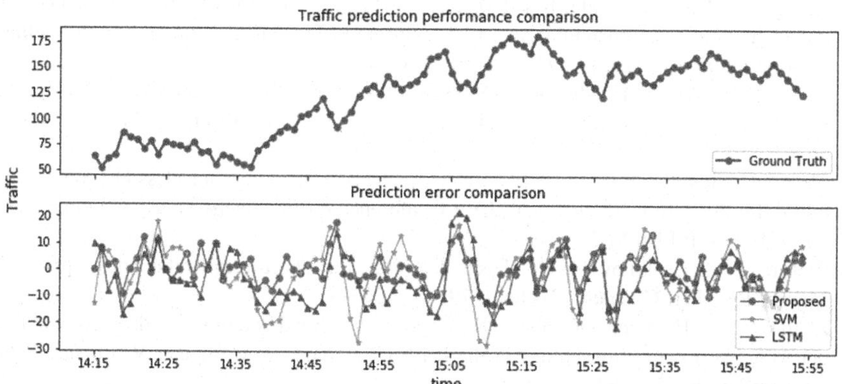

Fig. 7. Traffic prediction performance comparison at a 10 min prediction horizon.

5 Conclusion

In this paper, we explore the usage of vision based traffic estimation and spatial-temporal feature extraction for prediction. The proposed density based estimation method estimates traffic with higher accuracy. As the method outputs compact spatial density maps in time sequence, it gets convenient to process the information using convolutional LSTM neural networks for traffic prediction with lesser computational complexity.

References

1. Zeiler, M.D., Fergus, R.: Visualizing and understanding convolutional networks. In: Fleet, D., Pajdla, T., Schiele, B., Tuytelaars, T. (eds.) ECCV 2014. LNCS, vol. 8689, pp. 818–833. Springer, Cham (2014). https://doi.org/10.1007/978-3-319-10590-1_53
2. Lin, T.-Y., Goyal, P., Girshick, R., He, K., Dollár, P.: Focal loss for dense object detection. In: Proceedings of the IEEE International Conference on Computer Vision, pp. 2980–2988 (2017)
3. Redmon, J., Divvala, S., Girshick, R., Farhadi, A.: You only look once: unified, real-time object detection. In: Proceedings of the IEEE Conference on Computer Vision and Pattern Recognition, pp. 779–788 (2016)
4. Liu, W., Anguelov, D., Erhan, D., Szegedy, C., Reed, S., Fu, C.-Y., Berg, A.C.: SSD: single shot multibox detector. In: Leibe, B., Matas, J., Sebe, N., Welling, M. (eds.) ECCV 2016. LNCS, vol. 9905, pp. 21–37. Springer, Cham (2016). https://doi.org/10.1007/978-3-319-46448-0_2
5. Wang, X., Hua, X., Xiao, F., Li, Y., Hu, X., Sun, P.: Multi-object detection in traffic scenes based on improved SSD. Electronics **7**(11), 302 (2018)
6. Xingjian, S., Chen, Z., Wang, H., Yeung, D.-Y., Wong, W.-K., Woo, W.-C.: Convolutional LSTM network: a machine learning approach for precipitation nowcasting. In: Advances in Neural Information Processing Systems, pp. 802–810 (2015)
7. Toropov, E., Gui, L., Zhang, S., Kottur, S., Moura, J.M.: Traffic flow from a low frame rate city camera. In: 2015 IEEE International Conference on Image Processing (ICIP), pp. 3802–3806. IEEE (2015)
8. Zheng, Y., Peng, S.: Model based vehicle localization for urban traffic surveillance using image gradient based matching. In: 2012 15th International IEEE Conference on Intelligent Transportation Systems, pp. 945–950. IEEE (2012)
9. Chen, Y.-L., Wu, B.-F., Huang, H.-Y., Fan, C.-J.: A real-time vision system for nighttime vehicle detection and traffic surveillance. IEEE Trans. Ind. Electron. **58**(5), 2030–2044 (2010)
10. Chen, Z., Ellis, T., Velastin, S.A.: Vehicle detection, tracking and classification in urban traffic. In: 2012 15th International IEEE Conference on Intelligent Transportation Systems, pp. 951–956. IEEE (2012)
11. Polson, N.G., Sokolov, V.O.: Deep learning for short-term traffic flow prediction. Transp. Res. Part C Emerg. Technol. **79**, 1–7 (2017)
12. Zhang, C., Li, H., Wang, X., Yang, X.: Cross-scene crowd counting via deep convolutional neural networks. In: Proceedings of the IEEE Conference on Computer Vision and Pattern Recognition, pp. 833–841 (2015)
13. Zhang, Y., Zhou, D., Chen, S., Gao, S., Ma, Y.: Single-image crowd counting via multi-column convolutional neural network. In: Proceedings of the IEEE Conference on Computer Vision and Pattern Recognition, pp. 589–597 (2016)
14. Oñoro-Rubio, D., López-Sastre, R.J.: Towards perspective-free object counting with deep learning. In: Leibe, B., Matas, J., Sebe, N., Welling, M. (eds.) ECCV 2016. LNCS, vol. 9911, pp. 615–629. Springer, Cham (2016). https://doi.org/10.1007/978-3-319-46478-7_38
15. Zhao, Z., Li, H., Zhao, R., Wang, X.: Crossing-line crowd counting with two-phase deep neural networks. In: Leibe, B., Matas, J., Sebe, N., Welling, M. (eds.) ECCV 2016. LNCS, vol. 9912, pp. 712–726. Springer, Cham (2016). https://doi.org/10.1007/978-3-319-46484-8_43

16. Zhang, S., Wu, G., Costeira, J.P., Moura, J.M.: Understanding traffic density from large-scale web camera data. In: Proceedings of the IEEE Conference on Computer Vision and Pattern Recognition, pp. 5898–5907 (2017)
17. Okutani, I., Stephanedes, Y.J.: Dynamic prediction of traffic volume through Kalman filtering theory. Transp. Res. Part B Methodol. **18**(1), 1–11 (1984)
18. Xie, Y., Zhang, Y., Ye, Z.: Short-term traffic volume forecasting using Kalman filter with discrete wavelet decomposition. Comput.-Aided Civ. Infrastruct. Eng. **22**(5), 326–334 (2007)
19. Yu, G., Hu, J., Zhang, C., Zhuang, L., Song, J.: Short-term traffic flow forecasting based on Markov chain model. In: IEEE IV2003 Intelligent Vehicles Symposium. Proceedings (Cat. No. 03TH8683), pp. 208–212. IEEE (2003)
20. Zhang, Y., Xie, Y.: Forecasting of short-term freeway volume with v-support vector machines. Transp. Res. Rec. **2024**(1), 92–99 (2007)
21. Tan, H., Xuan, X., Wu, Y., Zhong, Z., Ran, B.: A comparison of traffic flow prediction methods based on DBN. In: CICTP 2016, pp. 273–283 (2016)
22. Bengio, Y., Lamblin, P., Popovici, D., Larochelle, H.: Greedy layerwise training of deep networks. In: Advances in Neural Information Processing Systems, pp. 153–160 (2007)
23. Ma, X., Tao, Z., Wang, Y., Yu, H., Wang, Y.: Long short-term memory neural network for traffic speed prediction using remote microwave sensor data. Transp. Res. Part C Emerg. Technol. **54**, 187–197 (2015)
24. Fu, R., Zhang, Z., Li, L.: Using LSTM and GRU neural network methods for traffic flow prediction. In: 2016 31st Youth Academic Annual Conference of Chinese Association of Automation (YAC), pp. 324–328. IEEE (2016)
25. Wang, J., Hu, F., Li, L.: Deep bi-directional long short-term memory model for short-term traffic flow prediction. In: Liu, D., Xie, S., Li, Y., Zhao, D., El-Alfy, E.-S. (eds.) ICONIP 2017. LNCS, vol. 10638, pp. 306–316. Springer, Cham (2017). https://doi.org/10.1007/978-3-319-70139-4_31
26. Lv, Y., Duan, Y., Kang, W., Li, Z., Wang, F.-Y.: Traffic flow prediction with big data: a deep learning approach. IEEE Trans. Intell. Transp. Syst. **16**(2), 865–873 (2014)
27. Huang, W., Song, G., Hong, H., Xie, K.: Deep architecture for traffic flow prediction: deep belief networks with multitask learning. IEEE Trans. Intell. Transp. Syst. **15**(5), 2191–2201 (2014)
28. Wu, Y., Tan, H.: Short-term traffic flow forecasting with spatial-temporal correlation in a hybrid deep learning framework, arXiv preprint arXiv:1612.01022 (2016)
29. Yu, H., Wu, Z., Wang, S., Wang, Y., Ma, X.: Spatiotemporal recurrent convolutional networks for traffic prediction in transportation networks. Sensors **17**(7), 1501 (2017)
30. Jagadish, D.N., Mahto, L., Chauhan, A.: Density based clustering methods for road traffic estimation. In: IEEE Region 10 Conference (TENCON), pp. 885–890 (2020)
31. Sochor, J., Herout, A.: Unsupervised processing of vehicle appearance for automatic understanding in traffic surveillance. In: 2015 International Conference on Digital Image Computing: Techniques and Applications (DICTA), pp. 1–8. IEEE (2015)
32. Ester, M., Kriegel, H.-P., Sander, J., Xu, X.: A density-based algorithm for discovering clusters in large spatial databases with noise. In: Kdd, vol. 96, no. 34, pp. 226–231 (1996)
33. Zapata-Impata, B.S., Gil, P., Torres, F.: Learning spatio temporal tactile features with a convlstm for the direction of slip detection. Sensors **19**(3), 523 (2019)
34. Grigorev, A.: Nevsky prospect traffic surveillance video (movement by the opposite lane cases hours). figshare, 25 December 2018. https://figshare.com/articles/Nevsky_prospect_traffic_surveillance_video_MOOL-cases_hours_/5841267/6. Accessed 25 May 2020

Deep Learning Based Stabbing Action Detection in ATM Kiosks for Intelligent Video Surveillance Applications

B. Yogameena[1](✉), K. Menaka[1], and S. Saravana Perumaal[2]

[1] Department of ECE, Thiagarajar College of Engineering, Madurai, India
ymece@tce.edu

[2] Department of Mechanical Engineering, Thiagarajar College of Engineering, Madurai, India
sspmech@tce.edu

Abstract. The role of computer vision algorithms for the analysis of human action as well as their behavior has been gaining more importance since they could be applied for detecting even the complex action of a person stabbing others. Instinctive detection of such violent action restricts the crimes and guarantees the protection of the public. To address this social threat, this paper presents an intelligent video analytics for detecting the stabbing action of ATM surveillance applications by assuming static camera environment. The dataset collection is the significant contribution towards this complex action detection framework. By means of MAMR (Motion Assisted Matrix Restoration) foreground extraction and labelling have been done, and then hierarchical-based You Look Only Once (YOLO) v3 detector has been employed for further detection of 'knife-in-hand' of the suspect. Further, Lucas Kannade (LK) and Weber Local Descriptor (WLD)-based motion detection is executed using the hybrid network YOLO v3 (Darknet-53) in this video analytics. Finally, in the proposed hybrid-based hierarchical, the results of these Two Stream (TS) detection results are concatenated by averaging their classification scores to confirm the stabbing action and they have been validated using the mean Average Precision (mAP) metric on ATM and Non-ATM surveillance videos.

Keywords: 'knife in hand' detection · Motion detection · Yolo v3 · Stabbing action detection · Two stream concatenation

1 Introduction

Human action analysis plays a vital role in detecting the abnormal action among individuals in the surveillance scenario. Violent action detection decreases the risk factor of safety in most of the surveillance scenario. Numerous algorithms on action analysis concentrate only on simple actions such as walking, running, bending and so on [1] rather than on complex actions. Detection of human aggressive action in surveillance applications is the ultimate challenge especially in airports, railway stations, and, largest gatherings of people in temples and so on. For example, more recently in the international airport at southwest Philadelphia, the suspect involved in

S. K. Singh et al. (Eds.): CVIP 2020, CCIS 1378, pp. 356–368, 2021.
https://doi.org/10.1007/978-981-16-1103-2_30

deadly stabbing of a victim has been identified and arrested. The stabbing attack of a person most often occurs in finance-based surveillance scenarios such as ATMs and banks. Similar incidents to such violent events happened in Bangalore ATM and China ATM. Such incidents which frequently take place across the globe mandate the necessity to take up a research on preventing such crimes and ensuring the safety of the public. It is very challenging to detect such stabbing attacks in a restricted environment like ATM. However, the process of identifying the assailants or stabbers is much complicated in sparse or most crowded banks and other financial surveillance surroundings. Hence, the aim of the proposed system is to develop an intelligent video analytics for ATM surveillance applications for detecting the stabbing action happening inside the ATM. The factors like illumination changes, human physique, clothing diversity, camera movement, and occlusions are some of the several challenges generally faced during the detection of the stabbers in video surveillance. While, focusing the problem with these constraints, the approach for the detection of the suspected stabber at the ATM scenario is structured as follows. The rest of the paper has been organized as follows. Literature review of related work and the contribution of proposed work are conferred in Sect. 2 and Sect. 2.1. Methodology is explained in Sect. 3. In Sect. 4, the results and the discussion with the evaluation of various surveillance and the web surveillance dataset are experimented and explored. Finally, the conclusions and the future research scope are presented in Sect. 5.

2 Related Work

Nowadays, the application of computer vision techniques towards human violent action detection has significantly been booming. It is inferred from the literature [1] that the focus and the experimentation on violent action detection in surveillance environment are lacking. The objective of this paper is to detect the stabbing action especially in ATM surveillance. It involves person detection, spotting the knife used for stabbing and violent action detection. Since person detection is the key step [2] for detecting the stabbing attack, the selection of moving object detection algorithms plays a significant role. In computer vision literature, there are numerous moving object segmentation algorithms. While detecting the stabbers, shadows and ghosts also add more complexity in this process. In this paper, the primary process foreground segmentation is completed using MAMR [2] for stabbing action detection since it is insensitive to gradual or sudden illumination changes and shadow as well as ghost effects, as compared to GMM [3] and ViBe [4]. It is also robust against camouflages, with varying lighting conditions, different types of motion and slow moving objects in the background. This experimentation has been carried on GMM, ViBe and MAMR has been carried out and based on the qualitative and quantitative analysis, MAMR has been adopted. Subsequently, labelling is also performed for the segmented foreground to identify whether the individual possesses knife or not. Consequently, appearance-feature based object 'knife-in-hand' detection plays a crucial role in the stabbing action detection. Several handcrafted features such as Active Appearance Model (AAM) and Geometric approaches [5, 6] are the familiar knife detection approaches. However, these approaches could process an image at the pixel level while facing a major limitation is the required accuracy could be attained only when the targeted knife is at the perfect perception level.

Recently, deep networks have gained much attention in complicated tasks such as detection of objects in real world scenarios. AlexNet, [7] a Convolutional Neural Network (CNN) has superior image representation. CNN [8] loads ample time during the training process. Subsequently, Region-based Convolutional Neural Network (R-CNN) proposed in [9], is slow since it carries out ConvNet forward pass for each and every region proposal without sharing computation. Consequently, Spatial Pyramid Pooling network (SPP-net) [10] increases the speed of R-CNN, and it is employed with fixed-length representation, yet the detection accuracy decreases. Compared to R-CNN, SPP-net, and Fast R-CNN [11], Faster R-CNN has the maximum speed and accuracy, yet, the performance is poor for low resolution videos. Yolo is faster compared to the other above mentioned state-of-the-art deep learning algorithms [12]. However, important localization errors create complexity and produce scarce false positives in the background. Yolo v2 improves the detection accuracy and produces increased recall values. However, it detects only 20 object classes whereas Yolo9000 detects more than 1000 class objects even though it suffers with model small objects like sun glasses [13]. Hence, Yolo v3 (Darknet-53) [14] an improved version of Yolo v2 has been proposed to detect small objects like faces, 'knife in hand', which often exists in surveillance scenario.

It is assured that no deep learning algorithm detects knife used for stabbing. This is one of the major contributions of this proposed work. The methodology of action analysis has been categorized into single-layered and hierarchical-based approach [1]. For simple actions like walking, boxing and hand waving that are found in bench-marked KTH [15] dataset, single-layered approaches [1] are suitable. Hierarchical-based approach [16] models the difficult structure of human activities and it is flexible for complex actions [1]. However, algorithms, based on these approaches have not dealt with complicated violent action like stabbing. Henceforth, for the first time, in this paper, a hierarchical-based approach has been adopted for stabbing action detection. Various local features such as histogram, Fisher vector discussed in [17, 18] are used for action detection but they rely on sliding window for localization. More recently, some literatures like [19, 20] have dealt with the action detection using deep learning methods. Subsequently in this paper, Here, TS concatenation of appearance as well as motion play a major role in action detection. Therefore, this paper proposes a hybrid-based hierarchical approach by combining appearance and motion features has been proposed for detecting the stabbing action. It is inferred that WLD provides sufficient motion information required for violent action recognition [20]. Accordingly, the 'knife-in-hand' detection and motion detection are concatenated through TS process in the proposed framework for stabbing action detection.

2.1 Contribution of the Proposed Framework

Motivation and Problem Statement. Due, to the rising number of indoor crimes at public places like ATMs, Banks etc., the researchers have started focusing on the wide range of applications of the CCTVs. This current issue across the globe has motivated the researchers to necessarily develop a framework for the detection of stabbing attacks on the real world surveillance videos, with a main focus on the security of the public. From the literature, it is inferred that the stabbing action detection at ATM kiosks has not yet handled especially using deep learning method. The existing appearance-based methods fail to handle this problem effectively. Hence, a hybrid-based hierarchical approach is required to discover the 'stabbing with knife' action.

Objective. To evolve a hybrid framework for the discovery of complex action like stabbing attacks in the real world ATM surveillance videos by focusing mainly on the public security.

Key Contribution. The proposed hybrid-based hierarchical stabbing action detection framework includes foreground segmentation, labeling an individual, 'knife-in-hand' detection using Yolo v3 (Darknet-53) and optical flow parameter estimation using LK and WLD methods. The dataset collection is the significant contribution towards this complex action detection framework. It comprises a large set of unconstrained stabbing action surveillance videos that are collected from YouTube, serial, etc. The challenges include varying illumination (gradual, sudden) conditions, camouflage, small object (knife), and blur. This dataset can help in detecting violent stabbing action in surveillance scenario to confirm the stabber during crime detection. From [19], it is observed that high- quality proposals have been obtained from motion RPN required for frame level action detection. In [19, 20], TS concatenation of appearance as well as motion plays a major role in action detection. Another significant contribution of this research is that the proposed hybrid-based hierarchical approach that combines 'knife-in-hand' and the motion detection results derived from Yolo v3 by averaging their detection scores to confirm the stabbing action. It is validated using the mean Average Precision (mAP) metric on ATM and Non-ATM surveillance videos.

3 Proposed Methodology

3.1 Methodology

The main objective of this paper is to develop an automated system that works out effectively to detect the stabbing action. The proposed method segments the foreground using MAMR and the segmented foregrounds are labelled. Consequently, the proposed hybrid-based hierarchical system adopts Yolo v3 for 'knife-in-hand' detection. The labeled person who is detected with the 'knife-in-hand' is the suspected one, who should have committed the crime. Then, the optical flow parameters are computed for each five consecutive frames by applying the LK and WLD methods. The information obtained from Flow 5 is stacked as a ground-truth for training. Following that, Yolo v3 detects the motion of the suspect. Finally, the stabbing action is detected by the concatenation of TS detection scores. The overview of the stabbing action detection method using Yolo v3 is depicted in Fig. 1. Yolo v3 is compared with Yolo, Yolo v2 and Faster R-CNN for validation.

3.2 Knife-in-hand Detection Using Yolo v3

Consequent to foreground segmentation using MAMR, blob detection and labelling, Yolo v3 [14] object detector has been adopted for 'knife-in-hand' detection. Yolo9000 struggles to model small objects, so in order and to eradicate this flaws, Yolo v3- an improved version of Yolov2 [13] has been introduced in [14] to detect small objects. The input is resized to 256 × 256 for effective computation. For accurate prediction of bounding boxes, YOLO v3 network determines the centre coordinates of the box respective to the filter location by utilizing a sigmoid function. It also estimates the coordinates of the bounding box, object detection score and class predictions. Yolov3 estimates the confidence score by means of logistic regression and it procedures the feature extraction Darknet-53 network comprising 53 convolutional layers to detect small objects better. Previous feature map is up sampled by the factor of two. The obtained up sampled features are merged through concatenation to obtain more significant information. Besides, for bounding box regression, the binary cross-entropy loss function is utilized for object classification to increase the detection accuracy. To evaluate the performance of the trained network on the test data, the confidence score is assigned as 0.5 for the target class of the object predicted by the Intersection over Union (IoU) of the target ground truth and the labelled box. As a result, the proposed framework adopts Yolo v3 with Darknet-53 to detect the moving objects such as 'knife-in-hand' of the suspect that often appears small in ATM surveillance.

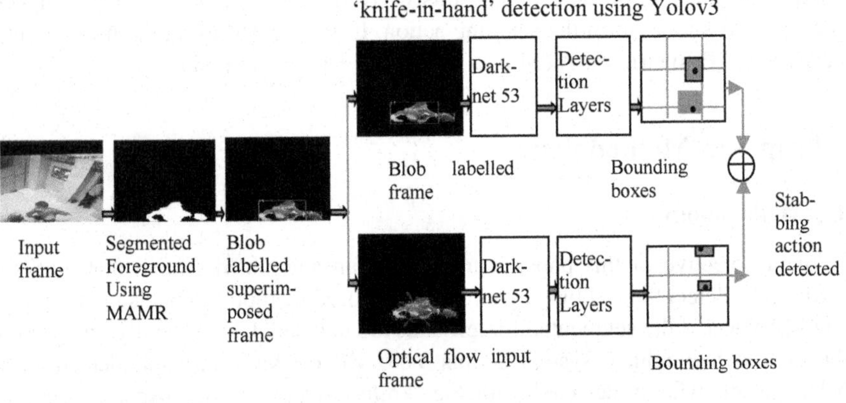

Fig. 1. Overview of the proposed hybrid stabbing action detection framework.

3.3 'Optical Flow Parameter Estimation for Motion Detection Using Yolo v3

The 'knife-in-hand' is primarily detected in the above Sect. 3.2. It is not sufficient to conclude the occurrence of stabbing action by simply the 'knife-in-hand' detection. Moreover, it is essential to confirm whether the stabber performs the significant motion to make it an action. High-quality proposals have been obtained from motion RPN using CNNs for accurate action representation. Hence, along with the detection of the 'knife in suspect's hand', the required optical flow parameters such as, ξ_m the WLD magnitude are estimated using

$$\xi_m(x_c) = \arctan(\alpha \sum_{i=0}^{p-1} \frac{(x_i - x_c)}{x_c}) \tag{1}$$

Here, x_c indicates the center pixel, x_i (i = 0, 1, 2, 3,…., p−1) to represent the neighboring pixel p of x_c. The arctangent function partially reduces the noise. The difference in the intensity among neighboring pixels is adjusted using the parameter α. The WLD orientation optical parameter ξ_0. Where $x_1 - x_5$ and $x_3 - x_7$ indicate the intensity

$$\xi_0(x_c) = \arctan(\frac{(x_1 - x_5)}{(x_3 - x_7)}) \tag{2}$$

Difference of two neighbouring pixels of x_c in the vertical and horizontal directions, respectively. The estimated parameters are stacked as a 3-channel image. Finally, if the motion is detected using the Yolo v3 detection module, then the corresponding labelled individual carrying a 'knife-in-hand' will be confirmed in the proposed hybrid-based hierarchical framework for the stabbing action.

3.4 Stabbing Action Detection by Concatenation of Two Frames

From [13] it is clear that the concatenation of two streams such as appearance and the motion improves the accuracy of stabbing action detection. Also, a person carrying a knife may not be a suspect for all the times. Therefore, along with the 'knife-in-hand' detection, the proposed work detects the motion of an individual to ensure whether the suspect performs stabbing or not. Finally, the obtained independent logistic regression scores of 'knife-in-hand' using Yolo v3 and the motion of the suspect using Yolo v3 are averaged for concatenation. It enables to confirm the detection of the stabbing.

4 Experimental Results and Discussion

Experiments have been carried out on visual surveillance dataset and the results are evaluated using MATLAB 2018b. Indoor as well as outdoor surveillance videos are used in this paper for stabbing action detection. Six thousand stabbing videos (ATM and Non-ATM) with approximately 900 s each are segregated and twenty percentage of the videos are used for testing to expose the performance of the proposed hybrid-based hierarchical stabbing action detection framework. Remaining videos are used for training and validation. The sample description of the videos is as follows. Various challenges of the dataset include camouflage in ATM1 dataset, for instance ATM2 has a very low resolution, at Non-ATM1, the object in the background is same as knife, Non-ATM2 image is blurred, and Non-ATM7 has an excessive blur. In particular, the footage of a woman stabbed over 22 times by a stalker in Delhi, collected from CCTV footage of Oneindia News, has been cited as an example with camouflages. Sample dataset specifications are given in Table 1. A few links of dataset used in this paper are as follows:

ATM 1: https://youtu.be/Yw-Apx06xrk
ATM 2: https://youtu.be/UfkcVFkvsQk,
ATM 3: https: //www.youtube.com/watch?v=anVFC81_mtc
ATM 4 YouTube stabbing action video
ATM 5 https://youtu.be/4LpebbNqiFo
ATM 6 https://youtu.be/eQVrCdh738c
Non-ATM 1: https://youtu.be/hrBh5x_3hW0
Non-ATM 2: https://youtu.be/kgvois3ZxxY
Non-ATM 3: YouTube stabbing action video
Non-ATM 4: https://youtu.be/qUB7Yc2ppNo
Non-ATM 5: https: //youtu.be/sgjgzews20A
Non-ATM6: https://www.youtube.com/watch?v=25bg9CI2ZJ8
Non-ATM 7: https://youtu.be/a9-fezMmm98
Non-ATM8: YouTube video
Non-ATM 9: https://youtu.be/w2g2fsoRJ2Y
Non-ATM10: https://youtu.be/2LQjvIOzTeA
Non-ATM11: https://www.youtube.com/watch?v=0lcWCFzI46Y
Non-ATM12: https://youtu.be/Gqsz3VATOhk
Non-ATM13: https://youtu.be/smbgjPVQkjQ
Non-ATM14: https://youtu.be/gRt77r1Uljc

The process initially starts with the frame conversion. Consequently, the foreground is segmented using diverse state-of-the-art background subtraction algorithms like GMM, ViBe, and MAMR. It is found that for ATM3 dataset, GMM and ViBe provide poor segmentation results, since these algorithms are sensitive to sudden illumination changes. Compared to GMM and ViBe, MAMR provides good results for all tested datasets by facing various challenges such as ghosts, camouflage and gradual as sudden illuminations. As a result, MAMR has been adopted for the present experimentation. The 'knife-in-hand' is detected using Yolo v3 (Darknet-53), floating point operations measured per second makes it robust against other object detectors.

Table 1. Stabbing action surveillance dataset and their specifications

Dataset	Time (t (s))	Frames/ second	Total No. of frames	Resolution	Challenging conditions	View angle
ATM1	129	15	1935	640 × 360	Camouflage	Profile
ATM2	20	30	600	1280 × 720	Varying Illumination	Profile
ATM3	278	25	6950	352 × 288	Sudden illumination	Front
ATM4	97	30	2910	480 × 360	Camouflage	Front
ATM5	32	8	256	1280 × 720	Small object	Front
ATM6	108	15	1620	448 × 336	Varying Illumination	Front
Non-ATM 1	734	30	22020	640 × 360	Small object	Front
Non-ATM 2	59	24	1416	480 × 360	Excess blur	Front
Non-ATM 3	10	30	300	640 × 360	Camouflage	Front
Non-ATM 5	178	25	4450	640 × 360	Camouflage	Profile
Non-ATM 6	10	30	300	640 × 360	Camouflage	Front
Non-ATM 7	7	25	175	1280 × 720	Motion Blur	Profile
Non-ATM 8	30	25	750	450 × 360	Varying Illumination	Front
Non-ATM 9	104	29	3016	1280 × 720	Varying Illumination	Profile
Non-ATM 10	42	24	1008	1280 × 720	Varying Illumination	Profile

The detected bounding box is annotated in red color to proceed further to ensure the suspect for the stabbing action. Before testing with region-based methods, the target is annotated as ground truth for 10,000 h videos and they are used for training. A sample of 10 × 10 image set from training videos is revealed in Fig. 2. After training, it is tested for 'knife-in-hand' detection using Yolo v3 and it provides better results for tested videos as compared to other deep networks. The failure cases are discussed in detail. The experimentation has been validated using the performance metric mAP (%) for the proposed Yolo v3 with Darknet-53 based 'knife-in-hand' detection and is compared with the existing deep networks such as CNN, Fast R-CNN, Yolo, Yolo v2 and Faster R-CNN. They are quantitatively illustrated in Table 2. These experimental results evidently show that Yolo v3 provides a higher accuracy even in real-world challenging conditions in stabbing action surveillance data.

Other than this quantitative analysis, the ablation study has been performed in accordance with foreground segmentation. In this work, 'knife-in-hand' detection has also been experimented directly on the frames without performing foreground segmentation. Interestingly, it is observed that if the foreground segmentation procedure is neglected, more False Positive (FP- knife like object in the background and foreground) results occur. They are qualitatively revealed in Non-ATM 8, and Non-ATM 9 datasets. In Non-ATM 10 dataset, knife like object in the background has been detected as knife and the results are depicted in Fig. 3a. This kind of FP can be certainly avoided by foreground segmentation which authenticates the significance of foreground segmentation before 'knife-in-hand' object detection for processing any videos. The proposed framework ensures whether the labelled individual possesses the knife and undergoes stabbing action. However, the 'knife-in-hand' detection fails in certain scenarios and hence further the detection of stabbing action could not further be achieved. Such failure cases obtained from ATM 6, Non-ATM1, Non-ATM6, and

Non-ATM7 are depicted in Fig. 3b. The appearance-based 'knife-in-hand' detection alone cannot confirm the stabbing action. Hence, to ensure the stabbing action detection by means of the knife detected frames, the motion can be detected using optical flow parameters such as magnitude and orientation that are estimated using LK and WLD methods. This optical flow information with their corresponding label is annotated as a ground-truth for Flow 5 superimposed frames. Finally, the motion is detected using Yolo v3 and the corresponding labelled suspect carrying a 'knife-in-hand' is noted. The significance of the combination of motion along with the appearance for stabbing action detection is discussed in Sect. 2.1. The sequence of the proposed framework, 'knife-in-hand' detection (blue-bounding box), the labelled individual who is suspected for stabbing action (red-bounding box), are illustrated in Fig. 4. The proposed TS concatenation framework estimates the stabbing action detection by averaging the independent mAP scores of 'knife-in-hand' and motion detections. The averaged mAP performance metric of stabbing action detection using the proposed TS concatenation framework is quantitatively illustrated in Table 3. It is observed that the averaged mAP logistic regression detection scores by combining 'knife-in-hand' using Yolo v3 and the motion (WLD based optical flow parameter) of the suspect using Yolo v3 produces better results than the LK based TS concatenation.

Various Conditions	Training Images for 'knife-in-hand' Detection
Target (Blurred)	
Targeting Left	
Targeting Right	
Targeting Obtuse	
Targeting Obtuse (Blurred)	
Targeting Reflex (Blurred)	
Targeting Reflex	
Targeting Downwards	
Targeting Upwards	
Target (Blur, Excess Blur, Normal)	

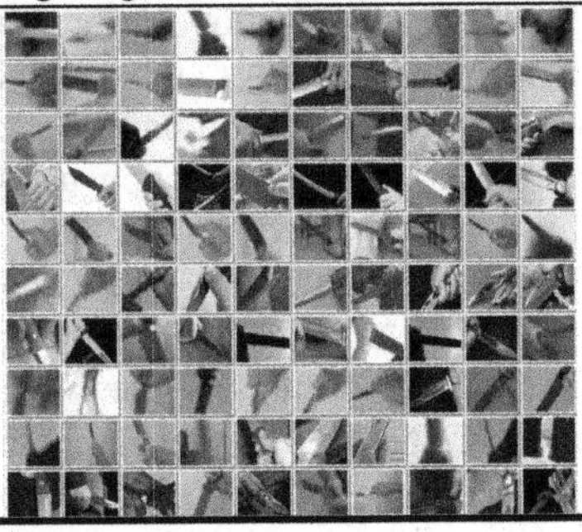

Fig. 2. Training images of 'knife-in-hand' acquired in challenging environments.

Table 2. mAP (%) of the 'knife-in-hand' detection using CNN, Fast R-CNN, Faster R-CNN (λ = 10), Yolo, Yolo v2 and Yolo v3

Dataset	CNN	Fast R-CNN	Faster R-CNN	Yolo	Yolo v2	Yolo v3
ATM 1	51.3	56.1	63.2	60.1	64	67
ATM 2	50.1	53.3	57.5	58.2	61.2	63.5
ATM 3	50.8	55.6	60.8	56.8	59	62.5
ATM 4	59.2	64.3	68.1	64	69.5	72
ATM 5	51	54	58.2	56	58.6	61
Non-ATM 2	52.6	58.7	62	59.1	60.3	64
Non-ATM 3	61	66	72.4	75	77	79
Non-ATM 5	69	74.8	79	77.4	78	83

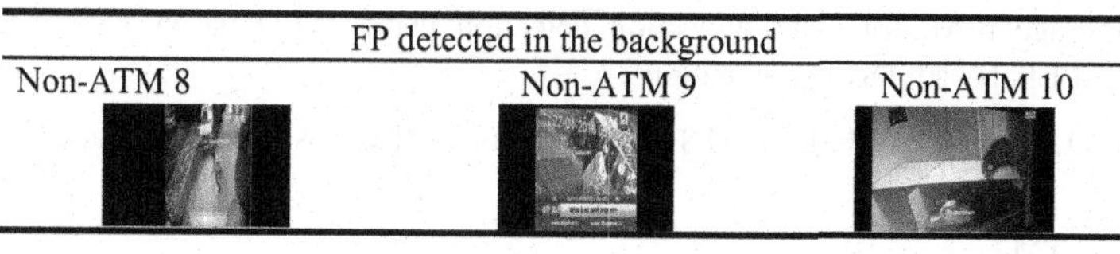

a

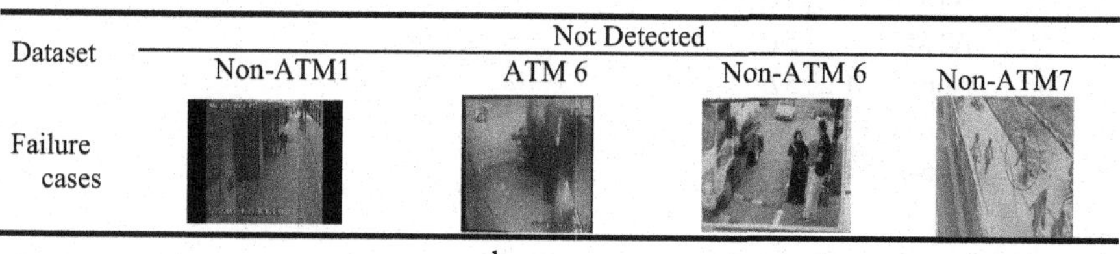

b

Fig. 3. False Positive and Failure cases of ATM and Non-ATM dataset. a) False Positive and Failure cases of ATM and Non-ATM dataset b) Failure cases of 'knife-in-hand' detection

Input Frame	MAMR	Superimposition/Label	Knife detection and Suspect Identification
244(ATM4)			
52(ATM5)			
575(Non-ATM2)			
1514(Non-ATM3)			
2925(Non-ATM5)			

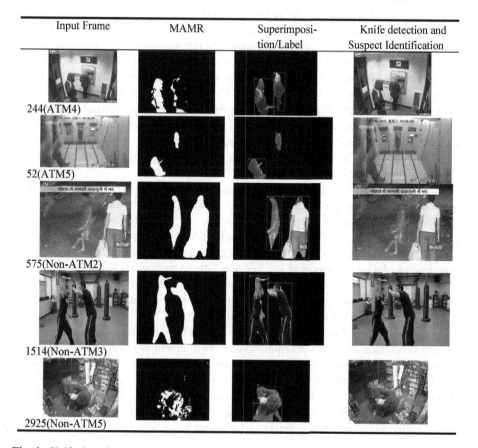

Fig. 4. Knife detection and suspect identification in tested ATM and Non-ATM scenario. (Color figure online)

Table 3. Average mAP for stabbing action detection using WLD based TS concatenation framework and LK based TS concatenation

S.No	Dataset	LK based TS concatenation	WLD based TS concatenation
1	ATM1	58	62
2	ATM2	52	53
3	ATM3	60	62.5
4	ATM4	73	75
5	ATM5	51	54
6	Non-ATM 2	57	58
7	Non-ATM 3	78	82
8	Non-ATM 5	79	81

5 Conclusion

The proposed Two Stream (TS) concatenation, a hybrid-based hierarchical framework is proficient of detecting violent stabbing action at ATM kiosks. If the foreground segmentation procedure is neglected, more FP results occur as in Non-ATM 8, Non-ATM 9 and Non-ATM 10 and it authenticates the significance of foreground segmentation. This framework includes foreground extraction using MAMR, labelling and 'knife-in-hand' detection by means of Yolo v3 with Darknet-53. Moreover, Lucas Kannade (LK) and Weber Local Descriptor (WLD) based motions are detected using Yolo v3 with Darknet-53. Finally, the Two Stream (TS) 'knife-in-hand' and motion detections are concatenated by averaging. The proposed system is the novel act for detecting the violent stabbing action that impacts the benefit to the social security in an ATM surveillance. The dataset collection is the significant contribution towards this complex action detection framework.

Consequently, it can afford an intact intelligent social security-based video analytics system. The proposed Yolo v3 with Darknet-53-based framework has been compared with the existing deep networks such as CNN, Fast R-CNN, Faster R-CNN, Yolo and Yolo v2. The Yolo v3 with Darknet-53 performs better in multifarious surveillance environments that have more challenges like camouflage, small object, very low resolution, excess and motion blur, strong and sudden illuminations, and frontal and profile views. The performance metric mean Average Precision (mAP) has been used for experimental validation. The proposed hybrid framework has been tested in sparse crowded rather than in huge crowded scenario. This work shall be extended for examining more datasets unrestricted to the ATM surveillance with excess challenging conditions such as occlusion, sparse environment containing more than two pedestrians. Further research shall be taken up on the estimation of the force and the speed of the suspect, and the recognition of the stabber's face expression during such violent stabbing attacks and hence, so that the number of false positives may be reduced in future. The research may also be focused on developing an interface to bring the instant notice to the concerned authority for social security.

References

1. Aggarwal, J.K., Ryoo, M.S.: Human activity analysis: a review. ACM Comput. Surv. (CSUR) **43**(3), 1–47 (2011)
2. Ye, X., Yang, J., Sun, X., et al.: Foreground background separation from video clips via motion-assisted matrix restoration. IEEE Trans. Circuits Syst. Video Technol. **25**(11), 1721–1734 (2015)
3. Zivkovic, Z., Van der Heijden, F.: Efficient adaptive density estimation per image pixel for the task of background subtraction. Pattern Recogn. Lett. **27**(7), 773–780 (2006)
4. Barnich, O., Droogenbroeck, M.V.: ViBe: a universal background subtraction algorithm for video sequences. IEEE Trans. Image Process. **20**(6), 1709–1724 (2011)
5. Glowacz, A., Kmiec, M., Dziech, A.: Visual detection of knives in security applications using active appearance model. Int. J. Multimedia Tools Appl. **74**, 4253–4267 (2015). https://doi.org/10.1007/s11042-013-1537-2
6. Yu, A.M., Kozlovskii, V.A.: Algorithm of pattern recognition with intra-class clustering. In: International Conference on Pattern Recognition and Information Processing, Minsk, Belarus, pp. 54–57, May 2011
7. Krizhevsky, A., Sutskever, I., Hinton, G.E.: ImageNet classification with deep convolutional neural networks. In: International Conference on Neural Information Processing Systems, Lake Tahoe, Nevada, USA, pp. 1–9, November 2012
8. Zeiler, M.D., Fergus, R.: Visualizing and understanding convolutional networks. In: Fleet, D., Pajdla, T., Schiele, B., Tuytelaars, T. (eds.) ECCV 2014. LNCS, vol. 8689, pp. 818–833. Springer, Cham (2014). https://doi.org/10.1007/978-3-319-10590-1_53
9. Girshick, R., Donahue, J., Darrell, T., et al.: Region-based convolutional networks for accurate object detection and segmentation. IEEE Trans. Pattern Anal. Mach. Intell. **38**(1), 142–158 (2016)
10. Zhao, W., Luo, H., Peng, J., et al.: Spatial pyramid deep hashing for large-scale image retrieval. Neurocomputing **243**, 166–173 (2017)
11. Ross, G.: Fast R-CNN. In: International Conference on Computer Vision, Santiago, Chile, pp. 1440–1448, December 2015
12. Redmon, J., Divvala, S., Girshick, R., et al.: You only look once: unified, real-time object detection. In: International Conference on Computer Vision and Pattern Recognition, Las Vegas, Nevada, USA, pp. 779–788. IEEE, June 2016
13. Redmon, J., Farhadi, A.: YOLO9000: better, faster, stronger. In: IEEE Conference on Computer Vision and Pattern Recognition, Honolulu, HI, US, pp. 6517–6525, July 2017
14. Redmon, J., Ali, F.: YOLOv3: an incremental improvement. Preprint, https://arxiv.org/abs/1804.02767, April 2018
15. Schuldt, C., Laptev, I., Caputo, B., et al.: Recognizing human actions: a local SVM approach. In: International Conference on Pattern Recognition, Cambridge, UK, pp. 32–36, September 2004
16. Yu, E., Aggarwal, J.K.: Human action recognition with extremities as semantic posture representation. In: IEEE Conference on Computer Vision and Pattern Recognition, Miami, Florida, USA, pp. 1–8, June 2009
17. Gaidon, A., Harchaoui, Z., Schmid, C.: Temporal localization of actions with actoms. IEEE Trans. Pattern Anal. Mach. Intell. **35**(11), 2782–2795 (2013)

18. Oneata, D., Verbeek, J., Schmid, C.: Efficient action localization with approximately normalized Fisher vectors. In: IEEE Conference on Computer Vision and Pattern Recognition, Columbus, OH, USA, pp. 254–2552, September 2014
19. Peng, X., Schmid, C.: Multi-region two-stream R-CNN for action detection. In: Leibe, B., Matas, J., Sebe, N., Welling, M. (eds.) ECCV 2016. LNCS, vol. 9908, pp. 744–759. Springer, Cham (2016). https://doi.org/10.1007/978-3-319-46493-0_45
20. Kalogeiton, V., Weinzaepfel, P., Ferrari, V.: Joint learning of object and action detectors. In: International Conference on Computer Vision, Venice, Italy, pp. 2001–2010, December 2017

An Algorithm for Semantic Vectorization of Video Scenes - Applications to Retrieval and Anomaly Detection

Komuravelli Prashanth, Yeturu Kalidas(✉), Jay Rathod Bharat Kumar, Sai Prem Kumar Ayyagari, and Aakash Deep

Indian Institute of Technology, Tirupati, Tirupati, India
ykalidas@iittp.ac.in

Abstract. Video scene retrieval and anomaly detection are important problems in the area of computer vision that share a common concept, of vectorization of the input image frames. We propose here a new vectorization approach and a fast object tracking algorithm. First step is to use any of the existing methods for recognition of objects in image frames. The subsequent step is our key contribution, to use information inside these objects, tracking and generation of semantic vectors for a sequence of image frames. We introduce a novel way of ultra high speed object tracking using a density based clustering of local vector representation of objects across video frames. The vectorization results in semantic features involve object types, their identifiers and movement information. The algorithm has been validated for its ability to retrieve scenes having the highest similarity, over a subset of the YouTube 8M data set on about 1200 videos having 36651 sub-scenes. One type of validation is, among the frames that were closest to the query scene, the fraction of them having common picture characteristics is 90%. The second type of validation is, among the successive frames with a little time gap, a similarity of more than 90% is recorded as desired. The vectorization algorithm is tested for its usefulness to a different problem scenario of anomaly detection in video frames. The vectorization performed well for qualitative and quantitative evaluation on standard and customized anomaly detection data sets of videos and results are reported here.

Keywords: Object tracking · Video scene indexing · Video scene retrieval · Anomaly detection · Scene vectorization · Density clustering

1 Introduction

Scene retrieval is an active area of research with applications to enhancing customer experience and surveillance scenarios [12]. The fundamental strategy in scene based retrieval involves vectorization of a sequence of frames.

The approach by Zhang and co-workers [20] involves Spatio-Temporal Independent Component Analysis (stICA) where each frame is represented as a

S. K. Singh et al. (Eds.): CVIP 2020, CCIS 1378, pp. 369–381, 2021.
https://doi.org/10.1007/978-981-16-1103-2_31

vector of pixel intensities. These vectors are used for identification of top few principal components in a given sequence of frames. The principal components are used as vectors. While this approach offers high speed and is applicable to static scenes, it has issues in capturing scenes having moving objects and different types of objects. The approaches in [9] involves segmentation of objects and background based on information positional changes between frames. These objects information is used for vector generation. However this approach does not handle object categories at finer levels as foreground and background objects may be of different types.

The approaches in [2,3,7,21] involves spatio-temporal segmentation of videos based on key point tracking across frames. Previous works mainly focused on key point detection and tracking across video frames based on features such as SIFT. However this traditional approach would be a computationally costly exercise when the number of key points is several times higher than the number of objects in a given frame. In our approach, we have described objects and tracked objects as against key points thereby potentially reducing computational costs. Content based scene retrieval algorithms consider properties such as colour, texture and spatial properties of objects present in each of the frames [12] and across frames. One example of content based retrieval approach is by Jawahar and co-workers [8] which involves detection and matching of textual information present in the frames of scene. However it is restricted to those videos where text is present. However these algorithms do not consider object category, tracking and movement as features which carry additional information.

A *KD-Tree* algorithm [4,5,11] is a region indexing mechanism where a high dimensional space in partitioned into hyper cuboids by partitioning along the dimensions. Given an input point in *d-dimensional space* a *KD-Tree* searches for proximal points of the same dimension by applying thresholds along each of the *d-dimensions* and narrowing down to a search region. Proximity queries are efficiently served using a *KD-tree* data structure. While KD-Tree is a standard paradigm for nearest neighbour search, the novelty in our work stems from the vectorization approach we have proposed. Object recognition is a major category of computer vision problems including recognition of sub-regions [16,17]. The formulation is essentially a supervised pattern mapping problem where input image is transformed to a tensor corresponding to labels for sub-regions. The dataset is composed of a set of $\{(x_i, y_i)\}$ points, where x_i is the input image having 3 channels and the output y_i is a tensor representation capturing sub-region category, position of the rectangle, its width and height. The most popular method is Yolo by Redmon and co-workers [16] which runs in near real time time scales. We have used this method for recognition of 80 common objects in image frames. Object recognition itself is not directly helpful in vectorization of a sequence of image frames, although it serves a tool to aid in the vectorization exercise.

In order to derive features such as movement of an object in a scene, the task requires tracking of object across scene and it is challenging due to discontinuities such as intermittent occlusion. However, considered across frames, an object leaves a trail of overlapping regions which are detectable by a clustering algorithm for arbitrary shapes. We introduce here a novel feature tracking algorithm by using a *KD-tree* data structure and performing repeated operation of *Kleene-closure* to deduce a cluster of presence of object across frames in a scene.

On the other hand, anomaly detection is an important category of problems [19]. In this problem statement, a sequence of image frames need to be studied and scored whether they are deviant from previous sequence of image frames. We have applied our scene vectorization technique and demonstrated that it outperforms simple features such as pixel intensity histogram and pixel vector representations. Anomaly detection problem scenario is peculiar class of algorithms where there is abundance of *nominal or normal data* and less of *anomalous data*. The requirement is to pose the problem is single class classification or detection of deviation from a given characteristic distribution of points. It can be considered a *semi-supervised* learning strategy with two phases where the first phase deals with learning of the distribution of normal data points and a human-in-loop second phase. The second phase deals with adjustment of parameters, thresholds or even the unsupervised learning strategy used in first phase based on quality of evaluation on the test data set. Some of the unsupervised learning algorithms used are Gaussian Mixture Models (GMM) [18], Hidden Markov Models and recent other deep learning based strategies [19].

2 Methodology

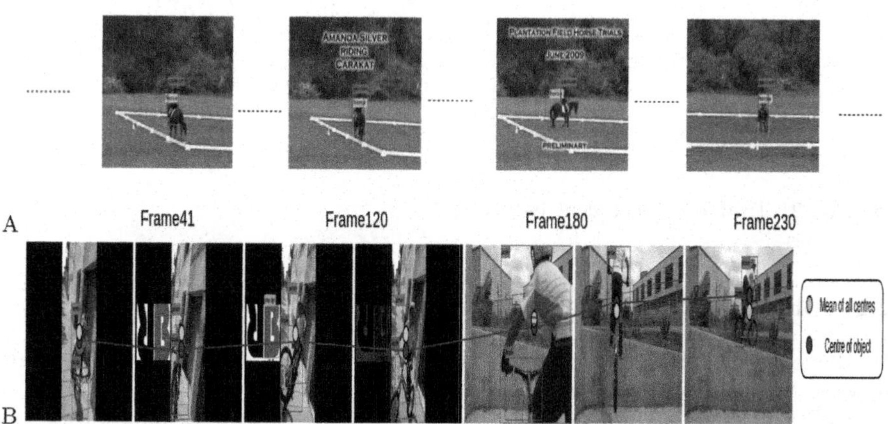

Fig. 1. An example of a scene showing 4 frames. The actual scene has 240 frames.

The algorithm for scene vectorization involves object recognition and efficient tracking across frames. The process involves forming a scene vector from several object vectors and use of density based clustering.

2.1 Scene Representation

A scene is represented by a sequence of frames. The number of frames is a hyper parameter that we have kept with a default value of 240 which corresponds to 8 s scene in a video recording of 30 frames per second. An example of a scene is shown in (Fig. 1A).

Algorithm 1. Tracking of objects for given scene

Require: $O[o_i]_{i=1...N}$ // O objects present across all frames.

$V = OneHotEncoding(O.label)$ //one hot encoding of all objects

$V = Concat(\gamma * V, O.xt, O.yt, O.xb, O.yb, O.hist)$,

//Where, $(xt, yt), (xb, yb)$ are top left and bottom right coordinates of O

//and γ is scaling factor

//and $hist$ is cancatenated histogram of pixel value across R,G,B channels.

$T = KDTree(V)$

$S = \{\}$

Let, $KC(\cdot)$ denote Kleene closure and T is the tree and r is the radius

return $(\forall v \in V) : S.append(KC(T.query(r, v))$

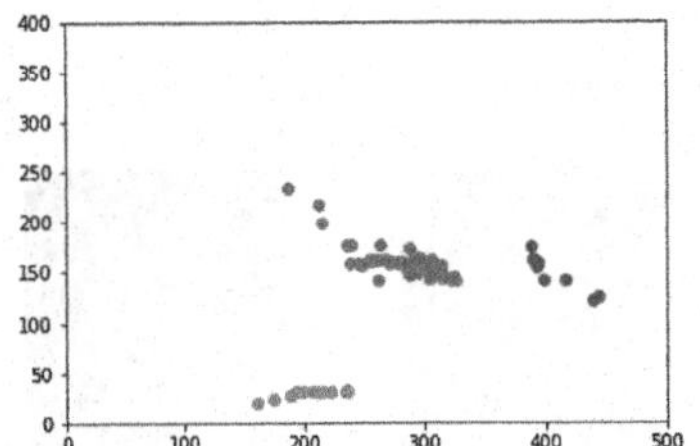

Fig. 2. Trail of object centres across frames

Algorithm 2. Scene Descriptor Algorithm

Require: $S = [f_i]_{i=1...N}$ //where f_i is the ith frame in scene S.

$O[o_i]_{i=1...N} = DETECT()$ //Detection of objects with YOLO across all frames, where o_i list of objects in i^{th} frame

$o_i = [r_{ij}]_{j=1...n_i}$ //where r_{ij} is j^{th} object information in i^{th} frame

$\chi = [C_k]_{k=1...n} = TRACKING(O)$ //where c_k is trail of kth object across frames in which it is available.

$C_k = [r_{ap}, r_{bq}.....]$ //objects across cluster k

$text = ""$

Let τ //threshold for moving objects

for $C \in \chi$ **do**

  $\mu = MEAN((\forall h \in C)\{(h.xt + h.xb)/2, (h.yt + h.yb)/2\})$

  $\sigma^2 = VARIANCE((\forall h \in C)\{(h.xt + h.xb)/2, (h.yt + h.yb)/2\})$

  $(xt, yt), (xb, yb)$ are top left and bottom right coordinates of h.

  if $\sigma > \tau$ **then**

    $(\exists h \in C) : text = text + "moving\_" + h.label$

  else

    $(\exists h \in C) : text = text + "non-moving\_" + h.label$

  end if

end for

$vector = vectorizer(text)$

2.2 Object Recognition

We have used Yolo [16] for recognition of 80 number of common objects in images. In each frame objects are recognized as shown in (Fig. 1A).

Yolo [16] is a high-speed object detection based on the formulation of loss function for regression over image sub-regions which works at a speed of 45 fps (frames per second) and able to detect 80 different objects. Another faster version of the algorithm called *tiny-yolo* that works at 244 fps and able to detect 20 different objects. We process videos with yolo as the first step to detect objects.

2.3 Object Vectorization

The object recognition formulation handles one frame at a time and does not keep track of temporal information across frames for identify of the object. In order to track objects across frames, the first step is to represent a recognized object by a vector. We propose a new vectorization approach where each object in the frame is represented by a vector having 4 components.

1. n-dimensional one-hot encoding of object category. Where n is number of different objects present in scene.
2. Positional features - coordinates of the top left corner
3. Positional features - coordinates of the bottom right corner
4. Histograms of red, blue and green channels of 20-dimensions per channel

The dense point representation of object o is given by following schema, $Concat(\gamma * OHE(o.label), o.xt, o.yt, o.xb, o.yb, o.hist)$. Where, the element, $OHE(O.label)$ denotes One hot encoding of object label, which will be an 80-dimensional vector where each dimension represents the different object as YOLO detecting 80 different objects. The elements, $(o.xt, o.yt)$ and $(o.xb, o.yb)$ are top left and bottom right coordinates of surrounding rectangle of an object in a frame. The element, $o.hist$ is concatenated histograms of red, blue and green channels of 20-dimensions per channel. The element, γ is the scaling factor of One hot encoding. where coordinates and label are obtained using *Yolo*.

2.4 Algorithm for High Throughput Object Vector Tracking Using KD-trees

Traditional tracking involves defining a feature vector for the region to be tracked and searching for proximal vectors in the adjacent frames in and around a neighbourhood area. However, this approach is time-consuming and not desirable in the context of generation of rough feature vectors for a scene. We have devised an approach based on considering all the object vectors as a set and building a *KD-tree* [4]. A KD-tree partitions and building an index for a *D-dimensional space* into sub-regions. Given a query vector, the vector is efficiently mapped to one of the unique sub-regions. Proximity queries are best served by *KD-tree* where nearest neighbour vectors are retrieved for the query vector within a given distance range.

The algorithm for tracking of objects across frames is shown in (Algorithm 1). A sketch of the algorithm is outlined below.

1. Consider a scene as a sequence of 240 image frames (this is adjustable), this corresponds to 8 s in a standard 30 frames per second video recording
2. Perform object recognition in each of the image frames
3. Obtain object vectors for each of the recognized objects across frames
4. Pool the vectors for all the objects in all of the 240 frames as a set
5. Build a *KD-Tree* for this set of vectors
6. For each object vector, determine proximal vectors

7. Cluster the vectors by repeated application of *Kleene-closure* operation to build a profile of object motion across frames
8. Use the cluster profile to derive scene vectorization.

The algorithm (Algorithm 1) takes a scene S which has N frames as input and performs object detection across all frames. All objects stored in a list O with frame id, label, and coordinates of a bounded rectangle. All objects are vectorized and clustered where each cluster corresponds to effectively *tracked appearances* of a particular object across different frames.

An illustration of the application of the (Algorithm 1) to randomly selected objects is shown in (Fig. 2).

2.5 Video Scene Retrieval

Video scene retrieval requires representation of a scene as a vector. Scene vectorization employs object vectors and tracking algorithm to arrive at semantics such as an object is present or absent, and whether it is moving or not moving across frames.

A Data Set of 1200 Videos from Youtube 8M. In order to build and test the algorithm, we have used for reference, Youtube 8M data set [1]. The data set has as many as 8 million short videos where each video is about for 5 min and is recorded at a rate of 30 frames per second (fps). As executing the algorithm on 8 million videos is both extremely time consuming and requires high end resources, we have chosen to demonstrate the workings of the algorithm on a small subset of 1200 videos from popular categories. We downloaded videos based on tags such as ‘person’, ‘car’, ‘horse’, etc.

Scene Vectorization and Retrieval Algorithm. The idea behind video scene retrieval is to represent a scene as a vector and similarity between two scenes is calculated by distance between corresponding vectors. A video scene is a sequence of image frames, given a query scene the algorithm has been designed to retrieve similar scenes based on the definition of visual context of the video scene. The method works by - (i) converting the video scene into vector and (ii) indexing vectors for high speed retrieval. The algorithm for scene vectorization is given in (Algorithm 2). A schematic description of the algorithm is shown in a flow chart (Fig. 3).

As a first step, the recognized objects in each of image frames are vectorized (Sect. 2.3). The vectors for all the objects from across all frames of a scene are considered a set and clustered (Sect. 2.4). Most often, for all practical purposes, each cluster corresponds to a single object across frames whether moving or stationary. In corner cases and not visually important cases, the movement of the object is too fast to form clusters. We chose to mainly address the majority cases where scene is understandable by a human and the intent is to retrieve similar scenes. Within each cluster, centroids of rectangular encapsulation of

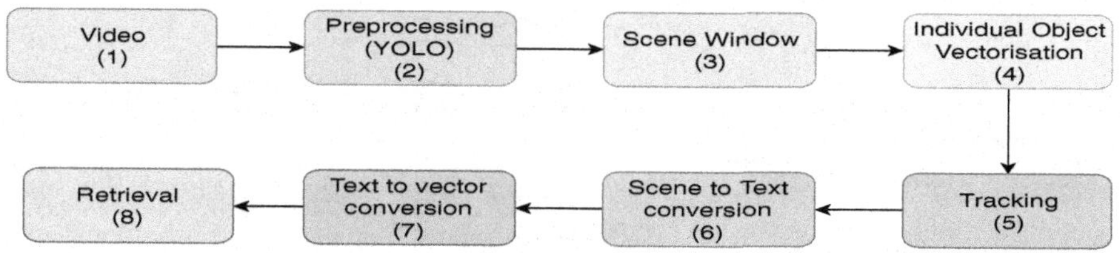

Fig. 3. Flowchart of the algorithm for retrieval of similar scenes

the objects are considered as a set of coordinates. From the centres of all the rectangles, mean and variance are determined for coordinate position. When the variance in coordinate position is above a threshold τ (100 in our case) then the object is considered to be in motion, otherwise stationary. For illustration a moving object and a chain of its appearance across frames in a cluster, is shown in (Fig. 1B). Semantic textual labels generated for the objects are for example, "moving-car, non-moving-person, moving-horse".

The semantic textual labels for a scene hence generated is essentially a paragraph description of activity in a scene. There are several existing text vectorization tools such as *Hashing, Count and TF-IDF vectorizers* that convert paragraphs to vectors.

Algorithm 2 is pseudo code representation of video scene to vector representation algorithm which takes video scene S of length n frames $[f_i]$ where $i \in 1 \ldots n$. As a first step, objects are detected and vectorized in each of the frames (Sect. 2.3). Here, O is list containing information about objects across frames of a video scene. We perform tracking of objects across scene with the Algorithm 1 discussed in previous section by giving O as input to the algorithm. Here, *text* is the textual representation of video scene which is initially empty. The Tracking algorithm returns set of sets(clusters) where each set is a trail of an object across video scene. The element, χ is returned set of sets returned by tracking algorithm which is $[C_k]$ $k \in 1 \ldots n$ and n denotes number of unique objects across video scene. We traverse through each $C \in \chi$ which is trail of an object which contains bounding box information of object across different frames in video scene. We find variance σ^2 of centroid of each bounding box and threshold it with τ. If $\sigma^2 \geq \tau$ then we append *text* with *moving_h.label* for some $h \in C$. The element, *text* will give textual representation of video scene after traversing through all $C \in \chi$, We then perform text to vector conversion using *vectorizer*. The *vectorizer* can be count vectorizer or TF-IDF vectorizer or any other text vectorizer. The element, *vector* is final vector descriptor of given input video scene.

Fast Scene Retrieval and Indexing. For each scene vector, obtaining closest scene vectors requires vector proximity search module to have been already deployed. We store the *KD-tree* model and use the same for retrieving similar scenes as shown in (Fig. 4A). We also propose a distributed mechanism of query

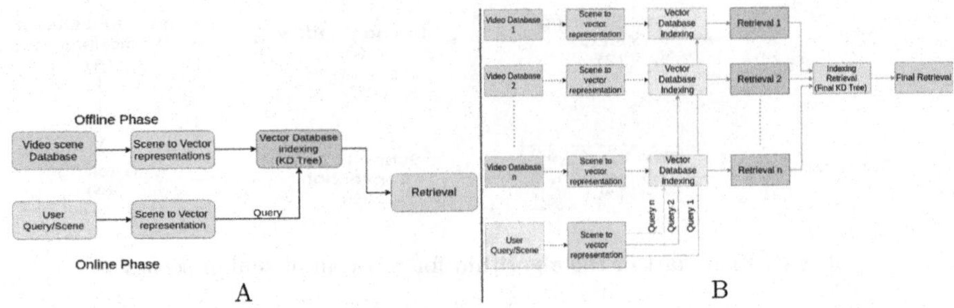

Fig. 4. Retrieval mechanisms in KD-Tree. (A) Shows a schematic of retrieval from a single data store while (B) denotes a schematic for s distributed scene retrieval system.

scene retrieval from *KD-tree* models scattered for each specific video repository. We build a *KD-tree* from query results of distributed *KD-trees* as shown in (Fig. 4B).

2.6 Semantic Vectorization - Application to Anomaly Detection in Videos

We have used the scene vectorization approach for anomaly detection in videos. The anomaly detection algorithm has two phases where in the first phase distribution characteristics of normal data are learnt and in the second phase qualitative and quantitative assessment of detection of anomalies is carried out. We have defined a scene as composed of 30 consecutive frames. Given a continuous and *un-specified* number of input frames arriving as a stream, the anomaly detection formulation requires certain assumptions on the number of input frames to define a context. A sketch of the algorithm is given below.

1. A scene is defined as a sequence of K frames (default K is 30) $S_i = [F_i, \ldots, F_{K+i-1}]$
2. A context is defined as the most recent set of M scenes (default M is 100) $C_i = \{S_{i-M+1}, \ldots, S_i\}$
3. First phase learns an unsupervised model on the context, $M_i = unsup(C_i)$ where $unsup(\cdot)$ indicates a function such as a GMM or HMM.
4. The second phase evaluates the model on test data, $\rho = Test(M_i, T)$ where ρ indicates a quality metric and $Test(\cdot)$ is a testing mechanism that emits a quality score
5. The whole process is repeated until best configuration of parameters and model performance is accomplished.

2.7 Evaluation Metrics

The scene retrieval algorithm is evaluated for its ability to recall known similar scenes. At present there is no database which provides a repository of known scenes. We proposed a simple way of determining known similar scenes by taking a given scene and its immediate neighbour.

Some of the definitions of scene, the next scene and metrics are given below.

1. A scene is defined as a sequence of K frames, $S_i = [F_i, \ldots, F_{i+K-1}]$, where F_j is j^{th} frame
2. A scene has associated description set of words, S_i^d such as "moving_car", "non-moving_person"
3. Similarity of a query scene S_q to a given scene S_g is given by $sim(g, q) = \frac{S_q^d \cap S_g^d}{|S_g^d|}$
4. A scene S_i is also vectorized using text vectorization algorithms such as Hashing, Count and TF-IDF methods and is denoted by S_i^v
5. A proximal j^{th} scene for a given query g^{th} scene is given by, $N(g) : j = \arg\min_{k \in KD(S_g^v)} |S_k^v - S_g^v|$
6. Here, $KD(v)$ gives indices of neighbourhood scene vectors for a given scen vector v
7. Accuracy of retrieval of a gth scene is computed as $acc(g) = sim(g, N(g))$

3 Results

3.1 Scene Retrieval

The algorithm is evaluated on two aspects - (1) quality of scene-vectorization and (2) ability to recall known similarities.

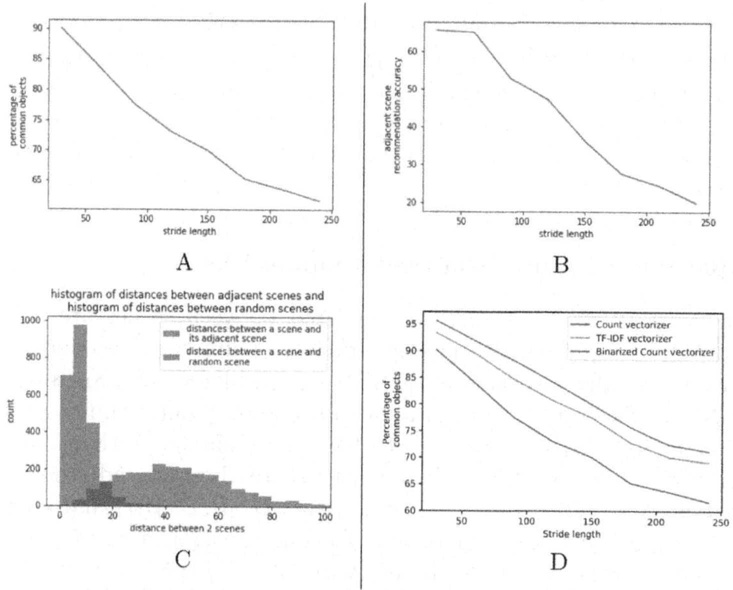

Fig. 5. Effect of stride length over performance - (A) Stride length vs similarity; (B) Stride length vs recall of subsequent scene; (C) similarity vs frequency; (D) Stride length-vs-similarity with different vectorizers (Color figure online)

Quality of Scene Vectorization. For evaluating the quality of scene vectorization, We have retrieved the closest similar scene to a given query scene and computed number of common objects. Each video frame sequence is traversed to generate scenes for a given stride length Γ. Stride corresponds to a jump in the number of frames between the previous and the current frame sequence. For example, $S_i, S_{i+\Gamma}, S_{i+2*\Gamma}$ are sequence of scenes with stride Γ. A data list of scene vectors is prepared for a given stride length $D^{\Gamma} = (\forall v \in V) : [Sv_1, \ldots, Sv_{Lv_k - \Gamma+1}]$. Here, the element V is the set of total set of videos under study, in this experiment it is 2346. The element Sv indicates v^{th} video and Lv denotes length of the video in terms of number of frames in it. A *KD-tree* is built on the data set D^{Γ} and accuracy of retrieval is computed for each and every scene in the data set. Accuracy for a given stride Γ is defined as, $acc^{\Gamma} = \frac{1}{|D^{\Gamma}|} \sum_{g \in D^{\Gamma}} acc(g)$. Accuracy scores are computed on the data set and shown in (Fig. 5A)and we can observe that as stride length increasing similarity score decreasing.

Retrieval of Known Similar Scenes. It is a very challenging exercise to obtain a data set of known similar scenes. One work around and highly effective way would be to consider two scenes which are just one frame apart to be highly similar. For all practical purposes we can assume S_i and S_{i+1} to be highly similar and this is the approach we have followed in preparing a data set of similar scenes. However, when scenes are taken with a stride length, the contents of the next scene tends to be different if the stride increases.

Given that D^{Γ} is a list of scenes taken at stride Γ, let us define $X_i = D^{\Gamma}[i]$ as i^{th} scene. Similarity between two successive scenes at a given stride as $sim(X_i, X_{i+1})$. We have computed average of similarity scores between successive scenes as mentioned in Sect. 2.7, $\frac{1}{|D^{\Gamma}|-1} \sum_{i=1,\ldots,|D^{\Gamma}|-1} sim(X_i, X_{i+1})$.

The neighbourhood scene similarity score versus various values of strides is shown in (Fig. 5B) and we can observe that as stride length increases the recall subsequent scene decreases. Fig. 6 is the example of ground truth scene as well as retrieved scene.

3.2 Ability to Capture Non-trivial Similarities

In order to assess if the similarities captured between scenes are non-trivial, we have computed similarities between random pairs of scenes and compared against known similar scenes. A scene we have considered is for 8 s in time which corresponds to 240 frames. Within a video frame of about 5 min recording, one can expect to find adjacent 8 s clips to have more similarity than any random scene within the video. A set of similarity scores between adjacent scenes is computed as, $X = \{(\forall i, j \in D^{240} : i < j) : sim(D^{\Gamma}[i], D^{\Gamma}[j])\}$ and a histogram is plotted (Fig. 5C) green colour region. To compare against any random scene, for every scene a random pair is chosen (without $i < j$ condition), $Y = \{(\forall i, j \in D^{240}) : sim(D^{\Gamma}[i], D^{\Gamma}[j])\}$ and the histogram is plotted (Fig. 5C) red colour region.

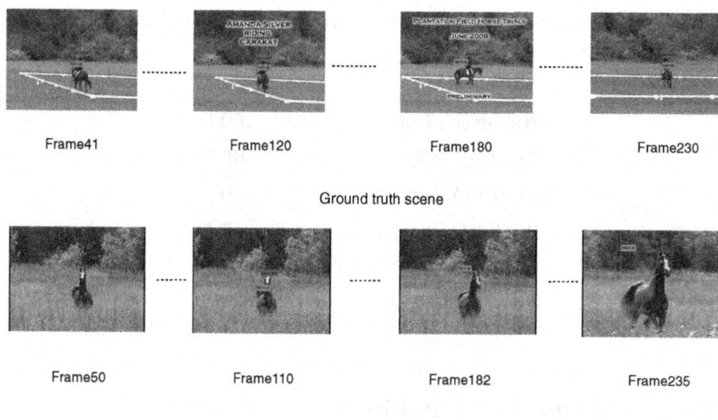

Fig. 6. Example of ground truth and retrieved scenes.

3.3 Effect of Scene Vectorization and KD-tree

In order to build the *KD-tree*, for each scene a vector needs to be prepared. Initially (Sect. 2.5) a scene is represented as a bag of words, such as for example, "moving_car". Effectively a scene can be considered now as a *paragraph.* In the text analysis realm, there are alternative ways of vectorization of a given paragraph. Some of the popular mechanism include Hashing vectorizer, Count and TF-IDF vectorizer. For various stride levels, performance of vectorization mechanisms is evaluated and shown in (Fig. 5D).

3.4 Evaluation of Performance of Semantic Vectorization for Anomaly Detection

A given video is partitioned into scene and vectors are determined (Sect. 2.6). We have chosen Gaussian Mixture Model (GMM) as the unsupervised mechanism for **Phase 1**. For **Phase 2**, synthetically anomalies are induced in the video scenes and are considered test set. Ability of the algorithm to detect anomalies as the number of scenes it is able to retrieve as anomaly is computed from the test data set. A stride of 1 is used in preparing the scene vectors from the video. We performed our experiments using proposed semantic vectorization on USCD pred1 dataset [14] and reported AUC score and bench-marked with other methods in (Table 1).

Regarding the anomaly detection part of the work, our intention is mainly to demonstrate the usefulness of the proposed scene vectorization in this additional setting than only retrieval scenario. Given that anomaly detection itself is a vast subject, we will carry out full scale benchmarking as future research.

Table 1. AUC comparison of various approaches in UCSD pred1 [14] Dataset

Methods	AUC
Hasan*et al.* [6]	50.6
Lu*et al.* [13]	65.51
MPPCA [10]	59
Social force [15]	67.5
Social force+MPPCA [14]	66.8
Our Method	78.6

3.5 Data and Methods Availability

We have uploaded subset of youtube8M dataset that we have used for carrying experiments in the following link https://drive.google.com/open?id=12fXuwMg9ZA3ARThWY4iFlAXqSUOe1lyb The code used to carried out experiments is available on https://github.com/prashanth4518/scene_retrieval.

4 Conclusions

We report here a novel approach for vectorization of video scene via density based clustering of object vectors across frames. We also report here application of such a vectorization for scene retrieval and anomaly detection in video sequences. The object vectorization itself is a new algorithm based on *KD-tree* and iterated *Kleene closure* applicable for high speed object tracking across image frames. A basic test for anomaly detection ability, indicated the algorithm performed satisfactorily on detection of induced known anomalies in video sequences and another standard data set. The algorithm is general purpose with future research directions including to expand to other sources of information such as sub-titles, audio information and applications including surveillance and time series sensor measurements.

Acknowledgements. Acknowledging herewith research grant and support from Toshiba software (India) Pvt. Ltd., as part of project RB/1920/CSE/001/TOSH/KALI hosted at IIT Tirupati.

References

1. Abu-El-Haija, S., et al.: Youtube-8M: a large-scale video classification benchmark. CoRR abs/1609.08675
2. Altadmri, A., Ahmed, A.: A framework for automatic semantic video annotation. Multimed. Tools Appl. **72**, 1167–1191 (2014). https://doi.org/10.1007/s11042-013-1363-6

3. Basharat, A., Zhai, Y., Shah, M.: Content based video matching using spatiotemporal volumes. Comput. Vis. Image Underst. **110**(3), 360–377 (2008). Similarity Matching in Computer Vision and Multimedia
4. Bentley, J.L.: Multidimensional binary search trees used for associative searching. Commun. ACM **18**(9), 509–517 (1975)
5. Buchanan, A., Fitzgibbon, A.: Interactive feature tracking using K-D trees and dynamic programming. In: VPR 2006, vol. 1, pp. 626–633 (2006)
6. Hasan, M., Choi, J., Neumann, J., Roy-Chowdhury, A., Davis, L.: Learning temporal regularity in video sequences, pp. 733–742, June 2016
7. Zhang, H.Z., Wang, J.Y.A., Altunbasak, Y.: Content-based video retrieval and compression: a unified solution. In: Proceedings of International Conference on Image Processing, vol. 1, pp. 13–16 (1997)
8. Jawahar, C.V., Chennupati, J.B., Paluri, B., Jammalamadaka, N.: Video retrieval based on textual queries (2005)
9. Jiang, R.M., Crookes, D.: Approach to automatic video motion segmentation. Electron. Lett. **43**(18), 968–970 (2007)
10. Kim, J., Grauman, K.: Observe locally, infer globally: a space-time MRF for detecting abnormal activities with incremental updates. In: 2009 IEEE Conference on Computer Vision and Pattern Recognition, pp. 2921–2928 (2009)
11. Kubica, J., Masiero, J., Moore, A., Jedicke, R., Connolly, A.: Variable KD-tree algorithms for spatial pattern search and discovery (2005)
12. Liu, Y., Zhang, D., Lu, G., Ma, W.Y.: A survey of content-based image retrieval with high-level semantics. Pattern Recogn. **40**(1), 262–282 (2007)
13. Lu, C., Shi, J., Jia, J.: Abnormal event detection at 150 fps in MATLAB. In: 2013 IEEE International Conference on Computer Vision, pp. 2720–2727 (2013)
14. Mahadevan, V., Li, W., Bhalodia, V., Vasconcelos, N.: Anomaly detection in crowded scenes. In: 2010 IEEE Computer Society Conference on Computer Vision and Pattern Recognition, pp. 1975–1981 (2010)
15. Mehran, R., Oyama, A., Shah, M.: Abnormal crowd behavior detection using social force model. In: 2009 IEEE Conference on Computer Vision and Pattern Recognition, pp. 935–942 (2009)
16. Redmon, J., Divvala, S., Girshick, R., Farhadi, A.: You only look once: unified, real-time object detection. In: 2016 IEEE Conference on Computer Vision and Pattern Recognition (CVPR), pp. 779–788 (2016)
17. Ren, S., He, K., Girshick, R., Sun, J.: Faster R-CNN: towards real-time object detection with region proposal networks. In: Advances in Neural Information Processing Systems 28, pp. 91–99. Curran Associates Inc
18. Reynolds, D.: Gaussian mixture models. In: Li, S.Z., Jain, A. (eds.) Encyclopedia of Biometrics, pp. 827–832. Springer, Boston (2009). https://doi.org/10.1007/978-0-387-73003-5_196
19. Zaheer, M.Z., Lee, J.H., Lee, S., Seo, B.: A brief survey on contemporary methods for anomaly detection in videos. In: 2019 International Conference on Information and Communication Technology Convergence (ICTC), pp. 472–473 (2019)
20. Zhang, X.P., Chen, Z.: An automated video object extraction system based on spatiotemporal independent component analysis and multiscale segmentation. EURASIP J. Adv. Sig. Process. **2006**, 1–22 (2006). https://doi.org/10.1155/ASP/2006/45217
21. Zhou, H., Yuan, Y., Shi, C.: Object tracking using sift features and mean shift. Comput. Vis. Image Underst. **113**(3), 345–352 (2009). https://doi.org/10.1016/j.cviu.2008.08.006. http://www.sciencedirect.com/science/article/pii/S1077314208001331. Special Issue on Video Analysis

Meta-tracking and Dominant Motion Patterns at the Macroscopic Crowd Level

Franjo Matkovic(✉) and Slobodan Ribaric(✉)

Faculty of Electrical Engineering and Computing, University of Zagreb, 10000 Zagreb, Croatia
{franjo.matkovic,slobodan.ribaric}@fer.hr

Abstract. This paper presents a method for crowd motion segmentation and generating dominant motion patterns at the macroscopic crowd level, where a crowd is treated as an entity. In this approach, the dominant motion patterns, as a base for behaviour analysis of a mass of people, are the focus of interest. Dominant motion patterns are generated based on meta-trajectories. A meta-trajectory is defined as a set of tracklets and/or trajectories of entities in the crowd. The entities are particles initially organized as a uniform grid which is overlaid on a flow field. To estimate the flow field, a dense optical flow is used. Based on advection of the particles, tracklets/trajectories are obtained. They are grouped by a graph-based clustering algorithm and meta-trajectories are obtained. By overlapping meta-trajectories with the quantized orientation of the average optical flow field dominant motion patterns are obtained. The preliminary experimental results of the proposed method are given for a subset of UCF dataset, a subset of Crowd Saliency Detection dataset, our own FER dataset and computer crowd simulation videos of characteristic behaviour.

Keywords: Macroscopic crowd level · Crowd analysis · Optical flow · Particle advection · Meta-trajectory · Dominant motion pattern

1 Introduction

Nowadays, video surveillance is widely used in ensuring security in places where large numbers of people gather. A large number of people situated in the same environment and sharing a goal is considered as a crowd [1]. Recently, automatic crowd analysis is getting more attention as a research area in computer vision [2–4]. Crowd analyses may be performed at the following levels: i) microscopic; ii) macroscopic and iii) mesoscopic [3]. Conventional computer vision methods are not appropriate for macroscopic level [3]. The solution are a continuum-based

This work has been supported by the Croatian Science Foundation under project IP-2018-01-7619 "Knowledge-based Approach to Crowd Analysis in Video Surveillance" (KACAVIS).

S. K. Singh et al. (Eds.): CVIP 2020, CCIS 1378, pp. 382–393, 2021.
https://doi.org/10.1007/978-981-16-1103-2_32

or physics-inspired approaches such as fluid dynamics, force models, energy and entropy-based [5].

A method proposed in the paper is crowd motion segmentation represented by meta-trajectories and generating dominant motion patterns at the macroscopic crowd level based on the flow field. The dominant motion patterns are obtained based on meta-trajectories – the sets of tracklets or trajectories of particles which are initially overloaded on the flow field. The flow field is estimated with dense optical flows. By the advection of particles in a video clip, tracklets/trajectories are obtained and these tracklets/trajectories are grouped into several meta-trajectories using the graph-based minimum spanning tree clustering. By combining the meta-trajectories and information extracted from a quantized orientation of the average optical flow (obtained from the video clip), dominant motion patterns are determined. The main novelties might be: i) a meta-trajectory generator that combines particle advection and particle tracklets graph-based minimum spanning tree clustering; ii) the determination of dominant motion patterns based on overlapping meta-trajectories with the quantized orientation of the average optical flow field; iii) the assignment of a velocity vector to each dominant motion pattern.

2 Related Work

A physics-inspired approach to treat a human crowd as a flowing continuum, and modelling crowds as a physical fluid with particles or a particle flow was proposed by Hughes [6]. The notation of a particle flow was introduced in computer vision-based crowd analysis by Ali and Shah [7]. They proposed a Lagrangian Particle Dynamics model for the segmentation of high-density crowd flows and detection of flow instability. Mehran et al. [8] combined particle flow and the Social Force Model (SFM) to detect and localize abnormal crowd behaviours. The regions of abnormalities in the frames were localized using interaction forces obtained based on the SFM. Solmaz et al. [9] used trajectories of particles that represent motion in a scene to locate regions of interest. Ullah and Conci [10] presented a method for crowd motion segmentation which combines foreground extraction based on a Gaussian mixture model, motion extraction by block-based correlation, and trajectories of particles (which are obtained by optical flow) on a foreground region. Motion segmentation is obtained by using the min cut/max flow algorithm. Jodoin et al. [11] proposed a meta-tracking method for surveillance video analysis to determine dominant motion patterns and to find the entry/exit areas. The method consists of 4-stages. At the first stage, a motion histogram is computed for each pixel using sparse optical flow. At the second stage, motion histograms are converted to orientation distribution functions. Third stage performs meta-tracking using particles to detect the dominant flow. Fourth stage clusters meta-tracks to find dominant motion patterns and the entry/exit points. Zhang Y. et al. [12] presented a procedure for constructing a group-level representation of a crowd which organized the crowd motion patterns based on graphs and provided characteristics to gain an insight into crowd behaviour.

They used particle advection for trajectory extraction and Mean Shift-based trajectory clustering. Bag of trajectory graphs is used for understanding behaviour patterns. Dehghan and Kalayeh [13] used a meta-tracking approach to understand pedestrian dynamics in crowded scenes. The method includes the steps: i) a scene is split into hexagon patches and two-dimensional orientation distribution functions are learned for each patch; ii) a Time Homogeneous Markov Chain Meta-tracking method is used to find sources, sinks and dominant paths in the scene; iii) based on the 3-term trajectory clustering method, the entry and exit prediction is made for each individual. Zhang L. et al. [14] presented an approach to crowd motion pattern segmentation based on trajectory tracking and prior-knowledge learning. The approach also used an orientation distribution function-based cumulative probability model to construct a particle flow field. Then, the obtained trajectories of particles are clustered, and the number of clusters is estimated by using prior knowledge. A. S. Hassaneina et al. [15] introduced a clustering method for the identification of motion pathways in highly crowded scenes. Pairwise similarities between motion tracklets, obtained based on particle advection, are estimated using a novel similarity measure inspired by line geometry. The similarity measure effectively captures the spatial and orientation similarity between tracklets. To obtain the motion pathways, the authors used two hierarchical levels of an adaptation of the distance-dependent Chinese Restaurant Process (DD-CRP) model. The authors extended DD-CRP clustering adaptation to incorporate the source and sink gate probabilities for each tracklet. In [16], the authors presented an approach to estimate the flow of people in crowded scenes by using a post-processing method that can be coupled with any baseline optical flow technique. Plane homography is used to project the calculated optical flow to world coordinates. Subsequently, the flow is filtered based on Generalized Social Forces and projected back to the image domain. The method was tested in conjunction with three baseline optical flow algorithms. The results showed that the post-processing method improved the crowd flow of all tested algorithms. The paper [17] presents survey of motion estimation (ME) methods using fluid dynamics (FD). The survey states that conventional ME methods fail at high-density crowds, while FD-particle flow and FD-streakflow are appropriate for high and very high crowd density. Recently, in [18], the authors described two approaches to common pathway detection in crowd scenes. The first approach is the conventional computer vision method based on collecting tracklets, and hierarchical clustering. The second proposed approach is based on deep learning to tackle the problems and limitations of the first approach. It is based on LSTM units, which detect scene common pathways. The LSTM approach assumes knowledge of the scene entrance segments and then predicts complete trajectories.

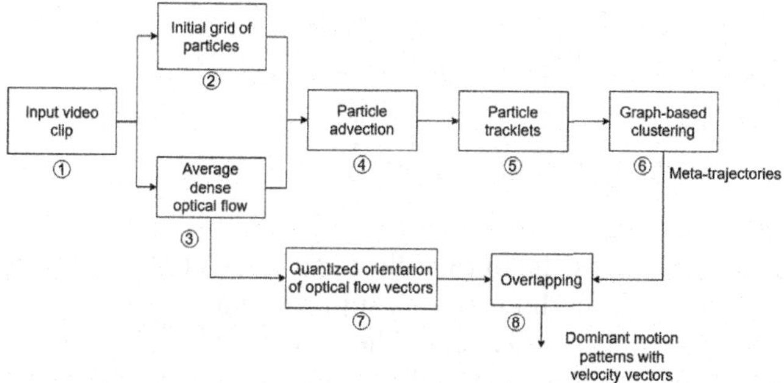

Fig. 1. Overview of the proposed method: flowchart of the entire method

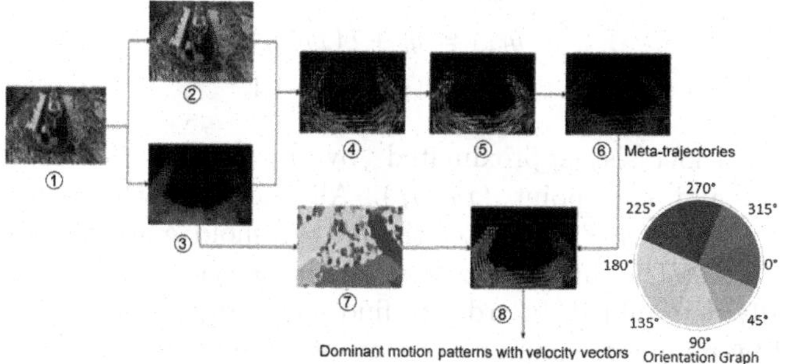

Fig. 2. Interpretation of each step of the method

3 Our Method

Figure 1 depicts a flowchart of the proposed method. It consists of eight main steps. Figure 2 illustrates the intermediate result of every step of the method. Initially, particles are uniformly distributed throughout a whole frame, creating a grid of particles $(\frac{W}{n}, \frac{H}{m})$, where W and H are width and height of an image (in pixels) respectively, m and n are steps which define density of particles, and they are experimentally set. A dense optical flow is calculated by using the method proposed in [19] for every pair of successive frames in the video clip. An average optical flow field is calculated over T frames in the video clip to minimize the influence of fluctuations and small errors in the optical flow. Particle advection, based on an average optical flow field, is used to create tracklets of particles in the video clip. The procedure for obtaining a tracklet based on particle advection is described below. Video sequence is split into video clips consisting of T consecutive frames. Each video clip is represented by a tensor of a size $T \times W \times H$, where T is the number of frames and $W \times H$ denotes the frame resolution. There are two matrices representing average values of the optical flow field components $\overline{u}(x, y)$, and $\overline{v}(x, y)$, where $x = 1, 2, .., W$ and $y = 1, 2, .., H$ respectively, i.e. the dimensions of the matrices correspond to the dimensions of a frame:

$$\overline{u}(x,y) = \frac{1}{T-1}\sum_{t=1}^{T-1} u(x,y,t)$$
$$\overline{v}(x,y) = \frac{1}{T-1}\sum_{t=1}^{T-1} v(x,y,t) \tag{1}$$

where $u(x, y, t), v(x, y, t)$ is the optical flow at time t at the position (x, y) computed by the Farnebäck method. Let us suppose that a particle is at the initial position $(x_t,\ y_t)$ at $t = 1$, i.e. $(x_1,\ y_1)$. The new position of the particle at $t = 2$ is obtained by $x_2 = x_1 + \overline{u}(x_1, y_1)$ and $y_2 = y_1 + \overline{v}(x_1, y_1)$. Iterative calculation of the final particle position at $t = T$ is based on:

$$\begin{aligned} x_{t+1} &= x_t + \overline{u}(x_t, y_t) \\ y_{t+1} &= y_t + \overline{v}(x_t, y_t) \\ 1 \le t &\le T-1 \end{aligned} \tag{2}$$

A particle tracklet is approximated by a straight line with starting point (x_1, y_1) and end point (x_T, y_T). All particles whose advected path $\sqrt{(x_T - x_1)^2 + (y_T - y_1)^2}$ is shorter than a threshold ρ are removed from further consideration. The threshold ρ depends on the type of video sequence and is experimentally determined. In order to find meta-trajectories, particle tracklets are grouped by minimum spanning tree graph-based clustering as follows:

i) Calculate the matrix of the HU distances [20] between all particle tracklets. This is computed as the average Euclidean distance between points on two trajectories:

$$D_{HU}(F_i, F_j) = \frac{1}{L}\sum_{k=1}^{L}\sqrt{(x_{i,k} - x_{j,k})^2 + (y_{i,k} - y_{j,k})^2}; i \ne j \tag{3}$$

where F_i and F_j are particle tracklets, $i,\ j = 1,\ 2,\ \ldots,\ N$, where N is the number of particle tracklets, k is the index of a point of a tracklet, x and y are the coordinates of a point of a tracklet, and L is the number of points of a tracklet. In our case, $L = 2$ and $k = 1, 2$. The HU distance function is selected because it relies on similar trajectories having the same point distribution with consecutive points in corresponding tracklets in spatial proximity.

ii) Based on the matrix of HU distances, construct a complete graph with weighted edges, where weight corresponds to the distance between the particle tracklets F_i and F_j; $i,\ j = 1,\ 2,\ ...,\ N$.

iii) Find a minimum spanning tree (MST). The MST is selected due to its close conformity to the proximity principle of perceptual organization.

iv) Build a histogram of the weighted edges of the MST and find the threshold value for the inconsistent edges [21]. A histogram is used to find a set of inter-cluster weighted edges and a set of intra-cluster weighted edges. The threshold value corresponds to the "valley" between the histogram's peaks.

v) Split the MST into subgraphs, which correspond to the clusters, by deleting the edges that have values higher than the threshold. This step of the clustering method is selected because it supports the Gestalt principles of perceptual 2D data organization.
vi) Delete clusters whose size is smaller than the predefined threshold τ. The reason for this step is to eliminate clusters with a small number of tracklets. The threshold τ is experimentally determined. In such a way, the clusters with a small number of tracklets are treated as the results of "noisy" particle trajectories which do not correspond to dominant motion patterns.

The subgraphs represent meta-trajectories. Orientations of the average optical flow field are quantized into eight different intervals shown as an orientation graph (Fig. 2). To obtain the dominant motion patterns with velocity vectors, overlap the meta-trajectories represented as a binary mask (1s correspond to the trajectories) with the quantized orientation of the average optical flow field. A velocity vector $\mathbf{v}_i = (\overline{u}_i[\frac{pixels}{Tframes}], \overline{v}_i[\frac{pixels}{Tframes}])'$ assigned to a dominant motion pattern i is obtained based on its average optical flow calculated for T successive frames in a video clip.

4 Preliminary Experiments

Experiments were preformed on the subsets of UCF dataset [7] and the Crowd Saliency Detection dataset [22], which are often used for crowd analysis, as well as, on our own FER crowd video sequences [23] and computer crowd simulation videos of characteristic behaviours [24]. The experiments setup details are given in Table 1.

Figure 3 depicts the comparative qualitative results of meta-trajectories for the Marathon video sequence. The Figure also includes the results of a recent technique based on the post-processing (filtering) of optical flow obtained by the Farnebäck method [16]. Figure 4 displays the comparative results of meta-trajectories with other methods [7,11,14]. The first four rows in Fig. 4 were taken from [14]. The last row represents the results of the proposed method. The meta-trajectories are displayed with different colours. The previously mentioned parameters ρ and τ are determined as follows. The value of the threshold ρ depends on the nature of a crowd scene and the camera position. For example, close-up crowd scenes require a bigger value of the threshold ρ. The values for ρ are given in Table 1. Figure 5 shows the results of the meta-trajectories for different threshold values ρ used in the testing. Clearly, this should be learned or experimentally specified for each type of scene, because this depends on the distances of the objects (people), camera movement, and zooming. The threshold τ is experimentally determined and is set on 5% of the biggest cluster size for all video clips. Figure 6 displays dominant motion patterns obtained by overlapping of the meta-trajectories with a quantized orientation of optical flow. Figures 7, 8 and 9 illustrate the obtained results for the video clips from the FER video dataset: Bottleneck, Two groups walking towards each other and

Split. The clusters of tracklets, i.e. meta-trajectories, correspond to the perception and interpretation of a human. The meta-trajectories for three clips of a video sequence of a computer crowd simulation are represented in Fig. 10. The last column in the Figure displays the dominant motion patterns with average velocity vectors.

Table 1. Experiment setup

	Number of frames	Frame resolution	Number of clips/number of frames T	Number of initial particles $(\frac{W}{n}, \frac{H}{m})$ $m = n = 10$	Advected path threshold ρ
UCF dataset video sequences					
Marathon	450	360 × 202	15/30	720	5
Mecca	200	360 × 202	6/30	720	10
Crowd Saliency video sequences					
Hajj	34	160 × 120	1/30	192	1
Bridge	450	240 × 180	15/30	432	5
FER crowd video sequences					
Bottleneck	1050	1310 × 736	35/30	2390	10
Two walking groups	480	1920 × 1080	16/30	5035	10
Split	330	1594 × 896	11/30	3537	15
Computer Crowd Simulation video					
Bottleneck	210	377 × 358	7/30	1295	10

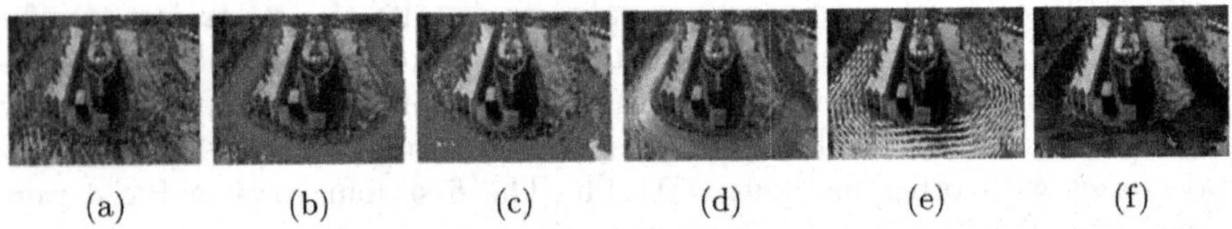

(a) (b) (c) (d) (e) (f)

Fig. 3. Comparative qualitative results of meta-trajectories for Marathon video sequence (a) original frame, b) [14], c) [7], d) [11], e) our method. The figure also includes the results of recent technique based on post-processing (filtering) of optical flow obtained by Farnebäck method f) [16].

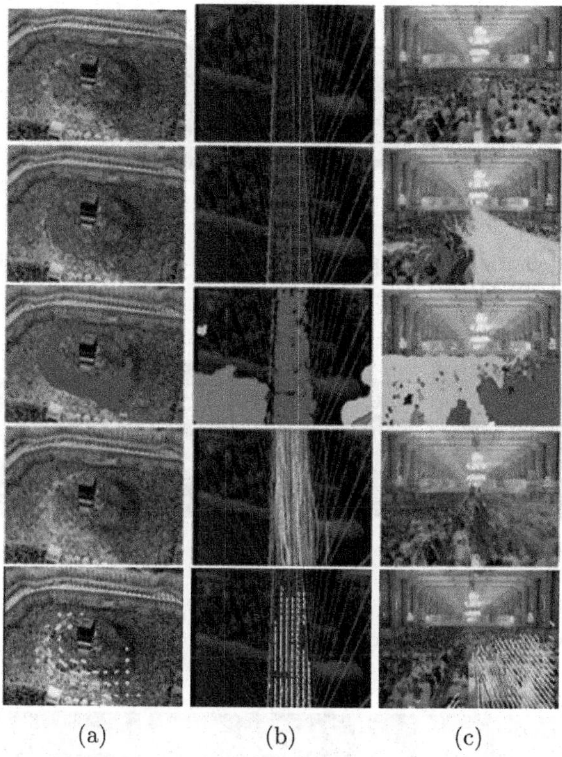

(a) (b) (c)

Fig. 4. Meta-trajectories: a) Hajj, b) Bridge, c) Mecca. Rows of the figure in the following order (from up to down) represent: original frames from the video sequences, results from [14], where the authors used trajectory tracking and prior knowledge learning, results produced by particle flow and FTLE field segmentation from [7], and results obtained by meta-tracking by [11]. The last row represents the results obtained by our method.

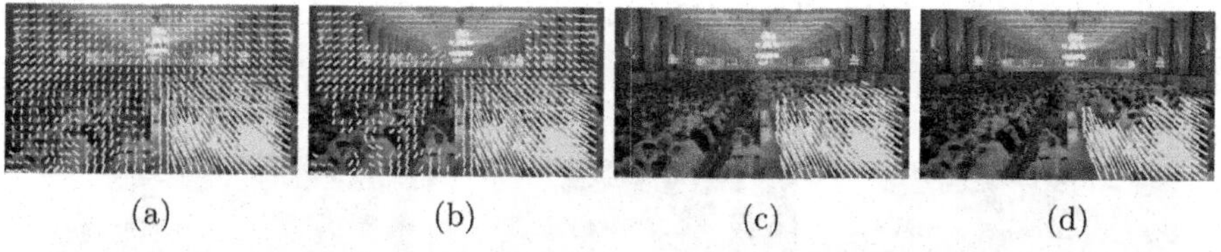

(a) (b) (c) (d)

Fig. 5. Meta-trajectories for different threshold values ρ; a) $\rho = 1$; b) $\rho = 5$; c) $\rho = 10$; d) $\rho = 15$

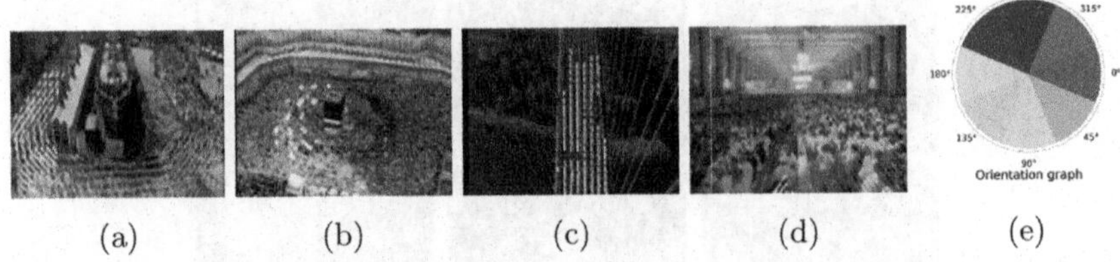

(a) (b) (c) (d) (e)

Fig. 6. Dominant motion patterns overlapped with the original frame: a) Marathon, b) Hajj, c) Bridge, d) Mecca

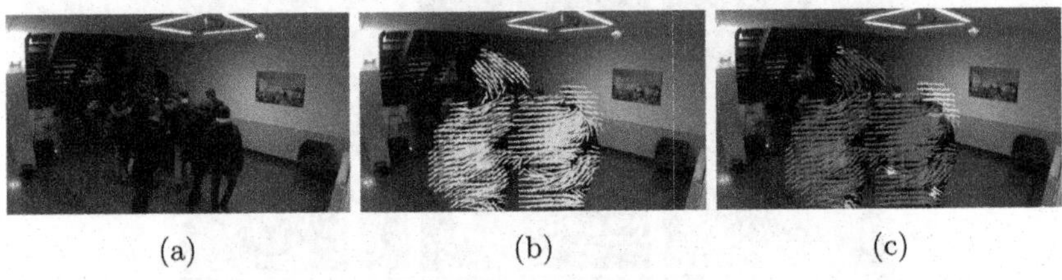

(a) (b) (c)

Fig. 7. Bottleneck sequence; a) original frame; b) meta-trajectories; c) dominant motion pattern with velocity vector $\mathbf{v} = [21, -7]'$ overlapped with a)

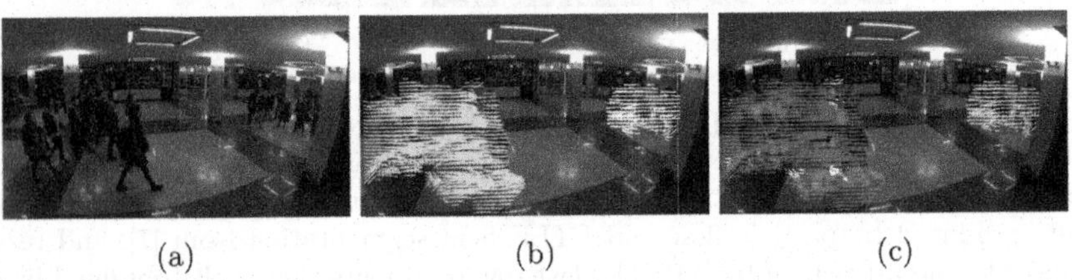

(a) (b) (c)

Fig. 8. Two groups walking towards each other; a) original frame; b) meta-trajectories; c) dominant motion patterns with velocity vectors ($\mathbf{v}_1 = [55, -2]'$ for blue meta-trajectory and $\mathbf{v}_2 = [-25, 1]'$ for white meta-trajectory) overlapped with a) (Color figure online)

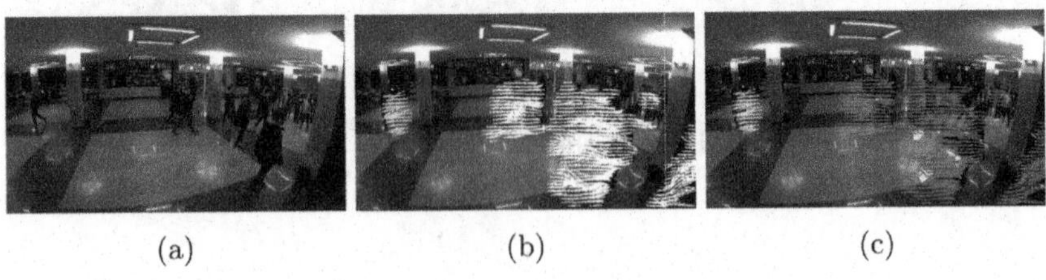

(a) (b) (c)

Fig. 9. Split sequence; a) original frame; b) meta-trajectories; c) dominant motion patterns with velocity vectors ($\mathbf{v}_1 = [-26, 6]'$ for blue meta-trajectory and $\mathbf{v}_2 = [38, 0]'$ for white meta-trajectory) overlapped with a) (Color figure online)

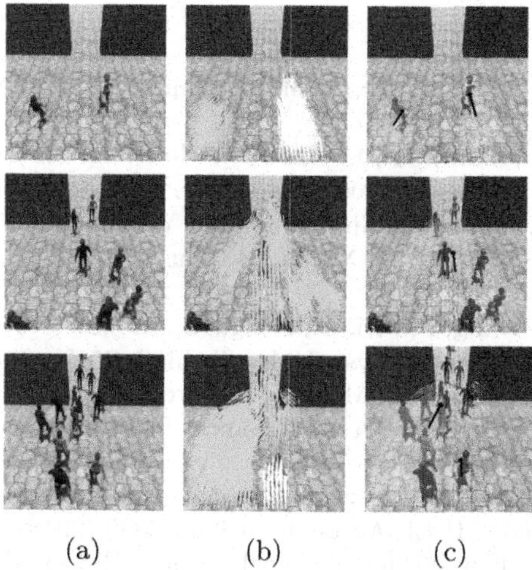

(a) (b) (c)

Fig. 10. Dominant motion patterns with velocity vectors for three clips of a video sequence of crowd simulation: a) original frames; b) meta-trajectories; c) dominant motion patterns with velocity vectors overlapped with original frame: first row - clip 3 (frames 61–0; $\mathbf{v}_1 = [22, -34]'$ for blue meta-trajectory and $\mathbf{v}_2 = [-15, -52]'$ for white meta-trajectory); second row - clip 4 (frames 91–20; $\mathbf{v}_1 = [-5, -45]'$ for blue meta-trajectory); third row - clip 6 (frames 151–80; $\mathbf{v}_1 = [27, -51]'$ for blue meta-trajectory and $\mathbf{v}_2 = [-2, -40]'$ for white meta-trajectory); (Color figure online)

5 Conclusion

The paper proposes a method for generating meta-trajectories of crowds and dominant motion patterns with velocity vectors at the crowd macroscopic level. The method uses particle advection, where particles are initially organized as a uniform grid which is overlaid on the optical flow field. Video sequences are split into video clips, each 30 frames. Based on the advection of the particles in the video clip, tracklets are obtained. To extract the meta-trajectories, the particle tracklets are grouped with graph-based clustering by using the HU distance and the minimum spanning tree algorithm. The clustering method is selected because it supports the Gestalt principles of perceptual 2D organization. Dominant motion patterns are obtained based on overlapping meta-trajectories with the quantized orientation of the average optical flow field. A velocity vector is assigned to each dominant motion pattern. The preliminary experiments were conducted on video sequences of real-world crowd scenes and computer crowd simulation dataset. The obtained results are compared with state-of-the-art methods.

In future work, the extracted meta-trajectories and dominant motion patterns with velocity vectors through a sequence of video clips will be used to infer crowd behaviours in scenes at the macroscopic level.

References

1. Adrian, J., et al.: A glossary for research on human crowd dynamics. Collec. Dyn. **4**, 1–13 (2019)
2. Ali, S., Nishino, K., Manocha, D., Shah, M.: Modeling, simulation and visual analysis of crowds: a multidisciplinary perspective. In: Ali, S., Nishino, K., Manocha, D., Shah, M. (eds.) Modeling, Simulation and Visual Analysis of Crowds. TISVC, vol. 11, pp. 1–19. Springer, New York (2013). https://doi.org/10.1007/978-1-4614-8483-7_1
3. Li, T., Chang, H., Wang, M., Ni, B., Hong, R., Yan, S.: Crowded scene analysis: a survey. IEEE Trans. Circuits Syst. Video Technol. **25**(3), 367–386 (2015)
4. Swathi, H.Y., Shivakumar, G., Mohana, H.: Crowd behavior analysis: a survey. In: International Conference on Recent Advances in Electronics and Communication Technology, pp. 169–178 (2017)
5. Zhang, X., Yu, Q., Yu, H.: Physics inspired methods for crowd video surveillance and analysis: a survey. IEEE Access **6**, 66816–66830 (2018)
6. Hughes, R.L.: The flow of human crowds. Annu. Rev. Fluid Mech. **35**, 169–182 (2003)
7. Ali, S., Shah, M.: A Lagrangian particle dynamics approach for crowd flow segmentation and stability analysis. In: IEEE Conference on Computer Vision and Pattern Recognition, pp. 1–6 (2007)
8. Mehran, R., Oyama, A., Shah, M.: Abnormal crowd behavior detection using social force model. In: IEEE Conference on Computer Vision and Pattern Recognition, pp. 935–942 (2009)
9. Solmaz, B., Moore, B.E., Shah, M.: Identifying behaviors in crowd scenes using stability analysis for dynamical systems. IEEE Trans. Pattern Anal. Mach. Intell. **34**(10), 2064–2070 (2012)
10. Ullah, H., Conci, N.: Crowd motion segmentation and anomaly detection via multi-label optimization. In: ICPR Workshop on Pattern Recognition, pp. 1–6 (2012)
11. Jodoin, P.M., Benezeth, Y., Wang, Y.: Meta-tracking for video scene understanding. In:10th IEEE International Conference on Advanced Video and Signal Based Surveillance, pp. 1–6 (2013)
12. Zhang, Y., Huang, Q., Qin, L., Zhao, S., Yao, H., Xu, P.: Representing dense crowd patterns using bag of trajectory graphs. SIViP **8**(1), 173–181 (2014). https://doi.org/10.1007/s11760-014-0669-9
13. Dehghan, A., Kalayeh, M.M.: Understanding crowd collectivity: a meta-tracking approach. In: Proceedings of the IEEE International Conference on Computer Vision and Pattern Recognition (CVPR) Workshops, pp. 1–9 (2015)
14. Zhang, L., He, Z., Gu, M., Yu, H.: Crowd segmentation method based on trajectory tracking and prior knowledge learning. Arab. J. Sci. Eng. **43**, 7143–7152 (2018)
15. Hassanein, A.S., Hussein, M.E., Gomaa, W., Makihara, Y., Yagi, Y.: Identifying motion pathways in highly crowded scenes: a non-parametric tracklet clustering approach. Comput. Vis. Image Underst. **191**, 102710 (2020)
16. Almeida, I., Jung, C.: Crowd flow estimation from calibrated cameras. Mach. Vis. Appl. **32**(1), 1–12 (2020). https://doi.org/10.1007/s00138-020-01132-y
17. Farooq, M.U., Saad, M.N.B.M., Malik, A.S., Ali, Y.S., Khan, S.D.: Motion estimation of high density crowd using fluid dynamics. Imaging Sci. J. **68**(3), 141–155 (2020). https://doi.org/10.1080/13682199.2020.1767843
18. Moustafa, A.N., Gomaa, W.: Gate and common pathway detection in crowd scenes and anomaly detection using motion units and LSTM predictive models. Multimed. Tools Appl. **79**, 20689–20728 (2020). https://doi.org/10.1007/s11042-020-08840-7

19. Farnebäck, G.: Two-frame motion estimation based on polynomial expansion. In: Bigun, J., Gustavsson, T. (eds.) SCIA 2003. LNCS, vol. 2749, pp. 363–370. Springer, Heidelberg (2003). https://doi.org/10.1007/3-540-45103-X_50
20. Hu, W., Xie, D., Fu, Z., Zeng, W., Maybank, S.: Semantic-based surveillance video retrieval. IEEE Trans. Image Process. **16**(4), 1168–1181 (2007). https://doi.org/10.1109/TIP.2006.891352
21. Zahn, C.T.: Graph-theoretical methods for detecting and describing gestalt clusters. IEEE Trans. Comput. **C–20**, 68–86 (1971)
22. Lim, M.K., Kok, V.J., Loy, C.C., Chan, C.S.: Crowd saliency detection via global similarity structure. In: International Conference on Pattern Recognition, pp. 3957–3962 (2014)
23. [dataset] Matković F., Marčetić, D., Ribarić, S.: FER dataset (2020). http://kacavis.zemris.fer.hr/datasets/FER_dataset.zip. Data retrieved from KACAVIS webpage
24. [dataset] Matković F.: Crowd simulation dataset videos (2020). http://kacavis.zemris.fer.hr/datasets/Crowd_simulation_dataset_videos.zip. Data retrieved from KACAVIS webpage

Digital Video Encryption by Quasigroup on System on Chip (SoC)

Deepthi Haridas(✉), D. Sree Kiran, Shivi Patel, K. Raghavendre, Sarma Venkatraman, and Raghu Venkatraman

Advanced Data Processing Research Institute (ADRIN), Department of Space, Government of India, Secunderabad 500009, Telangana, India
deepthi@adrin.res.in

Abstract. Video is the relied means of visual communication in a contactless manner. With personal, official and educational communication moving online, there arises a strong need of video encryption schemes, to maintain privacy and confidentiality. The current manuscript presents a novel Quasigroup Video Encryption Scheme (QuVench). Achieving the near real time encryption/decryption rate with very little latency while maintaining a small footprint is a challenge. Near real time secure processing of video data is achieved with the proposed encryption algorithm seamlessly, maintaining a small footprint. This algorithm is suitable for UAV and drone applications. The present work details the algorithm, its hardware implementation as well as the security analysis on Quasigroup Video Encryption Scheme (QuVench).

Keywords: Data encryption · Quasigroup · Pseudo-random numbers · Quadratic residue · Latin square

1 Introduction

Video communication is of immense importance for both civilian and defense activities. Unmanned Aerial Vehicles (UAVs) are predominantly used for various strategic purposes. Under all circumstances, there is prominent need to have real time encryption scheme without inserting additional artifacts on video data. In most of the scenarios, real time encryption is obtained forgoing the decrypted video quality.

State of art UAV or IoT applications, make use of IP/analogue cameras for the ease of handling video data. The applications encompass IOT applications to drones, for various purposes from surveillance to civilian/strategic communication. IP/analogue cameras being used in most of the current day applications like visual surveillance, UAV and drone. Prime concern with IP/analogue cameras is payload security. There are immense challenges involved in securing the bulky video data and congested network bandwidth. Fast, efficient and robust design of video encryption schemes are required, to realize real time secured

S. K. Singh et al. (Eds.): CVIP 2020, CCIS 1378, pp. 394–405, 2021.
https://doi.org/10.1007/978-981-16-1103-2_33

video communication. Suppose if the video data is communicated in plain, then any adversary can maliciously make use of data by sniffing the data in transit.

There have been sufficient number of works on cryptanalysis on video encryption algorithms [1–3]. Most of the video encryption methods are susceptible to known plaintext/ciphertext attacks and chosen plaintext/ciphertext attacks.

Video encryption requires speed as well as security, both the factors cannot be compromised and are mandatory. Hence the current work applies Quasigroup based algorithm towards video encryption. [4–8] Researchers have dwelled in working out crypto primitives based on quasigroups for the past four decades. Recent survey of quasigroups and their application is provided in [10]. Quasigroup is well suited for applications on resource constraint devices. Quasigroup based crypto primitives provide effective realization of both fast processing speed and data security, as compared to the conventional encryption algorithms. Cryptographic primitives based on quasigroups have been used in design of stream ciphers, block ciphers, hash functions and pseudo random number generators. Conventional ciphers require more resources and processing time. This hampers execution speed of conventional ciphers, introducing latency into video transmission. One of the most binding requisite for UAV application is small footprint. Hence conventional ciphers are not ideal solution for lightweight resource constraint devices. Current paper presents a novel Quasigroup Video Encryption Scheme (QuVench) for near real time encryption of high definition video data for IoT and UAV applications. QuVench provides both robustness as well as near real time encryption/decryption for video data. Current work elaborates the security analysis on Quasigroup Video Encryption cipher (QuVench), suited for both IoT and UAV applications.

The rest of the paper is organized as follows: Sect. 2 demonstrates Quasigroup video encryption cipher in detail. Section 3 present hardware implementation of QuVench as well as speed. Section 4 details the security analysis of Quasigroup video encryption scheme. Concluding remarks are covered in Sect. 5.

2 Quasigroup Video Encryption Cipher (QuVench)

Quasigroup Video Encryption Cipher (QuVench) is a Quasigroup based cipher to encrypt the video feed from analogue camera, and decrypt the transmitted encrypted video feed received at the base station. The analogue camera supports HD resolution with no encoding. Raw data is encrypted and transmitted across. The live transmitted video is decrypted in near real time and viewed at the display of the base station. The entire process takes place seamlessly as depicted in Fig. 1. Basic definitions of Quasigroup, latin square is available with [9] and Blum Blum Shub [15].

Utilizing our experience of working in the field of quasigroups we have observed, Quasigroups is mathematical paradigm that works well as a cryptographic primitive towards designing cryptotools like cryptographic ciphers towards block ciphers, stream ciphers and hashes etc. The current paper introduces a novel quasigroup video encryption cipher specially suited for designing

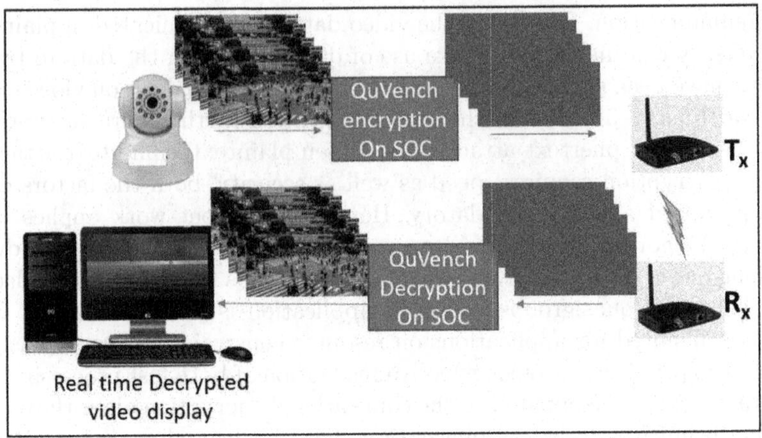

Fig. 1. Wireless encrypted video transmission flow

secured solution towards SOC platform. The current paper introduces the concept of quasigroup processing of video data before xoring it with pseudo random numbers. Our work uses quasigroup of the order 256. The current paper shows the encryption/decryption results on mixkit video frames [14]. Figure 2 [b], [c] depicts the resultant encrypted, decrypted frame for a series of 4 frames for visual interpretation. QuVench is initiated as follows:

- ⁎ **Setup**
  Let the computation be done on $\mathbb{Z}_{256}$. Let $\mathbb{Q}$ be a quasigroup s.t. $\mathbb{Q} : \mathbb{Z}_{256} \times \mathbb{Z}_{256} \longrightarrow \mathbb{Z}_{256}$, defined as $\mathbb{Q}(i, j) = i{*}j = k$, where i, j and $k \in \mathbb{Z}_{256}$ and $*$ is the binary operation defining the quasigroup $\mathbb{Q}$ of cardinality 256. $\mathbb{Q}_{par}$ denotes the parastrophe corresponding to Quasigroup $\mathbb{Q}$.
- ⁎ **Generation of Blum Blum Shub (BBS) Pseudo Random Bytes**
  Blum Blum Shub (BBS) Generator are Cryptographically Secure Pseudo Random Generator (CSPRNG). BBS generator generates BBS bytes equal to size of frame in bytes.

2.1 QuVench Encryption

Encryption in QuVench works as follows:

- ⁎ **QuasiProcessing of frames**
  Present paper introduces notion of quasi transformed frames to video encryption processing in following manner:

  Let us denote $\mathbb{F}_{m \times n}$ be single video frame of size $m \times n$ where m denotes number of scan lines of frame and n denotes number of pix columns of frame. $\tilde{\mathbb{F}}_{m \times n}$ be transformed quasiprocessed frame. As quasigroup considered here is of order 256. Hence input frame $\mathbb{F}_{m \times n}$ needs to be padded additional bytes

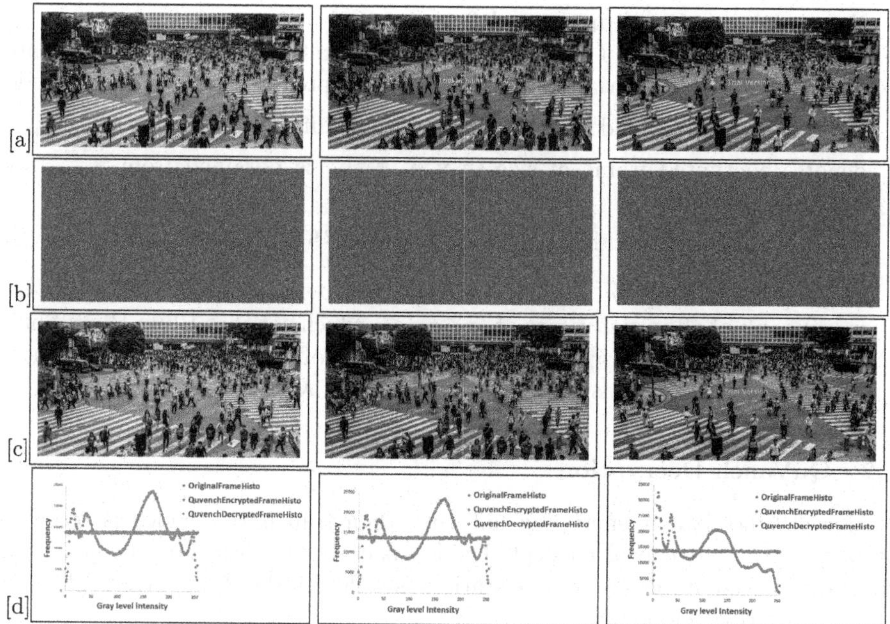

Fig. 2. [a] Three input mixkit [14] video frames [b] corresponding three QuVench encrypted video frames and [c] Resultant QuVench decrypted three video frames [d] Histogram of original frame Vs QuVench encrypted frame Vs QuVench decrypted frame corresponding to first, second and third frames

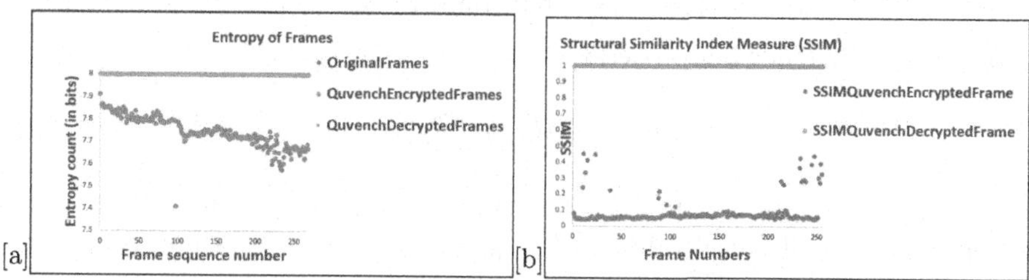

Fig. 3. [a] Plot of entropy of original frames vs corresponding QuVench encrypted frames as well as corresponding resultant decrypted frames, and [b] Scatterplot of SSIM vs frame numbers for QuVench encrypted frames as well as resultant decrypted frames, with original frame as reference frame

to make it a multiple of 256× 256.

$$\tilde{\mathbb{F}}(x+i, y+\mathbb{Q}(i,j)) = \mathbb{F}(x+i, y+j) = \mathbb{F}(x,y) * \mathbb{Q}(i,j); \tag{1}$$

where, $0 \leq x < m$, $0 \leq y < n$, $0 \leq i < 256$, $0 \leq j < 256$ and $0 \leq \mathbb{Q}(i,j) < 256$

* **Randomizing Quasiprocessed frames**
For every new session of video communication, initial values of (p_0, q_0, s_0) are different. Based on initial values (p_0, q_0, s_0) cryptographically secure pseudo random bytes generated are always going to be different. Let us assume $\tilde{\tilde{\mathbb{F}}}_{m \times n}$ denotes encrypted frame of size $m \times n$. $\tilde{\tilde{\mathbb{F}}}_{m \times n}$ is obtained from $\tilde{\mathbb{F}}_{m \times n}$ by following process:
$$\tilde{\tilde{\mathbb{F}}}(x, y) = \tilde{\mathbb{F}}(x, y) \bigoplus BBS[z]; \tag{2}$$
$\forall 0 \leq x < m, 0 \leq y < n, 0 \leq z < m \times n, z \in \mathcal{K}(p_0, q_0, s_0)$, where $\mathcal{K}(p_0, q_0, s_0)$ is key bank of all initial values of (p_0, q_0, s_0) which satisfies Blum Blum Shub generator conditions [15]. For every new session of video a refreshed z or new set of $z \in \mathcal{K}(p_0, q_0, s_0)$ is selected from key bank $\mathcal{K}(p_0, q_0, s_0)$.

2.2 QuVench Decryption

Near real time data is encrypted onboard, then transmitted video is received at base station. Received encrypted video packets are decrypted in near real time and viewed at display of base station as is depicted in Fig. 1. Decryption in QuVench works as follows:

* **DeRandomizing Quasiprocessed frames**
For every decrypted session processing of video communication, initial values of (p_0, q_0, s_0) are seeded with same seed values as was used during encrypting video transmission.
Let $\tilde{\tilde{\mathbb{F}}}_{m \times n}$ denotes received encrypted frame of size $m \times n$. $\tilde{\mathbb{F}}_{m \times n}$ is obtained from$\tilde{\tilde{\mathbb{F}}}_{m \times n}$ by following process:
$$\tilde{\mathbb{F}}(x, y) = \tilde{\tilde{\mathbb{F}}}(x, y) \bigoplus BBS[z]; \tag{3}$$
$\forall 0 \leq x < m, 0 \leq y < n, 0 \leq z < m \times n, z \in \mathcal{K}(p_0, q_0, s_0)$, where $\mathcal{K}(p_0, q_0, s_0)$ is key bank of all initial values of (p_0, q_0, s_0) which satisfies Blum Blum Shub generator condition [15].
* **DeQuasiProcessing of frames**
As in Quasiprocessing of frames, $\mathbb{F}_{m \times n}$ be single video frame of size $m \times n$ where m denotes number of scan lines of frame and n denotes number of pix columns of frame.
$$\mathbb{F}(x, y) = \tilde{\mathbb{F}}(x, y) * \mathbb{Q}_{par}(i, j) \tag{4}$$
where, $0 \leq x < m$, $0 \leq y < n$, $0 \leq i < 256$, $0 \leq j < 256$ and $0 \leq \mathbb{Q}_{par}(i, j) < 256$, $\mathbb{Q}_{par}$ is parastrophe of quasigroup.
Hence base station decrypts and obtains originally transmitted video.

3 Hardware Implementation of QuVench

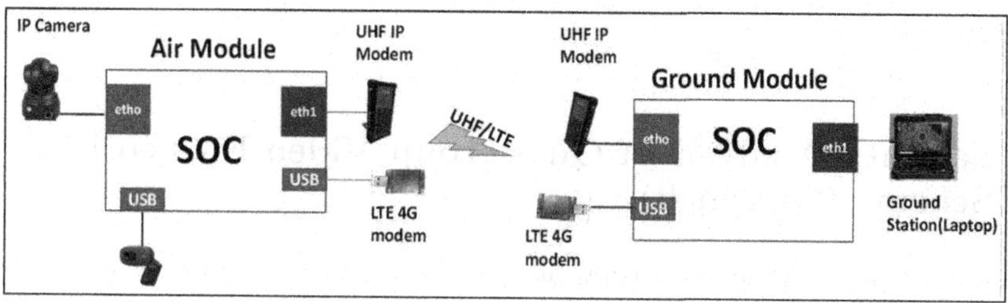

Fig. 4. Architectural diagram of Air and Ground modules of QuVench Secured Communication

Air and ground segment of QuVench Secured Communication scenarios are as explained in Sect. 2, hardware architectural diagram is displayed in Fig. 4. QuVench encryption resides on SOC of air module, whereas QuVench decryption resides on SOC of ground module. SOC device used is Tegra Nano Board, specifications of it are shown in [19].

SOC board contains following interfaces:

- IP Camera: connected through Ethernet Interface.
- USB Camera: Interfaced to USB 2.0/3.0.
- UHF I/P Modem: IP enabled Modem at UHF band of 450 MZ with a data rate of 2 Mbps.
- LTE modem: USB interfaced 4G LTE modem with a data rate of 5–12 Mbps.

The processing works as below.

Initially, keys are generated and exchange of key take place for the session. Such generated keys will be synced both at ground and air modules before the session get initiated/started. Time taken for pseudo random number generation is 2 min on Tegra Nano board. Foot print of encryption/decryption module is around 750 KB.

SOC rate of frame processing for an image of dimension 1280 × 720 is near real time, here each frame encrypted data at 13 msec against 40 msec of frame rate for an USB2.0 interface camera [20]. Rate of Processing of SOC is near real time, as processing of encryption/decryption occurs directly over raw data i.e. uncompressed video data (it can be extended to loseless compressed video data). At present, USB camera interface has been tested. Original frame dimension was 1280 × 720, for Quasi frame dimension is resized to 1280 × 768. Modified frame volume is 3 MB, this amounts to 60 MB for a camera of 20 fps. Data transfer rate required is approximately 480 Mbps. As shown is Table 1, processing is being carried out in near real time, however data transfer speed depends on available network bandwidth.

Table 1. Encryption Decryption Speed for each frame achieved on Tegra

Frame size (B)	Time taken (ms)	QuVench encryption/decryption processing	
		Speed (Gbps)	Footprint (KB)
$1280 \times 720 \times 3$	13	1.584	750

4 Security Analysis of Quasigroup Video Encryption Scheme (QuVench)

Video encryption cipher is acceptable for practical applications from security point of view, if cost and resources incurred in mounting a successful attack on it, is several times higher than value of encrypted video [1]. Aspects of security analysis are discussed as follows:

4.1 Security Analysis of Secret Key

The set $(\mathbb{Q}, p_0, q_0, s_0)$ forms secret key for QuVench, where $\mathbb{Q}$ corresponds to quasigroup of order 256, $(p_0, q_0, s_0) \in \mathcal{K}(p_0, q_0, s_0)$ is key bank of all initial values of (p_0, q_0, s_0) which satisfies Blum Blum Shub generator. This can further be divided into two categories:

Table 2. KeySpace of QuVench

Algorithm	QuVench	Muhammad et al. [11]	Huang et al. [13]	Xu et al. [12]
KeySpace	10^{58000}	10^{90}	10^{56}	2^{180}

Quasigroup Key Space. Total number of latin squares of order 256 [5] is:

$$0.753 \times 10^{102805} \geq LS(256) \geq 0.304 \times 10^{101724}$$

where $LS(256) =$ Total number of Latin squares of order 256.

Security of Blum Blum Shub (BBS). Security of Cryptographically Secure Pseudo Random Number Generators follows from intractability of number theoretic open problem of quadratic residuocity [17] as well as it being probabilistic polynomial algorithm [16] for Blum-Blum-Shub prng. For every session initial seed for BBS changes hence QuVench is probabilistic encryption scheme. Every time the session starts new BBS bytes would be used. Thereby changing encrypted data for every session.

Hence Keyspace for QuVench $\approx 10^{58000}$ (as depicted in Table 2.), which is more than total number of stars in our galaxy. Huge keyspace of QuVench, makes it secured against quantum and conventional computing. As keys in keyspace will never get exhausted, practically for every session a new key could be used.

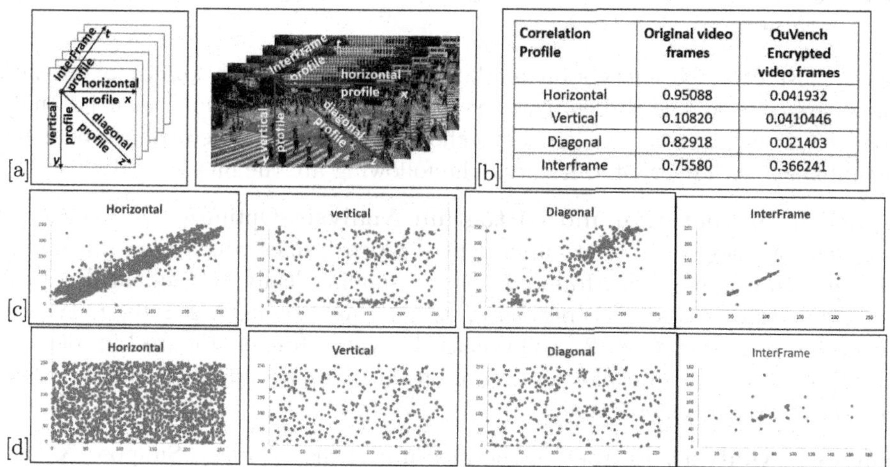

Correlation Profile	Original video frames	QuVench Encrypted video frames
Horizontal	0.95088	0.041932
Vertical	0.10820	0.0410446
Diagonal	0.82918	0.021403
Interframe	0.75580	0.366241

Fig. 5. [a] Visual representation of correlation profiles video frames, [b] Correlation coefficient of adjacent pixels in Original video frames Vs corresponding encrypted video frames [c] Horizontal Profile, vertical profile, diagonal and interframe correlation profile of original video frames [d] Horizontal Profile, vertical profile, diagonal and interframe correlation profile of QuVench encrypted video frames

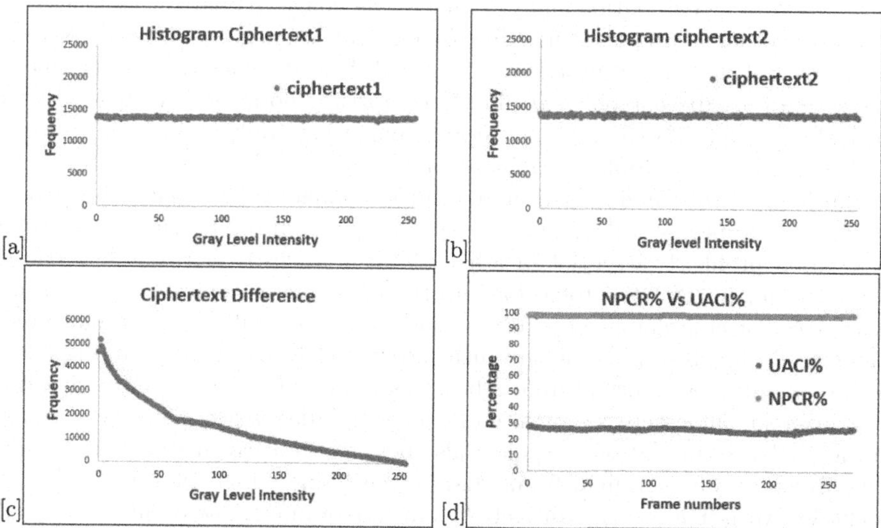

Fig. 6. Scatterplot of [a] Histogram of ciphertext of frame1 encrypted with key1, [b] Histogram of ciphertext of frame1 encrypted with key2, [c] Histogram of difference frame encrypted with key1 and key2 and [d] Comparison of NPCR and UACI scores for 270 sequence of frames

4.2 Qualitative Evaluation of Quvench Encrypted/Decrypted Frames

Since most of video encryption methods are susceptible to known plaintext/ciphertext attacks and chosen plaintext/ciphertext attacks. Under security analysis of Quvench, prime concern is to show that original video frames bear no resemblance with encrypted frames. The following are the measures discussed:

Visual Representation and Histogram Analysis. Optimized video encryption scheme should result in an encrypted video frames which bear no resemblance with original video frame, in fact it should ideally be random. Figure 2 depicts initial successive three Fig. 2 [a] original frame, Fig. 2 [b] QuVench encrypted frames and Fig. 2 [c] QuVench decrypted frames. Figure 2 [d] depicts superimposed histogram plot for original frame, corresponding encrypted frame and resultant decrypted frame.

Entropy Analysis. Entropy is the measure of disorderness. Suppose $\mathbf{X}$ is a random variable, let $p(\mathbf{X})$ be its probability distribution. In Fig. 3 Entropy of sequence of frames is plotted. Figure 3 depicts superimposed entropy plot for original sequence of frames, QuVench encrypted sequence of frames as well as QuVench Decrypted sequence of frames. Entropy is computed for sequence of 270 frames for all original, encrypted and decrypted frames.

Correlation Analysis. Current work illustrates correlation analysis with reference to video frames. Present work proposes a new correlation profile for video data. Performing correlation analysis on a single image compared to sequence of frames in a video, differs slightly. In case of a single image: horizontal, vertical profile as well as diagonal profile are computed. Within image the scatter plot of pixel values of adjacent pixels is plotted comprising horizontal, vertical as well as diagonal profile. For image encryption, comparing horizontal profile, vertical profile and diagonal profile of original image to encrypted image (with in image) is sufficient. With reference to minute change of adjacent pixels spanning across sequence of frames in video, current paper proposes introduction of interframe correlation profile. Scatterplot of adjacent pixel values in horizontal, vertical, diagonal and interframe profile for an original frame is depicted in Fig. 5 [c]. Scatterplot of adjacent pixel values in horizontal, vertical, diagonal and interframe profile for corresponding Quvench encrypted frame is depicted in Fig. 5 [d]. In case of video, sequence of frames bears lots of redundancy, variation of adjacent pixel spanning across sequence of frames in video is negligible as is shown in Fig. 5. Hence correlation coefficient also behaves similarly, it varies drastically with frame between original frame and Quvench encrypted frame. Correlation coefficient variation is comparatively less in case of interframe profile of original video frames than interframe profile of Quvench encrypted video frames.

Structural Similarity Measure Index (SSIM). SSIM is used for measuring similarity between two images. SSIM [18] index is the metric to measure image quality with reference to uncompressed/distortion free image as reference. Present paper considered SSIM measure as a quality metric to show structural similarity index of encrypted frame with original frame. SSIM is computed for a sequence of 270 original frames, 270 Quvench encrypted frames and corresponding 270 decrypted frames. Current work presents SSIM metric comparison of decrypted frames with Quvench encrypted frames, having original frames as reference frames, as is depicted in Fig. 3 [b]. SSIM=1 signifies that similarity of resultant frame with original frame is exactly same.

Diffusion Property Analysis. Diffusion Property implies ability of cipher to diffuse change in plaintext/ keys over its corresponding ciphertext. Weak diffusion property of cipher would result in successful differential attacks [15]. Number of changing pixel rate (NPCR) and unified averaged changed intensity (UACI) [21] are two metrics to evaluate degree of resistance against differential attacks provided by the cipher.

To analyze diffusion property of QuVench cipher, plaintext video frames is kept intact, while prngs are seeded differently for second set of encryption of same plaintext video frames sequence. For diffusion analysis, experimental results are obtained retaining same set of plaintext video frames and same quasigroup. Generated two different ciphertext video frames $\mathbb{C}_1$ and $\mathbb{C}_2$ resulted from application of QuVench on same video frames with different (p_0, q_0, s_0). Histogram of first ciphertext frame of corresponding $\mathbb{C}_1$ and $\mathbb{C}_2$ are depicted in Fig. 6 [a] and [b]. Both Fig. 6 [a] and [b] shows uniform distribution of ciphertexts with small variation of prng seeding. Histogram of absolute difference of first ciphertext frames i.e. $|\mathbb{C}_1 - \mathbb{C}_2|$ is plotted in Fig. 6 [c]. Figure 6 [d] depicts comparison of NPCR% to that of UACI% for a sequence of 270 frames of $\mathbb{C}_1$ and $\mathbb{C}_2$. After Processing 270 frames of $\mathbb{C}_1$ and $\mathbb{C}_2$ mean value for NPCR% is 99.63 and UACI% is 26.211.

5 Conclusion

Current paper presents novel Quasigoup based video encryption scheme Quasigroup video encryption scheme (QuVench). It achieves near real time encryption decryption for secure video transmission. Security is a prime requirement along with speed of transmission. Extensive security analysis is performed in present work to quantify security standard of current scheme. Probabilistic QuVench Cipher takes the advantage of using quasigroup for encryption. As total number of quasigroups of order 256 is a very huge number. Hence QuVench encrypted video data will be quantum secure with future computers with Qubit Processors. Qualitative assessment of QuVench concludes following:

- Histogram analysis: Decrypted frames have identical histogram as the original frame. Histogram of encrypted frame is uniform distribution, as is desirable for a perfect encrypted data.
- Entropy Analysis: Entropy plot of decrypted frames exactly superimposes with that of original frame. Entropy of encrypted frame is always 8bits per byte. Maximum possible entropy for any 8bit data is 8 bits per byte. Hence encrypted data poses highest level of disorderness.

- Correlation Analysis: Original video frames is not correlated to the corresponding encrypted sequence of frames in horizontal, diagonal, vertical and interframe direction.
- Structural Similarity Measure (SSIM) for decrypted sequence of frames with original frames as reference frames is 1 always. Which signifies decrypted frame is exactly same as original video frames. Demonstrating that in the process of encryption and decryption video data does not undergo any lose. On the other hand, SSIM measure of encrypted frames compared to that of original sequence of frames is very less. This metric demonstrates encrypted frames does not hold any similarity with original frames.
- Diffusion Property Analysis: QuVench cipher is secure against differential attack. Resultant ciphertexts obtained from applying QuVench to same plaintext video frames, same quasigroup but with variable prng seeds. QuVench is a probabilistic cipher wherein just varying seeds for prngs resulted in high scores of NPCR% and low scores of UACI%. Hence QuVench is secured against differential attack.

Current work has come up with QuVench cipher fulfilling requirement of near real time speed and secured video data transmission as well as at rest solution, while maintaining a small footprint. Future direction, QuVench to be tested on IP camera interface, implementation data rates as well computing time needs to be compared with present scenario.

Acknowledgment. Deepthi Haridas (DH) would like to thank Dr. Rallapalli Phani Bhushan and Dr. Pramod Kumar for their time and advice.

References

1. Seidel, T., Socek, D., Sramka, M.: Cryptanalysis of video encryption algorithms. In: Proceedings of The 3rd Central European Conference on Cryptology TATRACRYPT (2003)
2. Li, S., Li, C., Lo, K.-T., Chen, G.: Cryptanalysis of an image encryption scheme. J. Electron. Imaging **15**(4), 043012 (2006)
3. Arroyo, D., Li, C., Li, S., Alvarez, G., Halang, W.A.: Cryptanalysis of an image encryption scheme based on a new total shuffling algorithm. Chaos Solitons Fractals **41**(5), 2613–2616 (2009)
4. Dénes, J., Keedwell, A.D.: Latin Squares: New Developments in the Theory and Applications, vol. 46. Elsevier, Amsterdam (1991)
5. Koscielny, C.: Generating quasigroups for cryptographic applications. Int. J. Appl. Math. Comput. Sci. **12**(4), 559–570 (2002)
6. Gligoroski, D., Markovski, S.,Markovski, S.: Cryptographic potentials of quasigroup transformations (2003)
7. Shcherbacov, V.: Quasigroup based crypto-algorithms. arXiv preprint arXiv:1201. 3016 (2012)
8. Markovski, S., Gligoroski, D., Kocarev, L.: Unbiased random sequences from quasigroup string transformations. In: Gilbert, H., Handschuh, H. (eds.) FSE 2005. LNCS, vol. 3557, pp. 163–180. Springer, Heidelberg (2005). https://doi.org/10.1007/11502760_11

9. Markovski, S., Gligoroski, D., Andova, S.: Using quasigroups for one-one secure encoding. In: Proceedings of the VIII Conference on Logic and Computer Science, LIRA, vol. 97, pp. 157–162 (1997)
10. Chauhan, D., Gupta, I., Verma, R.: Quasigroups and their applications in cryptography. Cryptologia 1–39 (2020)
11. Muhammad, K., Hamza, R., Ahmad, J., Lloret, J., Wang, H., Baik, S.W.: Secure surveillance framework for IoT systems using probabilistic image encryption. IEEE Trans. Ind. Inform. **14**(8), 3679–3689 (2018)
12. Xu, L., Li, Z., Li, J., Hua, W.: A novel bit-level image encryption algorithm based on chaotic maps. Opt. Lasers Eng. **78**, 17–25 (2016)
13. Huang, X.: Image encryption algorithm using chaotic Chebyshev generator. Nonlinear Dyn. **67**(4), 2411–2417 (2012). https://doi.org/10.1007/s11071-011-0155-7
14. https://mixkit.co/free-stock-video/
15. Stinson, D.R., Paterson, M.: Cryptography: Theory and Practice. CRC Press, Boca Raton (2018)
16. Vybornova, Y.D.: Password-based key derivation function as one of Blum-Blum-Shub pseudo-random generator applications. Proc. Eng. **201**, 428–435 (2017)
17. Junod, P.: Cryptographic Secure Pseudo Random Bits Generation: The Blum-Blum Shub Generator. (Unpublished, August 1999). http://tlapixqui.izt.uam.mu/sem-cryipto/Sucesiones/CryptoRandomBits.pdf
18. Wang, Z., Bovik, A.C., Sheikh, H.R., Simoncelli, E.P.: Image quality assessment: from error visibility to structural similarity. IEEE Trans. Image Process. **13**(4), 600–612 (2004)
19. Tegra Nano Board. https://developer.nvidia.com/embedded/jetson-nano-developer-kit
20. Logitech USB C270 HD Camera. www.logitech/com
21. Chen, G., Mao, Y., Chui, C.K.: A symmetric image encryption scheme based on 3D chaotic cat maps. Chaos Solitons Fractals **21**(3), 749–761 (2004)

Detection Based Multipath Correlation Filter for Visual Object Tracking

Himadri Sekhar Bhunia[1(✉)], Alok Kanti Deb[2(✉)], and Jayanta Mukhopadhyay[3(✉)]

[1] Advanced Technology Development Centre, Indian Institute of Technology, Kharagpur, Kharagpur, India
hb.pku08@gmail.com

[2] Department of Electrical Engineering, Indian Institute of Technology, Kharagpur, Kharagpur, India
alokkanti@ee.iitkgp.ac.in

[3] Department of Computer Science and Engineering, Indian Institute of Technology, Kharagpur, Kharagpur, India
jay@cse.iitkgp.ac.in

Abstract. This paper presents a novel detection based multipath correlation filter (DT-MPT) for moving single object tracking from Unmanned Aerial Vehicles (UAVs). Most object trackers suffer under complicated situations such as the fast motion of objects, camera motion, similar objects, and occlusions, usually found in UAV videos. This paper utilizes a correlation filter based tracking algorithm along with a motion estimation block, a novel detection block, and a new multipath block to cope with those challenges. The detection block uses the concept of the difference image to detect moving objects, while the multipath block considers multiple positions for a few looks ahead frame for accurate localization of an object position. The performance analysis on three challenging benchmark datasets UAV123@10fps, UAV20L and DTB70 show that the proposed tracker DT-MPT outperforms its base tracker as well as most of the other top-performing state of art correlation filter-based trackers while running in almost real-time.

Keywords: Kalman filter · Detection network · Object tracking · Correlation filter · Multipath tracking

1 Introduction

Object tracking is one of the fundamental research problems in the field of computer vision. Recently, aerial video surveillance has become very popular in the field of object tracking. It has various applications in military, sports, to name a few. Aerial object tracking faces several more challenges due to small object size, low-quality images, abrupt illumination changes, and camera motion. In recent years, several discriminative correlation filter-based trackers such as KCF [11], SAMF [16] have shown good performance in terms of speed and accuracy due to

S. K. Singh et al. (Eds.): CVIP 2020, CCIS 1378, pp. 406–418, 2021.
https://doi.org/10.1007/978-981-16-1103-2_34

computation performed in the Fourier domain. The performance of those trackers are further improved by spatially regularized correlation filter-based trackers such as SRDCF [6] and ECO [4]. Lately, several deep feature-based tracking algorithms [14,19] have been introduced to improve accuracy and robustness, but they suffer in speed due to deep features computation. Nowadays, a two-stage tracking algorithm [10], such as tracking by detection, has become very popular. Unlike single-stage methods mentioned earlier, the two-stage algorithms generate proposals first and then classify them in the second stage. Detection-based tracker, as reported in [26], combines online and offline training to improve accuracy but suffers in speed due to using of multiple deep networks. Current developments in the object detection field such as YOLO [20] and Faster R-CNN [22], encourage using detection networks along with tracking networks. As mentioned by Dogra et al. [8], most of these methods often suffer in many challenging situations, such as presence of similar object, partial or full occlusion, which mostly found in aerial videos. The multipath approach [2,8] performs better in those situation by considering multiple locations for a few look ahead frames and then computes final object positions from multiple locations. Major drawback of the multipath algorithm is the exponential increse in the computation time. This paper proposes a modified multipath algorithm by utilizing non-maximum suppression (NMS) and a peak to sidelobe (PSR) based threshold technique. It improves the tracking speed and accuracy of the multipath algorithm. In this paper, a novel detection based multipath correlation filter (DT-MPT) has been proposed to improve tracking performance of a state of art correlation filter based tracker.

This paper is organized as follows; Sect. 2 describes the proposed methodology. Performance analysis is presented in Sect. 3 and conclusions are drawn in Sect. 4.

Fig. 1. Visualization of tracking results on UAV20L dataset. The proposed DT-MPT algorithm accurately tracks the target while ECO-HC fails.

1.1 Motivation and Contributions

The contributions of this paper are summarized as follows: First, we have proposed a novel detection based multipath correlation filter (DT-MPT). The algorithm consists of a novel difference image-based detection algorithm to localize possible moving objects within the search window. Rather than using the whole search region, the accuracy and speed of the tracking algorithm is improved by feeding only small size detected patches. The performance of the tracker is enhanced by applying a non-greedy search based modified multipath scheme combined with non-maximum suppression and peak to sidelobe based threshold technique in order to improve its speed and accuracy. Finally, the proposed novel tracker is used to improve the accuracy and robustness of the state of art based tracking algorithm ECO-HC [4]. Comprehensive studies have been carried out on various UAV datasets to analyze the proposed method's performance against different state-of-the-art trackers. The proposed tracker surpasses it's base tracker ECO-HC and the multipath based tracker ECO-MPT [2] significant amount in terms of precision and success rate while running in almost real-time under a limited hardware environment. Figure 1 shows the DT-MPT outperforms its base tracker ECO-HC under challenging situations such as, fast motion (top row), partial occlusion (middle row) and presence of similar objects (bottom row). The novel algorithm is a generalized framework, and it can be used with any other object tracking algorithm towards improving its performance significantly.

2 Proposed Approach

This section explains different blocks of the detection based multipath correlation filter (DT-MPT) in detail. Figure 2 shows a schematic diagram of the proposed approach.

The motion estimation block predicts a search region by using Kalman Filter [13] while considering constant velocity motion model and measurements from the previous frame. This estimation is important for accurate localization of fast moving targets often found in UAV videos.

The **detection block** uses a weighted subtraction layer along with deep convolution neural network and region proposal network to localize moving object candidates inside the search window. The detection block focuses on the moving target only and localize those object patches while removing most of the stationary backgrounds.

The **tracking block** consist of the correlation filter based base tracker ECO-HC [4]. Candidate patches are correlated with the object to be tracked to get an accurate location. Parameters of the filter are learned online to cope with small changes in the object appearances.

Multiple similar correlation score in correlation map are found due to presence of similar objects and occlusion, In those situation, the **multi-path block** update object location after considering multiple locations for a few looks ahead frames.

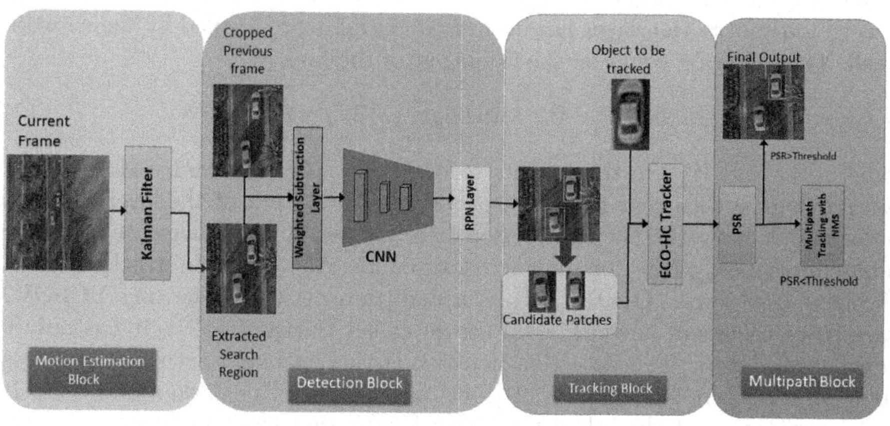

Fig. 2. Proposed method outline

2.1 Kalman Filter Block

The movement of most of the objects present in the UAV videos is nonlinear. However, motion between two frames can be considered to be linear with some uncertainty. In order to get a rough estimate of the object's position in the next frame, the Kalman filter [13] is used. Here, a simple linear motion model has been considered. State vectors are similar to [1] as shown in the Eq. 1.

$$\mathbf{x} = [p_x, p_y, s, a, \dot{p_x}, \dot{p_y}, \dot{s}]^T \tag{1}$$

Where p_x and p_y are horizontal and vertical pixel locations of the center of the target while scale s and a represents the scale and aspect ratio of the target bounding box, respectively. The aspect ratio is taken as constant. The Kalman filter predicts the states using the Kalman Filter framework [13]. Then, measurements are corrected via actual position and bounding box found in the final stage. If no object is found, the Kalman filter only predicts based on previous measurements.

2.2 CNN Based Detection Network Block

A novel CNN based detection method has been proposed here. The purpose of using this block is to detect all possible moving objects in the previously extracted sub-window.

Network Architecture. The inputs to the network are a combination of current and previous frames. The current frame image is cropped and scaled to the same size of previous frame. Difference of two corresponding frames in a video, can localize moving objects. Unlike feeding difference image to the deep network, a weighted subtraction layer has been used. Weights are learned by the network itself. The following equation shows output of the layer.

$$OutLayer = W_1 \times inLayer1 - W_2 \times inLayer2 \tag{2}$$

Where, W_1 and W_2 are the weights to be learnt. The $inLayer1$ and $inLayer2$ are previous and current frames respectively. The output of the layer is fed to a deep CNN network. The subtraction layer focuses on the moving objects only and reduces most of the non moving backgrounds. Along with subtruction block, We have used tiny YOLOV2 [21] as a detection network. The tiny YOLOV2 uses its own custom network architecture called Darknet53 [21]. It has only 9 convolution layers. The detection network is very fast and accurate. The loss function used here is similar to [21] but only for object or background class. It is a combination of three loss functions: localization loss, confidence loss and classification loss. The network output is the coordinates of the moving object in the current frame inside the search region.

Network Training. The Darknet53 is pre-trained on COCO [17] dataset. For finetuning, UAVDT [9] multi-object UAV dataset has been used. During training, two successive frames are cropped randomly and passed to the network. To avoid overfitting, affine transformation is used for data prepossessing.

2.3 Efficient Convolution Operator Based Tracking Block

In order to cope with scene changes and exactly localize the position of the single object to be tracked, each region proposals are correlated with the previous frame template using the high-performance efficient convolution operator with handcrafted features (ECO-HC). It is a state of art tracking algorithm and the base tracker for DT-MPT. The tracker is proposed by Danelljan et al. [4]. Unlike other correlation-based trackers, ECO-HC uses a factorized convolution operator. It reduces the dimensionality of the feature set and improves speed and performance. It is defined as,

$$J_{Df}\{x\} = Df * J\{x\} = f * D^T J\{x\} \tag{3}$$

The matrix D is a projection matrix or linear dimensionality reduction matrix of size $N \times M$, where $N > M$ and M is the filter dimension. The projection matrix D and filter f is learned jointly by solving a loss function using the Gauss-Newton method. Unlike updating filter parameters in every frame, ECO-HC uses a Gaussian Markov Model (GMM) which represents various target appearances.

Re-detection: In many cases, the detection network may not find any candidate patches. The reason could be no object present, partially occluded object or static or very slowly moving object. In those situation ECO-HC uses a cropped patch of the search region near the object's previous location as candidate patch for accurate localization of the target.

2.4 Multipath Based Tracking

Most of the tracking algorithm (Single path trackers) considers maximum location in the response map as object's accurate location. Under challenging situations such as presence of similar object, color, texture and occlusion these trackers often fails to track object due to considering single maxima. In those situations multipath based tracking methods performs much better due to considering multiple peaks of similar value nearby. Unlike the previously proposed algorithm [2], we have used Peak to Sidelobe Ratio (PSR) to compute threshold score. PSR is used for evaluation quality of response in the response map [3]. The expression equation is given by:

$$PSR = \frac{R_{\max} - \mu_{s1}}{\sigma_{s1}} \tag{4}$$

where $R_{\max}$ is the maximum scores of the response map. $s1$ is the side lobe region around the peak, and μ_{s1} and σ_{s1} are the mean value and standard deviation of the side lobe area. The PSR value reduces significantly due to inaccurate localization of the object often happens due to similar object or occlusion. In the proposed method, if the computed score of the current frame is greater than its respective historical average values with a certain ratio, the output is considered reliable. A threshold score T_{MPT} is chosen based on PSR for switching the algorithm between choosing single location (single path mode) and multiple locations (multi-path mode). Unlike the previous work [2], here we have used a non-max suppression (NMS) within a small window to filter out some peaks present in very close proximity. This process helps the multipath algorithm to explore the entire response map and reduce its computation time by considering less number of locations. An example of the proposed method is shown in Fig. 3. The same notations has been used as proposed in [2] for convenience. The condition, PSR between two successive frames, fails from frame $t+1$ to $t+2$ and the algorithm switches to the multipath mode. As a result, two locations are selected after applying NMS. In the next frame $t+3$, four locations are considered from each of the two locations. Continuing this process increases computational burden exponentially, a level threshold is used L_{max}. If for any frame, the current level L satisfies the condition $L > L_{max}$, algorithm switches to single-path mode. Now exact location in frames $t+2$, $t+3$ and $t+4$ are computed by finding the path that has maximum PSR from frame $t+1$ to $t+5$ by using the shortest path algorithm [7].

3 Experimental Analysis

3.1 Setup

The proposed method is implemented on a PC with processor Intel i5 3.2 GHz, 16 GB RAM and Nvidia GPU. Due to the abrupt movement of moving objects, the Kalman filter motion model measurement noise covariance is considered as 10. The process noise covariance is taken as 0.01. The search region bounding

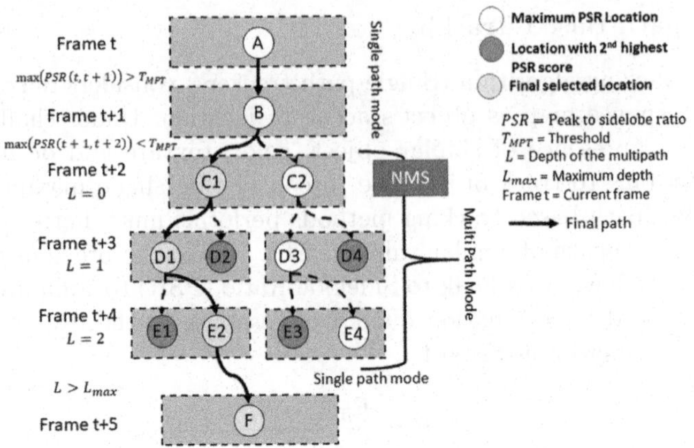

Fig. 3. Mutlipath based tracking method example

box size is taken as five times object size. The real-time tiny YOLOV2 detection network is used for fast detection. The anchor box size for the region proposal layer is taken as 5. To improve tracking speed, handcrafted features have been used in the ECO-HC tracker. Histogram of Oriented Gradients (HOG) and Color Names (CN) features and other parameters are taken same as in [2] for comparison. The tiny YOLOV2 is trained to detect any moving object. There may be some wrong background patch detection due to the movement of the camera. The tracking block rejects all those patches after correlation. During no object detection, the re-detection method in tracking block uses reduced (three times of object size) patch size to track the object. The threshold value (T_{MPT}) is estimated by trial and error and kept same throughout the experiment for each dataset. The maximum depth ($L_{\max}$) of the multipath block is taken as 4. A buffer network is used to store upto three frames for processing during multipath algorithm during real time implementation. In this implementation, a very few (two) local peaks are taken due to the inclusion of the NMS algorithm, which boosts its performance. The proposed algorithm runs in almost real-time ($\sim 20fps$) while achieving better accuracy and robustness.

3.2 Evaluation Metrics

Our tracker is evaluated using conventional precision and success plots as used in OTB 2013 benchmark [24]. Precision plot is calculated by measuring location error or the Euclidean distance between the estimated target center position and ground truth centers. The success plot measures an overlap score (OS). An overlap score is defined as,

$$OS = \frac{|B_t \cap B_g|}{|B_t \cup B_g|} \tag{5}$$

Where, B_t is the target bounding box and B_g is the ground truth bounding box. The precision plot measures the percentage of videos have location error less than 20 pixels whereas the success plot measures the percentage of videos have overlap score less than 0.5. All the trackers are ranked using the area under the curve (AUC).

3.3 Results on Different UAV Datasets

The DT-MPT is evaluated on three challenging benchmark datasets, UAV123@10fps, UAV20L and DTB70. The proposed traker is compared with its base tracker ECO-HC [4], multipath based ECO-HC tracker (ECO-MPT) [2] and several top performing deep learning and handcrafted feature based trackers, such as, SiamRPN [14], MDNet [19], SRDCF [5], MEEM [25], MUSTER [12] and SO-DLT [23].

UAV123@10fps [18]. The UAV123 dataset contains 123 short duration videos. UAV123@10fps is the downsampled version of the UAV123 dataset. The dataset is more challenging than UAV123 due to the large movement of objets to be tracked. The proposed DT-MPT algorithm excels all the other top performing trackers while achieving a significant boost of 5.52% for base tracker ECO-HC, 3.32% for multipath based tracker ECO-MPT and 1.84% for Deep tracker SiamRPN in terms of success rate, thus providing better robustness against large object motion. Figure 5 shows a comparison of overall precision and success plots. The success rates under various attributes are shown in Table 3. DT-MPT performs much better in most of the attributes.

UAV20L [18]. The UAV20L dataset contains 20 long-duration video sequences. In long duration sequences, object may get occluded, disappear and reappear again. Figure 4 shows a comparison of overall precision and success plots. The success rates under various attributes are shown in Table 2. The proposed method outperforms all the state of art trackers including ECO-HC by 14.49%, ECO-MPT by 7.97% and SiamRPN by 4.40% in overall success rate, thus proving its ability to handle drift and object reappearance.

DTB70 [15]. This dataset consists of 70 low resolution UAV videos. It has several challenging video sequences of small object, cluttered scenes. Our method outperforms ECO-HC and ECO-MPT by 8.55% and 2.77% respectively in success rates, thus providing better robustness in cluttered scenes and presence of occlusion. Figure 6 shows a comparison of overall precision and success plots. The success rates under various attributes are shown in Table 4. The tracker perform better in most of the attributes. The proposed tracker performance has some dependency over its base tracker performance. For some attributes, such as deformation, out plane rotation, the proposed tracker performance hampers due to the poor performance of ECO-HC.

Table 1. An ablation study on UAV20L dataset

Configurations	Precision	Success rates	Average FPS
DT-MPT (ours)	**0.682**	**0.474**	20
DT-MPT without MD	0.640	0.451	29
DT-MPT without MP	0.591	0.442	25
DT-MPT without MD and MP	0.549	0.414	36

3.4 Ablation Study

Here, a very brief analysis of the algorithm is given under different configurations. Considering different experimental settings following three configurations are made:
DT-MPT without motion-detection (MD) block uses linear interpolation for search window estimation and patch size is the same as the search window size.
DT-MPT without multipath (MP) block only excludes multipath block.
DT-MPT without MD and MP block uses only the tracking block.
Performance analysis is implemented on UAV20L dataset, as shown in the Table 1. The analysis shows that the tracker without MD and MP block performs worst. The MP and MD block increases some computation complexity but gives a significant boost in performance.

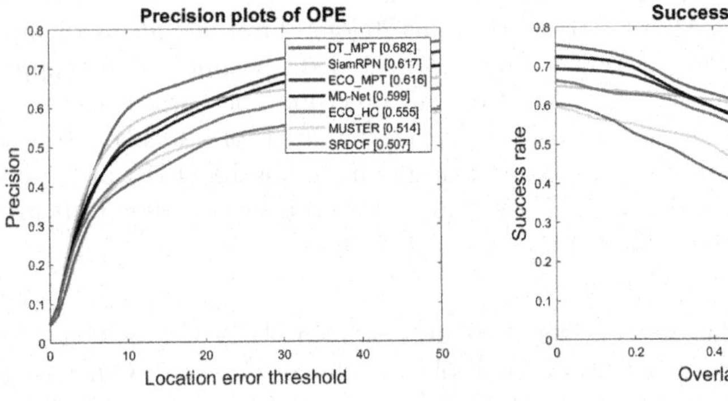

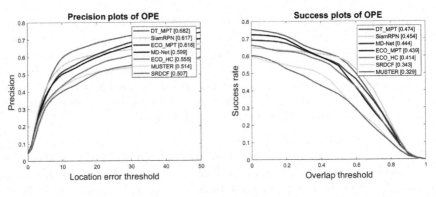

Fig. 4. A visualization of overall precision and success plots on UAV20L dataset.

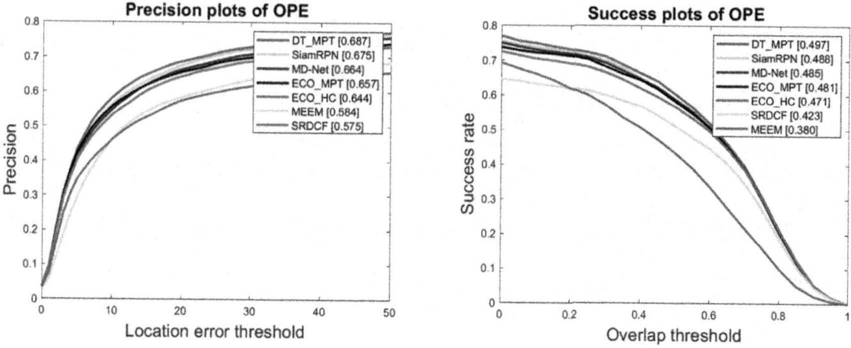

Fig. 5. A visualization of overall precision and success plots on UAV123@10fps dataset

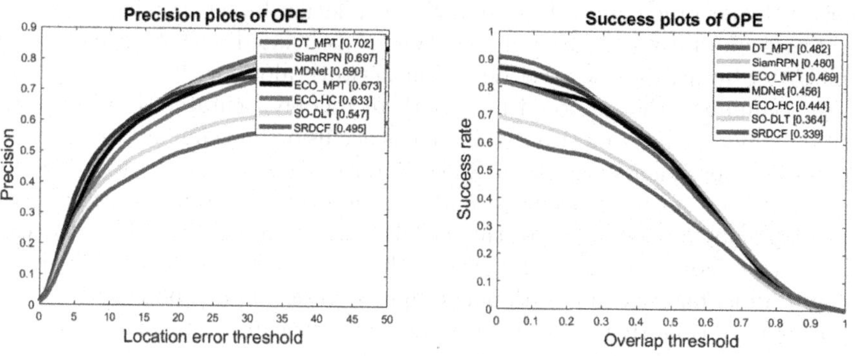

Fig. 6. A visualization of overall precision and success plots on DTB70 dataset

Table 2. Success rates comparison with other trackers on UAV20L dataset

Trackers	Camera Motion	Partial Occlusion	Full Occlusion	Scale Variation	Similar Object	Aspect Ratio Change	Background Clutter	Fast Motion	Illumination Variation	Low Resolution	Out of View	View point Change	**Overall**
DT-MPT	0.458	0.445	0.323	0.467	0.534	0.417	0.306	0.389	0.427	0.349	0.438	0.416	**0.474**
SiamRPN [14]	0.436	0.423	0.267	0.444	0.532	0.388	0.104	0.422	0.343	0.335	0.479	0.450	0.454
MDNet [19]	0.427	0.425	0.222	0.429	0.485	0.370	0.243	0.305	0.406	0.327	0.398	0.381	0.444
ECO-MPT [2]	0.421	0.418	0.267	0.430	0.476	0.376	0.250	0.325	0.372	0.325	0.411	0.386	0.439
ECO-HC [4]	0.396	0.391	0.248	0.399	0.440	0.337	0.250	0.278	0.372	0.301	0.385	0.366	0.414
SRDCF [6]	0.327	0.320	0.170	0.332	0.397	0.270	0.156	0.197	0.295	0.228	0.329	0.303	0.343
MUSTER [12]	0.307	0.305	0.200	0.314	0.342	0.275	0.230	0.206	0.242	0.278	0.301	0.318	0.329

Table 3. Success rates comparison on other trackers on UAV123@10fps dataset

Trackers	Camara Motion	Similar Object	Fast Motion	Out of View	Full Occlusion	Aspect Ratio Change	Background Clutter	Illumination Variation	Low Resolution	Partial Occlusion	Scale Variation	View Point Change	**Overall**
DT-MPT	0.496	0.432	0.289	0.464	0.525	0.430	0.359	0.357	0.426	0.326	0.437	0.458	**0.497**
SiamRPN [14]	0.476	0.428	0.287	0.455	0.504	0.427	0.376	0.343	0.428	0.318	0.422	0.447	0.488
MDNet [19]	0.475	0.426	0.268	0.451	0.494	0.420	0.355	0.348	0.396	0.331	0.412	0.420	0.485
ECO-MPT [2]	0.463	0.484	0.334	0.405	0.265	0.408	0.332	0.390	0.323	0.420	0.446	0.417	0.481
ECO-HC [4]	0.449	0.479	0.321	0.388	0.256	0.409	0.355	0.382	0.313	0.410	0.434	0.265	0.471
SRDCF [6]	0.399	0.421	0.311	0.368	0.229	0.346	0.263	0.333	0.237	0.355	0.390	0.356	0.423

Table 4. Success rates comparison on DTB70 dataset

Trackers	Camara motion	Similar object	Out plane rotation	Out of view	Occlusion	In plane rotation	Background clutter	Deformation	Scale variation	Overall
DT-MPT	0.510	0.509	0.317	0.407	0.505	0.642	0.430	0.415	0.453	**0.482**
SiamRPN [14]	0.495	0.487	0.336	0.393	0.487	0.438	0.377	0.433	0.503	0.480
ECO-MPT [2]	0.497	0.482	0.326	0.402	0.480	0.441	0.416	0.407	0.440	0.469
MDNet [19]	0.467	0.444	0.360	0.435	0.464	0.657	0.406	0.441	0.416	0.456
ECO-HC [4]	0.466	0.449	0.271	0.387	0.440	0.555	0.329	0.391	0.437	0.444
SO-DLT [23]	0.313	0.306	0.332	0.346	0.336	0.495	0.274	0.446	0.368	0.364
SRDCF [6]	0.360	0.330	0.162	0.343	0.289	0.421	0.233	0.227	0.331	0.339

4 Conclusions

In this work, a detection based multipath correlation filter has been proposed to improve the accuracy and robustness of a correlation based tracking algorithm. The tracker addresses some of the challenges associated with tracking objects from UAVs by utilizing a novel detection network along with a modified multipath technique. The proposed multipath technique accurately localize object position under challenging situations such as occlusion and similar objects. Comprehensive experiments on several UAV datasets show much-improved performance in terms of overall accuracy and precision than the top performing state of art single object tracking algorithms while running in real-time. The algorithm can be made more efficient by increasing the depth of the multipath block, but it may lead to higher computational complexity due to an exponential increase in the computation. However, the pruning technique can be considered to reduce the computational burden.

Acknowledgement. The first author was financially supported for carrying out part of the work from project IMPRINT 1, Ministry of Human Resource Development, Government of India.

References

1. Bewley, A., Ge, Z., Ott, L., Ramos, F., Upcroft, B.: Simple online and realtime tracking. In: 2016 IEEE International Conference on Image Processing (ICIP), pp. 3464–3468. IEEE (2016)
2. Bhunia, H.S., Deb, A.K., Mukhopadhyay, J.: Multipath based correlation filter for visual object tracking. In: Deka, B., Maji, P., Mitra, S., Bhattacharyya, D.K., Bora, P.K., Pal, S.K. (eds.) PReMI 2019. LNCS, vol. 11942, pp. 490–498. Springer, Cham (2019). https://doi.org/10.1007/978-3-030-34872-4_54
3. Bolme, D.S., Beveridge, J.R., Draper, B.A., Lui, Y.M.: Visual object tracking using adaptive correlation filters. In: 2010 IEEE Computer Society Conference on Computer Vision and Pattern Recognition, pp. 2544–2550. IEEE (2010)
4. Danelljan, M., Bhat, G., Shahbaz Khan, F., Felsberg, M.: Eco: efficient convolution operators for tracking. In: Proceedings of the IEEE Conference on Computer Vision and Pattern Recognition, pp. 6638–6646 (2017)

5. Danelljan, M., Hager, G., Shahbaz Khan, F., Felsberg, M.: Convolutional features for correlation filter based visual tracking. In: Proceedings of the IEEE International Conference on Computer Vision Workshops, pp. 58–66 (2015)
6. Danelljan, M., Hager, G., Shahbaz Khan, F., Felsberg, M.: Learning spatially regularized correlation filters for visual tracking. In: Proceedings of the IEEE International Conference on Computer Vision, pp. 4310–4318 (2015)
7. Dijkstra, E.W., et al.: A note on two problems in connexion with graphs. Numerische mathematik **1**(1), 269–271 (1959)
8. Dogra, D.P., et al.: Video analysis of Hammersmith lateral tilting examination using Kalman filter guided multi-path tracking. Med. Biol. Eng. Comput. **52**(9), 759–772 (2014)
9. Du, D., et al.: The unmanned aerial vehicle benchmark: object detection and tracking. In: Proceedings of the European Conference on Computer Vision (ECCV), pp. 370–386 (2018)
10. Held, D., Thrun, S., Savarese, S.: Learning to track at 100 FPS with deep regression networks. In: Leibe, B., Matas, J., Sebe, N., Welling, M. (eds.) ECCV 2016. LNCS, vol. 9905, pp. 749–765. Springer, Cham (2016). https://doi.org/10.1007/978-3-319-46448-0_45
11. Henriques, J.F., Caseiro, R., Martins, P., Batista, J.: High-speed tracking with kernelized correlation filters. IEEE Trans. Pattern Anal. Mach. Intell. **37**(3), 583–596 (2015)
12. Hong, Z., Chen, Z., Wang, C., Mei, X., Prokhorov, D., Tao, D.: Multi-store tracker (muster): A cognitive psychology inspired approach to object tracking. In: Proceedings of the IEEE Conference on Computer Vision and Pattern Recognition, pp. 749–758 (2015)
13. Kalman, R.E.: A new approach to linear filtering and prediction problems (1960)
14. Li, B., Yan, J., Wu, W., Zhu, Z., Hu, X.: High performance visual tracking with siamese region proposal network. In: Proceedings of the IEEE Conference on Computer Vision and Pattern Recognition, pp. 8971–8980 (2018)
15. Li, S., Yeung, D.Y.: Visual object tracking for unmanned aerial vehicles: a benchmark and new motion models. In: Proceedings of the Thirty-First AAAI Conference on Artificial Intelligence, pp. 4140–4146 (2017)
16. Li, Y., Zhu, J.: A scale adaptive kernel correlation filter tracker with feature integration. In: Agapito, L., Bronstein, M.M., Rother, C. (eds.) ECCV 2014. LNCS, vol. 8926, pp. 254–265. Springer, Cham (2015). https://doi.org/10.1007/978-3-319-16181-5_18
17. Lin, T.-Y., et al.: Microsoft COCO: common objects in context. In: Fleet, D., Pajdla, T., Schiele, B., Tuytelaars, T. (eds.) ECCV 2014. LNCS, vol. 8693, pp. 740–755. Springer, Cham (2014). https://doi.org/10.1007/978-3-319-10602-1_48
18. Mueller, M., Smith, N., Ghanem, B.: A benchmark and simulator for UAV tracking. In: Leibe, B., Matas, J., Sebe, N., Welling, M. (eds.) ECCV 2016. LNCS, vol. 9905, pp. 445–461. Springer, Cham (2016). https://doi.org/10.1007/978-3-319-46448-0_27
19. Nam, H., Han, B.: Learning multi-domain convolutional neural networks for visual tracking. In: Proceedings of the IEEE Conference on Computer Vision and Pattern Recognition, pp. 4293–4302 (2016)
20. Redmon, J., Divvala, S., Girshick, R., Farhadi, A.: You only look once: unified, real-time object detection. In: Proceedings of the IEEE Conference on Computer Vision and Pattern Recognition, pp. 779–788 (2016)
21. Redmon, J., Farhadi, A.: Yolo9000: better, faster, stronger. In: The IEEE Conference on Computer Vision and Pattern Recognition (CVPR), July 2017

22. Ren, S., He, K., Girshick, R., Sun, J.: Faster R-CNN: towards real-time object detection with region proposal networks. In: Advances in Neural Information Processing Systems, pp. 91–99 (2015)
23. Wang, N., Li, S., Gupta, A., Yeung, D.Y.: Transferring rich feature hierarchies for robust visual tracking. arXiv preprint arXiv:1501.04587 (2015)
24. Wu, Y., Lim, J., Yang, M.H.: Online object tracking: a benchmark. In: Proceedings of the IEEE Conference on Computer Vision and Pattern Recognition, pp. 2411–2418 (2013)
25. Zhang, J., Ma, S., Sclaroff, S.: MEEM: robust tracking via multiple experts using entropy minimization. In: Fleet, D., Pajdla, T., Schiele, B., Tuytelaars, T. (eds.) ECCV 2014. LNCS, vol. 8694, pp. 188–203. Springer, Cham (2014). https://doi.org/10.1007/978-3-319-10599-4_13
26. Zhang, Y., Wang, D., Wang, L., Qi, J., Lu, H.: Learning regression and verification networks for long-term visual tracking. arXiv preprint arXiv:1809.04320 (2018)

Graph-Based Depth Estimation in a Monocular Image Using Constrained 3D Wireframe Models

Bishshoy Das, H. Pallab Jyoti Dutta(✉), and M. K. Bhuyan

Department of Electronics and Electrical Engineering, IIT Guwahati, Guwahati 781039, India
{bishshoy,h18,mkb}@iitg.ac.in

Abstract. In this paper, the problem of estimating the depth of an object from its monocular image is addressed. Here, basically, an algorithm is developed, which performs shape matching, and as a result, achieve accurate depth maps of objects. In the algorithm, first, an optimal camera position is determined. Then, the 3D model is projected onto the image plane of the camera, yielding a projected 2D image of the 3D model. An objective function determines a score based on graph-based feature matching, and the depth map is extracted from the geometrical information of the 3D model. Finally, the depth map and the original image are combined to create a 3D point cloud simulation of the object. Experimental analysis shows the efficacy of the proposed method.

Keywords: Monocular image · Depth map estimation · Wireframe model · 3D reconstruction

1 Introduction

Depth estimation of a scene from monocular images is an elemental problem in computer vision. With the rapid development of machine learning, most of the recent techniques of depth estimation have focused on learning depth estimator models from pixel data [1], stereo cues [2] and semantic labels [3]. Markov Random Fields trained via supervised learning of depth cues has ramified Make3D [4], which yields excellent depth maps of unstructured scenes. These techniques are well suited for outdoor scenes, and also where there are lots of pixels belonging to separate object classes, *viz.,* sky, tree, road, grass, water, building, mountain and foreground objects [3]. Other works rely on stereo vision [5,11] or structure derived from motion [6]. Both of these methods require two or more images. Shape from shading [7] extracts photometric cues from a single image, which becomes challenging when surfaces have non-uniform color or texture. Geometric cues like vanishing points [8], horizon and surface boundaries [9] can only determine the affine structure of images.

In this paper, we present an algorithm to generate depth maps only from a single image that contains an object on a white background, using graph-based

S. K. Singh et al. (Eds.): CVIP 2020, CCIS 1378, pp. 419–433, 2021.
https://doi.org/10.1007/978-981-16-1103-2_35

image representation [10]. We focus on the very basic fact that an image is a projection of a 3D object on two dimensions of the image plane of a camera. The human brain assumes that the image of a hand-drawn cube is that of a cube because a 3D model of a cube exists well-defined in its memory. We make this assumption as the only explicit assumption in our algorithm. The proposed method is explained in the sections to follow.

2 Proposed Method

The algorithm flow is presented in Fig. 1. There are three computational blocks and one flowchart connecting all these blocks. In the graph feature extractor block, we take an image, use its corners and edges to determine a vertex list and an adjacency matrix of the graph representation of the image. In the score function block, we take two graph representations of two different images (the object image and the rendered image), and compute the distance between their representations in terms of the centroid, surface area, overlap area, vertex and edge scores. All these scores are then added together to form a combined score. In the optimization stage, we show the flow of the optimization algorithm. Finally, in the flowchart, we show how all the blocks are connected together.

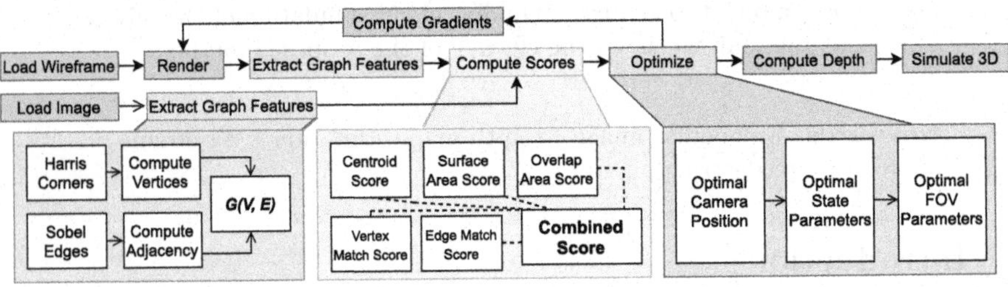

Fig. 1. Block diagram of the purposed algorithm

First, we load the object's monocular image. Then we extract its graph features using the graph feature extractor block. We also initiate a 3D model and feed it to the optimizer. The optimizer instantiates a state vector of the 3D model, feeds it to the renderer, which generates the image of the 3D model for the given state. Then the graph feature extractor extracts graph features from it. Both the graph representation of the object image and the rendered image of the 3D model is fed to the scoring function block, which computes all the different aforementioned scores and feeds it back to the optimizer. The optimizer performs gradient ascent and tweaks the state vector in a way to maximize the scores. After enough iterations, the optimal state vector is obtained which is used to extract the depth map and subsequently perform a point cloud simulation of the input object.

2.1 Graph-Based Features

Graph-based methods are used for structure detection, which also gives us an estimation of the depth map.

Graph Vertices: We set the corners of the image to be the vertices V of the graph G. The corners of the 2D object image (I_R-image) are extracted using the Harris corner detector.

Graph Adjacency Matrix: Adjacency matrix A_R is an $N \times N$ matrix, where $N = |V|$ and $A_R(i,j) = 0$ or $1, \forall\ 1 \leq i \leq N,\ 1 \leq j \leq N$ indicating the absence or presence of an edge, respectively, between v_i and v_j. To determine the values of the adjacency matrix A_R, we used the following approach. We extract the edge map image I_E of I_R using the Canny edge detector. We define a square mask image I_M of size $n \times n$ pixels. To determine $A_R(i,j)$, we center the mask on a corner point v_i. We traverse the mask I_M on a line connecting corners points v_i and v_j. We count the number of white pixels between them. If it is greater than 90% of the Manhattan distance between the two, then $A_R(i,j)$ is 1 or else 0.

2.2 Constrained 3D Wireframe Models

3D models of primitive shapes like cubes and spheres are created, adhering to the *OpenGL* format (homogeneous coordinate system). The vertices of the 3D model V and the edges E is defined as a graph $G = (V, E)$ in terms of adjacency matrix A. Centered around the origin, we allow the models to scale unconstrained in x, y and z directions. This consideration also allows higher level shapes to be taken into account using one single primitive model. A model of a cube may generate a family of cuboids. This generalization allows one model to encompass a larger number of 3D models while not explicitly changing the graph (wireframe). This imposes constraints on the 3D models and it reduces the number of possible solutions in the degenerate problem of finding a 3D model from a 2D image.

2.3 Operations on the 3D Models

Model-View-Projection Matrices: Our models are defined within the clip space specified by *OpenGL* specifications. So, the model matrix M is simply the identity matrix I_4. View matrix Λ models the camera's position $\overrightarrow{e}$, it's *look-at* direction $\overrightarrow{l}$ (from point $\overrightarrow{e}$) and it's orientation $\overrightarrow{u}$ (orthogonal to $\overrightarrow{l}$). In Sect. 2.6, we discuss our approach to find the optimal camera position. Direction at which the camera is pointing is fixed at $\overrightarrow{l} = [0\ 0\ 0]^T$, and orientation of the camera is fixed at $\overrightarrow{u} = [0\ 1\ 0]^T$ to reduce redundant camera movements. All the possible states of the wireframe model which can be generated by varying $\overrightarrow{l}$ and $\overrightarrow{u}$. These states can also be generated by varying $\overrightarrow{\theta}$. The projection matrix Pr models the field of view θ_{fov} of the *"lens"* mounted on the camera. We set the frustum's near plane (or the image plane) to be 0.1 unit from the camera and the far infinite plane to be 10 units away. θ_{fov} will be all also be optimized during gradient ascent. The above matrices are generated using the *OpenGL Mathematics* library. The model-view-projection matrix is therefore, can be represented as: $MVP(\overrightarrow{e}) = Pr \times \Lambda(\overrightarrow{e}) \times M = Pr \times \Lambda(\overrightarrow{e})$.

Affine Transformation: Affine Transformation is also applied in the order: Translation → Rotation → Scaling.

Thus, the Affine Transform matrix is defined as:

$$AT = \begin{pmatrix} s_x \cos\theta_y \cos\theta_z & -s_y \sin\theta_z \cos\theta_y & -s_z \sin\theta_y & t_x \\ s_x \sin\theta_x \sin\theta_y \cos\theta_z + s_x \cos\theta_x \sin\theta_z & -s_y \sin\theta_x \sin\theta_y \sin\theta_z + s_y \cos\theta_x \cos\theta_z & s_z \sin\theta_x \cos\theta_y & t_y \\ s_x \cos\theta_x \sin\theta_y \cos\theta_z - s_x \sin\theta_x \sin\theta_z & -s_y \cos\theta_x \sin\theta_y \sin\theta_z - s_y \sin\theta_x \cos\theta_z & s_z \cos\theta_x \cos\theta_y & 0 \\ 0 & 0 & 0 & 1 \end{pmatrix}$$

Note that the translation in z direction is redundant in the presence of scaling and hence eliminated. Finally the operations are combined as: $MVP \times AT$.

2.4 State Vector

The proposed state vector $\overrightarrow{X}$ is a *9-dimensional* vector, and it is represented as: $\overrightarrow{X} = [s_x\ s_y\ s_z\ \theta_x\ \theta_y\ \theta_z\ t_x\ t_y\ \theta_{fov}]^T$.

Projected Images: Each state vector $\overrightarrow{X}$ represents a state of the 3D model (first *8-dimensions*) and the camera parameter (θ_{fov}). Each state is rendered using the *OpenGL* API to generate the projected image I_X, which has a resolution of $R_X \times R_Y \times 3$ and 24-bit color depth. This projection operation is represented as: $P(\overrightarrow{X}) = I_X$. The corners of the 3D model are rendered as a square of 5 px width and blue color. Edges are rendered as white straight lines. Triangles are filled with red color, and the background is painted as black. In our tests, R_X =720 px and R_Y =720 px for all the images.

2.5 Score Functions

The score function $F(I_X)$ (or the combined score function), generates a numerical value based on the graph of $G_X = (V_X, E_X)$, (which is the graph of I_X) and other several sub-score functions. They are- Centroid score function $F_G(I_X)$, Vertex score function $F_V(V_X)$, Edge score function $F_E(E_X)$, Surface Area score function $F_S(I_X)$, Overlap Area score function $F_O(I_X)$.

Centroid Score: The centroid area score measures the closeness of the centroid of the two images, I_R and I_X. We define a function $L_X\left(\begin{bmatrix} x \\ y \end{bmatrix}\right)$ on image I_X and pixel coordinate $[x\ \ y]^T$ as: $L_X\left(\begin{bmatrix} x \\ y \end{bmatrix}\right) = \begin{cases} 0, & \bigwedge_{k=1}^{3} I_X(x,y,k) = 0, \\ 1, & otherwise \end{cases} \begin{cases} 1 \le x \le R_X \\ 1 \le y \le R_Y \end{cases}$.

Also, we define $L_R\left(\begin{bmatrix} x \\ y \end{bmatrix}\right)$ on image I_R and pixel coordinate $[x\ y]^T$ as: $L_R\left(\begin{bmatrix} x \\ y \end{bmatrix}\right) = \begin{cases} 0, & \bigwedge_{k=1}^{3} I_R(x,y,k) = 255, \begin{cases} 1 \le x \le R_X \\ 1 \le y \le R_Y \end{cases} \\ 1, & otherwise \end{cases}$. L_X indicates whether $I_X(x,y)$ is foreground pixel or background pixel. All background pixels in I_X are *black*. The same is performed by L_R except for all the background pixels in I_R which are *white*.

The centroids of I_X and I_R are computed respectively as:

$$C(I_X) = \left\lfloor \frac{\sum_{i=1}^{R_X}\sum_{j=1}^{R_Y} L_X\left(\begin{bmatrix} i \\ j \end{bmatrix}\right)\begin{bmatrix} i \\ j \end{bmatrix}}{\sum_{i=1}^{R_X}\sum_{j=1}^{R_Y} L_X\left(\begin{bmatrix} i \\ j \end{bmatrix}\right)} \right\rfloor, C(I_R) = \left\lfloor \frac{\sum_{i=1}^{R_X}\sum_{j=1}^{R_Y} L_R\left(\begin{bmatrix} i \\ j \end{bmatrix}\right)\begin{bmatrix} i \\ j \end{bmatrix}}{\sum_{i=1}^{R_X}\sum_{j=1}^{R_Y} L_R\left(\begin{bmatrix} i \\ j \end{bmatrix}\right)} \right\rfloor$$

Next, we define $C'(I_R)$ as the maximum possible distance from the centroid of I_R and the square bounded by $[0\ 0]^T$ and $[R_X\ R_Y]^T$. We use this value for normalizing the centroid score.

$$C'(I_R) = \max\begin{pmatrix} \left\|C(I_R) - [0\ 0]^T\right\|_2, \\ \left\|C(I_R) - [R_X\ 0]^T\right\|_2, \\ \left\|C(I_R) - [0\ R_Y]^T\right\|_2, \\ \left\|C(I_R) - [R_X\ R_Y]^T\right\|_2 \end{pmatrix}$$

The centroid score of I_X is calculated as: $F_G(I_X) = 1 - \frac{||C(I_X) - C(I_R)||_2}{C'(I_R)}$

Graph-Based Scores: Graph-based scores enable the optimization algorithm to select structurally, better-projected images. We compare the graph representation of the object image I_R (which is $G_R = (V_R, E_R)$) with the graph representation of the projected image I_X (which is $G_X = (V_X, I_X)$) to generate two sets on independent scores, the vertex score $F_V(V_X)$ and the edge score $F_E(V_E)$.

Vertex Score: Corners of the image I_X are set as the vertices of the graph representing I_X. Corners of I_X are detected by detecting patches of blue pixels and the coordinates are set as V_X. To compute the vertex score, we associate all vertices in V_X with some vertex in G_R (which is the graph for I_R, *i.e.*, $G_R = (V_R, E_R)$) and form a new vertex list, V_C. The ith item in the list V_C is defined as:

$$V_C^{(i)} = \underset{v\, \in\, V_R}{\arg\min} \left\|V_X^{(i)} - v\right\|_2$$

$V_C^{(i)}$ is, therefore, that vertex in G_R, which is closest to the vertex $V_X^{(i)}$; the vertex distance being measured as the Euclidean distance between the two pixels they represent. The proposed vertex score is then computed as:

$$F_V(V_X) = 1 - \frac{\sum_{i=1}^{|V_X|} \|V_X(i) - V_C(i)\|_2}{|V_X|\sqrt{R_X^2 + R_Y^2}}$$

Edge Score: The edge score measures the number of edges common in both graphs G_R and G_X. Calculation of *Edge score* is illustrated in Fig. 2.

Fig. 2. (a) Blue dotted line indicates an edge in G_R. Red dotted line indicates an edge in G_X. The corners are matched but edges are not. *Corner score* = 1, *Edge score* = 1. (b) Blue dotted line indicates an edge in G_R. Red dotted line indicates an edge in G_X. Both corners and edges are matched. *Corner score* = 1, *Edge score* = 2 (Color figure online)

On a global scale, a higher edge score means a better state vector of the 3D model. For example, in Fig. 3 both the configuration (3.b) and (3.c) yield very high centroid scores, surface area scores and overlap area scores, but (3.c) gives less edge score. Thus, structurally, configuration (3.c) is preferred over the configuration (3.b), in the optimization process. We use the algorithm used for Graph Adjacency Matrix to construct the adjacency matrix A_X of G_X (graph of I_X). Hereafter, we compare the adjacency matrices of the two graphs (V_C, A_X) and (V_R, A_R) to calculate the edge score by exploiting the fact that $V_C \subseteq V_R$. We create a list λ, the ith element of which is given by: $\lambda^{(i)} = j \mid V_C^{(i)} = V_R^{(j)}$.

Therefore, the mapping λ indicates the location in V_R at which a vertex in V_C is to be found out. Consequently, we can also get to know which row-column in A_X should be compared to row-column in A_R for an edge in A_X to be "matched" with an edge in A_R. Then, we count the number of edges "matched" in both the adjacency matrices. To avoid over-counting, we initialize a matrix ρ of dimensions $|V_R| \times |V_R|$ and initialize all the values in ρ as 0. We mark $\rho(\lambda(i), \lambda(j))$ to 1 to indicate that the edge $A_R(\lambda(i), \lambda(j))$ has been counted. Since A is symmetric, we also mark $\rho(\lambda(j), \lambda(i))$ as counted. We initialize a counting variable, $c = 0$, and apply the following formula to count the number of edge matches as:

$$\left.\begin{array}{r} c := c + 1 \\ \rho(\lambda(i), \lambda(j)) = 1 \\ \rho(\lambda(j), \lambda(i)) = 1 \end{array}\right\}, \text{ if } \left\{\begin{array}{c} A_X(i, j) = 1 \\ A_R(\lambda(i), \lambda(j)) = 1 \\ \rho(\lambda(i), \lambda(j)) = 0 \end{array}\right.$$

We formulate our proposed edge score as: $F_E(E_X) = 1 + c$

The addition of 1 doesn't allow the combined score to become zero if there are absolutely no edge matches, which may happen during the initial few iterations of optimization.

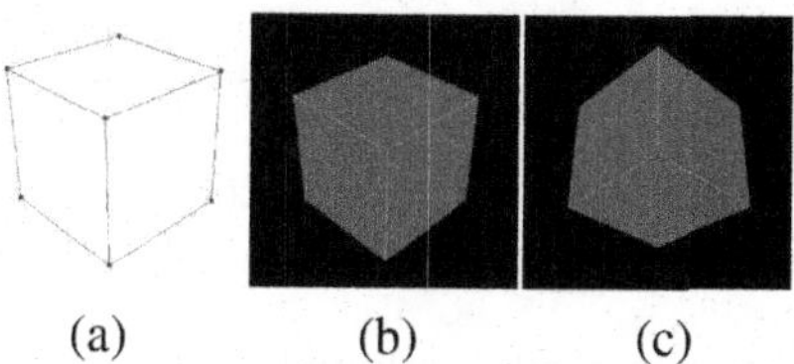

Fig. 3. (a) A graph of a cube object; (b) A configuration of a 3D cube model. *Edge score* = 10, since there are 9 matched edges with the graph shown in (a). The *centroid score, surface area score* and *overlap area scores* are very high; (c) A different configuration, which also has a very high *centroid score, surface area score* and *overlap area score,* but has a lower *Edge score* of 7, since there are only 6 matched edges.

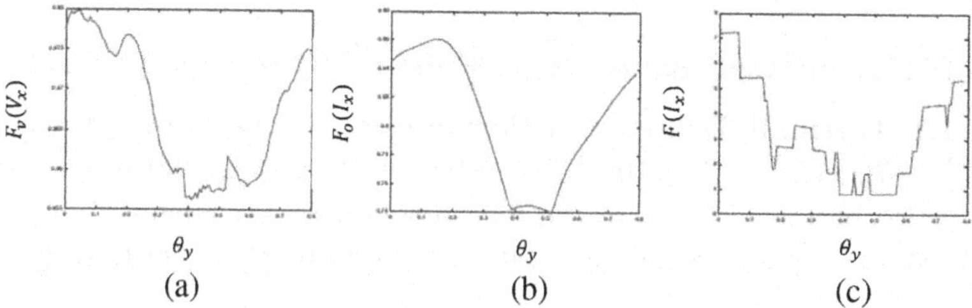

Fig. 4. Variation of different score functions in the optimization process of fitting a 3D wireframe model of a cube in a similar cube like 2D image (in this case, a Rubik's cube). All state parameters are determined at optimization stage 1, where a good camera position is obtained. Then the cube is rotated about the y-axis, and the following plots of various scores are noted. (a) Plot of $F_V(V_X)$ vs. θ_y ; (b) Plot of $F_O(I_X)$ vs. θ_y; (c) Plot of $F(I_X)$ vs. θ_y. This indicates that the overlap area score is a smoother function, and hence, it is well applicable for gradient ascent.

Surface Area Score: The surface area score measures the area footprint of I_X and compares to that of I_R. The surface area σ is calculated as:

$$\sigma(I_R) = \sum_{i=1}^{R_X} \sum_{j=1}^{R_Y} L_R\left(\begin{bmatrix} i \\ j \end{bmatrix}\right), \sigma(I_X) = \sum_{i=1}^{R_X} \sum_{j=1}^{R_Y} L_X\left(\begin{bmatrix} i \\ j \end{bmatrix}\right)$$

The proposed surface area score is defined as: $F_S(I_X) = 1 - \frac{|\sigma(I_X) - \sigma(I_R)|}{\sigma(I_R)}$

Overlap Area Score: The pixels common in I_R and I_X is calculated as (Fig. 4):

$$L_{X,R}\left(\begin{bmatrix} x \\ y \end{bmatrix}\right) = \begin{cases} 1, L_X\left(\begin{bmatrix} x \\ y \end{bmatrix}\right) = L_R\left(\begin{bmatrix} x \\ y \end{bmatrix}\right) \\ 0 \qquad otherwise \end{cases}$$

The overlap area $\Omega(I_X)$ is defined as: $\Omega(I_X) = \sum_{i=1}^{R_X} \sum_{j=1}^{R_Y} L_{X,R}\left(\begin{bmatrix} i \\ j \end{bmatrix}\right)$

The union area $\Gamma(I_X)$ is defined as: $\Gamma(I_X) = \sigma(I_R) + \sigma(I_X) - \Omega(I_X)$

The overlap area score is measured as: $F_O(I_X) = 1 - \frac{\Gamma(I_X) - \Omega(I_X)}{\Gamma(I_X)}$

Combined Score: The proposed combined score $F(I_X)$ is defined such that the effect of both overlap area score and the edge score are high and is given as:

$$F(I_X) = F_E(E_X) \times \frac{c_1 F_G(I_X) + c_2 F_V(V_X) + c_3 F_S(I_X) + c_4 F_O(I_X)}{c_1 + c_2 + c_3 + c_4}$$

2.6 Proposed Optimization Stages

Stage 1: Finding Optimal Starting Point for Gradient Ascent

Stage 1.1: Optimal Translation Parameters. We begin by optimizing the centroid score $F_G(I_X)$ over the translation parameters t_x and t_y of the state vector $\overrightarrow{X}$ for better accuracy in the following progressive stages. t_x^* and t_y^* are the optimal translation parameters and the operation is performed as: $\{t_x^*, t_y^*\} = \arg\max_{t_x,\ t_y} F_G(P(\overrightarrow{X}))$, subject to: $t_x \in \mathbb{R},\ t_y \in \mathbb{R}$

The update equation is defined as: $\overrightarrow{X} := \overrightarrow{X} + \eta \overrightarrow{\nabla} F_G(P(\overrightarrow{X}))$

The gradient operation is performed as:

$$\frac{\partial F_G(P(\overrightarrow{X}))}{\partial x_i} = \frac{F_G(P([x_1, \ldots, x_i + h, \ldots, x_9]^T)) - F_G(P(\overrightarrow{X}))}{h}$$

Stage 1.2: Initial Pass for Determining Scaling Parameters. This stage of the optimization process tries to obtain a good camera position for viewing the 3D model. We fix the camera at a distance of 20 units of clip space coordinates, invoke gradient ascent on the overlap area score, and restrict the search dimensions only to the scaling parameters $(s_x,\ s_y,\ s_z)$, such that $s_x = s_y = s_z$.

$$\arg\max_{s_x, s_y, s_z} F_O(P(\overrightarrow{X})), \text{subject to: } s_x \in \mathbb{R},\ s_y \in \mathbb{R},\ s_z \in \mathbb{R},\ s_x = s_y = s_z$$

The update equation is therefore be written as: $\overrightarrow{X} := \overrightarrow{X} + \eta \overrightarrow{\nabla} F_O(P(\overrightarrow{X}))$ The gradient operation is performed as:

$$\frac{\partial F_O(P(\overrightarrow{X}))}{\partial x_i} = \frac{F_O(P([x_1, ..., x_i + h, ..., x_9]^T)) - F_O(P(\overrightarrow{X}))}{h}$$

Based on the following criteria, η and h are adjusted with each iteration j. Let the mean combined score in the jth iteration be:

$$\mu^{(j)} = \left(\frac{1}{9} \sum_{i=1}^{9} \frac{\partial F(P(\overrightarrow{X}))}{\partial x_i}\right)\Bigg|_j$$

Then η_{j+1} and h are calculated as:

$$\eta_{j+1} = \begin{cases} \eta_j/2, \text{ if } \mu_j > \mu_{j+1} \\ 0.1, \text{ if } \eta_j < 0.01 \end{cases}, \quad h := \frac{h}{2}, \text{ if } \eta_j < 0.01$$

Stage 1.3: Optimal Camera Position and Scaling Parameters. We place the camera in several latitude-longitude intersections of an imaginary sphere. Denoting, latitudes as ϕ and longitudes as θ, we have limits $-90° \leq \phi < 90°$ and $0° \leq \theta < 360°$ to cover the entire sphere. We generate linearly spaced latitudes in set Φ and linearly spaced latitudes in set Θ. So for every element in set $\Phi \times \Theta$, we compute camera position vector $\overrightarrow{p}$ as:

$$\overrightarrow{p} = \begin{bmatrix} r\cos(\theta)\cos(\phi) & r\sin(\theta)\cos(\phi) & r\sin(phi) \end{bmatrix}^T$$

We update the view matrix Λ with camera position $\overrightarrow{p}$, and optimize the overlap area score function with the same constraints over the scaling parameter. The gradient ascent update is then performed as:

$$\underset{s_x, s_y, s_z}{\arg\max} F_O(P(\overrightarrow{X})), \text{subject to: } s_x \in \mathbb{R}, \ s_y \in \mathbb{R}, \ s_z \in \mathbb{R}, \ s_x = s_y = s_z$$

The update equation is: $\overrightarrow{X} := \overrightarrow{X} + \eta\overrightarrow{\nabla} F_O(P(\overrightarrow{X}))$
The optimal camera position $\overrightarrow{p^*}$ is that $\overrightarrow{p}$ which yields the highest combined score, and it is given by: $\overrightarrow{p^*} = \arg\max_{\overrightarrow{p}} F(P(\overrightarrow{X}) \mid \overrightarrow{p})$
The optimal scaling parameter s^* is therefore be written as:

$$s^* = \underset{s_x}{\arg\max} F(P(\overrightarrow{X}) \mid \overrightarrow{p^*}), \text{subject to: } s_x \in \mathbb{R}, s_y \in \mathbb{R}, s_z \in \mathbb{R}, s_x = s_y = s_z$$

Stage 2: Optimal Wireframe Model Parameters. After determining the optimal camera position $\overrightarrow{p^*}$ and the optimal scaling parameters s^*, we use this information to initiate gradient ascent on all the parameters of the state vector $\overrightarrow{X}$, except for the camera parameter θ_{fov}. As the first 8 parameters control the wireframe model alone, it would be computationally beneficial as optimization in one of the dimensions is excluded. We have chosen 30° or $\pi/6$ as the field of view of the camera's lens. To maximize the overlap area score, only 8 parameters of the wireframe model are taken into account. We optimize the overlap area score $F_O(I_X)$, but select the optimal state vector having the highest combined score $F(I_X)$. Thus, the optimization process and the update equations are defined as follows:

$$\underset{s_x, s_y, s_z, t_x, t_y, r_x, r_y, r_z}{\arg\max} F_O(P(\overrightarrow{X}) \mid \overrightarrow{p^*}) \text{ subject to: } s_x, s_y, s_z, t_x, t_y, r_x, r_y, r_z \in \mathbb{R}$$

$$\overrightarrow{X} := \overrightarrow{X} + \Psi \times \overrightarrow{\nabla} F_O(P(\overrightarrow{X}))$$

where, Ψ is a diagonal matrix. The ith diagonal element $\Psi(i,i)$ represents the step size for the ith dimension. We use the following approach to determine $\Psi(i,i)$.

$$\text{If } F_O(P(\overrightarrow{X})) < 0.9, \Psi(i,i) = \begin{cases} 0.1, \text{ if } \frac{\partial F_O(P(\overrightarrow{X}))}{\partial x_i} \geq \frac{1}{9}\sum_{i=1}^{9} \frac{\partial F_O(P(\overrightarrow{X}))}{\partial x_i} \\ 0.05, \qquad otherwise \end{cases}$$

$$\text{If } F_O(P(\overrightarrow{X})) \geq 0.9, \quad \Psi(i,i) = 0.05$$

Stage 3: Optimal Wireframe Model and Camera Model Parameters. In the final stage, we allow all the parameters of the state vector to be modified in order to improve the scores even further. Thus, we also find the optimal camera model parameter θ_{fov} in this stage. The optimization and update equations are:

$$\arg\max_{\overrightarrow{X}} F_O(P(\overrightarrow{X}) \mid \overrightarrow{p^*}) \text{ subject to: } s_x, s_y, s_z, t_x, t_y, r_x, r_y, r_z, \theta_{fov} \in \mathbb{R}$$

$$\overrightarrow{X} := \overrightarrow{X} + \eta \overrightarrow{\nabla} F_O(P(\overrightarrow{X}))$$

2.7 Depth Map Extraction

The actual depth values are normalized and all the non-object pixels are set to 0. The new depth values are: $D(i,j) = \begin{cases} \frac{d_{max} - Z(i,j)}{d_{max} - d_{min}}, \text{ if } Z(i,j) \neq 1 \\ 0 \qquad \text{otherwise} \end{cases}$

2.8 Combining Object Image and Depth Map

After we extract the depth map D, we combine it with object image I_R to simulate a 3D experience of what the real object actually was.

3 Experimental Results

We tested our algorithm on various images of different structures. A comparison of the ground truth depth maps, the depth maps generated by our algorithm and other methods are shown in Fig. 5. Also, optimal camera positions obtained after optimization stage 1 are shown, along with the final wireframe model output. A comparison of a 2D image and its depth map is shown by overlaying the 2D image on the depth map with 50% transparency. The scores are shown in Table 2. The RMS error between the ground truth and the depth map generated by our algorithm is given in Table 1.

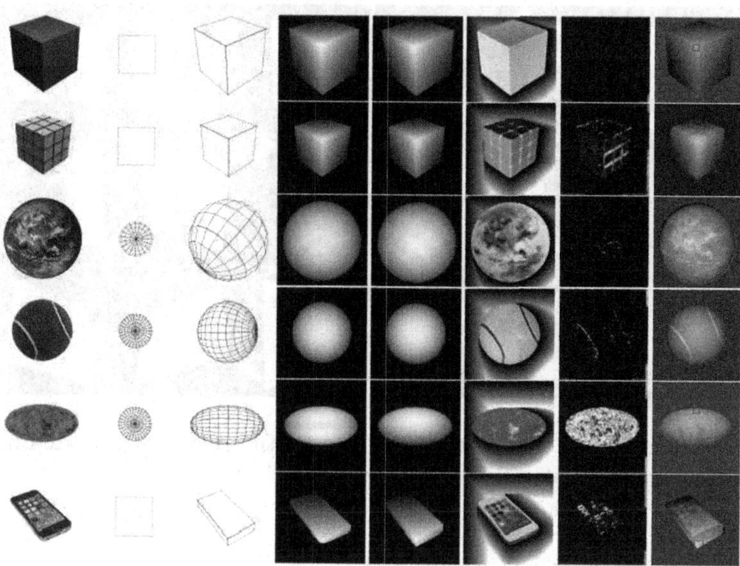

Fig. 5. Col 1 shows 2D object image; Col 2 shows corresponding 3D wireframe model and it's initial state; Col 3 shows final state of the wireframe model (i.e. output of optimization stage 3); Col 4 shows Ground truth depth map; Col 5 shows the depth map generated by our algorithm; Col 6 shows the depth map generated by shape from shading algorithm [12]; Col 7 shows the depth map generated by depth from defocus algorithm [13]; Col 8 shows overlay comparison of object and depth map. Red squared marks show erroneous areas. (Color figure online)

Table 1. RMS error between the ground truth and the generated depth map

Cube	Rubik's Cube	Earth	Tennis Ball	CMB Map	iPhone
2.892904	0.123181	3.420901	1.975758	5.801795	4.013128

Table 2. Comparison of 2D image and its depth map in terms of a matching score

Object image	Centroid score $F_G(I_X)$	Vertex score $F_V(V_X)$	Edge score $F_E(E_X)$	Surface area score $F_S(I_X)$	Overlap area score $F_O(I_X)$	Combined score $F(I_X)$
Cube	1	0.993406	10	0.998222	0.984951	9.89104
Rubik's Cube	1	0.993827	9	0.997169	0.983042	8.89238
Earth	0.983197	0.976024	107	0.999979	0.96473	103.92
Tennis Ball	0.998044	0.964645	369	0.999724	0.979267	360.614
CMB Map	0.998041	0.971926	404	0.99506	0.978407	395.369
iPhone	0.997234	0.992845	2	0.985505	0.955688	1.94163

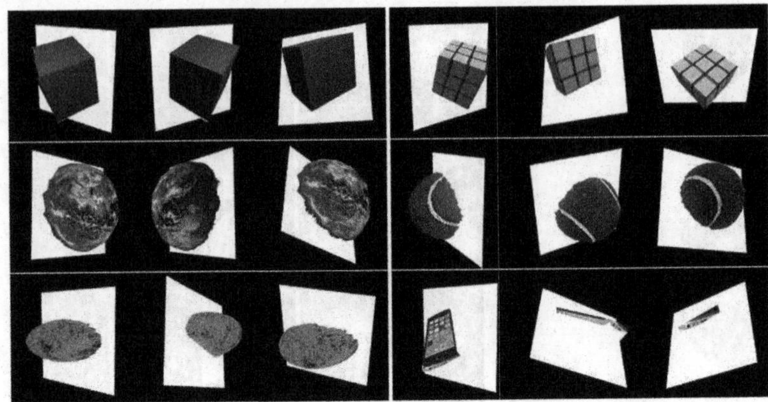

Fig. 6. 3D simulation of Cube, Rubik's Cube, Earth, Tennis Ball for 200 iterations each; CMB Map for 300 iterations; iPhone for 2500 iterations.

3.1 3D Simulation

The simulation of different images are shown in Fig. 6 for different angles. In Fig. 8, we show the transition of the 3D wireframe model from stage 1 (after optimal camera position has been computed) to the final configuration in the optimization stage 3. Even though the wireframe model gets close, but fails to improve after a certain point because of the rounded corners of the iPhone 5S. Figure 9 shows the plot of the RMS error of the depth map over 1200 iterations.

3.2 Facial Reconstruction

Our proposed algorithm can also be employed for 3D facial reconstruction. We demonstrate that using a generic wireframe model of a human face and images of human faces, the algorithm can be used to find the depth map of a human face. Thus, the image and the depth map can be combined to produce a reconstructed 3D model of a person's face (shown in Fig. 7). A part of the experimental simulation of our proposed 3D reconstruction algorithm is available at https://youtu.be/9sz1yvcGoBo.

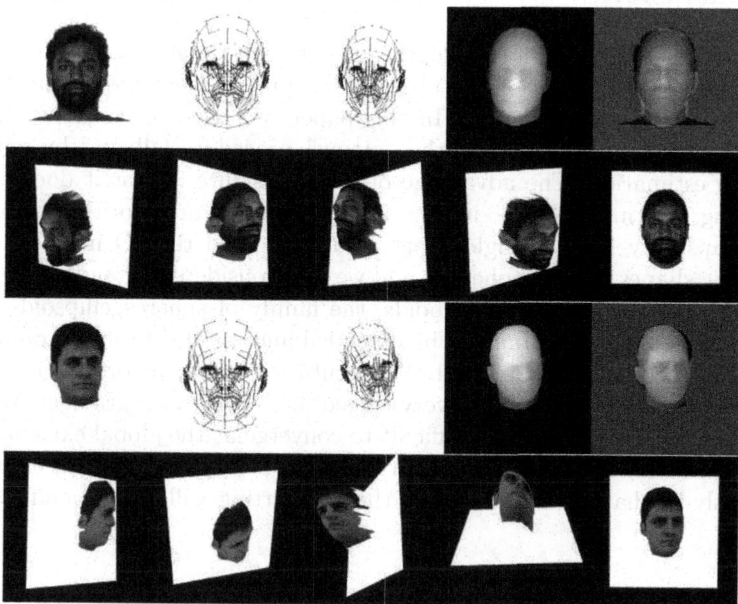

Fig. 7. Row 1 shows (a) Image from Yale Face Database; (b) Initial state of the face wireframe model; (c) Final state after optimization; (d) Depth map of the image of (a) Row 1; (e) Overlay of images (a) and (d) of Row 1. Row 2 shows 3D simulation of the images of Row 1. Row 3 shows (a) Image from FEI Face Database; (b) Initial state of the face wireframe model; (c) Final state after optimization; (d) Depth map of the image (a) of Row 3; (e) Overlay of (a) and (d) of Row 3. Row 4 shows 3D simulation of the images of Row 3.

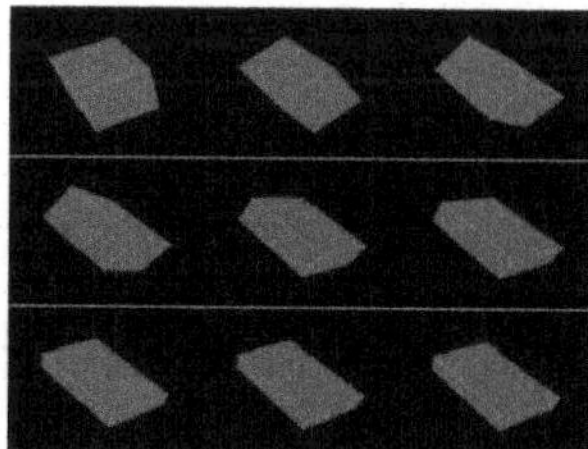

Fig. 8. States of the cube model during iterations of stage 3 optimization. Configuration of the wireframe model after (a) 0, (b) 100, (c) 200, (d) 300, (e) 500, (f) 600, (g) 800, (h) 1200, and (i) 2500 iterations.

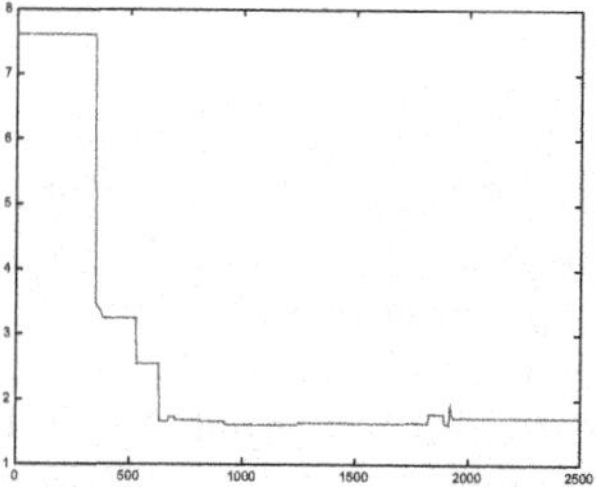

Fig. 9. Depth map RMS error vs. iteration in the estimation of iPhone.

4 Conclusion

When a human brain performs depth perception/estimation of a 2D image, it determines the 3D shape of the object from previous experience and the 3D model registered in its memory. In this paper, we tried to construct an optimization algorithm that mimics the "fitting" procedure followed by our brain for depth estimation. The advantage of this procedure is that it does not rely on shading, lighting, or stereo information. We present an algorithm to generate depth maps only from a single image. We considered the 3D model fitting of some basic shapes (cubes, spheres), and we also considered extended versions of these shapes (family of cubes/cuboids, the family of spheres/ellipsoids). However, our proposed algorithm can be extended and applied to more complicated shapes like face, tree, etc. as well. The limitation of our algorithm is that the objective function is non-convex, very jagged, with high value gradients throughout the search space. It is very difficult to converge at the global extrema. Also, another disadvantage of our algorithm is that if the object image has a structure not exactly as that of the 3D model, then the fitting will be bad and less than perfect.

References

1. Saxena, A., Chung, S.H., Ng, A.Y.: Learning depth from single monocular images. In: Advances in Neural Information Processing Systems, pp. 1161–1168 (2006)
2. Saxena, A., Schulte, J., Ng, A.Y.: Depth estimation using monocular and stereo cues. IJCAI **7**, 2197–2203 (2007)
3. Liu, B., Gould, S., Koller, D.: Single image depth estimation from predicted semantic labels. In: IEEE Conference on Computer Vision and Pattern Recognition (CVPR), pp. 1253–1260. IEEE (2010)
4. Saxena, A., Sun, M., Ng, A.Y.: Learning 3-D scene structure from a single still image. In: IEEE 11th International Conference on Computer Vision, ICCV 2007, pp. 1–8 (2007)
5. Scharstein, D., Szeliski, R.: A taxonomy and evaluation of dense two-frame stereo correspondence algorithms. Int. J. Comput. Vis. **47**(1–3), 7–42 (2002). https://doi.org/10.1023/A:1014573219977
6. Forsyth, D., Ponce, J.: Computer Vision: A Modern Approach. Prentice Hall, Upper Saddle River (2011)
7. Zhang, R., Tsai, P.-S., Cryer, J.E., Shah, M.: Shape-from-shading: a survey. IEEE Trans. Pattern Anal. Mach. Intell. **21**(8), 690–706 (1999)
8. Criminisi, A., Reid, I., Zisserman, A.: Single view metrology. Int. J. Comput. Vis. **40**(2), 123–148 (2000). https://doi.org/10.1023/A:1026598000963
9. Heitz, G., Gould, S., Saxena, A., Koller, D.: Cascaded classification models: combining models for holistic scene understanding. In: Advances in Neural Information Processing Systems, pp. 641–648 (2009)
10. Jain, A.K., Dubes, R.C.: Algorithms for Clustering Data. Prentice-Hall Inc., Upper Saddle River (1988)
11. Malathi, T., Bhuyan, M.K.: Asymmetric occlusion detection using linear regression and weight-based filling for stereo disparity map estimation. IET Comput. Vis. **10**(7), 679–688 (2016). https://doi.org/10.1049/iet-cvi.2015.0214

12. Ping-Sing, T., Shah, M.: Shape from shading using linear approximation. Image Vis. Comput. **12**(8), 487–498 (1994)
13. Chakrabarti, A., Zickler, T.: Depth and deblurring from a spectrally-varying depth-of-field. In: Fitzgibbon, A., Lazebnik, S., Perona, P., Sato, Y., Schmid, C. (eds.) ECCV 2012. LNCS, vol. 7576, pp. 648–661. Springer, Heidelberg (2012). https://doi.org/10.1007/978-3-642-33715-4_47

AE-CNN Based Supervised Image Classification

Ganduri Chandra(✉) and Muralidhar Reddy Challa(✉)

Indian Institute of Technology, Hyderabad, Hyderabad, India
{manichandra,ai19mtech11009}@iith.ac.in

Abstract. Point of Care Ultrasound (PoCUS) imaging is an important tool in detecting lung consolidations and tissue sliding, and hence has a potential to identify the onset of novel-CoVID-19 attack in a person. Of late, Convolutional Neural Network (CNN) architectures have gained popularity in improving the accuracy of the predictions. Motivated by this, in this paper, we introduce a CNN based Auto Encoder (AE-CNN) for a better representation of the features to get an accurate prediction. While most of the existing models contain 'fully connected' (FC) layers, in our work, we use only convolutional layers instead of FC layers before the output layer, which helps us in achieving a less training time of the model. Moreover, fully connected layers of a network can not learn the patterns in an image as much as convolutional layers can. This is the main advantage of our model over its existing counterparts. We demonstrate that our model detects the lung abnormalities in the ultrasound images with an accuracy of 96.6%.

Keywords: Convolution Neural Network · Extreme Gradient Boosting (XGBoost) · Image processing · Lung ultrasound · Machine learning

1 Introduction

In the recent months, novel corona virus (n-CoVID-19) has wrecked havoc across the world, impacting millions of lives and their livelihoods. As a result, curbing n-CoVID-19 has become a matter of primary concern for clinicians. Driven by the dire need in controlling this pandemic, several researchers have started putting in their efforts for early diagnosis and treatment at affordable costs.

In view of unknown nature of the n-CoVID virus, it is necessary to develop novel ways for evaluating patients who are suspected to be infected with it. Early computed tomography (CT) scanning of the patients might be beneficial, because patients may demonstrate radiologic findings before the onset of the symptoms. Lung ultrasound (LUS) imaging is a practical tool for detecting abnormalities in the lungs. Recent literature [1] (and the references therein) suggests that LUS diagnosis has its own advantages because of mobility and correlation with the radiological findings for the pneumonia.

Ultrasound imaging is purely based on the sound reflections, which occur at the surface of the lungs when the ultrasound waves cross the air-tissue interface.

S. K. Singh et al. (Eds.): CVIP 2020, CCIS 1378, pp. 434–442, 2021.
https://doi.org/10.1007/978-981-16-1103-2_36

Even to date, experience in handling the LUS is only limited to the pneumologists and the professionals working in the intensive care Units (ICUs). It has been shown [2,3] that the Lung Ultrasound technique has the ability to define the alterations affecting the ratio between the tissue and the air in the lungs. The surface of the normal lungs contains air. Incident sound waves mostly get reflected back when the lungs are healthy. The scattered waves produce artifacts characterized by the horizontal lines (A-lines) as shown in the Fig. 1(a).

In this work, we consider the severity of the n-CoVID-19 attack in four stages. In stage 1 of the abnormality, various types of vertical artifacts (B-lines, shown in Fig. 1(b)) appear in the ultrasound images in relation to the alterations of the pleura tissue. As a result, the ratio between the air and tissues starts reducing. In Fig. 1(c), it may be observed that the width of the B-Lines increases as the pleura line depletes. This is the stage 2 of the problem. Appearances of the B-lines so obtained from the ultrasound images are very heterogeneous.

Consolidations start accumulating into lungs, which is clearly visible in Fig. 1(d). This is the 3rd stage of severity. Most of the parts of pleura line get affected. In the 4th stage (final stage), lungs get filled with the consolidations. As a result, there would be no space for the flow of air inside lungs. This can be clearly seen in Fig. 1(e).

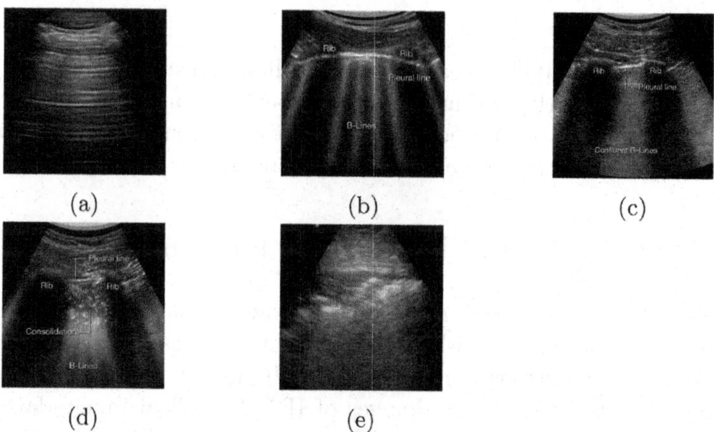

Fig. 1. Lung Ultrasound Images: (a). A-Lines, (b). B-Lines, (c). Confluent B-Lines, (d). Confluent B-Lines with Consolidations and (e). Consolidations.

There is an evidence that Ultrasound may be comparable to both radiology and CT in terms of detecting the abnormalities in the pleura line [4]. Lung ultrasound helps in both identification and subsequent monitoring of the suspected viral infections, even before the progression of respiratory symptoms in some cases.

Conventional methods, such as PCA-based feature extraction methods, have been widely used in many applications like face recognition, object identification etc. Any method whose architecture of the network is remarkably simple compared to the traditional architectures such as ResNet, DensNet, Inception, VGG-16 etc. seems to have great value for faster execution of classification problems. In view of the stated need, we propose a new Auto-Encoder, which is broadly an unsupervised neural network model learning compressed version of the input data. It can also use supervised learning methods while training the network. As a result, our auto-encoder may be termed as a 'self-supervised' learning method.

Most of the existing Auto-Encoder models involve few 'fully connected' (FC) layers in latent space. In this paper, we use only convolutional layers instead of FC layers. By this approach, we observe that using only convolutional layers and no FC layers takes less training time of the model. Moreover, fully connected layers of a network cannot learn the patterns in an image as much as convolutional layers can. This is the main advantage of our model over the existing ones. The contributions of this work are as follows:

1. Proposing an efficient Auto-Encoder model from which we extract global features for the classification of the Lung Ultrasound Image data.
2. Applying an ML classifier (XG-Boost, in particular) to the features of the labeled data, extracted from Latent space of our proposed model, to achieve a better accuracy.
3. Retrieving, additionally, the original images from the output of our model with minimum loss.

The rest of the paper is organized as follows. Section 2 presents a brief overview of related works and motivation for our work in more detail. Section 3 presents a summary of our proposed model. Section 4 contains our experimental results. Section 5 discusses some concluding remarks.

2 Related Works and Motivation for Current Work

A Deep Neural Networks based Autonomous model for both detection and localization of the abnormalities (B-lines) from a 'Lung Ultrasound video' has been introduced in [5]. A clustering method using dictionary learning has been proposed in [6], wherein the similar images of IRMA medical image database are grouped into clusters using K-SVD. The authors of [7] have introduced deep learning based localization and extraction of both A-lines and B-lines from the Ultrasound imaging. In this method, all the frames have been given as input source to the CNN to predict both the accuracy score and the severity of the disease associated to the input frame.

The work in [8] has proposed an approach using deep learning in the ultrasound imaging systems along with a domain-specific opportunities. Deep neural network model, in general, is designed to encode the input ultrasound data into a compressed latent space (bottle neck layer) using a series of multiple convolutional layers and maxpooling operations.

Detection of the corona virus signatures from a chest X-ray has been introduced in [9]. In which, the authors have used the traditional convolutional neural network model (VGG-16) for the chest X-ray classification and achieved 85% accuracy. As the size of the data set has been small (around 500 images), the authors have appended it by generating synthetic images through GAN Network. Finally, in detecting the signatures of corona virus in X-ray chest images, the authors have achieved an accuracy of 95% after training the model with both original and the synthetic images.

Identifying the abnormalities (B-lines) from Lung ultrasonic requires specific training. A novel method has been designed in [10] for detecting the lines from speckle images. In which it has been claimed that the lines can be restored via solving an inverse problem using the Radon transform. The approach proposed in [10] has divided the problem into a series of sub-problems. Additionally, it has included a blind deconvolution step in the Radon transform domain to obtain a better visualisation and also improve line detection accuracy, particularly, when convex or non-convex optimisation techniques are applied for the restoration of lines. Based on the results, authors have been able to identify B-lines from the images automatically and obtain an accuracy of more than 50% compared to its existing counterparts possessing similar objectives. Further, it has been claimed that above approach can be applied to other ultrasound applications where the detection of lines can help the diagnosis.

A novel method has been utilized in [11] for classifying the 2-dimensional fetal ultrasound planes using the CNN based decision fusion classification model. The traditional CNN architecture used in [11] is ALEX-NET.

In the present scenario, a more detailed study on detecting the signatures of n-CoVID-19 from Lung ultrasound images is very much undeniably needed. Further, the performance of the impact on increasing number of extracted features from the intermediate layers of our proposed network on the ML algorithm's detection is required. Lastly, more recent state-of-the-art ML as well as deep learning algorithms should be studied to extract more global features and further improve the accuracy. With these motivations, we now present below our proposed model 'Auto Encoder based CNN'.

3 Auto Encoder Based CNN

Broadly, Auto-Encoder model learns the representations of image data for dimensionality reduction, by training the network to ignore the noise content present in data.

Our motivation to construct an accurate AE-CNN model is to compress the original data and retrieve back with minimum loss, so that the weights of the network get optimized during the training phase. Block level representation and summary of our proposed model are presented in Fig. 2 and Fig. 3.

For effective utilization of both memory and the processing time during testing phase, we extract the features from the bottle neck layer (with the shape $16 \times 16 \times 16$) and apply the same as a feature vector for the Machine Learning based prediction.

Figure 4 and Fig. 5 depict the convolution layers that are added to the bottleneck layer of our AE-CNN model to further reduce the numbers of the features

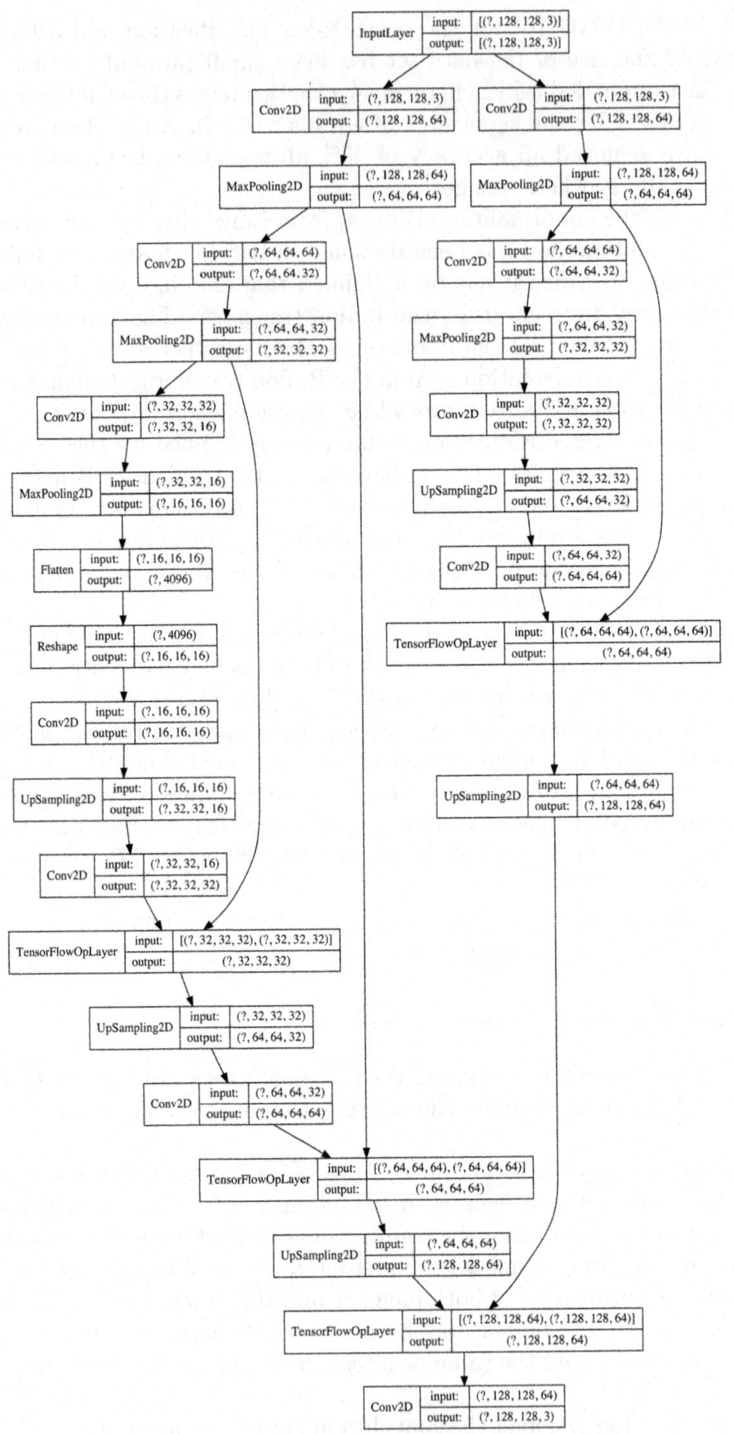

Fig. 2. Summary of our proposed Auto-Encoder model

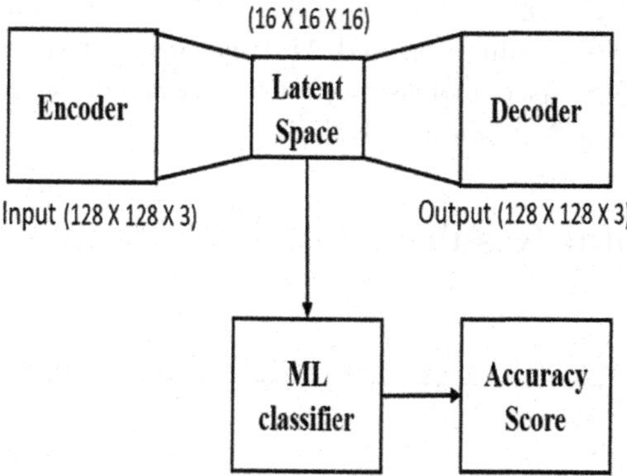

Fig. 3. Block level representation of our proposed model

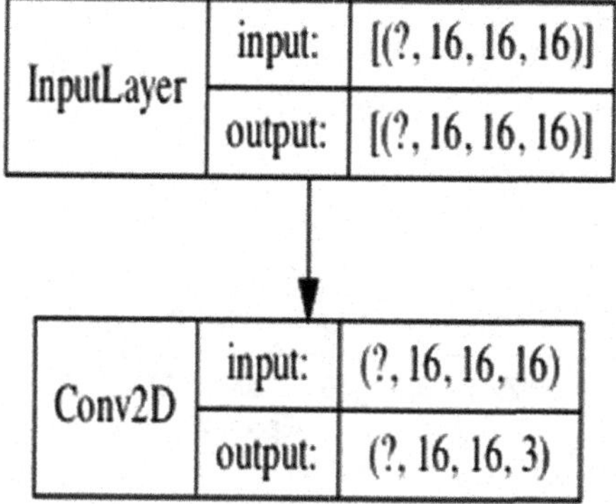

Fig. 4. Summary of the convolution layer added to the latent space of AE-CNN model to reduce the number of features to 768 features.

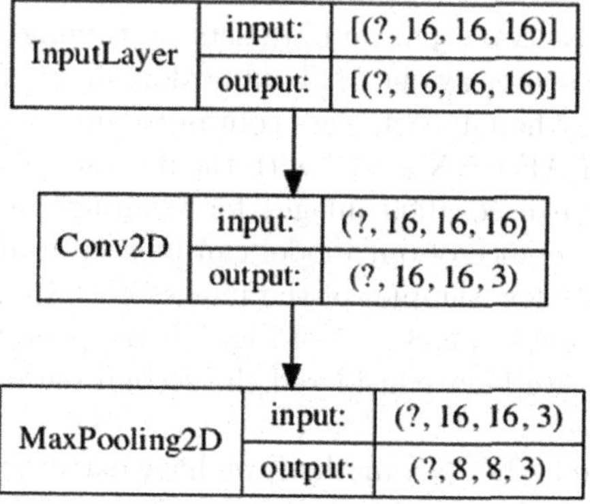

Fig. 5. Summary of the convolution layers added to the latent space of AE-CNN model to further reduce the number of features to 192 features.

to 786 ($=16 \times 16 \times 3$), 192 ($= 8 \times 8 \times 3$) from 4096 features which are extracted from bottle neck layer of our proposed Auto-Encoder model.

The ML classifiers used in this work are XG-Boost, Multilayer perceptron (MLP) and K-Nearest Neighbours (KNN).

4 Experimental Results

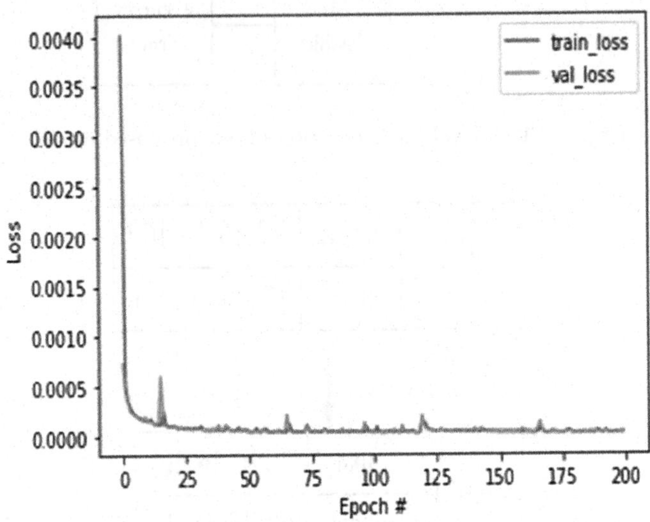

Fig. 6. Loss-Epochs

To begin with, we have developed a CNN based Auto encoder model to get the output same as the input with a minimum loss, as detailed below.

We have considered two separate data sets containing around 800 and 1900 images from the open source available in public domain[1,2]. We have divided these images into 5 classes, wherein each class contains a minimum of 150 images. We have then trained our AE-CNN model with the data set containing 1900 images. Out of these, we have used 1000 images for training leaving the rest for the validation. The performance of our model can be seen from Fig. 6.

Figure 7 represents few samples of the images corresponding to the data set we have considered. Rows 1, 2, 3, 4, 5 of Fig. 7 correspond to classes 1, 2, 3, 4, 5 respectively. Further, we have considered the second dataset containing around 800 images for testing.

Using our proposed AE-CNN method, we have extracted the features of each individual image from these 800 images to train the ML models for accurate

[1] https://www.grepmed.com/?q=covid19.
[2] https://www.butterflynetwork.com/covid19.

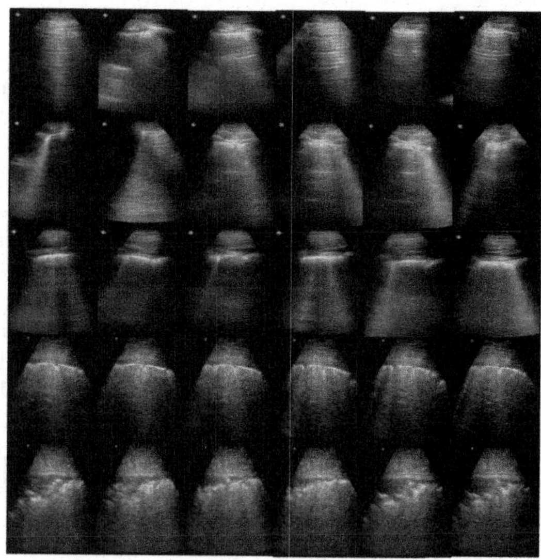

Fig. 7. Data set with images of 5 classes

prediction. We have also used these features as baseline while evaluating the performance of other classifiers. We present the classification results comparing the performance of various ML models in detection of n-CoVID-19 from the ultrasound images in Table 1.

Table 1. Accuracy table

Name of Classifier	4096 Features	768 Features	192 Features
XG-Boost	93.3%	96.6%	91.1%
MLP	92.5%	86.76%	76.15%
KNN	88.8%	88.8%	91.1%

It may also be seen in Table 1 that the accuracy of various classifiers is compared for varying number of input features. From Table 1, it can be concluded that the XGBoost classifier provides best accuracy value of 96.6% while MLP results in the next best performance of 92.5%.

5 Conclusion

In this work, we have introduced an efficient CNN based Auto-Encoder model, from which we have extracted features for the lung image classification. Also our proposed model (AE-CNN) has proven its good performance in the reconstructing the original image. By applying ML to features extracted from latent space we have achieved best accuracy of 96.6% using XG-Boost Classifier.

References

1. Smith, M.J., Hayward, S.A., Innes, S.M., et al.: Point-of-care lung ultrasound in patients with COVID-19 – a narrative review. Anaesthesia **75**, 1096–1104 (2020). https://doi.org/10.1111/anae.15082
2. Miller, A.: Practical approach to lung ultrasound. BJA Educ. **16**, 39–45 (2016). https://doi.org/10.1093/bjaceaccp/mkv012
3. Ioos, V., Galbois, A., Chalumeau-Lemoine, L., et al.: An integrated approach for prescribing fewer chest x-rays in the ICU. Ann. Intensive Care **1**, 4 (2011). https://doi.org/10.1186/2110-5820-1-4
4. Wolfram, F., Braun, C., Gutsche, H., Lesser, T.G.: In-Vivo assessment of lung ultrasound features mimicking viral pneumonia using a large animal model. IEEE Trans. Ultrason. Ferroelectr. Freq. Control. https://doi.org/10.1109/TUFFC.2020.3010299
5. van Sloun, R.J.G., Demi, L.: Localizing B-Lines in lung ultrasonography by weakly supervised deep learning, in-vivo results. IEEE J. Biomed. Health Inform. **24**, 957–964 (2020). https://doi.org/10.1109/JBHI.2019.2936151
6. Srinivas, M., Naidu, R., Sastry, C.S., et al.: Content based medical image retrieval using dictionary learning. Neurocomputing **168** (2015). https://doi.org/10.1016/j.neucom.2015.05.036
7. Roy, S., et al.: Deep learning for classification and localization of COVID-19 markers in point-of-care lung ultrasound. IEEE Trans. Med. Imaging **39**(8), 2676–2687 (2020). https://doi.org/10.1109/TMI.2020.2994459
8. Van Sloun, R.J., Cohen, R., Eldar, Y.C.: Deep learning in ultrasound imaging. Proc. IEEE **108**(1), 11–29 (2019). http://arxiv.org/abs/1907.02994
9. Waheed, A., Goyal, M., Gupta, D., Khanna, A., et al.: CovidGAN: data augmentation using auxiliary classifier GAN for improved Covid-19 detection. IEEE Access **8**, 91916–91923 (2020). https://doi.org/10.1109/ACCESS.2020.2994762
10. Anantrasirichai, N., Hayes, W., Allinovi, M., Bull, D., Achim, A.: Line detection as an inverse problem: application to lung ultrasound imaging. IEEE Trans. Med. Imaging **36**(10), 2045–2056 (2017). https://doi.org/10.1109/TMI.2017.2715880
11. Sridar, P., Kumar, A., Quinton, A., Nanan, R., Kim, J., Krishnakumar, R.: Decision fusion-based fetal ultrasound image plane classification using convolutional neural networks. Ultrasound Med. Biol. **45**, 1259–1273 (2019). https://doi.org/10.1016/j.ultrasmedbio.2018.11.016

Ensemble Based Graph Convolutional Network for Semi Supervised Learning

Rakesh Kumar Yadav(✉), Manikanta Moghili, Abhishek, Prashant Shukla, and Shekhar Verma

Department of IT, Indian Institute of Information Technology Allahabad, Prayagrai, India
{pcl2014003,mit2018004,rsi2016006,rsi2016502,sverma}@iiita.ac.in

Abstract. In this paper, an Ensemble based Graph Convolutional Network **(EGCN)** is proposed for relational datasets. **EGCN** encodes the pairwise similarity between data points for semi supervised learning and feature representation. The GCN model with Laplacian filter is not able to completely explore the local geometry of the data distribution as the null space of Laplacian remains constant along the manifold. This leads to poor extrapolating ability of the GCN model. In order to improve this GCN model, Hessian filter is introduced. The Hessian filter is more efficient and has richer null space. It can encode the relationship among the data points better by fusing structural properties with original features. In our **EGCN**, two parallel GCNs are executed, one with Laplacian filter and other with Hessian filter. In **EGCN** model Laplacian, filter accumulate the information from a data point to all its neighbors and Hessian filter gathers the information between adjacent data points that lie in the neighborhood of a data point. Extensive experiment conducted on various relational datasets indicates that **EGCN** out performs both Laplacian and Hessian filter based GCN models by a significant margin on various relational datasets.

Keywords: Graph Convolutional Network · Semi supervised learning · Laplacian · Hessian · Relational dataset

1 Introduction

Graphs [6,15] are an appropriate and effective way of data representation that can define the pairwise relationship between nodes. They can be utilized for various applications like social networks, recommendation systems, and molecular graph structured datasets [3]. Many other applications [13,14,19] with relational data can also be modeled as a graph for better information approximation. Machine learning model uses the structure of the graph to extract the underlying information. Even though a graph is the most efficient representation of data distribution as it can best describe the intrinsic structure of data. However, an important concern that needs to be addressed is to find an appropriate method to incorporate information about the structure of the graph into the machine learning techniques.

S. K. Singh et al. (Eds.): CVIP 2020, CCIS 1378, pp. 443–451, 2021.
https://doi.org/10.1007/978-981-16-1103-2_37

CNN extracts the common features from an input image by applying Convolutional operations using different filters. It determines the similarity of each pixel by considering its neighboring pixels (minimum of 3 for the corner pixels and a maximum of 8 for non corner pixels). This can be applied to the relational datasets by representing them as images. But, in a graph, the neighborhood may not be fixed or regular. In a connected graph, a node can have at least 1 neighbor and maximum of $n - 1$ neighbors.

For a better data representation for the relational datasets [12], Graph Convolutional Networks (GCNs) [17] is used. GCN is based on Laplacian filter that iteratively bundle the feature information from the local neighborhood graph using neural networks. Its convolution operation transforms and aggregates feature information from a node and its neighbors and propagates the information across the graph. Graph Laplacian on high dimensional manifold approximates the geometry by exploiting the data points in the local region. Graph Laplacian estimates the divergence of gradient of the data generating function. It uses the adjacency matrix to explore the similarity between a node and its neighboring nodes in a relational dataset. Graph Laplacian [1] while estimating the similarity between a node and its adjacent neighbor nodes discards the presence of similarity among the neighbors, which in turn leads to the poor intrinsic geometry estimation. The convolution operation with a filter over a signal on graph nodes can be computed by multiplying the signal and the filter (after transforming them to the Fourier domain) and then transferring the obtained value back to the discrete domain. But GCN [20] with this filter aggregates a comparably lesser number of relations among the node and its neighborhood. As the points lie on a local region, there is a high probability that the neighboring nodes might also be related to each other.

In this paper, we propose an ensemble GCN in which both, Laplacian and Hessian filters, are used for convolution separately. The outputs of the two parallel arms of EGCN are averaged to obtain a better classification result.

2 Ensemble Graph Convolutional Network

EGCN has two parallel GCN models are with Laplacian and the Hessian filters. This section proceeds with a brief detail GCN based on Laplacian filter and Hessian filter [4] followed by the explanation detail analysis how they can aggregated for best results.

2.1 Graph Convolution

Motivated from the spatial domain based on the Euclidean distance, Fourier analysis of the graph depends on the spectral decomposition of graph Laplacian. The graph Laplacian of undirected graph is given by $\mathcal{L} = D - A$, where D is the diagonal matrix. $\mathcal{L}$ is a symmetric positive definite matrix and its eigendecomposition, $\mathcal{L} = \mathrm{U} \wedge \mathrm{U}^T$, where $\wedge$ is diagonal matrix of eigenvalues and its corresponding orthonormal eigenvalues are represented by $\mathrm{U} \in \mathbb{R}^{N \times N}$. This eigenvalue decomposition of the graph Laplacian in the graph domain is equivalent to the Fourier transform in the spectral domain such that eigenvector values are considered to be equal to the Fourier modes and eigenvalue defines the frequencies of the graph.

Consider $x \in \mathbb{R}^N$ be a signal defined on the vertices of the graph. The Fourier transformation of x is defined as $\hat{x} = \mathrm{U}^T x$ and the corresponding inverse operation is given as $x = \mathrm{U}^T \hat{x}$. Based on this, graph convolution operation between x and filter g is defined as,

$$g * x = \mathrm{U}((\mathrm{U}^T g) \otimes (\mathrm{U}^T g)) = \mathrm{U}\hat{\mathrm{G}}\mathrm{U}x,$$

where $\hat{\mathrm{G}}$ is the diagonal matrix containing the spectral filter coefficient. Graph convolution can be approximated with k^{th} order polynomial of the Laplacian.

$$\mathrm{U}\hat{\mathrm{G}}\mathrm{U}^T x \approx \sum_{i=0}^{k} \theta_i \Delta^i x = \mathrm{U}\Big(\sum_{i=0}^{k} \theta_i \wedge^i\Big)\mathrm{U}^T x,$$

where θ_i are the coefficients. This filter coefficients corresponding to the polynomial of the Laplacian eigenvalues are defined as, $\hat{g}(\lambda_j) = \sum_i \theta_i \lambda_j^i$. It can also be defined as $\hat{\mathrm{G}} = \sum_i \theta_i \wedge^i$.

2.2 EGCN

GCN employ the affine approximation as shown in Eq. 1 ($k = 1$) and first two coefficient of the polynomial be $\theta_0 = 2\theta$ and $\theta_1 = -\theta$. Based on this the basic GCN convolution operation be defined as,

$$g \star x = \theta(I + D^{-1/2}AD^{-1/2})x, \tag{1}$$

In order to further refine this GCN model, matrix $D^{-1/2}AD^{-1/2}$ replaced with its normalized version $D^{-1/2}AD^{-1/2}$. The layer wise propagation rule for the GCN can be defined as,

$$H^{l+1} = \sigma(D^{-1/2}AD^{-1/2}H^l W^l), \tag{2}$$

where, σ defines the non linear activation function like $ReLU$. H^l is the feature matrix of the lth iteration, initially $H_1 = X$. The trainable weight is denoted by W. The identity matrix defined along the adjacency matrix to capture the self connections.

The GCN model with Hessian filter [4] is used based on the Hessian matrix. The Hessian filter identifies and explore the relations among the data points with form the neighborhood of the of a data point. In order to compute the Hessian matrix **B**, consider $N(x_i)$ denotes all the data points in the neighborhood of x_i. The independent coordinate system can be estimated by computing a local tangent space centered T_x at x_i. The local coordinate is obtained by PCA on $N(x_i)$ (Fig. 1).

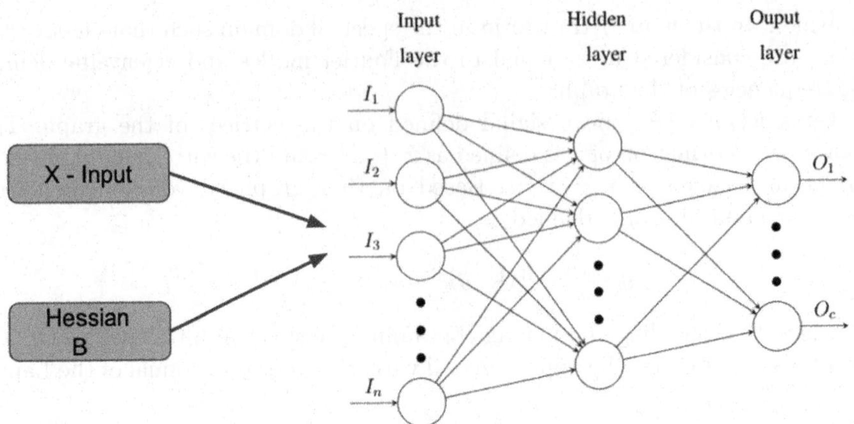

Fig. 1. GCN with Hessian filter

The Hessian approximation is obtained as,

$$\frac{\partial^2 f}{\partial x \partial x}\Big|_{x_i} \approx \sum_{j=1}^{N(x_i)} \mathbf{S} f(x_j), \tag{3}$$

where $\mathbf{S}$ is an operator that defines the relationship between the function values and its second derivatives. It is obtained from the second order Taylor expansion of f at $x_j \in N(x_i)$ by fitting a second order polynomial through least square method. The Frobenius norm of the Eells of f at x_i is obtained as,

$$||\nabla_a \nabla_b f||^2 = \sum_{r,s=1}^{d} \Big(\sum_{j=1}^{N(x_i)} \mathbf{s}_j^{(i)} f(x_j) \Big)^2 = \sum_{j,h=1}^{N(x_i)} f(x_j) f(x_h) \mathbf{B}_{j,h}^{(i)}$$
$$= \langle f^{(i)}, \mathbf{B}^i, f^{(i)} \rangle = \mathbf{f}^T \mathbf{B} \mathbf{f}$$

where , d spans the independent coordinate system using the leading eigenvector and $\mathbf{B}_{j,h}^{(i)} = \sum_{j,h}^{n} \mathbf{S}_j^{(i)} \mathbf{S}_h^{(i)}$ is the needed Hessian. The propagation rule defined by GCN with Hessian matrix filter can be defined,

$$H^{(l+1)} = \sigma(\mathbf{B} H^{(l)} W^{(l)}),$$

where, $H^{(l)}$ is the feature matrix at l^{th} layer, W is the weight matrix, and $\mathbf{B}$ is the Hessian filter obtained from the graph structured dataset.

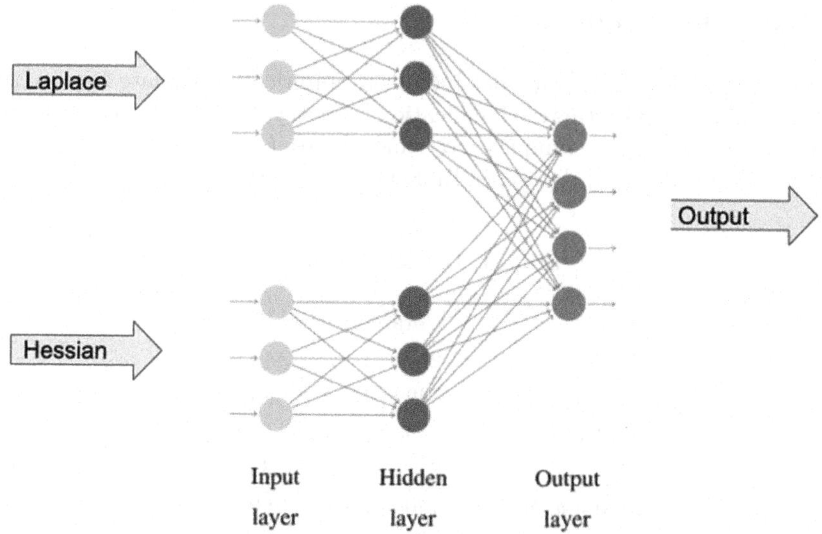

Fig. 2. EGCN model

As shown in the Fig. 2, the two GCN models, one with Laplacian filter and other with Hessian filter is executed to together as two arms of the EGCN model and output is obtained by averaged out for better results. Further the output of both models are concatenated together to form a single representation for EGCN model which is given as input to single softmax layer. The output obtained as passed into the softmax to get the final perception layer as $Z = \text{softmax}(H^{(l)})$. The final output $Z \in \mathbb{R}^{N \times C}$ denotes the label prediction for data points $x_i \in X$. Each row of Z_i contains the label prediction having the value between 0 and 1 for the ith node and C is the number of classes. The softmax function for this can be defined in the following form as,

$$f(Z_j) = \frac{e^{Z_j}}{\sum_{i=1}^{n} e^{Z_i}}$$

The loss from this final layer EGCN is back propagated to both models separately. This fulfill the aim of the ensemble method is to learn the optimal hidden representation by exploiting both Laplacian and Hessian properties of the underlying graph. This allows the model to propagate accurate labels to the unlabeled nodes and enables generalization to all data points In order to measure the error of the model the cross entropy loss function is applied for model.

$$CE = -\sum_{i \in \omega} \sum_{j=1}^{C} Y_{ij} \ln Z_{ij},$$

here, ω denotes the set of nodes having labels. $Y \in \mathbb{R}^{N \times C}$ is the label matrix and each row of Y_i denotes the ground truth for the ith node.

3 Experiment and Result

In this section, the EGCN model has been empirically evaluated and results have been reported in terms of classification accuracy. EGCN has been compared against many existing techniques. To demonstrate its effectiveness its has been executed on 3 real world datasets (Table 1).

Table 1. Dataset description

	Cora	Citeseer	Pubmed
Nodes	2708	3327	19,717
Edges	5429	4732	44,338
Features	1433	3703	500
Classes	7	6	3
Training Nodes	140	120	60
Validation Nodes	500	500	500
Test Nodes	1000	1000	1000

3.1 Dataset Description

- **Cora** - This dataset [9] is a collection of 2708 publications classified in 7 categories. It form a citation network of 5429 links between them. Each publication is presented as an node of the undirected graph.
- **Citeseer** - This dataset [5] composed of 3327 scientific publications from 6 classes. Each publication comprises of 3703 words which described by the 0/1 word vector.
- **Pubmed** - This dataset [10] comprises of 19717 diabetes publications with three classes namely diabetes mellitus type 2, diabetes mellitus experimental and diabetes mellitus type 1. It form a citation network of 44338 links and each publication is 500 dimensional vector.

3.2 Experimental Setup

The same experimental setup employed as mentioned in the [7]. For each of this dataset all nodes features are used and only 20 nodes per class as labelled in the networking training. The same hyperparameter optimization is followed as mentioned in [7]. The hyperparameter has been optimized on the citeseer dataset and same has been used for datasets.EGCN has been trained maximum of 200 epochs by employing the adam algorithm with a learning rate of 0.01. ReLU(.) activation function has been used for EGCN model.

Table 2. Classification accuracy comparison of EGCN, and other state-of-the-art semi supervised learning methods

Methods	Datasets		
	Citeseer	Cora	Pubmed
ManiReg [2]	60.1	59.5	70.7
SemiEmb [16]	59.6	59.0	71.1
LP [21]	45.3	68.0	63.0
DeepWalk [11]	43.2	67.2	65.3
ICA [8]	69.1	75.1	73.9
Planetoid [18]	64.7	75.7	77.2
GCN [7]	70.3	81.5	79.0
HesGCN [4]	60.6	59.7	80.5
EGCN	71.8	82.3	78.3

3.3 Result Analysis

In this section, we have analysis the classification results obtained on the relational datasets. The results have been summarized in the Table 2 and highest accuracies are highlighted in bold. The classification accuracies suggest that the EGCN consistently outperforms the baseline methods on all datasets by a considerable margin. The first important inference that can be concluded from the Table 2 the recently proposed method GCN, HesGCN and EGCN have a much higher classification accuracy than the existing traditional methods like ManiReg [2], SemiEmb [16], and LP [21] for all three datasets.

On Citeseer dataset EGCN has the significant accuracy of 71.8, it outperforms GCN by 1.2% and HesGCN by sufficient margin. The other traditional methods have have ≈10% less classification accuracy than EGCN. On Cora dataset, EGCN again out performs other techniques by a non negligible factor, EGCN has accuracy 82.3% and it leads from GCN by 0.8% and HesGCN by huge margin. On Pubmed dataset, EGCN lags behind both GCN and HesGCN by 0.7% and 2.2% respectively.

4 Conclusion

In this paper, Ensemble GCN with graph Laplacian and Hessian filters is proposed for semi supervised classification on graph structured relational datasets. EGCN is able to leverage the geometric structure of the data points and is able to perform better implicit regularization as compared to native GCN with Laplacian only. The Hessian is able to take into account the affinity between adjacent data points belonging to a neighborhood, which is not captured by the Laplacian. The Laplacian and Hessian filter co regularize each other and the ensemble classifier is able to achieve higher accuracy for most datasets by making the two sub classifiers agree with each other. The experiments on relational datasets validate its robustness and effectiveness as compared to other GCN models.

References

1. Belkin, M., Niyogi, P.: Laplacian eigenmaps and spectral techniques for embedding and clustering. In: Advances in Neural Information Processing Systems, pp. 585–591 (2002)
2. Belkin, M., Niyogi, P., Sindhwani, V.: Manifold regularization: a geometric framework for learning from labeled and unlabeled examples. J. Mach. Learn. Res. **7**(Nov), 2399–2434 (2006)
3. Duvenaud, D.K., et al.: Convolutional networks on graphs for learning molecular fingerprints. In: Advances in Neural Information Processing Systems, pp. 2224–2232 (2015)
4. Fu, S., Liu, W., Tao, D., Zhou, Y., Nie, L.: HesGCN: Hessian graph convolutional networks for semi-supervised classification. Inf. Sci. **514**, 484–498 (2020)
5. Giles, C.L., Bollacker, K.D., Lawrence, S.: Citeseer: an automatic citation indexing system. In: ACM DL, pp. 89–98 (1998)
6. Hamilton, W.L., Ying, R., Leskovec, J.: Representation learning on graphs: methods and applications. arXiv preprint arXiv:1709.05584 (2017)
7. Kipf, T.N., Welling, M.: Semi-supervised classification with graph convolutional networks. arXiv preprint arXiv:1609.02907 (2016)
8. Lu, Q., Getoor, L.: Link-based classification. In: Proceedings of the 20th International Conference on Machine Learning, ICML 2003, pp. 496–503 (2003)
9. McCallum, A.K., Nigam, K., Rennie, J., Seymore, K.: Automating the construction of internet portals with machine learning. Inf. Retrieval **3**(2), 127–163 (2000). https://doi.org/10.1023/A:1009953814988
10. Namata, G., London, B., Getoor, L., Huang, B.: Query-driven active surveying for collective classification. In: 10th International Workshop on Mining and Learning with Graphs, p. 8 (2012)
11. Perozzi, B., Al-Rfou, R., Skiena, S.: DeepWalk: online learning of social representations. In: Proceedings of the 20th ACM SIGKDD International Conference on Knowledge Discovery and Data Mining, pp. 701–710 (2014)
12. Schlichtkrull, M., Kipf, T.N., Bloem, P., van den Berg, R., Titov, I., Welling, M.: Modeling relational data with graph convolutional networks. In: Gangemi, A., et al. (eds.) ESWC 2018. LNCS, vol. 10843, pp. 593–607. Springer, Cham (2018). https://doi.org/10.1007/978-3-319-93417-4_38
13. Shahraki, F.F., Prasad, S.: Graph convolutional neural networks for hyperspectral data classification. In: 2018 IEEE Global Conference on Signal and Information Processing (GlobalSIP). pp. 968–972. IEEE (2018)
14. Wan, S., Gong, C., Zhong, P., Du, B., Zhang, L., Yang, J.: Multi-scale dynamic graph convolutional network for hyperspectral image classification. arXiv preprint arXiv:1905.06133 (2019)
15. Wang, Y., Meng, Y., Li, Y., Chen, S., Fu, Z., Xue, H.: Semi-supervised manifold regularization with adaptive graph construction. Pattern Recogn. Lett. **98**, 90–95 (2017)
16. Weston, J., Ratle, F., Mobahi, H., Collobert, R.: Deep learning via semi-supervised embedding. In: Montavon, G., Orr, G.B., Müller, K.-R. (eds.) Neural Networks: Tricks of the Trade. LNCS, vol. 7700, pp. 639–655. Springer, Heidelberg (2012). https://doi.org/10.1007/978-3-642-35289-8_34

17. Wu, Z., Pan, S., Chen, F., Long, G., Zhang, C., Yu, P.S.: A comprehensive survey on graph neural networks. arXiv preprint arXiv:1901.00596 (2019)
18. Yang, Z., Cohen, W.W., Salakhutdinov, R.: Revisiting semi-supervised learning with graph embeddings. arXiv preprint arXiv:1603.08861 (2016)
19. Yu, B., Yin, H., Zhu, Z.: Spatio-temporal graph convolutional networks: a deep learning framework for traffic forecasting. arXiv preprint arXiv:1709.04875 (2017)
20. Zhang, S., Tong, H., Xu, J., Maciejewski, R.: Graph convolutional networks: algorithms, applications and open challenges. In: Chen, X., Sen, A., Li, W.W., Thai, M.T. (eds.) CSoNet 2018. LNCS, vol. 11280, pp. 79–91. Springer, Cham (2018). https://doi.org/10.1007/978-3-030-04648-4_7
21. Zhu, X., Ghahramani, Z., Lafferty, J.D.: Semi-supervised learning using Gaussian fields and harmonic functions. In: Proceedings of the 20th International Conference on Machine Learning, ICML 2003, pp. 912–919 (2003)

Regularized Deep Convolutional Generative Adversarial Network

Adarsh Prasad Behera(✉), Sayli Godage, Shekhar Verma, and Manish Kumar

Indian Institute of Information Technology, Allahabad, Allahabad 211012, Uttar Pradesh, India
pwc2015004@iiita.ac.in

Abstract. The unique adversarial approach in training deep models of Generative Adversarial Networks (GANs) results in high-quality image synthesis. With minor tweaks in architecture, training methods, learning types, many variants of GANs are proposed. Despite the development of different variants of GANs, there is an absence of work on the comparison of GAN and its regularized variant. This work focuses on the analysis of DCGAN and Regularized DCGAN. First, we define two unique methods, such as direct and indirect classifications for performance evaluation of GANs using image classification through CNN. We compare both the models according to different parameters such as architecture, training methods, accuracy with CNN classifier, distribution of real and synthesized data, discriminator loss, and generator loss on the benchmark MNIST and CIFAR10 data sets. Comparison results show significant improvement in generated image quality, higher direct and indirect classification accuracy, and better learning of distributions in the case of Regularized DCGAN.

Keywords: GAN · Adversarial · DCGAN · Regularization · CNN classifier · Direct classification · Indirect classification · MNIST · CIFAR10

1 Introduction

GAN model consists of a pair of deep neural nets termed as Discriminator and Generator. The generative model takes input given as random uniform noise and tries to generate output (fake images) identical to real images. In contrast, the discriminative model takes real input data(images) and fake data(images) and tries to distinguish between them; its output is a scalar probability that the input belongs to genuine data distribution. The Generator and Discriminator are arranged in adversarial form against each other. The whole structure depicts a min-max game with two opponents (Discriminator and Generator) in which the Generator tries to minimize its loss by optimizing objective function while the Discriminator tries to maximize it. The ultimate intention of this game is given as: [2,3].

S. K. Singh et al. (Eds.): CVIP 2020, CCIS 1378, pp. 452–464, 2021.
https://doi.org/10.1007/978-981-16-1103-2_38

$$\min_{Gen}\max_{Disc} V(Disc, Gen) = E_{x\sim p_{data}(x)}[\log Disc(x)] + E_{z\sim p_z(z)}[\log(1 - Disc(Gen(z)))] \tag{1}$$

Deep Convolution GANs (DCGANs), a variant of GAN, uses CNN architecture in Discriminator. For Generator, simple convolutions are replaced by up convolutions so that it maps from low dimensional latent vector to high dimensional image [10].

Deep generative models can model representations of the complex world from unlabeled data in an unsupervised manner. Generative models can be estimated by minimization of the symmetric Jensen-Shannon divergence,

$$D_{\mathrm{JS}}(P\|Q) = \frac{1}{2}D_{\mathrm{KL}}\left(P\|\frac{1}{2}(P+Q)\right) + \frac{1}{2}D_{\mathrm{KL}}\left(Q\|\frac{1}{2}(P+Q)\right) \tag{2}$$

where D_{KL} denotes the Kullback-Leibler divergence.

GANs minimize JS divergence between target and generated distributions. A more general class of variational divergence estimation, called f-divergence, where a convex function `f` is included. Training a generative model is equivalent to **`f-divergence`** minimization. The choice of divergence functions varies according to training functions [8].

The problem that sometimes arises while training GANs is when the probability density functions P_{data}over real data x and generated data P_g do not overlap. In such situations, the divergences between real and generated data that GANs minimize are meaningless, as the Discriminator can be perfect, i.e., the gradient of the Discriminator irrespective of input is zero can lead to no further improvement in Generator and training stops.

Most of the research focused on stabilizing the training of GANs by targeting minimizing the divergences implicit in GANs. The Jensen-Shannon (JS) divergence is implicit in the vanilla GAN with alternative divergences, such as **`f-divergence`** in **`f-GAN`** and Wasserstein distance in WGAN [11]. The **`f-GAN`** objective can be defined as

$$F(\mathbb{P}, \mathbb{Q}; \psi) \equiv \mathbf{E}_{\mathbb{P}}[\psi] - \mathbf{E}_{\mathbb{Q}}[f^c \circ \psi] \tag{3}$$

where f^c is the `Fenchal dual of f` and $\Psi \ni \psi : \mathcal{X} \to \mathbb{R}$ used to get lower bound on `f-divergence`.

One of the major challenges of GANs while learning model data distribution is **Dimensional misspecification**. P_g and genuine data distribution P_{data} are embedded in low dimensions leading to no density overlap thus limiting support. To deal with this underlying limitation, a unique regularization technique that minimizes f-divergence between P_{data} and P_g. that yields a stable GAN training procedure with a lesser computational cost. The Regularized variant produces higher visual quality images and a stable training process for GANs. JS-Regularization added penalty terms on the norm of real gradients. When the Generator produces accurate data distribution, and Discriminator outputs 0 on such diffusion, the gradient penalty term ensures Discriminator does not deviate from Nash-equilibrium [7].

The comparison & evaluation of the images generated by GANs is a problematic task [2]. However, there exist some qualitative and quantitative measures for evaluating GAN models [5]. Qualitative measures involve user studies and studying the internals of models. Some of the qualitative methods like Nearest neighbor [15], rating and preference judgment [14] and rapid scene categorization [9] have been proposed to measure the performance of GANs on the quality of generated images. However, these methods are primarily biased towards over-fitting. Quantitative measures are seen as less subjective and may not agree to the human judgment of generated images. Lack of a perceptually significant image similarity metric, lack of variety of probability criteria have made evaluating generative models notoriously hard. Visual evaluation is a very crude way of assessing the quality of images. The interdependence of the elemental network architecture and the sample image formation steps of GANs needs substantial study. The decision to choose architectures most appropriate for GANs and produce highly realistic images needs to be explored.

Recent work in the past had begun to target this challenge through quantitative measures. The Inception Score (IS) metric was defined in [12], which is the most widely used metric for GAN performance evaluation. IS's fundamental idea is a pre-trained neural network used to store preferable GAN attributes generated images such as high diversity and classifiability. Though IS gives a fair correlation with diversity and quality of GAN generated samples, it can not detect over-fitting as it is biased towards Memory GANs. Memory GAN remembers the training image set and generates identical samples [1]. It also fails to detect "Mode collapse". Frechet Inception Distance (FID) was proposed as an improvement of IS in [4]. In FID, a sample of synthesized images is embedded in a feature space defined by a particular layer of Inception Net. The mean and covariance are calculated for both real and generated data assuming the embedded layer as a continuous multivariate Gaussian. The major drawback of FID is the assumption that the features will always be Gaussian.

2 Problem Formulation

Issues like dimensional misspecifications caused severe training failure for GANs. By addressing this concern with the help of JS-Regularization, an additionally stable DCGAN variant was presented. Despite the proven effectiveness of the regularized model, there is a lack of a substantial study based on comparative analysis of both regularized and un-regularized variants.

There is no unanimous measure which can be regarded as the best and most appropriate. Different methods cover different aspects. IS and FID guarantee statistical evaluation, but they suffer from two critical drawbacks. Firstly these methods heavily rely on previously trained deep neural nets. These pre-trained networks are invariant to transformations that occur during the image generation process. Most of the time, it uses ImageNet for training. ImageNet is an extensive data set with 14 million images and 1000+ classes. The architecture trained on it might not be well suited for small data sets from other domains. Secondly, these measures fail to compute the distance of generated images from data manifold in precision and recall. High precision value hints generated images are similar to those from real data. On the other hand, a high recall value suggests the generated images cover real distribution well.

3 Proposed Method

Several evaluation measures exist; however, there is no agreement as to which method is more likely to capture merits and demerits with unbiased comparability among all other models. We propose two novel metrics based on image classification through CNN for performance evaluation of generative models to overcome these inherent limitations with the ability to conduct an unbiased comparison of different variants of GAN. To distinguish images from different classes, a pre-trained CNN is used for predicting class labels for GAN generated images.

We introduce two novel methods i.e. **Indirect Classification & Direct Classification** based on generated image classification accuracy. We use CNNs to classify GAN generated images. If the GAN learns to fake data so well that CNN trained on such(GAN generated) data set can correctly classify real test images, we say GANs well preserve that diversity of images. Conversely, if CNN is trained on real images and performs better in classification, the accuracy of generated images is as good as validation accuracy; we can say that fake images are similar to the real images' training set. An optimally trained GAN will precisely capture the target distribution and generate fake images very similar to real ones [6,13]. Let us assume the following notations:
GAN set (generated images with labels predicted by CNN)- **SGan**
Original training images from data set - **SOrig**
Test images from data set - **SValid**
3 CNN models with similar architecture - **C1, C2, C3**

3.1 Indirect Classification - IC

The accuracy score of a CNN that has been trained on SGan and investigated on a test set of real pictures SValid is termed as Indirect Classification score. If the model is not good enough, the Indirect Classification score will be lower than the average validation accuracy of the CNN trained on SOrig. C1 Classifier is a CNN trained on original train data. It will be used to classify the synthetic data generated by DCGAN and regularized DCGAN.

The next step is to train DCGAN and Regularized DCGAN models for various epochs and save the results. GAN generated images are denoted as SGan. This SGan is passed through C1 to get labels for corresponding images. The output is SGan labeled data set.

C2 CNN is trained on SGan labeled data set, and SValid is tested on C2. The accuracy obtained after this testing is termed Indirect Classification accuracy. As the number of generated images increases, model C2 are trained better. When Indirect Classification accuracy is close to CNN's validation accuracy, it shows the diversity of generated diffusion. We conclude that generated pictures are almost like real ones if the CNN model, which learns options for discriminating pictures generated for various categories, will correctly classify real pictures. In different words, the Indirect Classification score is equivalent to the "Recall" measure. A decent Indirect Classification score validates the GAN generates samples with moderate diversity.

3.2 Direct Classification - DC

The accuracy score of a CNN trained on real images SOrig and investigated on generated images SGan is termed as Direct Classification score.

C3 CNN is trained on the original SOrig data set. SGan is tested on C3. The accuracy obtained after testing SGan on C3 gives us Direct Classification accuracy. "Precision" measures the fraction of relevant samples among the retrieved samples. Retrieved samples are the output of GAN, and relevant samples are those comparable to real images. Therefore by computing this fraction, we calculate the distance between images and data manifold. DC score is, therefore, similar to measuring "Precision" of the GAN model. If GAN happens to memorize the training set, i.e., the model overfits, making the Direct Classification score relatively higher. On the other hand, if GAN fails to learn the target distribution well, the generated images are of low quality, and the Direct Classification score is significantly lower. Ideally, the Direct Classification score would be approximately similar to the C1 validation accuracy.

4 Results and Analysis

For analysis purposes, we begin with observing individual performances of DCGAN and Regularized DCGAN models and conclude with a comparative performance assessment. The models are tested on MNIST and CIFAR10 data set.

4.1 Performance with Various No of Epochs

We assess the performance of the Discriminator model based on its accuracy to discern real and fake images. The generator model is assessed based on its loss and accuracy. DCGAN is trained for numerous epoch sizes and checked for performance.

Table 1. Generator and discriminator accuracy of DCGAN at various epochs

Epochs	Discriminator accuracy in %	Generator accuracy in %
50	Real: 99.7, Fake: 99.9	95
100	Real: 79.3, Fake: 68.3	93
500	Real: 68.6, Fake: 46.3	26
1000	Real: 61.1, Fake: 62.7	21
1200	Real:56.0, Fake: 59	23
1800	Real:56.0, Fake: 60.0	27
3000	Real: 57.9, Fake: 57.4	28
6000	Real: 58.3, Fake: 57.5	32
9000	Real: 56.9, Fake: 60.7	32

Table 1 shows the discriminator and generator accuracies at various epochs for MNIST data set. At the beginning of the training process, the images generated by the DCGAN are of low quality and easily distinguishable by the Discriminator. Hence, the accuracy of the Discriminator is high as it can easily distinguish between real and fake images. However, as the number of epoch increases, the Generator learns the images' pattern and produces high-quality images that are not distinguishable from the real images. Hence, the Discriminator's accuracy decreases, and a GAN is said to converge when the Discriminator cannot distinguish real and fake images, and the probability decreases to 50%. Training that results in stabilized DCGAN will have a Discriminator loss in the range of 0.5 to 0.8. The Generator loss is typically higher initially and hovers around 1.0, 2.0 when it becomes stable. This loss convergence would generally signify that the DCGAN model found some optimum, where it cannot improve more and has learned well enough to its ability. We can say that Discriminator and Generator models are approaching convergence.

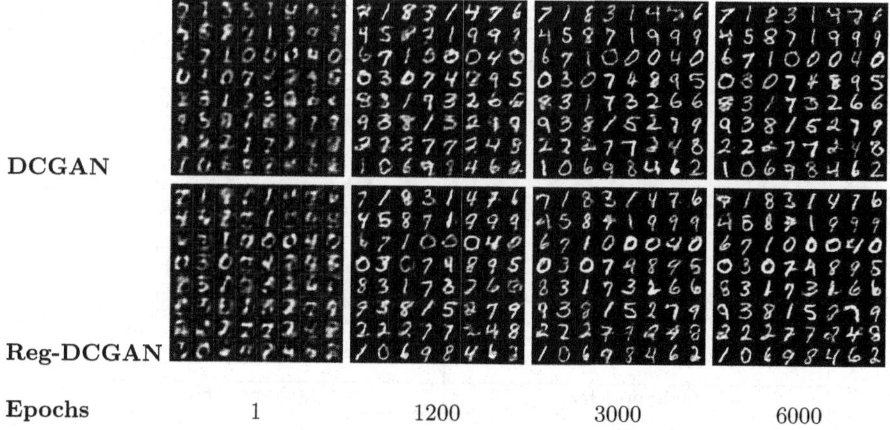

Fig. 1. The performance of generator can be visualised at various epochs for MNIST

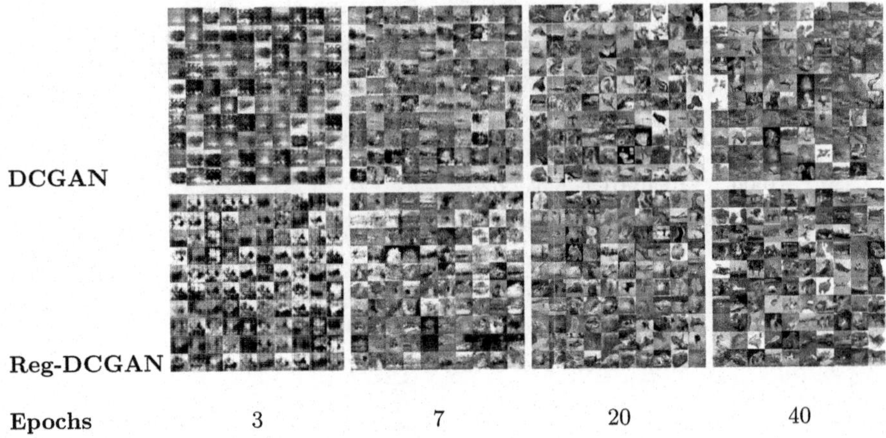

Fig. 2. The performance of generator can be visualised at various epochs for CIFAR10

Table 2. Discriminator, generator model losses and accuracy

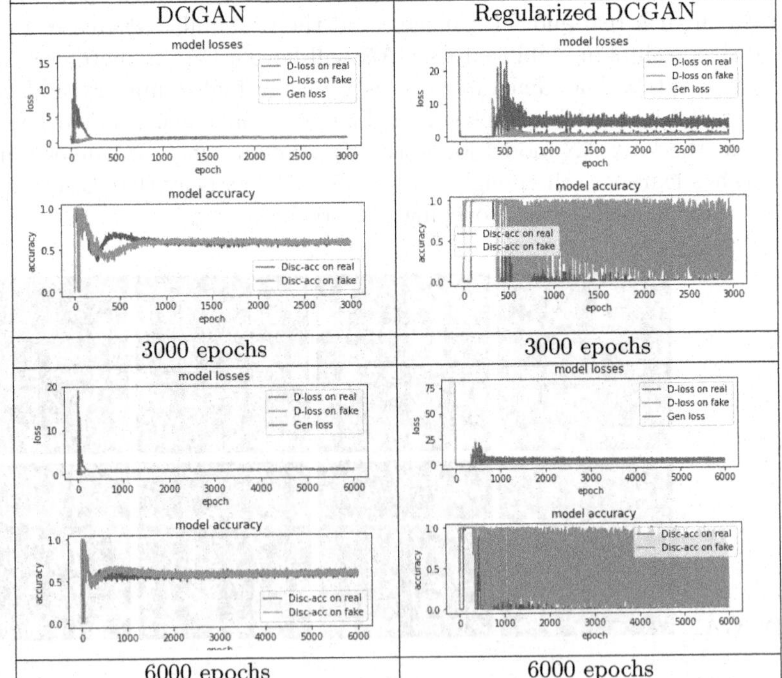

Loss and Accuracy plots at different epochs	
DCGAN	Regularized DCGAN
3000 epochs	3000 epochs
6000 epochs	6000 epochs

For the MNIST data set, DCGAN Generator can quickly learn features in the first few hundred epochs. After this, loss and accuracy remain mostly stable. The image quality generated by the two models does not show a considerable visual difference in Fig. 1. In the case of CIFAR10, while the DCGAN produced samples show collapse over a few modes, Reg-DCGAN generated samples are diverse and of higher quality than the unregularized variant in Fig. 2.

Table 2 shows the discriminator and Generator losses and accuracies at various epochs for the CIFAR10 data set. Loss and accuracy are cardinal when evaluating the performance of any model. Discriminator and Generator loss is recorded at each step during training. The Discriminator accuracy of classification on real and fake samples is also saved at each iteration. At the end of the training, these are used to create line plots for various epochs. Generator loss value peaks from 0 to 20 at the beginning and drops as learning begins. The final loss recorded with Generator is anywhere between 0 to 2. Discriminator loss on fake follows a similar pattern to that of Generator, while on real, it remains somewhere close to 0.

Considering accuracy as a parameter for analysis, it can be observed in Table 2 that the model is close to convergence when Discriminator accuracy for real and fake approaches 50%. i.e., The Discriminator is no more able to differentiate between real and fake data, and it produces results (real/fake) with 0.5 probability.

4.2 Generative Model Evaluation Through Indirect & Direct Classification

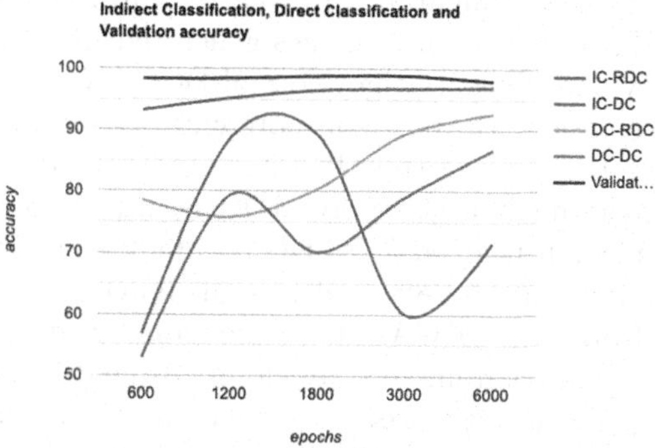

Fig. 3. Validation accuracy, indirect & direct classification scores on MNIST

To substantiate that DCGAN can easily reproduce a simple data set like MNIST ensuring high image quality and diversity, we conduct the following experiment on a three-layered CNN classifier. It can be observed in Fig. 3, we see the validation accuracy is 98%. The Indirect Classification scores on DCGAN(IC-DC)

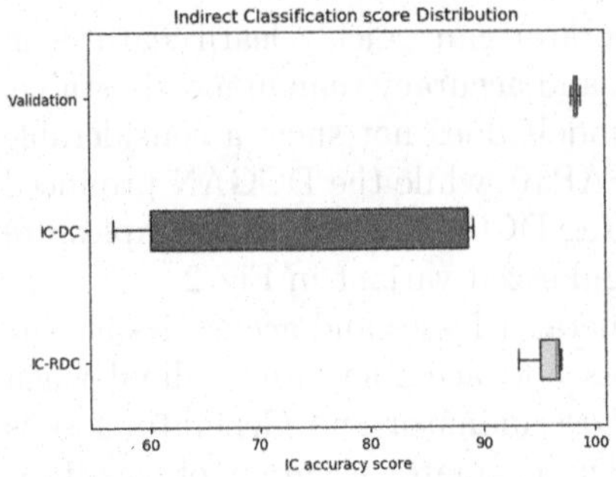

Fig. 4. Box plot representation of Indirect Classification

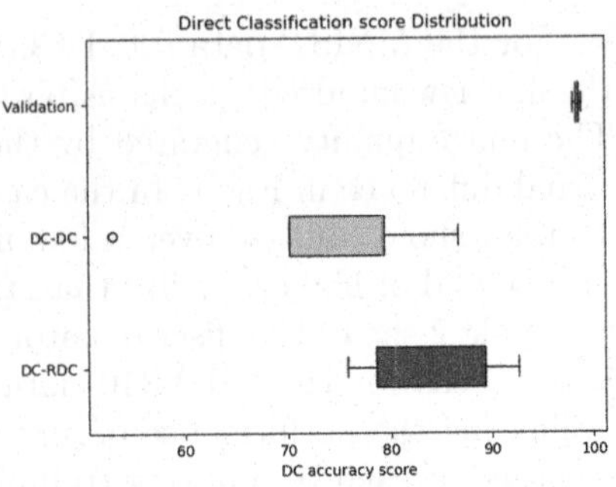

Fig. 5. Box plot representation of Direct Classification

exponentially increase until around 1500 epochs and drop sharply, suggesting training instability or collapse on few modes resulting in less diverse output. The Indirect Classification scores on Regularized DCGAN(IC-RDC) follow the validation scoreline and move closer to it as the number of epochs increases proving the inconsistencies were addressed by regularizing Discriminator, thus leading to smoother training. Although The Indirect Classification score gives a detailed portrayal of training irregularities, the Direct Classification scores on both models (DC-RDC and DC-DC) are making slow but steady progress towards the validation score. This validates that DCGAN can accurately extract MNIST features and generate samples with high resemblance to real ones. Thus precision of both models is comparable, Regularized proving still higher than the standard model. This confirms that images generated from stabilized DCGAN are of better quality and diversity than normal DCGAN.

Figure 4 and Fig. 5 shows the box plot representations of indirect classification and direct classification, respectively. In Fig. 4, the validation accuracy hovers around 98%, with the median at 98. IC-RDC accuracy scores range between 92–98%, with the median near 96%. IC-DC accuracy scores have a wide range distribution approximating 55–88% and median lying at 72. This shows that generated images from Reg-DCGAN have moderate diversity, and the model has better "Recall", as its parameters are closer to the original distribution.

Similarly, in Fig. 5, validation scores are fixed at 98%. Both DC-DC and DC-RDC have approximately equal box lengths and close medians. However, 75% of DC-DC scores lie below 80%, while more than half of DC-RDC scores lie in 80–90%. Reg-DCGAN samples illustrate better "Precision"and are more realistic than an un-regularized variant.

For the experiment on CIFAR10, we chose 6-layered convnet CNN architecture with pooling and Dropout set to 0.2. The learning rate fixed at 0.001, and the validation split of 0.2 gives 40k samples in training and 10k in the valida-

Table 3. Indirect & direct classification scores in % on CIFAR10

Epochs	IC-DC	IC-RDC	DC-DC	DC-RDC
10	10	10.30	57.4	66.01
20	15.3	17.33	63.04	70.71

tion set. Twenty-five epochs with SGD optimizer, the model, gives validation accuracy of 63%.

On observing the training data set size, there is a vast difference between those of the real set and the generated set. SOrig has 50k images in the training set, while SGan has only 10k. Thus it overfits the SGan data and performs poorly on the test set. CNN trained on greater input data size will be modeled better and classify desirably. A different perspective given by this experiment highlights an essential aspect of image generation, i.e., diversity. Reg-DCGAN generated images are diverse and learned from the entire set of training images for a particular class. While the results shown here are generated with 20 epochs and 10k generated images, they can surely improve by training 100+ epochs and generating around 50k image sets.

From Table 3, it can be observed that reasonable Direct classification accuracy, but very low Indirect Classification accuracy, testifies generated images are of decent quality but are not diverse enough to cover the entire distribution. This claim is supported by the metrics like IS = 1.001 and FID = 601 tested on 5k samples. By increasing the generated sample size, the randomness while shuffling is reduced, leading to a boost in scores.

4.3 Comparison of Distributions

For estimating the performance of GANs with finite sample sizes and finite discriminator size, there is no inherent estimate of how good the distributional fit is. We use subjective human evaluation of the distribution of generated images by DCGAN, Regularized DCGAN, against the distribution of the original Train set of MNIST.

In Fig. 6, we chose to plot label frequency distribution alternative to label data distribution as the sizes of the Train set and generated sets are bound to mismatch. We obtain the percent-wise distribution of each label of the MNIST Train set for unbiased comparison, and those from generated sets are plotted against this. The DCGAN distribution tends to overshoot for some labels (e.g., labels 4,8) at the beginning for around 600 epochs compared to Train distribution. This may happen due to mode collapse on a particular digit like '4'. The Generator has learned a few features and is not well trained to cover every mode. If we measure the distance between the generated distribution and target distribution, the gradients can point to more random directions if the distributions do not substantially overlap.

The Regularized DCGAN distribution overlaps substantially more with Train distribution than DCGAN distribution. This assumption is supported by the fact

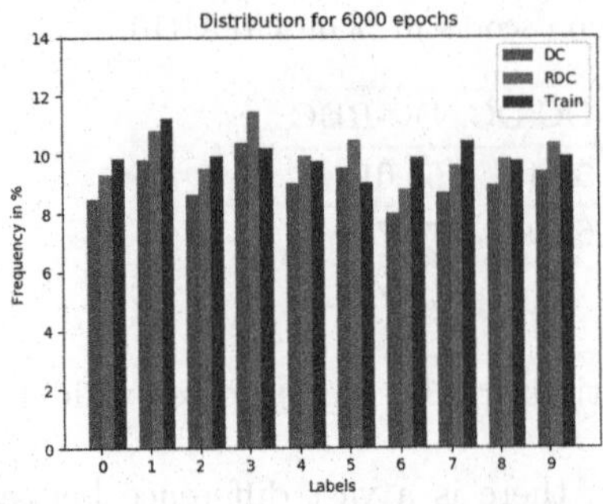

Fig. 6. Distribution comparison of DCGAN, Reg-DCGAN generated images for 6000 epochs

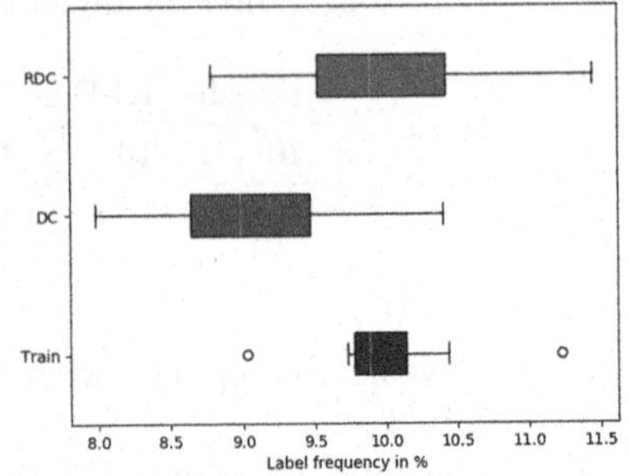

Fig. 7. Comparative box plot for distribution comparison of DCGAN, Reg-DCGAN and training data set

that there is no arbitrary spike in frequency for any of the labels. This is possible only when the generated data is diverse, with maximum modes covered and not focusing on a few ones. Training progresses iteratively refining the Generator and Discriminator. Both optimize the objective function until the real distribution is perfectly overlapped from the distribution induced by the Generator. While the DCGAN might collapse after around 50k iterations, the regularized variant makes Discriminator weak and can be trained smoothly for more than 200k iterations avoiding collapse [11]. We establish through visual assessment; the Reg-DCGAN distribution is close-packed with Train distribution of original data.

For comparing distributions between many groups, we use a box plot in Fig. 7. Key observations to note in Fig. 6 are the median of Train and Reg-DCGAN lie around 9.8, and that of DCGAN is much lesser at 8.9. The generated and target distribution of samples for Reg-DCGAN have a similar median. Although the box-plot for Train shows outliers at 9% and 11.4%, which correspond to labels 5 and 1 respectively, they are not one and just an imitation of the original distribution of MNIST labels. The broad range of dispersion of Train labels is quite similar to that of Reg-DCGAN if these outliers are included. Even though the interquartile range for DCGAN and Reg-DCGAN distributions are the same, the medians are well separated. Overall, both DCGAN and Reg-DCGAN data look they are generally distributed in the same way. Overall, half of the labels' frequency falls between 9.5 to 10.5 in Reg-DCGAN, but it also includes the entire dispersion of Train excluding outliers. In comparison, DCGAN dispersion is far from this range. With the exploration and careful observation from above, we can safely validate that Regularized DCGAN induces distribution that follows target distribution exhaustively.

5 Conclusion

In this work, we defined two novel metrics for quantitative performance evaluation of GANs through image classification using CNN. Then, we shifted our focus towards image synthesis in DCGAN and regularized DCGAN using pre-existing data sets. We reviewed the generated synthetic images qualitatively using human perception and the proposed methodology as well. We also compared the class distribution of real and generated images for DCGAN and regularized DCGAN for different epochs.

It can be concluded that though DCGAN works satisfactorily for simple data sets, its performance can be further enhanced by applying regularization. Regularized DCGAN outperforms DCGAN in qualitative and quantitative evaluation methods and in learning the distribution of real data. However, in the case of data sets with moderate complexity, DCGAN fails to generate impressive results. The performance of DCGAN can be calibrated to a great extent by applying regularization on it. Comparison results showed significant improvement in generated images in regularized DCGAN. Both Direct and Indirect classification accuracy and learning of distributions improved with regularized DCGAN.

References

1. Borji, A.: Pros and cons of gan evaluation measures. Comput. Vis. Image Underst. **179**, 41–65 (2019)
2. Cheng, K., Tahir, R., Eric, L.K., Li, M.: An analysis of generative adversarial networks and variants for image synthesis on MNIST dataset. Multimed. Tools Appl. **79**(19), 13725–13752 (2020). https://doi.org/10.1007/s11042-019-08600-2
3. Goodfellow, I., et al.: Generative adversarial nets. In: Advances in Neural Information Processing Systems, pp. 2672–2680 (2014)
4. Heusel, M., Ramsauer, H., Unterthiner, T., Nessler, B., Hochreiter, S.: Gans trained by a two time-scale update rule converge to a local nash equilibrium. In: Advances in Neural Information Processing Systems, pp. 6626–6637 (2017)
5. Hitawala, S.: Comparative study on generative adversarial networks. arXiv preprint arXiv:1801.04271 (2018)
6. Lucic, M., Kurach, K., Michalski, M., Gelly, S., Bousquet, O.: Are gans created equal? A large-scale study. In: Advances in Neural Information Processing Systems, pp. 700–709 (2018)
7. Mescheder, L., Geiger, A., Nowozin, S.: Which training methods for gans do actually converge? arXiv preprint arXiv:1801.04406 (2018)
8. Nowozin, S., Cseke, B., Tomioka, R.: f-gan: training generative neural samplers using variational divergence minimization. In: Advances in Neural Information Processing Systems, pp. 271–279 (2016)
9. Oliva, A.: Gist of the scene. In: Neurobiology of Attention, pp. 251–256. Elsevier (2005)
10. Radford, A., Metz, L., Chintala, S.: Unsupervised representation learning with deep convolutional generative adversarial networks. arXiv preprint arXiv:1511.06434 (2015)
11. Roth, K., Lucchi, A., Nowozin, S., Hofmann, T.: Stabilizing training of generative adversarial networks through regularization. In: Advances in Neural Information Processing Systems, pp. 2018–2028 (2017)
12. Salimans, T., Goodfellow, I., Zaremba, W., Cheung, V., Radford, A., Chen, X.: Improved techniques for training gans. In: Advances in Neural Information Processing Systems, pp. 2234–2242 (2016)

13. Shmelkov, K., Schmid, C., Alahari, K.: How good is my gan? In: Proceedings of the European Conference on Computer Vision (ECCV), pp. 213–229 (2018)
14. Snell, J., Ridgeway, K., Liao, R., Roads, B.D., Mozer, M.C., Zemel, R.S.: Learning to generate images with perceptual similarity metrics. In: 2017 IEEE International Conference on Image Processing (ICIP), pp. 4277–4281. IEEE (2017)
15. Theis, L., Oord, A.V.D., Bethge, M.: A note on the evaluation of generative models. arXiv preprint arXiv:1511.01844 (2015)

A Novel Approach for Video Captioning Based on Semantic Cross Embedding and Skip-Connection

Rakesh Radarapu(✉), Nishanth Bandari(✉), Satwik Muthyam(✉), and Dinesh Naik(✉)

National Institute of Technology Karnataka, Surathkal, India

Abstract. Video Captioning is the task of describing the content of a video in simple natural language. Encoder-Decoder architecture is the most widely used architecture for this task. Recent works exploit the use of 3D Convolutional Neural Networks (CNNs), Transformers or by changing the structure of basic Long Short-Term Memory (LSTM) units used in Encoder-Decoder to improve the performance. In this paper, we propose the use of a sentence vector to improve the performance of the Encoder-Decoder model. This sentence vector acts as an intermediary between the video space and the text space. Thus, it is referred to as semantic cross embedding that bridges the two vector spaces, in this paper. The sentence vector is generated from the video and is used by the Decoder, along with previously generated words to generate a suitable description. We also employ the use of a skip-connection in the Encoder part of the model. Skip-connection is usually employed to tackle the vanishing gradients problem in deep neural networks. However, our experiments show that a two-layer LSTM with a skip-connection performs better than the Bidirectional LSTM, for our model. Also, the use of a sentence vector improves performance considerably. All our experiments are performed on the MSVD dataset.

Keywords: Video captioning · Skip-connection · Semantic cross embedding · Sentence vector

1 Introduction

Humans are quite capable of giving a proper caption for a video clip without many semantic errors or misconceptions. Figure 1 shows the description given by humans for the video which is quite accurate. However, for machines it is not quite easy to identify the objects involved, the interactions among them and generate a fitting description. With the introduction of CNNs reading an image has become a feasible task for machines. The progress in Natural Language Processing, helped machines to understand human language in the form of

S. K. Singh et al. (Eds.): CVIP 2020, CCIS 1378, pp. 465–477, 2021.
https://doi.org/10.1007/978-981-16-1103-2_39

word embeddings. Word embeddings are used in applications like neural machine translation, text generation and information retrieval.

Video Captioning is processing the visual information to generate textual information. Processing videos is a challenging task because unlike an image, a video has both spatial and temporal information. CNNs are capable of capturing the spatial information in the images and the temporal information of the video is captured by the use of one or more LSTM layers.

Attention is a mechanism used for tasks related to language translation, visual content description, question-answering and became important in the Encoder-Decoder architecture which is used for all sequence-to-sequence related tasks. Soft attention is used in particular for these where the context vector for the Decoder is computed as a weighted sum of the encoder output states.

Fig. 1. Caption: a man is kneading a ball of dough

Thus the overview of our contribution is as follows:

I Word embeddings from pre-trained models like BERT base [3], GloVe, Elmo are used. Comparisons among these embedding approaches based on the performance of our model are made.

II Experiments are conducted with feature vectors for video frames taken from different CNNs like Inception-v3, VGG-16 and NASNet-Large.

III The use of Multi-Head attention for the Decoder to softly select the encoder states.

IV Employing the use of a skip-connection in the Encoder and comparing it to the Bidirectional model.

V The concept of a sentence vector to aid the Decoder. A sentence vector is a part of the caption space. We try to map the video information, which is in visual space, directly to its corresponding caption in the caption space.

2 Related Work

Initial works mostly concentrated on Image Captioning that were later extended to video captioning. Vinayals et al. [18] has proposed a deep-recurrent model that used latest advances in computer vision and machine translation to generate captions to images. His model was trained to maximize the likelihood of the target description sentence for a training image. You et al. [25] combines both top-down and bottom-up strategies to extract richer information from an image, and combines them with a RNN that can selectively attend semantic attributes detected from the image. Fang et al. [4] proposed a language model to generate captions and rank them using a dual-stream RNN model. The model learns to extract nouns, verbs, and adjectives from regions in the image. Using the above words the model generates a meaningful sentence describing the image.

Y. Pan et al. [9] proposed a novel deep learning architecture using Long Short-Term Memory with Transferred Semantic Attributes (LSTM-TSA). LSTM-TSA is used for transferring semantic attributes from the images and videos into the CNNs and RNNs in an end-to-end manner. In this, image and video semantics reinforce each other to boost video captioning. L. Gao et al. [6] proposed an Encoder-Decoder architecture with an attention LSTM in the Decoder to improve the context of caption and introduced a new loss function to improve the semantics of the caption. Song et al. [14] proposed a novel hLSTMat encoderdecoder framework, which integrates a hierarchical LSTMs, temporal attention and adaptive temporal attention. This model decides when to use visual information and semantic information on its own.

Xu et al. [22] used combination of convolutional neural networks and recurrent neural networks called RCN and combined it with a trainable vector of locally aggregated descriptor (VLAD) layer to develop a novel Sequential layer called SeqVLAD. They have tested this framework on video captioning and video action recognition task and proved its effectiveness. Ning Xu et al. [21] designed attention in attention network to hierarchically explore the attention fusion in an end-to-end manner. It specifically has multiple encoder attention modules and fusion attention modules.

Bin et al. [2] proposed a new LSTM called Bi-directional LSTM that processes videos in both forward and backward direction to gain information for decoding from future time steps as well. Also, a soft attention mechanism is proposed that focuses on targets with certain probabilities at every timestep. J. Song et al. [13] proposed a new end-to-end framework known as multi-model stochastic RNNs (MS-RNN) that takes uncertainty in the data into consideration by introducing stochastic variables. This approach combines BiLSTM and soft attention mechanism with a new LSTM called S-LSTM that introduces uncertainty in the training phase.

Y. Yang et al. [23] uses the concept of generative adversarial networks shortly known as GAN for captioning the videos. The generator is responsible for giving captions for videos where as the discriminator classifies the sentences into true or generated data thereby acting as an adversary to caption generator. Q. Zheng et al. [26] proposed a Syntax-Aware Action Targeting (SAAT) module which learns actions by simultaneously referring to the subject and video dynamics. First, they identify the subject by mapping global dependence among multiple objects and then decode action from a common space that fuses the embedding of the subject and the temporal feature of the video.

3 Proposed Approach

Our goal is to generate a natural language description for a given video. We propose a Semantic Cross Embedding (SCE) based Encoder-Decoder architecture with a skip-connection in the Encoder for this task. Our model takes feature vectors extracted from a 2D CNN as inputs and encodes them to capture the spatio-temporal information from the video. The overall architecture of our final model is shown in Fig. 2. We make use of the concept of a sentence vector which will be explained in Sect. 3.4.

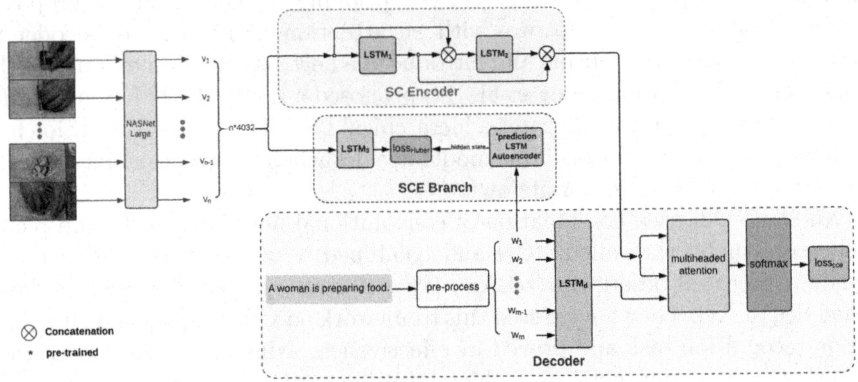

Fig. 2. The Architecture of our video captioning model with Semantic cross embedding and skip-connection (SCE + SC) has 3 main modules: a) Encoder with skip-connection b) Decoder with Multi-Head Attention c) Semantic Cross Embedding Branch.

3.1 Feature Extraction

The first phase consists of extracting feature vectors from the videos. The videos are broken down to frames, resized and re-scaled. Resize and re-scale are needed because the videos from the dataset are of varying frame sizes and also to suit the input needs of the pre-trained CNN model. The pre-processed frames are fed, in order, to a CNN model to extract feature vectors that are a high-level representation of videos. Three different models namely NASNet-Large, Inception-v3, VGG-16 are used to extract feature vectors.

NASNet-Large is a Convolutional Neural Network that takes an image of size 331×331 as input and outputs a feature vector of size 4032.

In NASNet-Large, though the overall architecture is predefined as in [27], the blocks or cells are not predefined by authors. Alternatively, they are explored by reinforcement learning search method i.e. the number of repetitions N and the number of initial convolutional filters are as free parameters and used for scaling. The variant used for our work is taken from the Tensorflow Hub and consists of 18 Normal cells, starting with 168 convolutional filters.

A Normal cell is a group of convolutional cells that return a feature map of the same dimension and a Reduction cell is a group of convolutional cells that return a feature map where the feature map height and width is decreased by a factor of two.

InceptionV3 [15] is a Convolutional Neural Network developed by Google for image captioning that takes a 299 $\times$ 299 sized image as input and outputs a feature vector of size 2048.

The basic unit of this network is an 'inception cell', which consists of multiple convolutions running in parallel and ultimately concatenating the output. The input channel depth is adjusted using 1×1 convolutions. Each inception cell uses 1×1, 3×3 and 5×5 filters to learn features at various scales from input. Max pooling is used with 'same' padding to retain the dimension for concatenation.

VGG 16 Visual Geometry Group [12] (VGG-16) was developed by Oxford that takes a 224 $\times$ 224 sized image as input and outputs a feature vector of size 4096.

VGG-16 uses only 3×3 filters with a stride of 1 in the convolution layers and 2×2 filters in the pooling layers with 'same' padding. All hidden layers use ReLU activation function and are followed by 3 fully-connected layers.

3.2 Terminology and Notation

Let the video for which a caption needs to be generated be denoted by V = $\{v_1, v_2, v_3...., v_n\}$, where n is the number of frames. Now the visual features extracted, from video V as described in Sect. 3.1, be X = $\{x_1, x_2, x_3...., x_n\}$ $\epsilon R^{d_i * n}$, where d_i is the dimension of the feature vector of a single frame. Let the caption be denoted by $W \epsilon R^{d_w * c}$, where d_w is the dimension of a word embedding and c is the number of words in the caption. The caption generated by the model be represented as $W' \epsilon R^{d_w * c}$.

3.3 Encoder-Decoder

The role of the Encoder is to capture the temporal features from the 2-D CNN features extracted at the frame level. We use Long Short-Term Memory Networks for this task. LSTMs are used to extract a fixed-dimensional vector representation for a series of frames. Our Encoder consists of a two-layer LSTM with a skip-connection.

The Decoder should learn to predict the caption given the video information. The caption is generated one word at a time. So given a current word and the output from the Encoder, the Decoder predicts the next word in the caption. We use multi-head attention for the model which takes the encoder output and the decoder state to attend to selective regions in the encoder output which determine the Decoder output. The loss that captures the translation from videos to words is computed as

$$loss_1 = -\sum_{t=1}^{N_w} \log P(w_t|E, w_1, w_2, ..., w_{t-1}) \tag{1}$$

where, N_w represents the number of words in the caption and Eq. 2 represents the probability of the predicted word w_t given the previously generated words $w_1, w_2, ..., w_{t-1}$ and the encoder output E.

$$P(w_t|E, w_1, w_2, ..., w_{t-1}) \tag{2}$$

3.4 Semantic Cross Embedding

The feature vector X from the video, as described in Sect. 3.2, is passed to an LSTM layer to generate a 768-D vector. During the training process, we compare it against the hidden state from an LSTM autoencoder, as shown in Fig. 3, trained on the caption set. Since this hidden state captures the content of the caption and is used in regenerating the caption, it gives extra information to the Decoder to predict the next word. Since this vector summarizes a caption we refer to it as a sentence vector.

Let the sentence vector from the language model be SV and the sentence vector generated by SCE branch be SV' then the Huber loss is computed as

$$e_k = \begin{cases} \frac{1}{2}(sv_k - sv'_k)^2 & for\ |sv_k - sv'_k| \leq \delta \\ \delta|sv_k - sv'_k| - \frac{1}{2}\delta^2 & Otherwise \end{cases} \tag{3}$$

$$loss_2 = \sum_{k=0}^{d_w} e_k \tag{4}$$

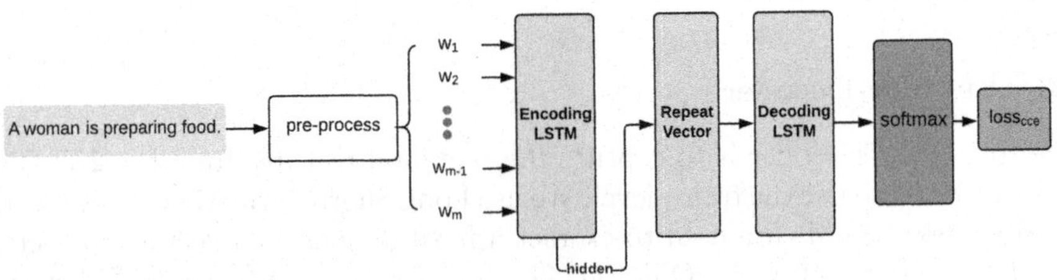

Fig. 3. LSTM autoencoder

3.5 Multi-head Attention

The encoder output contains information about the entire video. But for the Decoder to generate the next word given the current word it needs to select only a subset of the features. So scalar dot product attention [16] allows the Decoder to attend to only selective information from the Encoder. Consider Eq. 5, Query, Value represents the encoder output information, Key represents the decoder previous state information. Here the encoder output is weighted for different regions based on the current decoder states to produce a context vector for the next word. This constitutes one head of the multi-head attention. The use of multiple heads makes it possible for the Decoder to attend to the information from the Encoder at different positions from different representational spaces at the same time. Single head attention is computed as

$$Attention(Q, K, V) = softmax(\frac{QK^T}{\sqrt{d_n}})V \tag{5}$$

$$(Q, K, V) = (R_d W^Q, R_e W^K, R_e W^V) \tag{6}$$

where R_d is the decoder states, R_e is the encoder states, $\{W^Q, W^K, W^V\}$ $\epsilon R^{d_i * d_n}$ are the weights for multiple attention heads, where d_i is the dimension of the attention input and d_n is the number of units in an attention head.

3.6 Training

We train the language model initially to get the sentence vectors of all the captions. Then we train the proposed architecture, loading the pre-trained language model, as shown in Fig. 2 with an objective loss function built by integrating two loss functions which simultaneously consider video translation to words and sentence vector generation. The experimental setup can be found in Sect. 4.2

$$loss = \lambda loss_1 + (1 - \lambda) loss_2 \tag{7}$$

where λ is a hyper-parameter between 0 and 1.

4 Experimental Results and Discussion

4.1 Dataset

The Microsoft Video Description (MSVD) dataset has a total of 1,970 short video clips from YouTube, with attached human-generated descriptions. On average, there are around 41 descriptions per video. This dataset contains about 80,000 clip-description pairs, with each clip having descriptions in different languages. For our work we use the English descriptions only. We adopt the same data split as provided in [17], with 1,200 video clips for training, 100 video clips for validation and the remaining 670 clips for testing.

4.2 Implementation

Data Preprocessing and Evaluation. The average duration of the videos from the corpus is 10.2 s. So we sample only 28 frames per clip uniformly. These frames are pre-processed and passed to a CNN, here we consider NASNet-Large pre-trained model, to extract a 4032-D feature vector for each frame. So we have a 28*4032-D vector for each video from NASNet-Large. Every video has at least 28 frames and hence there is no need for padding here.

The captions provided for the videos are collected from different sources and are of varying lengths. Therefore we remove the punctuation from the captions, convert them to lower case and tokenize. The misspelt words and the least occurring words are filtered out from the vocabulary. Captions are adjusted to a length of 20. Any caption exceeding the size is truncated and a caption with less than 20 tokens is padded. Word Embedding techniques like BERT [3], GloVe, Elmo are used to obtain 768-D, 300-D or 1024-D vector for each token. We compare the performance of different word embeddings for our model in 4.4. The *bos*, *eos* tokens are used to mark the beginning and the end of the caption, *pad* as padding token and *unk* as unknown, for words not found in the vocabulary.

Experimental Setup. The 28*4032 feature vector represents the video to be processed. It is passed to the Encoder, which is a two-layer LSTM with a skip-connection. The number of units in the LSTM is taken as 512. So we get 28*512-D from layer 1 and 28*512-D from layer 2 that makes a 28*1024-D vector, from the Encoder. The SCE branch contains a single LSTM layer with 768 units and a pre-trained LSTM autoencoder. The number of units in the attention layers is set to 512. The number of units in the Decoder LSTM is taken as 1024. Adam Optimizer with a learning rate of 5e-4 is used for training and a batch-size of 64. Beam search with a beam-width of 3 is used during testing.

4.3 Evaluation Metrics

To evaluate the performance of the model we have considered 3 standard metrics: BLEU, ROUGE, CIDER and to compare the final results of our work with state-of-art papers on MSVD we have considered BLEU, METEOR and CIDER as the metrics.

- **BLEU (BiLingual Evaluation Understudy)** BLEU calculates the n-gram hit ratio of output caption against the ground truth. It is suitable for short sentences. We have used Bleu 1,2,3 and 4 scores for our performance analysis.
- **ROUGE (Recall-Oriented Understudy of Gisting Evaluation)** Rouge metric is based on the longest common subsequence. The longer the common subsequence the more similar the reference and candidate sentences.

- **METEOR (Metric for Evaluation of Translation with Explicit Ordering)** METEOR is a mean value of unigram-based recall and precision scores. The main difference between METEOR and BLEU is this metric combines both recall and precision.
- **CIDEr (Consensus-based Image Description Evaluation)** CIDER score for n-grams of length n is computed using the average cosine similarity between the generated sentence and the human annotated sentences, which accounts for both precision and recall.

4.4 Results and Analysis

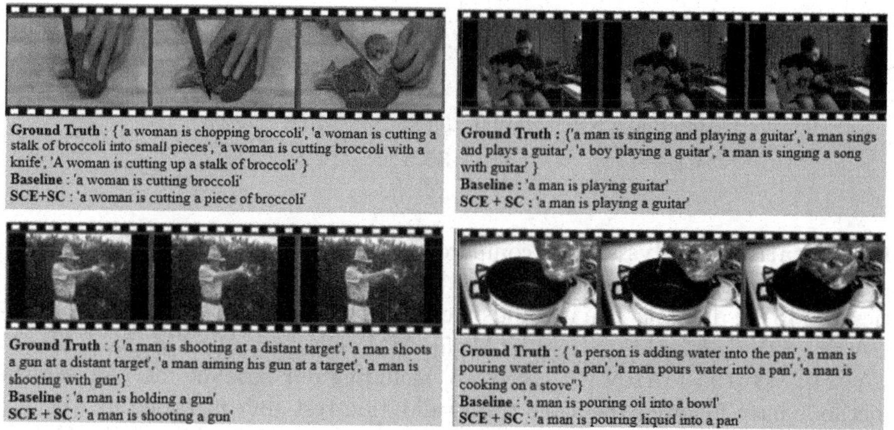

Fig. 4. The qualitative comparison of our proposed SCE+SC model, baseline and ground truth captions

Qualitative Analysis. Figure 4 shows the qualitative comparison of our proposed SCE+SC model against ground truth and baseline model captions. The video frames and ground truth shown in the figure are taken from MSVD dataset. Both the baseline model and our proposed SCE+SC model have given a good set of captions for the videos.

But the baseline model fails to identify the portrayed action and objects in few cases. The SCE+SC model has performed well in object and action identification. For example, the baseline model has given *holding* whereas the action *shooting* identified by SCE+SC model is more precise according to the context. Also, the word *bowl* is given by the baseline model whereas the word *pan* given by SCE+SC model is more appropriate. Therefore, it is clear that the semantic cross embedding helped in getting proper words.

Table 1. Performance comparison with various methods on the MSVD test dataset

Model	B@4	METEOR	Rouge	CIDEr
S2VT [17]	–	29.2	–	–
h-RNN [24]	49.9	32.6	–	65.8
V-ShaWei-GA [7]	47.9	30.9	–	–
S2VT+RL [11]	45.6	32.9	69.0	80.6
SCN-LSTM [5]	51.1	33.5	–	77.7
MMVDN [20]	37.6	29.0	–	–
aLSTM [6]	50.8	33.3	–	74.8
BAE [1]	42.5	32.4	–	63.5
TA [24]	41.9	29.6	–	51.7
M3 [19]	**52.8**	33.3	–	–
MARN [10]	48.6	35.1	71.9	**92.2**
S-VC [8]	35.1	29.3	–	–
Baseline	49.0	33.8	70.6	82.3
SCE+SC	52.1	**35.5**	**72.1**	85.7

Quantitative Analysis. We compare the performance of our method with state-of-the-art methods using BLEU@4, METEOR, ROUGE and CIDEr metrics on MSVD dataset. The methods include S2VT [17], h-RNN [24], V-ShaWei-GA [7], S2VT+RL [11], SCN-LSTM [5], MMVDN [20], aLSTM [6], BAE [1], TA [24], M3 [19], MARN [10], S-VC [8] including our baseline method. All the methods have followed the same train-validation-test split provided in [17].

Table 1 shows the metrics of various models. M3 [19] achieved the highest BLEU@4 score followed by our model which outperformed the rest in terms of BLEU@4 score. This shows that our proposed model has been able to identify the exact set of words in the dataset better than the other models which improved the BLEU@4 scores as it is measured by the n-gram hit ratio.

In terms of CIDEr metric, our proposed model ranked second. Our model achieved the highest Rouge and METEOR scores compared to others'. This trend shows that our SCE+SC model outperforms the state-of-the-art methods in video captioning. When compared to the baseline model, the proposed model achieved the highest scores. This shows that semantic cross embedding and skip-connection has boosted the performance of the model.

Table 2. Effect of various Word Embedding techniques on the model training

Model	B@1	B@2	B@3	B@4	METEOR	Rouge	CIDEr
BERT	**81.0**	**68.8**	59.1	49.0	**33.8**	**70.6**	**82.3**
Elmo	80.3	68.7	**59.3**	**49.7**	33.5	70.1	80.8
GloVe	80.6	67.0	55.7	47.8	33.1	70.3	80.3

Table 2 shows the effect of the use of different pre-trained word embeddings in our base model. With the use of BERT embeddings, the results are slightly better than Elmo and GloVe embeddings.

Table 3. Performance comparison of Bidirectional LSTM Encoder and Encoder with a skip-connection

Model	B@1	B@2	B@3	B@4	METEOR	Rouge	CIDEr
BiLSTM	81.1	69.5	59.8	49.1	33.8	69.7	79.1
LSTMs with SC	**82.8**	**71.0**	**60.9**	**50.9**	**34.2**	**70.3**	**82.4**

Table 3 compares the performance of Bidirectional LSTM Encoder and Encoder with a skip-connection. Encoder with a skip-connection performed slightly better for every metric.

Table 4. Comparison of different trained CNN models used for obtaining spatial features

Model	B@1	B@2	B@3	B@4	METEOR	Rouge	CIDEr
NASNet-Large	**75.8**	**61.9**	**50.7**	**41.1**	**31.4**	**68.4**	**76.8**
Inception-v3	72.6	57.9	48.9	39.2	30.8	60.5	66.4
VGG-16	69.8	54.5	43.1	31.4	29.3	64.6	55.4

Table 4 shows the comparison between the performances of a basic Encoder-Decoder model with a single-head attention using different 2-D CNN models. It is clear that NASNet-Large features have performed well when compared to VGG-16 and Inception-v3 based feature vectors. So, we have chosen to use NASNet-Large to extract feature vectors for the video/images.

Figure 5 shows BLEU@4 and METEOR scores for different values of the hyper-parameter λ in Eq. 7. We can observe that the model performs best when $\lambda = 0.9$.

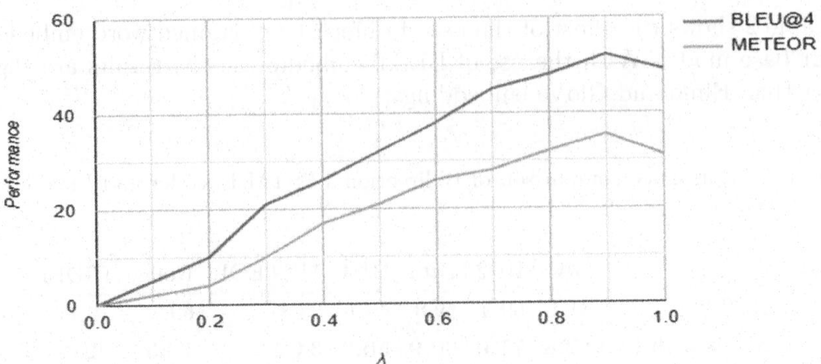

Fig. 5. BLEU@4 and METEOR scores for different values of λ

5 Conclusion

In this paper, we proposed semantic cross embedding and skip-connection in Encoder for Video Captioning. The SCE or sentence vector is a representation of the video in the caption space. It assists the Decoder to improve the performance of the model. The use of a skip-connection in the Encoder performs better than a Bidirectional Encoder. Experiments conducted on MSVD validate our approach and analysis. Our approach gave better results when compared to various other state-of-the-art techniques. Our future work would be to make use of 3-D CNNs along with 2-D CNNs to further boost the process of video captioning.

References

1. Baraldi, L., Grana, C., Cucchiara, R.: Hierarchical boundary-aware neural encoder for video captioning. In: 2017 IEEE Conference on Computer Vision and Pattern Recognition (CVPR), pp. 3185–3194 (2017)
2. Bin, Y., Yang, Y., Shen, F., Xie, N., Shen, H.T., Li, X.: Describing video with attention-based bidirectional LSTM. IEEE Trans. Cybern. **49**(7), 2631–2641 (2019)
3. Devlin, J., Chang, M., Lee, K., Toutanova, K.: BERT: pre-training of deep bidirectional transformers for language understanding. CoRR abs/1810.04805 (2018)
4. Fang, H., et al.: From captions to visual concepts and back. In: 2015 IEEE Conference on Computer Vision and Pattern Recognition (CVPR), pp. 1473–1482 (2015)
5. Gan, Z., et al.: Semantic compositional networks for visual captioning. In: 2017 IEEE Conference on Computer Vision and Pattern Recognition (CVPR), pp. 1141–1150 (2017)
6. Gao, L., Guo, Z., Zhang, H., Xu, X., Shen, H.T.: Video captioning with attention-based LSTM and semantic consistency. IEEE Trans. Multimed. **19**(9), 2045–2055 (2017)
7. Hao, W., Zhang, Z., Guan, H., Zhu, G.: Integrating both visual and audio cues for enhanced video caption (2017)

8. Li, G., Ma, S., Han, Y.: Summarization-based video caption via deep neural networks. In: Proceedings of the 23rd ACM International Conference on Multimedia, MM 2015, pp. 1191–1194. Association for Computing Machinery, New York (2015). https://doi.org/10.1145/2733373.2806314
9. Pan, Y., Yao, T., Li, H., Mei, T.: Video captioning with transferred semantic attributes. In: 2017 IEEE Conference on Computer Vision and Pattern Recognition (CVPR), pp. 984–992 (2017)
10. Pei, W., Zhang, J., Wang, X., Ke, L., Shen, X., Tai, Y.: Memory-attended recurrent network for video captioning. In: 2019 IEEE/CVF Conference on Computer Vision and Pattern Recognition (CVPR), pp. 8339–8348 (2019)
11. Rennie, S.J., Marcheret, E., Mroueh, Y., Ross, J., Goel, V.: Self-critical sequence training for image captioning. In: 2017 IEEE Conference on Computer Vision and Pattern Recognition (CVPR), pp. 1179–1195 (2017)
12. Simonyan, K., Zisserman, A.: Very deep convolutional networks for large-scale image recognition (2015)
13. Song, J., Guo, Y., Gao, L., Li, X., Hanjalic, A., Shen, H.T.: From deterministic to generative: multimodal stochastic RNNs for video captioning. IEEE Trans. Neural Netw. Learn. Syst. **30**(10), 3047–3058 (2019)
14. Song, J., Li, X., Gao, L., Shen, H.T.: Hierarchical LSTMs with adaptive attention for visual captioning. CoRR abs/1812.11004 (2018)
15. Szegedy, C., Vanhoucke, V., Ioffe, S., Shlens, J., Wojna, Z.: Rethinking the inception architecture for computer vision (2015)
16. Vaswani, A., et al.: Attention is all you need. CoRR abs/1706.03762 (2017)
17. Venugopalan, S., Rohrbach, M., Donahue, J., Mooney, R., Darrell, T., Saenko, K.: Sequence to sequence - video to text. In: 2015 IEEE International Conference on Computer Vision (ICCV), pp. 4534–4542 (2015)
18. Vinyals, O., Toshev, A., Bengio, S., Erhan, D.: Show and tell: a neural image caption generator. CoRR abs/1411.4555 (2014)
19. Wang, J., Wang, W., Huang, Y., Wang, L., Tan, T.: M3: multimodal memory modelling for video captioning. In: 2018 IEEE/CVF Conference on Computer Vision and Pattern Recognition, pp. 7512–7520 (2018)
20. Xu, H., Venugopalan, S., Ramanishka, V., Rohrbach, M., Saenko, K.: A multi-scale multiple instance video description network (2015)
21. Xu, N., Liu, A., Nie, W., Su, Y.: Attention-in-attention networks for surveillance video understanding in internet of things. IEEE Internet Things J. **5**(5), 3419–3429 (2018)
22. Xu, Y., Han, Y., Hong, R., Tian, Q.: Sequential video VLAD: training the aggregation locally and temporally. IEEE Trans. Image Process. **27**(10), 4933–4944 (2018)
23. Yang, Y., et al.: Video captioning by adversarial LSTM. IEEE Trans. Image Process. **27**(11), 5600–5611 (2018)
24. Yao, L., et al.: Describing videos by exploiting temporal structure. In: 2015 IEEE International Conference on Computer Vision (ICCV), pp. 4507–4515 (2015)
25. You, Q., Jin, H., Wang, Z., Fang, C., Luo, J.: Image captioning with semantic attention. CoRR abs/1603.03925 (2016)
26. Zheng, Q., Wang, C., Tao, D.: Syntax-aware action targeting for video captioning. In: Proceedings of the IEEE/CVF Conference on Computer Vision and Pattern Recognition (CVPR), June 2020
27. Zoph, B., Vasudevan, V., Shlens, J., Le, Q.V.: Learning transferable architectures for scalable image recognition. CoRR abs/1707.07012 (2017)

Dual Segmentation Technique for Road Extraction on Unstructured Roads for Autonomous Mobile Robots

Kethavath Raj Kumar(✉), D. K. Savitha, and Narayan Panigrahi

Centre for Artificial Intelligence and Robotics (CAIR),
Defence Research and Development Organization (DRDO), Bangalore 560093, India
rajkumark@cair.drdo.in

Abstract. Segmentation and delineation of road features from remotely sensed images find many applications including navigation. Road segmentation of mobile robots for autonomous navigation is further challenging because of illumination conditions of the scene varies as per the environment. The scene becomes more complicated in case of locations such as varying slope and unstructured or rural road conditions. We propose a novel technique called "Dual Segmentation" in which the image is pre-processed with modified RG chromacity based intensity normalization. The normalized image channels obtained are subjected to k-means clustering to find their cluster compactness. Based on the minimum cluster compactness one of the image channel is selected and Otsu segmentation is applied on it to obtain road segments. This segmented image is further processed with morphological operations to remove noise. Finally gray connected operation is applied to retain the single large road segment by removing many small unconnected regions. The outcome of the proposed Dual Segmentation technique gives pixel accuracy of about 99% with reference to ground truth images. The average execution time per image is 0.07 s when run on an Intel i5-M520 @ 2.40 GHz CPU.

Keywords: Dual segmentation · RG chromacity · Otsu segmentation · Morphological operations · Gray connected · Robot navigation

1 Introduction

Perception plays an important role in ground mobile robots for autonomous navigation of outdoor environments [1]. In perception, vision and Light Detection and Ranging (LiDAR) sensors are used for road segmentation, object detection and object tracking [2]. However, vision sensors are inexpensive and light weight as compared to Light Detection and Ranging (LiDAR). The image captured by vision sensors contains rich information such as texture, color and luminance. Segmentation of road from the Instantaneous Field of View (IFOV) of vision sensor capturing the scene from a perspective camera is very useful for autonomous navigation of unmanned ground vehicle. This problem becomes

S. K. Singh et al. (Eds.): CVIP 2020, CCIS 1378, pp. 478–489, 2021.
https://doi.org/10.1007/978-981-16-1103-2_40

challenging when the terrain is highly undulated with varying slope, lighting conditions and unstructured roads without proper marking of lane, median and signs of navigation aids.

Autonomous navigation of ground mobile robots in natural environments has many peculiarities. There are various deep-learning based state-of-the-art methods for road segmentation reported by [3,4]. Most of them have high computational requirements and training overheads. In this paper, we propose an algorithm called "Dual Segmentation" for segmentation of road regions in unstructured road environments using a mono-camera mounted on the ground mobile robot. We implemented a modified Otsu Thresholding method for road segmentation by using harmonic mean normalization as a pre-processing step. Further to improve the segmented image we applied morphological transformations and grayconnected in the post processing for better delineation of road data from perspective IFOV. The road segmentation results are experimentally verified for images containing different conditions like varying illumination, texture, colour and slope. The results of our proposed method are compared with varying ground truth data. The outcome of the computation has distinct advantages such as (1) It is computationally inexpensive i.e. it can work with low-end CPUs, (2) No training data is required to segment and classify the roads from the images, and (3) It is economical in terms of memory requirements and human effort.

2 Related Work

In general, vision sensors are used in many applications for mobile robots such as object detection, identifying traffic signals, object tracking, road detection, etc. Xu et al. presented vision based road detection algorithm in unstructured environment [5]. In recent years, extensive study has been conducted in vision based road detection and segmentation. There are various methods based on texture and color features. Rotaru et al. [6] uses the features extracted using the HSI color space for road segmentation, while Christopher et al. [7] uses a combination of color and texture features. Deb et al. converts the RGB image into the YCbCr colorspace and applies thresholding and detection of the road on the Luminance(Y) plane of the image [8]. However, in unstructured environments, the texture and color features are complex and these methods suffer due to changing lighting conditions. Lu et al. proposed superpixel based road segmentation [9]. Alvarez and Lopez depict the illumination invariance by converting it in the log chromaticity scale normalized in the G plane [10].

Another school of thought for road segmentation is based on road boundaries. He et al. [11] proposed to fit a road curvature based model using road boundaries for road segmentation. However, this method fails in unstructured environments which do not have appropriate road boundaries. Kong et al. [12] used vanishing points for road segmentation. This approach fails in presence of a curved road or a slope. Alvarez et al. [13] uses prior information for road segmentation obtained from geographic information systems (GIS) in combination with road cues which are estimated from the image. This however fails for most cases which don't have GIS database.

Isafiade et al. segments the road using line model matching(LMM) and road model matching(RMM) along with the ISODATA clustering [14]. S. Beucher et al. uses watershed algorithm for extracting road regions which detects shadows as obstcales [15]. Chen shows a concept of preprocessing using Sobel operator for detecting edges and removing the pixels which are not relating to the road part of the image and then applying Machine Learning [16]. However, this algorithm doesn't converge well enough and is dependent on the annotated dataset.

Lyu et al. uses Convolutional Neural Networks (CNN) based algorithm for road segmentation using 3D point-cloud data from LiDAR [17]. This requires annotations of point cloud data which is quite tedious in itself.

3 Theory

Techniques used in our road segmentation approach are as described in Fig. 1. They contain resizing, normalization, clustering, thresholding, morphological operations and gray-connected. Each one of them are explained in detail.

3.1 RG Chromaticity

The RG Chromaticity color space is known to be intensity invariant. Any pixel of an image will have three colors, Red, Green and Blue within it. In RG colorspace, the pixel values are represented by the relative proportion of these values rather than their absolute intensity values. This has many known advantages for applications of computer vision and image processing. Since in this colorspace, the intensity information is not present, lighting changes does not produce major effects. Moreover this colorspace is less prone to intensity based noises arising due to external lighting conditions [18, 19].

3.2 K-Means Clustering

Clustering is a popular method in data analytics. The aim of this process is to cluster the data points into various partitions. One such unsupervised method for clustering is k-means clustering. It tries to divide the data points into k clusters.

The k-means clustering algorithm minimizes the objective function, in this case a squared error function given by:

$$J = \sum_{i=1}^{k} \sum_{j=1}^{n} ||x_i(j) - b_j|| \tag{1}$$

where $x_i(j)$ are the intensity values of pixels; b_j is the cluster centre (the centroids); n is the number of data points; k is the number of clusters [20].

3.3 Otsu Thresholding

Thresholding is a very crucial operation in image segmentation. It is through this step that we can classify the pixels of image in separate classes. There are various methods for this but most of them require thresholds to specify manually. This is quite tedious and cumbersome process. There is one such thresholding technique called Otsu's method which does not require to manually specify the threshold limits. It automatically identifies the threshold values [21,22].

Otsu's algorithm divides the image into 2 classes. The threshold t is chosen so as to maximize the inter-class variance which in turn minimizes the intra-class variance simultaneously. The individual class probabilities P are:

$$q_1(t) = \sum_{i=1}^{t} P(i) \quad q_2(t) = \sum_{i=t+1}^{l} P(i) \tag{2}$$

The class means are given by:

$$\mu_1(t) = \sum_{i=1}^{t} \frac{iP(i)}{q_1(t)} \quad \mu_2(t) = \sum_{i=t+1}^{l} \frac{iP(i)}{q_2(t)} \tag{3}$$

The aim of the algorithm is to minimize the intra-class variance which are given by:

$$\sigma_1(t) = \sum_{i=1}^{t} [i - \mu_1(t)]^2 \frac{P(i)}{q_1(t)} \quad \sigma_2(t) = \sum_{i=t+1}^{l} [i - \mu_2(t)]^2 \frac{P(i)}{q_2(t)} \tag{4}$$

And the weighted intra-class variance is:

$$\sigma_w(t) = q_1(t)\sigma_1(t) + q_2(t)\sigma_2(t) \tag{5}$$

where $\mu_1(t)$, $\mu_2(t)$ are means of the road and non road class and $\sigma_1(t)$, $\sigma_2(t)$ are the variances of the class.

3.4 Morphological Transformations

Morphological operations are post processing steps applied after the thresholding operations. The mask obtained after thresholding are often distorted by texture and contain noise. A well known operation for noise removal is opening. This involved erosion followed by dilation. Erosion switches the pixel off which were previously on. This would remove the pixels that were wrongly classified. Dilation operation does the reverse by switching the pixel on which was classified wrongly. This would classify some foreground pixels which was wrongly classified as background [23].

3.5 Grayconnected

Grayconnected is connected component based algorithm for image classification. It takes into account the pixel values of neighbouring pixels and classifies accordingly. This works on the fundamental principle that objects belonging to a specific class having similar gray values will be present in the connected form [24].

4 Proposed Method

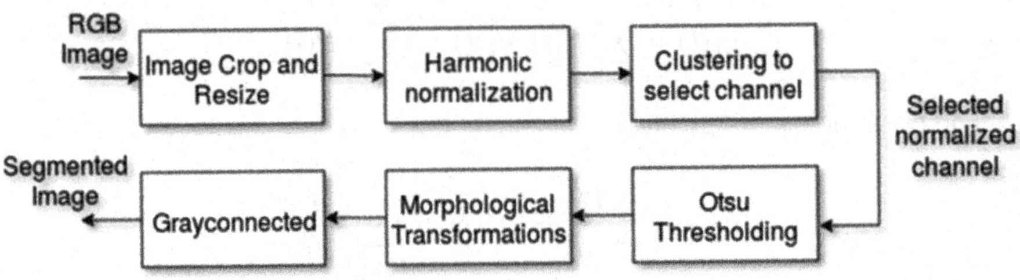

Fig. 1. Block diagram of Dual Segmentation methodology

The first step is to preprocess the image to remove the region above horizon and resizing the image for easier computations. In our robot, the camera was placed on the ground robot in such a manner that the sky region constitutes the upper half of the image.

In certain cases, the camera individual Red, Green and Blue components were obtained from the image and then we converted the RGB image to a chromaticity invariant colorspace normalized by harmonic means of the individual r, g and b values as shown below:

$$c1 = \frac{\frac{1}{r}}{\frac{3}{\frac{1}{r}+\frac{1}{g}+\frac{1}{b}}} \quad c2 = \frac{\frac{1}{g}}{\frac{3}{\frac{1}{r}+\frac{1}{g}+\frac{1}{b}}} \quad c3 = \frac{\frac{1}{b}}{\frac{3}{\frac{1}{r}+\frac{1}{g}+\frac{1}{b}}} \tag{6}$$

This method was inspired by the concept of rg chromticity [18,19]. Normalizing R, G and B values of an image gets rid of distortions caused by excess illumination and shadows in the image. This makes the image satisfy the normal distribution which reduces effects due to poor contrasts and removes glares in the image. Thus the quality of the image is improved making it easier for further processing.

In most of the cases, the road region was visually observed to lie on the plane constituted by the normalized blue image. However, in some cases it was observed that the normalized green image visually contained better segregation of the road region and the non-road region. A weighted average of all images was also considered, but pre-determining the weights for every image is difficult. It is not possible to manually select the road component for further processing of the image. To avoid this human intervention, each of the three normalized components of the image are passed through a k-means clustering algorithm with k = 2. One underlying assumption behind implementation of k-means clustering is that the entire road region has similar intensity values and is contained within a single cluster. This would segregate each image component (namely c_1, c_2 and c_3) into two clusters with similar intensity values within the cluster. The values of centroid for each cluster were computed. The normalized component containing a better contrast between the road and non-road region has considerable difference between the centroid values of the two clusters. This component with greater difference between the centroids is then chosen for further processing. An example to illustrate the working and importance of k-means clustering is produced below. Figure 1 shows the input image, its equivalent image c_2, and its subsequent clusters obtained by applying k-means clustering. As observed, the difference in the cluster intensity is minor and hence the clusters are showing non-road region in the road-part clusters and vice-versa. This proves that the c_2 image is not the appropriate choice for segmentation.

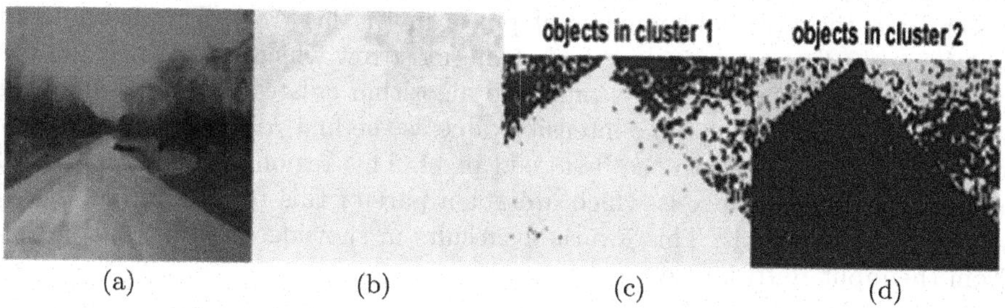

(a) (b) (c) (d)

Fig. 2. The images from left to right are (a) input image, (b) c_2 image, (c) cluster 1 and (d) cluster 2.

Here, Fig. 2 shows the input image, its equivalent c_2 image and its subsequent clusters obtained by applying k-means clustering. Unlike in c_2 image, the difference in the cluster intensity is quite apparent and hence the clusters are distinctly different, with very little noise. Thus we use c_3 for further processing for this particular image. The average intensity of each cluster is given by the centroid value (Fig. 3).

The next step of the algorithm involves thresholding the monochrome image into a binary image using otsu's thresholding.

The output binary image then undergoes a series of morphological operations where the regions having an area lesser than a predetermined threshold are eliminated. The output of these operations is found to segment the road region in the image with satisfactory accuracy. However, some non-road regions are also classified as road regions. To eliminate this error, a novel Dual Segmentation method is developed that determines the false positives and discards them. In

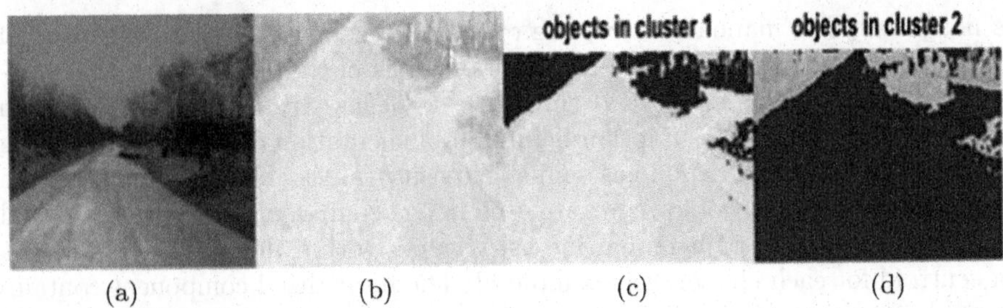

Fig. 3. The images from left to right are (a) input image, (b) c_2 image, (c) cluster 1 and (d) cluster 2.

this Dual Segmentation method, it is assumed that the robot lies on the road and the image taken by the monocular camera mounted on the robot contains road pixels in its bottom-most row. Our aim is to identify the first road pixel in the bottom-most row. A region in the bottom-most row is considered as a road if it contains more than a threshold number of pixels continuously classified as road. To obtain this, we eliminate pixels (wrongly classified as road) containing lesser than the threshold number of pixels in the last row. This helps us in obtaining the first road pixel in the bottom-most row which is further fed to the grayconnected algorithm. Grayconnected algorithm creates a region containing all the pixels having the same intensity value as the first road pixel and directly or indirectly connected to the first road pixel. This region is classified as road region. All the other pixels which are not a part of this region are considered as the non road pixels. This invariably results in showing only the road region from the input RGB image.

5 Experiments

5.1 Thresholding on Various Channels

Here we present the results of thresholding on the channels normalized using Arithmetic Mean (AM), Geometric Mean (GM) and Harmonic Mean (HM). As we clearly see the red channel of harmonic mean produces best results. Hence we chose this channel for further processing. The k means clustering approach quantifies this. Henceforth we will perform harmonic normalization and select the red channel for the next step.

5.2 Thresholding Without Harmonic Normalization

We can clearly observe that thresholding after harmonic mean normalization has improved the results significantly.

5.3 Morphological Transformations After Thresholding

Morphological Transformation removed the unwanted noise (Fig. 5).

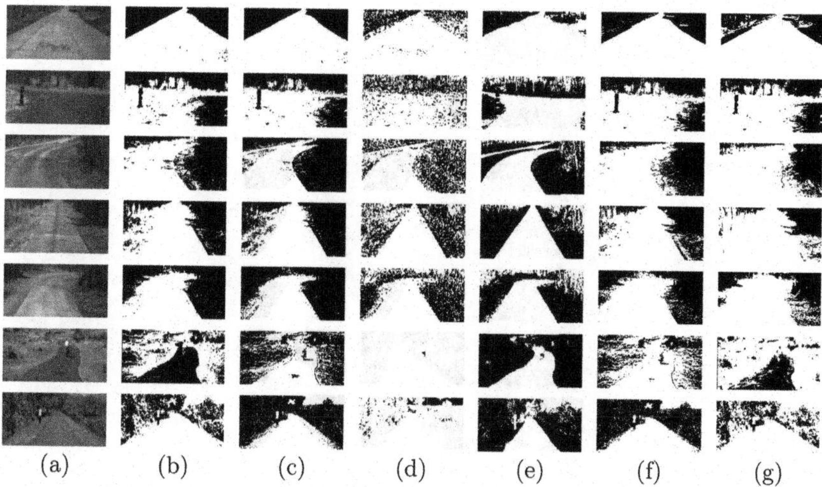

Fig. 4. The columns from left to right are (a) input images, (b) Otsu thresholding on green channel and (c) Otsu thresholding on red channel (d) Otsu thresholding on Harmonic Mean's green channel and (e) Otsu thresholding on Harmonic Mean's red channel (f) Otsu thresholding on Geometric Mean's green channel and (g) Otsu thresholding on Geometric Mean's red channel (Color figure online)

5.4 Grayconnected Operation

The grayconnected operation removed the unwanted sections. We assume that from the camera view all the parts of the road would be connected. This helped in removing some misclassified portions of the image (Fig. 6).

6 Results

In order to compute the accuracy, the ground truth of an image is necessary which has a clear observation of the road and non-road region. The ground truth was created using MATLAB 2017b Image-Segmenter application by treating all the road pixels as 1's and the non-road pixels as 0's i.e. the road region was colored with white color manually and the non road region, that is the left out pixels were read as 0's. Each pixel of the obtained binary image was compared with the corresponding pixel of the ground truth image and the accuracy was calculated based on the pixel accuracy [25] using the formula given below:

$$\eta = \frac{Total\ Number\ of\ Pixels\ Matched\ with\ Ground\ Truth}{Total\ Number\ of\ Pixels} \tag{7}$$

Dice Coefficient was computed according to the formula given below

$$DSC = \frac{2|X \cap Y|}{|X| + |Y|} \tag{8}$$

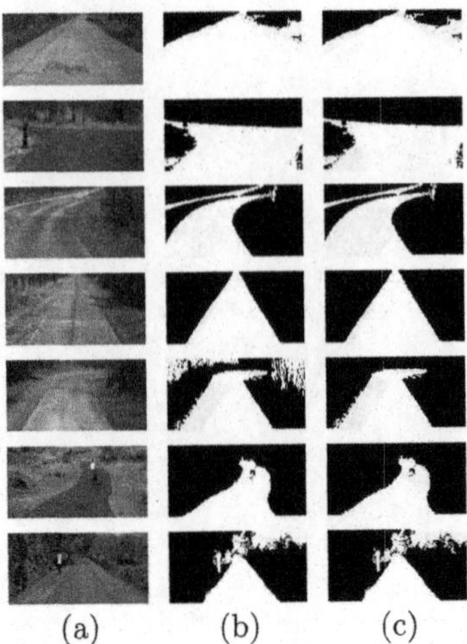

Fig. 5. The images from left to right are (a) input image and (b) outputs of morphological transform operation (c) output of grayconnected operation

Here the X and Y are predicted mask and groud truth mask respectively. We also computed Jaccard Index according to the formula given below

$$JC = \frac{|X \cap Y|}{|X \cup Y|} \tag{9}$$

Similary here the X and Y are predicted mask and groud truth mask respectively [26].

The dataset for testing our algorithm was captured from a camera mounted on a mobile robot. The images in the dataset were particularly taken from a known campus area with presence of unstructured roads and less maintained roads. Of these images, we chose images present in Column 1 of Fig. 4 for the purpose of the paper to prove the validity of the proposed algorithm based on the inclusion of all the possibilities which one may encounter in a unstructured roads road condition. The dataset includes images with differences in texture, illumination and presence of objects commonly found in unstructured roads settings. Roads observed in this settings are unstructured roads without availability of delineated markings. Table 1 describes the results in various metrics including pixel accuracy, dice coefficient and jaccard index. The Dual Segmentation algorithm clocked an average execution time of 0.07 s per image when run on an Intel i5-M520 @ 2.40 GHz CPU.

The state of the art deep learning based methods require high computational resources including Graphic Processing Units (GPUs) with dedicated GPU RAM. For instance, state of the art semantic segmentation networks require GPU RAM in the order of 16 GB for training and more than 8 GB for inference [3].

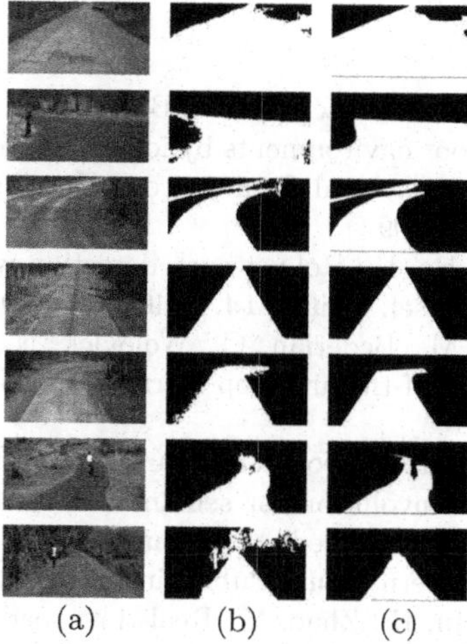

Fig. 6. The columns from left to right are (a) input images, (b) dual segmentation output and (c) ground truth

Table 1. Evaluation results on dataset

Metric name	Otsu thresholding	Dual segmentation
Pixel accuracy	0.9532	0.9903
Dice similarity coefficient	0.8872	0.909
Jaccard index	0.7982	0.8452

7 Conclusion

The proposed segmentation method called Dual Segmentation gave efficient results, in terms of the time taken to run the algorithm as well as accuracy of results. The outcome of the proposed segmentation technique for test images gave pixel accuracy of about 99% with reference to their ground truth images. It is concluded that the Dual Segmentation method is able to segment the unstructured roads and less maintained roads for navigation of mobile robot. The algorithm is computationally inexpensive and economical. Since it only needs a camera and a low-end CPUs. Also, it does not require the exercise of training the data, thus saving time and energy. The mask generated from this algorithm can be used as ground truth for machine learning based solutions.

Acknowledgment. The authors would like to thank Director, CAIR and Shri V C Ravi for helping us in procuring resources and publishing these results.

References

1. Wurm, K.M., Kümmerle, R., Stachniss, C., Burgard, W.: Improving robot navigation in structured outdoor environments by identifying vegetation from laser data. In: 2009 IEEE/RSJ International Conference on Intelligent Robots and Systems, pp. 1217–1222, October 2009
2. Tan, J., Li, J., An, X., He, H.: Robust curb detection with fusion of 3D-lidar and camera data. Sensors (Basel, Switz.) **14**, 9046–9073 (2014)
3. Guignard, M., Schild, M., Bederián, C., Wolovick, N., Vega, A.J.: Performance characterization of state-of-the-art deep learning workloads on an ibm "minsky" platform, January 2018
4. Chen, L.-C., Zhu, Y., Papandreou, G., Schroff, F., Adam, H.: Encoder-decoder with atrous separable convolution for semantic image segmentation. In: Hebert, M., Sminchisescu, C., Weiss, Y. (eds.) Computer Vision - ECCV 2018, vol. Ferrari, pp. 833–851. Springer International Publishing, Cham (2018)
5. Xu, W., Zhuang, Y., Hu, H., Zhao, Y.: Real-time road detection and description for robot navigation in an unstructured campus environment. In: Proceeding of the 11th World Congress on Intelligent Control and Automation, pp. 928–933, June 2014
6. Rotaru, C., Graf, T., Zhang, J.: Color image segmentation in HSI space forautomotive applications. J. Real-Time Image Process. **3**(4), 311–322 (2008). https://doi.org/10.1007/s11554-008-0078-9
7. Rasmussen, C.: Combining laser range, color, and texture cues for autonomous road following. In: Proceedings 2002 IEEE International Conference on Robotics and Automation (Cat. No. 02CH37292), vol. 4, pp. 4320–4325, May 2002
8. Kaushik, D., Suny, A.: Shadow detection and removal based on YCbCr color space. Smart Comput. Rev. **4**, 02 (2014)
9. Lu, K., Li, J., An, X., He, H.: Vision sensor-based road detection for field robot navigation. Sensors **15**, 29 594–29 617 (2015)
10. Alvarez, J.M., Lopez, A.M.: Road detection based on illuminant invariance. IEEE Trans. Intell. Transp. Syst. **12**(1), 184–193 (2011)
11. He, Y., Wang, H., Zhang, B.: Color-based road detection in urban traffic scenes. IEEE Trans. Intell. Transp. Syst. **5**(4), 309–318 (2004)
12. Kong, H., Audibert, J., Ponce, J.: General road detection from a single image. IEEE Trans. Image Process. **19**(8), 2211–2220 (2010)
13. Alvarez, J.M., Lopez, A.M., Gevers, T., Lumbreras, F.: Combining priors, appearance, and context for road detection. IEEE Trans. Intell. Transp. Syst. **15**(3), 1168–1178 (2014)
14. Falola, O., Osunmakinde, I., Bagula, A.: Supporting drivable region detection by minimising salient pixels generated through robot sensors, June 2019
15. Murou, W.: Image segmentation: a watershed transformation algorithm, January 2016
16. Chen, K.-H., Tsai, W.-H.: Vision-based autonomous land vehicle guidance in outdoor road environments using combined line and road following techniques. J. Robot. Syst. **14**(10), 711–728 (1997)
17. Lyu, Y., Bai, L., Huang, X.: Real-time road segmentation using lidar data processing on an FPGA. In: 2018 IEEE International Symposium on Circuits and Systems (ISCAS), pp. 1–5, May 2018
18. Martinkauppi, J.B., Pietikäinen, M.: Facial skin colormodeling, pp. 113–135. Springer, New York (2005). https://doi.org/10.1007/0-387-27257-7_6

19. Gevers, T., Gijsenij, A., van de Weijer, J., Geusebroek, J.: Pixel-BasedPhotometric Invariance, ch. 4, pp. 47–68. John Wiley Sons, Ltd. (2012). https://doi.org/10.1002/9781118350089.ch4
20. Kanungo, T., et al.: An efficient k-means clustering algorithm: analysis and implementation. IEEE Trans. Pattern Anal. Mach. Intell. **24**, 881–892 (2002)
21. Otsu, N.: A threshold selection method from gray-level histograms. IEEE Trans. Syst. Man Cybern. **9**, 62–66 (1979)
22. Yousefi, J.: Image binarization using Otsu thresholding algorithm, May 2015
23. Anuar, K., Jambek, A., Sulaiman, N.: A study of image processing using morphological opening and closing processes. Int. J. Control Theory Appl. **9**, 15–21 (2016)
24. Wang, Y., Bhattacharya, P.: Image analysis and segmentation using gray connected components. In: 1996 IEEE International Conference on Systems, Man and Cybernetics. Information Intelligence and Systems (Cat. No. 96CH35929), vol. 1, pp. 444–449, October 1996
25. Zhang, Y.J.: A review of recent evaluation methods for image segmentation. In: Proceedings of the Sixth International Symposium on Signal Processing and its Applications (Cat. No. 01EX467), vol. 1, pp. 148–151, August 2001
26. Taha, A.A., Hanbury, A.: Metrics for evaluating 3d medical image segmentation: analysis, selection, and tool. BMC Med. Imaging **15**(1), 1–28 (2015)

Edge Based Robust and Secure Perceptual Hashing Framework

Satendra Pal Singh(✉) and Gaurav Bhatnagar

Department of Mathematics, Indian Institute of Technology Jodhpur, Jodhpur, India
pg201383504@iitj.ac.in

Abstract. In this paper, a novel hashing framework is proposed using edge map and image normalization. In the proposed method, the input image is normalized using geometric moments and an edge map is then employed using the canny edge detector. The estimated binary image is divided into non-overlapping blocks and a chaotic map is used for random block selection. The singular value decomposition is carried out on the selected blocks for extracting the significant features followed by generation of hash value. The simulation results support the contention that the proposed technique is secure and considerately robust against a variety of image manipulations.

Keywords: Perceptual hashing · Image normalization · Singular value decomposition · Edge map

1 Introduction

In today's world where rapid development in communication technology and widespread availability of internet increases the pervasive multimedia data sharing through social network websites such as Facebook, Linkden, Instagram etc. Simultaneously, unethical practices and digital forgery of digital content reached up to significant level due to easily available software tools. Therefore, identification and authentication of digital content are of paramount importance. As a result, several solutions have been developed to address these issues in past few years but perceptual hashing is superior among image security applications.

Generally, hashing techniques can be categorized in two groups namely perceptual image hashing and cryptographic hashing technique respectively. The former technique allows limited perceptible changes whereas the latter is very sensitive to single bit changes of the input data. Due to this fact, traditional hash functions such as SHA-1 [1] are not appropriate for image authentication. Typically, an image hash is a kind of unique identifier that represents the respective image. An ideal hash function should preserve three important property namely robustness, secure and discrimination respectively. 'Robustness' implies that similar image content should result in a similar hash value. The security of hash function can be described in two ways. Firstly, the entity with correct

S. K. Singh et al. (Eds.): CVIP 2020, CCIS 1378, pp. 490–500, 2021.
https://doi.org/10.1007/978-981-16-1103-2_41

secret key can generate the exact hash value. Secondly, the image hash must be able to detect the malicious manipulations. Finally, 'discrimination' imply that different images should generate the different hash value corresponding to input content.

A number of image hashing approaches [2–7] have been designed and proposed in the existing literature. However, to achieve the desired level of robustness and security for a universally optimal scheme remains a challenging task. Swaminathan et al. [2] developed a image hashing technique based on Fourier-Mellin transform and controlled randomization process. This method is rotation invariant and provides better robustness against geometric distortions. Khelifi et al. [3] computes image hash based on virtual watermark detection using weibull distribution, but the method is unable to detect the small change in area of the content. Lv et al. [4] proposed a hashing method on the basis of SIFT feature and Harris corner detector. In this approach, key points are obtained using SIFT detector, from which most stable points are then retained using Harris corner detector. Tang et al. [5] presented an image hashing technique based on tensor decomposition. This method shows limited robustness against geometric operations, specifically for large degrees of rotations. Monga et al. [6] proposed a two-stage framework for perceptual image hashing using feature points, where end-stopped wavelet transform is employed for feature detection. Then, an iterative process is followed to obtain the final hash value. An extending approach has been discussed in [7]. An image hashing approach based on the combination of local and global features is developed by Ouyang et al. [8]. These features are obtained by SIFT detector and Zernike moments respectively. This method is resilient to geometric operations but less sensitive against content manipulation. Neelima et al. [9] proposed a hashing technique based on SIFT features and singular value decomposition. This technique shows poor performance against rotations. Singh et al. [10] proposed a hashing framework based on discrete cosine transform and SVD. The technique show good performance against geometric manipulation. In addition, Singh et al. [11] proposed a novel security framework for medical images, in which author generate the perceptual hash value using SIFT features.

In this work, a new perceptual hashing framework based on image normalization and edge map is proposed, which is robust enough for numerous image processing operations as well as geometric distortions. The basic idea is to extract the invariant feature from the test image and convert into the hash value using the hash generation process. For this purpose, the input image is normalized using geometric moments and an edge map is employed using the Canny edge detector. The binary image is then divided into non-overlapping blocks and a random block selection process is employed using piece-wise linear chaotic map. The significant coefficients are extracted from the each selected block using the singular value. The obtained vector is quantized to generate the final hash value. Finally, attack analysis and comparative analysis demonstrate better robustness and reliability of the proposed scheme against intentional or unintentional attacks.

The rest of the paper is organized as follows. Section 2 describes the Singular value decomposition, Edge detection process and Piecewise linear chaotic map. Section 3 presents the proposed hashing framework. Experimental results and analysis is discussed in Sect. 4. Finally, concluding remarks are summarized in Sect. 5.

2 Mathematical Preliminaries

2.1 Piece-Wise Linear Chaotic Map (PWLCM)

In a chaotic system, a piecewise linear chaotic map (PWLCM) [12] is a 1D linear map that is composed of multiple linear segments. It has versatile dynamical properties such sensitivity to initial condition in comparison to chaotic map with single segment. Mathematically,

$$Z(\ell+1) = M[Z(\ell);k] = \begin{cases} \frac{Z(\ell)}{k}, & \text{if} Z(\ell) \in [0,k) \\ \frac{Z(\ell)-k}{0.5-k}, & \text{if} Z(\ell) \in [k,0.5) \\ M[1-Z(\ell);k], & \text{if} Z(\ell) \in [0.5,1) \end{cases} \tag{1}$$

where k is a real constant such that $k \in (0, 0.5)$ and $Z(\cdot) \in (0, 1)$. This map contains four line segments. The main benefit of this is that it has large key space with no periodic window in the approximated region.

2.2 Singular Value Decomposition

Singular value decomposition (SVD) is an efficient matrix decomposition method, which is useful in many signal and image processing applications. Recently, SVD is used in perceptual hashing technique due to its stable feature. Let $\mathcal{I}$ be a matrix of size $m \times n$, then Singular value decomposition (SVD) of $\mathcal{I}$ can be express as: $\mathcal{I} = USV^T$, where U and V are unitary matrix of size $m \times m$ and $n \times n$ respectively. S is a diagonal matrix of $m \times n$ where the leading diagonal contains the non-negative elements.

2.3 Edge Detection Process

Edge detection is a mathematical approach that extracts the points of high contrast by estimating the intensity difference in the image. All these points combinedly constitute an edge map of the corresponding image. The edges represent the object boundary in an image and therefore considered as an important feature. The edge detectors namely Sobel, Prewitt and canny edge detectors are used to generate the edge map, but its low error rate and strong de-noising ability makes it superior among all. In the proposed hashing framework, the canny edge detector is applied to extract edges in the test image.

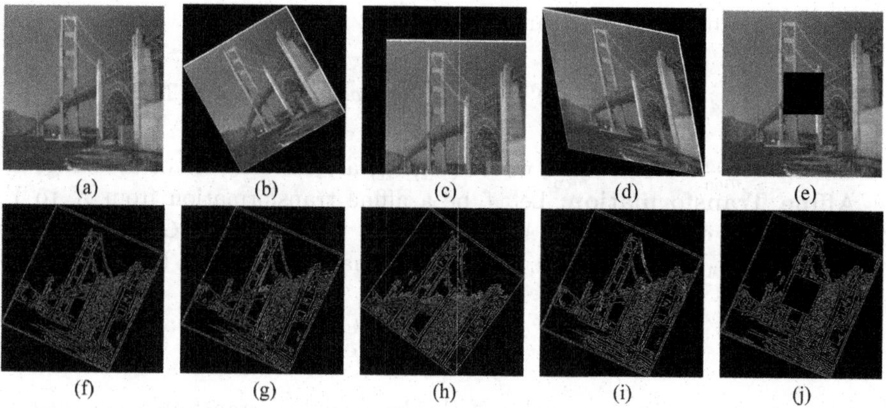

Fig. 1. (a) Original image, (b) Rotation, (c) Translation, (d) Shearing, (e) Cropping; Second row shows the edges after normalization.

3 Proposed Hashing Framework

Without loss of generality, assume that I is an original gray-scale image of size $M \times N$ and H be the corresponding hash value of length L. In order to generate hash value, the input image is preprocessed, then normalization and edge map is applied on the resultant image. An illustration is depicted in Fig. 1. The details of designing steps used in the hash generation process is given below.

3.1 Image Pre-processing

The input test image may be of different size, but the length of the generated hash should be same. Therefore, all the images are resized to the same standard size of $M \times N$ to ensure the fixed length hash value.

3.2 Image Normalization

The determination of invariant features plays a crucial role in various image analysis applications. These features retain the relevant configuration information under a class of appropriate transformation such as affine transformation which includes the rotation, scaling and translation information of an image. The image normalization can be achieved by utilizing the geometric and central moments. The whole process can be summarized as:

- **Image Moments:** Let $\mathcal{H}(u, v)$ be a gray-scale image of size $M \times N$. Then its geometric moments $m_{r,s}$ of order $(r+s)^{th}$ can be defined as:

$$m_{r,s} = \iint_C u^r v^s \mathcal{H}(u, v)\,du dv \quad r, s = 0, 1, 2 \ldots \tag{2}$$

The central moments $\mu_{r,s}$ can be defined as:

$$\mu_{r,s} = \iint_c (u - u_\alpha)^r (v - v_\beta)^s \mathcal{H}(u,v) du dv \quad r,s = 0,1,2\ldots \tag{3}$$

and $u_\alpha = \frac{m_{10}}{m_{00}}$ $v_\alpha = \frac{m_{01}}{m_{00}}$, where (u_α, v_α) are the centroid of the image H.

- **Affine Transformation:** Let f be a affine transformation from X to Y. Then, there exist a matrix M with respect to linear map G and vector B such that $\mathcal{H}_A(u,v) = G[\mathcal{H}(u,v)] + B$. Schemantically, it can be written as

$$\begin{bmatrix} u_a \\ v_a \end{bmatrix} = \begin{bmatrix} a_{11} \ a_{22} \\ a_{33} \ a_{44} \end{bmatrix} \begin{bmatrix} u \\ v \end{bmatrix} + \begin{bmatrix} t_1 \\ t_2 \end{bmatrix} \tag{4}$$

where $a_{11}, a_{22}, a_{33}, a_{44}, t_1$ and $t_2 \in R$. The geometric transformations such as rotation, scaling, translation and shearing transform can be derived from this transformation. The combination of these transformation are used in image normalization as follows:

1. For translation invariance, center the image $\mathcal{H}(u,v)$ using Eq. (6), matrix G_t and vector (t_1, t_2) such that:

$$G_t = \begin{bmatrix} 1 \ 0 \\ 0 \ 1 \end{bmatrix}, t_1 = \frac{m_{10}}{m_{00}}, \quad t_2 = \frac{m_{01}}{m_{00}} \tag{5}$$

The transformed coordinate can be obtained as:

$$(u_a, v_a)^T = (a_{11} - t_1, a_{44} - t_2)^T \tag{6}$$

2. For shear invariance, apply the share operator on the resultant image in x-direction followed by y-direction. The matrix correspond to these operator are given below:

$$G_x = \begin{bmatrix} 1 \ \beta \\ 0 \ 1 \end{bmatrix}, G_y = \begin{bmatrix} 1 \ 0 \\ \gamma \ 1 \end{bmatrix} \tag{7}$$

where β and γ can be obtained by the following relation:

$$\beta^3 \mu_{03}^{(t)} + 3\beta^2 \mu_{12}^{(t)} + 3\beta \mu_{21}^{(t)} + \mu_{30}^{(t)} = \mu_{30}^{(x)} \tag{8}$$

$$\mu_{11}^{(x)} + \gamma \mu_{20}^{(x)} = \mu_{11}^{(y)} \tag{9}$$

3. For scaling invariance, scale the resultant image in x and y direction to achieve similar size to the original image. The matrix corresponding to scaling operator is give as:

$$G_s = \begin{bmatrix} \alpha \ 0 \\ 0 \ \delta \end{bmatrix} \tag{10}$$

3.3 Hash Generation Process

1. Apply normalization to the preprocessed image I^P as described in the Sect. 3.2. Let I^N be the normalized image.
2. Obtain a binary image I^B using edge map on normalized image I^N.
3. Partition the image I^B into non-overlapping blocks $\{B_j|j = 1, 2 \dots L\}$ of size $r \times r$, where $L = (M \times N)/r^2$.
4. Select the random blocks using the secret key S_{key} and PWLCM as described in Sect. 2.1.
$$B_s = \{B_j|j = 1, 2 \dots S_k,\ \ k = 1, 2 \dots L\} \tag{11}$$
5. Apply SVD on the selected blocks B_s.
$$B_s = U_s S_s V_s^T \tag{12}$$
6. Select the maximum singular value from each block and generate the intermediate hash value.
$$I_F = \{S_i|i = 1, 2 \dots S_k,\ \ k = 1, 2 \dots L\} \tag{13}$$
7. Obtain the binary sequence as follows.
$$H_F = \begin{cases} 1, & \text{if } I_F \geq T \\ 0, & \text{otherwise} \end{cases} \tag{14}$$
Where threshold T is a mean value of the vector I_F.
8. The vector H_F is randomly permuted to generate the final hash value H.

4 Results and Discussion

To assess the performance of the proposed technique, an extensive experimental analysis has been conducted using various gray-scale images. The benchmark images such as Bridge, Lena, Eline, Lake and Car of size 512×512 are considered as the experimental images and depicted in Fig. 2. Each image is divided into non-overlapping blocks of size 32 and length of the generated hash value is 256 bit.

Fig. 2. Experimental Images: (a) Bridge, (b) Lena, (c) Eline, (d) Lake, (e) Car.

The similarity between the hash is measured using Normalized Hamming Distance (NHD). The NHD is computed for a pair of image hashes and normalized it with respect to the length of the hashes. Mathematically, NHD can be defined as follows

$$NHD = \frac{\sum_{i=1}^{L} H_k(i) - H_m(i)}{L} \tag{15}$$

where L is the length of the hash value of the kth and m^{th} image respectively. The normalized hamming distance is inversionally proportional to similarity between the image pairs. A prefixed threshold value τ is used to classify the visually similar or dissimilar image. If NHD between the hash pairs is less than τ then the image is considered as the visually similar image otherwise the different ones. Another important criteria is that perceptually hashing technique should be completely secure. Therefore, the proposed scheme employed the random block section process using Piece-wise linear chaotic map. The seed value is 0.18 for the proposed hashing technique. The performance of the proposed technique is evaluated based on perceptual robustness and comparative analysis. The details are discussed in the following sections.

4.1 Perceptual Robustness

Various content preserving operations such as additive Gaussian noise, Median filter, Rotation, Scaling, and JPEG compression are applied on the test images to measure the robustness of the proposed technique. The NHD is computed between the hashes extracted from the original and attacked images, and its distribution are shown in Fig. 3. It can be observed that NHD below the value threshold $\tau = 0.20$ is safe. In the first experiment, robustness of the proposed technique is examined against additive Gaussian noise. For this purpose, Gaussian noise is added to the test images with different variance varying from 0.02 to 0.12 with step size 0.02. Then NHD is determined between the original and Gaussian noisy images and its distribution is depicted in Fig. 3(a). The effectiveness of the proposed scheme is tested against median filtering. The median filter with varying filter size from 3×3 to 13×13 is applied on the test images and then NHD is computed between the hash pairs corresponding to the test and median filtered image respectively. The obtained NHD is depicted in Fig. 3(b). All NHDs are much smaller than the prefixed threshold value $\tau = 0.20$, which indicates that the proposed technique is highly robust against median filter attack.

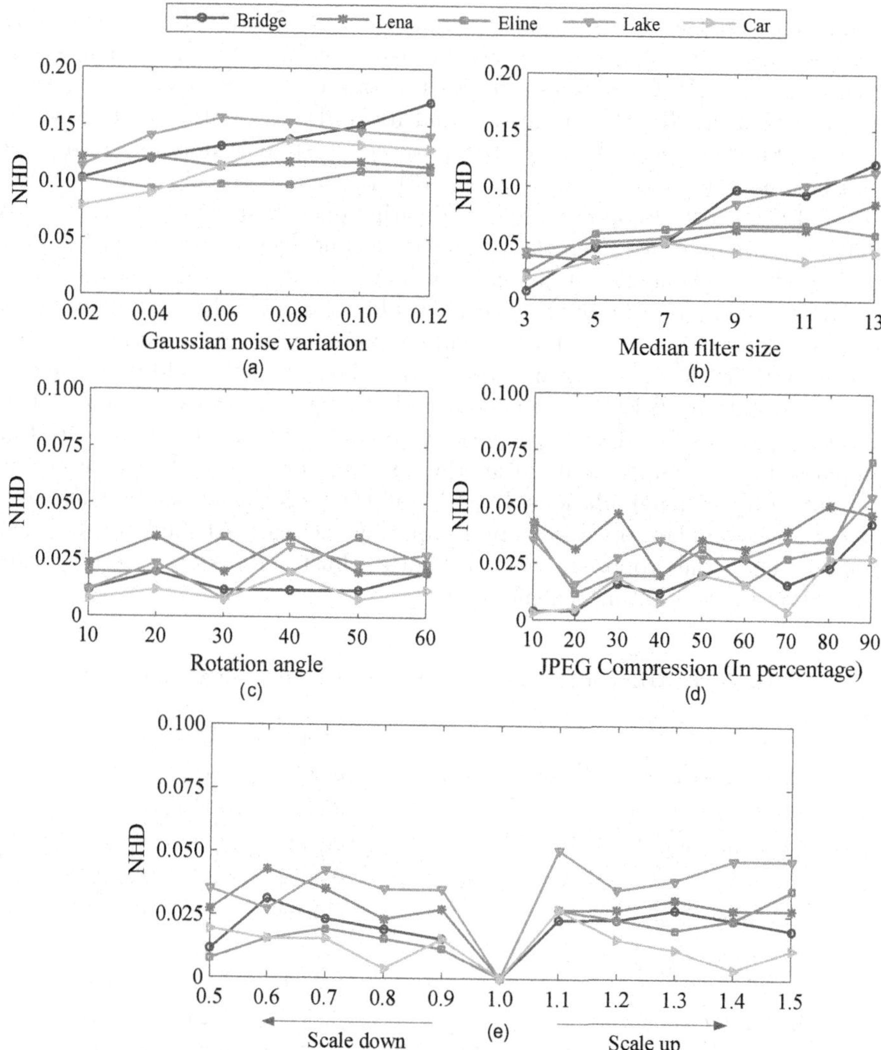

Fig. 3. Robustness validation based on standard experimental images.

The effectiveness of the proposed scheme is also tested against geometric attacks. For this purpose, the test images are rotated from 10° to 60°, and then NHD is computed between rotated and original images. The NHD distribution with respect to rotation is shown in Fig. 3(c). It is found that NHD is much smaller than threshold value for smaller angle rotation as well as for large rotation. Hence, the proposed technique preserved higher robustness against image rotation. The experiment is further extended to another geometric operation image scaling. The size of the test images is reduced from scale factor 1 to

0.5 and increased by the scale factor from 1 to 1.5. The NHD corresponding to scaled images are shown in Fig. 3(e). Finally, performance evaluation is also checked against JPEG compression. All the test images are compressed from 10% to 90% using JPEG compression and its NHD distribution is depicted in Fig. 3(d). Further, the validity of the proposed system is illustrated through Gaussian blurring, Average filter (13×13), Histogram equalization, Resizing ($512 \rightarrow 128 \rightarrow 512$), Cropping (20%), Shearing operations.

The results obtained from the proposed hashing scheme are compared with existing schemes Monga et al. [6] and Neelima et al. [9]. For this purpose, average NHD is computed between hash pairs obtained from the content preserving images and original test images, and compared with existing schemes. The average NHD is estimated against zero-mean Gaussian noise addition, Median filtering, Rotation, JPEG compression, and scaling operations, as depicted in Fig. 4(a–e). It was found that, proposed technique estimates the lower NHD in comparison to the comparison of the other existing schemes [6, 9] against all the considering image manipulations. In addition, the performance is also compared against other standard operations by computing average NHD and are shown in Table 1. Hence, the proposed scheme is highly robust and performs better in the comparison to the existing scheme.

Table 1. NHD for the set of different image processing attacks.

Attacks	Proposed	Ref [6]	Ref [9]
Salt & pepper noise (Density = 0.10)	0.0664	0.1821	0.2201
Speckle noise (30%)	0.0390	0.1501	0.1861
Gaussian blur (11×11)	0.0507	0.2115	0.2810
Average filter (11×11)	0.0622	0.1881	0.3312
Cropping (20%)	0.0664	0.2417	0.3211
Shearing	0.0117	0.2013	0.3896
Resizing ($512 \rightarrow 128 \rightarrow 512$)	0.0430	0.2124	0.3156
Histogram equalization	0.0547	0.2371	0.3321
Contrast adjustment (Increased by 50%)	0.0781	0.3691	0.4214
Brightness adjustment (decreased by 50%)	0.0508	0.3711	0.4527

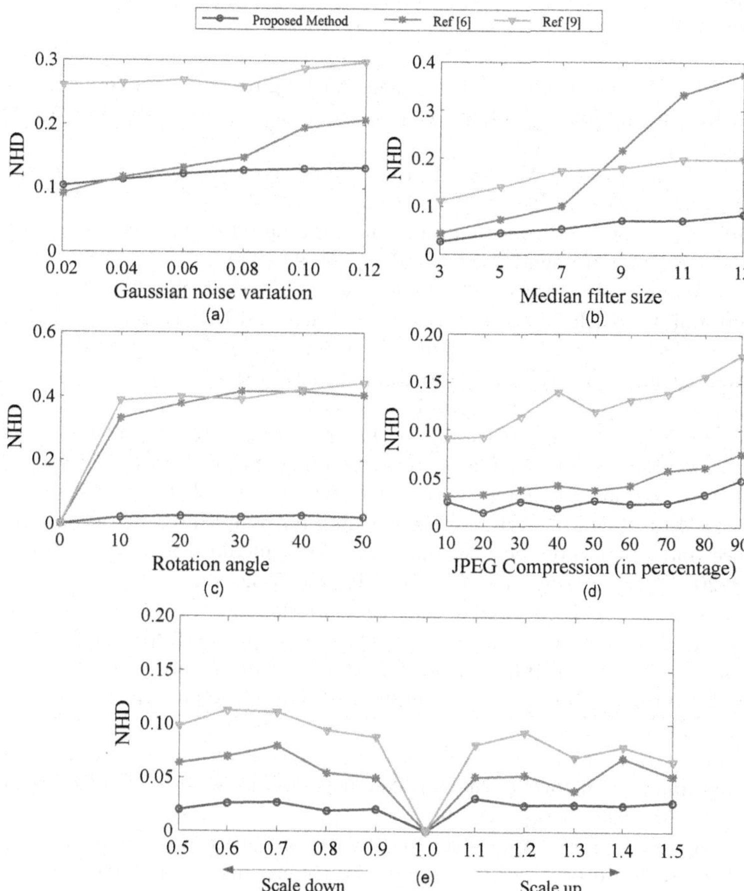

Fig. 4. Robustness comparison between proposed scheme and existing schemes: (a) Additive Gaussian noise, (b) Median Filtering, (C) Rotation, (d) JPEG Compression, (e) Image scaling.

5 Conclusion

In this paper, a new edge based perceptual hashing scheme has been proposed, which provides solution to the problems of geometric manipulation. In this hashing technique, invariant features are extracted using image normalization and edge map. The obtained hash value has excellent ability to classify the image as well as useful in the authenticate of the image. The efficiency of proposed scheme is tested against several geometric and signal processing operations. The simulation results show that the proposed scheme can resist several content preserving operations and provide better robustness.

References

1. Singh S.P., Bhatnagar G.: A robust image hashing based on discrete wavelet transform. In: International Conference on Signal and Image Processing Applications (ICSIPA), pp. 440–444 (2017)
2. Swaminathan, A., Mao, Y., Wu, M.: Robust and secure image hashing. IEEE Trans. Inf. Forensics Secur. **1**(2), 215–230 (2006)
3. Khelifi, F., Jiang, J.: Perceptual image hashing based on virtual watermark detection. IEEE Trans. Image Process. **19**(4), 981–94 (2009)
4. Lv, X., Wang, Z.J.: Perceptual image hashing based on shape contexts and local feature points. IEEE Trans. Inf. Forensics Secur. **7**(3), 1081–1093 (2012)
5. Tang, Z., Chen, L., Zhang, X., Zhang, S.: Robust image hashing with tensor decomposition. IEEE Trans. Knowl. Data Eng. **1**, 1 (2018)
6. Monga, V., Evans, B.L.: Perceptual image hashing via feature points: performance evaluation and tradeoffs. IEEE Trans. Image Process. **15**(11), 52–65 (2006)
7. Monga, V., Evans, B.L.: Robust perceptual image hashing using feature points. In: IEEE International Conference on Image Processing, vol. 1, pp. 677–680 (2004)
8. Ouyang, J., Liu, Y., Shu, H.: Robust hashing for image authentication using SIFT feature and quaternion Zernike moments. Multimedia Tools Appl. **76**(2), 2609–2626 (2016). https://doi.org/10.1007/s11042-015-3225-x
9. Neelima, A., Singh, K.M.: Perceptual hash function based on scale-invariant feature transform and singular value decomposition. Comput. J. **59**(9), 1275–1281 (2016)
10. Singh, S.P., Bhatnagar, G.: A chaos based robust and secure image hashing framework. In: Indian Conference on Computer Vision, Graphics and Image Processing, pp. 1–7 (2018)
11. Singh, S.P., Bhatnagar, G.: Perceptual hashing-based novel security framework for medical images. In: Intelligent Data Security Solutions for e-Health Applications, pp. 1–20. Academic Press (2020)
12. Zhou, H.: A design methodology of chaotic stream ciphers and the realization problems in finite precision, Ph.D. thesis, Department of Electrical Engineering, Fudan University, Shanghai, China (1996)

Real-Time Driver Drowsiness Detection Using GRU with CNN Features

Ayush Srivastava[1], K. S. Sangwan[1], and Dhiraj[2](✉)

[1] Birla-Institute of Technology and Science (BITS, Pilani), Pilani Campus, Pilani, Rajasthan, India
f2016616@pilani.bits-pilani.ac.in

[2] CSIR - Central Electronics Engineering Research Institute (CSIR-CEERI), Pilani, India
dhiraj@ceeri.res.in

Abstract. There are many visual characteristics linked with drowsiness like eye closure duration, blinking frequency, gaze, pose, and yawning. In this paper, we propose a robust deep learning approach to detect a driver's drowsiness. We start by extracting the mouth region from incoming frames of the video stream using Dlib's frontal face detector and a custom dlib landmark detector. Then, a deep convolutional neural network (DCNN) is used to extract deep features.. Lastly, yawning is detected using a yawn detector consisting of 1D-DepthWise Separable-CNN and Gated Recurrent Unit (GRU) which learns the mapping or patterns from temporal information of the sequence of features extracted from frames and predicts yawning/not yawning. Yawn detector was able to reach training and validation accuracy of 99.99% and 99.97% respectively. We were able to achieve an inference speed of ~30FPS on our host machine on live video recording and ~23 FPS on an embedded board for the same. To check the robustness of our model, testing was done on the YawDD test set where we were able to detect yawning successfully. On the other hand, while testing NTHU data many false positive was observed. Thus, our approach can be effectively used for real-time driver drowsiness detection on an embedded platform.

Keywords: Drowsiness detection · Convolutional neural networks (CNN) · Recurrent neural networks (RNN) · Gated Recurrent Unit (GRU)

1 Introduction

Road accidents are caused because of various reasons, one of them being driver drowsiness. After continuous driving for a long time, drivers can easily get tired resulting in driver fatigue and drowsiness. Research studies have shown that most accidents occur due to driver fatigue. Developing technology for detecting driver drowsiness to reduce accidents is one of the main challenges. According to [1], India recorded more than 150,000 fatalities in the year 2018 due to road accidents. American National Highway Traffic Safety Administration (NHTSA) [2] published a report which indicated that 803 casualties were reported in 2016 because of drowsy drivers. For instance, trucks and tempos which transport bulk products are mainly driven at

S. K. Singh et al. (Eds.): CVIP 2020, CCIS 1378, pp. 501–513, 2021.
https://doi.org/10.1007/978-981-16-1103-2_42

night. The drivers of such vehicles who drive for such continuous long periods become more susceptible to these kinds of situations. Detecting the drowsiness of drivers is still ongoing research to reduce the number of such miss-happenings and accidents. Therefore, the drowsiness of drivers is a crucial problem that requires an efficient and effective solution. Typical methods used to identify drowsy drivers are physiological based, vehicle-based, and behavioral-based. Physiological methods such as heartbeat, pulse rate, and Electrocardiogram [3, 4], etc. are used to detect fatigue levels. Vehicle-based methods include accelerator pattern, acceleration, and steering movements. Behavioral methods [5–8] include yawn, Eye Closure, Eye Blinking, etc. In this paper, we propose a behavioral method to detect yawn and thus detect drowsiness. Yawning is one of the major indicators to detect drowsiness, tiredness, and fatigue.

Our model is inspired by the works presented in [9, 10]. In [9] the author tries to detect activity like a man performing a high jump in a sequence of input images while in our approach we detect yawning in a sequence of images. In [10] the authors have implemented a Convolutional neural network model trained on ImageNet [11] database, whereas we have used AffectNet database for the same purpose i.e. to train our Deep Convolutional neural network from scratch and then use it to extract deep features from the region of yawning on the face. Secondly, the author in [10] has used a stacked LSTM [12] network for handling temporal information of yawning, but we use a combination of 1D-Depthwise Separable-CNN and Gated Recurrent Unit (GRU) for that purpose. In our method, a camera is installed in front of the driver which captures the video of the driver while he is driving. We use this video stream to extract frames, detect faces in it using Dlib's frontal face detector then detect landmarks of the mouth using our custom Dlib shape predictor. Using these landmarks, we make a bounding box and crop the mouth region which is sent to the feature extractor (pre-trained DCNN). Features are extracted in groups of 32, and these features of 32 frames are fed to a yawn detector which is a combination of 1D-Depthwise Separable Convolution and Gated Recurrent Unit(GRU), it detects whether there is a yawn in this sequence of frames or not. The next sections elaborate on our approach, results, and datasets used.

2 Proposed Algorithm

As shown in Fig. 1, our method consists of three steps, firstly detecting the mouth region using a combination of Dlib's frontal face detector and a custom Dlib shape predictor. Second, use our pre-trained Deep convolutional network to extract spatial features from the mouth region, and finally, we detect yawn in temporal information extracted from the mouth region using a combination of 1D-Depthwise Separable-CNN and Gated Recurrent Unit (GRU).

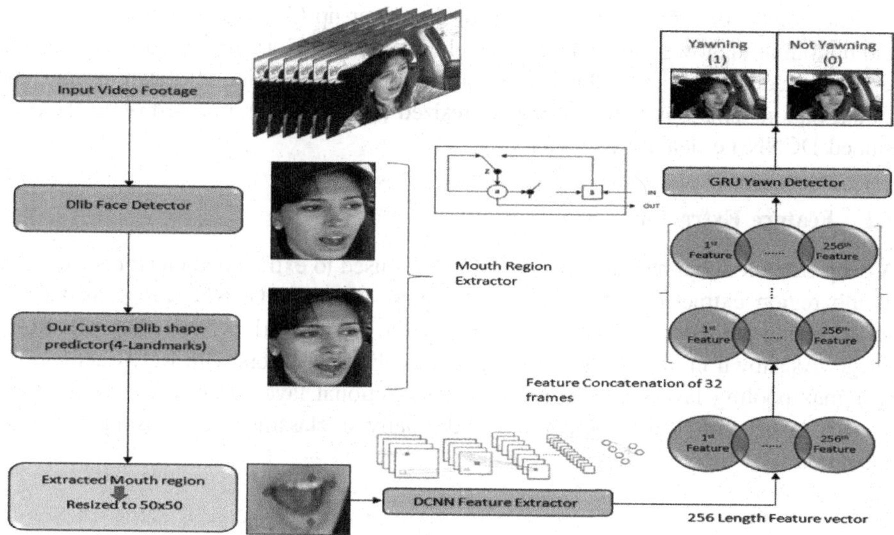

Fig. 1. Proposed method

2.1 Mouth Region Extractor

Firstly, we use Dlib's HOG [13] + Linear SVM [14] frontal face detector to detect faces in frames, it is significantly more accurate than Haar cascades [15] with less false positives. Fewer parameters to tune at test time and is faster than DNN based facial detector. Secondly, we use a Custom Dlib's shape predictor which predicts just 4 landmarks on the mouth instead of calculating all 68 facial landmarks in which the traditional Dlib's shape predictor present in [16] predicts. Using our custom shape predictor significantly decreases the time taken and computation performed. We were able to decrease the model size from 99.7 MB (standard facial landmark detector) to 7.20 MB (custom Dlib shape predictor). Comparison of standard dlib shape predictor and custom dlib shape predictor is shown in Fig. 2.

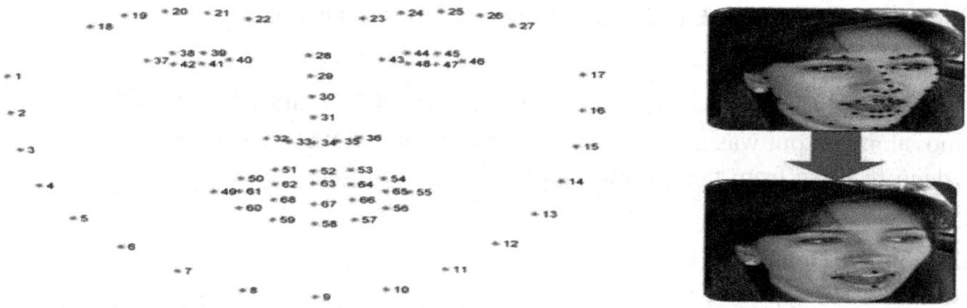

Fig. 2. Standard Dlib shape predictor (left), Custom Dlib shape predictor (right)

The points corresponding to the top of the upper lip (52), lip corners (49 and 55), and bottom of the lower lip (58) which can be seen in Fig. 2 are then used by the mouth region extractor to estimate the size of the bounding box which is drawn around the mouth region. This box is then cropped, resized to (50, 50), and passed on to the pre-trained DCNN i.e. feature extractor.

2.2 Feature Extractor

A deep convolutional neural network (DCNN) is used to extract deep features from the mouth region extracted using the mouth region extractor. DCNN was trained from scratch using the AffectNet database [17]. Input to the network is 50 × 50 pixels RGB image. As shown in Fig. 3, there are eight convolutional layers with ReLU activation, four max-pooling layers after every two convolutional layers, one dense (fully connected) layer with ReLU activation, and finally a classifier layer using SoftMax activation.

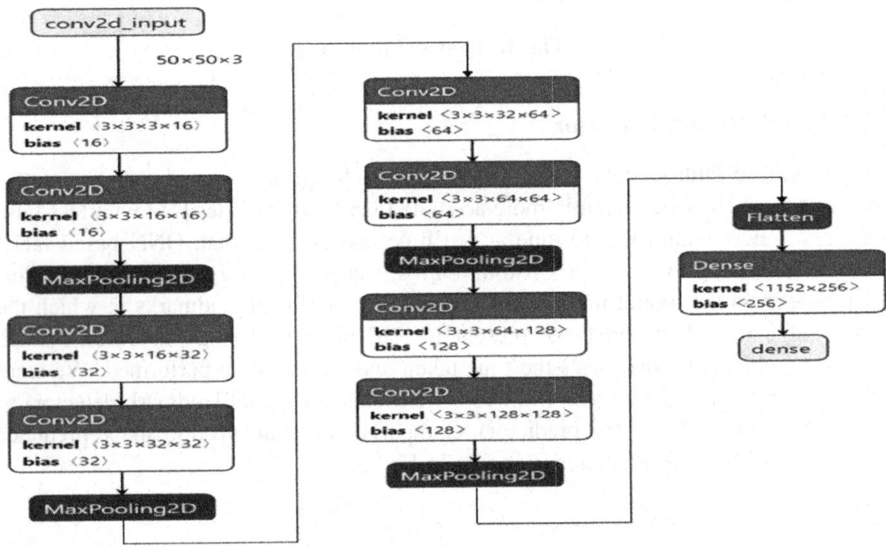

Fig. 3. Deep feature extractor architecture

We removed the SoftMax layer from our DCNN after training it, thus after removal, its output was a 256-length feature vector that was used to spatial information or deep features from the mouth region.

2.3 Yawn Detector

Yawn is a combination of various mouth movements like a person opening his/her mouth, then comes a prolonged state of open mouth and finally its closing, this process usually takes about 2–3 s. Thus, to classify the sequence of frames into yawning or not yawning we use a variation of recurrent neural network (RNN) called Gated Recurrent Unit (GRU). Recurrent neural networks not only uses the output of a single data point but also takes into consideration the output of previous data points, thus in our case it will use temporal information in a set of 32 frames to predict one value Simple RNN suffers from vanishing gradient and exploding gradient problem [18], these occur during backpropagation in the training of a deep neural network. In vanishing gradient problem, the gradients which come from deeper layers go through a large number of calculations due to the chain rule used in gradient descent, and as they approach the initial layers, if they have small values (say < 1), they diminish exponentially and hence vanish and make it impossible for the model to learn. While on the other hand if they have large values (say > 1) then they get exponentially larger and blow up crashing the model, causing the exploding gradient problem.

To counter these, special types of RNNs, like Long Short-Term Memory Networks (LSTM) and Gated Recurrent Units (GRU) [19] are used in place of traditional RNN. LSTM has memory cells that are used to store information and input & forget gates to control its flow, which helps them to learn long-range temporal dependencies, while on the other hand GRU lacks a memory unit and thus has fewer parameters than LSTM. GRU is shown in Fig. 4.

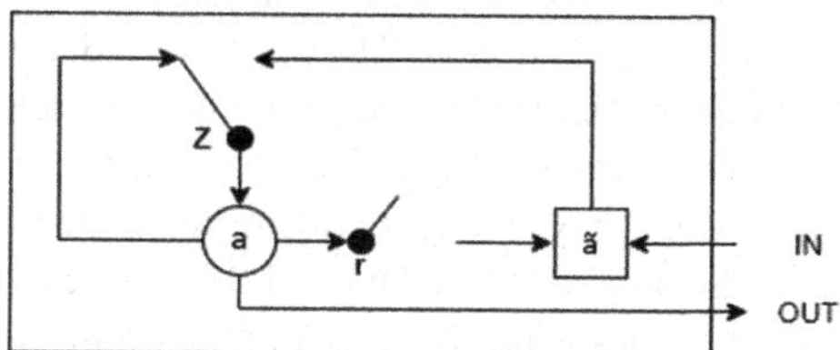

Fig. 4. Gated Recurrent Unit [19]

The activation a_t^j at a time t is a linear interpolation of the previous activation a_{t-1}^j and present activation $\tilde{a}_t^j$:

$$a_t^j = \left(1 - z_t^j\right) a_{t-1}^j + z_t^j \tilde{a}_t^j \tag{1}$$

Next, update gate z_t^j decides how much activation is updated by the unit.

$$z_t^j = \sigma(W_z x_t + U_z a_{t-1})^j \tag{2}$$

Next, the candidate activation is computed.

$$\tilde{a}_t^j = tanh(W x_t + U(r_t \circ a_{t-1}))^j \tag{3}$$

Where r_t is a set of reset gates and $\circ$ denotes element-wise multiplication. When r_t^j is close to 0, the unit does not remember the previous values, thus the units work as if it is reading the first symbol of an input sequence. Reset gate is computed as follows

$$r_t^j = \sigma(W_r x_t + U_r a_{t-1})^j \tag{4}$$

We have used a combination of 1D-DepthWise Separable-CNN and GRU shown in Fig. 5.

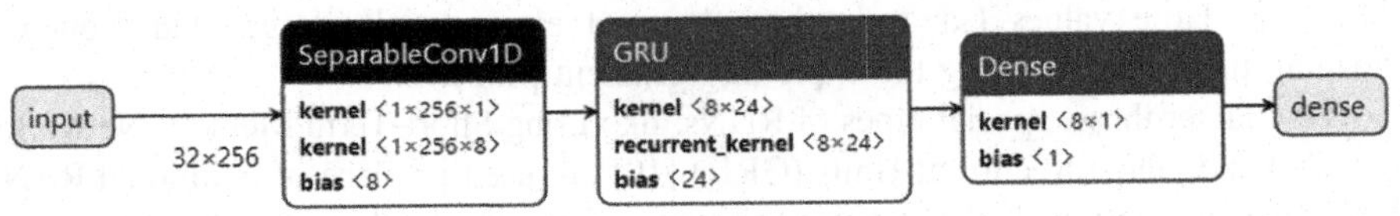

Fig. 5. Yawn detector architecture

As GRU works well for short term dependencies and contains lesser parameters then LSTM, they are computationally more efficient then LSTM. As we are planning to execute our models on an embedded board with an application for driver drowsiness testing so we preferred the combination of 1D-Depthwise Separable-CNN and GRU which is having a smaller computational footprint than stacked LSTM. Our model detects a yawn in 32 continuous frames thus GRU is a better option than LSTM as they contain fewer parameters, thus they would perform better in real-time on embedded systems. 1D- DepthWise Separable CNN layer (1 filter size * 8 units, padding the same) convolves on the 32 frames. The collection of 32 frames is given together as an input to yawn detector with each frame having a 256-length feature vector and performs the operations on them and adjusts its weights according to our data using backpropagation. Our model collects the latest 32 frames from the incoming video and inputs them into the yawn detector for prediction. It predicts whether there is yawning in those sequences of 32 frames or not and provides us with one output for 32 frames. Two threshold values (A) and (B) were kept, if the sigmoid output of our yawn detector is above (A) then it is concluded that there is yawning in 32 frames and if the number of time yawning is detected crosses (B) then yawning is detected and the driver is alerted else he/she is not.

3 Experimental Results and Discussions

This section explains datasets used, experiments performed and hyperparameters used in our study.

3.1 Description of Datasets

We have used three widely used datasets particularly AffectNet, YawDD [20] and iBUG-300W [21–23] were used in this study. The iBUG-300W dataset is used to train a shape predictor to identify 68 pairs of distinct integers, (x, y)-coordinates of the facial structure depicted in Fig. 2 above. These pairs of integers or landmarks include the eyes, eyebrows, nose, mouth, and jawline. The iBUG-300W dataset consists of 7,764 labeled images. Few sample images depicting different types of environments in which images were shot are shown in Fig. 6.

Fig. 6. Sample images from iBUG-300W dataset

We used labels corresponding to points 49 (left corner of the lip), 52 (top of the upper lip), 55 (right corner of the lip), 58 (bottom of the lower lip) to train our shape predictor which reduced our model size and training speed significantly. AffectNet database of facial expressions in the wild has around 1M facial images collected which have been gathered from the Internet. Around 440,000 are manually annotated, while the rest are annotated using two baseline deep neural networks to classify into seven different expressions which are Surprise, Happy, Neutral, Fear, Disgust, Sad, Anger. In our work, we have considered five expressions Fear, Surprise, Neutral, Sad, Happy to pre-train our DCNN. Out of 440,000 images, there were many which could be classified in two different classes thus a total of 23,500 images (4700 for each class) which strictly belong to one class, were manually selected to train our model. These images were split into train and validation sets in an 85:15 ratio. The images in the dataset were of variable size thus all each image was resized to 50 $\times$ 50 RGB images.

Few sample images showing diversity in terms of different facial expressions are shown in Fig. 7.

Fig. 7. Sample images from AffectNet database (left to right: fear, happy, neutral, sad, surprise)

YawDD dataset contains two video datasets of drivers with various facial characteristics, it has been widely used for yawning detection. There are two different forms of this dataset available, one being in which a camera is installed on the side mirror which is used in our study while the other is a camera installed on the dashboard. The variant of the database which we have used contains 322 videos of male and female drivers of different ethnicities with/without glasses/sunglasses. We used a selected number of videos in our study. The videos have been recorded using an RGB camera at 30 FPS at a resolution of 640 × 480 pixels in AVI format without audio. Videos are divided into three classes, normal driving (no talking), talking, and yawning. We have used normal driving and yawning while driving classes in our study. We extracted a total of 52,794 frames. Few sample frames from one male subject of YawDD dataset used to train our model are shown in Fig. 8.

Fig. 8. Frames of normal class and Yawning from YawDD dataset

3.2 Model Training

A host machine with Ubuntu OS, 32 GB RAM, NVIDIA GPU was used to train our models using Keras deep learning library with TensorFlow backend. The custom Dlib shape predictor was trained on the iBUG 300-W dataset. The trained custom dlib shape predictor provides accurate facial landmarks on test facial frames. Landmarks chosen in our shape predictor are shown in Fig. 2. While training the feature extractor we used Keras inbuilt ImageDataGenerator (with random rotation within the range of 20°, random zooming by x0.15, width shift by x0.2, height shift by x0.2, horizontal flip, and fill_mode ='nearest') to avoid overfitting. Adam optimizer with learning rate 1e − 4, batch size 8 was used. The loss function used was categorical cross-entropy. Early stopping utility in Keras callbacks was used, patience level was kept to 20. After 94 epochs, we were able to achieve a training accuracy of 81% and a validation accuracy of around 79%. Variations of accuracy and validation accuracy, loss, and validation loss are shown in Fig. 9. Validation accuracy could have been improved by considering more data from the AffectNet dataset as we only used 23,500 images, but 80% validation accuracy was sufficient to extract spatial information from extracted mouth images.

From all the selected videos in our YawDD dataset, we extracted 12185 yawning frames and 40,609 non-yawning frames which comprise clips of 30 males and 30 females of the YawDD dataset. a sliding window approach was used on this array of frames to create various windows having a window size of 32. Then these collections of windows were shuffled randomly and split into training and validation set with an 80:20 ratio. We were able to create a total of 42,208 windows (samples) for training and 10553 windows for validation where each window consisted of 32 consecutive frames. The trained DCNN was used to extract a 256-length feature vector from each frame resulting in a final shape of 32 × 256 for each window. This was then used to train GRU based yawn detector. Adam optimizer with a learning rate of 1e − 3 and a batch size of 512 was used. The loss function is used for binary cross-entropy. The model performance in terms of loss and accuracy is shown in Fig. 9. After 20 epochs, a training accuracy of 99.99% and validation accuracy of 99.97% was obtained.

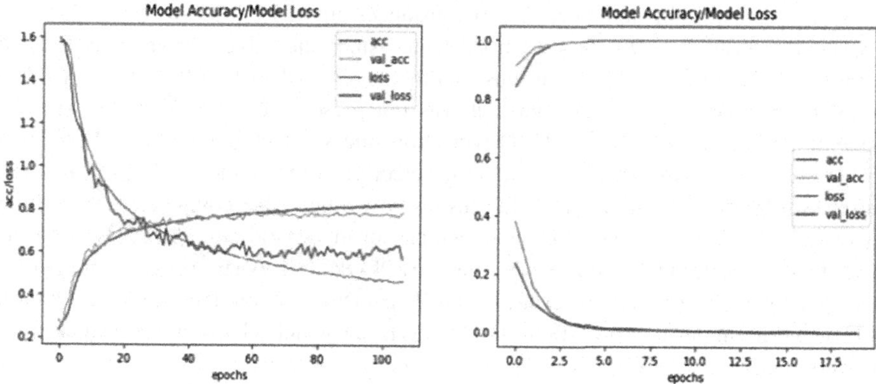

Fig. 9. Learning curve for Feature Extractor (Left), Yawn detector (Right)

3.3 Inference

The inference model was tested on a host computer and embedded board platform with test data consisting of randomly selected clips from custom test split created from YawDD dataset, live video feed and NTHU dataset.

a) Host Computer

The testing of the end-to-end model (face detector + feature extractor + yawn detector) was done on a windows laptop having an Intel i7 processor with 16 GB RAM. We were able to achieve an inference speed of $\sim$30 FPS (frames per second) on a 3 min 11 s long live video of a subject. Our model was successfully able to detect all 16 Yawning instances with a few false positives. Detection results from our end-to-end model for yawn detection are shown in Fig. 10. Experiments were also done on several clips in the YawDD dataset recorded in daylight on male and female subjects with and without glasses achieving an inference speed of $\sim$28 FPS as shown in Fig. 11.

Fig. 10. Prediction from our model

Fig. 11. Prediction from our model on YawDD dataset

Our model was able to detect 12 yawn instances out of 13 in 10 yawning clips of an average duration of 19.9 s, one wasn't detected since the subject brought his hand in front of his mouth while yawning thus mouth wasn't visible. It also gave a few false-positive i.e. predicted yawning when it was not present. Testing of model was also done on random clips from NTHU Driver Drowsiness detection dataset [24] as shown in Fig. 12. Though our model was able to detect yawning frames at ~28FPS, it also misclassified many non-yawning frames as yawning. The count of false-positive increased. There can be few reasons for which our model did not perform well on this data. Firstly, our model is trained on the YawDD dataset where an RGB camera has been used while the NTHU dataset uses an IR camera. Second, the videos recorded in NTHU are at angles that are different than angles at which videos are recorded in our training data i.e. YawDD.

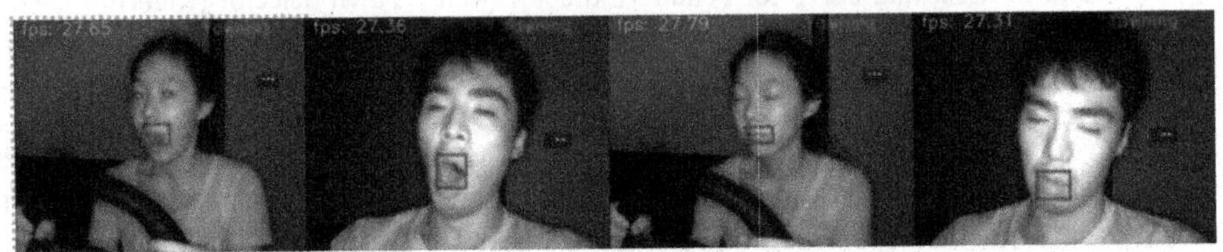

Fig. 12. Predictions from our model on the NTHU dataset

b) Embedded Board

The inference model was also tested on a latte panda embedded board having ubuntu 18.04 OS, intel core m3 processor, Intel HD graphics 615, and 8 GB RAM. The yawn instance detection accuracy remained the same as that of the host machine but the FPS decreased, we were able to achieve inference speed of ~23 FPS on a live video of a subject recorded video achieving real-time performance as shown in Fig. 13. Experiments were also done on YawDD and NTHU dataset in the same conditions on the same clips as on the host computer. Here also, there were a few false positive in YawDD and live recording which increased in the case of NTHU data as shown in Fig. 14 and Fig. 15. FPS decreased as compared to the host computer which is expected as an embedded board is computationally weaker.

Fig. 13. Prediction from our model on embedded board

Fig. 14. Prediction from our model on YawDD data on embedded board

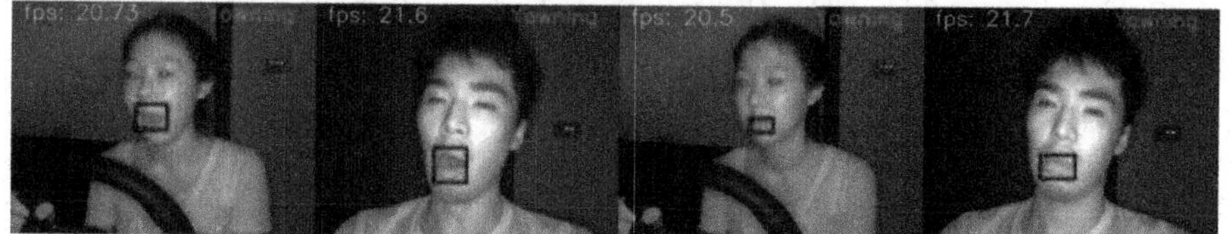

Fig. 15. Prediction from our model on NTHU data on embedded board

4 Conclusion

In this paper, we present a deep learning algorithm for drowsiness detection. Our algorithms pipeline consists of a face detector, a custom Dlib shape predictor, a deep convolutional neural network, and a yawn detector which is a combination of 1D-Depthwise Separable-CNN and Gated Recurrent Unit (GRU). Dlib's frontal face detector is one of the fastest face detectors while maintaining accuracy, our custom Dlib shape predictor is of a significantly smaller size than the standard Dlib shape predictor and our yawn detector contains only two layers with a total of 2,729 parameters. Yawn detector achieved a training and validation accuracy of 99.99% and 99.97% respectively. With these parameters and accuracy, we were able to get the real-time performance of ~30FPS on the host machine and ~23FPS on an embedded board on a live video of a subject. Experiments were done on testing clips from the YawDD dataset which was shot in the daytime of male and female subjects with and without glasses, we were able to achieve ~28FPS on the host machine while ~22FPS on the embedded board. It also gave many false-positive i.e. misclassified many frames of non-yawning as yawning on NTHU data but that is expected given our yawn detector is trained on YawDD. Thus, our approach can be effectively used for real-time driver drowsiness detection on an embedded platform. We hope to devise a platform that motivates a safe driving environment and reduces on-road accidents. In the future, we plan on optimizing our model and implementing it on embedded boards like Raspberry Pi along with edge devices like Intel Neural Compute Stick.

References

1. https://timesofindia.indiatimes.com/india/over-1-51-lakh-died-in-road-accidents-last-yearup-tops-among-states/articleshow/72078508.cms. Accessed 17 July 2020
2. National Center for Statistics and Analysis: 2016 fatal motor vehicle crashes: Overview. (Traffic Safety Facts Research Note. Report No. DOT HS 812 456), October 2017. National Highway Traffic Safety Administration, Washington, DC

3. Stanley, P.K., Prahash, T.J., Lal, S.S., Daniel, P. V.: Embedded based drowsiness detection using EEG signals. In 2017 IEEE International Conference on Power, Control, Signals and Instrumentation Engineering (ICPCSI), pp. 2596–2600. IEEE, September 2017
4. Purnamasari, P.D., Hazmi, A.Z.: Heart beat based drowsiness detection system for driver. In: 2018 International Seminar on Application for Technology of Information and Communication, pp. 585–590. IEEE, September 2018
5. Mehta, S., Dadhich, S., Gumber, S., Jadhav Bhatt, A.: Real-time driver drowsiness detection system using eye aspect ratio and eye closure ratio. In: Proceedings of International Conference on Sustainable Computing in Science, Technology and Management (SUSCOM). Amity University Rajasthan, Jaipur, February 2019
6. Rahman, A., Sirshar, M., Khan, A.: Real time drowsiness detection using eye blink monitoring. In: 2015 National Software Engineering Conference (NSEC), pp. 1–7. IEEE, 2015, December 2015
7. Jie, Z., Mahmoud, M., Stafford-Fraser, Q., Robinson, P., Dias, E., Skrypchuk, L.: Analysis of yawning behaviour in spontaneous expressions of drowsy drivers. In: 2018 13th IEEE International Conference on Automatic Face and Gesture Recognition (FG 2018), pp. 571–576. IEEE, May 2018
8. Al-sudani, A.R.: Yawn based driver fatigue level prediction. In: Proceedings of 35th International Conference, vol. 69, pp. 372–382 (2020)
9. Donahue, J., et al.: Long-term recurrent convolutional networks for visual recognition and description. In: Proceedings of the IEEE Conference on Computer Vision and Pattern Recognition, pp. 2625–2634 (2015)
10. Zhang, W., Su, J.: Driver yawning detection based on long short term memory networks. In: 2017 IEEE Symposium Series on Computational Intelligence (SSCI), pp. 1–5. IEEE, November 2017
11. Deng, J., Dong, W., Socher, R., Li, L.-J., Li, K., Fei-Fei, L.: Imagenet: a large-scale hierarchical image database. In 2009 IEEE Conference on Computer Vision and Pattern Recognition, pp. 248–255 (2009)
12. Hochreiter, S., Schmidhuber, J.: Long short-term memory. Neural Comput. **9**(8), 1735–1780 (1997)
13. Dalal, N., Triggs, B.: Histograms of oriented gradients for human detection. In: 2005 IEEE Computer Society Conference on Computer Vision and Pattern Recognition (CVPR 2005), vol. 1, pp. 886–893. IEEE, June 2005
14. Cortes, C., Vapnik, V.: Support-vector networks. Mach. Learn. **20**(3), 273–297 (1995)
15. Viola, P., Jones, M.: Rapid object detection using a boosted cascade of simple features. In: Proceedings of the 2001 IEEE Computer Society Conference on Computer Vision and Pattern Recognition. CVPR 2001, vol. 1, p. I. IEEE, December 2001
16. King, D.E.: Dlib-ml: a machine learning toolkit. J. Mach. Learn. Res. **10**, 1755–1758 (2009)
17. Mollahosseini, A., Hasani, B., Mahoor, M.H.: Affectnet: a database for facial expression, valence, and arousal computing in the wild. IEEE Trans. Affect. Comput. **10**(1), 18–31 (2017)
18. Grosse, R.: Lecture 15: Exploding and Vanishing Gradients. University of Toronto Computer Science (2017)
19. Chung, J., Gulcehre, C., Cho, K., Bengio, Y.: Empirical evaluation of gated recurrent neural networks on sequence modeling. arXiv preprint arXiv:1412.3555 (2014)
20. Abtahi, S., Omidyeganeh, M., Shirmohammadi, S., Hariri, B.: YawDD: a yawning detection dataset. In: Proceedings of the 5th ACM Multimedia Systems Conference, pp. 24–28, March 2014

21 Sagonas, C., Antonakos, E., Tzimiropoulos, G., Zafeiriou, S., Pantic, M.: 300 faces In-the-wild challenge: database and results. Image Vis. Comput. (IMAVIS) **47**, 3–18 (2016). (Special Issue on Facial Landmark Localisation "In-The-Wild")
22. Sagonas, C., Tzimiropoulos, G., Zafeiriou, S., Pantic, M.: 300 faces in-the-wild challenge: the first facial landmark localization challenge. Proceedings of IEEE International Conference on Computer Vision (ICCV-W), 300 Faces in-the-Wild Challenge (300-W). Sydney, Australia, December 2013
23. Sagonas, C., Tzimiropoulos, G., Zafeiriou, S., Pantic, M.; A semi-automatic methodology for facial landmark annotation. In: Proceedings of IEEE International Conference on Computer Vision and Pattern Recognition (CVPR-W), 5th Workshop on Analysis and Modeling of Faces and Gestures (AMFG 2013), Oregon, USA, June 2013
24. Weng, C.-H., Lai, Y.-H., Lai, S.-H.: Driver drowsiness detection via a hierarchical temporal deep belief network. In: Asian Conference on Computer Vision Workshop on Driver Drowsiness Detection from Video, Taipei, Taiwan, November 2016

Detection of Concave Points in Closed Object Boundaries Aiming at Separation of Overlapped Objects

Sourav Chandra Mandal(✉), Oishila Bandyopadhyay(✉), and Sanjoy Pratihar(✉)

Indian Institute of Information Technology, Kalyani, India
{oishila,sanjoy}@iiitkalyani.ac.in

Abstract. Separation of overlapping objects is one of the critical preprocessing tasks in biomedical and industrial applications. Separation of the attached objects is necessary, aiming at some qualitative research analysis or diagnosis of some existing behavior. It has been observed that a partial overlap between two or more convex shape objects introduces concave regions over the boundary. Here, in this paper, we present a novel approach for detecting the concavities along the overlapped object boundaries. The proposed algorithm works by computing the visibility matrix concerning the boundary pixels, which works as a variant of the chord method. Furthermore, our proposed method selects strong boundary candidates using the visibility matrix to ignore smaller concave-zones. Some distance thresholds introduced by us guide the selection. These detected concave points might be used subsequently for the separation and counting of objects. Experimental results show the degree of correctness and usefulness of the proposed method.

Keywords: Concavity detection · Separation of overlapping objects · Visibility graph

1 Introduction

Various machine vision applications like medical imaging, agro-applications, surveillance applications, etc. require the separation of overlapped objects. Images related to such vision applications are shown in Fig. 1 as examples. The separation in such applications aims to identify the hidden boundaries, grouping contour belonging to the same object, and estimating the dimensions of partially visible objects. Objects with overlapping parts introduce considerable complexity to the separation process. Moreover, it becomes more complicated if the input image contains many objects of various sizes and shapes. Overlapping of the objects creates concave regions, and the detection of the concave regions helps in the separation of overlapped objects [17,35,36].

Several works have been reported in the literature which addresses the separation of attached convex objects like food grains, coins, blood cells, etc. in images.

S. K. Singh et al. (Eds.): CVIP 2020, CCIS 1378, pp. 514–525, 2021.
https://doi.org/10.1007/978-981-16-1103-2_43

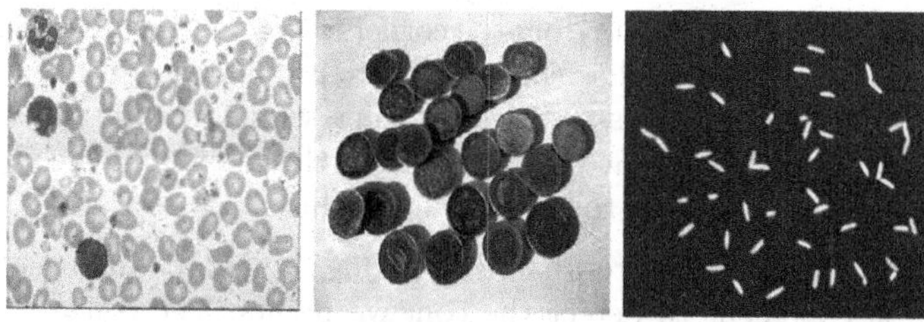

Fig. 1. Applications: medical image analysis to diagnose some behavior (left); coin counting from tray images (middle); quality estimation from rice samples (right).

In applications, the count of these objects is often required for some quantitative analysis. Most of the works are watershed transform [6,15,30], mathematical morphology and granulometry [3,14,23,32] based. The watershed transform is a common approach to understand overlapping during cell segmentation. A stochastic watershed is commonly used to improve the performance of watershed based segmentations [1]. This technique has been applied in various field like medical image analysis [5,7,25], computer vision [24], bio-medicine [9,16], signal processing [20], industrial applications [11,21], remote sensing [19], computer-aided design [26], and video coding [33]. In case of highly overlapped objects, the watershed transform still faces difficulties in proper segmentation. Morphological operations are introduced to improve the separation of overlapping objects. Park et al. [23] proposed an automated morphological analysis model for overlapping object segmentation. Works are there for separation of touching and overlapping objects based on digital geometry. The idea of outer isothetic cover (OIC) [3,4] has been presented and used to identify the joining points of the edges coming from two different objects. These joining points are matched in pairs for a suitable separation. These joining points are usually the concave points on the contour. information. Recently, Convolutional neural network (CNN) [13], multi-scale CNN [31], and graph partitioning-based frameworks have been introduced to solve the separation of overlapping particles. But the main drawback of the CNN approach is that it requires huge training to achieve high performance and accuracy. Concavity detection and analysis have a vital role in separation or splitting. Many methods are available which applied concave point detection techniques in object separation problem. These methods find the concavity points to determine the possible split lines. Several methods have been proposed for the same. Commonly used approaches for concavity detection are categorized into the following four groups, namely, curvature method, skeleton detection, chord method and the polygonal approximation method. They are discussed below in detail.

Curvature Method: In curvature-based approaches edge information are extracted first [22]. Then all corner points, $C = c_1, c_2, \ldots, c_n$, are identified from the image contour and finally following the rotation types at the corner points concave points are understood. One popular curvature method approach for finding all the concave points from the corners is Vector Triangle Area Method [10]. Corner points are treated as concave points if the area of the triangle made of the points (c_{i+1}, c_i, c_{i-1}) is positive. In some works, the detected dominant points are referred to as concave if the values of the maximum the curvature at those points is greater than a threshold value [34].

Skeleton Method: In skeleton-based methods, boundary information of the objects is a key element to detect the concave points. The concave points are also understood as the intersections between the skeleton and contour points of the object, as proposed in [28].

Chord Method: In the chord-based approach, the concave points are extracted as points with the maximum distance to the concave area chord [12]. In another method [18], the concave points are identified using concave regions' boundaries and their corresponding convex hull chords. The concave points are understood as the points on the boundaries of concave pockets with maximum perpendicular distance from the convex hull chord [27].

Polygonal Approximation: Polygonal Approximation is a well-known method for representation of the digital curves as a collection of smaller straight pieces or segments. A dominant point divides two consecutive segments. Dominant points (c_i) are detected first and then the concave points are selected from the set of dominant points [2,36] . The Dominant point $c_i \in C_{dom}$ is considered to be a concave point if $\overline{c_{i-1}c_i} \times \overline{c_i c_{i+1}}$ is positive.

Our Contribution: To address the issue of separation of overlapped objects, we require the following steps: contour extractions, concave point detection, concavity analysis and fixing splitting lines for separation. An analysis of the concave regions can understand the splitting lines. In this paper, we have proposed a method for detecting the concavities along the overlapped object boundaries. These concave points may be used for the separation of objects subsequently. Our proposed algorithm works by computing the visibility matrix concerning the boundary pixels. Furthermore, we have tuned the algorithm by introducing different thresholds, which helps us report strong concave-zones by ignoring smaller concave regions.

2 Proposed Methodology

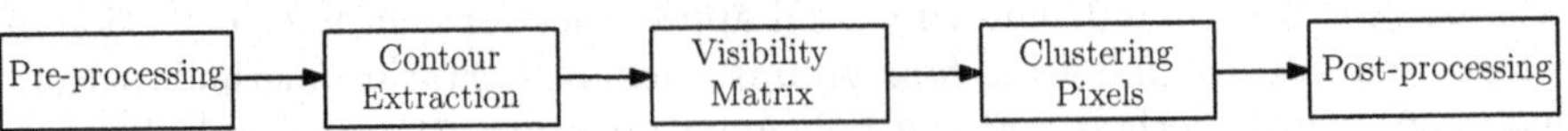

Fig. 2. The proposed method: steps of computation.

We propose here a method to detect and analyze the concave-zones in the boundary of overlapped objects. The diagram shown in Fig. 2 represents the methodology of the proposed approach.

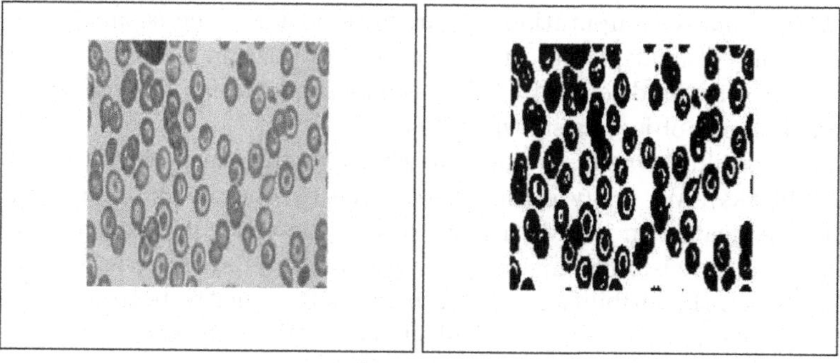

Fig. 3. Binarization for contour extraction.

Binarization is one of the key-task in the pre-processing stage in our work, so that the contour extraction becomes fast and easier (see Fig. 3). We have used adaptive binarization techniques for image binarization [29]. Contour extraction is done through boundary pixel extraction and subsequent thinning and filling [8]. Individual objects are understood as a separate connected component and processed separately. An example is shown in Fig. 4. The contour Matrix CM is a 2-D matrix which holds N points where $CM(i, 1)$ represents the x-coordinate value of the i-th point and $CM(i, 2)$ represents the y-coordinate value of the i-th point. The contour points are traversed clockwise from the top-right position.

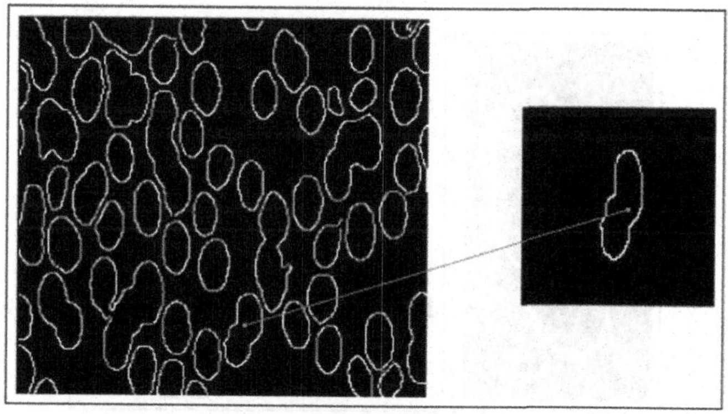

Fig. 4. Isolated single object and its contour.

2.1 Visibility Matrix and Analysis of Clusters

The *Visibility matrix (VM)* is a $N \times N$ binary matrix where N is the number of points in the contour of the object, The visibility matrix holds the values 0 and 1. For every point pair (p_i, p_j) from the contour, consider the chord p_ip_j. If cord p_ip_j is fully inside the object then we set $VM[i][j]$ to 1 else it is set to

0. Visibility matrix computation and management is done separately for each object contour. If multiple objects are present in the image they will be treated one after another as discussed earlier. Demonstration has been given in Fig. 5 for a single image object as shown in Fig. 4.

In the visibility matrix, we are interested in the black-pixel clusters (connected 0-blocks). We analyze the clusters one by one for the detection of the prominent concave zones and then we detect the exact concave points within the zones. As the visibility matrix is (approximately) symmetric, we can think of a diagonal in the visibility matrix from top-left corner to bottom-right corner that divides the matrix in two equivalent parts. We can process either of them. With respect to the contour shown in Fig. 5, there are two major clusters in the visibility matrix (in one side of the diagonal).

The primary observation is that the cluster-points, which are local minimums in terms of horizontal distances from the diagonal, are the peaks of the concavity zones. Algorithm 1 calculates the horizontal distances from all diagonal points to the first black point it hits in the clusters. If it does not hit (from the diagonal), then we set the distance equal to N. The algorithm's input is a visibility matrix VM, and it reports the distance matrix, DM, as output. The distance matrix entry $DM(k,3) = j - i$ if the horizontal line from the diagonal point (k,k) hits a 0-block pixel at (i,j). The values $DM(k,1)$ and $DM(k,2)$ designates i and j respectively. The peaks of these concavity zones are identified by analyzing the distance matrix DM. For example, in the object shown in Fig. 5, three concavity peaks are found. The peaks are shown as green boxes in Fig. 6. It has been shown how the cluster peaks in the visibility matrix map with the object contour pixels.

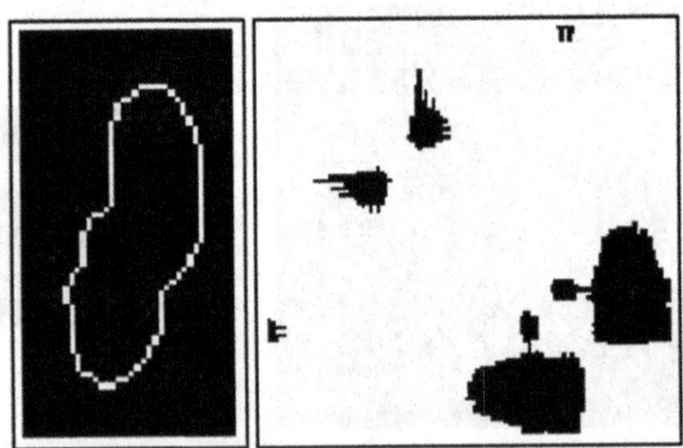

Fig. 5. Object boundary (left) and its visibility matrix (right).

Algorithm 2 describes the process of finding the cluster peaks. The cluster peaks are the local minimums in the distance matrix DM. The input to Algorithm 2 is DM, and the output is *result matrix (RM)*, which contains only peaks extracted from DM. Algorithm 2 uses a threshold value (th_{d1}) (empirically the value of th_{d1} lies in between 10 and 13 for input images of resolution 250 by 250, approximately) to find out all such peak points.

Algorithm 1: Distance-From-Diagonal

```
Result: Input: Visibility Matrix (VM), Output: Distance Matrix (DM)
DM ← Zeros(N,3);
k ← 1;
while i ← 1 to N do
    FLAG = 0;
    while j ← i to N do
        if VM[i][j]) == 0 AND FLAG == 0 then
            DM[k][3] ← (j-i);
            DM[k][1] ← i;
            DM[k][2] ← j;
            FLAG ← 1;
            k ← k+1;
        end
        if j==N AND FLAG == 0 then
            DM[k][3] ← N;
            DM[k][1] ← i;
            DM[k][2] ← j;
            k ← k+1;
        end
    end
end
```

The last conditional block uses another threshold th_{d2} in the algorithm, which is applied to avoid the local ignorable concavities. Like th_{d1}, the other threshold th_{d2} (values lies in between 16 to 19 for images of resolution 250 by 250, approximately) is also set based on the size of the image objects empirically. For further tuning, we can check some (approx 10–12) neighboring distance values around the peak point to eliminate local concavity. Another observation from the clusters is that the cluster size determines the degree of the concavity. Higher concavities form larger clusters, and the local smaller concavity zones create small clusters in the visibility matrix.

Peak points of the clusters in the visibility matrix are the concavity peaks in the contour. After the execution of Algorithm 1 and 2, the result matrix (RM) contains all the peaks. Figure 6 demonstrates the fact. The peaks stored in the result matrix (RM) are now mapped to the contour matrix (CM) to mark the points with concavity.

3 Experiments

To do experiments, we have used two types of data images. The first type of images are synthetically generated, and the second type of images is a collection of real images targeting some applications. The synthetic data set contains images with overlapped ellipse-shaped or circular objects. Overlapped objects are randomly scaled, rotated, and translated. These data sets are arbitrarily

Algorithm 2: Peak-Point-Extraction

```
Result: Input - Distance Matrix (DM), Output - Result Matrix (RM)
RM ← Zeros(k,3);
FLAGV ← Zeros(k);
r ← 1;
i ← 1;
while i ≤ N do
    if DM[i][3] ≤ th_d1 AND FLAGV[r] == 0 then
        RM[r][1] ← DM[i][1];
        RM[r][2] ← DM[i][2];
        RM[r][3] ← DM[i][3];
        FLAGV(r) ← 1;
    end
    if DM[i][3] ≤ th_d1 AND FLAGV[r] == 1 then
        if RM[r][3] > DM[i][3] then
            RM[r][1] ← DM[i][1];
            RM[r][2] ← DM[i][2];
            RM[r][3] ← DM[i][3];
        end
    end
    if DM[i][3] ≥ th_d2 AND FLAGV[r] == 1 then
        r ← r + 1;
    end
end
```

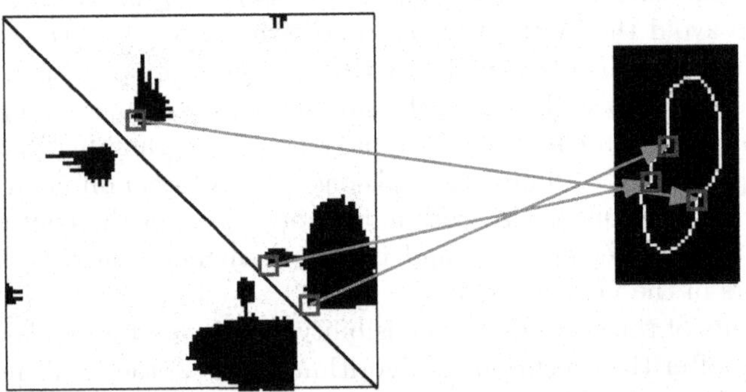

Fig. 6. Mapping from visibility matrix to contour concavity peaks.

created to test our proposed algorithm. The real images are captured by ourselves using a mobile camera. For rice-grains images, the objects are sometimes touching each other. Grains are dropped from a certain height using tea-spoon as samples. This application's objective may be considered as separation of the touching objects and then analyzing the percentage of broken or half rice units in the sample. Without doing the separation task, we cannot apply the size and perimeter information for proper classification. Also, to be noted that automated grading from the captured images can lead to controlled husking in rice mills. Secondly, we have captured touching and overlapped coins kept in a tray. Counting coins from images is the objective in this part. The amount of overlapping of these image objects is 30% to 40%. Mostly, the shapes in synthetic images are irregular.

3.1 Results

We experimented on 90 different overlapping or touching objects with different shapes (sometimes similar shames) consisting of both synthetic and real captured images as discussed in the beginning of the section. Synthetic images consist of varied and variegated shapes whereas for the the camera captured images the individual objects have mostly uniform shape and sizes. But, for the rice images many units are broken. A set of sample rice component images and results are shown Fig. 7. A full-tray image is shown in Fig. 8. Another set of results for camera captured coin images is shown in Fig. 9.

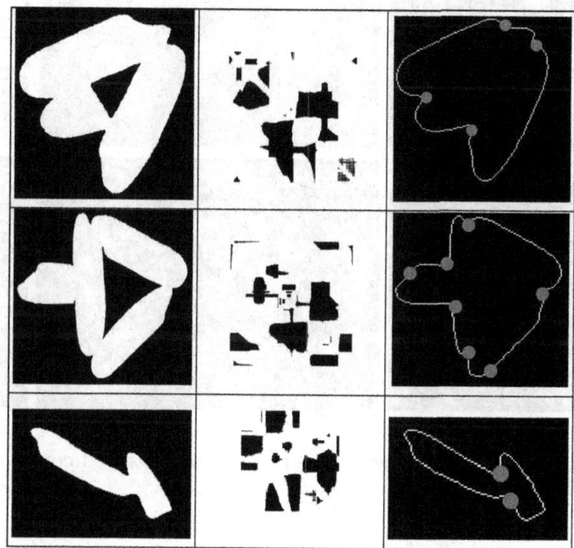

Fig. 7. Sample touching rice units in rice tray images (cropped), visibility matrix, and detected concave points (only the outer curve is considered).

$$TPR = TP/(TP + FN) \tag{1}$$

$$PPV = TP/(TP + FP) \tag{2}$$

$$ACC = TP/(TP + FP + FN) \tag{3}$$

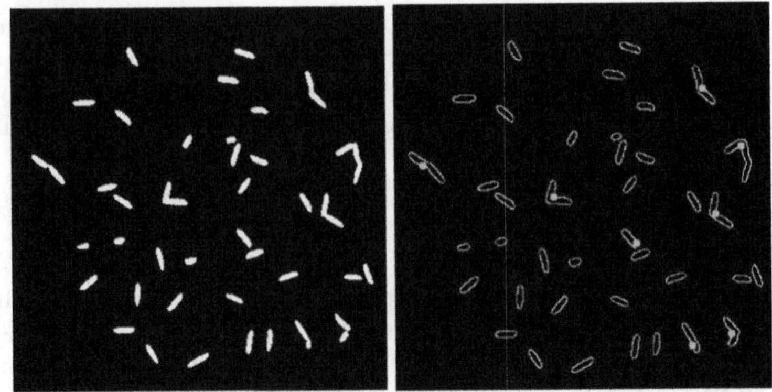

Fig. 8. Sample touching rice units and detected concave points.

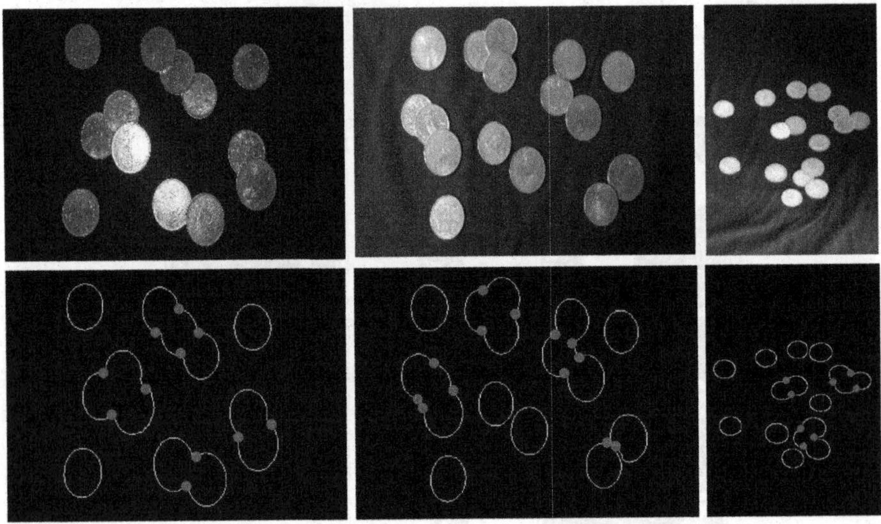

Fig. 9. Sample images of overlapped coins and detected concave points.

The performance metrics for evaluation of our proposed method are presented using *true positive rate (TPR)*, *positive predictive value (PPV)* and *accuracy (ACC)* which are defined as shown in Eq. 1, 2, and 3. Here, TP, FP, and FN represents *true positives*, *false positives*, and *false negatives* respectively. The TP, FP, and FN are observation values concerning the image ground truth and the results obtained by our proposed method. Respective detection results are shown in Table 1. Experimental results show that for camera captured images, we obtain detection accuracy of 83% and for synthetic images the figure is above 90%. Comparative results with respect to some existing well-known methods are shown in Fig. 10 for a synthetic image. The results shown here, clearly express the merit of our proposed method for detection of concavities in irregular boundaries.

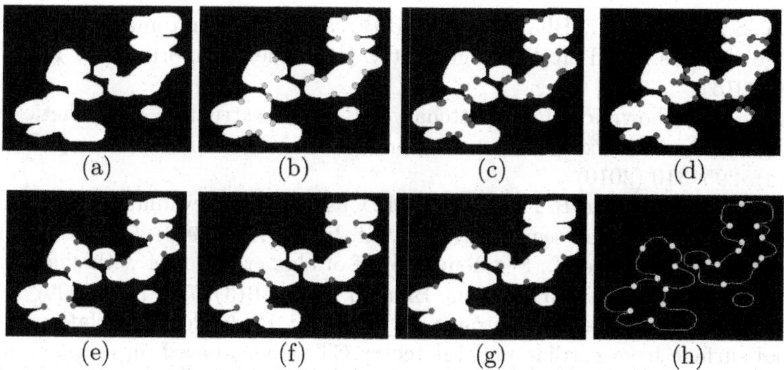

Fig. 10. Comparative results: (a) Original image (b) Ground truth, (c) Zhang et al. [36], (d) Bai et al. [2], (e) Dai et al. [10], (f) Zafari et al. [35], (g) Kumar et al. [18], (h) **Proposed method.**

Table 1. Comparison of the performance of concavity detection on a synthetic image data set.

Method	Technique	TPR (%)	PPV (%)	ACC (%)	Avg. Time (S)
Zhang [36]	Avg. distance deviation	84	38	35	2.28
Bai [2]	Line fitting	79	40	36	2.52
Dai [10]	Curvature method	54	87	50	2.50
Zafari [35]	Curvature method	65	**95**	64	2.48
Kumar [18]	Cord method	33	94	31	8.17
Proposed method	Visibility matrix	**95**	86	**83**	**2.24**

4 Conclusion

In this paper, we proposed an approach to detect concave points. This detection of concave points is a necessary task in separation of objects in a partially overlapping set of convex objects. The contribution lies with the use of the visibility matrix as a variant of the chord method, which is tuned to detect only the significantly meaningful concave-zones ignoring the smaller concave segments. The basic chord-based method does not employ this tuning. This enhancement can improve the object separation process where weak concave zones will be ignored.

References

1. Angulo, J., Jeulin, D.: Stochastic watershed segmentation. In: Proceeding of the 8th International symposium on Mathematical Morphology, pp. 265–276 (2007)
2. Bai, X., Sun, C., Zhou, F.: Splitting touching cells based on concave points and ellipse fitting. Pattern Recognit. **42**, 2434–2446 (2009)

3. Bera, S., Biswas, A., Bhattacharya, B.B.: A fast and automated granulometric image analysis based on digital geometry. Fundamenta Informaticae **138**(3), 321–338 (2015)
4. Biswas, A., Bhowmick, P., Bhattcharya, B.B.: Construction of isothetic coves of a digital object: a combinational approach. J. Vis. Commun. Image Represent. **21**(4), 295–310 (2010)
5. Cates, J.E., Whitaker, R.T., Jones, G.M.: Case study: an evaluation of user-assisted hierarchical watershed segmentation. Med. Image Anal. **9**(6), 566–578 (2005)
6. Cheng, J., Rajapakse, J.: Segmentation of of clustered nuclei with shape markers and marker function. IEEE Trans. Biomed. Eng. **56**(3), 741–748 (2009)
7. Cristoforitti, A., Faes, L., Centonze, M., Antolini, R., Nollo, G.: Isolation of the left atrial surface from cardiac multi-detector CT images based on marker controlled watershed segmentation. Med. Eng. Phys. **30**(1), 48–58 (2008)
8. Canny, J.A.: Computational approach to edge detection. IEEE Trans. Pattern Anal. Mach. Intell. **8**(6), 679–698 (1986)
9. Charles, J.J., Kuncheva, L.I., Wells, B., Lim, I.S.: Object segmentation with in microscope image of palynofacies. Comput. Geosci. **34**(6), 688–698 (2008)
10. Dai, J., Chen, X., Chu, N.: Research on the extraction and classification of the concave point from fiber image. In: IEEE 12th International Conference on Signal Processing (ICSP), pp. 709–712 (2014)
11. Do, C.J., Sun, D.W.: Automatic measurement of pores and porosity in pork ham and their correlations with processing time, water content and texture. Meat Sci. **72**(2), 294–302 (2006)
12. Farhan, M., Yli-Harja, O., Niemisto, A.: A novel method for splitting clumps of convex objects incorporating image intensity and using rectangular window-based concavity point-pair search. Pattern Recognit. **46**, 741–751 (2013)
13. Fleet, D., Pajdla, T., Schiele, B., Tuytelaars, T. (eds.): ECCV 2014, Part IV. LNCS, vol. 8692. Springer, Cham (2014). https://doi.org/10.1007/978-3-319-10593-2
14. Iwanowski, M.: Morphological boundary pixel classification. In: Proceedings of the International Conference on "Computer as a Tool' EUROCON 2007. IEEE (2007)
15. Jung, C., Kim, C.: Segmenting clustered nuclei using H-minima transform-based marker extraction and contour parameterization. IEEE Trans. Biomed. Eng. **57**(10), 2600–2604 (2010)
16. Jalba, A.C., Wilkinson, M.H., Roerdink, J.B.: Automatic segmentation of diatom images for classification. Microsc. Res. Tech. **65**(1–2), 72–85 (2004)
17. Kothari, S., Chaudry, Q., Wang, M.: Automated cell counting and cluster segmentation using concavity detection and ellipse fitting techniques. In: IEEE International Symposium on Biomedical Imaging, pp. 795–798 (2009)
18. Kumar, S., Ong, S.H., Ranganath, S., Ong, T.C., Chew, F.T.: A rule-based approach for robust clump splitting. Pattern Recognit. **39**, 1088–1098 (2006)
19. Karantzalos, K., Argialas, D.: Improving edge detection and watershed segmentation with an isotropic diffusion and morphological levelling. Int. J. Remote Sens. **27**(24), 5427–5434 (2006)
20. Leprettre, B., Martin, N.: Extraction of pertinent subsets from time-frequency representations for detection and recognition purpose. Signal Process. **82**(2), 229–238 (2002)
21. Malcolm, A.A., Leong, H.Y., Spowage, A.C., Shacklock, A.P.: Image segmentation and analysis for porosity measurement. J. Mater. Proces. Technol. **192**, 391–396 (2007)
22. Pal, N.R., Pal, S.K.: A review on image segmentation techniques. Pattern Recognit. **26**(9), 1277–1294 (1993)

23. Park, C., Huang, J.Z., Ji, J.X., Ding, Y.: Segmentation, inference and classification of partially overlapping nanoparticles. IEEE Trans. Pattern Anal. Mach. Intell **35**(3), 669–681 (2013)
24. Park, S.C., Lim, S.H., Sin, B.K., Lee, S.W.: Tracking non-rigid objects using probabilistic Hausdorff distance matching. Pattern Recognit. **38**(12), 2373–2384 (2005)
25. Pratikakis, I.E., Sahli, H., Cornelis, J.: Low level Image partitioning guided by the gradient watershed hierarchy. Signal Process. **75**(2), 173–195 (1999)
26. Razdan, A., Bae, M.: A hybrid approach to feature segmentation of triangle meshes. Comput. Aided Des. **35**(9), 783–789 (2003)
27. Rosenfeld, A.: Measuring the sizes of concavities. Pattern Recognit. Lett. **3**, 71–75 (1985)
28. Samma, A.S.B., Talib, A.Z., Salam, R.A.: Combining boundary and skeleton information for convex and concave points detection. In: IEEE Seventh International Conference on Computer Graphics, Imaging and Visualization (CGIV), pp. 113–117 (2010)
29. Sauvola, J., Pietikäinen, M.: Adaptive document image binarization. Pattern Recognit **33**, 225–236 (2000)
30. Shu, J., Fu, H., Qiu, G., Kaye, P., Ilyas, M.: Segmenting overlapping cell nuclei in digital histopathology images. In: 35th International Conference on Medicine and Biology Society (EMBC), pp. 5445–5448 (2013)
31. Song, Y., Zhang, L., Chen, S., Ni, D., Lei, B., Wang, T.: Accurate segmentation of cervical cytoplasm and nuclei based on multi scale convolutional neural network and graph partitioning. IEEE Trans. Biomed. Eng. **62**(10), 2421–2433 (2015)
32. Vincent, L.: Fast granulometric methods for the extraction of global image information. In: Proceedings, 11 Annual Symposium of the South African Pattern Recognition Association
33. Wang, D.: Unsupervised video segmentation based on watersheds and temporal tracking. IEEE Trans. Circuits Syst. Video Technol. **8**(5), 539–546 (1998)
34. Wen, Q., Chang, H., Parvin, B.: A delaunay triangulation approach for segmenting clumps of nuclei. In: Sixth IEEE International Conference on Symposium on Biomedical Imaging: From Nano to Macro, pp. 9–12, Boston, USA, 2009
35. Zafari, S., Eerola, T., Sampo, J., Kälviäinen, H., Haario, H.: Segmentation of partially overlapping nanoparticles using concave points. In: Bebis, G., et al. (eds.) ISVC 2015, Part I. LNCS, vol. 9474, pp. 187–197. Springer, Cham (2015). https://doi.org/10.1007/978-3-319-27857-5_17
36. Zhang, W.H., Jiang, X., Liu, Y.M.: A method for recognizing overlapping elliptical bubbles in bubble image. Pattern Recognit. Lett. **33**, 1543–1548 (2012)

High Performance Ensembled Convolutional Neural Network for Plant Species Recognition

S. Anubha Pearline(✉) and V. Sathiesh Kumar

Madras Institute of Technology, Anna University, Chennai 600044, India
anubhapearl@mitindia.edu

Abstract. Recognition of plant species is challenging due to variation in leaves such as its arrangement, color variation, leaf venation, varying margin, inter- and intra-similar species. Photographed images possess difficulties in recognition due to differing lighting conditions, rotations, viewpoints, and color backgrounds. To minimize these issues, a Bi-channel Convolution Neural Network (CNN) involving two pre-trained CNNs (VGG-16 and SqueezeNet) is adopted. The networks are trained individually and their predictions are fused to obtain the final prediction scores. The Bi-channel CNN is evaluated on three datasets, namely, Flavia, Swedish leaf, and Leaf-12 datasets. The optimal γ values obtained for the three datasets (Flavia, Swedish Leaf and Leaf-12) are 0.5, 0.9 and 0.5, respectively. The performance metrics (accuracy, precision, recall and f1-score) obtained with the models trained on Leaf-12 dataset are 97.70%, 0.98, 0.98 and 0.98, respectively. The above-specified values are obtained for a γ value of 0.5.

Keywords: Plant species recognition · Deep learning · Bi-channel architecture · Late fusion

1 Introduction

Plant species recognition [1] using leaves is challenging, as it has different shapes, simple or compound structure and color variations (due to aging or seasonal conditions). Computer vision challenges such as camera viewpoint variation, illumination changes, scale variation and background clutter also prevail as a hindrance in plant species classification.

Convolutional Neural Networks (CNN) are prominent since 2012, as it performs both feature extraction and classification with the aid of convolution, pooling and fully connected layers (FC). Also, in recent times, the fusion of multiple CNNs are carried out to significantly boost the performance of the system. Hence, in this paper, a dual network is adopted for plant species recognition. In the following subsections, related works, methodology, experimental details and the results are discussed.

S. K. Singh et al. (Eds.): CVIP 2020, CCIS 1378, pp. 526–538, 2021.
https://doi.org/10.1007/978-981-16-1103-2_44

2 Related Works

Figueroa et al. [2] proposed a Convolutional Siamese Network (CSN) for plant species recognition. The method is tested on smaller datasets (No of Images/Class = varied between 5 to 30). CSN method consists of twin CNNs. Each CNN holds 3 sets of convolution with ReLU activation function, Maxpooling followed by a global average pooling and 2 fully connected layers. The similarity metric, Euclidean distance is utilized to find the similarity between the pairs of leaves.

Dual Deep Learning Architecture (DDLA) [3] is a feature extraction method incorporated for plant species recognition. The authors integrated two deep learning architectures, namely, MobileNet and DenseNet-121 for DDLA. The extracted features from DDLA are classified using machine learning classifiers. DDLA is evaluated on four leaf datasets (Flavia, Swedish leaf, Folio and custom created Leaf-12).

Rizk [4] proposed a dual path Convolutional Neural Network (CNN) for plant species recognition. Dual-path CNN incorporates two simple CNNs. Each path consists of four sets of convolution and max-pooling layers. The first path extracts the shape features and the second path extracts the venation features. The feature maps from each path are merged and forwarded to a fully connected layer. The augmented Flavia dataset is used in the evaluation of the method.

Siamese-Inception (S-Inception) network [5] is suggested for plant species recognition. It incorporates a technique called few-shot learning. S-Inception architecture utilizes two Inception CNNs connected in a parallel fashion. Spatial Structure Optimizer (SSO) metric is constructed for enhancing the performance of S-Inception. Then, the plant species are classified using K-Nearest Neighbor. The efficacy of S-Inception is determined using Flavia, Swedish leaf, and LeafSnap datasets.

Lee et al. [6] designed a hybrid fusion methodology, Ensemble CNN for recognition of plant species. It includes two networks, namely, Hybrid-Generic Convolutional Neural Network (HGO-CNN) and Plant-StructNet. HGO-CNN integrates the organ and generic knowledge gained from single plant images. Plant-StructNet modelling comprises of Recurrent Neural Network (RNN) emphasizing on multi-images. PlantCLEF 2015 dataset is used for assessing the methodology.

He et al. [7] proposed a bi-channel network for plant species recognition. VGG-16 and SqueezeNet pre-trained CNNs form the Bi-channel system. A stacking layer is used for fusing the predicted probabilities attained from the two pre-trained CNNs. The collected web-crawled images of Orchidaceae plant family is used in the evaluation of the method. The integrated technique achieved an accuracy of 96.81%.

Hu et al. [8] proposed a Multi-Scale Fusion Convolutional Neural Network (MSF-CNN) for plant species recognition. MSF-CNN utilized multiple CNNs for different image size and concatenated the output feature maps from the two consecutive CNNs. Experimental results are reported by using the MalayaKew leaf and the LeafSnap datasets.

Ghazi et al. [9] integrated two pre-trained fine-tuned CNNs (GoogleNet and VGG) for plant species recognition. Also, the authors explored the pre-trained CNNs such as GoogleNet, VGGNet and AlexNet architectures. LifeCLEF 2015 plant dataset is experimented on the integrated CNNs and attained an accuracy of 80%.

Pre-trained CNN models such as GoogleNet and VGG-16 are used in plant species classification. Similarly, pre-trained CNN models are employed in plant disease prediction. Mukherjee et al. [10] recommended early classification of plant disease through GoogleNet to preserve plant species from damage. Wang et al. [11] suggested VGG-16 fine-tuned model for identifying disease in apple leaf.

From the extensive literature survey, it is observed that there is a large number of research works focusing on either hierarchical, early or late fusion of deep learning networks. In recent years, the bi-channel framework gained attention because of its fusion methodology. Hence, in this paper, a bi-channel framework is adopted for plant species recognition. This approach is tested on three leaf datasets, namely, Flavia, Swedish leaf, and Leaf-12 (custom-developed).

3 Methodology

A Bi-channel Convolutional Neural Network (B-CNN) framework with the late fusion approach is proposed for plant species recognition [7]. The following subsections, details about the image preprocessing, bi-channel method and training algorithm.

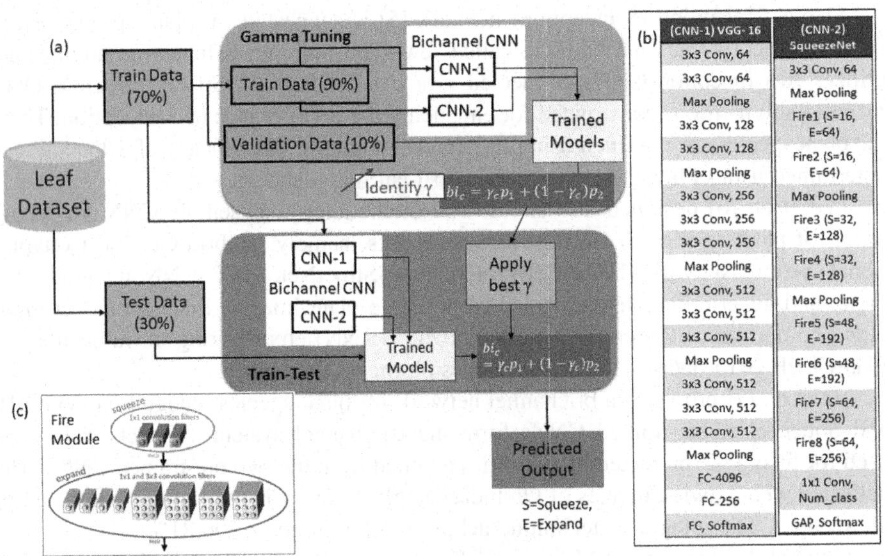

Fig. 1. Workflow for Bi-channel Convolution Neural Network. (a) Workflow (b) CNN-1 and CNN-2 (c) SqueezeNet's Fire Module [11]

Figure 1 illustrates the workflow of Bi-channel Convolution Neural Network. The leaf dataset is split as train (70%) and test (30%) data. The training data are passed to B-CNN architecture. B-CNN architecture consists of two CNN (CNN-1=VGG-16, CNN-2=SqueezeNet) architectures connected in a parallel manner. The two CNN frameworks are trained and validated individually to obtain prediction scores (p1, p2).

Based on the prediction, the weights (γ) are assigned to the individual architecture. It is performed to obtain the overall prediction of the bi-channel architecture. Optimal γ is identified from the Gamma tuning segment. The best Gamma value is used in the retrain process cum test data evaluation mechanism. Finally, performance metrics are estimated and reported.

3.1 Image Preprocessing

Three datasets, namely, Flavia, Swedish leaf and Leaf-12 are used. B-CNN method is also experimented on augmented datasets. The augmentation operations employed in this paper include horizontal flip, vertical flip and Gaussian blur. Also, the augmented dataset comprises the existing images from the dataset.

The images from each of the datasets are reconstructed to 300 × 300 using image resizing function by maintaining the aspect ratio and image quality. Hence, the images are further resized to 100 × 100 × 3 for saving computational time.

3.2 Bi-channel Convolutional Neural Network

Bi-channel CNN [7] is adopted for processing the leaf images. Bi-channel CNN includes two pre-trained CNNs, VGG-16 (CNN-1) and SqueezeNet (CNN-2) architectures. The prediction score from the two architectures is fused, as stated in Eq. (1).

$$bi_c = \gamma_c p_1 + (1 - \gamma_c)p_2, c = 1, 2, \ldots C \quad (1)$$

Where bi_c represents the final prediction score

γ_c is the weight
p_1 is the prediction score of CNN-1
p_2 is the prediction score of CNN-2
c is the leaf classes 1,2….C

CNN-1. VGG-16 [12] architecture is used in one of the branches of bi-channel CNN. It consists of thirteen 3 × 3 convolutions followed by three fully connected (FC) layers. This architecture comprises of five max-pooling layers inserted in between two convolution layers as shown in Fig. 1(b). The number of filters is increased from 64 to 512 as the architecture is deepened.

CNN-2. SqueezeNet [13] architecture is used in the second branch of the bi-channel framework. It consists of a convolution layer, followed by eight fire modules. The last fire module is followed by 1 × 1 convolution and Global Average Pooling (GAP). Fire module consists of operations such as squeeze and expand as shown in Fig. 1(c). Squeeze operation includes of 1 × 1 convolutions. The outputs from the Squeeze operation is fed into the expand operation. The expand operation consists of 1 × 1 and 3 × 3 convolutions. 1 × 1 Convolutions decrease the number of feature maps and functions similar to an FC layer.

3.3 Training of Bi-channel CNN

Bi-channel CNN is trained using SGD (Stochastic Gradient Descent) optimizer [14] with a learning rate of 0.001 and 50 epochs. The results deteriorated when the optimizer (Adam with different learning rates 0.001 and 0.0001) is varied. Algorithm 1 shows the procedure for Bi-channel CNN. The optimal γ is identified by incorporating Manual search mechanism. After training the data, the prediction score (validation data) obtained from CNN-1 and CNN-2 i.e. p1 and p2 are fused for each class by utilizing the equation represented in Step 4 of the algorithm.

The arbitrary weight γ is varied from 0, 0.1, 0.2, 0.3….1 and the final accuracies are predicted. Based on the highest accuracy, optimal weight γ_c is fixed. The best γ obtained is used in the final prediction process.

Algorithm: Late Fusion in Bi-channel CNN

Inputs: Images, I; Models, *m1* and *m2*; prediction score, p_1 and p_2; arbitrary weight, γ; Number of epochs, ep=50, Number of classes, $c \in 1,2..C$

Output: Predicted label, *l*

Step 1: Resize the Input Images, I to 100x100 pixels

Step 2: Train the images using the Model, *m1* for *ep* number of epochs and obtain the prediction score, p_1 using the validation data.

Step 3: Train the images using the Model, *m2* for *ep* number of epochs and obtain the prediction score, p_2 by using the validation data.

Step 4: Using p_1 and p_2, find the optimal arbitrary weight, γ by employing equation (1).

$$bi_c = \gamma_c p_1 + (1 - \gamma_c) p_2, c = 1, 2, \ldots C$$

Step 5: Retrain the bi-channel CNN architecture with best γ value acquired from validation data and evaluate the method by using the test data.

Step 6: The performance metrics are estimated and reported.

4 Experimental Results and Discussion

The experiments on plant species recognition system are implemented using Windows 10, 64-bit OS, CPU with Intel i7 processor 20 GB RAM and NVIDIA Titan X GPU with 3584 CUDA cores. The code implementation is carried out using Python 3.5, supporting python packages such as Keras with Tensorflow backend, OpenCV, scikit-learn, and os. Three leaf datasets (Flavia [15], Swedish leaf [16], and Leaf-12) are used in the experimental investigation.

4.1 Flavia Dataset

Flavia [15] is a standard leaf dataset consisting of 32 plant species. For each class, 50 images are utilized. The performance metric (Accuracy) of the individual CNN models is obtained by varying the size of input images in the dataset. The dimensions of the input images considered in the studies are 100 × 100 × 3 and 224 × 224 × 3. The estimated results are listed in Table 4. It is observed that the accuracy in the prediction of plant species is improved for larger input images (224 × 224 × 3) compared to smaller images (100 × 100 × 3). It also results in increased computation time for larger images. Also, the model utilizes parameters on a high scale for larger images. Hence, to save computational time and easier model reuse, image size of 100 × 100 × 3 is further employed for experimental evaluation (Table 1).

Table 1. Results obtained by varying input image size

Image Size	Number of parameters	Individual model training time (s)	B-CNN accuracy (%)
100 × 100 × 3	**CNN-1: 34, 650, 208**	**CNN-1: 74.91**	**94.38%**
	CNN-2: 722, 496	**CNN-2: 26.24**	
224 × 224 × 3	CNN-1: 118, 536, 288	CNN-1: 285.76	96.88%
	CNN-2: 738 ,912	CNN-2: 81.34	

The augmented dataset consists of 6400 images with 200 images per each class. Using train-validation set, the optimal γ value is identified as $\gamma = 0.5$ (validation accuracy = 97.99%) and is depicted in Fig. 2. The non-augmented dataset (Number of images = 1600) resulted in an optimum γ value of 0.7.

The accuracies achieved by using the augmented dataset (97.71%) is higher compared to the dataset without augmentation (94.38%). Other metrics such as precision, recall and F1-score are 0.98, 0.98 and 0.98, respectively. Also, Fig. 3 shows the confusion matrix curve plotted for the augmented Flavia dataset.

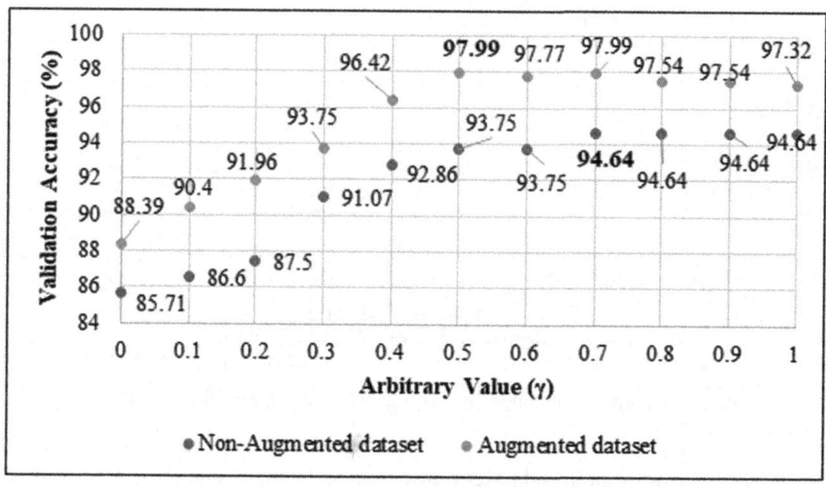

Fig. 2. Accuracies obtained by varying γ for Flavia dataset

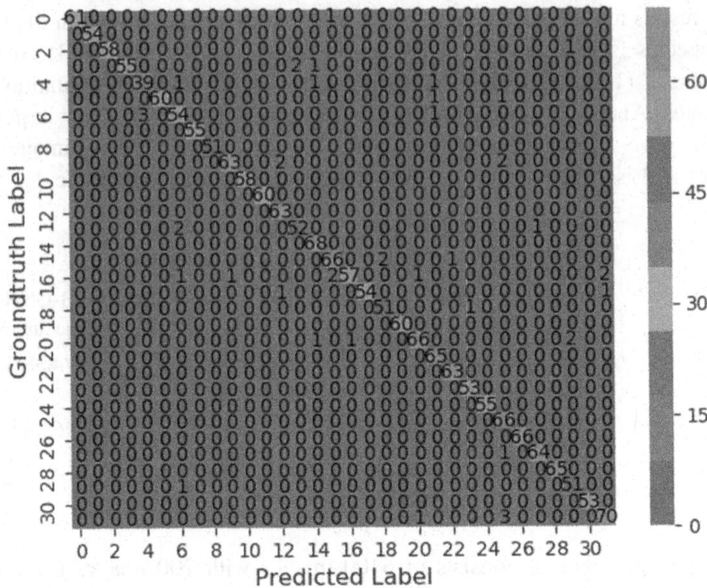

Fig. 3. Confusion matrix for Augmented Flavia dataset

4.2 Swedish Leaf Dataset

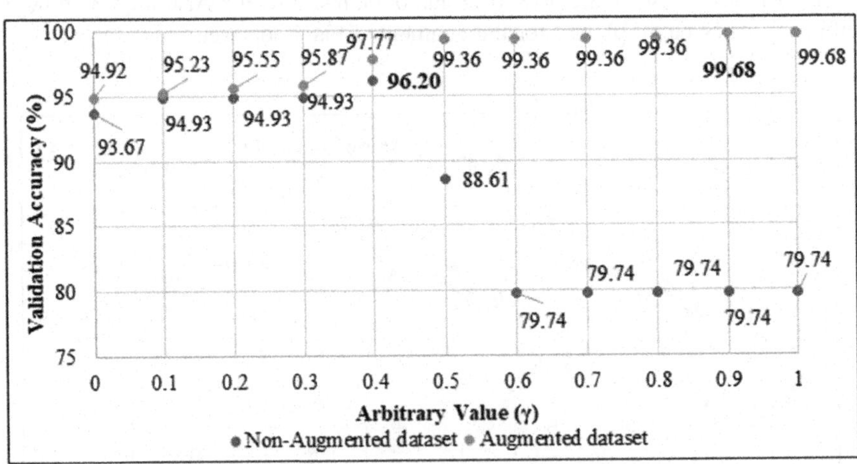

Fig. 4. Accuracies obtained by varying γ value for Swedish leaf dataset

Swedish leaf [16] is a standard dataset consisting of 15 plant species. Each of the plant species contains 75 images. The augmented dataset consists of 4,500 images with 300 images for each class. The optimal γ is estimated to be 0.9 (validation accuracy = 99.68%) from validation data and it is shown in Fig. 4. Similar to Flavia dataset, the dataset with and without augmentation resulted in different optimum γ values.

The augmented dataset resulted in an accuracy, precision, recall and F1-score values of 98.67%, 0.99, 0.99 and 0.99, respectively. The accuracy of Swedish leaf dataset without augmentation is 94.97%. Confusion matrix obtained by using the augmented Swedish leaf dataset is represented in Fig. 5.

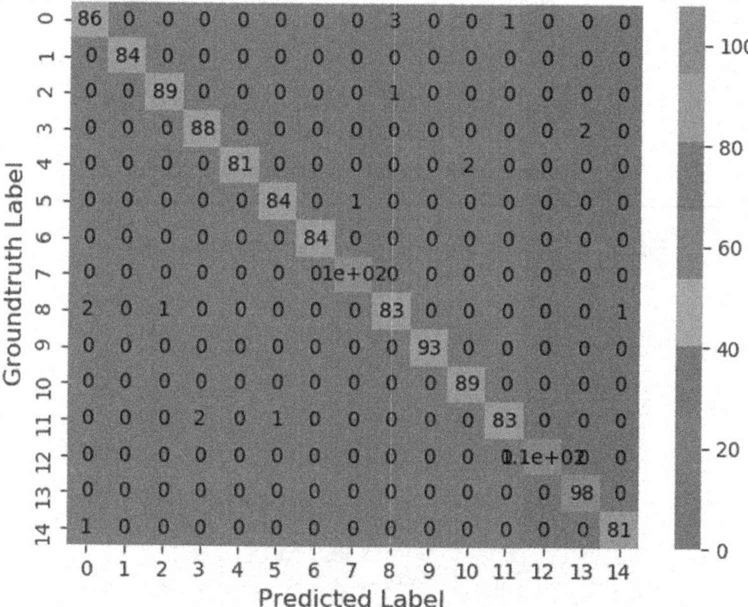

Fig. 5. Confusion matrix for Augmented Swedish leaf dataset

4.3 Leaf-12 Dataset

Leaf-12 is a self-collected real-time dataset. It consists of 12 leaf classes and 320 images per class. The total number of images in the augmented real time dataset is of 15,360. From the train-validation data, the optimal γ is estimated to be 0.5 (validation accuracy = 97.76%). Figure 6 shows the accuracies obtained on varying γ (train-validation). For Leaf-12 dataset, the γ value remained the same for non-augmented as well as the augmented dataset.

For the train-test data, the estimated accuracy, precision, recall and F1-score are 97.70%, 0.98, 0.98 and 0.98. The non-augmented dataset resulted in an accuracy of 95.49%. Confusion matrix obtained for the augmented Leaf-12 dataset is shown in Fig. 7.

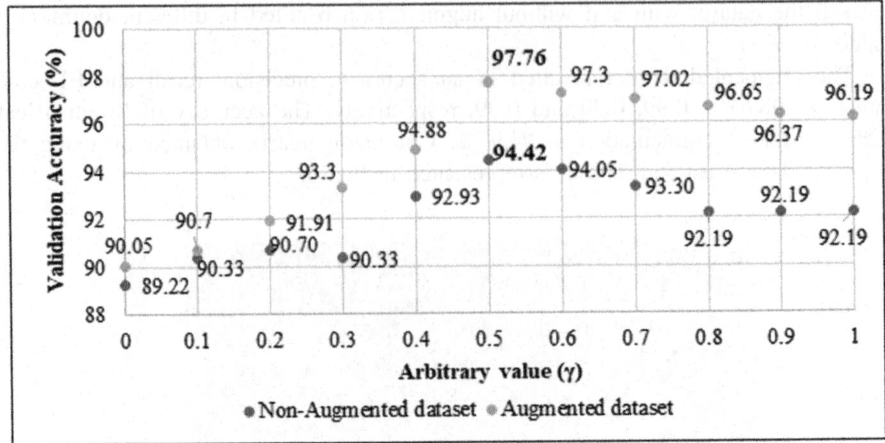

Fig. 6. Accuracies obtained by varying γ for Leaf-12 dataset

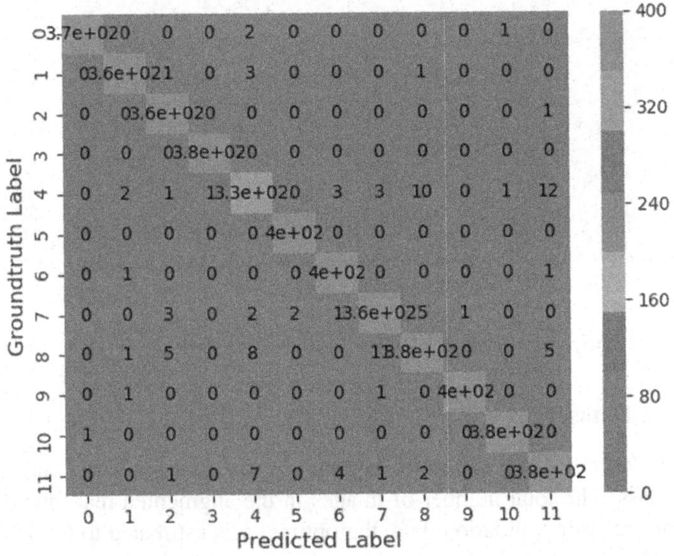

Fig. 7. Confusion matrix for Augmented Leaf-12 dataset

4.4 Discussion

Table 2 shows the estimated performance metrics for plant species recognition using a Bi-channel CNN. Accuracies of plant species recognition obtained from augmented Flavia, Swedish leaf and Leaf-12 datasets are 97.71%, 98.67% and 97.7%, respectively. The augmented datasets showed improved accuracies for standard and real-time datasets. Even though the accuracies proved to be better for the augmented datasets, it is proportionately increasing the computational time. The computational time increased four folds as the dataset size is increased by 4 times. Table 3 shows the computation time for CNN-1 (train and test time), CNN-2 (train and test time), gamma identification time and B-CNN prediction time.

Precision, Recall and F1-score for Flavia and Leaf-12 datasets obtain a similar value of 0.98. Whereas, for the Swedish leaf dataset, the obtained precision, recall and F1-score values are 0.99, 0.99 and 0.99, respectively. Using the Scikit-learn package, the weighted metrics (Precision, Recall and F1-score) are considered. In the experimental studies, the number of images per class is equal, eradicating the class imbalance problem. In addition to it, the weighted metrics manages the class imbalance problem for randomly distributed dataset between the train and test data groups.

Table 2. Results of Bi-channel CNN for standard and real-time dataset

Metrics	Flavia		Swedish leaf		Leaf-12	
	Without augmentation	With augmentation	Without augmentation	With augmentation	Without augmentation	With augmentation
Number of images	1,600	6,400	1,125	4,500	3,840	15,360
Accuracy (%)	94.38	**97.71**	94.97	**98.67**	95.49	**97.7**
Precision	0.95	**0.98**	0.95	**0.99**	0.95	**0.98**
Recall	0.94	**0.98**	0.95	**0.99**	0.95	**0.98**
F1-Score	0.94	**0.98**	0.95	**0.99**	0.95	**0.98**
Gamma	0.7	**0.5**	0.4	**0.9**	0.5	**0.5**

Table 3. Computation time for Bi-channel CNN

Computation Time (in seconds)	Flavia		Swedish leaf		Leaf-12	
	Without augmentation	With augmentation	Without augmentation	With augmentation	Without augmentation	With augmentation
i) CNN-1 Train time	77.65	289.42	53.77	209.83	181.32	699.34
ii) CNN-1 Test time	0.48	1.66	0.38	1.22	1.07	3.79
iii) CNN-2 Train time	26.44	106.36	19.41	74.52	63.07	250.88
iv) CNN-2 Test time	0.22	0.59	0.19	0.46	0.43	1.28
v) Gamma Identification time	0.04	0.07	0.04	0.06	0.04	0.15
vi) B-CNN Prediction time	0.01	0.02	0.01	0.01	0.01	0.04

From Table 4, it is observed that the accuracies obtained by using the Bi-channel CNN are higher compared to other methods such as conventional [17, 18], single deep learning architectures [17, 19] and double deep learning techniques [5].

Table 4. Comparison of accuracies between Bi-channel CNN framework and reported literatures

Methods	Flavia	Swedish leaf	Leaf-12
Conventional Method [17]	89.17%	88.46%	82.38%
Multiscale Distance Matrix [18]	90.33%	93.60%	–
S-Inception [5]	92.34%	91.67%	–
Inception-V3 [17]	92.50%	94.67%	90.28%
End-to-End CNN [19]	91.08%	96.06%	–
B-CNN	**97.71%**	**98.67%**	**97.70%**

The real-time images are collected and tested with the bi-channel CNN method (Trained model with the best gamma value of 0.5 on Leaf-12 dataset). The prediction results are shown in Fig. 8.

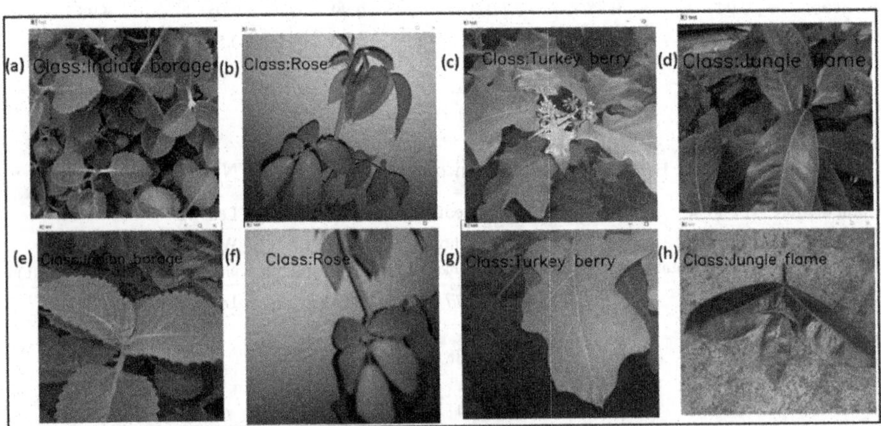

Fig. 8. Prediction of real-time images from Leaf-12 dataset using Bi-channel CNN. (Predicted class is mentioned over the image in Red font.) (a) Groundtruth: Indian Borage (b) Groundtruth: Rose (c) Groundtruth: Turkey Berry (d) Groundtruth: Jungle Flame (e) Groundtruth: Indian Borage (f) Groundtruth: Rose (g) Groundtruth: Turkey Berry (h) Groundtruth: Jungle Flame

5 Conclusion

Plant species recognition is performed using Bi-channel CNN. The proposed architecture consists of two CNN parallel branches (CNN-1 = VGG-16, CNN-2 = SqueezeNet). Both the CNNs are trained individually and prediction scores are obtained. The weighted prediction from each of the branches is fused (late fusion approach) to obtain the final predicted score. The weight γ parameter is optimized to achieve the highest performance metrics. The Bi-channel CNN method is assessed on three datasets namely, Flavia (94.38%), Swedish leaf (94.97%), and Leaf-12 (95.49%). Augmented datasets provided better performance for Bi-channel CNN. The accuracies of Flavia, Swedish leaf, and Leaf-12 datasets are 97.71%, 98.67%, and 97.70%, respectively.

Acknowledgment. The authors would like to thank NVIDIA for providing NVIDIA Titan X GPU under the University Research Grant Programme.

References

1. Wäldchen, J., Rzanny, M., Seeland, M., Mäder, P.: Automated plant species identification—trends and future directions. PLoS Comput. Biol. **14**(4), e1005993 (2018)
2. Figueroa-Mata, G., Mata-Montero, E.: Using a convolutional siamese network for image-based plant species identification with small datasets. Biomimetics **5**(1), 8 (2020)
3. Raj, A.P.S.S., Vajravelu, S.K.: DDLA: dual deep learning architecture for classification of plant species. IET Image Process. **13**(12), 2176–2182 (2019)
4. Rizk, S.: Plant leaf classification using dual path convolutional neural networks. Doctoral dissertation, Notre Dame University-Louaize (2019)
5. Wang, B., Wang, D.: Plant leaves classification: a few-shot learning method based on siamese network. IEEE Access **7**, 151754–151763 (2019)
6. Lee, S.H., Chan, C.S., Remagnino, P.: Multi-organ plant classification based on convolutional and recurrent neural networks. IEEE Trans. Image Process. **27**(9), 4287–4301 (2018)
7. He, G., Xia, Z., Zhang, Q., Zhang, H., Fan, J.: Plant species identification by bi-channel deep convolutional networks. In: Journal of Physics: Conference Series, vol. 1004, no. 1, pp. 1–6 (2018)
8. Hu, J., Chen, Z., Yang, M., Zhang, R., Cui, Y.: A multiscale fusion convolutional neural network for plant leaf recognition. IEEE Signal Process. Lett. **25**(6), 853–857 (2018)
9. Ghazi, M.M., Yanikoglu, B., Aptoula, E.: Plant identification using deep neural networks via optimization of transfer learning parameters. Neurocomputing **235**, 228–235 (2017)
10. Mukherjee, S., Kumar, P., Saini, R., Roy, P.P., Dogra, D.P., Kim, B.G.: Plant disease identification using deep neural networks. J. Multimedia Inf. Syst. **4**(4), 233–238 (2017)
11. Wang, G., Sun, Y., Wang, J.: Automatic image-based plant disease severity estimation using deep learning. Comput. Intell. Neurosci. (2017)
12. Simonyan, K., Zisserman, A.: Very deep convolutional networks for large-scale image recognition. arXiv preprint arXiv:1409.1556 (2014)
13. Iandola, F.N., Han, S., Moskewicz, M.W., Ashraf, K., Dally, W.J., Keutzer, K.: SqueezeNet: AlexNet-level accuracy with 50x fewer parameters and <0.5 MB model size. arXiv preprint arXiv:1602.07360 (2016)
14. Ruder, S.: An overview of gradient descent optimization algorithms. arXiv preprint arXiv: 1609.04747 (2016)
15. Wu, S.G., Bao, F.S., Xu, E.Y., Wang, Y.X., Chang, Y.F., Xiang, Q.L.: A leaf recognition algorithm for plant classification using probabilistic neural network. In: IEEE International Symposium on Signal Processing and Information Technology, pp. 11–16. IEEE (2007)
16. Söderkvist, O.J.O.: Computer vision classification of leaves from Swedish trees. Master's thesis, Linkoping University (2001)

17. Anubha Pearline, S., Sathiesh Kumar, V., Harini, S.: A study on plant recognition using conventional image processing and deep learning approaches. J. Intell. Fuzzy Syst. **36**(3), 1997–2004 (2019)
18. Wang, X., Du, W., Guo, F., Hu, S.: Leaf recognition based on elliptical half gabor and maximum gap local line direction pattern. IEEE Access **8**, 39175–39183 (2020)
19. Kaya, A., Keceli, A.S., Catal, C., Yalic, H.Y., Temucin, H., Tekinerdogan, B.: Analysis of transfer learning for deep neural network based plant classification models. Comput. Electron. Agric. **158**, 20–29 (2019)

Author Index

Printed in the United States
by Baker & Taylor Publisher Services

Printed in the United States
by Baker & Taylor Publisher Services